AN UNCOMMON
Journey

Book One in the Quaternion
of
The History of Old Dawson County,
Montana Territory

The Biography of Stephen Norton Van Blaricom

A True Story of the
First Settlers of the Last West

BY H. NORMAN HYATT

To Sarah Susan

Hardcover:
ISBN 10: 1-59152-057-6
ISBN 13: 978-1-59152-057-3

Sotfcover:
ISBN 10: 1-59152-056-8
ISBN 13: 978-1-59152-056-6

Published by H. Norman Hyatt

Cover photo: Stephen Norton Van Blaricom, 1914.
Photo courtesy of Ann Van Blaricom Falor.

To purchase autographed books directly from the author, write UCJ, 5102 Scenic Drive, Yakima WA 98908; call (509) 248-7379; or e-mail uncomjourney@aol.com.

Cataloging-in-Publication Data is on file at the Library of Congress.

Produced by Sweetgrass Books, PO Box 5630, Helena, MT 59604; (800) 821-3874; www.sweetgrassbooks.com.

a division of Farcountry Press

Printed in the United States.

15   14   13   12   11   10   09   1   2   3   4   5   6   7

Table of Contents

Appendices:

List of Maps:

Photographs and Portraits:

Preface

IN SEARCH OF SARAH SUSAN

ALISTAIR MACLEAN ONCE WROTE OF CAPTAIN JAMES COOK, the great explorer of the eighteenth century, "We know all about Cook and we know nothing about him."[1] I have always remembered MacLean's quote, for it described so well the condition of my own family.

My mother and my father were born in cabins in remote locations in the panhandle of northern Idaho—my father in 1909, my mother in 1910. While they knew and dearly loved their siblings (my father's father had seventeen children from two marriages; my mother was one of a family of seven sisters and one brother) they knew little about their respective families. They knew nothing of their ancestral origins, nor did they know how or when their predecessors had arrived in North America... or Idaho, for that matter. My mother had been told that her father was a "bastard" child who, although he knew his biological father, deliberately avoided any mention of him to his children. My father never met any of his four grandparents and knew only three of their four family names: Hyatt, Vess, and Van Blaricom. He knew that his grandfather's name was Newton Franklin Hyatt. He knew that his grandmother Hyatt's name was Elizabeth and that she was a Vess. And, while he knew his mother's maiden name was Alice Janette Van Blaricom, he knew neither the surname of her mother nor the given names of either of her parents.

I was eleven years old in the summer of 1951, driving my father's new 1950 Ford Club Coupe down a highway in eastern Montana, when I learned that Sarah Susan had been missing for all these years. Her memory had been hidden for three score and ten by that cloak of silence with which death inevitably surrounds its victims. The sexton of the Dawson County cemetery atop the hill in Glendive said there was no record of an interment

---

[1] *Captain Cook,* Alistair MacLean, Doubleday, New York, 1972.

of any "Mrs. Van Blaricom." There was no tombstone. We had searched for it diligently. Yet all nine of her children attested that, following a sunrise service on a crisp morning late in September of 1882, she had been buried at the very top of the hill of the "new" cemetery. They had recalled it clearly despite the fact that the oldest child, Stephen Norton, was but thirteen when the traumatic event occurred. Sarah Effie, the baby at three months, had been held in the arms of her grandmother, Mariah, during the brief graveside eulogy. The other seven children, ranging in age from the two-year-old toddler, Dora May, to eleven-year-old David, had stood clutched, huddling together in their loss. My grandmother, Alice, then a five-year-old, was among them. They were mere children and they trembled not from the chill of the dawn but from the growing realization that death had taken their mother from them forever and they feared the uncertain future.

My father, "Holly" Hyatt, was not a formally educated man but he was well read in those subjects in which he had an interest: Native Americans ("Indians," he called them) and the history of the American West. He had nearly memorized the works of two of the Yakima area's more well-known writers of history, L. V. McWhorter, the biographer of Chief Joseph in *Hear Me, My Chiefs,* and A. J. Splawn, the author of *Kamiakin.* Holly was a friend of Roscoe Sheller, the Sunnyside, Washington journalist who was the biographer of Ben Snipes, the local area's early cattle king.[2] My father admired these men for their abilities to "put pen to paper." I believe my father yearned to write but it was, unfortunately, a journey never taken.

It was New Year's Eve, 1923, when Harold Chandler Hyatt and two of his older brothers, Fred and Norton, went to a dance in the northern Idaho sawmill town of St. Maries. He would turn fifteen in a couple of weeks and, as his brothers duly noted, "His hormones had recently kicked in." Harold spent the evening dancing with various girls and flirting on the side with the young lady playing the piano. At the stroke of midnight he was standing by the doorway above which the fabled sprig of holly

---

[2] *Ben Snipes, Northwest Cattle King,* Roscoe Sheller, Binfords & Mort, Portland, Oregon, Fourth Edition, 1966.

was attached. The band struck up "Auld Lang Syne" and the entire crowd started singing—except for the piano girl, who jumped up and yelled, "Stay away from the one under the holly! He's mine!" His brothers both swore that she kissed him so hard and so long that he turned blue, either from a lack of oxygen or the ardor and strength with which she pressed home her surprise attack. "We nearly lost him," they claimed. He survived, however, and from that point on it was said that he could always be found right by the holly at every New Year's celebration. The family started out teasing him as "the Holly-Boy" and "Holly-Bug." It soon got shortened to just plain "Holly," and it stuck. "Holly" wasn't much of a stretch from "Harold," and so it was that my father was known the rest of his life to his family and friends as Holly Hyatt.

Born in a cabin near Sagle, Idaho (across the Pend Oreille River, south of Sandpoint) in January of 1909, my father had attended school from time to time. He believed he had reached a level roughly equivalent to the sixth grade. From the age of twelve, he and his brother, Norton, who was two years older, had worked in the vast and wild timberlands of the Idaho panhandle and northeastern Washington. Their father, Lee, was a severe asthmatic, a condition that precluded full-time employment but which had no apparent effect on his ability to conceive. With a brood of fourteen children, nine girls and five boys born between 1894 and 1919, twelve years old seemed to be the age of majority when it came to helping support the greater family.

In 1919, seeking drier weather for Lee, the family moved to the desert near Kennewick, Washington. In order to make ends meet they had a five-acre plot on which they raised asparagus and my grandmother, Alice, took in laundry. The smaller girls helped with the laundry work while the older ones took housekeeping jobs and worked as waitresses. Roy, the oldest child, had married in Sandpoint in 1913 and, in 1918, had taken a job in Seattle as a fireman in the Ballard station. The three middle boys, Fred, Norton, and Holly, kept at what they had been raised with and that was cutting down trees or skidding logs in the area of the "shadowy St. Joe" River in northern Idaho. Ray, as the youngest male (born near Coeur d'Alene in 1916), enjoyed the luxury of living at home until he graduated from high school (the only one of the boys to do so) in Yakima in 1934 and went off to the University of Washington on a swimming scholarship.

In 1927, at the respective ages of eighteen and seventeen, Holly and my mother, Daisy, ran off to Republic, Washington, and married. Legend has it that Holly's mother had the marriage annulled since Daisy was not of legal age and had no "permission slip" from her parents. In 1928, at the more auspicious ages of nineteen and eighteen, they again eloped to Republic and married a second time. I learned of this "twice-married" business when I was about five years old. At that tender age and for a few years thereafter, I would proudly proclaim that both of my parents had each been married before and that I was the product of a second marriage. It just seemed to make things so much more exotic. When I was about ten, my mother got absolutely sick of explaining this second marriage business to the neighbor ladies— "no," she wasn't divorced, and "no," her first husband hadn't died or left her. She threatened me with my life if I didn't stop telling "that story" and so, more or less, I reverted back to the more drab tale that my parents were married for some time—about eleven years—before I was born.

Soon after their second marriage, Holly accepted a job offer from Jimmy Bronson, one of the owners of the Cascade Lumber Mill in Yakima, to be the company's union organizer. It was a fairly common practice in those days for companies to sponsor their own unions in order to keep out other, less savory organizations, such as the Industrial Workers of the World (the "IWW" or "Wobblies"). Over the next twelve years my father taught himself to type, took several night courses at the local business college, and became a great believer in the Dale Carnegie school of "How to Win Friends and Influence People." On the other side of the coin, the story is told that he never went to work during the first five years of his job without the accompaniment of a baseball bat or an ax handle. It was a fairly rough crowd, and things got tougher in the early years of the Depression of the 1930s. How you won friends and how you influenced people clearly meant different things to different folks, and things could change quickly depending on the circumstances of the moment.

In 1936, my parents had their first child, a son later described to me as a "blue baby" born with a leaking heart valve. He died soon after birth. I came along in November of 1939 and, since my mother could have no more children, I was raised as an "only" child, a human condition that was somehow socially contraindicated according to many of my parents' acquaintances. The only imperfection I ever discovered about being an "only child" in a family otherwise composed of adults was that I frequently called my father "Holly." My mother always remained "Mom" or "Mother," never "Daisy." But Dad, Father, Harold, and Holly were completely interchangeable to me. I was a teenager before I noticed that the other kids never called their dads "Fred" or "Bob," but by that time I was too far down the road to care.

By the time World War II started in December of 1941, my father was a very active member of the American Federation of Labor, "the AF of L." Boeing Aircraft was expanding rapidly to meet the production needs of the American military, so his union experience and his skill at managing people soon landed Holly a job in their personnel department as an assistant vice president. We spent the next four years sequestered, more or less, in the Boeing "projects," a large housing tract built to handle the rapidly expanding personnel needs of the company during World War II. Vibernum Court, our address, was just past Emil Sick's Rainier Brewery baseball stadium on Empire Way, located in the south end of Seattle, just north of Columbia City.

In 1943, during the war, my parents bought a forty-acre pasture outfit about three miles northwest of Prosser, Washington. The huge, old, dilapidated three-story house on it came complete with a rubble foundation from the 1890s and a full dirt-floored basement. Sporting a footprint about forty-two feet wide and some thirty-two feet long, it was known locally as "the old ghost house." Jack Andrews and his wife, Winifred, had lived there for a number of years, occupying only the kitchen and a small back porch on the first floor. It was clear they had participated heroically in some war effort since the rest of the first floor was entirely filled from floor to ceiling with bundles of newspapers and magazines. A narrow trail wending through the stacks allowed the Jacksons to navigate to the front door and access the stairs leading to the upper floors. Old white-bearded Andy had nailed some screen across the holes left when he had removed the windows from the second and third stories. That allowed him to raise a few turkeys on the second floor and pursue his hobby of training homing pigeons from the cote provided by floor number three. The four old car bodies stashed in the huge front yard weren't too noticeable since the weeds were so high you couldn't see anything but the tops of the cars anyway. All in all, to my way of thinking, the place was quite a find.

The property wasn't far from my mother's parents, Grandpa and Grandma Myers, who had established a dairy farm near Prosser in 1929. When World War II wrapped up, we left Seattle and moved into an old, unpainted, two-bedroom shack on my grandparents' place in the fall of 1945. My father took a job as a "field rep" for Carnation Milk Company so we might have enough cash over a period of years to remodel the monstrous old "ghost house," build new fences, and otherwise "feed the farm."

After some three years, my father and Grandpa Myers finished remodeling to the point where the old "ghost house" was fit to live in. They removed the third floor entirely and replaced all of the poultry-damaged wood. With that distasteful task accomplished, they built a large balcony and three bedrooms on the second floor. They spent weeks removing the old car bodies, and truckloads of newspapers. Mr. and Mrs. Trusley hauled in dozens of truckloads of hand-shoveled dirt they took from the tailings of the recently constructed Roza canal, and we planted a huge lawn. My mother came up with a nice first-floor plan that included a spacious entry hall with a spiral staircase, a large living room, an office, and a large kitchen with a small porch and an attached dining room. She even left room for a future bathroom and toilet. My mother found a huge oak front door with extravagant brass fittings at an old church being demolished about five miles away in Grandview. Finally, they installed a shingle roof and sided the house with twelve-inch cedar shakes. They painted it all white with a forest-green roof and trim. When we moved in during the winter of 1948, it was absolutely the most beautiful thing I had ever seen.

Just after we moved in, the seven dairy cows arrived. I was eight years old when I discovered the meaning of the word "Purgatory." At first, I couldn't believe that those creatures had to be milked every morning at 5 a.m. and every evening at 5 p.m. After a couple of months, however, it became clear that that was the routine and we (and "we" included me) were stuck with it. For my own part, I made it clear to my parents that I didn't need to consume any dairy products at all in order to grow up. Further, I pledged that if I were paying the bills, I would never once complain about the price of milk, butter or cheese—if only we could get rid of those accursed milk cows. My bargaining fell on deaf ears. Every trip to that old dairy barn was as painful to me as a crossing of the River Styx. They did leave, finally, but it took five long years.

In 1949, Holly purchased a dozen registered Aberdeen Angus heifers. They became the nucleus for what eventually grew to be a substantial beef herd. And those Angus, as soon as they had a calf, became a complete self-sustaining unit. They provided their own little four-legged milking machines—the calves—who absolutely enraptured themselves three or four times a day by consuming all of momma's milk. None of that 5 a.m. and 5 p.m. business here! I wasn't a slow learner, and it took me only about one whole day to realize which end of a cow I wanted to be close to, and that was being out there supervising, making sure that those Angus calves were nursing their mothers like they were supposed to.

For all its exterior comeliness, the house suffered from some omissions. There was no insulation, and the only heat source was the Monarch wood stove located in the kitchen. The basement floor was dirt, and the foundation, which doubled as the basement's walls, was the original rubble from the 1890s. During the irrigation season, which lasted from mid-April through mid-October, the basement would fill with about two feet of water. It was a great site for black widow spiders, garter snakes, and chirping water dogs, and it provided a fertile breeding ground for mosquitoes. As children, my cousins and I would dare each other to see who had the nerves of steel required to wade around in that dark old basement with the mud oozing up through our toes and around our ankles.

The domestic water source for the house was an outside well about twenty feet from the kitchen. It was set up with a huge old iron hand pump that had formerly seen many years of service watering my grandpa's horses. The hand pump meant there was no indoor plumbing, no hot or cold water taps, and no toilet. The outhouse was wisely located quite some distance from the back porch. You quickly learned not to drink a drop for a couple of hours before you went to bed.

For whatever reason, no one got around to installing the plumbing until 1952. Finally—no more outhouse! And no more baths in that accursed laundry tub! I clearly remember soaking up the luxury of my first hot shower. I swore that I would never again take a bath in a tub of any kind! But the mosquitoes were still there and air conditioning hadn't yet found its way to rural America by 1952, so I'd try to sleep during those sweltering summer nights with the sheet pulled up over my face to keep those miserable mosquitoes from carting me off.

In 1951 (the year before the plumbing arrived) Holly decided to visit Kitty Clover Farms, an Angus outfit located across the highway from Boy's Town near Omaha, Nebraska. He needed to buy a bull or two for his small but growing Angus herd. I was eleven years old and, aside from a few trips to nearby Oregon, it was my first time to travel out of state. I was especially excited when Dad put me behind the steering wheel and let me drive the first sixty miles or so from our farm to the next town, out across the rural roads of the Horse Heaven Hills from Prosser to Hermiston, Oregon. Forty or forty-five miles an hour suited Mom okay, but when I hit seventy once, she threw a regular fit and I had to slow it down after that. Dad let me drive again in Idaho and Montana and then in the Dakotas and Nebraska. It was the same on the way back when we came through Wyoming and Utah. By the time we got home, highway driving at forty-five or fifty miles-an-hour was old hat.

It was on our way east that we stopped overnight in Glendive, Montana. We arrived in the midst of a tremendous dust storm and, finding our way to the first motel we spotted, the Derrick Inn, we spent the night chinking the doors and windows with towels and clothing in an unsuccessful attempt to keep out the fine sand and the grit. When we awoke the next morning, my father unexpectedly announced that his mother's mother, "Grandmother Van Blaricom" (he didn't know her first name) had died here in Glendive back in the 1800s and he would like to find her grave.

Our effort was unsuccessful. There was no record of her. "But," the sexton said, "that's not unusual for the early settlers. Maybe her remains were among the bones found when the footings for the new high school were being excavated." The sexton also pointed out that it would have been helpful if my father had known Mrs. Van Blaricom's husband's name, but that probably didn't matter too much since there was no record of any Van Blaricom burials anyway.

The following morning, Mom and I were already in the car when Holly shut the trunk and got behind the wheel. That's when he went philosophical on us. "You know, we think we know everything about this country, but the truth is that the people who really knew this country are dead. The ones living now have either forgotten or never knew what was known by their own people before them." That said, he turned the key in the ignition of our 1950 Ford Club Coupe and pressed the starter button on the dashboard. We left Glendive and headed east toward Bismarck.

I knew my grandfather, Lee Hyatt, had died in Yakima in 1928, shortly after the family's arrival. I knew all thirteen of my Hyatt aunts and uncles and all of my forty-three Hyatt first cousins. But ancestry had never crossed my eleven-year-old mind until that moment when the Glendive sexton referred to my great-grandmother's missing bones. I later asked my father when and where his own father had been born. "He was born in 1858 in Raleigh,[3] North Carolina," he answered. Like me, my father had never met his paternal grandfather, but he knew his name was Newton Franklin Hyatt and that he had died "somewhere in Idaho" before my father was born. Newton Franklin's wife, Elizabeth, was a Vess who was buried "up around Spokane." He knew his mother, my Grandma Alice, was a Van Blaricom, that she had

---

[3] Citing "North Carolina" as Lee's birthplace was correct enough, but the ancestral Hyatt family never lived anywhere near Raleigh. They had been residents of western North Carolina from sometime between 1765 and 1770, when Edward Hyatt, Lee's great-great grandfather, migrated from Maryland as a teenager. [HVBG, pp. 22–24.]

been born in Long Prairie, Minnesota, in 1875[4], and that was it. He said I should ask her about her family. It was, after all, her mother whose grave we had just tried to find. Perhaps she could throw some light on the mystery and, my father surmised, "Maybe she will remember her mother's name."

Like the country surrounding Glendive, my father's abbreviated responses to my queries left me feeling as if I were living in a relatively desolate geography. Grandparents had to have parents. Who were they? Where did they come from? And why had they picked remote Glendive as a place in which to put down roots?

I must have been old enough that some of my father's "philosophical" thoughts were starting to germinate in my own mind. It was clear enough. We knew all about our immediate Hyatt family, yet we knew nothing about "the Hyatts," our ancestry, or our heritage. And now that I was getting interested in it, those people who knew the truth were, of course, either gone or going.

When I was thirteen, I purposefully sat down with my Grandmother Hyatt in Yakima and, pad in hand, performed my first "interview." I still have the complete notes:

> August, 1953. Grandma Alice. Born in Long Prairie, Minnesota, on Dec. 16, 1875. Moved to Glendive in 1882. Traveled in "immigrant cars" on the Northern Pacific railroad. Mother died there the first year. Her maiden name was Sarah Susan Johnson. (Note: What's a "maiden name"?) Moved from Glendive to Victor, Montana, in 1887. Their wagons were filled with their household goods and supplies, so they walked almost all of the way. Grandma thought it was about five hundred and fifty miles. Father's name was Levi Van Blaricom. He served in the Civil War with the 4th Minnesota Infantry. He was lame in one hip from the war. He died in Victor in 1902 at the age of 60.

---

[4] Following the death of their mother in Glendive in 1882, at least two of the younger children thereafter approximated their own birth years. Alice and her immediately older brother, Freddie (born 18 May 1875 but who believed himself to have been born in 1874), both somehow got it wrong by a year. Alice was, in fact, born in 1876, and she and Fred both lived out their lives believing themselves to be one year older than they really were. Unknown to them, their births had been registered in Long Prairie with the Todd County authorities and the records show Fred born 18 May 1875 and Alice's birth date as 16 December 1876.

Such a simple task, yet, obviously, the question had never been asked. "Sarah Susan" was the name of my father's grandmother. It was Sarah Susan's grave that remained undiscovered. And, as a bonus, I had learned that her husband's name was "Levi" and that he was buried in a cemetery in Victor, Montana. I now knew more than my father knew about his own ancestors.

I was surprised when my grandmother thanked me for asking the questions about her family. She then gave me an old, worn-out book entitled *History of the Fourth Regiment Minnesota Infantry Volunteers* and said, "This book tells of my father and his brothers." To my consternation, children had scribbled in pencil throughout the book but, while several pages were torn, the text was all there and it was readable. That interview and my grandmother's gift of the book provided the beginning of my lifelong interest in genealogy.

I set out after the Hyatt family in 1954 and have worked on them and their collateral lines since then. In 1975, I got seriously interested in my grandmother's Van Blaricom family. A year later my father shared with me his last bit of philosophy. As was his custom, the comments came from out of the blue. "You know," he said, "the Japanese are going to leave us in the dust."

"What do you mean?" I asked.

"Well," he responded, "in Japan the grandparents essentially raise the children. Here, the grandparents now live away from the extended family. Each generation has to experience the same mistakes made by the previous generation. We expend a lot of time and effort continually re-inventing the wheel. The Japanese don't have to do that. That generation overlap gives them an understanding of their family histories and life experiences we don't have. We're missing the boat."

Three years later my father died.

I had long known about the two memoirs stored in my mother's keepsake trunk. They had been written by two of Grandmother Alice's brothers, Stephen Norton ("Nort" or "Norton") Van Blaricom and Frederick Alfred ("Fred") Van Blaricom. My mother passed away in 1981 and, upon her death, I fell heir to her treasured trunk. A few months later I browsed the two Van Blaricom manuscripts and discovered that, while they provided some information about the family, they really focused on the personal lives and adventures of the brothers as children and young men in Glendive and Dawson County between 1882 and 1900. I took notes pertinent to the greater family and put the manuscripts back in the trunk.

In 1990, while working on the Van Blaricom genealogy, I decided to go on a research trip to Minnesota. On the way, I would spend a couple of days in Glendive to see if I could have any better luck than my father had in 1951 in finding Sarah Susan (Johnson) Van Blaricom's grave. I took a copy of the brothers' manuscripts with me.

I walked into the Glendive Public Library, where Gail Nagle, the chief librarian, was very helpful and showed me the library's excellent collection of Montana history, her thoughtful accumulation of local "old-timers'" personal memoirs, and the facility's superb collection of both of Glendive's early newspapers, the *Glendive Times* and the *Glendive Independent*. However, the cemetery's early burial records were incomplete, and I had no better luck than my father in finding the gravesite of his grandmother. The location of Sarah Susan Van Blaricom's grave remained a mystery.

I inquired if there were any substantive histories of the original Big Horn and Dawson counties. Gail conceded there was, in fact, no "History of Dawson County" per se. The old vanity book titled *An Illustrated History of the Yellowstone Valley* gave some important details but was primarily a recitation of biographies of early residents who had the resources to pay for their own articles. There were the old, massive histories of Montana by Leeson, Stout, Miller, and others. There was the modern *Montana, A History of Two Centuries* by Malone, Roeder, and Lang. Mark Brown's excellent *The Plainsmen of the Yellowstone* covered the history of the entire Yellowstone River basin and, of necessity, concentrated on the highlights of the greater area, not the specifics of the original Dawson County.

Gail told me of two voluminous books, *Our Times, Our Lives* and *Courage Enough,* that recounted the family histories of lower Yellowstone River residents and told of many of the early immigrants of the area. I scrounged around and found and bought a copy of each. No mention of any Van Blaricoms there. She also referred me to Marie MacDonald's *Glendive, The History of a Montana Town,* a well-written booklet of excellent content that was, however, broad of scope and short of pages.

I decided to try the old newspapers. The Stephen and Fred memoirs, although they disagreed as to the exact date, placed the death of their mother in the fall of 1882. I started with the *Glendive Times* in August of 1882 and within an hour or so, in the edition of Thursday, September 28, 1882, I found her: "On Monday morning the wife of Levi Van Blaricon *[sic]* died of typhoid fever. This is a sad case as she leaves a family of 9 or 10 children." That placed her death on Monday, September 25, 1882. At last I knew when and where and how Sarah Susan had died. Now, where was she buried?

A small article in the *Glendive Times* printed on Thursday, August 17, 1882, gave me the first clue: "Mr. Frank Johnson's little two-year-old boy was buried last Saturday in the new cemetery."[5] Everyone I had spoken to had said there was only one cemetery in early Glendive, the one up on the hill now known as the Dawson County Cemetery. But, if there was a "new" cemetery in August 1882, that meant there was an "old" cemetery, too. I started going back through earlier editions of the weekly paper.

An article in the *Glendive Times* dated Thursday, June 15, 1882, solved the cemetery problem: "On behalf of the owners of the property in Blocks 174 and 175 of the town of Glendive, the undersigned hereby gives notice that no more burials will be permitted in said Blocks. Signed, N. E. Lawrence, Agent."[6]

Blocks 174 and 175 lie in what was the southeast end of the original townsite and are today bounded by Nowlan and Taylor, and Hughes and Mann.[7] Now covered by houses, there is no evidence

[5] The child referenced in the *Glendive Times* article was little Harry Johnson, the son of Frank Johnson and his wife, Carrie (Tuttle) Johnson. Frank Johnson was the brother of Sarah Susan (Johnson) Van Blaricom. The article described how Harry had died of "mountain fever" and, curiously, how his life "had been sustained by artificial means" over the past several days.

[6] N. E. Lawrence was Nelson E. Lawrence, the man erroneously identified by Dr. Lorman L. Hoopes as "N. C. Lawrence" who, in 1881, became the first postmaster of Glendive. Lawrence was also the original Glendive land agent for both the Northern Pacific Railroad and the Yellowstone Land and Colonization Company (that group formed by Colonel Lewis Merrill of the U.S. 7th Cavalry which platted the original townsite). [TLW, p. 197. NFM, p. 120.]

[7] *The Last Leaf,* Volume III-2. Also see the *Ranger Review,* 20 August 1992.

that a cemetery ever existed—except for the lady I met at city hall whose home was on the site and, upon learning of the existence of the "old" cemetery, insisted she had "always heard noises" beneath her house. She told how her alarm clock would often be mysteriously turned on or off during the middle of the night. Now she wasn't sure that she would ever return to the house.

With sexton Bruce Raymond's help, the issue of the old cemetery was soon put to rest. As Bruce pointed out, there is an "old" section of the Dawson County Cemetery that does contain a few graves whose markers have dates preceding June 15, 1882. Clearly, somewhere along the line the graves from Lots 174 and 175 had been moved to the "new" cemetery.

A few days later, in *The Independent Voice of Eastern Montana* dated November 14, 1935, I found mention of another, even older cemetery. It was in an article written by Glendive's first resident historian, Grace Marron Gilmore: "The first cemetery in Glendive was located on a little hill back of the Hatterscheid residence,[8] but only a few soldiers and railroad graders were buried there temporarily. The bodies were later shipped east."

This article omitted any mention of the cemetery located in Blocks 174 and 175. Clearly, there had been three cemeteries in use in early Glendive: the temporary affair for "soldiers and railroad graders" located "on a little hill back of the Hatterscheid residence"; the one on Lots 174 and 175 after the town was platted by Lewis Merrill late in 1880; and, finally, a third, the "present beautiful cemetery, on the hill overlooking our city" which went into service on or about June 15, 1882, when N. E. Lawrence precluded any future burials in Lots 174 and 175.

In the process of reviewing the old newspapers, I found many references to my family: Frank Perry and his Blue Jacket Coal Mine, Jay Orr Woods and his furniture store and taxidermy shop, which also sold polished buffalo horns, and Sheriff Henry Tuttle and

---

[8] The residence described was that of "Doc" Hatterscheid who, in 1935, lived at 501 S. Nowlan Avenue. That address was on the north corner of the block bounded by Barry Street, Taylor Avenue, Hughes Street, and Nowlan Avenue. Dr. Charles Albert Hatterscheid (1877–1940) was the state veterinarian for Dawson County. The hill described is in the block immediately to the southeast. That located the first cemetery between Barry, Rosser Avenue, Hughes, and Taylor. It was thus adjacent to and immediately southeast of the second cemetery that was later located on Lots 174 and 175 (and included the block on which the Hatterscheid residence was later situated). [Interview with John Steffen, 15 January 2006. See Map 1 on the following page for the locations of the three Glendive cemeteries.]

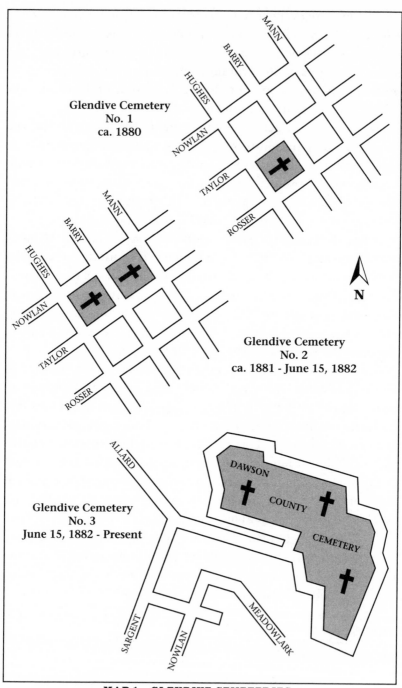

MAP 1—GLENDIVE CEMETERIES

his 1885 prohibition against men wearing sidearms when coming into town. There was an article recounting that Frank Johnson chased a few cows and was a Dawson County deputy sheriff as well. The "County Commissioner's Notes" in the *Glendive Times* contained repeated references to large Dawson County checks being issued to my great-great-grandmother, Mariah Scribner,[9] for the "care of the poor." The newspaper also reported the issuance of county checks to my great-grandfather, Levi Van Blaricom, for escorting prisoners to the jail in Miles City, for nursing wounded prisoners in the Dawson County Jail, for digging graves, and for cleaning flues at the jail and at the school. He got a county check for digging the hole for the septic tank for the first Dawson County Courthouse built in 1883 by general contractor W. S. Hurst.[10] The children's names from these families were repeatedly published in the newspapers as being "in attendance" at the Glendive public school and for being on the school's honor roll. But there was no mention of these people in *Our Times, Our Lives* or *Courage Enough*. Aside from the old newspapers and Stephen and Fred's manuscripts, they were nowhere else to be found.

A number of early Dawson County settlers' surnames were readily traceable: Harpster, Dion, Haskell, Herrick, Douglas, Mead, Jordan, Krug, O'Brien, Obergfell, Lovering, Cheney, and others. These names fell into three basic groups: First, the individuals of means in the town or the county who paid or who had a descendant who paid to have biographies written about them. These people could be found in the "vanity" books such as the *Illustrated History of the Yellowstone Valley*. Second, the early settlers whose names were given recognition because their families continued to live in the lower Yellowstone Valley or other "progeny" counties of the original Dawson County when various local societies published their centennial or other anniversary

---

9 Frank Perry was married to Mary Jane Johnson, Sarah Susan's sister. Jay Orr Woods was married to another of Sarah Susan's sisters, Maud Martha ("May" or "Muz") Johnson. Frank Johnson was Sarah Susan's brother. Dawson County Sheriff Henry ("Hank") Tuttle was Frank Johnson's brother-in-law. (Carrie Tuttle Johnson, Frank's wife, was Hank's sister.) Mariah Janette (Beardsley) (Johnson) Scribner was the Johnson siblings' mother.

10 GT, 30 June 1883: "County Commisioners let the contract for the courthouse to W. S. Hurst of the Bank of Glendive for $19,200. It is to be completed by October 1st [1883]." William S. Hurst was the father of Joe Hurst, who was hanged in Glendive in 1900 for the murder of Dawson County Sheriff Dominic Cavanaugh. [See THWT for that story.]

books—*Courage Enough, Footprints in the Valley, Roosevelt County's Treasured Years, Our Times, Our Lives,* and so on. Finally, there were a very small number of individuals named in the anniversary books only because someone affiliated with that particular publication somehow knew of them and had taken the time to research them. Thus it was that an early settler had to be associated with one of three conditions in order to be documented and thereby be given recognition as "an early settler": money, an inert descendancy, or luck. My ancestors had fallen into none of those categories.

Many names referenced in both of my great-uncles' manuscripts were also mentioned in the old newspaper accounts but couldn't be found elsewhere. Stephen and Fred had frequently spelled the names incorrectly, but with a little research I discovered that the "Surwines" were the Sirrine family; the "Bicycle Brothers" were the Biseigel brothers of Dickinson, Dakota Territory; Tom "Cushing" was Tom Courchene; and Bill "Break" was William Brake—and so the list of errata went. Other colorful characters in the manuscripts and the newspapers, such as Vic Smith, "Doc" Zahl, Eben Slawson, George Grant, Henry ("Hank") Tuttle, Gilman R. ("Bill") Norris, Jimmy Crain, and many others had played significant roles in the early development of old Dawson County but were either missing or given only passing mention in other published sources.

Perhaps, with a little research to correct the phonetically misspelled names, the two manuscripts written by Stephen and Fred Van Blaricom could make significant contributions to the history of the original Dawson County. I promptly donated a copy of each of the manuscripts to the Glendive library so Gail Nagle could add them to her collection of local memoirs. Maybe some researcher, some day, would find them useful. In the meantime, I was beginning to get interested in the history of the place. Jimmy Crain was a real character. The tombstone for Johnny Burns' young son, Charlie, was one of the most interesting and moving markers I'd ever seen. Andrew "Glendive" Smith was a quiet, unassuming man who had lived an exciting life as an army courier and mail carrier—yet no one recalled who he was. I started to build files on these men and their families. As with many undertakings, the solution to one question led to two more questions, and so I kept on collecting data.

Ten years later, several storage boxes of Dawsonia had accumulated and I was gaining some appreciation of the early settlement of northeastern Montana. I was also beginning to feel as if I knew many of the characters in the play. Finally, partially driven by the fact that eastern Montana, the fabled "Big Open" and, more specifically, the greater "old" Dawson County, had never had the story of its early settlement recounted in any singular cohesive format, I decided to present the results of my research in book form.

It quickly became clear that the story of the original Dawson County could not be told without understanding developments in Fort Buford, the Little Missouri River country, and "old" Custer (Big Horn) County. Events frequently occurred in those locales and others that directly influenced what went on in Dawson County. The contents of this book have, therefore, been expanded to include enough history and explanation of pertinent events that occurred immediately outside Dawson County so the reader can understand the "cause and effect" relationship to events occuring inside the county's defined political boundaries. As will be seen, "old" Dawson County was not an island unto itself.

This book has been purely a labor of love. I make no claim to being a professionally trained historian or writer. History is, of necessity, a somewhat subjective undertaking. Consequently, footnotes, author's notes, and a complete bibliography have been provided for three purposes: first, to give credit where credit is due; second, to note the sources of information that led to a given conclusion, and, finally, to provide further illumination of a subject not conveniently includable in the text. I would be pleased to receive notice of whatever errors might be discovered so they might be corrected in any future printings. I hope the book has been presented in a fashion that is, on the one hand, interesting to the lay reader and casual observer of the lower Yellowstone River country and, on the other hand, useful to the more serious historian.

This book is dedicated to the memory of Sarah Susan (Johnson) Van Blaricom and the other forgotten early settlers of northeastern Montana Territory. I am sure my father, Holly, would have assessed the situation this way: "Our predecessors knew all about this lower Yellowstone country and the people who settled it. Today, however, we know little of the common people who came early to this place or of the events that occurred here...for we have forgotten, misinterpreted or ignored that which was known."

I believe Stephen Norton Van Blaricom would be pleased that his observations have been used as the platform from which to resurrect knowledge of the activities and personalities of the early settlers of northeastern Montana.

It will never be known how Sarah Susan would have felt about this work. She was, I believe, a very private person who likely adhered to the social mores of her time. In that sense, the book probably tells far too many personal details about her and her family. I am sure she would be pleased, however, by the tombstone placed atop the hill of the "new" Dawson County Cemetery. The precise location of her burial was never discovered. Relying on the memoirs of her two sons, and with the gracious cooperation of the Dawson County Cemetery and sexton Bruce Raymond, a memorial marker was placed there in 1991. Now, at least, her existence can be recognized from time to time by her descendants and by the local folks who venture to the cemetery. The epitaph makes no claim to the fact that Sarah Susan gave birth to the second child born in Glendive proper, nor does it state that hers was almost certainly the first grave of a woman in the "new" cemetery on the hill.

The wording on the tombstone is simple. Her descendants believe that she was not an ostentatious woman and would have wanted it that way.

Sarah Susan Johnson

Wife of Levi Van Blaricom

Born   Died

Dec. 5, 1849   Sept. 25, 1882

Amherst   Glendive

Ohio   Montana

A Special Thank You

SPECIAL THANKS MUST BE GIVEN TO JOHN STEFFEN of Glendive for his unswerving and dedicated on-site research delivered upon request over a decade of involvement with this project. The results of his well-documented and meticulous labors were always most appreciated. The assistance of Charlene Porsild and the staff at the library of the Montana Historical Society, and especially the aid of research librarian Brian Shovers, was always willingly and professionally given. Four others—Pat Darling of Dillon, Montana; Ada Powell of Hamilton, Montana; May Bopp of Cogswell, North Dakota; and Jordan Burkart of Los Angeles—gave generously of their time and research regarding Deputy U.S. Marshal Alex Ayotte, Dawson County Sheriff Henry Tuttle, ranchman John Burns, and pioneer Mary ("May") (McDonald) Jordan and their respective families.

Various members of the greater Van Blaricom family provided oral histories and documents. Six of them provided particularly useful information. Ann (Van Blaricom) Falor, Norton and Maud's youngest child, gave generously of her time in a series of interviews in Akron, Ohio, in 1993 and 1994; she also produced all of the newspaper clippings regarding Stephen Norton Van Blaricom as well as newpaper articles he had written. Ann's daughter, Elizabeth (Falor) Carducci of Auburn, California, provided valuable information and news clippings regarding her grandmother, Stephen Norton's wife, Maud (Griselle) Van Blaricom, and Maud's brother, Paul Hunt Griselle. Norton's grandson, David Van Blaricom, of Charlotte, North Carolina, was in possession of Norton's voluminous diaries (1914–1945) and he laboriously copied and shared these valuable reference materials. Emma (Van Blaricom) Freeze, Norton's niece of Hamilton, Montana, proved a veritable fount of stories regarding the family, and she provided many newspaper clippings regarding the family as well as letters and other memorabilia. Emma's sister, Merle (Van Blaricom) O'Brien of West Seattle, had devotedly kept and then shared all three of her father Fred's memoirs (handwritten on Red Ryder school tablets in the early 1940s) which helped fill many of the gaps in Norton's story. Fred's son, Jim Van Blaricom of Lake Mary Ronan, Montana, was able to straighten out much of the confusion regarding the large Van Blaricom family due to his intimate knowledge of the whereabouts and fate of Norton's siblings.

Rose Wyman and Sylvia Mickelson, both of Glendive, provided valuable research materials and direction regarding original settlers of the lower Yellowstone River valley. The staff at the Dawson County Courthouse and the staff at Glendive City Hall were especially cooperative and helpful in that regard as well. Ardelle Adams, Dawson County Clerk of the Court, gave her support and guidance and allowed Karen and me to conduct dozens of hours of research in the court records of "Old" Dawson County. Gail Nagle and the Glendive Public Library staff graciously tolerated my presence for days as I reviewed the newspaper collection and scoured the contents of the library's excellent Montana Room. Gail also deserves kudos for her impressive collection of local memoirs. The Frontier Gateway Museum, under the direction of Louise Cross, has also assembled a significant and useful collection of photographs, memorabilia, and other items of historical importance. Thank you to Fayette Miller, assistant curator of the museum, for her several hours of assistance helping us sort through the voluminous documents and photographs stored there. Sexton Bruce Raymond was of great assistance in resolving the mystery of whether or not the remains interred in the two earlier cemeteries in Glendive had been moved to the present Dawson County Cemetery.

Special thanks to Elizabeth Edwards of Seattle, whose review and comments on the first draft of this book were most helpful and to Maria Fischer Jaime, whose expertise in computers helped solve innumerable formatting and other technical problems. The true tests of kinship and friendship were put to my cousin, Bruce Craven, my granddaughter, Audre Hyatt, and my friend, Ron Foster, all of whom accepted the trying and often monotonous task of proofreading.

Of course, none of this could ever have come to fruition without the assistance and direction of the professionals. Thank you, Kathy Springmeyer, for the hours spent on this project over the last two years and for the assistance of her professional staff at Sweetgrass Books, who handled so well all of the technical aspects of maps (Eric Hanson), design and production (Shirley Machonis), and permissions and other assistance (Theresa Rush). And to editors Beverly Magley and Jessica Solberg, a special "Thank You" to both for your guidance, your command of the English language, and your patience in trying to get some of it to "rub off" on me.

Finally, Karen Hyatt deserves special recognition. Over the past thirteen years she has served as a special and most competent research assistant, editor, sounding board, and critic. She has also been an amazingly tolerant wife and partner. Without her organizational skills and her determination, this book would never have been completed.

—Norman Hyatt, 2009

Introduction

MONTANA TERRITORY CAME INTO BEING WITH THE SIGNATURE of President Abraham Lincoln on May 26, 1864. Big Horn County, essentially the eastern third of Montana Territory, was created when the original nine counties of the territory were described by the territorial legislature on February 2, 1865.

On January 15, 1869, the legislature divided Big Horn County by approving an east–west line that followed the 47th Parallel. The southern half retained the "Big Horn" designation; the northern was given the name "Dawson." These two vast counties, covering some 61,000 square miles, constituted the country that Dr. Lorman Hoopes of Miles City aptly described as "This Last West." The northern half of that immense triangle of land between the Missouri, the Yellowstone, and the Musselshell rivers—also known as "The Big Open"; the vast area extending north from the Missouri River to Canada and east from the Milk River to the Dakota border; and, finally, the "Bad Lands" lying east of the Yellowstone and north of the mouth of O'Fallon Creek to the Montana–Dakota boundary line were all found within old Dawson County.

Old Dawson was 25,000 square miles of tough, dry country. It was, however, almost evenly bisected on a west–east line by the Missouri River. The Yellowstone River also flowed in a northeasterly direction from the southwest corner of the county to the confluence with the Missouri near Fort Union and the Dakota border. Both of these lifelines originated hundreds of miles away in the Rocky Mountains and for hundreds of years they had sheltered the Native American people and maintained the vast inventory of buffalo, elk, deer, and antelope that fed, clothed, and housed them. In 1805 and 1806, the two rivers became the highways for Lewis and Clark and the fur traders who followed. In 1860, the first two steamboats made it to Fort Benton, and, thereafter, small clusters of woodcutters established themselves along the upper Missouri west of Fort Union. Finally, following

Custer's defeat in 1876 and the Great Sioux War of 1876–1877, the Missouri and the Yellowstone valleys provided the natural shelter and the materials for the homesites of the first white settlers.

Notorious for its alkaline water away from the rivers, old Dawson County could be "hot as Hades" in the summer and subject to bitter Arctic conditions in the winter. Hail the size of grapefruit could (and did) kill man and beast alike, and sudden lightning storms took the lives of many a cowboy who found himself out on the unprotected prairie. Late frosts and unpredictable weather could devastate a crop or a garden, and fortunes were made and lost by the sudden arrival of either a frigid, howling blizzard or a warming chinook.

It took a hardy breed of men, women, and children to put down the first roots of settlement in such a harsh and unforgiving landscape. Many of their stories, like that of Sarah Susan, Stephen Norton Van Blaricom's mother, have been undeservedly lost or forgotten. Hopefully, this book will place them, for good or for bad, into the written history of old Dawson County. These people were, after all, the "first settlers" and, of necessity, each and every one of them was a participant in a singular and uncommon journey.

STEPHEN NORTON VAN BLARICOM

An Uncommon Journey is based on the personal correspondence, two memoirs, and various newspaper articles written by Stephen Norton Van Blaricom. That core of knowledge was supplemented by interviews with members of two generations of his family, data gathered from many "first settler" family descendants, as well as newspaper and other articles published about or during that era.

"How did he spell his name?" I asked his youngest daughter, Ann Falor, in a 1994 interview. "S-t-e-v-e-n? S-t-e-p-h-e-n? S-t-e-p-h-a-n?"

"I don't know that he really knew how to spell it himself," she responded. "If he did, he never told anyone. He always delighted in people guessing at it. To me, of course, he was always 'Papa' and to my children he was always 'Grandpa Norton.' To his friends he was 'Van' or 'Norton' or 'Stephen Norton.' If he wrote something, however, he always signed it 'S. N. Van Blaricom,' so I suppose for your purposes 'Stephen Norton' or just plain 'Norton' would work fine."[11]

Born in Minnesota in 1869, Stephen Norton Van Blaricom was thirteen years old when his mother died in Glendive in the late summer of 1882. As the eldest of nine children, he soon took employment with Hank Ward's cattle outfit, the **101,** whose range was on the east side of the Yellowstone between Cottonwood Creek and the Missouri River. Over the next six years he worked as a young cowhand for the **101** and for Pierre Wibaux at his **W** (W–Bar) and, on the west side of the Yellowstone, for E. P. Lovejoy and his **Diamond L** on Sevenmile Creek and the Redwater River, and for Johnny Burns at his **JB** ranch on Burns Creek.[12] He took odd jobs in Glendive whenever he was temporarily laid off from one of the ranches. In the spring of 1888, about the time he turned nineteen, he went to work for the Northern Pacific (NP) as a car man, a brakeman, a fireman and, finally, he worked his way up through the ranks to become a train driver or engineer. Later, about 1898, he became the hostler[13] in charge of the engines and rolling stock coming in and out of Glendive.

During his days as an engineer, around 1896, Norton met an attractive young telegrapher who worked at the NP station in Forsyth. Born and raised in Ohio, Maud Griselle was a graduate of the Philadelphia Academy of Fine Arts. Although raised a

[11] Interview with Ann (Van Blaricom) Falor, 4 February 1994. Stephen Norton Van Blaricom was a man of many names. To his brothers and sisters, he was "Stephen" or "Norton." He invariably signed his correspondence "S. N. Van Blaricom." He penned his memoir as "Stephen Norton Van Blaricom." To his immediate family—his wife, in-laws, children, and grandchildren—he went only by the name "Norton." Likewise, prior to 1900, there are mentions of him in the Forsyth newspaper as "Nort" and "Norton" Van Blaricom. As he grew older, his acquaintances in the Ohio farming community called him "Mr. Van." Both before and after his death, his wife, Maud, was routinely referenced in newspaper articles as "Mrs. S. N. Van Blaricom." For purposes of consistency, his full name of "Stephen Norton" or the familial "Norton" has been used throughout this text.

[12] The **"Diamond L"** reference came from page 6 of the original handwritten Fred Van Blaricom memoirs: "My oldest brother [Norton] was a cowboy riding the range for the Box L outfit..." Others, including the *Montana State Brands Directory,* described the brand as the "Diamond L." Joe Widmyer wrote that "E. P. Lovejoy is of the Diamond L Brand" (GI, 15 October 1887) and Norton specifically mentioned E. P. Lovejoy in his article published by the *Dawson County Review,* 15 February 1923. The other ranches described were mentioned or referenced by Norton in his memoir.

[13] The hostler took charge of a locomotive after a run and was responsible for its maintenance. He was charged with keeping an engine in constant use, mechanically ready, and physically located for its next run. He was also charged with servicing, maintaining, and re-shuffling the rolling stock of the railroad. In general, a hostler's job was to keep the trains serviced and moving. [TID, p. 1094.]

Presbyterian, she also attended, in deference to her maternal grandfather, the weekly meetings of the Society of Friends, the Quakers. Maud's mother had been a telegraph operator during the Civil War and she taught Maud and her brother Morse code as a childhood hobby, a "secret" way of communicating between themselves in a fashion their elementary school classmates couldn't understand. Over the years, their proficiency grew and eventually they could tap out lengthy and detailed messages to each other. Maud started working as a telegrapher on April 19, 1891, in the remote whistle-stop of Rosebud, Montana. In 1898, the Northern Pacific transferred her to their Glendive station. She and Norton became re-acquainted and romance bloomed.

Eighteen years in Glendive proved to be enough of the adventurous life for Norton. In March of 1900, both he and Maud gave notice to the Northern Pacific and returned to her previous home near Salem, Ohio. There they were married on April 5, 1900, the day after Norton's thirty-first birthday. He immediately went to work as a master mechanic for the McKeefrey Ironworks in nearby Leetonia, a position he held for a number of years. In 1903, they purchased a small farm not far from Maud's parents, and there they lived out their lives.

Norton's circumstances changed remarkably following his wedding. He and Maud joined the Presbyterian Church. The pace of his life slowed and he was able to devote time to his many academic and social interests. He first joined the local chapter of the Sons of Veterans and the Oddfellows Lodge. He was a charter member and, later, master of his Perry Township Grange. He then helped organize the Columbiana County Farm Bureau and became its first president. Always interested in the welfare of children, he was a member of the county visiting board to see if there were children or other residents of the area going without adequate food or clothing. He became the presiding judge of the township's voting precinct and, for the last twenty-six years of his life, took an active role in the township's election affairs. Delivering addresses to his fellow Farm Bureau members and Grangers in Columbiana County, he soon developed a reputation as a good public speaker. In 1917 and 1918 he was given a federal appointment to help organize, under the auspices of Ohio State

University, the County Extension Agencies for the state of Ohio. After a while he became a featured speaker on various subjects: soil conservation, his own story of being a pioneer child, ethics, history, astronomy, and paleontology.

"Astronomy?" one asks. "Paleontology?"

As a young man in Dawson County, Norton had become fascinated with the night skies while riding "nighthawk" for some of the ranches. Through the years he had read what he could on the subject, but it wasn't until around 1912 that he met some unnamed associate, an astronomer from Carnegie Tech in Pittsburgh, and his expertise blossomed. The man had come to visit Norton at his home for a day or two. The two men hit it off and the visit extended more than two weeks. Amazed by Norton's voracious appetite for the subject, the man gave him access to fairly technical treatises on the subject and, perhaps more important, made available for his use a large telescope on the university campus.

This relationship continued for many years. "My father would spend many weekends at the university," his daughter, Ann Falor, reported. "He would often take the train to Pittsburgh on Friday night and return on Sunday evening." Around 1926, Norton wrote, "From this man I got the start I had wanted for many years. While I lay no claim to being an astronomer in a mathematical sense, I am not ashamed of my knowledge of the geography of the heavens. My general knowledge has become sufficient that when I read what the scientists have to say I know what they are talking about."

It was during one of Norton's trips to visit his friend at the university that he wandered into the paleontology department. He noticed a large "joint bone" and commented to one of the department's staff that he had seen a specimen of that bone before. The exchange between the two men lasted another twenty years. Norton was fascinated by the history of the fossilized creatures, and the staff at the university was intrigued by his many encounters "in the wilds" of Dawson County with the counterparts of so many of their specimens. Where had he seen that specimen before? Could he find the location again? He would never claim that his skills in paleontology developed to a point where they could compete with his interest or proficiency in astronomy. "But," he claimed, "I came to know a great deal about these ancient reptiles...where and how they lived, the different species and where, when, how, and why they came to extinction."

Norton had some of the writer in him and he penned a few articles and letters that various newspaper editors saw fit to print.[14] After he arrived in Ohio, he began a diary in which he made frequent entries until his death in 1945.[15] He was a faithful correspondent and regularly wrote to his siblings, especially his brother, Fred, in Victor, Montana, and he kept in touch with old friends in Glendive. Sometime around 1926, he wrote a brief autobiography for the Salem News. That document served as the basis for his larger memoir written in 1940. In between those activities he penned his "speeches and talks," studied English, honed his spelling, polished his vocabulary, and researched his "pet" subjects of government, soil conservation, astronomy, and paleontology.[16] It was on April 12, 1939, that he addressed the Ohio State Senate Committee on Agriculture, "and," he proudly noted in his diary of that date, "I was complimented on my remarks by the Chairman of the Committee."

Norton was blessed with another worthy characteristic: he remembered things—people and events—and he wrote them down. Norton's remarkable memoir has served well as the foundation for this book. His life was truly *An Uncommon Journey*. In his various writings (the diary, the two versions of his memoir, his personal correspondence, and newspaper articles) and in newspaper articles written about him were recorded the names of people and descriptions of personalities and events long forgotten.

Using Norton Van Blaricom's forty-three-page memoir[17] as the structural vehicle, An Uncommon Journey expands upon his original telling and delves into the personalities and events

---

14 See the *Dawson County Review*, 15 February 1923. Also see the *Salem News* column, Salem, Ohio, undated but about 1926.

15 The diary is in the possession of Stephen Norton Van Blaricom's grandson, David N. Van Blaricom.

16 The information contained in this and the five preceding paragraphs was the product of an interview with Ann Falor, 4 February 1994.

17 The more expansive 1940 memoir incorporated the 1926 version. All of the page numbers referenced as "SNVB" coincide to the 1940 version of the memoir on file in the Glendive Public Library.

broached by that manuscript, his other writings, as well as pertinent newspaper articles and other contemporary sources. Please note that throughout the text, the phrase "the present day" or the words "today" or "modern" refer to the era of 1926 through 1940, the years in which Norton wrote the two versions of his memoir.[18]

Although the story that follows is written in the first person, the words are not exclusively those of Stephen Norton Van Blaricom. It simply became too detrimental to the flow of the text to bounce back and forth between first person quotes and third person narratives. For the sake of continuity, care has been taken to tell the story in the style Norton had written it (or would have had he related that particular story). Some readers might complain that such an approach makes the book one of historical fiction. In order to overcome that deficiency, special attention has been given in the footnotes and author's notes to attribute to the various sources the facts as they have been stated. A list of abbreviations identifying the sources of the information follows this preface and introduction. A complete bibliography follows the appendices.

---

[18] Copies of the two SNVB manuscripts (1926 and 1940) are in the author's possession as well as in the possession of other Van Blaricom family members. One of the later versions of the manuscript is in the Montana collection of the Glendive library. Stephen Norton Van Blaricom kept a diary the last thirty-one years of his life (1914–1945). His entry for Saturday, March 2, 1940, read: "I finished my memoirs today. Mr. Lower (a local land surveyor) and Miss Guy are editing and typing them for me." [Diary of S. N. Van Blaricom, 1914–1945.]

List of Abbreviations Used in Footnotes and Text

Key to the Bibliography:
(1) Unpublished Materials. (2) Published Materials.
(3) Newspapers. (4) Articles. (5) Books.

ABTW	*As Big as the West* (5)
AHJ	*Audubon and His Journals* (5)
AIR	*As I Remember* (2 volumes) (5)
ANAI	*Atlas of the North American Indian* (5)
AVBH	Interviews with Alice Janette (Van Blaricom) Hyatt (1)
AWY	*The American West Year by Year* (5)
B&S	*Boots and Saddles* (5)
BAC	*Bozeman Avant–Courier* (3)
BG	*Billings Gazette* (3)
BHND	*A Brief History of North Dakota* (5)
BLC	*Bad Lands Cowboy* (3)
BMH	*Bury My Heart at Wounded Knee* (5)
BSGSW	*Battles and Skirmishes of the Great Sioux War* (5)
BT	*Bismarck Times* (3)
BTrls	*Bitterroot Trails, Vol. I* (5)
CB	*Circle Banner* (3)
CE	*Courage Enough* (5)
CEnc	*Compton's Encyclopedia, 1972* (5)
CGL	*Crossing the Gender Line* (4)
CMM	*The Career of the Marquis de Mores* (2)
COM	*The Conquest of the Missouri* (5)
CPEnc	*Compton's Pictured Encyclopedia, 1945* (5)
CVR	*Cashmere Valley Record* (3)
CY	*Chronicles of the Yellowstone* (5)
CYRC	*A Chronological Record of Events at the Missouri...* (2)
DCR	*Dawson County Review* (3)
DCR&YM	*Dawson County Review and Yellowstone Monitor* (3)
DFIT	*Five Indian Tribes of the Upper Missouri* (5)
DJ	*50 Years in the Saddle* (5)

DT	*The Dig Tree* (5)
EBDC	*Empty Boots–Dusty Corrals* (2)
FBMF	*Fort Buford and the Military Frontier on the Northern Plains* (2)
FBWIP	*Fort Benton: World's Innermost Port* (5)
FIV	*Footprints in the Valley* (5)
FLP	"O.S.B. Eli Washington John Lindesmith: Fort Keogh's Chaplain in Buckskin" (4)
FTAW	*The Fur Trade of the American West* (5)
FVBM	Frederick Alfred Van Blaricom manuscripts (1)
GARDB	"Grand Army of the Republic, Descriptive Book of the Thomas Kean Chapter" (1)
GDR	*Glendive Daily Ranger* (3)
GG	Grace Gilmore, "Biographical Sketch of Henri J. Haskell" (1)
GHMT	*Glendive, the History of a Montana Town* (5)
GI	*Glendive Independent* (3)
GI&DCR	*Glendive Independent and Dawson County Review* (3)
GMNPDP	*Glendive, Montana: Northern Pacific Division Point* (2)
GT	*Glendive Times* (3)
GTHG	*A Guide to Historic Glendive* (5)
GTY	*A Ghost Town on the Yellowstone* (5)
H4M	*History of the Fourth Regiment of Minnesota Infantry Volunteers...* (5)
HABS	*Hanging Around the Big Sky* (5)
HAST	*The History of the Assiniboine and Sioux Tribes of the Fort Peck...* (5)
HBM	"The Harpster Brothers" manuscript (1)
HD	*Haskell Descendants Elected...* (2)
HH	Harold ("Holly") Chandler Hyatt tapes and manuscripts (1)
HML	*History of Montana* (5)
HMS	*History of Montana and Biographical Sketches* (5)
HNH	Harold Norman Hyatt notes (1)
HNPR	*History of the Northern Pacific Railroad* (5)
HOG	*Harvest of Grief* (5)
HOM	*History of Minnesota* (5)
HOMW	*History of the Mexican War* (5)
HVBF	*The History of the Van Blaricom Family* (2)

HVBG	*Hyatt and Van Blaricom, A Brief History and Genealogy...* (2)
HYCW	*Hoofprints from the Yellowstone Corral of the Westerners* (2)
HYV	*An Illustrated History of the Yellowstone Valley* (5)
IVEM	*The Independent Voice of Eastern Montana* (3)
JEN	*Jennie: The Life of Lady Randolph Churchill* (5)
JCIS	*Joseph Culbertson's Indian Scout* (5)
JLC	*The Journals of Lewis and Clark* [Bernard DeVoto, Ed.] (5)
KL	*Kaleidoscopic Lives* (5)
LOD	*Land of the Dacotahs* (5)
LPL	*Long Prairie Leader* (3)
MAG	*Montana Atlas & Gazetteer* (2)
MC	*Montana.* Map by George F. Cram. 1883. (2)
MCIW	*Minnesota in the Civil and Indian Wars* (5)
MDM/PR	*Minnesota, Dakota and Montana: The Pioneer Route* (2)
MGFC	*Map Guide to the U.S. Federal Censuses, 1790–1920* (5)
MISB	*Montana, Its Story and Biography* (5)
MLP	*Montana, The Land and the People* (5)
M/M	*Montana, A History of Two Centuries* (5)
MMC	*The March of the Montana Column* (5)
MRM	*Montana.* Map by Rand McNally. 1898. (2)
MSD	*Montana Stockgrowers Directory...* (5)
MT	*Morris Tribune* (2)
MTMN	*Montana Man* (5)
MWP	*The Mystic Warriors of the Plains* (5)
MYMR	*Map of the Yellowstone and Missouri Rivers...* (2)
NDAG	*North Dakota Atlas & Gazetteer* (2)
NFM	*Names on the Face of Montana* (5)
NG	*National Geographic* (4)
NP	Northern Pacific Railroad Company
NPMS	*The Northern Pacific, Main Street of the Northwest* (5)
NPRR	Northern Pacific Railroad Company
NYR	"Naming of the Tributaries and Sites of the lower Yellowstone" (1)
OD	"Old Dawson" (1)
OTOL	*Our Times, Our Lives* (5)
PA	*POST-AGE* (2)

PBSD/1	Proceedings of the Board, School Dist. No. 1, Dawson County (1)
PMM	*Progressive Men of the State of Montana* (5)
POY	*The Plainsmen of the Yellowstone* (5)
PW	*Pierre Wibaux and the W-Bar Ranch* (4)
RBL	*Roosevelt in the Bad Lands* (5)
RCTY	*Roosevelt County's Treasured Years* (5)
RL	*Rangelands* (4)
RLR	*Riel, A Life of Revolution* (5)
RR	*Ranger Review* (3)
RRRG	*Ranchers, Railroaders and Retailers of Glendive* (2)
RVR	*Ravalli Republican* (3)
SE	*Strange Empire* (5)
SGJC	*Senator George J. McCone* (2)
SN	*Salem News* (3)
SNVB	Memoirs and letters of Stephen Norton Van Blaricom (1)
SP	*The Splendid Pauper* (5)
T&T	*Trials and Triumphs* (5)
TABC	*Tales Along Beaver Creek* (5)
TCA	*Todd County Argus* (3)
TCS	*They Came and Stayed* (5)
TDE	*Terry Does Exist* (2)
TGN	*The Great Northwest* (5)
THWT	"The Hero Was Throw'd...But the Horse Was Tamed" (1)
TID	*Third International Dictionary* (Webster) (5)
TLW	*This Last West* (5)
TM	*Typhoid Mary* (5)
TNC	*The Negro Cowboy* (5)
TRP	Tom Ray papers (1)
TSMFF	*The Story of the Malakand Field Force* (5)
TT	*Terry Tribune* (3)
UMA	*Up the Missouri with Audubon* (5)
USC	*United States Census* (year and location identified in citation) (2)
USMHR	*U.S. Congressional Medal of Honor Recipients* (5)
VS	*The Champion Buffalo Hunter, Memoirs of Vic Smith* (5)
WAMP	*Wheels Across Montana's Prairie* (5)

WFRF	*The Woods Family and Related Families* (2)
WN	*Western News* (3)
WPTN	*We Pointed Them North* (5)
WTW	*The West That Was* (5)
WTW–TM	*The West That Was—From Texas to Montana* (5)
YC	*Yellowstone Country* (5)
YComm	*Yellowstone Command* (5)
YJ	*Yellowstone Journal* (Miles City) (3)
YLCC	Yellowstone Land and Colonization Company
YP	*Yellowstone Press* (Glendive) (3)
YR	*Yellowstone Red* (5)

STEPHEN NORTON VAN BLARICOM, 1914
PHOTO COURTESY OF ANN VAN BLARICOM FALOR

CHAPTER ONE

The Family
Van Blaricom

I WAS BORN IN THE LOG CABIN of my parents on the 4th day of April in the year 1869. The cabin was near the small village of Waterville, Minnesota, in Le Sueur County, about one mile to the north and maybe two miles to the east of the townsite itself. My father and mother lived all their lives as pioneers.[19]

During the Civil War, my father, Levi Van Blaricom, enlisted in the 4th Minnesota Volunteer Infantry Regiment. He volunteered in 1861 at the age of nineteen years. He returned to Minnesota from the South in 1865 having served, among other places, at the siege and surrender of Vicksburg under General Grant, with General Sherman on his famous March to the Sea and then, still as one of Sherman's "bummers," up the Atlantic seaboard to Washington, D.C.[20] He and my mother, whose maiden name was Sarah Susan Johnson, were married in Waterville in March of 1866, about a year after he came back from the war. My mother told me that when they were married my father was twenty-three and she was sixteen.[21]

Father had never attended school a day in his life but, cabin-taught by his mother, Grandma Mary Ann, he could read and write some. His spelling was of the original phonetic reform method. My mother, however, had what would pass as a sixth- or

---

[19] Unless otherwise noted the source for Chapter 1 is the SNVB manuscript, pp. 1–2.

[20] For a more detailed summary of the military service record of Levi Van Blaricom, see Appendix 1, *"Levi Van Blaricom and the 4th Minnesota Infantry."* Also see HVBG, pp. 96–105. For the complete history of the Fourth Minnesota Infantry Regiment, see H4M.

[21] Levi Van Blaricom and Sarah Susan Johnson were married 25 March 1866 in Waterville, Le Sueur County, Minnesota. Sarah Susan was born in Amherst, Lorain County, Ohio, on 5 December 1849, the daughter of Dr. Stephen Norton Johnson, a physician, and Janette Mary (Beardsley) Johnson. Levi was born 12 September 1842 in Shelby County, Ohio, the son of David Van Blaricom and Mary Ann (Reed) Van Blaricom. [HVBG, pp. 96–105 and p. 174.]

**LEVI VAN BLARICOM, CIRCA 1862,
FATHER OF STEPHEN NORTON VAN BLARICOM**
PHOTO COURTESY OF ELIZABETH FALOR CARDUCCI

seventh-grade education in the schools of today. She was, in any case, possessed of a wisdom and intelligence far in excess of her educational opportunities.

While here on the subject I might as well clear up the matter of us children's educational opportunities. My father was a nomad. There were always greener pastures in other fields. He was always searching for the pot of gold at the end of the rainbow, and the gold he sought most could only be found with a gun and a dog. As a result we were never very long in any one place, so I got what learning I could from schools in little dribs. I never got more than four months' schooling in any one year and, at the age of thirteen, just after we had immigrated to Glendive in Montana Territory in the spring of 1882, I wrote *finis* to my school life. Whenever I had attended, it had always been in a single-room affair with a single teacher and children of all ages mixed together. Never having thus attended a grade school, I am at a loss to say where I might have been graded. My guess would be that I was somewhere about the sixth grade.

I have been told that we are of Dutch descent, with our immigrant Van Blaricom ancestors coming from Holland with the Dutch West Indies Company in the early 1600s. That was back when New York City was New Amsterdam and Albany, New York—our family's "landing place"—was Fort Orange, New Netherland. The family soon settled in New Jersey, where they lived for several generations. Immediately following the American Revolution, my ancestors moved to the backwoods of Northumberland County, Pennsylvania. Around 1805, my great-grandfather Samuel moved his family again, this time to the newly opened land around Chillicothe, Ohio.[22]

My father, through no fault of his own, was raised as a vagabond. He once told me he had lived in at least five locations in Ohio, Indiana, Iowa, and Minnesota by the time he was thirteen years old. His parents, my Grandpa David and Grandma Mary Ann,

---

[22] Stephen Norton Van Blaricom's immigrant ancestors were Lubbert Gijsbertzsen (pronounced "Gysbertsen"), born in 1601 in the village of Blaricum, North Holland, his wife, Divertje Cornilesse, and their three sons, Gysbert, Thys, and Jan. Lubbert and his family arrived in North America in July of 1634. For the story of how the surname changed from Gijsbertzsen to Van Blaricom, a description of the generations from Lubbert Gijsbertzsen through Stephen Norton Van Blaricom and the family's continual westward migration from North Holland to Minnesota, see Appendix 2, *"The Van Blaricom Immigrants of 1634 and Their Descendants."*

moved to Kilkenny, Le Sueur County, Minnesota, along with that great flood of forty-thousand or so immigrants who invaded the former "Suland" in 1855.[23] A year or two later, they settled a little farther south, near Waterville. There were few whites in that part of Minnesota when they arrived in the Great Forest. This continual motion was a normal event well within the tradition of the Van Blaricom family's perennial, never-ending search for free land on the frontier. All of those "moves" continually placed the Van Blaricom family on the very forefront of the country's western expansion. And so it was that my father, born in Ohio in 1842, came by his natural nomadism.

I have seen old records in Shelby County, Ohio, from the 1820s and 1830s that show bounty payments made to my Grandfather David and his brothers, Henry and Phillip. During that era, Shelby County was plagued by wolves, and wolfers were paid four dollars per wolf scalp when they turned them in to county authorities.[24]

I also once ran across a book entitled *The History of Western Ohio and Auglaize County*. Written by C. W. Williamson in 1905, the text mentioned the activities of my grandfather, David, his brothers, and their father, Samuel. While not particularly complimentary, it gives a bit of the flavor of the circumstances in which the Van Blaricom family lived.

> From 1820 to 1833, Wapakoneta contained but few people who had been accustomed to mingle in the circles of polite society. The adventurers who came here to barter with the Indians were destitute of character, and indulged in all the vices of corrupt society. Drinking and gambling were inseparably connected with business and amusements of all kinds. Nearly every trader dealt in whiskey. The order from the War Department, prohibiting the sales of intoxicating liquors to the Indians, was not observed. The Van Blaricomes [sic] and others made money enough by secretly selling whiskey to the Indians to enter [and pay for] farms for themselves.

My mother's family was a far cry from the Van Blaricoms. The Johnsons were descended from Captain John Johnson, who

---

[23] See *"The Suland"* in Author's Notes following this chapter.

[24] HVBF, p. 127.

had settled in the Massachusetts Bay Colony a little while after the Pilgrims landed at Plymouth Rock in 1620.[25] This family essentially stayed put over the next two-hundred years, and they prospered. Sometime around 1820 my mother's grandfather and his sister became pioneers when they left Massachusetts and settled in Amherst, Ohio. My mother's father, Stephen Norton Johnson (I am named after him), and my mother's mother, Mariah Janette Beardsley,[26] were both born in Amherst. They were wed there about 1848. My grandfather had the pioneering blood among the Johnsons, and he and his family ended up on the Minnesota frontier at the same time as the Van Blaricoms. Grandfather Johnson had received medical training somewhere for he was both the Waterville village physician and the local veterinarian by the time the Civil War came in 1861.[27]

Grandpa Johnson enlisted in the 4th Minnesota Volunteer Infantry Regiment at the same time as my father. At that time, of course, they didn't know they would become son-in-law and father-in-law some five years later. In any case, the Army mustered both of them, along with one of father's cousins, into the regiment at Fort Snelling in December of 1861.[28] My grandfather Johnson, in addition to being a physician, was also quite an accomplished musician. While participating in a parade as a member of the band, he contracted pneumonia and died within mere days of his enlistment. And so it was that my grandmother, Mariah Janette (Beardsley) Johnson, was widowed at the age of thirty-three, and my mother, Sarah Susan, and her brother, Frank, and two sisters, Mary Jane and Martha, became fatherless in January of 1862.[29]

---

[25] For a discussion of the descendants of Stephen Norton's 1630 English immigrant ancestor, Captain John Johnson, see Appendix 3, *"The Johnson and Norton Lines."*

[26] See *"Maria ('Mariah') Janette (Beardsley) (Johnson) Scribner"* in Author's Notes following this chapter for the circumstances leading to Mariah's name.

[27] See *"Dr. Stephen Norton Johnson"* in Author's Notes following this chapter regarding Dr. Johnson's medical credentials.

[28] For the service records of Levi Van Blaricom's brothers and cousins during the Mexican War and the Civil War, see HVBG, pp. 94–95.

[29] Dr. Stephen Norton Johnson, "age 35," enlisted in the 4th Minnesota Infantry on 9 December 1861. He was mustered into the regiment at Fort Snelling, Minnesota, on 23 December 1861 and died of pneumonia on 2 January 1862, only ten days after going on active duty. [H4M, p. 543. MCIW, Vol. 1, p. 239. HVBG, p. 172.] Mariah (Beardsley) Johnson was pregnant at the time of her husband's death on 2 January 1862. About six months later,

Grandpa Stephen Norton Johnson was buried at the Fort Snelling cemetery. Over the years, however, the army moved the graveyard twice and the remains of those old soldiers lost their identities. They are now all buried in separate graves in the Fort Snelling National Cemetery near Minneapolis, but each of their tombstones simply reads "Unknown U.S. Soldier."[30]

Five or six years later, about the same time that my mother and father were married, my grandmother Johnson married an older man, a widower I believe, by the name of Zachariah Scribner.[31] I think he had an adult son by his previous marriage. That son was never around, however, and so Zachariah became the stepfather to Grandpa Johnson's children, my mother included. I, of course, only knew my mother's mother and stepfather as "Grandma and Grandpa Scribner."[32]

In later life, I have often wondered how it was that my father and mother ever paired. The Johnsons were, by Minnesota's frontier standards, relatively well off and well educated, a stable, traditional kind of family. That was not the case with the Van Blaricoms. In my memory, Grandpa David lived with my Uncle David Van Blaricom (Jr.) and his wife, my Aunt Martha Jane, near Waterville. Grandma Mary Ann, my "Irish" grandmother (her maiden name was Reed),[33] lived in her later years with another of my father's brothers, Uncle Phillip, up in Todd County. The "VBs," as they were referred to within the family, were quite the rough-and-readys one would associate with the frontier, living in their windowless log cabins with the loose-shingled roofs and, when

---

on 21 June 1862, a fifth child, a son she named Norton Stephen Johnson, was born at her home in Waterville. [HVBG, p. 173 and p. 177.]

[30] See "Unknown U.S. Soldier" in Author's Notes following this chapter for the story of how the remains of Dr. Stephen Norton Johnson and many of his comrades lost their identities.

[31] In a second marriage for both, Zachariah Scribner and Mariah Janette (Beardsley) Johnson were wed 6 February 1867 in Waterville, Le Sueur County, Minnesota. Although they were thirty-nine (Mariah) and forty-eight years old (Zachariah) on the date of their marriage, they were undeterred by their respective ages and they proceeded to have five more children. For details of the marriage of Zachariah Scribner and Mariah Janette (Janette Mary) (Beardsley) Johnson and a listing of Mariah's ten children from her two marriages, see Appendix 4, "Zachariah and Mariah Scribner."

[32] HVBG, pp. 176–177.

[33] Mary Ann Reed could trace her mother's lineage directly back to Sir William Hinton, one of England's wealthiest private citizens. Hinton was the Director of the Virginia Company and one of the financial founders of Jamestown. For the ancestry of Mary Ann Reed, see Appendix 5, "The Families of Reed and Hinton."

they had them, the rough-hewn split rail floors. More often, the floors were simply compacted dirt, elevated above ground level about a foot or so, so when the spring thaw came they wouldn't turn to mud like the ground outside.

The Van Blaricoms had lived so for generations. They were certainly not a family of wealth. Quite to the contrary, I believe they were historically "dirt poor" with little, if any, education and with no prospects in their futures. That comparison between the families of my two parents has always remained very clear whenever I think back as to how we children witnessed our mother and father and how they lived their lives.[34]

I can only attribute my mother's attraction to my father to the circumstances following the Civil War. Young, eligible men were scarce in Le Sueur County, Minnesota, in the spring of 1866. My mother had just turned sixteen some three months before the marriage, and she had been fatherless for the preceding four years, those being the tumultuous years of the Great Rebellion. Nor should we forget the stressful effects of the Great Sioux Uprising of 1862 and the accompanying massacres that whirled around the settlers of Minnesota while so many of the young men were gone off to the war in the South.[35]

The Minnesota Sioux opened their uprising on the 18th day of August 1862, with numerous raids on trading posts and settlements in the vicinity of the Fort Ridgely Reservation, less than seventy miles from Waterville. On the first day alone, around four-hundred white settlers were massacred. Panic hit the entire state. My mother told us children many times how father's youngest sister, Arlinda, who was seventeen or eighteen at the time, disappeared. It was never proven who carried her off or what became of her, but she was taken and was never seen nor heard from again.[36]

About a week later, a large war party of Sioux stormed the village of New Ulm.[37] They were driven off after about one-hundred

---

[34] HVBG, pp. 173–174.

[35] HVBG, pp. 94–95 and p. 173.

[36] HVBG, p. 81.

[37] Various battles and skirmishes occurred at New Ulm, Minnesota, on 19, 23, and 24 August 1862. [MCIW, Vol. 2, pp. 207–208.]

Indians were killed. It was in December of 1862 that over three-hundred Sioux were tried, found guilty of murder and sentenced to be hanged in Mankato. Only some twenty-five miles west of Waterville, Mankato was where my mother, Sarah Susan, and her sister, Mary Jane, were boarded for school. While President Lincoln commuted most of the sentences, it still resulted in the largest mass execution in American history. On the day after Christmas of 1862, thirty-eight Sioux were simultaneously hanged there in Mankato, only blocks from my mother's school. While my mother and her siblings didn't witness the actual executions, they knew exactly where they occurred and never forgot the event.[38]

In addition to the emotional distress suffered by my mother from the loss of her father, the tumult of the War of the Rebellion, and the terror of the Sioux uprising, it cannot have been comforting to her that Zachariah Scribner was busily courting her mother. I doubt there was ever any kind of a rift between them due to my grandmother's courtship and re-marriage, for my mother remained close to her mother and her siblings for the rest of her life. I have always surmised, however, that, certainly by 1866, my grandmother was involved with Grandpa Scribner and that provided some incentive for my mother to start her own nest. My father returned from the Civil War, perhaps seen by her as the wounded hero, the survivor of a regiment that had sustained tremendous losses in the South and which had led Sherman's victory parade down Pennsylvania Avenue in Washington City, the nation's capital. For whatever reason, my parents were attracted to each other and they were wed there in Waterville in 1866.[39]

Nine children were eventually born to this union. I was the oldest, followed by four brothers and four sisters. The three oldest, myself, David, and Mary Martha, were born in the log cabin near Waterville.[40] The next three, Jim, Fred, and Alice, were birthed in the log cabin in Reynolds Township outside of Long Prairie, Todd

---

[38] See *"Mary Jane (Johnson) Perry"* in WFRF. See *"The Mankato executions"* in Author's Notes following this chapter.

[39] H4M. HVBG, p. 104 and p. 174. See *"...perhaps seen by her as a wounded hero..."* in Author's Notes following this chapter for the consequence of Levi's Civil War wound.

[40] See *"Reynolds Township"* in Author's Notes following this chapter.

County, Minnesota. The next two children, Levi Perry and Dora May, were born at Grandma Scribner's house on the shore of Lake Jefferson. The last child, our baby sister, Sarah Effie, was born in our modest accommodation shortly after our arrival in Glendive, Montana Territory, in 1882.[41]

Here, in relation to the births of these children, allow me to record two of the most outstanding differences between the past and the present. There were then no doctors involved in the births nor were there any of these now-so-popular synthetic rubber nipples used to rear me or any of my eight siblings. At the time and place that most of these children were born, there were simply no doctors available. Grandma Scribner was the midwife to my mother at the three births near Waterville (me, David, and Mary), the first one, Jim, born in Reynolds Township, Perry's birth and Dora May's at Lake Jefferson, and the birth of Sarah Effie in Glendive. I recall very well that Grandma Mary Ann, who came to live with Uncle Phillip's family in 1874, assisted with the two other babies, Freddie and Alice, born while we were pioneering near Long Prairie.

At that time Todd County was a wilderness of lakes, swamps, and timber. I have absolutely no recollection of ever seeing or hearing of a doctor in the six years we lived there. There couldn't have been a doctor nearer than twenty miles, and I doubt if there was one that near. The roads were built by simply clearing the timber from the meandering wagon tracks. The only power anyone had was oxen, and, of course, telephones and telegraph were non-existent.[42] If, indeed, a frantic father had started for a doctor, a boy baby would have been sporting a mustache before dad got back!

As the account stands, the nine births never cost my father or mother a thin dime, and every one of the children lived to attain their maturity. All but two are living today, with an average age of well over sixty years.

---

[41] See *"The nine children of Levi and Sarah Susan Van Blaricom"* in the Author's Notes following this chapter for the birth dates and locations of the children.

[42] See *"Telephones and telegraph"* in Author's Notes following this chapter.

CHAPTER 1–AUTHOR'S NOTES

"The Suland": In 1855, Minnesota was the frontier: The 1840 census of St. Croix County, Wisconsin Territory (which contained that area which became northeast Minnesota) tallied 351 souls. Folwell estimated "the whole number of whites, and half-breeds living apart from the Indians, on the area of Minnesota in that year could not have been more than double that number, counting in the garrison at Fort Snelling [established in 1819], the missionaries, and the people about the trading stations." [HOM, Vol. I, p. 351.] Minnesota became a territory in 1849, and the census taken that year enumerated 4,852 people, including 317 military at Fort Snelling (plus a civilian population of 200) and Fort Gaines. The decennial census of 1850 gave the population as 6,077. The Sioux treaties that affected much of Minnesota were signed in 1851. By the end of 1853 the former "Suland" was nearly vacated but the 1841 preemption laws permitted only the occupation of surveyed lands. The Minnesota surveys did not begin until 1853, and "it was not until 1855 that the first installment of lands was offered for sale." [HOM, Vol. I, pp. 353–354.] In the spring of 1855 "a flood of immigration, perhaps without precedent, poured into Minnesota. Joseph A. Wheelock [estimated] there must have been forty-thousand people in the territory by the close of 1855." The territorial census taken in 1857 recorded a population of 150,037. [HOM, Vol. I, p. 359.] On 11 May 1858, Minnesota was admitted to the Union as the thirty-second state. [CEnc, p. 355.]

Maria ("Mariah") Janette (Beardsley) (Johnson) Scribner: Janette Mary Beardsley was born at Amherst, Lorain County, Ohio, on 2 April 1826. As a child and young woman, her parents and family called her "Janetta." Following her marriage to Stephen Norton Johnson (Jr.) in Akron, Ohio, on 29 October 1848, she called herself and signed legal documents as "Janette M. Johnson." [HVBG, pp. 171–173 and p. 176.] After being widowed in 1862 and, sometime before or at the time of her marriage to Zachariah Scribner in 1867, she changed her name to "Maria Janette." Although spelled "Maria," she pronounced her adopted name as "Mariah." [HVBG, p. 176.] Stephen and the rest of her grandchildren never knew her by any name other than "Mariah." For the sake of consistency, the phonetic spelling of "Mariah" has been used throughout this text. Her immigrant ancestors, William and Mary (Harvey) Beardsley, came with their three children to the Massachusetts Bay Colony in 1635. William was, in 1639, among the founders of Stratford, Connecticut. [HVBG, pp. 109–110.] Mariah's mother, Sarah (Hanchett) Beardsley, was also from a line of early Connecticut settlers. For a discussion of Mariah's Beardsley and Hanchett ancestors, see Appendix 6, *"The Beardsley and Hanchett Families."*

Dr. Stephen Norton Johnson: Where Stephen Norton Johnson attended medical school has never been discovered. That he was a physician there is no doubt. The most helpful documents in this regard are connected with the disposition of his estate in 1862. The estate itemized surgical instruments, medical books and his listing of accounts receivable. The court-appointed appraisers noted that there were substantial accounts receivable "which the doctor might have collected had he lived" but which were assumed to be uncollectable under the circumstances. [See the 1862 records of the inventory and disposition of the estate of Stephen Norton Johnson, Le Sueur County Courthouse, Le Center, Minnesota.]

"Unknown U.S. Soldier": The "Old Cemetery" at Fort Snelling was located on a small hill on the edge of the bluff above the Mississippi River. Originally located in a somewhat isolated site, the "Old Cemetery" eventually came to lie between one of the barracks, the stables and one of the ordnance warehouses. In 1904, in order to make way for the Fort Snelling History Center, whose construction was to commence in 1905, the graves at the "Old Cemetery" were removed to the "New Cemetery." During World War I, the area adjacent to the "New Cemetery" became a temporary marshaling area for incoming and outgoing troops. Between 1939 and 1940, in order to make way for what later became the Minneapolis International Airport, the U.S. Government started the Fort Snelling National Cemetery and the graves were moved a second time. Somewhere along the line, 149 of the graves from the "Old Cemetery" lost their identification. The remains were all reburied individually in a section located on the southwest side of the cemetery. Each grave is marked with a tombstone that simply reads: "Unknown U.S. Soldier." Dr. Stephen Norton Johnson rests in one of those graves. [HVBG, pp. 172–173.]

The Mankato executions: Sarah Susan Johnson attended the Mankato boarding school beginning with the fall term of 1856.

Mary Jane accompanied her there in the fall of 1858. When her husband, Dr. Stephen Norton Johnson, died of pneumonia at Fort Snelling in January of 1861, Janette Johnson allowed her two daughters of school age to remain at the boarding school in Mankato until the end of term in May of that year. Following that, the financial condition of the family along with the birth of a fifth child (Norton Stephen Johnson, born 21 June 1862) required that all of the children remain at home with their mother. All of the members of the family were in Waterville when the Sioux uprising started on 18 August 1862, and that is where they remained through the executions in Mankato on December 26 of that same year. The events of the Minnesota Sioux uprising of 1862 were traumatic enough that all four of the older children remembered them clearly. Sarah was thirteen years old, Mary Jane was ten, and Frank was eight when the uprising began. Even little "Muz" (who was nearly three) could remember sheltering at the Waterville church and at neighbor's houses for more than a month during the beginning of hostilities. Sarah and Mary Jane especially remembered the executions, because the gallows in Mankato were erected only a block or two from their boarding school. [ANAI, p. 155. HOM, Vol. II, Ch. VII: "The Punishment of the Sioux." HOM, Vol. II, p. 196, Footnote 12. MCIW, Volumes 1 and 2. See "Old Dawson" for a more complete telling of the story of the Sioux uprising. Also see "Mary Jane (Johnson) Perry" in WFRF.]

"...perhaps seen by her as the wounded hero....": Levi's hip had been dislocated when he was bucked off a "liberated" mule near Huntsville, Alabama, in December of 1863. Although he spent nearly four months in a hospital in Washington City (now Washington, D.C.), the dislocation never completely repaired. He walked with a limp for the rest of his days. The wound ultimately cost him his life. He was thrown from a horse near Victor, Montana, around the first of September 1902 and landed on the "bad" hip. The hip became infected, and he died on September 22, just ten days after his sixtieth birthday.

Reynolds Township: Citing a "township" to designate one's place of birth or residence was rather common during the 1800s and early 1900s. It is still occasionally used. Note that there was (is) no "town" necessarily present in a survey "township." The thirty-six square-mile townships (six miles by six miles containing thirty-six sections of one square mile each) were frequently given names. That was easier than referring to the legal survey designations (as in, for example, "Township 19 South, Range 23 East of the Willamette Meridian" or, as would be the standard abbreviation, "T 19 S, R 22 E of the WM"). Jim, Fred, and Alice were all born in the family's cabin in Reynolds Township, Todd County, Minnesota. Levi and Sarah Susan's farm was about a mile east of the school and meetinghouse located at a road intersection still known as Gutche's Grove, a few miles southwest of the town of Long Prairie.

The nine children of Levi and Sarah Susan Van Blaricom and their birth dates and birth locations:

Child	Birth Date	Location
Stephen Norton (Norton)	4 Apr 1869	Waterville, Le Sueur Co., MN
David Cass (Dave)	25 Apr 1870	Waterville, Le Sueur Co., MN
Mary Martha (Mary)	7 Mar 1872	Waterville, Le Sueur Co., MN
James Madison (Jim)	11 Jun 1873	Long Prairie, Todd Co., MN
Frederick Alfred (Fred)	18 May 1875	Long Prairie, Todd Co., MN
Alice Janette (Alice)	16 Dec 1876	Long Prairie, Todd Co., MN
Levi Perry (Perry)	18 Aug 1878	Lake Jefferson, Le Sueur Co., MN
Dora May (Dorie)	18 Aug 1880	Lake Jefferson, Le Sueur Co., MN
Sarah Effie (Effie)	9 July 1882	Glendive, Dawson Co., Mont. Terr.

[HVBG, Appendix B, Section II: Family Group Sheet, Levi Van Blaricom and Sarah Susan Johnson.]

Telephones and telegraph didn't exist: Stephen was referring to the fact that there were no telegraph services available in Todd County, Minnesota, in 1872. Samuel F. B. Morse filed his patent on the telegraph in 1837. The first commercial application was operating in 1844 between Washington City and Baltimore. [CEnc, Vol. TUV, p. 30.] The telegraph was commonly in use by the time of the Civil War (1861–1865). The telephone, however, was not invented by Alexander Graham Bell until 1876. The first commercial telephone switchboard was installed in 1878 in New Haven, Connecticut. [CEnc, Vol. TUV, p. 34 and p. 37.]

CHAPTER TWO

Long Prairie, Minnesota:
1872–1878

I N THE FALL OF 1871, my parents decided to leave the Waterville area and move up into Todd County, Minnesota, to homestead a quarter section of public land under the Soldier's Homestead Act.[43] My father had served four years in the Civil War and, as an ex-soldier, he took advantage of an act of Congress permitting veterans to homestead one-hundred-and-sixty acres of government land anywhere in the United States. He chose to go into a heavily wooded country located near the center of Minnesota. We moved there in the spring of 1872, father and mother with two sons and a baby daughter.[44] Father, in his characteristic fashion, simply yoked up the two oxen, stretched the canvas over the wagon bows, loaded mother, the three of us children, and the family's goods into the wagon, and away we went. Except for the many lakes and marshes, the country into which we moved was densely timbered. It was, indeed, a land new and primeval in the last degree.

My father and his brother, my Uncle Phillip, had each claimed quarter sections in the south half of Section 34 in Reynolds Township, about two miles south and four miles west of the village of Long Prairie. My father had the west quarter and Uncle Phillip the east. Section 34, on the northwest corner, bordered the settlement called Gutche's Grove. I am cautious about using the term "settlement" since I do not wish to give the wrong impression. Gutche's Grove was simply a single small building with a few rows of split-log benches inside. During the winter

---

[43] Unless otherwise noted, the source for Chapter 2 is the SNVB manuscript, pp. 2–6, and the SN article ca. 1932.

[44] See *"1872–The move to Todd County"* in Author's Notes following this chapter.

months it was the schoolhouse, except on Sunday when it was the church and Saturday when it was the meetinghouse. That building was the "settlement." Nor was there even an outhouse for either gender, a condition that gave pause for thought from those a little short on the pioneering spirit. But more on that subject later.

When we first arrived we moved into a kind of half-dugout, half-shack left by some pre-Civil War tenant who had perhaps been associated with the earlier Winnebago Indian settlement at Long Prairie.[45] In any case it was in a terribly dilapidated and forlorn condition but it at least provided shelter of some sort. My father and Uncle Phillip, my father's brother with whose family my Grandma Mary Ann later lived, set about immediately to build each family a new cabin on their respective homesteads.[46]

Our new home was built of logs and I am sure that there were not five pounds of nails in the whole structure. The sidewalls were all joined and fitted and then chinked. The floorboards were laid loose on the joists and the roof was made of what was called "shake" (much larger than what you think of as "shake" today) bound with rows of small logs lying on top. It was no uncommon experience for these fourteen- to eighteen-inch shake pieces, about two inches thick, to slip out from under the logs and fall to the floor or to the ground. On these occasions that portion of the roof had to be re-laid. Of course, it leaked some (for all of the old coarse shake roofs did), but a leaky roof was truly only a minor matter in the pioneer's life. What was of serious consequence, something of a tragedy, was for the fire to go out. A single box of sulphur matches cost ten cents in cash, and in our family's budget ten cents in cash was a serious matter.

---

[45] The Winnebago had left the Long Prairie reservation in 1855, some seventeen years before the two Van Blaricom brothers settled their families there. For a more complete story of the U.S. government's continuous and lamentable gyrations regarding the re-settlement of the Winnebago following the negation of the 1825 treaty at Prairie du Chien, see Folwell in HOM, Vol. I, Chapter XI: "Chippewa and Other Indian Affairs," pp. 308–320 and map following p. 324. Also see HOM, Vol. II, pp. 258–259.]

[46] Born in 1840, Phillip was Levi's immediately older brother. Mary Ann (Reed) Van Blaricom, Stephen's grandmother, moved north from the Waterville area to live with Phillip's family in Todd County in 1874. Mary Ann's move coincided with the death of Phillip's first wife, Roxie (Bailey), in March of that year. Mary Ann continued to live with her son, Phillip, and his family until her death on 14 April 1884 at the age of 81. She is buried in the Long Prairie cemetery. For a brief biography of Phillip Van Blaricom, see Appendix 7, *"Phillip E. Van Blaricom, Levi's brother."*

After our home was up, the next thing to be done was to clear enough timber from the land so that we might grow something to supplement our supply of fish and game. There was no way to transport this timber, and there was no market for it anyway so it was just cut and burned. I saw literally millions of board feet of as fine a hardwood as ever stood simply slashed and burned by the early settlers of Todd County. All they had for tools was an ax, a wedge, and a saw, and that was all that slowed them down. There was necessarily much cooperation between the sparsely settled neighbors in this work of preparing that timbered land for tillage.

Native game and fish were plentiful in this country, and we depended on them for our daily living. There were no industries of any kind, however, and that in turn made cash money very scarce. The family needed money for clothing and such food staples that could not be raised and for the necessities of gunpowder and lead. Hunting and trapping supplied most of the cash needs. Wild game was very abundant, for we were among the first settlers in that part of the state. Muskrat skins brought five to ten cents each. A good coon hide would bring from twenty-five to fifty cents. Deer and black bear skins were likewise cheap. We had to endure the usual privations of frontier life, but withal were very happy and contented.

Father soon cleared enough land on which he could raise food for the family. The virgin soil of the country was very fertile. Everything planted grew abundantly. There was, however, little or no market for surpluses, so it didn't take much acreage to produce all that we needed for food. But the winters were long and hard. I remember seeing snow four feet deep on the level, with drifts against some of the denser treelines three to four times that deep. There were no snowplows to open the roads. Snowplows couldn't have opened the roads anyway due to the ever-present stumps that had been left in the roadsteads. We just waited for Nature's thaw to perform the road-clearing service. And a long, tedious wait it often was, for we had no radio, no newspapers, or magazines. We had simply to depend on our own resources for amusement.

The tedium was not as bad as one might think, for we never

miss the things we have never had or have not seen others have. It is a peculiarity of the human condition that the absence of something, if that absence is common to all and it is not known except by reputation, does not create the symptom of envy or need. Let only one person in the community possess it, however, and then watch how quickly the wheels must move!

In our case, my father and Uncle Phillip would spend the winter months up north at the Pigeon River working for logging contractors so that we might have some cash. At home there were lakes nearby where Mother and us children could spend enjoyable and productive winter hours fishing through the ice. Also, once the school was open and I was old enough, I spent much of my time in those winter-bound months getting to and from and in attendance at school. The other children, with the exception of my brother, David, were too young to go to school but at home Mother would make up games in which we would memorize such things as the alphabet, arithmetic, poetry, and stories.

Besides fish there was abundant other game, especially squirrels, and an occasional deer. Father had a gun, but ammunition was always a problem. Ammunition was available, but it cost money and that commodity was always extremely scarce.

I remember one fall when Father went out on a hunt and did not return the same day. This did not worry Mother, for often he would hunt all day and be so far from home come evening that he would build a campfire and rest until morning, getting home the next day. On this occasion he came home with five coons hanging about him. They had denned and were fat as butter. Mother rendered the fat from the five and there was enough to furnish our spit for all of that long winter.

We were fortunate in that my parents had a stove. Consequently, our cabin was always snug and warm. The stove, however, took away the need for a fireplace with the result that, during all of those long winter months, our windowless home was completely dark except for a flickering spit. The spit was nothing more than one of my mother's cups with some of the grease taken from the game with a home-braided cotton string stuck in it. Mother would occasionally pull one of the two burner tops off the small stove to let it help light the room but usually the top of the stove was covered with water tubs heating for tomorrow's needs. Perhaps it is this history that has always allowed me to appreciate a good fireplace, not so much for the little heat it generates but for the warm and friendly glow of light with which it fills a room.

There was abundant wild fruit in the fall, especially cranberries. The bog marshes around the lakes were bountiful with them and many other small fruits. Mother, of course, always gathered a generous supply of these and the cranberries. We never saw, though, any of the larger fruits such as apples, nor an orange or banana. I was nine years old, back at my Grandma Scribner's house near Waterville, when I saw my first apples. I believe I was about eleven before I saw an orange. That tangy curiosity had come down to Waterville with a shipment of things from St. Paul.

The woods had a great number of sugar maple trees and it was from these that we got most of our sweets. There was no such thing as granulated sugar at that time, and brown cane sugar was ten pounds for a dollar. Father and Mother would make barrels of maple sugar in the spring and, of course, some maple syrup. When we children got to have a piece of syrup pie or berry pie it was an occasion of no mean importance. It mattered very little what the pie might be made of; it was a royal treat nevertheless.

In my own family today, Mother chooses the choicest viands, the most delectable morsels, and compounds a pie fit for the gods. These wonderful but pampered urchins of ours will look at it and query, "Ma, what kind of pie is this? Oh. Well, I don't think I like that kind." I am wondering who is the winner in this case. I had and continue to have a keen appreciation of my pie. I got a kick out of it as a child that lingers with me to this day. My children will never know such satisfaction for they have been surfeited on the common good things of life. I think I shall prefer to keep my memories and my appreciation for pie over theirs.

The same is true with other phases of child-life. As children we never had toys of any kind. I remember when I was about five years old I had a stick about two feet long that had been turned by a lathe. The simple fact that it was machined and was smooth and straight set it apart as a prized possession. A neighbor boy took a fancy to it and tried to take it from me. He might as well have tried to take meat from a hungry dog! I suspect, however, that I could buy a good-sized section of the World's Fairgrounds in New York City and present it to my children and they would utterly fail to get the same emotional satisfaction that I got out of my prized smooth stick.

Aside from visiting our few neighbors, our social life consisted of washing our faces, combing our hair, and putting on a clean shirt to go to a little Sunday school in attendance with fifteen or twenty other people. The Sunday school and church were both held in the nearby log schoolhouse that had been built by the various neighbors. It was here in Long Prairie that my brother, David, and I were introduced to our first schooling. It was nearly a mile from our house to the school and the path was through a deep wood. Father went with us on the first day, blazing a trail so we would not get lost on our daily journey. "Blazing a trail" consisted of chopping a strip of bark from the trees along the trail close enough together so that the "blazes" were always in sight to us as we traveled back and forth from home to school.[47]

The schoolhouse was a one-room log affair, primitive in the extreme. I recall that the class benches were made of split basswood logs. Plumbing, of course, was out of the question since there was none in central Minnesota. Additionally, however, this schoolhouse was also wholly innocent of anything resembling an "outside closet" (as an outhouse was politely called in those days). Built as it was on the edge of a dense wood, at Nature's call the students and the teacher were at liberty to take to the tall timber. You were, of course, subject to your own responsibility to be aware of where you stepped.

Modern health science makes much ado about sanitation. Please understand that I am not criticizing the learned knowledge of the scientists, but it has always seemed to me that there is one thing that needs explaining. Every time the bell rang for class to recommence from recess, every boy in the school (he might even be a hundred yards from the building) would cut a bee-line straight for the back of the school house, there to relieve himself of all his surplus bodily fluids. If that old building still stood

---

[47] The school's location assumed the name of "Gutche's Grove." Gutche's Grove is still noted on present-day maps and is a local reference point to the citizens of Long Prairie and Todd County.

after these sixty years, I could, at surprising elevations, indicate the marks of Will, Sam, or Henry. The terms of the school were never for more than four months and those, thankfully, were in the winter. I have often thought how fortunate that was for, had they held the school term over into warmer weather, they surely would have had to move the school. Notwithstanding the unsanitary conditions rendered by the lack of the outhouse and the ritualistic "markings" on the school's exterior walls, I cannot recall attending a single funeral involving any of the students or the teacher during the six years we lived there near Long Prairie.

CHAPTER 2–AUTHOR'S NOTES

1872–The move to Todd County: Whenever Stephen Norton Van Blaricom recalled the move to Todd County (in his memoir and in an interview with the *Salem News* in 1932), he cited 1871 as the year of the move. Phillip Van Blaricom (Levi's brother and Stephen Norton's uncle), however, who moved his family to Todd County at the same time, consistently stated the family moved to Todd County in 1872. After interviewing Phillip for an article regarding his daughter's wedding, a reporter for the Todd County Argus wrote: "They came to Todd County in 1872 and settled on the homesite in Southern Reynolds [Township near Long Prairie], where they still reside." [TCA, Thursday, 27 June 1907.] The same date was given in Phillip's obituary, some eighteen years later: "Mr. and Mrs. Van Blaricom moved to Todd County in 1872 settling on a farm in Reynolds township where he continued to make his home until his death." [LPL, Thursday, 9 July 1925.] One has to credit Phillip for the more accurate recollection of the year of the move from Waterville to Long Prairie. When the move occurred, Phillip was thirty-two years old and along with his brother, Levi, was co-planner and co-leader of the trek. Norton, on the other hand, was recollecting an event that took place when he was two or three years old.

The other piece of compelling evidence for the 1872 date was that Mary (Van Blaricom) Eddy (born 7 March 1872), the third child of Levi and Sarah Susan, always cited Waterville as her birthplace. She also maintained that the family moved to the Long Prairie area of Todd County when she was "a babe in arms."

CHAPTER THREE

Crossing the Rubicon:
July 1876 to March 1878

WE HAD LIVED IN LONG PRAIRIE the first four years as pioneers must, meeting the problems of each day and always anticipating better things. Today, as I look back at our years in the wilderness Todd County then was, I can understand the motives that caused those hardy settlers to push out into a primitive and isolated environment filled with danger and uncertainty. First came the firm belief that the condition they were leaving could soon be improved in this new land. Second, they were necessarily possessed of a total faith in themselves and their families, for there was no one else to depend upon. Finally, there was a long-term hope for the future, that the condition of their new environment would change as more people came and settled, that a broader sense of community and security would develop.

This life of pioneering did have one other requirement, however, and that was the survival of some of the old "Adam" in us—the human's ability to "go native" and shed civilization's culture as a snake would its skin. Some people could not adapt to the primitive lifestyle required of a pioneer and they failed. In our case, however, there was no undue unhappiness or longing, for, after all, what had been left behind? We did not wish or pine for the aesthetic things of life, for certainly my father's family had never had them, nor his father nor grandfather before him. It might have been otherwise in my mother's family for they were accustomed to a fair degree of urbanity in their lives. In my mother's case, however, she quickly accepted and adapted to the lesser expectations of my father after their marriage and she was never one to look back and show regret. As a family in Long

Prairie we lived close to Mother Earth and we were as happy in that element as a frog in his pool.[48]

Squirrel was certainly the most prolific source of our red meat supply. The squirrels in central Minnesota were of the small red variety, although larger in size than you find here in Ohio. The woods were simply alive with them and they were fat as little pigs due to the presence of numerous oak and butternut trees from which they gathered and stored their winter nuts. We would catch them in traps, thus saving what ammunition we had for larger game. The trouble in Long Prairie was that eating squirrel every day came to be awfully monotonous. As a child there wasn't much one could do about it, though, except keep on eating the succulent little things. I can attest to the fact that squirrel will keep a young lad both going and growing. It must be confessed, however, that as a young child I sometimes wondered if a growing boy should eat that much squirrel. I honestly feared, having been so told, that it might register on a boy's IQ and that the boy might grow up a little "squirrelly." Nobody ever commented on the "succulent" part.

Tea, coffee, and sugar were luxuries in which my parents rarely participated. Mother devised many substitutes for coffee, usually from cereal grains, but they were infrequently used. A wild mint that grew along the edges of the marshes made a fair substitute for tea. I find some of it here in Ohio and still enjoy it on some occasions.

Mother made all of our clothes with a hand needle. I am still mystified, however, concerning her source of supply of the fabric from which she made our garments. The only fabrics I remember were the ubiquitous grain and flour sacks. We must have brought them into the Long Prairie country with us. Be that as it may, we had them and wore them. One sometimes still sees or hears a joke about women's wear made of muslin sacking. It was no joke with my mother nor any of the women of that time and place, nor was there any undue shame or modesty about it. It was simply hazardous to loan your neighbor an Amoskeg grain bag, for there was better than a fifty-fifty chance that it would fall victim to his

---

[48] Unless otherwise noted, the source for Chapter 3 is the SNVB manuscript, pp. 6–10, and the SN article ca. 1932.

wife's shears to make him a pair of pants before he could return it. The women justifiably considered it quite an accomplishment to fashion a pair of trousers out of two grain bags and keep the "Amoskeg" brand name hidden.

But no matter who you are, what you are, or how well you fit, sooner or later you will encounter your Rubicon. In 1876 we met ours.[49] It happened on a July day when everything was lovely. I distinctly remember that it was midday with a fair, gentle breeze. The sun was shining brightly in a sky that had only wisps of cloud. At first we could faintly hear a distant sound emanating from the west or northwest. Looking skyward toward the source of what we heard, we could see enormous clouds of what first appeared to be vast but oddly undulating snow storms that had appeared from nowhere.[50] We children, well taught about the vagaries of weather in that part of the country, immediately headed for the safety of our log cabin and our parents. We stood outside the door, however, drawn by the curious event of a storm that late in the season and the unusually rapid oscillations of the approaching clouds. As they neared, you could see upon closer examination that they were not snow storms at all but were, instead, millions upon millions of minute animated specks, their bodies and wings glittering in the sun as they performed darting scintillations similar to those performed by flocks of starlings or blackbirds. At first a few grasshoppers started dropping from the sky. In a couple hours the country was alive with them. During the rest of the afternoon they kept increasing until by nightfall the stumps and fences, the trees and crops, and our cabin and outbuildings were literally covered with them. That night they went to roost like chickens on anything that was warm.[51]

---

[49] Although Stephen Norton wrote in his memoir that the first "hopper" invasion occurred in 1875, local records and other sources show that Todd County was not infested until the summer of 1876. See HOM, Vol. III, p. 102 and p. 106 and map following p. 106. Also see HOG, maps on pp. 16, 18, 20, 25, and 28.

[50] See *"The Rocky Mountain locust"* in Author's Notes following this chapter.

[51] The years 1873 through 1877 saw large areas of Minnesota infested with the Rocky Mountain locust. Because the Minnesotans victimized by the swarms thought it looked like the familiar grasshopper, they commonly referred to it as such in conversation and in print. To entomologists, however, the teeming insects were more properly identified as locusts. [Charles V. Riley, *The Locust Plague in the United States; Being More a Treatise on the Rocky Mountain Locust,* cited as Footnote 1, HOM, Vol. III, pp. 93–94.]

For the first day or two we didn't realize what was happening, but within a few days we knew we were in trouble. Massive visitations of hoppers had been reported in other areas of Minnesota starting in 1873, and again in 1874 and 1875. We had heard horror tales of them but had no real idea of the immensity of the swarms or the devastation they could cause. Difficult as it may be to believe, the sound of millions of grasshoppers eating is audible, and I have but to recall it and the hair stands on the nape of my neck. Many people likened the sound of the millions of munching hoppers to that of a wild prairie fire or the sound of the wild ocean during a storm. We saw our garden and other crops disappear, and soon everything we had planted that spring had been eaten. Our winter food supply was taken, consumed by the hoppers. How we got through the following winter I can barely remember, but I am sure that it remained vividly etched in the minds of my mother and father for the rest of their lives.[52]

I simply cannot describe nor could but few people alive today understand or appreciate what such a situation was like. One has no conception of the desolation that can be wrought upon a country by such a plague. Nor can one who has not experienced it conceive of the sense of desperation caused by such a cataclysmic event. There was no one, no industry, no government to which we could turn for help. There were no social organizations such as we have now, no help of any kind. There was only you, your immediate family, your extended family, and, to the extent you could help each other in a sense of desperate community, your neighbors. If you missed one meal, you hustled and struggled a little harder or you would miss two.

As our meager resources depleted, it is still a mystery to me how my mother ever managed, for to her must go the credit for our survival. The summer, fall, and early winter of 1876 passed and we always managed to have enough to eat, such as it was. Corn meal certainly constituted the source of our principal bread supply.

---

[52] It is nearly impossible to visualize the enormity of the swarms. "In 1887 [some ten years after the massive visitations of 1873–1877] a small swarm of locusts appeared in Otter Tail County [immediately west of Todd County] and deposited eggs" over an area roughly ten miles square. The following spring, not wanting the unwelcome moniker of having become a "new grasshopper county," the local farmers "attacked them vigorously. Thirty-five-thousand bushels of eggs and young hoppers were captured and destroyed and but few eggs were left for another season." [HOM, Vol. III, p. 111.]

All we had was corn bread in all of its known (and previously unknown) forms along with a few squirrels, a lot of fish that had grown huge and fat during the hopper plague, and the native wild fruits and the maple syrup that Mother had preserved. The hoppers had long since driven away the deer by stripping off what would have been their winter forage.

The spring of 1877 came, and everyone busied themselves again planting crops and gardens, thinking that last year's plague of locusts was gone for good, a freak occurrence never to return. I can remember my father commenting that they would need a crop this year in order to replenish their seed for the next year. It was not to be. In the early summer of 1877 the grasshoppers returned in full force but, for some reason I cannot explain— for it was certainly an act of Providence—our garden corn escaped destruction. I clearly remember my mother making a grater by punching holes in a piece of tin with a nail. With this crude tool she prepared the corn while it was still in the milk to make us corn bread. This she continued to do until the corn became too hard, and then she literally cracked it and ground it to powder with two stones. By the end of summer, the shoe really began to pinch.[53]

In 1876 there had been two cows we had raised from calves. These had been a big help in the first year of our troubles, but one died during the winter of 1876. The next summer, my parents were forced to sell the other one. I still remember the price: $12.00. Oh, how my mother husbanded that $12.00! But it just wouldn't stretch for a family of two adults and six children. It would have been ten or eleven months and another winter before the next crop season, for that year's crop and garden was gone, consumed by the hoppers.

It is my honest belief that my parents did not have in cash any more than $25.00 during the twenty-five months preceding March of 1878 when they decided to leave Long Prairie. I should have mentioned that these were the days following the terrible panic of 1873, when the whole country was in sore financial straits from the Jay Cooke scandal. Barter, not cash money, was the

---

[53] HOM, Vol. III, p. 102, p. 106 and map following p. 106. HOG, maps on pp. 16, 18, 20, 25, and 28.

prevalent means of trade in the frontier areas. Without cash and with nothing to barter the people had no means whatsoever.[54]

There did seem to be one crop, however, that the grasshoppers curtailed not in the least and that, of course, was the Long Prairie baby crop. Jim was born there in June of 1873. Freddie was born in May, 1875, and Alice arrived just before Christmas Day, 1876. Our collective mouths to feed were increasing almost in direct proportion to our parents' decreasing ability to feed them, no thanks to the hoppers.

During the winters of 1876–1877 and 1877–1878, we children had no shoes. For those of us old enough to go outdoors, Mother made Indian moccasins out of several layers of coarse grain sack material and then lined the insides of them with two or three layers of the muslin sacking. They were more than adequate and kept our feet quite warm during the freezing weather. Whenever the weather thawed, however, our moccasins were worthless for the simple reason that they were not impervious to moisture. In that case our "mocs" stayed in the cabin, safe and dry, and we children, being impervious to moisture (and mud!), would bound about barefoot until it again froze sufficiently to allow us to appreciatively put our great "mocs" back on again.

Finally came the month of March in the spring of 1878. We had fought through the last months of winter on what must have been the limits of privation. One morning, just when the ground was beginning to show through the snow, Mother came face-to-face with the realization that there was no food in that windowless log cabin with which to feed her babies. In all of the hardships and privations I had seen her endure, this was the first and only time I ever saw her courage fail. I remember her yet, sitting in the gloom away from the stove, quietly weeping in despair. Father went out on skirmish and sometime later that day returned home with food in a sack. I never knew where he got it or how, and I have no recollection of what it was, but it was food. We never came to that extremity again, although for some time it was touch and go.

---

[54] See *"The people had no means"* in Author's Notes following this chapter regarding the "Jay Cooke scandal."

CHAPTER 3–AUTHOR'S NOTES

The Rocky Mountain locust: The home of the locust was determined to be in the eastern foothills and bordering plains of the Rocky Mountains, extending from a point roughly in the center of Colorado to the northern tree line of Canada. Precisely what conditions caused the billions of locust eggs to hatch remains a mystery. What was known, however, was that following five rapid molts (all of which occur within six to eight weeks after hatching), the locust had a fully developed set of wings. It was then that some new impulse would set in and the horde would rise, circle around, and then set off, guided by some unknown force toward feeding grounds that could be hundreds of miles away. Folwell wrote: "[They] have been known to extend [their flights] two- or three-hundred miles without alighting." [HOM, Vol. III, pp. 93–94.] The only salvation was that the Rocky Mountain locust had a short life span. Once the creature developed wings, it only had two to four weeks of life. They would mate and lay their eggs in the territory they had recently invaded and "thus the billions of locusts which have lived in the season perish from the earth." [Charles V. Riley, *The Locust Plague in the United States; Being More a Treatise on the Rocky Mountain Locust,* cited as Footnote 1, HOM, Vol. III, pp. 93–94. The story of the locust plague in Minnesota is told by Annette Atkins in her book *Harvest of Grief.*]

The people had no means: The panic of 1873 was preceded in Minnesota and some other states by the first of five successive years of the locust disasters in the middle of June. The economies of those states were, therefore, already in the doldrums. On 18 September 1873, the collapse of the national banking house of Jay Cooke and Company precipitated fiscal panic throughout the country. Cooke had been heavily involved in the highly leveraged financing arrangements of the Northern Pacific Railroad (NP). Minnesotans, in particular, were heavily hit because so much employment was dependent on the NP construction in their state. With the banking collapse, cash quickly became almost impossible to find and debtors discovered that their creditors were loath to exchange commodities in lieu of money with which to meet their obligations. By the fall of 1877, there were few commodities to trade in many Minnesota counties, anyway. Depending on where the swarms had landed, the locusts had consumed everything for five consecutive years.

CHAPTER FOUR

The Trek Back to Lake Jefferson:
April and May, 1878

A S SOON AS THE WEATHER MADE IT POSSIBLE for Father to travel on foot he declared that the hoppers had won and we would leave the field of victory to them.[55] We would return to the southern part of the state whence we had come. The plan was for father to return by himself and, as soon as he could make a little money, to send for Mother and the six of us children. When he set off I don't believe my father had a penny in his pocket and I am sure my mother had not a penny in the house. Having no horse, and leaving the two oxen and the wagon for us to follow in later, father would walk back to Waterville. It was one-hundred and-sixty-five miles.[56]

As desperately as we all wanted to depart together, it was simply impossible. Father had a pair of ancient oxen and a fairly good wagon, but the oxen were in such poor condition that they looked absolutely hopeless. One of the old fellows, Whitey, was so thin and weak from lack of feed that he had to be helped up every morning. We had nothing to feed them during that winter but marsh hay, which is very poor in nutrients. While I do not remember the specific date of father's leaving, I well remember the feeling of impending loneliness and insecurity his departing would surely bring. I recall clearly the near panic caused by the

---

[55] As it turned out, both Levi and the hoppers gave up on Todd County at the same time. See *"The end of the plague"* in Author's Notes following this chapter. Phillip Van Blaricom, Levi's brother, stayed when Levi and his family left. Phillip became one of Todd County's prosperous farmers.

[56] Unless otherwise noted, the source for Chapter 4 is the SNVB manuscript, pp. 8–11.

uncertainty of us being left, perhaps forever, as he walked out through the door of the cabin. And I remember the fear that touched my heart as he slowly trudged out of sight.

Looking back on this event there was, indeed, cause for concern. We had no food in the cabin except for three sacks of corn meal and part of a small barrel of maple syrup. Mother had just turned twenty-eight and was pregnant with her seventh child (our brother, Perry, was born in August). I had my ninth birthday shortly after father left. David turned eight about the same time. Mary had just turned seven. Jim would be five in about two months, and little Freddie would shortly turn three. Alice was only about eighteen months. People in those days never made much fuss over birthdays or children's ages. It was just sort of an expectation that there were older heads on younger shoulders. Due to the times, perhaps, that expectation often became a reality. In any case, with Father gone and not to return, we were definitely responsible for trapping our own squirrels and catching our own fish. Our survival depended on it.[57]

About six weeks after Father had started south, he sent Mother a ten-dollar bill. The first thing she did was buy a generous supply of grain for those oxen. They were our only means of returning to Waterville and connecting back up with father. As soon as old Whitey could hoist himself up unaided in the morning and Mother thought he could make a short drive each day, she got my Uncle Phillip to come over and help her fix the wagon. He helped put the bows over the wagon box and they stretched the canvas over them. On the day we departed, late in May, Uncle Phillip came back again and helped Mother disassemble our stove pipe and load it and our small wood stove in the wagon. She then gathered our pitifully few belongings, assembled us six children, bundled us in our warmest clothing, and we left.

The days were warm, and the road was in fair shape. The country through which we traveled for the first fifty miles, however, was sparsely settled, and it was plain to see from their poverty that all the people had suffered from the hoppers as we had. We were quite well off, comparatively speaking, for my mother had at least half of that ten dollars left yet. The oxen were improving daily

---

[57] HVBG, p. 181.

and, all things considered, we got along very well, camping each night by the roadside and sleeping in the wagon.

After we had been on the road a week or more, it looked very much as if there would be a bad storm. We were passing through a Norwegian settlement at the time, and mother thought she would see if we could get accommodations at a farmhouse. The first one we came to was a one-room log cabin, as most of them were at that time. Inside the cabin were eight or ten people, young and old. To provide insulation and additional heat, most of the room had been banked up with a crib three to four feet tall and about a foot wide. It was filled with a compost of fermenting barnyard manure mixed with straw. This was a fairly common practice among the Norwegians, and I had seen and smelled this effective heat source before. I could not figure out, however, why it had not been removed this late in the season—until I realized that it was a handy location to store their tableware, for that's where it was at the time. Be that as it may, they spoke very little of our language so we backed on out and took our chances with the storm.

Looking back on that brief meeting in that crowded Norwegian log cabin, I can see it displays a great portrait of America and her opportunities. The second and third generations of those Norwegian pioneers are now occupying the governor's chair and filling the halls of the Minnesota legislature.

The storm passed and we were getting along swimmingly by this time. Mother had unsparingly fed and cared for the oxen. They were gaining in condition and strength, and we were beginning to step off the miles. We were soon down in the well-settled country that had not been plagued by the grasshoppers, meeting great numbers of settlers heading for the Red River of the North to take up claims there. One night, after we had camped, two men with a rather light team of horses camped near us. After they had eaten their supper they came over to our camp. They soon made it known that they were interested in our oxen. These cattle of ours were quite large of frame and had they been in any kind of flesh they would have been attractive animals. The country where the two men were going had a heavy virginal sod that was hard to break and they knew their small horses could not do it. And so it was they struck mother up for a trade.

Well, my mother was pretty much stumped. She had never handled horses in her life. She knew, though, that she could make much better time with them, and that was becoming a big objective now, for that ten dollars was fading fast. If I had that old tenner today, I would take it out of circulation and retire it to a glass case for the rest of its existence, for I doubt if any other bill of that denomination ever did such a heroic job. She asked the two men to let her think over the deal until morning and said she would talk it over with me, her nine-year-old son. Of course, to me, the opportunity to get a team of horses in place of the slow oxen was like asking a boy whether he would rather push a wheelbarrow or drive a Cadillac. The next morning Mother agreed to the trade—horses and harness for yoke and oxen.

The men left the horses and harness, yoked up the oxen, thanked us again for the trade, and started on their way before we broke camp. When we were ready to start, we found ourselves in a real dilemma. Mother had never harnessed a horse before in her life and she found it a problem she could not solve. I was no help, for I had less experience around horses than she did—and she had none. As luck would have it, there was a farm not far from our camp, and in the distance she could see the farmer out in the field plowing. Mother promptly decided to walk out and ask if he would come and show her the ropes about harnessing a team. Fortunately for us, the farmer proved a willing teacher, and from him she learned the trick. After that we had no further difficulty on that score, and the team turned out to be very satisfactory. They were in good condition and easy to handle, and we made twice the distance in a day that we could with the oxen.

Father had started out to meet us and had made his calculation of a meeting point on an ox-team basis. We had had the horses for a few days, however, and were much farther along than he had anticipated. And of course he was looking for a team of oxen. He was riding in the company of another man when we met. The two of them were talking and I remember that my father nearly passed us by. Mother had not recognized him, for he was riding some distance off to the side of the wagon track. We children only recognized him from the back of the covered wagon after he had passed. In any case, we had a joyous reunion and continued on our way. We camped out two more nights before we reached Grandma Scribner's house on Lake Jefferson.

And so ended the trials of the last two years of my earliest childhood.

CHAPTER 4–AUTHOR'S NOTES

The end of the plague: The locust plague did not re-appear in Todd County or anywhere else in Minnesota in 1878. Following the scourge of 1877, which ended around 1 July, there then occurred an unanticipated and, as yet, unexplained change in the behavior of the creatures. In previous years the locusts would appear, devour everything in sight and then proceed to lay their eggs in that location. In 1877, the flights appeared to be on eating forays only and made no preparations for laying their eggs. Even the direction of the departing flights seemed to be random in nature. Some, in fact, flew back toward the west and northwest, "but," Folwell wrote, "the conjecture that they were return migrations to the original home of the locust in the Rockies has not been verified." In any case, despite small outbreaks in later years, the massive plagues of destruction seen in 1873–1877 never recurred. [HOM, Vol. III, p. 110.] From 1878 on there were abundant crops throughout Minnesota, and the economy of the state rapidly took a turn for the better. By the fall of 1882, with the close of Governor Pillsbury's term, Minnesotans were realizing that better days had arrived. [HOM, Vol. III, pp. 72, 97, 126, and 143.] Ironically, it was the spring of that same year, after twenty-six years residency in Minnesota, that the Scribner, Johnson, Woods, Perry, and Van Blaricom families chose to depart for the "greener pastures" of the arid eastern plains of Montana Territory.

CHAPTER FIVE

Lake Jefferson and Waterville:
May 1878–April 1882

WE PROCEEDED STRAIGHT AWAY TO LIVE with my maternal grandmother until my father could get us established somewhere. Well, we ended up staying almost three years, and it was there that I enjoyed the only normal child life I ever knew. Grandpa and Grandma Scribner's farm bordered on a large lake, Lake Jefferson, about midway between Le Center and Mankato and about fifteen miles northwest of our previous home near Waterville. The lake was full of fish, and Grandma had good boats. There were also excellent bathing beaches. We four boys—myself, David, Jim, and Freddie—lived either in or on the water all summer, and when winter came we had skating, and fishing through the ice. We had plenty of aunts and uncles and cousins to play with as well.[58]

Grandma Scribner had already had five children with Doctor Johnson when she married Zachariah Scribner in 1867. At the time of their marriage, her Johnson children ranged in age from four years to seventeen (the oldest being my mother, who was already married to my father at that time). Thirty-eight-year-old Grandma Mariah and forty-seven-year-old Grandpa Zachariah proceeded to have five children together, born between 1868 and 1874. (Grandma Scribner was forty-five years old when the last of her ten children was born.) Their first child, a boy, was born and died in 1868. Clarence ("Cad") was born in 1869 (the same as me), Charles in 1870, Charlotte in 1872, and Minnie in 1874.

---

58 Unless otherwise noted, the source for Chapter 5 is the SNVB manuscript, pp. 11–13.

David, Mary, Fred, Alice, and I were born between 1869 and 1876. It always felt a little strange that our aunts and uncles were the same ages as us, their nieces and nephews.

Frank Perry had married our mother's sister, Mary Jane, and they had associated themselves with Grandma and Grandpa Scribner. They had three children when we showed up: Buhrl, Roy, and Enola.[59] At four, three, and one, they were a little younger than the rest of us, but all-in-all, the twelve of us aunts, uncles, nieces, nephews, and cousins became fast friends and good playmates.

It was a little confusing when we first showed up because Grandma Scribner's youngest son from her marriage to Doctor Johnson was still living at home. He was my uncle and his name was Norton Stephen Johnson. Well, I was nine years old and my name was Stephen Norton Van Blaricom. Both of us, however, went by the name of "Norton." We finally got it sorted out when everybody decided that since he was the oldest (sixteen), they would call him "Nort" and me "Norton." That worked fine and, to our families, we have always remained "Nort" and "Norton."[60]

There at Lake Jefferson I got another eight months of schooling during two of the four-month winter sessions, and they were the best of my checkered academic career. Two more babies were born there at Grandma Scribner's, Perry in August of 1878 and Dora May in August of 1880.

In the spring of 1881, father moved us to a forty-acre place back near his Van Blaricom family outside of Waterville. Some of the land had been cleared and it already had an old, windowless log cabin on it. My parents cleaned up the place and we moved in and planted our garden. It was near enough that Dave, Mary, Jim, Freddie, and I had to go to the school in town that winter, our first experience in such a situation. It was two miles to town, one mile through a dense wood and another mile that took us across a frozen lake. Oftentimes when we made that trip through the woods, the four of us left just three tracks: one for each foot

---

[59] See *"The Perry Family"* in WFRF.

[60] By 1878, the other two Johnson children of Mariah were married and gone from the nest. Frank Johnson had become a cooper (barrel maker). He married Carrie Tuttle in 1873, and they were living up north in Todd County near the settlement of Little Sauk, where the Tuttle family resided. Martha May ("Muz") Johnson had married Jay Orr Woods in 1876, and they were located in Cleveland, Minnesota, where Jay Orr worked as a carpenter for the railroad.

and one for the seat of our pants. The only trouble was that once we got to town and the school, we found ourselves quite outside of our element.

All of our previous school experience in Todd County had been in the company of children who lived in relatively primitive conditions and whose economic circumstances were similar to ours. In Waterville, however, most of the children attending the school were the sons and daughters of merchants and other tradesmen, from homes of an affluence we had never known or been associated with. Don't ever minimize this condition they call an inferiority complex, for in a child's life it is a deadly thing. We were in such distressed circumstances that people would often give Mother articles of clothing that we children would wear. Someone, for example, had given my mother a coat that, with some imagination, fit me. It was far better than anything else I had, so I wore it to school one day. During a recess I overheard a boy, the son of a local merchant, telling his companions that his mother had given my mother the coat I was wearing. I am sure I bear the scars of that humiliation today.

My sister and brothers also had similar experiences befall them at our winter sojourn at the Waterville school. We grew more quiet and, with the exception of a couple of friends, withdrew from the others into our own little group of five by the time the four-month session had ended. I believe the usefulness of that school was completely nullified to us because of that series of unpleasant experiences.

Fortunately, at least from the view of our having to continue on in the Waterville school, our father's feet were beginning to itch. We couldn't have been there too long, for no babies were born there.

One day, long before the snow was gone in the spring of 1882, Father came home all enthused about a new country that was just being opened up to settlers. He had a brochure that told how the Northern Pacific Railroad was building their great transcontinental line from St. Paul to the Pacific coast. They had an enormous land grant from the government by which the railroad held title to every odd-numbered section in a strip, which, I believe, extended twenty miles in each direction from the track. In any case, it

**MARIAH JANETTE (BEARDSLEY)(JOHNSON) SCRIBNER,
CIRCA 1905**
PHOTO COURTESY OF JAMES E. VAN BLARICOM

ZACHARIAH SCRIBNER, CIRCA 1879
PHOTO COURTESY OF JAMES E. VAN BLARICOM

embraced hundreds of thousands of acres. The railroad company was anxious to colonize these lands, for they needed the money from the land sales and the business that settlement along the railroad would bring. I do not believe that any man, unless he had been paid for it, would lie like the men who wrote of the "fabulous" opportunities that country held for those who would come and take them.

Most of the articles and advertising claims were ridiculously absurd, but my father and his associates were ever primed for adventure (or misadventure) and the solvency of a tale or rumor of new and greener fields never got a hearing. Ah, yes! Glendive, Montana Territory! Soon to be the Western Hub of the NP! (It was briefly, in the mid-summer of 1881, the western end of the line.[61]) And the lower Yellowstone River valley! A country of fabulous opportunity! Cattle could graze year-round without hay, and corn would grow better than in Ohio! The grass of Montana was better than Kentucky blue grass, and, as a consequence, the wool grown there was softer and the beef was juicier! Wheat would grow in perfection wherever it was cultivated! "The winters," the brochure stated, "are far from rigorous and nearly every day is fit for out-door work."[62] Well, it was just a regular Garden of Eden!

Surely the author of the descriptive my father got hold of is president of the Ananias Club[63] in whatever clime he happens to now reside. I would expect it is someplace low in elevation and extremely hot.

On a more personal side, I know that my father's sister, Marthie, and her husband, Ben Wyant, had taken their five children and headed west in 1881. They traveled by train to the end of the track in western Dakota Territory and then went on by wagon to Miles City and Fort Keogh. There they met a young fellow by

---

[61] After the roundhouse was finished, Glendive did become a division point between and a primary maintenance and repair site for the railroad's Missouri (Bismarck to Glendive) and Yellowstone (Glendive to Billings) divisions. [TLW, p. 377.]

[62] MDM/PR. The Northern Pacific also pushed books written by authors who were favorably disposed to the settlement of the areas the NP tracks passed through. One of the most popular writers on this subject was Major James Sanks Brisbin, an officer with the 2nd Cavalry stationed at Fort Keogh. In 1881 he penned *The Beef Bonanza, or How to Get Rich on the Plains*. Brisbin was so enthusiastic on the subject of agriculture that his men referred to him as "Grasshopper Jim." [TLW, p. 34.]

[63] "Ananias was an early Christian who, according to Acts 5:1-11, was struck dead for lying to the Apostle Peter." [TID, p. 77.]

the name of Tom Alexander. Alexander, a U.S. Army Major by the name of Brisbin, and a couple of other men had decided to start a town about fifty miles west of Miles City. They thought for sure that the Northern Pacific would build right through their site and they would be able to profit by starting a town there. Tom Alexander married my cousin, Melissa, early in 1882, so the Wyants had hooked up with Alexander and had started a cattle ranch just outside the new town that they called Forsyth.[64]

I recall that two of my Uncle Frank Johnson's brothers-in-law, Hank Tuttle and his brother, Will, had worked on the railroad construction crews for two or three years as the track was laid west from Bismarck. Once the railroad got to the new settlement of Glendive in July of 1881, the two men let the track go on by. They hunted a few buffalo at first and then settled in the town. Both of them eventually took work as deputy sheriffs in Dawson County. Will wasn't married, but somewhere along the line Hank's wife, Anna, put herself and their two kids on the train and moved from Minnesota to Glendive late in 1881 or early in 1882. I'm sure that Grandma and Grandpa Scribner had kept up with the reports being sent by the Tuttle boys to their sister, Carrie, who was Uncle Frank Johnson's wife.

Although they weren't frequent writers, the Wyants had sent back word to the Van Blaricoms (who were Aunt Marthie Wyant's family) about the "boom" that was going to occur in the vicinity of the railroad towns as the railroad reached them. I am quite sure that the combination of the Wyant's stories to the Van Blaricoms, and the Tuttle's stories to the Johnsons and Scribners, had a great deal to do with the collective family decision to sell everything they had accumulated in Minnesota and move some seven-hundred miles north and west to the remote frontier of Glendive in the lower Yellowstone valley.

A further inducement was the fact that the railroad was offering very attractive rates to immigrants. Had it been otherwise, my immediate family could not have gone, for it took everything my parents could scrape together to pay the fares to our destination. I remember that the one-way freight rate charged to "emigrants"

---

[64] TLW, p. 3, p. 34, p. 67, p. 117, and p. 376. See *"Benjamin Franklin and Mary Martha Wyant"* in Author's Notes following this chapter.

or "land settlers" from St. Paul to Glendive was $20 per person for a second-class seat and $100 per freight car, including a ticket for one man if the car contained livestock.[65]

The irresponsible, adventurous nature of my father is well illustrated here. He took the risk of abandoning his established home, leaving an area that he knew and in which he was well-acquainted, and going nearly seven-hundred miles into a new country. He took with him his wife and eight children and another he knew would be born within a few months of arriving in Glendive—and he knew he would be practically without any funds when we landed at our destination. Every cent my parents could scrape together had been used to pay our fares.

Our father's vocation was that of a subsistence hunter. He had been lamed in one hip during his role in the War of the Rebellion and, aside from his service in the Army and being paid for occasionally helping a neighbor, I don't believe he had held more than two paying jobs in his adult life. We would be utterly dependent on him finding some source of income immediately upon our arrival in a raw frontier town that was little more than a year old. The only redeeming feature to this whole undertaking was that we would be in the company of several families of our near relatives.[66] They could extend help if the need arose. This fact, considering the events that transpired, ultimately proved to be our Saving Grace, especially for three of my four sisters and my youngest brother, Perry.

---

[65] The "emigrant" passenger fare of $19.90 secured a seat in "a Clean, neat, Second Class Car with upholstered seats." The Northern Pacific was quick to point out to their first class and Pullman passengers that they could never be assigned to a slow-moving emigrant train, since the NP settlers and their cars were attached to the regular express trains, not vice versa. [MDM/PR.] Since the NP "express trains" in 1882 averaged less than eighteen miles-per-hour (see Chapter 6), it is difficult for a modern traveler to appreciate what was meant by "a slow-moving emigrant train."

[66] See "We would be in the company of several families of our near relatives" in Author's Notes following this chapter.

CHAPTER 5–AUTHOR'S NOTES

Benjamin Franklin and Mary Martha (Van Blaricom) Wyant: One year before their move to Montana Territory in 1881, the Wyant family was shown on the 1880 census as residing in Spruce Hill, Douglas County, Minnesota:

Name	Age	Occupation	Birthplace
Benjamin Wyant	49	Laborer	Kentucky
Mary M.	49	Keeping House	Iowa
Melissa	15	At home	Minnesota
Julia ("Ella")	13	At Home	Minnesota
Benjamin F.	11	At Home	Minnesota
Joshua	9		Minnesota
George F.	7		Minnesota

[USC, Spruce Hill, Douglas County, Minnesota, p. 5, dwelling number 41, 4–5 July 1880.]

From the census record and other family records, it is apparent that, within her own Wyant family, Mary Martha Wyant went by the name of "Mary" or "Mary Martha." To the Van Blaricoms, however, she was routinely referenced as "Marthie" or "Aunt Marthie." That may have been a Van Blaricom "pet" name that stuck with her as she grew up.

On 7 March 1882, the Wyant's daughter, Melissa, age seventeen, married Tom Alexander, age twenty-six, in Forsyth. Around the same time a young stagecoach driver married Julia ("Ella") Wyant, fifteen. The Wyants also had three sons, Benjamin Franklin ("Frank"), Joshua, and George ("Finn"). Frank and Finn both worked as cowboys for the famed FUF ranch for a number of years. The FUF was a Minnesota outfit, The Green Mountain Stock Ranching Company, owned by Henry F. Fletcher and A. L. Belknap of Minneapolis. In 1882 the ranch was originally located some twelve miles north of Forsyth. Thomas W. "Whit" Longley was the early day foreman. The ranch quickly grew to cover three other locations, including Cannibal Island, some five miles west of Forsyth, where their horse ranch was situated. [TLW, p. 52, p. 143, and p. 208] Frank Wyant reportedly became the manager of the FUF some time after the turn of the century.

Tom Alexander was born in 1856 in Farmiston, New Brunswick,

Canada. His family soon moved to Idaho and he was raised there. He was known to have been a prospector and miner in the Boise area by 1873 at the young age of seventeen. By 1876 he was at the Tongue River Cantonment (which later became Fort Keogh) where he worked as a clerk for the U.S. Army. Alexander went on to serve in the Nez Perce campaign in 1877. That same year, he started operating a two-hundred-acre ranch on the south side of the Yellowstone River some forty-seven miles west of Miles City. In 1880, the NPRR surveyors determined that his site would make a good station. Alexander then brought in Major James S. ("Grasshopper Jim") Brisbin and Lieutenant Edmund Rice (both of the 2nd U.S. Cavalry stationed at Fort Keogh) and Robert L. Edwards of Miles City and they platted the town of Forsyth. By July of 1882, the railroad had arrived and the population was reckoned to be about five-hundred people. Captain Galbraith of the 11th U.S. Infantry (garrisoned at Fort Custer) took the train from Forsyth to Glendive. He reported that Forsyth was "mostly canvas houses and tents. Drinking and gambling were something fierce." Of some eighty-nine structures in town, Galbraith estimated that sixty-nine of them were gambling places. [TLW, p. 3 and p. 117.] The place soon calmed down and began to assume the appearance of a more normal town. When Father Lindeman visited Forsyth in April of 1883, he wrote in his diary, "everything I saw made a favorable impression on me. As they say, 'I fell in love with the people and the place.'" [Cited in TLW, p. 117.]

Although young Melissa (Wyant) Alexander died in childbirth in Forsyth in 1883 at the age of eighteen, her daughter, Mae Alexander, lived. Mae later married "a Hollenbeck boy" and descendants from that marriage continue to reside in Forsyth. In 1885, Tom Alexander married Mary Fitzpatrick (1858–1955). Benjamin Franklin Wyant and Mary Martha (Van Blaricom) Wyant lived out their lives on their ranch near Forsyth. Benjamin Wyant died in 1900 at about the age of sixty-nine. Mary Martha died in 1913 at about the age of eighty-two. Both of them and their daughter, Melissa (Wyant) Alexander, are buried in the Forsyth cemetery. In September of 1918, Tom Alexander, at the age of fifty-two, was killed by lightning. [TLW, p. 3, p. 67, and p. 376. TCS, pp. 2–3 and p. 360. T&T, p. 19.]

It is of some interest to note that Hiram M. Marcyes, one of Forsyth's earliest settlers, was a comrade-in-arms with Levi Van Blaricom during the Civil War. They both served all four years of the Civil

War as members of Company "I" of the 4th Minnesota Infantry Regiment. Born in Maine about 1843, Marcyes had enlisted with Levi in 1861. When Marcyes re-enlisted with the regiment on 1 January 1864, he was transferred to the "Non-Commissioned Staff as Principal Musician." In 1865, he returned to Minnesota, where he farmed and worked in a flourmill. In 1876, he married Louise Leffelmaker. By 1882 they were settled in Forsyth, where Hiram started out simply enough by selling peanuts and candy. He soon opened a general merchandise store and became one of Forsyth's more successful citizens. Marcyes became Forsyth's justice of the peace in 1883. [H4M, p. 544. MCIW, Vol. I, p. 239. TLW, p. 215.]

We would be in the company of several families of our near relatives: Every living descendant of Mariah Janette (Beardsley) (Johnson) Scribner made the move from Waterville and Le Sueur County, Minnesota, to Glendive in 1882. Twenty-eight members of the Scribner, Van Blaricom, Johnson, and Perry families participated in the April 1882 migration. Brothers Henry C. ("Hank") and William Tuttle (brothers-in-law to Frank Johnson) and Hank's wife and family had preceded them in 1881. Jay Orr Woods was married to Sarah Susan's sister, May Martha ("Muz") Johnson. Woods worked as a carpenter for the NPRR in Minnesota. He arranged for a transfer to Glendive and arrived in June or July of 1882. His wife, "Muz," and their three children followed Jay Orr to Glendive in April of 1883. An enumeration of the specific family members and their dates of arrival in Glendive follows:

Note: Large number (e.g., "1") tallies an adult
Small Roman numeral (e.g., "xiv") tallies a child
The letters "ca." abbreviates the word "circa" or "about"

Name	Approximate age on date of arrival
(Arrived in Glendive with the NP late in 1880. Settled in Glendive in June/July of 1881)	
1. Hank Tuttle	34
2. Bill Tuttle	25
(Arrived in Glendive in the fall of 1881)	
3. Anna Tuttle (wife of Hank)	30
i. Child of Hank and Anna	6
ii. Child of Hank and Anna	3

Name	Approximate age on date of arrival
(Arrived in Glendive 22 April 1882)	
4. Zachariah Scribner	57
5. Mariah (Johnson) Scribner	55
iii. Norton Stephen Johnson	19
iv. "Cad" Scribner	13
v. Charles Scribner	10
vi. Charlotte Scribner	9
vii. Minnie Scribner	8
6. Levi Van Blaricom	39
7. Sarah Susan (Johnson) V. B.	32
Died in Glendive, 25 September 1882.	
viii. Stephen Norton V. B.	13
ix. David Van Blaricom	11
x. Mary Van Blaricom	10
xi. Jim Van Blaricom	8
xii. Freddie Van Blaricom	6
xiii. Alice Van Blaricom	5
xiv. Perry Van Blaricom	4
xv. Dorie Van Blaricom	1
8. Frank Perry	31
9. Mary Jane (Johnson) Perry	30
xvi. Buhrl Perry	8
xvii. Roy Perry	7
xviii. Enola May Perry	5
xix. Kendrick Perry	3
10. Frank Johnson	28
11. Carrie (Tuttle) Johnson	28
xx. Bertha Johnson	7
xxi. Grace Flora Johnson	3
xxii. Harry Johnson	2
Died in Glendive, about 9 August 1882.	
(Arrived in Glendive in June/July of 1882)	
12. Jay Orr Woods	27
(Arrived in Glendive in April of 1883)	
13. "Muz" (Johnson) Woods	23
xxiii. Myra Woods	5

Name	Approximate age on date of arrival

(Arrived in Glendive in April of 1883 cont.)

xxiv. Inez Woods	3
xxv. Harry Woods	2

(The following children were born in Glendive to the above-named families after their arrival.)

xxvi. Sarah Effie Van Blaricom	b. 9 July 1882
xxvii. Frank Herschel Woods	b. 15 June 1883
xxviii. Frank Perry, Jr.	b. 1883
xxix. Wilbur Tuttle	b. 11 November 1883
xxx. Edwin Jay Woods	b. 15 January 1885
xxxi. John Perry	b. 1885
xxxii. Ray Arthur Woods	b. 4 September 1886

[To reference the Tuttles, see USC, 1880, Billings County, North Dakota. OTOL, p. 2. TLW, p. 352. For the general family, see GT, 25 September 1885. HVBG, pp. 179–182. GT, 17 August 1882. GT, 28 September 1882. WN, 14 August 1961. For Jay Orr Woods and his family, see WFRF, p. 23 and p. 27 and "Additions and corrections as of December 1976." For the family of Frank Perry, see WFRF, pp. 47–50 and "Additions and corrections as of December 1976."]

On the immigrant railroad cars that arrived on 22 April 1882 were four families with eight married adults and twenty children, all related through Mariah Scribner. In addition, there were "all of their horses, oxen, cattle, pigs and chickens, their furniture and flatware, their tools, harness, farm implements, sacks of seed for planting and sacks of feed for their animals, their wagons and their weapons and whatever else they had or could think of and afford." [HVBG, p. 179.]

By April of 1883 (following the birth of Sara Effie, the deaths of Sarah Susan Van Blaricom and young Harry Johnson and the arrival of Jay Orr and "Muz" Woods and their three children), this greater family assemblage of Mariah Scribner and her husband, their children, all of her Johnson children and their spouses and children as well as their Tuttle in-laws, Hank and Bill, and Hank's wife and children tallied a group of twelve adults and twenty-four children. At least seven children were born after the family's arrival in Glendive. Starting with the original group of eleven adults and twenty-two children in April of 1882 and with the twelve adults and thirty-one children all living in Glendive or the immediate area by the winter of 1886–1887, research has found no larger family group living in Dawson County from the time they arrived until they left in the spring of 1887. (Levi, his son, David, his daughter, Mary, and Mary's baby, Emma Mabel, born 16 December 1887, left Glendive in 1888. Stephen Norton stayed in Glendive until he married and moved to Ohio in 1900.)

CHAPTER SIX

Glendive, Montana Territory: 1882

I T WAS ABOUT SEVEN-HUNDRED MILES from Waterville to Glendive. First, from Waterville to St. Paul was about seventy miles. Then it was about two-hundred-and-thirty miles from St. Paul to Fargo, two-hundred miles from Fargo to Bismarck, one-hundred from Bismarck to Dickinson, and another one-hundred miles from Dickinson to Glendive.

Our westbound train left St. Paul at 7:30 P.M. on April 20, 1882. That was the first time many of us had ever been on a train. We soon discovered that, unless there was a pretty fair breeze, the cars clacked along inside the smoke emanating from the engine. All of us children quickly learned not to poke our heads outside the windows. The hot embers discharged from the engine could settle on you and leave a burn mark on your skin or a hole in your clothes. Between the embers and the smoke, we kept our windows shut that whole night.

We arrived in Fargo about 8:00 the following morning. Our train simply switched to a new engine in Fargo. We probably weren't there an hour and we were off for Bismarck. I remember we were scheduled to arrive in Bismarck at 7:00 P.M., and we got there pretty much on time. We spent the night in Bismarck and left early the next morning for Dickinson and Glendive. Arrival in Glendive was scheduled for 7:30 that same night.[67]

Well, our Northern Pacific immigrant train arrived in Glendive,

---

[67] According to the Northern Pacific's schedule, one night on the train and one night in Bismarck got the traveler from St. Paul to Glendive in thirty-five hours and twenty minutes of actual "on the road" travel time. The distance between St. Paul and Glendive was six-hundred-and-twenty-three miles. The train was thus averaging 17.65 miles per hour, including the "whistle stops" for passengers, mail, water, and fuel. The eastbound train from Glendive departed for Dickinson and Bismarck at 6:45 A.M. [MDM/PR.]

Montana Territory, late in the evening of April 22, 1882.[68] For those of you who have some interest in the history of the area, I should point out that our train crossed the Missouri between Bismarck and Mandan on a ferry. That continuous band of steel from St. Paul to Glendive didn't then exist. There was no railroad bridge across the Missouri at Bismarck until October of 1882. It was during the winter of 1878–1879 that General Rosser[69] built his famous "ice bridge." He simply laid ties on the ice, spiked the track, and away they went all winter. They transported tons of supplies across to the west side of the Missouri during that winter.[70] They later built a ferry large enough to transport supplies and railroad cars, and that operated until the bridge was finished in the very late fall of 1882. Thus, between completion of the line and beginning of commercial service to Glendive in July of 1881 until November of 1882, the ferry at Bismarck kept the railroad running.[71]

It was also between Bismarck and Glendive that we passed Sentinel Butte. The conductor pointed it out and said that the railroad threw a big party when they finished laying the track to that point in 1880. That was, after all, the boundary between Montana Territory and Dakota Territory. What that conductor didn't know in 1882 when he told me about Sentinel Butte was that their jubilant celebration had been ten miles premature. Sometime around 1885 or 1886, when they did the land surveys for settlement of that part of the country, they discovered the error—and there were more than a few embarrassed railroad surveyors.[72] On the other hand, if you've ever crossed that desolate stretch of country, it's easy to understand the mistake when one considers that, aside from Sentinel Butte, there were no "Welcome

---

[68] Unless otherwise noted, the source for Chapter 6 is the SNVB manuscript, pp. 13–15. See *"Glendive"* in Author's Notes following this chapter for a brief history of the town.

[69] Former Confederate General Thomas L. Rosser was the chief engineer for construction of the Northern Pacific Railroad from Bismarck through eastern Montana. He was a former West Point roommate of George A. Custer and an erstwhile adversary of Custer during the Civil War. Custer once chided Rosser for not leaving behind clothes that would fit him (Custer) when one of Custer's forays forced Rosser to flee his headquarters and leave his baggage. [B&S, p. 72.]

[70] HNPR, pp. 395–396. The "ice bridge" at Bismarck was first utilized on 12 February 1879. [NPMS, p. 25.] For a more detailed discussion of the famed structure, see *"The ice bridge"* in Author's Notes following this chapter.

[71] The Missouri River bridge was opened on 21 October 1882. [NPMS, p. 37.]

[72] HML, p. 549.

to Montana" signs present at the time of their arrival. No "Burma Shave" signs either. That second set of surveyors finally did mark the true boundary. They simply placed a tall pole by the railroad track upon which was nailed a fine pair of deer antlers. No sign. No nothing. Just the antler pole.[73]

The morning following our arrival in Glendive was chilly, with a drizzling rain. All about was the hurry and bustle of a raw frontier town. Tin cans and animal bones lay about and sagebrush grew speckled about the streets. "Where you from?" was the common salutation our first few days in town.[74]

Glendive was platted where the Northern Pacific Railroad formed a junction with the Yellowstone River, about eighty miles upriver from Fort Buford.[75] From Dickinson, Dakota Territory, to Glendive is one-hundred miles of what is probably some of the most godforsaken country in the United States. Unless you count the Little Missouri at Medora, there is not a cup of good water in the whole distance. Especially to the north and on the western half of this route, the Indians called the country "Bad Lands" with good reason. Intensely hot in summer and deadly cold in winter, they were dry as the bottomless pit most of the time.[76]

In the region around Glendive, our only source of potable water in 1882 was the Yellowstone River. Water from the alkaline wells in Dawson County was not fit for domestic use. Sweet-water springs were a rare find. The Yellowstone has its source in the Rocky Mountains, and the water is of the melted snows of the mountains and the run-off of all the country in between until it joins with the Missouri River at Fort Buford. There are those today who would have you believe that the river got its name from the French-Canadian fur trappers who supposedly called it the *Roche Jaune* or the "yellow rock." Nothing could be further from the truth. The river gets its name from the fact that from the time the ice goes out in the spring until some time in the latter part of June it is nothing more than a roiling stream of light brown silt. I have always surmised that it was named the "Yellow

---

[73] HNPR, p. 136. See *"Nice party. Wrong place."* in Author's Notes following this chapter.

[74] Newspaper article by Stephen Norton Van Blaricom, DCR, Thursday, 15 February 1923.

[75] TLW, p. 399. See *"How far is it?"* in Author's Notes following this chapter.

[76] See *"The Bad Lands"* in Author's Notes following this chapter.

Stone" by the Northern Pacific Railroad because if they had called it the "Light Brown Mud River" they never would have had any takers for all their land.[77]

During all of the years I lived in Glendive, we were obliged to buy our water from a water peddler who charged twenty-five cents for a single fifty-two-gallon barrel. We were often the recipients of a barrel of water, which, when it settled, would have two inches of solid silt in the bottom of the barrel. I can assure you that Glendive was no place for people who were unduly particular or finicky. Nobody waited for the water to settle before we drank it, for it was a considerable wait of several days to get the sediment to settle at all. Death by thirst would have been the fate of anyone waiting for the last particle of sediment to fall from that liquid solution of Yellowstone water and put itself to its final rest on the bottom of that barrel.[78]

When your income is meager and you pay twenty-five cents for a barrel of water, you quickly learn something about economy. A housekeeper was considered extravagant if she used more than eighty gallons a week and that included drinking water, cooking, bathing, and doing dishes and laundry. In our family of ten, that quota worked out to eight gallons per week for each of us. Our scientific friends have told us that most people drink about a quart of water a day. That left us about six gallons per person per week for the rest of our needs. I am told that about five gallons of water flow each minute when a modern shower is in use. The average person in the United States today requires more than fifty gallons of water per day for personal and household use. I am also told that a bath in a modern tub requires about twenty-five gallons of water.[79] Well, you just didn't get many bathtubs sold in a place like Glendive in 1882. You learned that you could just take a basin of water with the usual cloth and a bar of soap and do a pretty fair job on old John B.O. And, depending on weather conditions, if you really wanted to do a bang-up job there was always the Yellowstone at no charge whatsoever.

---

[77] The *Roche Jaune* or "Yellowstone" was so-named long before Lewis and Clark first saw the river in 1805. For a detailed discussion of the history of the name, see POY, pp. 14–15.

[78] See *"Water was twenty-five cents a barrel"* in Author's Notes following this chapter.

[79] "Water," CEnc (1972), Vol. 22, p. 66.

Aside from the Yellowstone River and its tributaries, eastern Montana can be pretty dry. I have looked up the government meteorology reports and they show an average precipitation of but ten to eleven inches per year. If you then exclude the snowfall and the hailstones, that means it doesn't rain much in the average year. In addition, the weather report shows that Miles City, Montana, has the record for the widest variation of temperature of any place in the United States, with recorded readings of sixty-four degrees below zero and one-hundred-and-twelve above. Glendive is no different. They just didn't start recording there as soon as they did in Miles City due to the early presence of a weather station at Fort Keogh.

Like most of the early railroad towns along the Yellowstone, the main street of Glendive was laid out parallel with the railroad. There was room enough for a good-sized two-way wagon road between the front door of the first saloon and the ends of the ties. That placed the commercial part of town and, eventually, the better residences between the track and the river. On the other side of the tracks, between the railroad and the big hill, were the small remnant structures of the old abandoned military post, Camp Porter, that had been built before the town came along, put there to guard the railroad construction.[80] Within a couple of years, the Northern Pacific's roundhouse and other shops, the stockyard, and the cottages of the less affluent were also built over there. Not that there was social difference between one side of the tracks and the other. Do not misunderstand me in thinking that there was a "right side of the tracks" or a "wrong side of the tracks" in Glendive, for there wasn't. People moved freely with absolutely no "class" distinction between them.[81]

---

[80] Norton erred in stating that "the old abandoned military post" was built before the town of Glendive was platted. Camp Porter was built after the town of Glendive was platted. See *"'The old military post' in Glendive"* in Author's Notes following this chapter.

[81] Alice (Van Blaricom) Hyatt, in an interview in August of 1953, also remarked on the absence of "class distinction" in the frontier towns of Montana Territory.

CHAPTER 6–AUTHOR'S NOTES

Glendive: When Stephen Norton Van Blaricom and his family arrived in April of 1882, Glendive was an unincorporated town situated in unorganized Dawson County. The official plat for the town, initially called "Yellowstone," had been filed on 20 August 1880. [GT, 19 May 1883.] The town was first laid out in October of 1880 with the final surveys completed in June of 1881. [GT, 19 May 1883, 19 April 1884, and 27 June 1886.] Even after Dawson County was organized on 27 September 1882 and Glendive was named the county seat, the town remained unincorporated for another twenty years. The citizens of Glendive failed to incorporate the town until 6 October 1902, when ninety-nine of the one-hundred-and-twenty-four voters (representing the city's twelve-hundred-and-fifty-four men, women, and children) decided that Glendive should "be and is Incorporated as a City of the Third Class." [GHMT, p. 46.] It took until 27 April 1903 for elections to be held and for the charter itself to be issued. So it was that from the time Glendive was platted late in 1880 until it was chartered in 1903, there was no city government or city services of any kind. The three county commissioners and the county sheriff ran everything in the town. (The situation was the same in Sidney, where incorporation didn't occur until 1911.)

One of the unfortunate yet fairly common problems then seen in the small, new towns of the West was that thieves would resort to arson to either cover their tracks or to provide a diversion for their escape. Often, the smell of coal oil would betray the fact that a store was being burgled in the middle of the night. A few newspaper snippets told of some of these events:

> Prescott's drug Store just about burned as Gallagher and Kelley's Building was drenched with kerosene, but it was caught in time. [GT, 2 August 1885.]

> Wm. Lowe's hardware store was burglarized. Lost cutlery and revolvers. Fire was attempted. [GI, 4 June 1887.]

Just because the county didn't provide various services, however, didn't mean the citizens of Glendive simply stood by and let the world fall in on them. Very early on (sometime late in 1882 or early in 1883) the merchants banded together and hired their own night watchman. A second watchman was added in 1885. [GT, 10 May 1885.]

While credit should be given where credit is due, the more pressing problem was to have enough sober men present to man the bucket brigades, especially late at night. Among those who did show up, it wasn't uncommon to see the fire fighting force dwindle rapidly if there was any liquor, wine, or beer being "saved" from the structure on fire. Invariably, if a saloon or "tasting room" was involved, the inventory was rarely found in the morning and the building was almost invariably reported as a "total loss."

> At 3 AM the old Merrill House caught fire and burned. Could have been "set" or maybe the laundry room fire wasn't out. [GT, 13 December 1885.]

> Many of the young sprigs got gloriously drunk on the spirits they found in the basement. [GT, 20 December 1885.]

> The Dion Block...caught fire and all furnishings were removed. On the main floor all of the saloon items were removed. Henry Dion suffered a $500 loss in his stock [since the] spirits were mostly drank by the rescuers. [GI, 9 January 1886.]

The county never responded to the merchants' and citizens' calls for a fire department. It simply wasn't in the budget and, the commissioners pointed out, the Northern Pacific had a water line that ran from the Yellowstone to the tracks to provide water to the locomotives. The problem was that somebody had to start up the pump when a fire was in progress. Even if the pump was started, it was a high-volume, low-pressure rig. There were no hoses long enough to service the town, and the water pressure was insufficient to fight a fire with them anyway. The citizens voiced their frustration:

> Yellowstone Hotel suffers $1,000 in fire damage. We have no fire protection! [GI, 19 February 1887.]

It was later in the year of 1887 that the merchants formed their own volunteer fire and bucket brigade so they could respond to fires in the town—if they could find and deliver enough water to fill enough buckets to put out a fire. In the end it was brick construction (used to replace the businesses as they burned down) that solved Glendive's fire problem. Work began on a community water system in 1905. The pressurized system built of wooden water mains was completed in 1907. [GTHG, p. 14.]

The ice bridge across the Missouri River at Bismarck was first utilized on 12 February 1879. [NPMS, p. 25.] The Missouri River bridge was opened on 21 October 1882. [NPMS, p. 37.] In 1968, Charles R. Wood stated in his book *Northern Pacific, The Mainstreet of the Northwest* that the ferry and ice bridge systems were used in combination until the bridge opened in the fall of 1882: "From 1879 to 1882 operation of trains across the Missouri River...was accomplished by laying tracks on the ice in the winter as soon as it would bear the load and by ferry boat when it had broken up." [NPMS, p. 25 and p. 37.] Since the ice bridge was first utilized during the winter of 1878–1879, four winter seasons, according to Wood, would have passed with the ice bridge periodically in use (the winters of 1878–1879, 1879–1880, 1880–1881, and 1881–1882).

Without specifically mentioning the famed ice bridge, Eugene V. Smalley, the author of *History of the Northern Pacific Railroad,* wrote in 1883: "The Missouri Division, from Mandan on the west bank of the [Missouri] river to the Yellowstone, was operated for two years in connection with the road east of the Missouri by means of a transfer boat which carried trains across, not without considerable difficulty in times of high water and floating ice." [HNPR, p. 390 and pp. 394–397.] Thus, according to Smalley, the ice bridge was utilized during the winter of 1878–1879, and the ferry was used exclusively during the winters of 1880–1881 and 1881–1882.

Between the two accounts, one published in 1883, the other in 1968, it is not clear as to how many years the "ice bridge" was kept in service. In any case, passenger train and commercial service to Glendive opened 5 July 1881. The bridge between Mandan and Bismarck was not put into service until October of 1882. Between those two dates, according to Smalley, all commercial traffic moved across the Missouri via the Northern Pacific's "transfer boat" in both summer and winter. When Stephen Norton Van Blaricom and his family made the move to Glendive in April of 1882, they utilized the ferry to cross the Missouri River at Mandan.

Nice party. Wrong place. As late as 1885, the boundary line between North Dakota and Montana had not been precisely surveyed. "[From Glendive] to the eastern boundary of Montana is about fifty miles, the location of the boundary line never having been accurately determined." [HML, p. 549.] The problem rested with the surveying instruments of the day. The earth revolves at the speed of fifteen degrees per hour. If one knows the precise time difference between the surveyor's location and some fixed point, say the Greenwich meridian, it is a relatively simple task to calculate longitude. However, as Sarah Murgatroyd explained in her book *The Dig Tree,* "it was a tall order to expect a watch to function without error throughout the rigors of a desert expedition." [DT, p. 162.] The calculation required a precisely functioning chronometer and the expert use of a sextant to calculate local time by determining when the sun reached its highest point. Due to the inaccuracy of the early explorers' and surveyors' timepieces, exact longitudinal fixes were always difficult well into the twentieth century. (The history of determining longitude is recounted in *Longitude* by Dava Sobel, Walker and Company, New York, 1995.) To compound the problem, Montana's eastern boundary was legally described as "the twenty-seventh degree of longitude west of Washington [City]." By the time the boundary surveys were being done, however, the United States had agreed to the use of longitudes west of Greenwich, England, and some cartographers and others frequently cited Montana's eastern boundary as located at one-hundred-and-four degrees west of the Greenwich meridian. The two sets of longitudes didn't (and, it should be pointed out to some modern cartographers, still don't) match. The Greenwich meridian is slightly more than two miles east of the Washington meridian. For a more detailed discussion of the problem of establishing the boundaries of Montana and its counties, see that subject in "Old Dawson."

The precise location of the party mistakenly thrown at "Sentinel Butte" on 10 November 1880 is unrecorded in the history books. However, Sentinel Butte (the "butte," per se) is about ten miles east of the actual Montana boundary, and that generalized term ("Sentinel Butte," whatever or wherever that meant) rested in everyone's memory as the site of the premature celebration. Some people have suggested that "Sentinel Butte," the old Northern Pacific Railroad station only one mile east of the North Dakota–Montana boundary, was the site where the party took place. The problem with that scenario is that the station wasn't built until 1881. That makes one believe that Sentinel Butte Station was part of the track laying and construction that only commenced the year following the big border-crossing party.

According to local historian Tom Ray, the NPRR surveyors did, in fact, make a ten-mile mistake: "First to set foot on Montana soil were the track layers from the east and they were officially welcomed not by a Montana official, but by a North Dakota lawyer! Through error the Dakota–Montana line was believed to be ten miles east of the true line and at the mistaken point a celebration was held on November 10, 1880. Two silver spikes connected with two silver links were driven into the track and on them were inscribed: 'Welcome, Northern Pacific Railroad, Dakota to Montana.' General Manager H. E. Sargent of the railroad officiated. Drafted to represent Montana, [was] George F. Flannery, Bismarck attorney...." Ray continued: "Actual entry of the [track-laying] crews into the [territory] took place on May 14, 1881. On that day they crossed the real line near Wibaux, then known as Beaver." [TRP, pp. 32–33.] *The Montana Atlas and Gazetteer* shows the eastern boundary of Montana to be almost exactly seven miles east of downtown Wibaux.

It took the telegraph (to accurately transmit the time) and the land settlement surveys of 1885, 1886, and 1887 to finally locate the true Montana–Dakota boundary. (Homesteads couldn't be filed or "proved up" without proper survey descriptions.) The time at the Naval Observatory in Washington City was telegraphed to the surveyors in Wibaux and then the distance back to the boundary was physically measured. In order to embarrass the Northern Pacific, the survey crew simply planted a tall pole topped with a large pair of deer antlers to mark the boundary line where the railroad track crossed it. The train crews not only took the joke in stride, they turned it around and promoted it as an embarrassment to the surveying community. In any case, the "antler pole" soon gained popular recognition as marking the Montana–Dakota border. It remained in place and was the only border "sign" for a number of years, generating innumerable stories regarding the "pole-and-antler" marker. [HNPR, p. 136.]

How far is it? The circumstances and equipment available on the Montana frontier prior to the more accurate land surveys meant that measured distances between points were not precise. "Glendive is otherwise described [in a railroad brochure] as resting on latitude 47 degrees and 3 minutes north, and longitude 105 degrees and 45 minutes west. It is eighty-five miles or more on the river from the [Northern Pacific] roundhouse [in Glendive] to the confluence of the Yellowstone and the Missouri, and eighty-one miles by the old stage road...." [GTY, pp. 10–11.]

In 1881, T. P. McElrath had recorded the "old stage road" distances measured with an odometer: "Glendive to Burns Ranch, 22.98 miles; Burns Ranch to Crane [sic] Ranch, 22.66 miles; Crane Ranch to Gorman's Ranch, 5.96 miles; Gorman's Ranch to Twelvemile Creek, 12.88 miles; Twelvemile Creek to Missouri River [Ferry], 9.70 miles; and Missouri River Ferry to Fort Buford, 3.18 miles. Total Road Miles, Glendive to Missouri River: 74.18 miles." [*Yellowstone Valley*, T. P. McElrath, 1881, cited in TLW, p. 399.] Thus, McElrath's computations placed Fort Buford at 77.36 road miles distant from Glendive plus the width of the Missouri River crossing.

Measuring the distances down the Yellowstone River itself was another matter: "A table of distances on the Yellowstone River [from its confluence with the Missouri River] as recorded by steamboat Captain Grant Marsh: Glendive [Creek], 126 miles" or, say, about 128 miles to the center of downtown Glendive—a site that didn't exist when Marsh did his measuring in 1873 and 1875. [BT, 6 August 1877. TLW, p. 380.] Marsh had developed his own system for measuring distances. The top or "hurricane" deck of his sternwheeler, the *Josephine*, was exactly 150 feet long. He would station three men there, one situated aft to record and the other two started out forward. The first of the two men stationed forward would pace along with some fixed object on the shore as they passed. When he reached the stern, he would signal and the second man would start to pace it off while the first man would return to the bow. The recorder simply tallied each trip and then multiplied times 150 feet. And thus were the distances traveled each day computed. "While not to be compared in accuracy to a survey," wrote Joseph Mills Hanson in his biography of Marsh, *The Conquest of the Missouri*, "this method established the distances along the river with approximate certainty, and from that day to the present [the book was originally published in 1909] the measurements taken by the Key West and the Josephine [in 1873 and 1875] have been regarded as the standard ones for the Yellowstone, no regular survey of the river having ever been made." [COM, pp. 205–206]

The "Bad Lands": The English term "bad lands" (or "badlands") was simply a translation of the French-Canadian voyageur's description of *mauvaises terres. The Great Northwest,* a Northern Pacific Railroad publication written by Henry J. Wisner (Putnam and Sons, New York, 1883, p. 181), explained in greater detail: "The designation 'Bad Lands' is derived from the times of the old French voyageurs, who, in their trapping and hunting expeditions in the service of the great fur companies, described the region as *'mauvaises terres pour traverser,'* meaning that it was a difficult region to travel through. This French descriptive term was translated and shortened into 'bad lands.'" [TGN, p. 181.] The Sioux Indian word for that kind of country was "maco sica" (hence "Makoshika" State Park which borders Glendive today). On the other hand, "The first white men to see the badlands often used the word 'Hell.' 'Hell cooled over' they called them. General [Alfred P.] Sully remarked...'Gentlemen, there is Hell with the fires put out.'" [GHMT, p. 6.] In some cases, the fires hadn't been (couldn't be) put out. The underground lignite coal fires could burn for long periods, sometimes years. Marie MacDonald noted the last of the underground fires in Dawson County were not extinguished until the 1930s. [GHMT, p. 5.]

"Water was twenty-five cents a barrel." Any resident of Glendive who needed water put out a red flag to signal the drayman. There were often so many red flags out that travelers went right on through thinking the town was under quarantine for one kind of disease or another. While the red water flags seem humorous in retrospect (they really could have picked another color), the quarantine thing was not a joke in Glendive. "Barrels [of water from the Yellowstone River] and [hand-dug, shallow] wells were, indeed, a source of epidemics, and Glendive desperately needed a reliable, uncontaminated water supply." The water issue is what finally forced the town to incorporate in 1902. The water treatment plant didn't arrive, however, until 1917. [GTHG, pp. 13–14 and photo caption, p. 61. Also see this subject in "Old Dawson."]

"The old military post" in Glendive: In his memoir (on p. 15), Stephen Norton erred in writing that "Camp Porter was an abandoned military post...built before the town came along." It is true that the Glendive area had been a beehive of various short-lived military establishments through the years 1873 through 1881. The only fortified structure on the east (south) bank of the Yellowstone, however, was Stanley's Stockade, located about eight miles upriver from the mouth of Glendive Creek. Built under the supervision of Colonel David Sloane Stanley during the Northern Pacific surveying expedition of 1873, the area surrounding the stockade also saw brief service during the Sioux campaigns of 1876–1877. Two early locations were both named Camp Canby. The first had been built at the mouth of Glendive Creek on the east side of the Yellowstone and was occupied for less than two weeks in 1873. The other, located on Deer Creek and utilized for only days in 1876, was sited on the west side of the Yellowstone near the future site of the Glendive Cantonment. The Glendive Cantonment was built late in 1876 on the west side of the Yellowstone, slightly downstream from and on the opposite side of the Yellowstone from Glendive Creek. In the summer of 1880, Camp Hargous (a.k.a. "Camp Thorington") was initially located on the plateau immediately south of and above Glendive Creek. In September of 1880 Camp Thorington was then moved a couple of miles south to a site on the Yellowstone River that was centered on the newly platted town of Glendive. Finally, Camp Porter was built on the southeast corner of the platted townsite and replaced Camp Thorington during the winter of 1880–1881. The Camp Porter site was abandoned and auctioned off to the highest bidder on 5 December 1881. Contrary to popular belief, the "old" military post of Camp Porter was built on the opposite side of the tracks from the town, not vice versa. In other words, Camp Porter was built in the town after the site was platted. [See "Old Dawson" for a complete discussion of the military establishments in the Glendive area.]

CHAPTER SEVEN

Dawson County, Montana Territory: 1882

WHEN WE ARRIVED IN GLENDIVE late in April of 1882, Custer County comprised all of the Montana Territory running north to south, a distance of about three-hundred miles, and extending west from the border of the Dakota Territory about two-hundred miles.[82] There was an old Army trail worn in by foot, horse, and wagon traffic that connected Fort Buford to Fort Keogh, but there was not a single mile of surveyed or built road in all of the 55,000 or 60,000 square miles of the county. In all of that territory I believe there were but two schoolhouses in existence, the small private one of Miss Harpster's in Glendive and one in Fort Keogh (now Miles City).[83]

Just a few months after we arrived, in September I believe it was, Custer County was split in half. The southern half retained the name of "Custer County," while the northern half was designated "Dawson County."[84]

There couldn't have been fifteen-hundred men, women, and children in Dawson County, with about a thousand living in and about Glendive. Most of the town's residents were there because of the railroad. If the Northern Pacific hadn't gone ahead and

---

[82] Unless otherwise noted, the source for Chapter 7 is the SNVB manuscript, pp. 13–16.

[83] There were, in fact, three schools in Dawson County and six schools in Custer County in 1882. See *"First schools"* in Author's Notes following this chapter for a brief history of the early educational facilities in both counties.

[84] Stephen Norton Van Blaricom and many others were erroneous in their belief that Dawson County didn't exist until September of 1882. Dawson County had been created in 1869. It wasn't organized with its own slate of officers and county commissioners, however, until September of 1882. See *"Dawson County"* in Author's Notes following this chapter.

built the roundhouse in Glendive, there wouldn't have been two-hundred people remaining once the graders and the track-building crews and the people who supplied them had left.[85] Aside from the railroaders, the rest of the country was just inhabited by cattle and cowhands—thousands of Longhorns and dozens of cowhands, though neither of the two species came to town much—when the cattle were being shipped in or out or the cowhands were out of work or had some time off for whoopee.

Geologists say that at one time the Gulf of Mexico extended north along the eastern side of the Rocky Mountains to the Arctic Ocean. One doesn't have to be a geologist to know that the region for hundreds of miles in Wyoming and Montana had been under water for many centuries. The evidence is everywhere in the form of specimens of extinct sea life. As a boy, while wandering through the hills of Dawson County, I used to find fragments of bones of ancient reptilian life. I always wondered what kind of animal could have bones such as I found, joint bones, for example, as large as a twelve-quart pail. I lived in and around Glendive for eighteen years, from April of 1882 until May of 1900, but as long as I lived there I never met a local man or woman who could offer a suggestion as to their origin. In later years, however, museums of the East have found and collected for their display many fine specimens of the reptilian age.[86]

When that great prehistoric sea dried up, it left the chemicals of the water deposited in the soil, and through the years they formed alkali. Of all the vile things on earth, to me, alkali water is one of the worst. If you are ever forced to drink it, and sooner or later all of the early Dawson County inhabitants were, your lips will soon dry out and crack and bleed. Another feature of alkali water is that the first dose you get of it will provide the most violent laxative you have ever experienced. Survive that first encounter—which you will, although you think you won't at the time—and thereafter you will be more or less immune to its purgative effects.

This is my personal memoir, and I reserve the right to express my opinion on anything that occurs to my mind as I have

[85] See *"No Roundhouse, no Glendive"* in Author's Notes following this chapter.

[86] See *"Evidence of the 'reptilian age'"* in Author's Notes following this chapter.

understood or appreciated it. I do know that if some of those old-timers from Dawson County should see or hear what I have to say in the next few paragraphs, they would come here to Ohio, or telegraph to have me shot.

First, the government and the Army corralled the Indians so the Northern Pacific Railroad could pass through. The government and the railroad then took title to all the land so they could sell it for a profit to settlers who believed their wild claims of it being the Land of Milk and Honey. At the same time the hunters, with the silent approval of the U.S. government, were slaughtering the buffalo to extinction for their hides, humps, and tongues. A few people (like my Uncle Jay Orr Woods) even polished their horns and made furniture of them: chairs, beds, and divans. The Easterners participated in this heedless act by buying everything that was sent their way and then they asked for more. And so it was that the massive commercial slaughter performed by the buffalo hunters was fully supported by the government, the railroad, and the public. When the cattlemen and the other settlers showed up, they jumped right in and finished the grisly work.

With the buffalo gone, the Indians had to become entirely dependent on the government for their food resource. They couldn't leave their shrinking reservations and return to the land. The native peoples were ill-served in this regard. They were assigned agents early on who were nefarious, parsimonious with the food rations and other supplies, and who were responsible, along with the government, for unconscionable misery and suffering and many deaths on the reservation. I never blamed Gall or Sitting Bull or Joseph or their people one whit for not wanting to be pulled into the reservation system.[87] Likewise the wolves and the grizzlies disappeared, mostly hunted to death, but the survivors slowly dwindled to extinction along with their natural meat supply, the buffalo. The elk, the deer, the antelope and the beaver weren't far behind.

---

[87] The betrayal of treaty covenants and the disjointed maladministration of the various Indian agents, the U.S. government's agency supervisors, and the U.S. Army presented the Fort Peck Indian Reservation (and other reservations) with a series of rolling disasters. Conditions were absolutely brutal, and countless Native Americans died of disease and starvation well into the late 1880s. See *"The History of the Assiniboine and Sioux Tribes of the Fort Peck Indian Reservation, Montana, 1800–2000"* for a more complete telling of the early days of the Fort Peck Reservation.

After the winter of 1886-87 the cattlemen saw they couldn't survive winter on an open range basis without stored supplies of feed. Even without over-grazing—even if the winter grass had been there—the cattle wouldn't paw through the snow cover to get to the feed like the bison or the horses would.

Within two decades the big open range outfits followed the trail of the Indians and the buffalo. The land surveys were complete and deeds or leases were then required to control the grazing areas. There were exceptions, men of vision like Pierre Wibaux of the **W** (W-Bar) and Henry Boice at the **777** (Three Sevens) who understood the value of both assemblage and conservation. And there were a few ranches like the **W** and the **XIT** that lasted longer than the twenty years.[88] Even before all of the big cattle outfits pulled out, however, the farmer-settlers (the "honyockers") came in and started fencing it all and, where they could, they plowed up the native grass and replaced it with tilled crops.[89]

And now you old sourdoughs can get ready to shoot, for I am about to do my stuff. In my opinion, it is an absolute tragedy that the white people ever invaded eastern Montana. Eastern Montana and western Dakota territories should have all been left to the Indians and the buffalo and the elk, the grizzly and the wolf, the coyote and the antelope, the beaver and the curlew—and the rattlesnakes. It was a land of deer and jackrabbits and birds by the thousands. These creatures and the Indians were the natural inhabitants of eastern Montana and western Dakota. All of that country west of the Missouri and north of the Platte clear up to Canada and then to the eastern foothills of the Rockies should have been left to them. I have always understood the necessity for the railroad to connect the rest of the country to the east. Transcontinental transportation was a necessary thing. I also understand the necessity of having to build a centrally located roundhouse in such a place as Glendive or Forsyth or Billings so that the long-distance trains might have some point of repair. Beyond that we should have built those rails straight through

---

[88] The **XIT** ceased their operations in Montana in 1909. Wibaux shut down in Dawson County in 1905 or 1906. See *"The XIT and the W"* in Author's Notes following this chapter.

[89] See Chapter 9 for a discussion of the development of tillage agriculture in Dawson County.

from Bismarck and kept right on going until they got to Bozeman and Helena.

Up to the time I left Glendive in 1900, Dawson and Custer counties were nothing more than graveyards for the burial of lost hopes and failed dreams. It may be more inhabitable than the steppes of Russia—but not much. (To my Dear Wife: In the event of my sudden demise you will find my last will and testament in the upper right-hand drawer of my desk.)

CHAPTER 7–AUTHOR'S NOTES

First schools: The first school in Dawson County opened in 1875 and was operated by L. A. Fitch in conjunction with the "Indian farm." It was located on the Indian reservation on the north side of the Missouri River at the Fort Peck trading post and agency. [RCTY, p. 39.] In 1879, the agency was moved to Poplar River with a sub-agency located at Wolf Point. Gilbert Hedenberg, age twenty-five, managed the farm at Wolf Point and, in the evenings, taught Indians of all ages and sexes "to read, write and cypher." [FIV, Vol. 2, p. 663. GT, 2 March 1882 cited in VS, p. 176. USC, Dawson County, 1880.] The first agency school utilized specifically for children was a boarding school opened in Poplar in 1882. Attendance was compulsory, and the children were not allowed to leave. Enrollment, however, was limited to sixty students. Due to the lack of similar educational facilities on the north side of the Missouri, many of the Assiniboine and Sioux children were sent all over the United States, some as far east as the Carlisle Indian School in Pennsylvania. This situation was not relieved until 1893 when Camp Poplar was abandoned by the Army and the old Army buildings were converted to school use. Three-hundred children then attended the Poplar boarding school. [FIV, Vol. 2, p. 663. See HAST for a more complete account of the school system on the reservation.]

During the winter of 1880–1881, Miss Hettie Harpster opened her private school in Glendive on the northeast corner of Benham Street and Meade Avenue (now the site of Sacred Heart Church). She taught one five-month session that began in 1880 and another five-month session in 1881. At its peak there were twelve students, each of whom paid fifty cents per month to attend. [OTOL, p. 370.] Dawson County built the county's first public school, located on the same corner of Benham Street and Meade Avenue as Hettie Harpster's location, during the late fall of 1881. The public school (Dawson County School District No. 1) opened in December of 1881. The first teacher was Miss Mary Vunk. Ten students enrolled in the first session. [GMNPDP, p. 3.] Hettie Harpster, however, didn't stray too far. The *Bozeman Avant-Courier,* on 19 January 1882, reported, "the Glendive school is to open [its January session] with 29 pupils. Miss Hattie *[sic]* Harpster is the teacher."

Starting in 1881, Charlie Adams, age thirty-four, used his cabin in Newlon (located at Fox Creek on the west side of the Yellowstone between Glendive and Fort Buford) as the location to teach his fifteen-year-old wife, Anna (Sartin), his daughter, Mabel (from a previous marriage), three of neighbor William Newlon's children, and two of his wife's Sartin siblings. Four years later, in 1885, the men of the Newlon neighborhood built a small log school in the village. The Newlon men were not renowned for their carpentry skills. The small structure was known for many years as the "Sway Back School." [CE, p. 794. USC, Dawson County, 1880.]

In Custer County, the first school had been organized in "Old Town" on 24 June 1878. The first classes were held from 18 July through 1 September. There were six white children (all girls) and "a black boy named George Mercer" in attendance. The *Bozeman Avant-Courier* reported in 1879 that "there are three private schools [now being] taught at the [two] military posts [of Fort Keogh and Fort Custer]." Housing for the post teacher(s) at Fort Keogh was included in the plans (dated 1 September 1878) for additions to the fort in 1879. By December of 1880, there were schools in "Pease Bottom" (on the north side of the Yellowstone about eight miles below the mouth of the Big Horn River) and "Big Porcupine" (later "Forsyth") as well. The number of school age children in Custer County grew exponentially and left Dawson County "in the dust." The "school report" for Custer County in 1879 said "the number of persons of school age is thirty-seven." On 30 December 1880, the *Bozeman Avant-Courier* reported "sixty-three out of one-hundred-and-four children [in Miles City] are old enough to attend school" and, of the "229 [children] in the district [Custer County?], forty-nine are too young to attend school." On 6 December 1882, the Yellowstone Journal reported there were "453 children of school age (four colored)" in School District No. 1 (which included Miles City and extended northeast through O'Fallon Creek to the county line with Dawson County). [TLW, p. 117, pp. 243–244 and p. 280.]

Dawson County: Although Dawson had been a separate legal entity from Custer County since 1869, it had never been organized due to the lack of any significant population. (There were about one-hundred-and-eighty men, women, and children in both the 1870 and 1880 Dawson County censuses.) At the time Norton and his family arrived in April of 1882, all of Dawson County's affairs were administered from Miles City, the county seat of Custer

County. Additionally, Glendive had a Custer County deputy sheriff assigned to it (Morris Cain, the Glendive blacksmith), a Custer County constable for the "Township of Glendive" (Jim Taylor, the Glendive sutler and saloonkeeper), and a Custer County justice of the peace for the "Township of Glendive" ("Judge" Joseph "Wolf" Allen). If it looked liked Custer County and it acted like Custer County, it must have been Custer County. Norton was not alone in erroneously believing that Glendive was a part of Custer County. Many of the earliest inhabitants perceived it that way as well.

While Stephen Norton Van Blaricom may have had the practical effects right, the history was quite a bit different. When the Territory of Montana was organized on 2 February 1865, that area which later became Dawson County was the northern half of Big Horn County. For administrative purposes, the immense Big Horn County (the easternmost third of Montana) was attached to Gallatin County, where Bozeman was the county seat. Dawson County was created by the territorial legislature on 15 January 1869 by dividing Big Horn County on an east–west line at the 47th parallel, with the trading post of Fort Peck named as the "administrative" center. The new county remained unorganized, however, so while Big Horn County remained attached to Bozeman, the control of Dawson was shifted to Chouteau County and Fort Benton. No functions of any substance or record ever emanated from Fort Peck. Chouteau County courts administered justice (such as it was) in Dawson County, while, in theory, "the law" came from the sheriff of Chouteau County and the U.S. Deputy Marshals located in Fort Benton and Fort Buford, Dakota Territory.

On 14 June 1877, Big Horn County was organized and renamed "Custer County" and Miles City declared the county seat. Although the administration of Dawson County was not formally moved from Fort Benton in Chouteau County to Miles City in Custer County, the Custer County authorities quickly went about expanding their de facto jurisdiction in thinly populated Dawson County. In August of 1880, with their formation of "Glendive Township," the Custer County Commissioners usurped control over all of Dawson County east of the Yellowstone River. On 18 February 1881, the Montana Territorial Legislature formally transferred administration of all of Dawson County from Fort Benton, Chouteau County to Miles City, Custer County. The residents of Dawson County, however, viewed the management of Custer County as completely corrupt and the linkage was seen to have "increased...the political disabilities under which the citizens of Dawson County labored." [HML, p. 541.] On 9 September 1881, a group of Dawson County citizens met and petitioned Governor Benjamin F. Potts to allow the organization of the county. A year later, on 27 September 1882, Dawson County was officially organized, the governor appointed county officials, and Glendive was named the county seat. The first election in Dawson County took place on 7 November 1882. The elected officials took office in January of 1883. [See "Old Dawson" for a more detailed description of the political history of the county.]

In 1882, there were about 25,000 square miles in Dawson County and about 30,000 square miles in Custer County. Their respective areas did fluctuate substantially between 1869 and 1890, depending on where county boundaries were periodically relocated and what portion of the Crow Reservation was included in or excluded from Custer County. When the Montana Territorial Legislature changed the name from Big Horn County to Custer County on 16 February 1877, for example, Custer County alone comprised a huge land mass of some 45,210 square miles. [TLW, p. 82.] In February of 1883, Dawson County was expanded slightly (the border was moved south ten miles) to comprise an area of 25,992 square miles while Custer County, with the formation of Yellowstone County and the shrinkage of the Crow Reservation, had diminished to about 30,000 square miles. [GHMT, p. 33 and GT, 29 December 1883. TLW, p. 82. MGFC, pp. 200–203.]

In addition to Glendive, the early locations with enough white population or importance to be perceived as "settlements" in Dawson County were Poplar River Agency and Wolf Point (both north of the Missouri River on the Fort Peck Indian Reservation), Morgan Ranch, Burns Ranch, and Newlon (all three on the Yellowstone between Glendive and Fort Buford), Beaver Creek and Keith (side by side at the future location of Wibaux), and (by 1883) the derelict remnant of the once-bustling Carroll (located a few miles west of the Musselshell's confluence with the Missouri River). [GHMT, p. 33.] Discounting the transient military personnel on the Fort Peck Reservation and with the possible exception of Newlon, there were no more than twenty permanent white residents at any location. Morgan Ranch and Burns Ranch each had fewer than ten inhabitants, including the children at the Johnny Burns place. (See Map 2 on page 75 for the locations of these early settlements.)

There was also the issue of inaccurate descriptions of the longitudinal boundaries used to determine what country was in Dawson County and what wasn't. The act of the United States dated May 26, 1864, that organized the Territory of Montana, described the eastern boundary of Montana (and Dawson County) to be 27 degrees of longitude west from Washington City. On the other hand, the act of the Legislative Assembly of the Territory of Montana dated January 15, 1869, which established the County of Dawson, defined the county's eastern boundary as 104 degrees of longitude west from Greenwich. The problem was that 27 degrees west from Washington City would be 104 degrees, 3 minutes and 2.30 seconds west of the Greenwich meridian. Thus the 1869 territorial description placed the line between two and three miles east of the federal description of 1864. Not that it mattered too much. With few exceptions, the early surveyors couldn't accurately determine their longitudinal positions anyway. To further confuse matters, the various mapmakers also guessed at where the longitudinal lines should go. The mapmakers also routinely merged the longitudinal lines west of Greenwich and Washington City. Thus, 104 degrees of longitude west from Greenwich was displayed as the same as 27 degrees west from Washington City.

A couple of examples serve to illustrate the confusion:

1. The western boundary of Dawson County. The first attempt to survey eastern Montana was the military expedition under the supervision of Captain William F. Raynolds in the years 1859 and 1860. The map resulting from the Raynolds survey incorrectly portrayed the locations of 108 degrees of longitude west of Greenwich and 31 degrees of longitude west of Washington City. In 1864 the Montana Territorial Legislature used that longitude to legally describe the western boundary of Big Horn County and, in 1869, Dawson County. The Raynolds maps were modified in 1876 but only by adding physical features that had been identified during the intervening sixteen years. Both the 1860 and 1876 maps showed the confluence of the Musselshell and the Missouri to be about ten miles west of the incorrectly mapped longitude. The famed 1883 map by George F. Cram then incorrectly moved the location of "108 degrees west of Greenwich" some thirty miles or so to the west of the location for that longitude as displayed on the Raynolds maps. Cram thus displayed the confluence of the Musselshell and the Missouri some twenty-two miles east of 108 degrees of longitude, and that placed what had been the settlement of Carroll (1874–1877) well inside Dawson County. Finally, the 1898 map issued by Rand McNally dropped the "degrees west of Washington City" labels, expressed itself in degrees west of Greenwich, and correctly located the longitudinal line of 108 degrees west of Greenwich. The 1898 Rand McNally map approximates modern surveys that show the center of the Musselshell confluence to be almost exactly four miles east of 108 degrees.

It mattered little that the mapmakers kept moving the locations of the longitudinal lines. The occupants of Carroll told the U.S. Post Office (1874–1877) that they were in Dawson County when the town was first up and running. The Carroll freight road ("the Carroll Trail") that ran from the Missouri River to Helena was last used in 1875 and the town started to dwindle away. There was a small settlement that re-started the post office (1880–1882), this time registered as being located in Chouteau County. The problem was that Carroll had technically been in Meagher County all along. Meagher had been formed in 1867 and included what had been all of Chouteau south of the Missouri River to the Big Horn (later Dawson) County line. But the maps didn't show it that way, and Montanans didn't see it that way. They thought Carroll was in Dawson County from 1874–1877. Sometime after 1879 they believed Carroll was in Chouteau County through 1882. After that, it didn't matter too much anyway since the abandoned townsite was swept away by the Missouri later in the 1880s. [NFM, p. 43 and pp. 180–181. MYMR. MC. MRM. MAG, p. 75.]

2. The eastern boundary of Dawson County (and Montana Territory). In 1864, the federal government described the eastern boundary of Montana Territory as being 27 degrees of longitude west of Washington City.

That line is just a few feet west of the old Fort Union site (1828–1865) on the Missouri River. In 1869, the Montana Territorial Legislature described the eastern boundary of Dawson County as being 104 degrees of longitude west of Greenwich. That line essentially runs through the center of Fort Buford (1866–1895). The two longitudinal lines are almost exactly two miles apart at the confluence of the Missouri and Yellowstone rivers.

In 1880, the Northern Pacific surveyors had initially declared a point at or near Sentinel Butte (now some ten miles inside North Dakota) as the border of Montana. In 1881, that error was discovered and the line was moved west to approximate a point about 104 degrees west of the Greenwich meridian, thus matching, more or less, the description given by the territorial legislature. That line left what is now Beach, North Dakota, inside Montana. Cram's 1883 map showed the Greenwich and Washington City longitudes as one, but his map moved the Montana border about three miles to the west and thus compensated to match to the federal description. Cram, however, then moved Beach right along with the boundary and left it in Montana. While Cram moved the boundary on the map, the physical boundary wasn't moved to its proper location of 27 degrees of longitude west of Washington until 1885, at which time they also discovered that Beach was really on the Dakota side of the line. So it was that Beach was "administered" (to the extent it was administered at all) from Miles City from 1880 through September of 1882 when Dawson County was organized. It then stayed part of Dawson County until that area of the country was physically surveyed in 1885. The actual boundary was perfected in 1885 by a telegraphic time trans-mission from Washington City to Mingusville (now Wibaux) and then physically measured back east from the Mingusville telegraph office to the boundary. [POY, p. 75 and p. 85. FBMFNP, p. 41. CE, pp. 345–346. NDAG, p. 20. MYMR. MC. MRM.]

Ultimately it wasn't so much an issue having to do with the technical accuracy of what was described as "Dawson County." It was, instead, what the settlers and other contemporaries perceived. If it looked like a duck and walked like a duck and quacked like a duck, then it must have been a duck. (See Map 2 on the following page to see the boundaries of Dawson County as they were perceived circa 1880–1882. Also see Map 5 in Chapter 9 for a portrayal of today's counties that were formed from the original Dawson County of 1869.)

The 1870 census for the twenty-five-thousand or so square miles that Dawson County then encompassed tabulated one-hundred-and-seventy-seven souls, including Jane ("Jenny") Smith, the wife of Frank Smith, "woodcutter," the only white woman recorded prior to 1877 (which saw the presence of white families at Fort Keogh) in all of eastern Montana. The 1880 census of one-hundred-and-eighty was little different than that of 1870 except there were a few more white women and the population had shifted from total residency on the Missouri River in 1870 to the vast majority residing in the Yellowstone River valley in 1880. Indian Agent Nathan S. Porter, however, reported 5,829 Sioux (of whom 1,116 were Sitting Bull followers who had recently surrendered) and 1,450 Assiniboine living on the Fort Peck Indian Reservation in 1880. [HAST, p. 123.] (That compares to a total population of 2,104 (1,404 Yankton Sioux and 710 Assiniboine) reported in 1905. See HAST, p. 188.) There also was a permanent band of Gros Ventres (Hidatsas) located on the Yellowstone between Glendive and Fort Buford (until their forcible removal in 1894) that numbered about two hundred depending on the time of year. The latter group shows on maps (at around forty tepees or "lodges") but is never mentioned in any census data. There were also small groups of "Indians" (presumably Métis) scattered along the Milk River who, like the Gros Ventres (Hidatsas), were not included in any of the 1870 or 1880 census data; they may have numbered another couple of hundred or so. [USC, Dawson County, 1870 and 1880 and USC, Valley County, 1900. See the biography of George McCone in the Glendive Public Library and FVBM for mention of the permanent Gros Ventre (Hidatsa) encampment. For more details regarding Dawson County, Valley County, and the Fort Peck Indian Reservation see those subjects in "Old Dawson" and HAST.]

No Roundhouse, no Glendive: Glendive probably owes its long-term development to the foresight of Henry F. Douglas. Fully understanding the necessity of making the townsite important to the railroad, Douglas "offered to furnish the bricks for a roundhouse if the railroad would make Glendive a division point." Fortunately

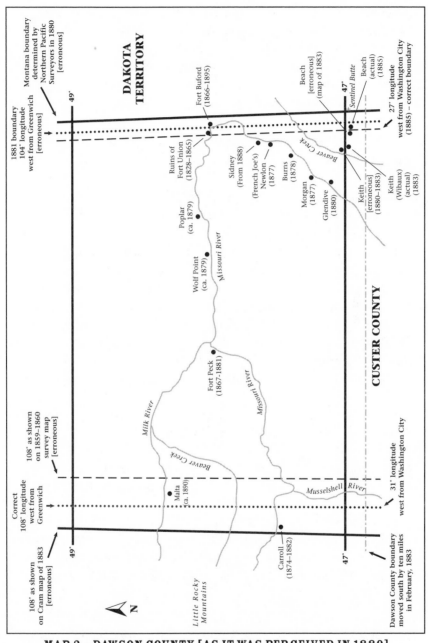

MAP 2—DAWSON COUNTY [AS IT WAS PERCEIVED IN 1880]
[NOT TO SCALE]

for Glendive, the railroad accepted his generous offer. Douglas had been the post trader at the Standing Rock Reservation since 1874. By 1880, he was supplying both the NPRR construction crews and the adjacent military posts between Bismarck and Glendive. [GHMT, p. 14.] In 1882, he also became a late-comer participant in Major Lewis Merrill's Yellowstone Land and Colonization Company which, late in 1880, platted the Glendive townsite. [OTOL, p. 11.] See Author's Notes following Chapter 24 for the biography of Henry Douglas.

Evidence of the "reptilian age": Geologists and paleontologists accompanied almost all the military surveying and exploratory expeditions following Lewis and Clark. By the 1870s, certainly, knowledge of the geological formations and that large fossils existed in the plains east of the Rocky Mountains was relatively common among scientific circles. That knowledge was gathered often to the frustration of the military leaders of the expeditions. Their missions were often juxtaposed. Lieutenant Colonel (Brevet Brigadier General) James W. Forsyth and famed steamboat captain Grant Marsh were accompanied by a group of scientists from the Smithsonian and elsewhere during their navigation and exploration of the Yellowstone River in 1875. Forsyth queried Marsh about what it was that he was always putting down in his little book. Marsh replied that the book contained his navigational notes about the Yellowstone: mileage, depths, landmarks, and so forth. Forsyth said that he had looked high and low for that kind of information and never had been able to find it. Marsh told Forsyth the he supposed his "little notes" wouldn't be of any value compared to the data being compiled by the men from the Smithsonian. Forsyth then replied to the effect that he didn't give a whit about the geological formations or the traces of the Mesozoic. "I want to know," he said, "about this river for the transportation of [troops and] supplies, and all the engineers and professors on earth can't give me what you have in that book." [As reported by Joseph Mills Hanson in COM, p. 208.]

To the settlers of the 1880s, however, it was the fields of coal that provided the most immediately visible proof of the repeated prehistoric flooding of eastern Montana. "Great swamps were formed east of the mountains and were later buried to become coal and oil fields." [M/M, p. 5.] What geologists now describe as "the Glendive Basin" had once evolved into a great swamp. The evidence of sedimentary layering that occurred over the eons are readily visible in the bad lands where erosion has exposed sedimentary rocks layered with veins of coal and containing the fossilized remains of prehistoric plants, trilobites, dinosaur bones, and petrified figs. The country near Glendive also contains magnificent displays of rosy red scoria, the result of the interminable burning of the area's ubiquitous coal. [GHMT, pp. 5–6.] Dinosaurs also roamed the plains of eastern Montana. Colonies of the duck-billed *Maiasaura* and fossils of baby dinosaurs have been unearthed in the eastern part of the state. One of the most impressive skeletons of *Tyrannosaurus Rex* was discovered near Jordan in 1908. [M/M, p. 5.] During the Ice Age, great sheets of ice extended as far south as Glendive. [M/M, p. 5.] Near Lindsay, about midway between Glendive and Circle, an expedition from the University of Calgary unearthed one of the most complete mammoth skeletons ever discovered. [GHMT, p. 6.]

The XIT and the W: Although it remained in business some nineteen years, the **XIT** was a relative latecomer to eastern Montana. The ranch didn't arrive from Texas until 1890 and it operated until closing out its Montana holdings in 1909. [GHMT, p. 22. See Author's Notes following Chapter 16 for the story of the **XIT**.] With a twenty-two or twenty-three year run, Pierre Wibaux and his **W** perhaps lasted longer than any of the other early cattlemen. He showed up in June of 1883 and raised cattle in Dawson County until 1905 or 1906. Of all the original outfits that operated on a commercial scale, however, nobody lasted as long as Mr. and Mrs. Harvey Hall, who established their sheep ranch, the Glendive Livestock Company, north of Wibaux on CS Creek in 1880. The Halls sold out in 1910 or 1911 after a thirty-year run. [See Author's Notes following Chapter 21 for the biography of Pierre Wibaux. The Hall story is told in Chapter 24.]

CHAPTER EIGHT

Crime and Punishment and the Horse in the Coffin

P EOPLE WHO HAVE NEVER VENTURED OUTSIDE of and away from civil governance cannot appreciate how thin is this veneer of civilization in man's nature. And man will shed it just as sure as a snake sheds its skin. There was no law or civil government whatsoever when we first arrived in Glendive. The only law we saw or knew was that old primeval one of survival of the fittest. I will not go into the matter of the social conditions in Glendive that resulted from this tumultuous lawlessness, but I am glad I saw it, for it has left me always with a keen sense of appreciation for the value of government to society.[90]

If there was a mistake to be made in early-day Glendive, it was to be made by affectations of either of the extremes of society. That person who affected the "airs" of being better than the next was as sure to be called to task as that man who had made the self-determination, either real or imagined, that he was a "bad" man. It is truly amazing how polite a rough society can be when the law is absent and each man is directly and immediately accountable for his actions and words only to those present. Justice could and would be dispensed just as rapidly and to the same degree that injustice was incurred.[91] Glendive was the sort of typical frontier

---

[90] SNVB, p. 15. Glendive was frequently cited by early travelers as the toughest town of all in eastern Montana. One of the few men to have been interviewed who came very early into northeastern Montana was Henry Bolter: "By that time [the spring of 1881], Glendive had gotten almost worse than Miles City. A man had to be tough just to survive." [YC, p. 106.] "Glendive [by the spring of 1882] had become the roughest town of all. It was not safe to go downtown." [YC, p. 107.]

[91] Justice sometimes had its own peculiarities in a frontier town like Glendive. See *"The early Glendive court system"* in Author's Notes following this chapter for a story related by Vic Smith in his memoir.

town where "middle-of-the-road," whatever that was, defined the most successful course of social behavior.[92]

The heavy influx of immigrants to eastern Montana in the spring of 1882 made it necessary that civil government be established. Glendive, located in the southeastern portion of Dawson County, contained the vast majority of the sparse population so it became the county seat. Miles City, which had been the administrative center, continued to be the county seat for Custer County. After this was done, the necessary complement of Dawson County officers was appointed and some semblance of order began to be established.

Glendive could be a fairly tough place and justice was necessarily dispensed quickly. It didn't take months or years in those days to decide a case nor to mete out appropriate punishment. I can remember a few incidents that occurred in or around Glendive and the reader might find it interesting if I relate a few of them at this time.

When that French Count was tried for murder over in Dakota Territory it took the jury all of ten minutes to decide he wasn't guilty of anything except self-defense.[93]

One morning they caught some vagrant swiping a coat from a store in Glendive. N. L. Davis gave chase and whacked the culprit over the head with his revolver. The thief took offense at this and pulled out a razor and was going to give old Davis a working over. Hank Tuttle showed up and arrested the man. They gave him a hearing before noon that same day and his sentence was to leave town in thirty minutes. He did and he never came back and everybody was happy.[94]

In the winter of 1884–1885, a fellow by the name of Jack Dempsey got a little tipsy during the New Year's Eve party and, on New Year's Day, he decided to shoot up the town. He shot

---

[92] Hermann Hagedorn observed that Theodore Roosevelt took note of this same phenomenon during his tenure on the Little Missouri between 1883 and 1887: "There was very little quarreling or fighting, due, Roosevelt suspected, to the fact that all the men were armed; for, it seemed, that when a quarrel was likely to end fatally, men rather hesitated about embarking upon it." [RBL, p. 282.]

[93] GT, 27 September 1883. The "French Count" was the Marquis de Mores of Medora. While the jury was only out for ten minutes, the trial lasted a week "from September 12, 1885, to September 19, 1885, inclusive." [CMM, p. 61.]

[94] GI, 18 August 1887.

out a few windows, busted a couple of bar mirrors and plugged holes in some of Glendive's downtown buildings including the sheriff's office. He was arrested and within the week he had been tried, found guilty, fined $100 and sentenced to six months in the county jail.[95]

This deal of being put in jail was no small thing, especially during the winter. Bill Tuttle used to tell a story about Hank, his brother, when Hank was the sheriff of Dawson County: "It was the dead of winter and we had sixteen Injuns down in the jail all charged with horse-stealin' and was they ever a-raisin' a ruckus. Hank and his wife and family lived in the jail upstairs. I was pullin' jail duty that night. I went up and told Hank: 'Them damn Injuns down in the jail are a-dancin' a Death Dance–and they won't quit. You better do somethin'...and quick!' He and I went out and in a few minutes we went back upstairs and Hank flung his sombrero on the floor and sat down. His wife asked if everything was all right down in the jail. 'Death Dance...Hell!' he said. 'They're just a-tryin' to keep warm!' "[96]

The other side of the jail deal was that this was a place where, in the 1880s, some hard characters were put together and you really didn't want to be there. I always thought the best expression of this was voiced by a middle-aged rowdy from Texas who was being carted off to the Glendive hoosegow following a fracas in one of the Glendive saloons. "Hold up here, boys," he yelped out. "You're a-tryin' to take a good monkey an' put him in the wrong box!"

A young railroad town like Glendive that was also a livestock shipping point full of cowboys and railroaders wasn't exactly a society that took tea and crumpets for breakfast. When somebody got incarcerated they were put into cells with some pretty rough folks and the result could be a high "suicide" rate. Of course, people never really knew if they were suicides at all.[97]

The gravest error anyone could make was to be seriously impolite to the lady-folks of a man's family. Women were few and

---

[95] GT, 3 January 1885 and 10 January 1885. The *Yellowstone Journal* reported on 10 January 1885 that Jack Dempsey was "a well known tough about Glendive."

[96] MTMN, p. 8.

[97] "There have been five suicides in the Miles City Jail within a short time!" [GT, 5 May 1883.]

far between and, in general, they were treated with the utmost propriety. If you were the fool who decided to "get smart" with or demean a man's wife or daughter you were really playing with fire. In the summer of 1883 a fellow by the name of Bill Rigney and a pal of his had stayed up all night drinking in Miles City. That next morning, still drunk, they barged in to Ed Campbell's[98] home where the family was sitting down to breakfast with a boarder, George McKay. Rigney used some very ugly language on the family in general but especially to Grace Campbell, Ed's young daughter who was about thirteen years old. Ed and the boarder, George, succeeded in wrestling Rigney and his pal out of the house but Rigney wouldn't shut up even then. About that time, however, a neighbor, Charlie Brown,[99] joined in the fray with the handle of a pickaxe. That quieted Rigney down and he was hauled off to jail. That night, around midnight, the jailer was "overcome" by a quiet but determined group of some forty citizens. They removed Rigney, took him to the Northern Pacific railroad bridge that crossed Tongue River, tied a rope around his neck and flung him off. Rigney had picked the wrong house, the wrong girl, the wrong father, the wrong neighbor, and the wrong town. And that was the end of that.[100]

The other capital crime of the Territory of Montana was to steal a horse. If they got you for that, the end of a lariat and the limb of a tree was your penalty. You might shoot a man or pull off a burglary and get a hearing, but steal a horse and it was a shortcut to your finish.[101] The very least I ever heard of a horse thief getting was ten years at hard labor in Deer Lodge and that was because he was lucky and got caught by the county sheriff. With the Stranglers of '84, however, rustlers simply weren't treated that

---

98 Ed Campbell's full name was Robert Edward Campbell. He reportedly went by "Ed" Campbell. He and his boarder, George McKay, were both blacksmiths in Miles City. [TLW, p. 52.]

99 Charlie Brown was a German immigrant born in Stuttgart, Germany, in 1828. A man of about fifty-five years when this incident occurred, he was described as "five feet eleven inches, weight about 220 lbs., healthy and tough." Variously a paymaster and wagonmaster for the Terry expedition in 1876, he and his family were early Miles City settlers. He opened his famous saloon, "Charlie Brown's," in Miles City in June of 1878. [TLW, pp. 37–38.]

100 The Rigney affair wasn't quite as simple as Norton portrayed it. See *"The hanging of Bill Rigney"* in Author's Notes following this chapter.

101 AVBH notes. Also see FVBM.

politely. In northeastern Montana and the Little Missouri River country of western Dakota Territory, Floppin' Bill Cantrell and his vigilante posse hanged, shot, or otherwise killed somewhere between seventy and a hundred horse and cattle thieves between June and November of 1884. No judge. No jury. Sometimes, maybe, not even the right man. But the thieving took a real dip and things calmed down for a while after they gave the country a good cleaning.[102] Even three years later, in 1887, I remember that the citizens of the Judith Basin organized a Vigilance Committee whose purpose they said, "was to dispose of Indian horse thieves without the interference of the forms of justice."[103]

People have frequently asked me, especially in later years, why the theft of a horse would lead to such dire consequences. Today people live in an increasingly impersonal society in which one only knows that individual transportation is by automobile. Automobile insurance is available and man well understands the bounty of cash. If your car gets stolen today, you hitch a ride home, notify your insurance company of the theft, and buy another car the next day. You certainly wouldn't hang a car thief, even if the police, especially in today's big cities, bothered to try to catch him. Why, then, one might ask, were horse thieves so frequently hanged before the automobile came into common use?

There are about five answers to that question and, if you put them all together, the hangman's hemp might be easier to understand. First of all, in 1882, a working cowboy, for example, made about twenty dollars a month plus room (if there was one) and board.[104] A decent horse was worth between fifty dollars and one-hundred dollars. A cow was worth eight dollars to twelve dollars. A calf wasn't worth anything except that two years later, as a mature steer, it would bring you a ten-dollar bill. Thus it was that you would have to steal a small herd of cattle before you

---

[102] See Chapter 13 and Author's Notes following Chapter 13 for details on the "Montana Stranglers" of 1884. While the secretive "Stranglers" were active, the press sometimes took note of their activities—and sometimes not. Even when they did, it was very low key: "Three men hung on Beaver Creek. They were rustlers." [GT, 25 October 1884.]

[103] GI, 11 June 1887.

[104] Norton's observations on a cowboy's pay and livestock values were a little light. See *"The value of labor and livestock"* in Author's Notes following this chapter.

had the value of one good horse. The second reason was that there was little cash and no such thing as "horse credit" or "horse installment payments" or "horse insurance." If you stole a man's horse, you put him afoot and the average man might well have no means with which to replace it except after several months of menial labor. A third reason, and perhaps the most important, was that if a man's horse were taken from him out in the country, he could die from the elements, wild animals, hostile Indians, or another "bad man." A horse thief literally put a man's fortune and life at risk when he stole the man's transportation. The fourth reason was that a good horse was hard to come by. Quality horses tend to improve with age, and the owner and mount come to know each other's ways. They develop an emotional attachment one to the other that the owner of a favorite pet, a cat or a dog, would understand. Finally, life was simpler then. There was a universal moral commitment in those days that a serious crime really should be punished. It wasn't anything nearly as complicated as today where you hear all these arguments about whether punishment is a deterrent or whether there was something in the social background of the criminal that should or could excuse his behavior. Steal a horse and get caught by the sheriff: ten years in Deer Lodge. Steal a horse and get caught by the Stranglers, the owner, a rancher, or his cowboys—you probably wouldn't make it to town.[105]

I mentioned the emotional association between horse and rider and how that attachment grew with time. There aren't many stories that tell of a horse being buried in a coffin, but that really did happen in Dawson County. Bill Cheney had been a wagon master with General Sully when they campaigned from Minnesota to the Yellowstone in pursuit of the Sioux in 1864. It wasn't but a few years and old Bill returned to this country. In the fall of 1877, in company with a buffalo hunter and former Army scout by the name of "Glendive" Smith,[106] Cheney departed Fort Buford to

---

[105] AVBH notes. Also see FVBM.

[106] The most likely candidate to have been with Cheney was a local man, a former Army scout, dispatch rider, and mail carrier known in 1877 as "Glendive" Smith. The quiet, unassuming Andrew Smith who, many years later (in 1892) was elected to the Dawson County Board of Commissioners (1893–1897), was almost certainly the same man described by contemporaries as "Glendive" Smith.

return to his own woodhawk camp up the Yellowstone.[107] When they left Ft. Buford, the commandant, Colonel Charles Gilbert, asked Smith and Cheney to keep an eye out for two dispatch riders overdue from Ft. Keogh. Upriver, in the vicinity of what is now Sidney, Smith and Cheney found the two missing men dead, castrated, scalped, and stripped, and not necessarily in that order. They quickly decided to return to Buford and let Colonel Gilbert know the fate of his men. There was another small problem, however. The dozen or so Indians who had perpetrated this grisly act were camped in a cottonwood grove there on the river near what became known as Cheney Point.

Cheney was riding a beautiful bay horse, a seven-year-old Morgan, "Nig" by name. Nig snorted a warning to Smith and Cheney about the same instant the Indians spotted them. Well, the horse race was on. They went north and west for several miles at a dead gallop. Seeing they couldn't make a stand on the flats on the west side, Smith and Cheney headed down to the Yellowstone. Alternately lunging and swimming, they made it to the east side of the Yellowstone. Smith's horse fell dead on the other side. That left the two men with one horse and about fifteen miles and a Missouri River crossing to go. To make a long story short, suffice it to say that "Glendive" Smith and Bill Cheney made it, thanks to Nig.[108]

Cheney wasn't bashful about telling people that he had promised the horse that he would take care of him the rest of his life if only Nig could get them out of this scrape in one piece. Bill Cheney later settled a place near Ridgelawn where Nig lived to

---

[107] See HYCW, Vol. 22, No. 2, pp. 9–12. This article states that in 1877 Cheney was operating a woodhawk site on the Yellowstone near present-day Sidney. "Woodhawks" were hardy individuals who located themselves near cottonwood groves and chopped, dried, and sold wood to the riverboats as they traversed up and down the river. On the Yellowstone, this activity began soon after Custer's demise at the Little Big Horn in the summer of 1876, with the subsequent river traffic related to troop movements and to the construction of Fort Keogh and Fort Custer. Many of these men woodhawked to the river traffic in the spring, summer, and early fall, hunted buffalo or "wolfed" in the winter, and chopped wood the rest of the time. See "Old Dawson" for a discussion of the hazardous career of being a woodhawk.

[108] There are at least two versions of this well-known story. The tale of the pursuit by the Indians and the subsequent escape directly attributable to Nig are consistent between the stories. The main variants relate to Bill Cheney's role and who the "Smith" was who accompanied Cheney. For a comparison and analysis of the two stories see "Vic Smith or Andrew Smith: Who rode with Cheney?" in Author's Notes following this chapter.

the ripe old age of forty-two years. I was told that when Nig died in 1912, old Bill had a man who worked for him, Andrew Hanto, build a coffin for Nig. Covered in two new blankets, the horse was buried on Bill's ranch near Ridgelawn and that's where he rests to this day.[109]

---

[109] For the Hanto reference see CE, p. 897. Cheney's woodhawk site was near the confluence of Lone Tree Creek and the Yellowstone (now the location of Sydney). Sometime in the 1880s he moved north and started a ranch not far from Aleck and Jennie Ayotte's place at Ridgelawn. Cheney lived there until he died in December of 1920.

CHAPTER 8–AUTHOR'S NOTES

The early Glendive court system: Vic Smith recounted in his memoir a tale of justice regarding arson, assault, and battery that occurred in Glendive in the spring of 1882. That was before Dawson County was organized, and the law was enforced by officials appointed by Custer County. A man by the name of Parsons owned the land across the Yellowstone from Glendive. In the fall of 1881, Parsons allowed Don McArthur to build a place he called "The River House" for buffalo hunters and other travelers. [GT, 4 May 1882.] Even when things were booming, the ferry only made two round trips a day. [GT, 7 April 1883: "Glendive is booming! The ferry between Glendive and West Glendive plys across twice a day!"] That meant that the people waiting on the ferry had plenty of time to imbibe in McArthur's refreshments and, as a result, McArthur did a good business that fall and winter.

In the spring of 1882, Parsons decided that there was enough traffic for two shops and told McArthur that, while McArthur could stay on, he (Parsons) was also going to put up a saloon in that location. One day Parsons delivered all of the materials for the building. That same night, according to Smith, McArthur's bouncer, a man named Jensling, set the building material on fire and destroyed it. When Parsons saw Jensling, he accused him of burning the property. Jensling then proceeded to beat up Parsons. The next morning, Jensling crossed the river and went into Glendive, where he just happened to run into Judge Olson of the justice court just as the judge was headed in to one of the saloons for his morning shot of whiskey (as was his custom). Omitting the fact that Parsons had accused him of arson, Jensling told Olson that he had a little "dust-up" with Parsons and that he didn't want to have his reputation sullied by being hauled into court. Vic Smith told the rest: "The judge thought a minute and said, 'Jensling, I will fine you a dollar and costs.' Jensling pulled out a pint of whiskey and said, 'Judge, keep this; it's good.' The judge, in a burst of generosity, said, 'Jensling, I remit the fine,' and that settled the case." [VS, pp. 99–100.] Thus was a case involving the issues of arson, assault, and battery and bribing a judge resolved in Glendive in the spring of 1882.

The hanging of Bill Rigby followed the fracas at Ed Campbell's house (which occurred about 7:00 A.M. of 21 July 1883). Around midnight of that same night a group of about forty men appeared at the Miles City jail. They disarmed Jim Conley ("the keeper of the pokey"), took his keys, and grabbed Rigby. They then hustled Rigby, "the offender of the public safety," to the Northern Pacific bridge that crossed the Tongue River, slipped a loop around his neck, and threw him off. The rumor was, however, that Rigby was already dead; that Rigby had died in the jail as the result of Charlie Brown's blow with the pickaxe handle; and that the "hanging" was simply a cover-up by the local vigilantes to protect Charlie from a charge of murder or manslaughter. There were enough people who believed the rumor that, on the night of the 23rd, a "tremendous fire" occurred in downtown Miles City that wiped out the entire block on the south side of Main Street between Fifth and Sixth. Many suspected that the fire was an act of revenge by Rigby's friends but nothing was ever proved. [TLW, p. 298.] Ed Campbell's blacksmith shop was not destroyed by the fire and Charlie Brown's Saloon, right across the street from the conflagration, escaped the flames as well. [TLW, p. 392.]

The value of labor and livestock: At "twenty dollars a month plus room and board," Stephen Norton may have been describing his own modest circumstances as a young and inexperienced ranch hand. He was about fourteen when he went to work on the east side of the Yellowstone for the Griffin Brothers and Ward Cattle Company for "ten dollars a month and keep." (See Chapter 11.) McElrath, in his booklet, *Yellowstone Valley* (1880), stated: "Should a cattle rancher desire 'herders' [they] could be hired for about $40.00 per month plus room and board." [Cited in TLW, p. 59.] McElrath's wage levels seem to be confirmed by most of the contemporary literature. The **777**, a Kansas outfit that came into the Beaver Valley country in 1883 and headquartered at Mingusville, was reported as paying "$40 a month whether they were [common] wranglers or top hands." [TABC, p. 18.] While prices on livestock varied widely, Norton was also a little bit light when he quoted the value of a horse at "between fifty dollars and a hundred dollars" and steers for "a ten-dollar bill." James S. Brisbin in *The Great Yellowstone Valley* (1882) reported "$200–$300 per pair for a 'fair' team of horses [for one-hundred to one-hundred-and-fifty dollars each] with mules somewhat higher. Horned cattle $10–$35 per head. Stock cattle $18–$20, depending on quality." [Cited in TLW, p. 401.]

Vic Smith or Andrew Smith. Who rode with Cheney? Vic Smith and Andrew Smith were contemporaries in northeastern

Montana and both men were, at various times, Army scouts, couriers, and buffalo hunters. Vic Smith was also a marksman of some note, an erstwhile journalist, and by far the better known of the two men.

There are two basic versions of the Bill Cheney–Nig story. The interpretation by Kathryn Wright is probably best known and it refers only to "a buffalo hunter who called himself Smith":

> In the fall of 1877, Bill Cheney was at Fort Buford. Preparing to go back to his woodyard on the Yellowstone, he encountered the commandant of the post, Colonel Charles Gilbert. Gilbert said, "I am expecting dispatches from Fort Keogh. The riders are overdue. Keep an eye out for them, will you?" Cheney agreed and, as he was trotting his horse across the fort's grounds, a buffalo hunter who called himself "Smith" decided he would saddle up and ride along. They departed Fort Buford, crossed the Missouri and rode to Cheney's cabin which was located some fifteen miles or so up the Yellowstone on the west bank. They spent the night at Cheney's place. The next morning, Smith intended to ride further south and Cheney decided to accompany him, stating, "Those dispatch riders ought to be showing up. I'll ride out a ways with you. Maybe we'll run into them." They found the mutilated dispatch men just west of present-day Savage, encountered the Indian slayers and, riding for their lives, they made a mad dash north for Fort Buford. After a chase of some twenty-four miles, they headed for the Yellowstone at a point somewhat north of present-day Sidney. During this prolonged pursuit, Cheney promised Nig: "Get me out of this scrape and I'll take care of you for the rest of your life." Upon swimming the Yellowstone, Smith's horse fell dead of exhaustion. Calling upon a super reserve of strength and will, Nig then carried both riders on down the Yellowstone another sixteen miles or so to the south bank of the Missouri opposite Fort Buford. The men at the fort saw them and they were saved. [See CE, pp. 897-897.]

The other version of the story, as related in 1945 by Tom Ray on page 263 of his historical novel *Yellowstone Red* is a simpler, less heroic tale, but it specifically names Vic Smith as the rider who accompanied Cheney. Ray told it this way:

Departing from Fort Buford, "Uncle Bill" Cheney was mounted on Nig, riding along to protect Vic Smith, the dispatch carrier..."but this time they may not get through." The two men were attacked by Indians and they narrowly escaped by swimming to the opposite side of the Yellowstone, where Vic Smith's horse fell dead of exhaustion. Soldiers from Fort Buford heard the shots and appeared in time to save the two men.

Clearly, the two stories are significantly different. In the Wright story, Cheney was a woodhawk on his way back to his camp on the Yellowstone, and "Smith" was a buffalo hunter who decided to accompany him. In the Ray version, Vic Smith was a dispatch rider and Cheney went along to protect Smith.

Despite the fact that Tom Ray took a great deal of interest in the history of the lower Yellowstone valley, his telling leaves the biggest holes. There are four major problems with the Tom Ray story and they leave little doubt that Vic Smith was not the man who accompanied Bill Cheney:

1. Tom Ray's book *Yellowstone Red* is a work of fiction that utilizes some real local characters to lend color and authenticity to his tale. The book's historical facts, however, were not always the most accurate: "Below and sharply to his right lay the meadow where one day the wagon master for General Whistler, W. H. Cheney (Uncle Will) was to homestead and build his home...[I]t is in the summer of 1864...." [YR, pp. 261–262.] Here the tale mixed two events and put Cheney in the wrong outfit: Cheney was a wagon master for the Sully expedition of 1864. The Whistler expedition took place in 1871, but Cheney had no part in it. Following the Sully expedition of 1864, Cheney did accompany the Stanley–Custer expedition of 1873 from Fort Abraham Lincoln to Pompey's Pillar and return, but in 1871, during the Whistler venture, Cheney was freighting for the Canadian Pacific construction between Winnipeg and St. Cloud. [See the biography of William Cheney in "Old Dawson."]

2. Both Kathryn Wright and Vic Smith's biographer, Jeanette Prodgers, placed Cheney's "ride for life" as having occurred

in the fall of 1877. [VS, p. xiv.] Vic Smith did confirm that he was a mail carrier riding for "Major Pease, the contractor," between Fort Buford, the Glendive Cantonment, and Fort Keogh in May of 1877 for two-hundred dollars per month. He then stated, however, that he departed that employment after only two trips "as he could make more money at something else." [VS, pp. 82–83.] Vic's first trip was "on the first of May" and, being paid by the month, it certainly didn't take until "fall" to make the second. The fact is that when the Cheney–Nig event occurred, Vic Smith was not "a dispatch carrier" as described by Ray.

3. Bill Cheney died on 13 December 1920 at the age of eighty-one. He never married. Sometime around 1900 Cheney's niece, Susan Harrison, moved out from the East to keep house for him. Tom Ray interviewed Ms. Harrison in 1935 and she related the "Vic Smith" version as retold by Ray. The interview occurred some fifteen years after the death of Bill Cheney and some fifty-eight years following an event that had occurred in 1877, some twenty-three years before Ms. Harrison's arrival in the country. Everybody knew it was a man named "Smith" who had accompanied Cheney from Fort Buford. Either Ms. Harrison or Tom Ray (or both) filled in the fifty-three-year-old blank by recalling the well- known Vic Smith and forgetting the lesser-known Andrew "Glendive" Smith (if they knew of him at all).

4. A fourth problem with the Harrison-Ray version is Vic Smith himself. Vic Smith was a rather accomplished writer (he left his memoir, which was later discovered and edited by Jeanette Prodgers and published in 1997 as *The Champion Buffalo Hunter*) and an erstwhile journalist who, in the mid-1880s, frequently wrote for the local newspaper, the *Glendive Times*. An avid self-promoter, Vic Smith never mentioned his participation in the well-known and oft-told tale of Bill Cheney and his beautiful Morgan, Nig. Vic described his first hazardous trip as a mail rider in May of 1877 in some detail. Had his second (and last) trip been the heart-pounding Cheney escape, he would have certainly told of his role in it.

ANDREW "GLENDIVE" SMITH
ENGRAVING FROM THE *GLENDIVE INDEPENDENT*, JUNE 20, 1896

VIC SMITH, 1880
PHOTO COURTESY OF THE MONTANA HISTORICAL SOCIETY RESEARCH CENTER PHOTOGRAPH ARCHIVES, HELENA

Born in New York City in 1855, Andrew Smith and his parents moved to Wisconsin when he was a year old. In 1866, the Smith family moved to Woodbury County, Iowa. About 1874, Andrew went to western Wyoming for a year and spent the following year (1875) in the Black Hills in search of his "El Dorado." Sometime in 1876, he hooked up with the U.S. Army as a scout and dispatch rider in Montana. The dispatch riders in 1876 and 1877 rode from Fort Buford to the Glendive Cantonment and on to Tongue River and Fort Keogh. Somewhere along the line, Andrew Smith apparently picked up the "handle" of "Glendive" Smith. It was Vic Smith himself who identified "Glendive" Smith as the man who, in the fall of 1876, helped him catch Wesley ("Yank") Brockmeyer's horse a couple of months after Brockmeyer had been killed by Indians in August of 1876 at the mouth of Powder River. [VS, pp. 63–66 and p. 84.] Joe Culbertson also identified "Glendive" Smith as a scout for Miles in the winter of 1876:

> I pulled out my field glasses and...noticed a horseman coming on the trail...I thought I would waylay him and kill him if I could. Just before getting to the spot [to ambush him] I noticed...he was a white man. He jumped off his horse and pulled his gun from the holster. I rode up to him, and it was "Glendive Smith," one of General Miles' scouts. [JCIS, p. 86 and p. 138.]

Finally, Andrew Smith was known to have been carrying the "horseback mail" between Fort Buford, the Glendive Cantonment and Fort Keogh "for a year" in 1877. [OTOL, p. 285.] Andrew Smith was also known to have periodically partnered up with Ed Marron and hunted buffalo in the lower Yellowstone from 1877. [TLW, p. 215.]The circumstantial evidence is such that there can be little doubt that "the buffalo hunter" (or "the courier" if you prefer the Ray version of the story) who accompanied Bill Cheney on his "ride for life" was Andrew "Glendive" Smith.

CHAPTER NINE

We Settle In:
Buffalo, Beef, and the
Blue Jacket Mine

T HE RAILROAD WAS OF TREMENDOUS IMPORTANCE to the early
Glendive settlers. It was, in general, the main source of
everyone's livelihood, for without it their employment
or abilities to function as merchants or tradesmen would have
ceased to exist. It also represented, for most of them, the only
avenue of escape back to whatever higher level of civilization
they had previously known. Many of them were more than just
a bit frightened at the vast emptiness they found all about them.
They were inclined to cuddle up to that iron rail, the only thing
in common between this boundless rugged land and what they
had known in their earlier homes.[110]

Some of the early settlers in Glendive took temporary possession
of the shacks left by the contracting railroad construction crews.
These were built stockade fashion, the timbers placed upright
side by side, their ends buried in a trench, and then crudely
chinked. In some cases, the "timbers" were cull railroad ties, but
more often they were simply the ubiquitous soft cottonwood tree
trunks and limbs found along the Yellowstone. These shacks had
dirt floors and dirt roofs and were generally windowless. A single
opening with a wood-hinged door allowed ingress and egress.
These shacks sat over on the east side of the tracks, strung out
between the roundhouse site and Camp Porter. We were more
fortunate since my father was able to rent one of the Camp Porter
structures left by the soldiers. They were of better construction

---

[110] Unless otherwise noted, the source for Chapter 9 is the SNVB manuscript, pp. 15–18 and
pp. 30–31.

and had wood floors and roofs, and they had a window in them. Ours was about fourteen feet square, for which my father had to pay ten dollars per month.[111] He only got that after about a month's wait, with us living in some spare warehouse space the railroad allowed our group to use until we got ourselves located.[112] We had a good-sized tent we had brought with us and between the two accommodations we got along very well.

It was in this modest circumstance, on July 9, 1882, about two months after we had arrived in Glendive, the last of my siblings, Sarah Effie, was born. Despite the rather primitive environment into which she entered this life she matured into a happy and healthy adult. I believe her to be the second child to have been born in the town of Glendive proper. Grant Brown, Nathan Brown's son, was born there the year before we arrived. Despite the fact there were other claimants, he was certainly the first child born in Glendive.[113]

Game was abundant. Although certainly not in the magnitude of the previous half decade, scattered herds of buffalo remained on the prairie when we arrived in April of 1882.[114] There were still large herds of antelope and deer, lots of prairie chickens and sage hens, and countless jackrabbits. Despite the fact there was a small meat shop in Glendive when we arrived, it suited no one in our family to use it. Whenever we needed meat, someone in the greater family, usually my father, simply went out on a hunt and got what we needed. There was no refrigeration, but we didn't need it in any case. So long as it was properly cut into strips, you could hang a strip of meat ten feet up from the ground in the dead of summer and it would dry without tainting in the least. I have always thought the explanation for that was in the fact

---

[111] The "structure" the Van Blaricom family acquired "after about a month's wait" was one of the quarters built for the enlisted men sometime around December of 1880. [TLW, p. 51.] The buildings at Camp Porter had been made of sawed lumber hauled in by steamboat from Bismarck. Some of the Camp Porter buildings were occupied well into the twentieth century. [John Steffen interview, 3 July 2008.]

[112] See *"The railroad allowed us..."* in Author's Notes following this chapter.

[113] Letter from Daniel Brown, November 1984. See *"Grant Brown"* in Author's Notes following this chapter.

[114] The buffalo count was still substantial when Norton and his family arrived in Glendive in April of 1882. William T. Hornaday was told by hide buyer J. N. Davis that, on the rail line between Miles City and Mandan, there were about 200,000 hides and robes shipped by white hunters in 1882. [Hornaday as cited by Prodgers in VS, Part IV, Footnote 4.]

that the air was so clear and dry that the fermenting bacteria could not live in it. Whatever the reason, spoiled meat was never a concern. In the winter, of course, Dawson County itself became the refrigerator. Then the cooking instructions were easy: "Boil to thaw then cook to taste."

On a day in mid-June of this first summer, Father and four other men decided they would go after some buffalo meat and they let me join them. This was my first "buff" hunt. I had just turned thirteen. Taking a team and wagon, two saddle horses, and enough grub for two or three days, we took the ferry across the Yellowstone, went up Deer Creek about a half-day's drive, and set up camp. The next morning at daybreak we could hear buffalo bulls drumming on the ground. They were over a hill to the north, about a half-mile from us. We immediately made preparations to stalk them.

Leaving the team tied to the wagon and leading the two saddle horses, we crept to the top of the ridge and peeked over. There, within easy range, were about thirty-five "buffs." Most of the men had .45-60 Winchester rifles, a good gun firing a .45 caliber round loaded with 60 grains of powder. This was a mighty fine rifle even though not of the power of the larger .45-150s and .50-160s used by the professional buffalo hunters. Giving me the saddle horses to hold, all five of them started shooting. They stopped three on the spot. Two of the men mounted their horses and started in pursuit. They overtook two more and killed them. The last two were nothing but a wanton waste, for the three we had would have presented us with more meat than we could possibly have used. No one, however, thought of economy in killing anything at that time. It simply wasn't a part of the mentality of that time and place. It wasn't an issue of killing what was needed. It was being able to return to town and tell about how many of what kind were killed.

One of the animals stopped on the first shooting was a big bull. He was badly wounded, too sick to charge, but he was still getting up, falling down, and rolling around. As soon as the herd had disappeared, father handed me his gun and asked me to go over and finish off the wounded animal. While I was but thirteen years old, I was a good shot, having been trained from infancy.

That, after all, was a commonplace and very important part of a young man's education on the frontier. But I was soon to learn that dispatching a buffalo was something different.

At that moment the old fellow was lying down. I went out about fifty feet in front of him and took aim, intending to shoot him between the eyes. I saw the dust fly out of his hair but it didn't seem to disturb the bull at all. I looked around and all five of the men were smiling at me. Well, I pulled up and let him have it once again. And again nothing happened. I decided I would try once more. I might as well have been shooting into a sandbank, for that was exactly what I was doing. The bull buffalo has a tuft of hair between his horns that is six or seven inches deep. In the summer, while fighting flies and gnats, this hair becomes completely compacted with sand, dirt, and water. No .45-60 round made by man will go through it. They all had a good laugh at my confusion and then Father suggested I go out to the side and put a shot in the region of his heart. This I did and the thing was done.

We selected as much meat as we would need from the first three that had been shot. We took only the choicest parts, the best of which were the humps. A buffalo has very high withers, and on either side there are some twenty pounds of choice meat. It has no particular muscular development and is very tender, always considered the choicest part of the animal. We took only the humps from the last two the riders had shot. We skinned all five and departed for home. We left far more for the wolves and coyotes than we took.[115]

I have often been asked about the quality of buffalo meat compared to beef. Let me relate a circumstance that illustrates the point very well. During the winter of 1882–1883, I was doing chores and otherwise helping out at the Glendive butcher shop. The proprietor went out hunting buffalo for hides that winter, leaving the shop in the charge of his wife. He would send in the humps and the hindquarters of the animals that he killed to supply the shop with meat. We stored them in an outbuilding where they froze hard as rock. When needed, we would bring them in, thaw them, and skin them out. If they skinned out and looked fresh, as some would,

---

[115] See *"The demise of the buffalo"* in Author's Notes following this chapter.

we hung them on one side of the shop and called them "Dawson County Shorthorn." If, as sometimes happened, they came out a little dark or dingy we hung them on the other side and called them "buffalo." A customer would come in and say, "Oh, I'm tired of buff. Give me some beef." We would take a cut from the fresh-looking "Shorthorn" side of the store and charge him two cents a pound more for it. We never heard a word of complaint and we had not one pound of beef in that store all winter.[116]

In truth, the longhorned cattle that roamed the ranges of Dawson County were no great treat once you put them on your plate. They spent all of their time grazing in order to grow and survive the one winter and two summers they were usually kept on the prairie. Well, walking and growing frame was no way to put any kind of tender in that Longhorn's steak. It was fine if you boiled it like a Yankee pot roast but it never provided any competition for the buffalo's hump. That quality issue was a tough deal for the stockmen to overcome and it nearly broke everybody who tried to ship directly from Montana to the Eastern markets. One time there was a scheme put forth by the Count over there at Medora to sell Longhorn meat to the poor people in the Eastern cities at discounted prices but even that didn't work.[117]

With the exception of my father, my people had always been farmers, and they had come to Montana and the Yellowstone valley with the intention of taking homesteads and carrying on as farmers. The railroad had a very large warehouse in Glendive, and they gave us permission to stay there until we could locate. It was very evident to most of the party that we had been misled as to the possibilities of agriculture in the country. There was some talk of going back, but most of them couldn't have gone back if they had wished. They had nothing to go back with and nothing to go back to. It was finally decided that there they were and so they settled into a pattern of systematically prospecting the

---

116 The "butcher shop" Norton referenced was The Glendive Meat Market. Started by Nick Comford in 1881, the place was owned by R. W. Snyder and Benjamin A. Savignac when Norton worked there in 1882 and 1883. See *"In 1882, the Glendive Meat Market..."* in Author's Notes following this chapter.

117 The "Count" referred to by Norton was the Marquis de Mores, an ambitious and somewhat eccentric member of the Orleans family in France. He was remotely in line for the French throne. See *"The Marquis de Mores and the Medora abattoir"* in Author's Notes following this chapter.

country for locations. In this they enjoyed unlimited privilege, for there were millions of acres from which to choose.

They finally selected a location on the west side of the Yellowstone about six miles below the town, with Deer Creek to the south and Threemile Creek to the north. This Threemile, Sevenmile, and Thirteenmile Creek business threw a lot of Glendive newcomers for a loop. They always thought the names signified that those creeks were three, seven, and thirteen miles from Glendive but that wasn't the case. Captain Grant Marsh[118] had named the creeks in recognition of their distances down the Yellowstone from the Glendive Cantonment. The cantonment was located on the west side of the river fully three miles downstream from the ferry at Glendive which is where everybody, after the town was laid out, crossed the Yellowstone to get to the road on the west side. To confuse the matter even further, the measure described was the steamboat distance on the river—including the meanders—not the land route the road ultimately followed. Thus, by road, it was truthfully about six-and-a-half miles from the Glendive ferry to Threemile Creek, about eleven miles from the ferry to Sevenmile Creek, and some fifteen-and-a-half miles to Thirteenmile Creek.[119]

All of the extended family moved out there between Deer Creek and Threemile Creek and started clearing what land they could, first for the gardens and then for some sort of cash crop, in our case some wheat and some corn. Mother being quite with child and due sometime in July, Father left mother at the shanty in town with the little ones and he and I would then go out and work. We oftentimes stayed out there at the family camp. We primarily helped the others build their dwellings and our communal gardens.[120]

The other exception to the Deer Creek settlement was my

---

[118] See "Old Dawson" for the biography of legendary steamboat master Captain Grant Prince Marsh.

[119] The same story about the naming of Threemile, Sevenmile, Ninemile (Morgan), and Thirteenmile creeks was related by local historians Walter D. Kemmis and Ira L. Bendon in an undated newspaper clipping found in the Mondak Heritage Center in Sidney, Montana. Bendon was known to have come into the Yellowstone country in 1880. [CE, p. 882.] Walter Kemmis died on 29 June 1955. [CE, p. 942.]

[120] See Map 3 on the following page for the *"Geography of the Missouri–Yellowstone Confluence."*

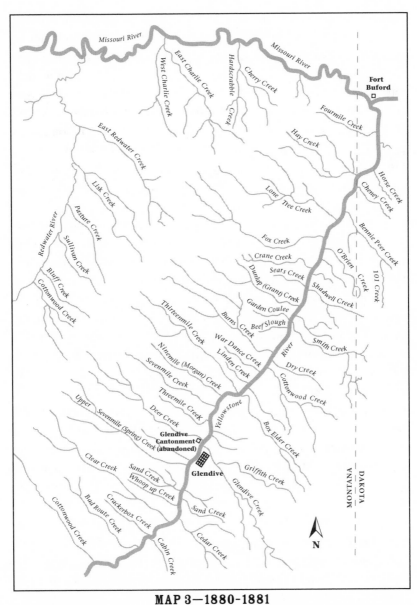

MAP 3—1880-1881
GEOGRAPHY OF THE MISSOURI-YELLOWSTONE CONFLUENCE
[NOT TO SCALE]

Uncle Frank Perry and his family. Shortly after our arrival, Uncle Frank bought a substantial coal vein about three miles up Griffith Creek. He took this over from Judge Wolf Allen and soon developed the Blue Jacket Mine. This was a large tunnel mine with huge rooms that Frank Perry and his men carved out over the years. It supplied most of the coal to Glendive during the time Uncle Frank was there from the fall of 1882 through the spring of 1887. Uncle Frank sold the mine to Charlie Bowers when our family left in 1887. I recall that Morris Cain owned it from 1890 until he moved to Washington State in 1900. What became of the mine after that, I don't know.[121]

My father was definitely not a farmer. He was a hunter by nature and he busied himself providing meat to the family settlement which, even by itself, was sizable for that country. Aside from that, he was quite good with his hands and was a rough carpenter of some skill. Father was a good horseman and, in Minnesota, he had also enjoyed no small reputation for being able to handle oxen, especially when skidding logs. He would make lengthy hunting forays and supply fresh meat to the soldiers at Fort Buford[122] in exchange for that ever-scarce commodity, cash money. It didn't matter too much that Father wasn't a farmer by nature. That very first season proved that farming without irrigation was hopeless anyway. Not one of them even got his seed back from the planting. The real irony of it was that the soil, indeed, was very fertile. It was capable of growing almost anything if it had water. The ten or eleven inches of natural precipitation, however, simply wouldn't do the trick.

A compounding factor to the failure was that they had brought their seed inventory with them from Minnesota. The Minnesota seed had probably come with them from Indiana in 1855. The Indiana seed had probably come from Ohio in the 1840s and, in all likelihood, the Ohio seed had come with Great-Grandpa Samuel from Pennsylvania around 1800. In any case, and wherever they had come from, those seeds simply weren't meant for the small

---

[121] This particular coal vein was first worked by Judge Joseph "Wolf" Allen during the winter of 1881–1882. Frank Perry bought the vein from Allen in 1882 and named it the Blue Jacket Mine. See *"The Blue Jacket Mine"* in Author's Notes following this chapter.

[122] See "Old Dawson" for a discussion of the significant role played by Fort Buford (1866–1895) in the development of northeastern Montana and northwestern Dakota.

amounts of moisture encountered in eastern Montana. Nobody then living in or around Glendive knew anything at all about irrigation. That was something you heard about the Mormons doing down in Utah.

It was George Grant and Emmet Dunlap who got the first irrigation project going on a small scale up on Grant's Prairie in 1883. They built a ditch and diverted Grant Creek into it. George and Emmet only had about ten acres apiece under water, but, over time, Emmet kept enlarging his area until it covered nearly a full quarter section. Because of Emmet's success, the locals took to calling the creek "Dunlap Creek," and "Grant Creek" eventually fell into disuse. The agency farmer at Wolf Point up north on the Fort Peck Reservation got some irrigation water going there in 1884.[123]

In any case, there wasn't a soul in Dawson County who had either the knowledge or the wherewithal to tackle the taming and diversion of the mighty Yellowstone. So there we sat the whole late spring and summer of 1882, trying to farm right by one of the great and reliable water sources of Montana, and we watched while our crops withered away from drought. Water, water everywhere, nor any drop to drink!

Nobody in Dawson County, Montana, in 1882 knew anything about the hybridized strains of cereal grains that exist today. It took the coming of the hardy German-Russian immigrants who were fleeing "Mother Russia" about a decade after the turn of the century to make the association between the plains of eastern Montana and the steppes of Russia. The country looked familiar to them and they knew what to do with it. They knew how and when to till it and when to seed it and when and how to harvest it. Most important, they knew what kind of seed to use and they knew that crops native to the eastern part of the United States would not survive the climatic conditions encountered in eastern Montana. To them and to our durable Scandinavian neighbors must go the credit of the development of successful dryland wheat farming in western America. That era, however, was not

---

[123] George Grant and Emmet Dunlap developed the first irrigation project in Dawson County by diverting Grant Creek (now "Dunlap Creek") in 1883. James P. Jones, the "farmer in charge" at the Fort Peck Reservation's sub-agency at Wolf Point, was the creator, designer, construction supervisor, and "water master" of the Wolf Creek irrigation project that started in 1884. See *Early irrigation projects* in Author's Notes following this chapter.

even to commence in Dawson County until a full three decades after our family had stepped off the train and decided to stay.[124]

Two incidents of our brief residence on the river downstream from Glendive might be of some interest. I have already mentioned that there were still quite a few buffaloes left in the country. It wasn't covered by the vast herds of the preceding decade. Instead they were to be found in small isolated groups and the occasional lone bull. One morning of that first spring an uncle, on getting up in the morning, was amazed to see an old bull buffalo standing in his garden not fifty yards from the house. My uncle rushed for his gun and, of course, killed him, only to discover that the buff was so old and flea-bitten that he was only fit for wolf bait. The old boy had been hooked out of the herd by the younger bulls, for he bore several fresh wounds from the struggle and he had a great deal of difficulty in moving at all. He was so old he was senile and he had simply wandered away to die. I can remember that when my uncle approached him, he just stood there not moving a muscle or blinking an eye. I wondered later if that old bull hadn't deliberately walked into my uncle's garden in order to be put away. It was, perhaps, a kind of buffalo suicide. Whatever was true, the killing was a mercy to him.

On another occasion Father and I had just gotten up one morning. The sun was not yet up when we heard what proved to be a two-year-old heifer bawling in great distress. Her bellows were of such magnitude that they were carrying from over a hill about a half-mile from the house. Father immediately got his gun and we started off in that direction to see what the trouble was. As we topped the rise, we saw three gray wolves disengage themselves from their breakfast and make off for the hills. They had put the heifer down by the expedient of disemboweling her. They had slit her abdomen through, leaving her entrails to fall out. The wolves had accomplished this handy bit of surgery just as clean as though it had been done with a knife. They had then proceeded to literally eat her alive. I have never forgotten that heifer's panic-stricken call of distress nor have I ever forgotten the agonizing results of the wolves' activities.

---

[124] GHMT, p. 39 and p. 42. See *"The growth of wheat farming in Dawson County"* in Author's Notes following this chapter.

Father immediately went up and put the poor heifer out of her misery. We then returned to the house. The settlers all kept some strychnine on hand for the very purpose of dispatching wolves. We then returned to the carcass and, slashing into the meaty parts, we put the poison inside the cuts. The next morning we found one of the wolves right by the carcass and another about fifty feet away. The third one we never found but his tracks showed that he was one sick wolf. We pelted the two and on the next trip to town father took them in and got his bounty.[125]

One of the peculiarities of the time worthy of mention was the money used in trade. Through 1881 and 1882 there were no one-cent, five-cent, or ten-cent pieces used in Glendive. If they were in circulation at all, nobody in Glendive would accept them. The smallest coin used was two bits silver.[126] It was also a fact that during the entire year of 1882 dollar bills were also taboo. They were out there but nobody in Glendive would accept them. Silver dollars were okay. Why this was the case, I do not know. I simply state it as a fact.

---

[125] See *"Dispatching the wolves"* in Author's Notes this chapter.

[126] See *"Two bits silver"* in Author's Notes this chapter.

CHAPTER 9–AUTHOR'S NOTES

"The railroad allowed us to live in some spare warehouse space when we first arrived in April of 1882." The land where the railroad warehouse was built in Glendive no longer exists. Few people realize how drastically the channel of the Yellowstone has changed over the years. Stephen Norton Van Blaricom revisited Glendive in 1923 and, during his stay, wrote an article the local newspaper published: "Our first camp [in April of 1882] was made in a big [N. P.] R. R. storehouse that stood about where the main channel of the river now runs just above the bridge." [DCR, Thursday, 15 February 1923, article by S. N. Van Blaricom.] John S. Truscott, a sergeant in the 5th U.S. Infantry (Mounted), had been stationed at Camp Hargous and Camp Thorington, the latter being located "near where the bridge now crosses the Yellowstone at Glendive." Late in October of 1880, the unit had been ordered back to Fort Keogh from which post they were sent off to Poplar River. In March of 1881 they were ordered back to Fort Keogh and they returned via Glendive. "We were indeed surprised to find a new comfortable town where only a few months ago there had been nothing. The rain [and ice break-up had] washed away considerable land between the town and the river. I would think about 500 feet or more was washed away, the main channel [now] being more to the north [or west] side of the river." [Undated letter from John S. Truscott to Mrs. Frank P. Fleming of Glendive, probably written in the 1920s or '30s.] Thus, the Northern Pacific had built a large warehouse in 1881 on the east (south) side of the Yellowstone on land bordering the new channel that had been formed when the river shifted from east to west (south to north) during the winter of 1880–1881. Sometime between 1882 and 1890, the river had shifted east (south) again and completely destroyed the warehouse site reported in the Van Blaricom article. (The U.S. Government built some navigational structures and steamboat docking facilities in Glendive during the 1880s. That stopped the erosion of the river toward the town.)

"Grant Brown, First White Child born in Glendive, Montana, April 23, 1881 in Small house that Sat on the Bank of the Yellowstone About where the Elevator is now above the iron bridge that crosses the Yellowstone. Fathers name was Nathan Brown; Grant was one of 12 children in that family, He was raised on a Horse Ranch on Belle Prairie in the Area where the road that the Louis Crest Family Called the Snake Trail. Above the Area called Frenchman Island where the Intake Dam is. Grant Died in 1951 of a Heart Attack. The last of this family of children Miles Brown, Died in 1961. Dan M. Brown of Miles City, The only living son of Grant, Has two Sons, Dan G. Brown, Bremerton, Washington an [sic] Clifford F. Brown, Miles City, Montana. No Male Grandchildren. [Signed] Daniel M. Brown–1003 Truscott, Miles City, Mt." [A copy of the undated Brown letter, dated as having been received by some third party in November of 1984, is in the possession of the author.] Nathan Brown, the baby Grant's father, is certainly the same Nathan "Squaw" Brown with whom the Harpsters left their horses on Belle Prairie during the winter of 1879–1880 and who later filed a homestead claim on part of the land platted by Colonel Merrill and the Yellowstone Land and Colonization Company for the townsite of Glendive. [See Nathan Brown in "Old Dawson."]

While there have been other claimants to the "first born in Glendive" title (in the Glendive press and in OTOL), only Grant Brown's birth date precedes the 9 July 1882 birth of Sarah Effie Van Blaricom. [HVBG, Family Group Sheet of the children of Levi Van Blaricom.] "The first child born in Glendive was Lettie Blake [sic] Bradshaw [Lettie Brake Bradshaw], born November 16, 1882. This honor has [also] been claimed for Josephine Halverson Hilliard, but as both babies arrived about the same time each one deserves honorable mention." [Grace M. Gilbert in IVEM, 14 November 1935.] However, there is evidence that Lettie Brake was born not in Glendive but at her father's ranch on the lower Yellowstone about fifteen miles south of the Fort Buford ferry crossing: "Early in 1884 [probably 1883] a cowboy [Will Brake] came riding into the area [Glendive] carrying a six-week-old baby girl [Lettie Brake] wrapped in a blanket." According to William Harpster, the Harpster biographer, Hettie Harpster "took this baby in," educated her, and raised her. [OTOL, p. 370.]) Forest Edward Burns, born 21 September 1879 in his parent's (John L. and Alice Burns) home on Burns Creek, was the first documented white birth in the lower Yellowstone country.

Grace Gilbert attributed the first white birth on the lower Yellowstone to being that of Lilly Leiper, "the wife of Judge Leiper." [Grace M. Gilbert, IVEM, 14 November 1935.] Judge Frank Leiper's obituary (5 June 1959, RR) stated that he was married to Lillian C. Sartian in Helena on 24 August 1905. Her surname has been variously spelled as "Sartian," "Sartain," and "Sartaire." The only family who settled early in the lower Yellowstone with a name spelled in that fashion was that of William A. Sartin and his wife, Eliza. Sartin had been a bugler for "I" Company of the 6th Infantry Regiment at Fort Buford. Following his discharge, the Sartin family followed William Newlon to the Newlon settlement in March or April of 1880. If Lillian was the child of William and Eliza Sartin she does not show on the 1880 census and would have to have been born, therefore, later than the mid-summer (June–July) of 1880. That places Lillian as born in the lower Yellowstone valley after Forest Edward Burns (21 September 1879) but perhaps before Lettie (Brake) Harpster (16 November 1882). The records would place Grant Brown (born 23 April 1881) and Sarah Effie Van Blaricom (born 9 July 1882) as the first and second children born in the town of Glendive with Josephine (Halverson) Hilliard, born about November 1882, a close third.

The demise of the buffalo: The bulk of the early northern buffalo hunting for trade was done by the various Indian tribes, especially the Sioux, Crow, Assiniboine, and Gros Ventres (of the North or Atsina), armed with spears, bows and arrows, muskets or breech-loading rifles. The tribes consumed the meat and traded in the relatively small market for finished robes that were shipped downriver to Bismarck. The Blackfeet did the same but they much preferred dealing with the Canadians. "In 1871, however, tanners discovered a method of treating buffalo hides for use as marketable leather" to fabricate shoes, harness material and coats. [M/M, p. 153.] "By the mid-1870s the hide hunters on the Southern Plains were looking for new hunting grounds and there was only one place left to look. That was eastern Montana and adjacent sections of Dakota and Wyoming Territories. Sitting Bull's defeat and Miles' vigorous campaigning along the Yellowstone in the years immediately following 1876 left no question" about where to head. [POY, p. 363.]

By 1880, Miles City was considered to be the geographical center of the remnant of the northern buffalo herd, an estimated 500,000 bison in a 150-mile radius. The rapid killing of this herd began about 1880. It was the coming of the railroad in 1881 that led to the demise of the northern buffalo herd centered in Montana. The estimates of the slaughter of the central Montana herd are: 125,000 in 1881; 250,000 in 1882; 60,000 in 1883; and "in 1884, when the last trainload of hides pulled out of Dickinson, Dakota Territory, it carried only enough hides to fill part of one car." [M/M, p. 154.] Those estimates, however, may have been low. During the winter of 1881–1882, Henry F. Douglas and David Mead bought and shipped over 250,000 buffalo hides from Glendive alone. [TLW, p. 96.] The last commercial "stand" of buffalo reportedly occurred in September, October, and November of 1883 between the east side of the Little Missouri over to the headwaters of the Cannonball River in what is now the southwestern part of North Dakota. There were about 10,000 bison in that herd. [VS, p. 190. POY, pp. 362–369.] According to Vic Smith and others, Sitting Bull and about 1,100 Sioux from the Standing Rock Reservation participated in this last slaughter. [VS, p. 190.] Almost all authorities seem to agree that this event put an end to commercial buffalo hunting. There weren't enough buffalo left to occasion any more than chance encounters with small groups. Even then the locals killed buffalo whenever they could. By 1889, the bison total remaining in all of North America was estimated at 535 animals. [MLP, p. 307.]

The waste associated with the slaughter of the buffalo herds was astounding. The Santa Fe Railroad reported in 1873 the shipment (from the southern plains) of 251,443 buffalo robes, 1,617,600 pounds of buffalo meat, and 2,743,100 pounds of bones. It was estimated that it took somewhat more than two kills to produce one hide of sufficient quality to ship. Thus about 500,000 buffalo were killed to ship 1,617,600 pounds of meat (or about three pounds of meat for each buffalo killed). A tongue alone weighed about 4 pounds. The hump and hindquarters were usually sold locally, if at all. In 1870, the value of a buffalo hide was $2.50; the tongue was worth twenty-five cents; the meat of the hindquarters and the hump, about two dollars; the bones, horns and hoofs, about twenty-five cents total. After the Northern Pacific Railroad showed up in Montana, the animals were often slaughtered for their hides alone, while the carcasses were left to rot on the plains. [MLP, pp. 305–307.] Following the killer winter of 1886–87, the cowboys and settlers of the northern plains were financially strapped. In an attempt to make ends meet, they gathered up the skeletons of the thousands of cattle that had died during the winter and the hundreds of thousands of bison killed over the previous decade. First loaded onto wagons and then hauled to the closest rail line, the bones were subsequently ground up for fertilizer or cattle feed (bone meal). [See Chapter 20 for a more detailed discussion of the winter of 1886–1887.]

In 1882, the Glendive Meat Market was owned by R. W. Snyder and Benjamin A. Savignac. Nicholas W. Comford, who had started the shop in the summer of 1881, sold the business to Snyder and Savignac in March of 1882. [TLW, p. 309 and p. 324.] Snyder was a known buffalo hunter and, "in addition to buffalo hunting, Mr. Snyder operated the...butcher shop in Glendive." [Article by Fred Dion, Jr., OTOL, p. 89.] Norton worked in the meat market during the winter of 1882–1883. The Snyders had met and married in Washington, D.C. in 1880 and had moved shortly thereafter to Miles City. They moved to Glendive in the spring of 1882. [OTOL, p. 297.] Since Ben Savignac didn't marry until 30 September 1883, the "proprietor" and "his wife" Norton referenced was undoubt-edly Mr. and Mrs. R. W. Snyder. [See the Marriage Certificate of "B. Savignac and Ada [Adelia] V. Gates, Glendive, Dawson County, Territory of Montana, September 30th, 1883. J. M. Cataldo, S. J., Cath. Pr." Recorded on 1 October 1883, Book 1, page 5, Marriage Records of Dawson County.]

The Marquis de Mores and the Medora abattoir: Intending to corner the market in all of the livestock being shipped to consumers in the East by the Northern Pacific Railroad, the Marquis de Mores arrived in the village of Little Missouri (known as the "Bad Lands Cantonment" during the railroad construction days), Dakota Territory, in March of 1883. He announced his intention to build a community there that would rival Omaha. "I am going to build an abattoir. I am going to buy all of the beef, sheep, and hogs that come over the Northern Pacific, and I am going to slaughter them here and then ship them to Chicago and the East," the twenty-five-year-old marquis announced.

Backed by the millions of his father-in-law (he had recently married Medora von Hoffman, the red-haired daughter of a wealthy New York banker of German extraction) and unwelcome in the village of Little Missouri, the marquis moved immediately across the Little Missouri River and, on April Fool's day, 1883, started his own town. He named it "Medora" after his wife. In partnership with the Haupt brothers, he quickly formed the Northern Pacific Refrigerator Car

Company to transport the vast commodities he planned to ship, and set about building his abattoir.

A few people asked the marquis if he realized the scale of his undertaking, his intent to slaughter all of the thousands upon thousands of head of livestock to be shipped by the Northern Pacific. According to Hermann Hagedorn, de Mores replied: "It doesn't matter! My father-in-law has ten-million dollars and can borrow ten-million dollars more. Do you think I am impractical? I am not impractical. My plan is altogether feasible. I do not merely think this. I know. My intuition tells me so. I pride myself on having a natural intuition. It takes me only a few seconds to understand a situation that other men have to puzzle over for hours. I seem to see every side of a question at once. I assure you, I am gifted in this way. I have wonderful insight." [RBL, pp. 59–61 and p. 71.]

On the surface, the idea was simple enough: it was a lot cheaper to ship refrigerated carcasses than it was to ship live beef. The carcass took a lot less room, it only weighed about fifty-five percent of the animal's live weight and it never had to be off-loaded for food or water. Additionally, carcasses didn't "shrink"; live cattle did, losing about ten percent of their weight being transported by rail from Montana to Chicago or Omaha. [RBL, p. 71.] The typical arrangement was to ship the cattle east and fatten them for a short period of ninety to one-hundred-and-twenty days just prior to slaughter. The marquis' idea resulted in shipping low quality beef very economically but he had no way to improve the quality of the meat prior to slaughter.

Once completed, the Medora abattoir could handle only twenty-five head of cattle per day. [RBL, p. 331.] Replaced with a new abattoir in June of 1885, capacity increased to one-hundred head per day. [RBL, p. 332.] The western cities along the Northern Pacific route acclaimed the Marquis de Mores' project enthusiastically, thinking it would mean cheaper beef in their storefronts. [RBL, p. 71.] From Chicago on east, however, the meat produced by the range cattle proved to be of such poor quality that the wholesalers could only dispose of it with difficulty and, finally, the retail dealers refused to buy it. Their consumers were used to the corn-fed beef of the Midwest and, even at a savings, they simply refused to buy the meat products being shipped to them straight off the grasslands of the plains of Montana, Wyoming, and the Dakotas. [RBL, pp. 332–333.]

The marquis then developed a scheme to buy all of the hops produced on the Pacific coast. He intended to contract his monopolized hops to the brewers of St. Louis and Milwaukee with the proviso that all of their by-product malt had to be shipped back to Medora in tank cars to be used as cattle feed. "It is the most concentrated and fattening food to be bought." [RBL, p. 333.] The brewers didn't see it his way and the scheme failed. Following that, the marquis decided he could sell his beef direct to consumers. He opened a multitude of shops in New York and other Eastern cities, but stores where only one kind of low-quality meat (grass-fed three- and four-year-old Longhorns) could be purchased didn't appeal to the public. "The Marquis had all the figures in the world to prove that the public should buy, but human nature thwarted him." [RBL, p. 448.]

In 1887, the marquis announced that he and his wife were going off on a short trip to India to hunt tigers. The Medora abattoir was shut down and that was the end of it. For information regarding the fate of the Marquis de Mores, see Author's Notes following Chapter 21. Also reference the marquis in "Old Dawson."

The Blue Jacket Mine: The Blue Jacket was the source of the coal that fired the hearths of Glendive during its earliest years. Precisely when the Blue Jacket shut down and exactly where the mine was located became lost with the passage of time. Finally, in a February 2002 interview with correspondent John Steffen, Mr. Clarence Starr stated that the earliest major coal mine in the area was up Griffith Creek about eight miles from town, somewhat upstream from the confluence with Glendive Creek. He stated that it was an underground mine with "rooms" (chambers) and noted "the mine's entrance was sealed up many years ago." It was Mr. Starr's opinion that this mine was the old Blue Jacket. Mr. Starr, ninety-two years old at the time of the interview, was born in Morrison County, Minnesota, in 1909, and came to Dawson County in 1910. He spent ten of his earliest working years in the area as a coal miner and coal broker. Mr. Starr took Mr. Steffen to the mine and Mr. Steffen reported that the indentations to the entrance of the old sealed mine could still be discerned. Just weeks after the Starr interview, Mr. Ray Autsby, then eighty-two years old, stated to Mr. Steffen that he had been raised on the ranch where the mine identified by Mr. Starr was located. He confirmed the site and stated positively that the mine located there was the lost "Blue Jacket Coal Mine." Of course, to Mr. Autsby, the Blue Jacket Mine had never been "lost." He had always known where it was. See Map 4 following this page for the location of the "lost" Blue Jacket Mine.

Among his many skills—soldier, prospector, lawyer, Justice of the Peace, homesteader, and land speculator—Joseph "Wolf" Allen was also a coal miner. "J. W. Allen is opening a coal mine in the [Glendive] area, and finds a ready market." [BT, 9 December 1881 cited in TLW, p. 4.] Frank Perry and his family arrived in Glendive in April of 1882, and by the fall of that year he had purchased the Blue Jacket from Judge Allen. [Various articles and advertisements, GT, 1883–1887.] Following the "killer winter" of 1886–1887, Perry moved on to the Bitter Root Valley south of Missoula and left Charlie Bowers in charge of the mine. [GI, 9 April 1887.] By 1888, Charlie had purchased the Blue Jacket. [GI, 13 October 1888.] In 1890, Bowers sold the Blue Jacket Coal Mine to Morris Cain. Cain became one of Glendive's first settlers when he opened his blacksmith shop in the town in 1880. Cain was an old Montana hand. He had been one of Major Reno's troopers who survived the battle at the Little Big Horn in 1876. In 1890, he sold his blacksmithing business and opened a saloon in town. His extra cash went into the Blue Jacket. Ten years later, in 1900, Morris Cain sold all of his interests in Glendive and moved to Meyers Falls, Washington (near Kettle Falls north of Spokane), where he started a large orchard. Cain died there two years later at the age of forty-five following an operation related to appendicitis. A 1903 article in an unidentified Glendive newspaper (probably the GI) stated: "W. J. Simms, the contractor who purchased the Blue Jacket coal mine from Morris Cain, is working the mine with a force of men and has two teams hauling. Orders will be promptly filled at $2.75 a ton delivered by telephoning No. 73." ["100 Years Ago," RR, 21 December 2003.]

Early irrigation projects: The Grant–Dunlap irrigation scheme near Tokna on Grant's Prairie was the first commercial irrigation scheme developed in the original Dawson County. George Grant was a buffalo hunter who came into Montana in 1873. [CE, 1045.] He had settled on the lower Yellowstone in 1878, originally locating about a mile south of John Burns on Burns Creek. In 1879 he moved

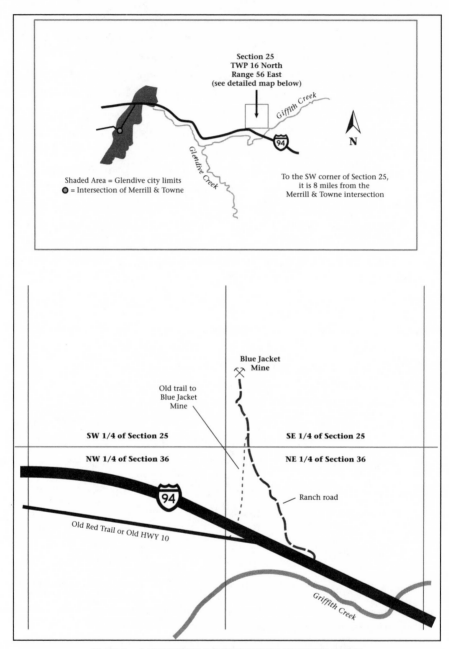

MAP 4—LOCATION OF THE BLUE JACKET MINE

to the flat adjoining what is now the settlement of Savage. The area was early known as "Grant's Prairie." George Grant was the son-in-law of Eben and Louisa P. Slawson. He was married to their daughter, Imogene, who, after marrying Grant in Minnesota in 1873, accompanied her parents to Dawson County in 1879.[In Courage Enough and contemporary newspaper accounts, Mrs. Grant's first name is seen spelled as "Emogene" or "Emigene." Her tombstone in the Cashmere, Washington, cemetery, however, reads: "Imogene Grant, May 17, 1853–July 18, 1898." Consequently, the spelling of "Imogene" has been used throughout this text.]

Emmet Dunlap had worked on the construction of the NPRR between Bismarck and Glendive. In 1881 Grant met Dunlap in Glendive and encouraged Emmet to move himself and his family to Grant's Prairie. Dunlap liked the idea and the location and took Grant up on the proposition. By 1883, the two men had completed a diversion dam on what became known as Dunlap Creek (on Grant's Prairie) and initially built a small canal from which they could collectively irrigate perhaps one-hundred acres between them. Shortly after completing their canal, Grant and Dunlap got into Dawson County's first "water fight" and wouldn't speak to each other for a number of years. Their wives, however, stayed relatively close and they served as the "water mediators" until Mrs. Dunlap's death in 1888. Following her death, the two men seem to have worked out the water rights deal and were good neighbors thereafter.

By 1889 Emmet Dunlap had enlarged his end of the small canal and was irrigating one-hundred-and-sixty acres. Grant, whose irrigated property in 1884 was reported to cover an eight-acre garden and a small orchard, was stated to have been "using water from the same ditch." [CE, pp. 716, 728–729, 731–734, 1042, & 1047.] Emmet Dunlap was still residing on his home place as late as 1897. In 1974 the Dunlap ranch was owned by Bob and Ida Seeve. [CE, p. 1044.]

The Grant family sold their place to Augustus Alfred Fredrickson, the Glendive-Ridgelawn mail carrier and stagecoach driver, late in 1896. On 1 January 1897 they departed the lower Yellowstone and moved to Old Mission (now Cashmere), Washington. This move put them back near Imogene's parents, Eben and Louisa Slawson, who had sold out along the Yellowstone and had gone to Old Mission in 1888. Imogene (Slawson) Grant died in Old Mission, Kittitas

County, Washington, on 18 July 1898 at the age of forty-five. [CE, pp. 716, 728–729, 731–734, 1042, & 1047.]

The second irrigation development in old Dawson County was the product of pure desperation. This was the Wolf Creek irrigation project started in 1884 on the Fort Peck Indian Reservation at Wolf Point. New Jersey-born James P. Jones, fifty-three, had arrived at Wolf Point in July of 1879 as the "farmer-in-charge." He had formerly been attached to the Poplar Agency as the post's butcher. There had been a drought during the 1883 growing season so the Indians had suffered a total crop failure. The winter supplies and annuities were late being delivered and the people in his charge were starving. Suddenly, the weather turned particularly harsh. Some have estimated that over three-hundred Native Americans died in the vicinity of Wolf Point during the winter of 1883–1884. The only newspaper in the area, the *Glendive Times,* hinted at the grim conditions but never laid out the full extent of the disaster. "Major Whipple, the paymaster at Fort Keogh, returned from Poplar Creek and Fort Buford. He says that the Indians have eaten all of their dogs and they are in a pitiful condition." [GT, 91 January 1884.] "We have received a letter from Wolf Point, Montana, in the Fort Peck Reservation that says the Indians there are starving." [GT, 9 February 1884. See HAST, pp. 126–146, for more details on the abominable conditions prevalent at the Fort Peck Reservation in the 1870s and 1880s.]

Desperate to adequately feed his famished charges (salvaging the floating beef and buffalo carcasses out of the Missouri River during spring break-up had already become an annual ritual), sub-agent Jones promoted his irrigation idea to "the powers that be" in charge of the Poplar Agency. His plan was approved and he started his undertaking in the spring of 1884. A diversion dam in Wolf Creek was built of rock hauled to the site by oxen pulling "stone boats" (small but heavily-built wood-runnered sleds). The oxen then pulled plows, following the anticipated path of the ditch. The Native American residents in the vicinity of Wolf Point, both men and women, then removed the plowed dirt with hand shovels. This process was repeated and repeated until the small canal was deep enough to carry the water where it was needed just west of the agency site at Wolf Point. While work continued on the ditch, the agency served lunch to the workers at noon. They were paid fifty cents per day with a coupon that could be used at the agency store. "This small project proved a great success and each year more acreage was added. Gardens and hay were raised in abundance." [RCTY, p. 35. FIV, Vol. 2, p. 663.]

The growth of wheat farming in Dawson County: It took the Germans from Russia and the Scandinavians to finally master cereal grain production in old Dawson County. An analysis of the area's population growth tells much of the tale of the increase in tillage farming as opposed to livestock ranching. The irrigation "boom" and the huge expansion in dryland farming had nearly simultaneous beginnings. In 1902, the National Reclamation Act was passed. Surveying for the sixty-five-mile Main Canal of the Lower Yellowstone Irrigation Project commenced in 1904. The canal was to run from a dam to be constructed some twenty miles downstream from Glendive (a site now called "Intake") to Fort Buford at the confluence of the Yellowstone and Missouri rivers (the canal ends at a site on the Missouri River now called "Nohly"). [GHMT, p. 39. MAG, p. 65 and p. 79.]

In conjunction with their livestock operations, a few of the early ranchers had started experimenting with dryland crops. They "would brag around town about their crops and after 1900 they began to make homestead claims, they and their sons and daughters." [GHMT, p. 39.] In 1904, a group of Germans from Russia settled in what became the Bloomfield area on the west side of the Yellowstone River. That proved to be only the tip of the immigration iceberg. The federal land surveys were late in coming to Dawson County and, without them, homesteads could not be deeded. Finally, in 1906, surveying on a large scale was undertaken. When Congress passed the Homestead Act of 1909 (which allowed 320-acre holdings and reduced the residency requirement to three years) the era of the eastern Montana homesteader began. With the passage of the Homestead Act of 1909, a group of three-thousand Polish citizens announced their intention to establish a colony near Glendive in 1910. While the Poles didn't show up, their announcement was a precursor of the "boom" that was soon to follow. [GHMT, p. 39 and p. 42.]

On 1 January 1910, the project was declared to be "96% complete. It eventually watered about 66,000 acres in Montana and North Dakota." [GHMT, p. 38.] The interest in dryland farming had been increasing over the past decade. Now, the dryland boom in conjunction with the opening of the massive Lower Yellowstone Irrigation Project, caused "the East" to become "Montana mad." [GHMT, p. 42.] In July of 1910, Joe Widmyer, the owner of the *Glendive Independent,* editorialized, saying the cattlemen, the horsemen, and the sheepmen "have moved to town and gone into the land business. [Instead of cattle, sheep and horses,] they [now] round up the land-seeker from the East and brand him as the owner of a small portion of their formerly vast ranges. They have abandoned the bronco for the automobile." [GI, 16 July 1910 cited in GHMT, p. 42.]

Excluding the "new" area of Valley County (created from Dawson in 1893), the population of the remnant Dawson County south of the Missouri River in 1900 was 2,443 people. Of that number, about 1,900 were residents of Glendive proper. Only about 543 people lived in the rest of the county. In 1910, the population of Dawson County was 13,231. [GHMT, p. 39.]

In 1912 alone, Dawson County (which then excluded all of the country north of the Missouri River) had over two-hundred-thousand acres go under the plow for the first time. In September of 1913, the U.S. government opened up five-hundred-thousand acres of the Fort Peck Reservation for white settlement. Forty-thousand people registered for seven-thousand claims. In 1913, the Dawson County Clerk of the Court reported that two-hundred-and-twenty-eight foreign-born citizens, more than half bearing Scandinavian surnames, were naturalized in that year alone. [GHMT, p. 39 and p. 42.] That was forty more than the number of men, women, and children reported for the entire county on the 1880 census. Known to the earlier settlers as "honyockers," these were the people, many of them new immigrants to America, who fleshed out the actual "settlement" of Dawson County.

After 1913, Dawson County was again divided into several smaller progeny counties (or parts thereof): Richland County and the northern half of Wibaux County in 1914 (the southern half of Wibaux County was taken from Custer County); the northern part of Prairie County in 1915 (like Wibaux County, the southern half of Prairie County was taken from Custer County); and Garfield and McCone counties in 1919. The remnant Dawson County boundaries have not changed since 1919. [See GHMT, p. 29, for McCone County; for all others including McCone, see GHMT, p. 34. Also see MGFC, pp. 203–205.] "By 1920 the same area [meaning that part of old Dawson County south of the Missouri River], now chopped into six counties, had a total [census] of 25,000. The farming of the open range and the plowing up of the benchlands caused the increase." [GHMT, p. 39.]

By 1881, that small corner of Dawson County lying west of the Musselshell River and south of the Missouri River had already been transferred to Meagher County. Recall that Valley County, all of that area of old Dawson County north of the Missouri River, had "spun off" in 1893. During the dryland boom era, Valley County itself produced three more progeny counties: Sheridan in 1913, the eastern half of Phillips in 1915, and Roosevelt County in 1919. Thus, it came to be that the original Dawson County that Stephen Norton Van Blaricom and the other early settlers knew in 1882 had been diced up into ten counties or parts thereof by 1919. An eleventh county, Daniels, was formed in 1920 from parts of Sheridan and Valley counties. [MGFC, p. 205.] See Map 5 on the following page for the progeny counties derived from the original Dawson County. (That part of old Dawson County that transferred to Meagher County prior to 1881 became part of Petroleum County when it was organized in 1924. Thus, the original Dawson County, as formed and described in 1869, is now scattered among twelve counties.)

Dispatching the wolves: The eradication of the wolf from the northern prairies occurred in two phases. "The pelts of these animals were not considered of much value until 1868, and not until 1870 did the trappers make a business of killing them." [CY, p. 89.] From the winter of 1870 through the winter of 1875 (or until the Great Sioux War) the professional wolfers spent their winters poisoning wolves. They would then return and skin them with the first spring thaw. E. S. Topping told of one group of six wolfers who, by themselves, accounted for "seven or eight-thousand" wolves during the winter of 1871–1872. [CY, p. 90.] After the Great Sioux War, the commercial buffalo hunters invaded northeastern Montana. When the bison were eradicated from the northern plains, the wolves that were left lost one of their primary food sources. As white settlement increased, pressure was also put on the elk, deer, and antelope

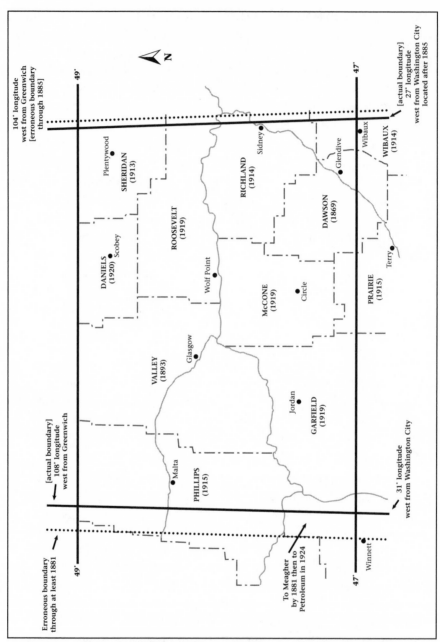

**MAP 5—THE ELEVEN PROGENY COUNTIES AND THE ONE REMNANT
COUNTY OF THE ORIGINAL DAWSON COUNTY OF 1869**

[NOT TO SCALE]

populations. The wolves naturally turned toward the thousands of cattle, calves, and sheep that were pouring into the country. Young horses didn't escape their attention either. Many of the livestock men didn't think that hunting alone was enough to rid them of the perceived scourge. Practically every rancher had his own supply of strychnine with which he would load the carcasses of dead cattle, sheep, deer, elk, and antelope. The Indians absolutely hated the strychnine because if they were out hunting, their own dogs would consume it if they found a stray carcass. Immediately after Dawson County was organized a bounty was placed on wolves. "The bounty on wolves should be raised." [GT, 12 January 1884.] "The wolf bounty should be increased." [GT, 8 February 1884.] "Like us, northern Wyoming is suffering from coyotes and wolves. We need a high bounty." [GT, 11 October 1884.] Various ranchers imported packs of wolfhounds to pursue and destroy the wolves. Even ten years later, Pierre Wibaux and others perceived the wolf issue to be unsatisfactory. "Pierre Wibaux now has two wolfing outfits. He is personally paying $3 per wolf. [That sum] plus the $3 bounty [paid by the county]…it pays." [GI, 15 June 1895.]

"Two bits silver": "Two bits silver" was used to describe twenty-five cents or a "quarter" of a silver dollar. This expression came into North American usage prior to the American Revolution when a common unit of international currency was the Spanish peso. The coin was too valuable to be used in everyday trade, so it would be cut into smaller units of eighths. An eighth of a Spanish peso was called a "bit." Thus, each piece of a Spanish peso cut into four parts was "two bits." The American usage then evolved to where any monetary unit worth one-fourth or a "quarter" of the coin of the realm (in this case, the peso; later the silver dollar) was called "two bits" or "two bits silver." [TID, p. 222.] The idiom has remained in use in America to the extent that a twenty-five-cent piece (one-quarter of a dollar) is still called "two bits," a fifty-cent piece is "four bits," and the sum of seventy-five cents is "six bits."

As the railroad was being built, the sutlers had to laboriously haul all the goods from Bismarck to the railhead and to the military posts. Although there were intermittent runs by steamboats to the forts Buford, Keogh, and Custer, river freight was still expensive. Consequently, beer that sold for a nickel in Bismarck sold for a quarter to the captive market of "swaddies" (soldiers) and buff hunters at the forts and to the isolated railway construction crews. When the towns of Dickinson, Miles City, Glendive, and Forsyth were started, it was these same sutlers and purveyors who set up shop and their pricing habits came right along with them. The minimum charge of a "quarter" for an item was so commonplace that the merchants didn't even carry smaller coins to use as change. The *Yellowstone Journal* in Miles City noted that the coming of the railroad put "the community at once in touch with the more concise and narrower [and less expensive] life in 'The States.'" It was a cheap and knowledgeable crowd of cowboys and settlers that followed the rails into town and they took on the saloons first. They were "stubbornly insistent on the acceptance of a nickel as adequate recompense for a glass of beer." The saloonkeepers (for obvious reasons) were strict adherents to the "two-bit theory." This hotly contested debate finally resulted in a compromise that established "two for a quarter" as the going rate. Thus it was the coming of the railroad that robbed the "high cost of freight" argument of "its honored plausibility [and, over a period of time] the 'nickel' displaced the 'quarter' as the smallest coin in use, and prices shrunk accordingly." [HYV, p. 345.]

CHAPTER TEN

Disaster Strikes:
September of 1882

I HAVE KEPT A FEW NEWSPAPER CLIPPINGS pertinent to our family or about people with whom our family was close. It is probably appropriate to share a few of them now. It may be of some interest to see the writing style then in vogue and to note in the first article the advertising of Mickey Farrell, a saloonkeeper who was a friend of the family. My father, my younger brother, Fred, and I all worked at Mickey's place at one time or the other. Fred and I would cut and carry firewood, swamp the place out in the mornings and do dishes. Father would do the same, plus he cleaned Mickey's flue and would work as a kitchen helper or pour a few "suds" once in a great while. Mickey was a big, gregarious Irishman who had arrived in Glendive following a stay in Miles City where he worked on the construction of Fort Keogh. He and Jim Butler built the first building in Glendive after the town was platted. They called the place "Jim's Opera House."[127]

M. FARRELL
Dealer in Fine Wines
Liquors & Cigars
Milwaukee Beer
RESTAURANT
A First Class Restaurant
and the best
LODGING HOUSE
in Glendive
Call and be Convinced [GT, 13 July 1882.]

---

[127] Jim's Opera House is pictured in the oldest known photograph of Glendive. Taken in 1881, the photo is shown in OTOL, p. 11. Fred Van Blaricom, one of Norton's younger brothers, was given a great deal of assistance from Mickey Farrell and his black housekeeper. See that story in THWT. Unless otherwise noted, the source for Chapter 10 is the SNVB manuscript, pp. 18–19.

I have always kept the second article because it reminds me of conditions in a frontier town that people today never consider. Life in those early days wasn't always a bowl of cherries. There were sights, sounds, and smells that differed substantially from what one encounters today.

> The health committee ought to look after the stench that is every evening wafted on the coursing zephyrs from down Valentine Street and from a certain hennery and pig pen between Glostner's old place and the Merrill buildings.[128] [GT, 17 August 1882.]

The third item is the obituary for my young cousin, Harry Johnson.[129] Little Harry was the son of Frank L. Johnson and Carrie Tuttle Johnson. Uncle Frank was my mother's brother and Aunt Carrie was the sister of Hank Tuttle, the third sheriff of Dawson County who served from January of 1885 through New Year's of 1889.[130]

> Mr. Frank Johnson's little two year old boy was buried last Saturday in the new cemetery. He has suffered for six long weeks, with mountain fever,[131] slowly wasting away and for the past three or four weeks has been kept alive by artificial means. [GT, 17 August 1882.]

The final article presents the event in my life that I have dreaded to attempt to describe. I would have to be a much better joiner of words than I am in order to build or paint a picture from which you might get some idea of what happened to our family.

---

[128] Despite the romance associated with the west, life in frontier towns did come with some drawbacks. Many residents maintained a chicken coop, a pig sty, a dairy cow or two, and their saddle and buggy horses. In many cases, however, the chickens were maintained without the coop and the pigs without the sty. See *"Chickens, pigs, and cows"* in Author's Notes following this chapter.

[129] See *"The death of young Harry Johnson"* in Author's Notes following this chapter.

[130] Saloon-owner Henry Dion was the first sheriff of Dawson County (1882–1882). He was appointed by Governor Potts when Dawson County was organized. Saloon-owner James Taylor was the first elected sheriff (1883–1884). Henry Tuttle, a former tracklayer and laborer for the Northern Pacific, was the third sheriff and served four years from January of 1885 through 1888. [OTOL, p. 2.] Frank Johnson, Hank's brother-in-law, served as one his deputies from time to time. Both Hank Tuttle and Frank Johnson had been deputy sheriffs under Sheriff Jim Taylor. See Author's Notes following this chapter for a listing of *"The early sheriffs of Dawson County."*

[131] See *"Mountain fever, typhus, or typhoid fever?"* in Author's Notes following this chapter.

There were then nine of us children, of which I was the oldest
and but thirteen years of age. Our sweet mother, who loved us all
dearly, contracted mountain fever. Lying there in that one-room
shanty and with no semblance of the care we can give the sick
today, she departed this life and went to her long rest.

> On Monday morning the wife of Levi Van Blaricon [sic]
> died of typhoid fever. This is a sad case as she leaves a
> family of 9 or 10 children.[132] [GT, 28 September 1882.]

From what has already been told of conditions in this
new country, you will understand that there were no social
organizations of any kind to take care of a situation such as this.
There was no Red Cross, no Salvation Army, and no children's
home. There were no welfare set-ups, and I doubt if there were
fifteen-hundred people in all of Dawson County to have funded
something like that even if it had been there.[133]

It started out with us two older boys, myself and David, living
with our father and doing odd jobs around town and trying to
fit some school in once in a while. By the spring of '83, however,
we were off on our own, and, being the ripe old ages of fourteen
and thirteen, we were able to find and keep jobs most of the
time. By October of 1882, however, the rest of the children were
scattered to wherever the winds of opportunity sent them to be
raised. Our maternal grandmother and her husband, Grandma
and Grandpa Scribner, took the two-month-old baby, Sarah
Effie, and four-year-old Perry. Mother's sister, Aunt Mary Jane,
and her husband, Frank Perry, took the next youngest, Dora May
(she was only two years old). My sister Mary, who was ten years
old when our mother died, eventually went down to Eben and
Louisa Slawson's stagecoach stop and road ranch and lived there

---

[132] Sarah Susan (Johnson) Van Blaricom was born 5 December 1849 in Amherst, Ohio, and
died 25 September 1882 in Glendive, Montana Territory, at the age of thirty-two. She
left nine children, five boys and four girls, who ranged in age from two months to
thirteen years. Death on the frontier was not generally viewed as any sort of remarkable
or newsworthy event. The passing of Sarah Susan was reported in the *Glendive Times* in
a kind of *pot pourri* column, a combination of news snippets, gossip, household hints,
and one-line items regarding the goods or personalities of the merchants who routinely
purchased advertising space in the newspaper. This was a typical "obituary" for the
newspaper of a small frontier town. Very rarely would the death of even a local celebrity
gather more than a line or two.

[133] See *"Charitable care"* in Author's Notes following this chapter.

with them. She helped with dishes and housekeeping chores and tended to the travelers who frequently stayed there. Jim, Fred, and Alice were initially sent down to my Aunt Marthie Wyant's place near Forsyth, some hundred-and-twenty-five miles distant, on west up the Yellowstone from Miles City. My aunt then sent Alice and Fred to live with a daughter of hers who had recently been married at the age of fifteen. That whole Forsyth thing didn't work out, so all three were returned to Glendive that winter. In the spring of 1883, Jim (who was then nine, about to turn ten) and David (thirteen) took off together and ended up in the Deadwood and Rapid City country, where they worked trimming railroad ties, swamping saloons, cleaning stables, loading freight, or whatever job they could find. Within a year or so, Jim ended up in Yellowstone National Park with a tourist company and spent most of the rest of his working life there. Alice, who turned six years old up in Forsyth, went to Uncle Frank Johnson's and stayed with them until the family moved to Victor in 1887. She then went to live with Grandma Scribner, and she worked in Grandma and Grandpa Scribner's restaurant at the Curlew mine until she married Lee Hyatt in 1892.

After fleeing Forsyth in the winter of 1882–1883, Freddie became the family's little nomad. Sometimes he stayed with our father and went to school in Glendive. Most often, he didn't. Just seven years old when our mother died, Fred would stay short periods with the Slawsons or the Grants or the Loverings down on the lower Yellowstone. He lived with John and Lottie La Combe up in the Redwater Divide country for quite a while. He stayed about a year with Alf White and his wife over in Dickinson. I remember he spent the killer winter of 1886–1887 with the Harpsters out on Belle Prairie. Indeed, with the singular exception involving Fred and Alice in Forsyth, the people caring for my siblings were all very kind. But all of them, if not poor, were in very modest circumstances.[134]

And now there is a question in your mind about the father of this family who let his children be scattered to the wind and, in many cases (especially myself, David, Mary, Jim, Fred, and, early

---

[134] AVBH notes. HVBG, pp. 178–192. See THWT for the biography and adventures of "Freddie" Van Blaricom.

on, Alice) left to their own devices among people who were not immediate family. I think it is better to all concerned that we clear this up as I see it. If you differ with me then clear it up to suit yourself. With mother there to guide and direct him I would say that our father was about thirty percent efficient as a provider. Without her, he was of little more use than a tomcat. It would, of course, be very unfair of me to leave the matter here, with this accusation, without some justification. Psychologists have rated the human intellect in points from zero to two-hundred, with an average intellect at one-hundred-and-thirty-five. On that basis I would rate my father at about seventy-five. Society, like the psychologists, is in the habit of judging everyone by the same standards, so today's intelligence quotients or IQs are a convenient measure. That standard, however, disregards the individual's capacity to perform, his ambition, and the level of educational opportunity. It also gives no accounting for our prenatal composition that so affects the individual's personality. One might be born with an ambition that burns him out in middle life, another has no ambition anywhere in his veins. One is born a great natural musician, another with some all-consuming passion. And then there are others who couldn't hatch an egg if they sat on it for three months. There are some things for which we are not responsible and about which we can do nothing.

That great Genius, the Creator of all things, had purpose in creating no two of us exactly alike. Humanity has not advanced to the point where we can understand that there is a harmony in His plan. My father as a family man became an instant and terrible flop with the death of my mother, and the world will judge him harshly. I do not, for I feel that I probably could have done no better had I nothing more than he had to make do with. His failure as a father and a provider was just a fact, not the product of deliberate intent. Peace be to his ashes.

The life and experiences of my mother, however, and those of other pioneer mothers were heroic. They were necessarily imbued with the spirit of the West, the spirit of the pioneer. The price these women had to pay never deterred them from making the attempt. They lived and died truthfully, fighting their own battles for survival and battling for their children's survival. Medical care for these women and children was the exception, not the rule, and there was no one to whom they might resort if they missed a meal.[135]

Not until recently has there been any worthy monument to that army of heroic pioneer mothers, who made it possible for those of us who came after to enjoy the great natural wealth that lay hidden in our vast country. E. W. Miland has caused to be erected in Ponca City, Oklahoma, a statue dedicated to "The Pioneer Mother." It is the figure of a woman dressed in plain homespun, shod in rough shoes, a sunbonnet shading the eyes that look out unafraid on future and distant places. In one hand a book, and she leads with her other her son, a lad of perhaps six years. This statue, by the sculptor Bryant Baker, fairly breathes that indomitable spirit which knows no defeat, and so typifies the spirit of my mother as I knew her. It is my wish to some day go and stand in the presence of that statue and remember her. To this day I rue my mother's death and that we could do naught but put her to rest in a dusty grave on that desolate and lonely hill overlooking Glendive. She has long since been gathered to her ancestors, and may God rest her deserving soul.[136]

---

[135] Unidentified and undated news article of a speech delivered by SNVB. Probably from the SN, ca. 1926.

[136] Newspaper article written by SNVB, probably the SN, ca. 1926.

CHAPTER 10–AUTHOR'S NOTES

The death of young Harry Johnson: As was then common practice, the next male child born into Frank and Carrie (Tuttle) Johnson's family after Harry's death in 1882 was also named Harry Johnson. The second Harry was aboard the passenger ship *Lusitania* when it was torpedoed by a German U-boat and went down off the coast of Ireland on 7 May 1915. One of the greatest of the sea's disasters, 1,198 people perished when the liner exploded and sank. Despite German warnings to U.S. citizens not to travel on British ships, 128 Americans were among the dead. Harry Johnson, however, was one of the few survivors. He later returned safely to the United States, married and lived out his life in Okanogan County, Washington. [WFRF, p. 46. SM, p. 48.]

The early sheriffs of Dawson County, from its organization in September 1882, through 1902 were:

> (Dates displayed are dates of appointment or election. Through the early years of the county, territory and state, commencement and termination dates of service varied widely compared to the date of election or appointment. In general, however, elected officials took office sometime the first week or two in January of the year following the year in which the election took place. There were two notable exceptions to this rule: The state-mandated election of October 1889 and the appointment of Joseph C. Hurst in 1898 immediately followed by the appointment of A. E. Aiken about a week later. [See below for details. For election data, see HML, pp. 377–381. For years served, see OTOL p. 2.]

Henry Dion	Appointed during organization. Served 27 September 1882 to January 1883 (i)
James Taylor	Elected 7 November 1882 (served to January of 1885) (ii)
Henry C. Tuttle	Elected 4 November 1884 (term was 1885 through 1886)
	Elected 2 November 1886 (1887 through 1888)

Joel Gleason	Elected 6 November 1888–1 October 1889 (iii)
	Elected 1 October 1889
	Elected 4 November 1890
	Elected 8 November 1892
Dominic R. Cavanaugh	Elected 6 November 1894
	Elected 8 November 1896
	Elected 8 November 1898 (iv)
Joseph C. Hurst	Appointed 30 December 1898 through about 7 January 1899 (iv)
A. E. Aiken	Appointed about 7 January 1899 (term was 1899 through 1900) (iv)
John Kennedy	Elected: 4 November 1900

(i) Henry Dion was appointed by the Governor of the Territory of Montana when Dawson County was organized.

(ii) Some of the men who were deputies to Sheriff Jim Taylor during his two-year tenure were John ("Jack") Conley, Henry C. ("Hank") Tuttle, William Tuttle, Frank L. Johnson, Morris Cain, and Gilbert ("Slim") Burdick.

(iii) After admission to the Union and the organization of the state of Montana in 1889, all of the individuals who had been public office holders in the territory had to stand for re-election. A special statewide election was held on 1 October 1889. [HML, p. 379.]

(iv) On the night of Christmas Eve, 24 December 1898, Dominic Cavanaugh was murdered, his skull fractured by a person or persons unknown. On 30 December 1898, his Republican opponent in the November election, Joseph C. Hurst, was appointed by the county commissioners to fill the seat. The Democrats of the county raised a tremendous fuss, maintaining their candidate, a Democrat, had won the election and the appointee should be of their party. On or about 7 January 1899, the Hurst appointment was rescinded and Alfred E. Aiken, a Democrat, was appointed to serve out the term. On 13 January 1899, Joe Hurst was indicted for the murder of Dominic Cavanaugh. Hurst was found guilty of the crime and, avowing his innocence to the end, he was hanged on the gallows at the Glendive jail on 30 March 1900. [FVBM, pp. 7–8. BG, 25 December 1898, 30 December 1898, 13 January 1899, 24 January 1899, 3 March 1899, 24 March 1899, 30 March 1899, and 30 March 1900. For a summary see BG, 21 April 1935. For a more complete recounting of the Cavanaugh-Hurst episode see THWT and see HABS, pp. 262–268.]

Mountain fever, typhus, or typhoid fever: Who died from what? "Mountain fever: 1: Any of various febrile diseases occurring in mountainous regions, as a) Colorado Tick Fever; b) Rocky Mountain Spotted Fever. 2: Infectious Anemia." [See mountain fever, TID, p. 1477.] Body lice or fleas served to transmit typhus while ticks generally acted as the transmitter of the "mountain fever" illnesses. Typhoid fever, however, "is transmitted by food or water that has been contaminated with human feces or urine. Polluted water is the most common source of the infection." [TM, p. 15.]

Usually, the symptoms of typhus were high fever, stupor alternating with delirium, intense headache, and a dark red rash. Typhoid fever was characterized by fever, severe inflammation of the intestines and diarrhea, headache, prostration, and the eruption of rose spots. Typhus and typhoid fever were known well enough to warrant their own descriptives since the "dark red rash" and the "rose spots" gave them away. [See typhoid / typhoid fever and typhus, TID, p. 2476.] Before the development of antibiotics during and following World War II, there was no "cure" for typhoid. The best a doctor could do was prescribe bed rest, try to control the patient's temperature and discomfort, and then hope for the best. About ten percent of the people who contracted typhoid fever died from it. [TM, pp. 27–29.]

Especially in the West, laymen of the day (Stephen Norton Van Blaricom among them) commonly referred to any disease causing a high fever as "mountain fever." Notice how he later described his mother as stricken with "mountain fever," yet the newspaper was more specific in its use of "typhoid fever." One suspects Harry Johnson really died of typhoid fever, the result of drinking contaminated water from the Yellowstone River. If a family member relayed the news to the paper, the death was frequently ascribed to "mountain fever." If the newspaper learned of the death from the local doctor, he was more specific and it was more accurately described as "typhoid fever." If one quickly scans the early local newspapers of the Yellowstone River towns, deaths attributed to typhoid fever or mountain fever were remarkably frequent well into the twentieth century. Typhoid fever was the great hidden killer of the Yellowstone.

Even though it had been common scientific knowledge for several decades that clean water alleviated the scourge of typhoid fever, Glendive was a real latecomer to the idea of water sanitation. From the beginning of the town in 1880, water was simply carted from the river in barrels and delivered to businesses and homes. That went on until 1907, when the town's first waterline construction project was completed. [GTHG, p. 14.] Despite the fact that the 1907 construction included a 250,000-gallon settling pond to help with the silt problem, no water filtration or treatment facilities were added. It was in 1915 that Dr. Donohue of the Montana State Board of Health reported he had found typhoid germs in Glendive's tap water. Marie MacDonald wrote that the newspaper "pooh-poohed the danger, saying that there had only been eight cases of typhoid" and "only two attributable deaths" that year. The town was evenly split on the issue and the fight was bitterly fought. Finally, with a narrow vote of sixty-three "for" and sixty-one "against," a bond was passed to pay for a water filtration and purification system. [GHMT, p. 50.] The water treatment plant was finally completed in 1917. [GTHG, photo caption, p. 61.] One can only speculate about the substantial number of victims who succumbed to typhoid fever during the thirty-seven years between the founding of Glendive and the installation of the water treatment facility.

Even after the development and continuing improvements of antibiotics, typhoid continues to be a major menace, especially in less developed countries. Seventeen-million cases were reported worldwide in 1997, with about 600,000 resultant deaths. [TM, p. 29.]

Chickens, pigs, and cows. All of these creatures living together inside the "city limits" of frontier towns could often make for a "gamey" atmosphere. There were repeated complaints about "smelly henneries" and "uncleaned pigstyes" polluting the air in Glendive.

Another common complaint concerned the owners of pigs who allowed their creatures to roam loose in the streets, plundering the garbage behind the restaurants, hotels, and saloons. Occasionally, the sheriff would act: "L. J. Kee was fined $23.40 for leaving his hogs to run around town." [GI, 21 May 1887.] The sheriff, however, would never let the situation get totally out of hand. Whenever any of the huge "boar hogs" (they could weigh several hundred pounds) would get aggressive and chase the ladies of Glendive off the boardwalk on Merrill Avenue, as they did on at least two occasions, somebody would go to jail. No man-or-woman-chasing boar hogs allowed!

Cows were less offensive. People were more or less used to them. Except for old "Daisy," an extraordinarily smart Glendive cow who, during her wanderings around town, learned how to open people's gates with her nose so she could enter their residential compounds and lay havoc to their flowers and their vegetable gardens. Then there was the time William Peoples' cow died. Bill took the death in stride but the *Glendive Independent* reported: "Bill thinks the cow was poisoned." He just doesn't understand it because "the cow never signed any of those petitions knowingly" and "she seemed to be on good terms with everybody." [GI, 7 April 1900.]

Charitable care: Quite aside from Stephen Norton Van Blaricom's perception that there were no "welfare set-ups" such as the Red Cross or Salvation Army in 1882, Dawson County did have, by 1883, a "home for the poor." Zachariah and Mariah Scribner, Norton's grandparents, operated it. They cared for individuals adjudged incompetent or who were so physically disabled or elderly to be incapable of earning a living or otherwise caring for themselves. The "home for the poor" cost the county about one-hundred dollars a month. With one exception, the county's early checks or drafts were invariably made out to "Mrs. Scribner." Later checks were written to "Zachariah Scribner." [GT, County Commissioner's Notes, 1882–1886.]

There was also an early county-funded "pest house" in Glendive where people suffering from communicable and dangerous diseases could be isolated if they were not quarantined in their own homes. As was then common throughout North America, Europe, and much of the rest of the world, Dawson County was quick to require the home quarantine of the victims of other serious diseases of the day, among them mumps, measles, head lice, and fleas. Residents afflicted with these or other types of communicable illnesses could (and usually would) be consigned to the "pest house." [See County Commissioner's Notes, GT and GI, 1882–1887. "George Willis is the first case of smallpox [in Glendive this year]. He was put in the pest house on Barry Island." GI, 2 February 1901.]

It is true that few areas of the frontier had any semblance of an organized "safety net" for those individuals or families who fell on hard times. There were no food banks nor clothing banks per se nor were there other types of organized charitable organizations such as the Red Cross or the Salvation Army in the early days of a frontier town. One can find, however, fairly frequent articles in the newspapers telling of dances or other types of socials being sponsored by immediate neighbors for the benefit of the elderly and the needy. As local churches organized, they, too, provided varying degrees of social and economic services. The Catholic priest, Father Eli Washington John Lindesmith, arrived in the Yellowstone country in 1880. Working out of Fort Keogh, he started serving the Glendive area in 1881. [TLW, pp. 203–204. OTOL, p. 19.] "Brother Van [W. W. Van Orsdel] made a visit to your locality in June, 1882, and got the [seven] men together who formed [in September of 1882] the society [of the Methodist Episcopal church]." [1932 letter from the Rev. G. C. Stull cited in OTOL, p. 18.] The Reverend G. C. Stull was the group's first preacher. Also formed in 1882 was the Congregationalist church society. They built the first church in Glendive that opened for worship in June of 1883 with services delivered by the Reverend O. M. McDuff. The Methodist Episcopal church was built in 1884. "The Catholics of Glendive purchased a Protestant meeting house [the Congregationalist building] on April 6, 1886." After minor remodeling, according to Grace Gilmore, "Holy Mass was celebrated for the first time on May 10, 1886 by Rev. Father Pauwlyn." [IV, 21 November 1935.] Others remembered it differently: "The first Mass was said in the church by Bishop John B. Brondel the day after the purchase" (or 7 April 1886). [OTOL, p. 19.]

CHAPTER ELEVEN

Glendive and the Lower Yellowstone: 1883

BETWEEN THE EFFORTS OF MY FATHER AND ME, the shanty where the family had been living was kept open for the rest of the fall of 1882 and through the winter. That way, any of the children who might be dispossessed of their newly found homes would have some place to come. I did such odd jobs as I could find, and we got through the winter.[137]

The following spring our folks, with the exception of Grandma and Grandpa Scribner and Frank Perry, all abandoned their land claims. They spread out to make their livings as best they could. Glendive was developing quite rapidly on a hunting and cattle-raising basis, and the railroad continued to expand its facilities there so they were able to make fair livings. At one time or another, every one of the men worked for the Northern Pacific. Grandpa Scribner kept a few cattle running the **ZS** brand and worked on county bid jobs obtained by my uncle, Jay Orr Woods.[138]

Henry Tuttle, my Aunt Carrie Johnson's brother, went to work as a deputy sheriff and later became the second elected sheriff of Dawson County.[139] Grandma Scribner opened her house to care

---

[137] Unless otherwise noted, the source for Chapter 11 is the SNVB manuscript, pp. 20–22 and p. 31.

[138] Also see WFRF and FVBM. The **ZS** brand in Dawson County is recorded to Zachariah Scribner in MSD, p. 163.

[139] Henry ("Hank") Tuttle later became one of America's first U.S. Forest Rangers. He and another ranger built the first ranger station in the United States at Alta, Montana, near the Bitter Root Valley in 1899. Born in Glendive on 11 November 1883 (while the family resided in the sheriff's apartment above the Dawson County Jail), Wilbur Tuttle (Hank and Dineen Tuttle's son) became a well-known writer. While living in Hollywood during the 1930s and 1940s, Wilbur authored several motion picture screenplays. For the biographies of Henry and Dineen Tuttle and their son, Wilbur Tuttle, see *"Hank Tuttle, sheriff of Dawson County"* in Author's Notes following this chapter.

for the poor, and the county gave her a substantial check for her services every month. Uncle Frank Perry continued to operate his Blue Jacket Mine,[140] and sold coal all over town. He also ran a few cattle with Grandpa Scribner. Uncle Frank Johnson ran some cows, did construction work, and, along with Hank Tuttle, worked part-time as a deputy sheriff.

Uncle Jay Orr Woods stayed on working as a carpenter for the railroad and opened a furniture store run by my aunt. He also did a fair amount of bid construction work on bridges and roads for the county. In addition to that, my aunt started polishing buffalo horns and sold hundreds of them to locals and travelers, and she sent them back East as curiosities as well. Sometimes they would be incorporated into hall trees as coat hooks, or several horns would be put together to act as the arms and legs on stuffed chairs. They also did taxidermy, mounting buffalo heads and other game as well.[141]

My Uncle Nort Johnson was one of those people you occasionally meet who is a natural-born musician. Nort worked at all kinds of jobs but he was always a centerpiece at the many dances and parties. He was an accomplished fiddler, a piano player and a singer and dance-caller. He could also play the harmonica and the Jew's harp[142] and he could do a pretty fair job on the banjo. Despite all of Uncle Nort's social exposure, he never married.[143]

It was in late winter 1882–1883, around March, that my father got relocated into a small cottage built of sawed lumber. It was less

---

[140] A little more than a year after the family left Glendive, the Blue Jacket Mine was described in an article in the *Glendive Independent:* "Yesterday we paid a visit to the Blue Jacket coal mine, and under the guidance of two miners made a complete tour of the various rooms being worked in the mine. There is enough coal in sight almost to supply Glendive for the next twenty years." [GI, 8 October 1888.]

[141] "J. O. Woods & Co., dealers in mounted heads, polished buffalo horns. Glendive, Montana Territory." [GT, 12 October 1882.] "Woods & McMillan, furniture. Merrill Avenue, Glendive, Montana Territory." [GT, 13 December 1884, cited in TLW, p. 375.] The partner in the furniture venture was Alan J. McMillan, the Canadian-born hotelier who was elected Dawson County treasurer in November of 1882. The GT on 17 August 1882 announced that Ray and A. J. McMillan "are the new managers of the Glendive Hotel." [TLW, pp. 231 and 232.]

[142] A "Jew's harp" was "a small lyre-shaped instrument placed between the teeth that gives a variety of tones from a metal tongue when struck by the finger. Perhaps so-called from their being purveyed by Jewish peddlers." [TID, p. 1,215.] Infrequently seen today, the instrument is now referred to as a "mouth harp" or a "jaw harp." [HNH.]

[143] HVBG, pp. 178–181. Also see WFRF.

than a year old, and it had a shingle roof, wooden floor, and some windows. It was a vast improvement over the accommodation we had previously occupied. It was small, though, so he continued to pitch the tent to use for storage.[144]

Father continued to hunt for Fort Buford and the Glendive meat shop,[145] but the buffalo were fast playing out. By the summer of '83 it was apparent that commercial buff hunting was a thing of the past. He bagged elk, deer, antelope, and birds, but not in sufficient quantity to make a living. He soon developed a business of cleaning flues and chimneys and did part-time work at the railroad roundhouse. He also did road work, and I remember one time he successfully bid on installing the septic system for the new county courthouse. It took him more than two weeks and he dug the whole thing by hand. Father once ran for county road superintendent but lost by a handful of votes. He was elected as Quartermaster of the Glendive branch of the Grand Army of the Republic,[146] but that position paid nothing. Father was an occasional gravedigger charged with burying people for the county. This didn't happen often because most people, if there was family, buried their own. Father's tasks in this regard were usually related to prisoners from the jail or the occasional drowning victim who floated down the Yellowstone. He also had infrequent work nursing wounded prisoners, and more frequent work transporting prisoners to other jurisdictions, primarily Miles City. Basically, father took whatever work he could get when he needed it.[147]

In the spring of 1883, just after I turned fourteen, I got a chance to go on a ranch on the east side of the Yellowstone for my keep and about ten dollars a month. This ranch, the **101**, was on the east side of the Yellowstone River some forty miles or so below Glendive. Their range extended from the Cottonwood

---

[144] AVBH.

[145] The history of "the Glendive meat shop" demonstrates the problem of determining "the first" of this and "the first" of that when attempting to reconstruct the settlement and development of frontier towns. Descendants of early settlers who continue to reside in the area frequently lay claim to the "fact" that their ancestor or some other distant relative did or built "the first" of this or that. It is only infrequently that research bears out these claims. See *"Who's on first?"* in Author's Notes following this chapter.

[146] See Author's Notes following this chapter for a brief discussion of *"The Grand Army of the Republic"* in Glendive and Montana.

[147] HVBG, pp. 178–192. Also see references to Levi Van Blaricom in FVBM.

Creek drainage on down to what is now known as Bennie Peer Creek. It then extended east from the Yellowstone over into the One-O-One Creek country in Dakota Territory. In any case, from the line shack where I was located it was seven miles up the river to our nearest neighbor and forty miles down to Fort Buford, the nearest settlement below us.[148]

The Sioux and Assiniboine were north of the Missouri River at Fort Peck. The Gros Ventre Indian Reservation[149] was below us near Fort Buford and the Crow Reservation was up the river some one-hundred-and-fifty miles, near the site where the Custer massacre had taken place some seven years before. The Fort Berthold Reservation was only about seventy miles to our east and the big Standing Rock Reservation was just south of Bismarck. The Indians belonging to all of these reservations used to visit and trade back and forth, and they invariably used our side of the river as their route. Old Chief Sitting Bull had surrendered at Fort Buford in 1881, only the year before our arrival. This was several years before the Battle of Wounded Knee. Prior to that event it was never safe to meet a band of Indians, especially Sioux, where they could "do" you and get away with it.[150]

The plains tribes, especially the Sioux, had not yet given up the idea that some day they would drive the whites out of that country and reclaim it. The Ghost Dance movement came into being about 1888 with the ideas of an Indian rebirth and the permanent expulsion of the white man. Rebirth meant literally

---

[148] This was the Griffin and Ward Cattle Company owned by brothers M. A. and Arnold Griffin and Henry Ward. Hoopes reported that Griffin and Ward brought in 3,000 head "in the early 1880s." The ranch was "some 25 miles to the northeast of Glendive. R. H. (Henry) Ward is the foreman." [TLW, pp. 144–145.] See MSD, p. 154, for the recorded **101** brand of "Griffin Bros. & Wood [sic]." See Author's Notes following Chapter 12 for a brief history of the **101** ranch.

[149] Stephen Norton Van Blaricom was simply in error on this point. There was neither a "Gros Ventre Indian Reservation" nor any other Indian reservation at Fort Buford in 1882 or later. For a brief history of the Gros Ventres (Hidatsas) and the Fort Buford military reserve see *Fort Buford, the Indian reservation that never was* in Author's Notes following this chapter. For the history of the Fort Peck Reservation, see that subject in "Old Dawson" and HAST.

[150] Crows traded with the Gros Ventres (Hidatsas) along the Yellowstone and at Fort Buford, and the Hidatsas reciprocated. The Hidatsas at Fort Buford and the Crows traded with the Hidatsas, Mandans, and Arikaras at Fort Berthold and vice versa. The Sioux went back and forth between the Fort Peck Reservation and Standing Rock and the other Sioux reservations in South Dakota. Almost all of these travelers passed through the lower Yellowstone area on the east side of the river.

that, with the return of all the Indian dead to a heaven right here on Earth. They also believed they would be impervious to the white man's bullets. Decades of hunger, broken treaties, and continued relocations had driven the Indians to a widespread acceptance of this dreamtime. The Battle of Wounded Knee in 1890 finished the Ghost Dancer sect and settled forever in the minds of the Indians the question of reclamation.[151]

I was often left alone at the ranch's line shack, sometimes for as much as a week. One hot day in August of 1883 I was by myself, so after dinner I saddled up my horse and rode back into the hills on some errand. This horse was a treacherous little rascal. Although he wasn't much bigger than a Rocky Mountain canary[152] he had the temperament of a mule. Whenever he took the notion, he would do his very best to dump me off. If he was successful (and he frequently was) he became an absolute artist about not letting me catch him again.

We were well away from the ranch when I saw a big gray wolf running at a right angle to my course and I could see clearly that it wasn't me and my horse he was running from. The wolf had hardly disappeared when a white-tailed deer did the same thing. This intrigued me, for I could not figure out what could have alarmed them. Below us was a piece of badlands that, so far as was known, no white man had ever been through, and they were considered impassable. The situation must have intrigued my companion, too, for suddenly he decided to do his best to leave me there to look out for myself.

Well, to make a short story shorter, that pointy-eared devil was again successful, but, as I left the saddle looking for a more stable situation, I grabbed the horn and pulled the saddle under his belly. For exactly this purpose I had long since learned not to cinch up that little stick of dynamite too tight. This always defeated the last half of his perpetual plan, for he never could run away with that big-seated cowboy saddle with its stirrups flopping around under him. I picked myself up and was trying to catch him when I heard a sound from downriver in the direction of those "impassable" badlands.

---

151 See *"Wounded Knee, the last gasp of the plains Indians"* in Author's Notes following this chapter for a discussion of Wounded Knee and the "Ghost Dancer" phenomenon.

152 "Rocky Mountain canary" was slang for "burro." The term was also applied occasionally to small-statured men, e.g. "Canary Tom" in lieu of "Shorty."

The day was very hot, and there was a considerable mirage that kept distant objects skittering about so they could not be plainly seen. But I could see moving objects. At some distance there was a deep coulee between me and these objects, and I could see them disappear into the far side of the coulee and then bob back up on my side. The mirage flickered a couple more times and then, in less time than it has taken me to tell it, they were near enough for me to see that these "objects" were Indians! They were coming just as hard as their horses could run and they were yelling as only Indians can yell! I judged there were about thirty-five of them. I am here today as a living example that totally denies the assertion that people's hair turns white on being badly frightened. Mine stood straight up, but it never changed a shade. If I had known what tribe they were, it would have helped some. The Gros Ventre and Crow I was not much afraid of, but it might have been Sioux and they were bad medicine.

There was a coulee close behind me that led to the river, about a half or three-quarters of a mile distant. Where this coulee emptied into the river were several acres of a sand bar that was densely covered with wild rose bushes and thickets of bullberry bush. Well, I hit the bottom of that coulee traveling, and brother I mean I was traveling. I am quite sure that if Glenn Cunningham, the Olympic games track star of today, had been started in front of me he would have been very much in my way and would have seen the back side of my dust trail in short order. I figured if I could make it to the brush at the river it would take some tracker to find me. I remember later realizing what a ridiculous thought that was, for those were Indians behind me. They were the natural-born trackers of the plains. They could track a prairie dog after the sun went down!

As I came near the river I was beginning to have some doubts about my fright. Those Indians could surely have overtaken me had they wished to. They knew I was in that coulee. I couldn't be anywhere else without them seeing me. Nevertheless, I didn't let up until I was in the brush. I lay there until I got my wind, but heard no one. I knew Indians well enough to know that if they were after me to do me any harm, I would have heard them long before this. I would have to crawl up a steep bank to gain the flat so I could see where they might be. This I did (after I had untangled myself from a veritable jungle of wild rose bushes) and there, not a hundred feet from where I cautiously stuck my head up, was the whole bunch.

There were all thirty-five of them, looking straight at me, and there I was, my eyes just clearing the edge of the bank, peering back at them. I was drenched with the sweat of my exertions and covered with dust. The two had combined together to make me look like the perfect mud-man—except for the hundreds of red dots. The rose bush thorns had done their work well. A fourteen-year-old mud-man with measles! They had my horse and saddle and were quietly waiting for that kid to come up and get his horse. Their leader came over, looked down at me from on top of the bank, and said, "Danger lose horse in big country." At the same time he handed me that devil rascal's reins. I thanked them profusely, and they went on their way. I doctored those thorn wounds for two weeks and never complained, not even once.[153]

It was also in the summer of 1883, the same month, perhaps, as my Indian adventure, when I saw my first steamboat stuck on a sandbar in the Yellowstone. I had been told the Yellowstone had been quite an active arterial for the paddle wheelers. We actually witnessed a few of them traversing the river after our arrival in April of 1882. From the time of the Great Sioux War in 1876 and 1877 until the railroad arrived in 1881, the military more or less claimed the Yellowstone as one of their own roads.[154] The Army even built some check dams and installed a levee at Glendive. After the NP got to the Yellowstone, however, the river traffic fell away pretty fast and, after 1882, the paddle wheelers became infrequent visitors.[155] A few boats would come up as far

---

[153] Emma Van Blaricom Freeze interview, August, 1992.

[154] For a discussion of the military "laying claim" to the Yellowstone River, see *"The military laid claim..."* in Author's Notes following this chapter.

[155] Joel Overholser (FBWIP, pp. 156–157) tallied the steamboat traffic on the Yellowstone and estimated the tonnages shipped: 6 boats and 700 tons in 1876; about 44 boats and 9,500 tons in 1877; 8 boats and 2,230 tons in 1878; 4 boats and 800 tons in 1879; 8 boats and 1,580 tons in 1880; 20 boats and 4,410 tons in 1881; 4 boats and 700 tons in 1882; 6 boats and 1,200 tons in 1883. Overholser kept no tally for 1884 and beyond. Lorman Hoopes (TLW, p. 380) stated that 1882 saw the last of the river traffic (six trips made by four boats) beyond Glendive to Miles City and Fort Keogh. Glendive, however, continued to see the occasional steamboat until the dam was completed at Intake in 1908. [GHMT, p. 38.]

STEAMER *HELENA* DISPLAYING "GRASSHOPPER" SPARS, 1880
PHOTO COURTESY OF HAYNES FOUNDATION COLLECTION, MONTANA HISTORICAL SOCIETY, HELENA

as Glendive every year, but in my memory I don't believe a single steamboat went up the Yellowstone any farther than Glendive after 1882.

In any case, one day I was riding on the east bank of the Yellowstone, the same area where I had met my Indian friends. Traveling north, I had just topped a bluff when I could see that ahead and off to my left were the chimneys[156] of a steamboat—and she clearly wasn't moving. Staying on the high ground as I

---

[156] Norton's contemporaries routinely used the word "chimneys" to describe what would now be called "smokestacks" or "funnels."

approached, I could see that, although headed downstream, she was certainly stranded, her back broken, and that the crew had done all they could to fashion a pair of poles up toward the bow to help keep her afloat.

Well, I couldn't have been more mistaken. The crew was busily involved in what was apparently, to them, just another day on the river. I was witnessing, for my first and only time, the odd practice of "grasshoppering." I had heard that the Indians referred to a steamboat as the "Fireboat-That-Walks-On-Water," but I had always thought that was some oblique reference to the splashing of the paddle wheel in conjunction with the smoke and sparks belching from the chimneys. It became abundantly clear, however, that this boat was actually inching its way across a sandbar with the help of two giant spars powered by large manila hemp cables drawn around the boat's own capstan. Additionally, the keel wasn't broken at all, but was flexing as the top of the sandbar passed under it.[157]

I sat there on the bluff and watched, fascinated by the precision and speed with which the crew worked to dislodge the huge boat.[158] It was also easy to understand why the steamboats never traveled at night—they could get into enough trouble with snags and sandbars in the daylight. Both the Yellowstone and the Missouri rivers were notorious for rapidly shifting courses and the sudden emergence of sandbars. The boats could get in a lot more trouble going downstream simply because their speed would ram them into hidden obstacles much harder than when they were traveling against the current.[159] As it was, the boat I was watching extricated itself within a couple of hours of my arrival and, none the worse for wear, went smoking down the river toward Fort Buford.

---

[157] LOD, p. 102. See "Grasshoppering" in Author's Notes following this chapter.

[158] FBWIP, p. 154. LOD, p. 100.

[159] YComm, p. 24. TLW, pp. 215–217. COM, pp. 130–131. See "The Missouri River boats rarely traveled at night" in Author's Notes following this chapter.

CHAPTER 11–AUTHOR'S NOTES

Hank Tuttle, sheriff of Dawson County: Henry C. Tuttle was born 18 July 1847 in Connecticut. Henry Tuttle, age eighteen, and George D. Tuttle (an apparent brother), age nineteen, both enlisted in Company E of Hatch's Battalion of Minnesota Cavalry in August of 1864. They both served about two years and were mustered out in May of 1866. Their unit was used in frontier garrison duty at various forts in Minnesota and Dakota Territory. [MCIW, Vol. I, p. 610.]

The Tuttle family was shown on the 1870 census (Round Prairie, Little Sauk [Township], Todd County, Minnesota, p. 2, dwelling number 17, 6 August 1870) as follows:

Name	Age	Occupation	Birthplace
William W. Tuttle	53	Farming	Connecticut
Elizabeth A.	43	Keeping House	Connecticut
Henry C.	23	Works on farm	Connecticut
Corintha E.	19	At Home	Connecticut
Carrie	16	At Home	Minnesota
William W.	14	At home	Minnesota
Bertha A.	12	At home	Minnesota
Alice C.	8		Minnesota

(The parents and Henry and Corintha were born in Connecticut, while the remaining children were born in Minnesota. That means the Tuttles were early Minnesota settlers, arriving from Connecticut sometime between 1851 and 1854.)

Around 1873 Henry married a German-born girl, Anna Dineen (the June 1900 census showed them married for twenty-seven years). Over the next twenty-five years they had eight children, six of whom lived to adulthood. Shortly after the NPRR restarted its construction from Bismarck in 1877, Henry and his brother, William, took jobs as common laborers. They usually worked the railroad construction from May until it shut down in December or January and then returned to their families in Minnesota during the winter.

Henry C. Tuttle can be found on page 14 of the 1880 census for Billings County, Dakota Territory, working as a "labourer" on the

NPRR construction crew: "Age 33, born Connecticut." His brother, "William Tuttle, age 24, herder, born Minnesota," was shown residing in the same dwelling. Soon after his arrival in Glendive in 1881, Henry associated himself with the sheriff's office, where, by 1882, he was working as both deputy sheriff and clerk to the Dawson County sheriff, James Taylor. [TLW, p. 352. OTOL, p. 307.] Bill Tuttle, Henry's brother, was also employed as a deputy sheriff.

In 1884, James Taylor, the first elected sheriff of Dawson County (November of 1882), decided not to run for a second term. In the election of 4 November 1884, "Hank" Tuttle ran as a Republican against Democrat Nick Comford. While Tuttle won the election, the actual returns "have been lost to history." [HYV, p. 378.] Wilbur Tuttle, Hank's son, noted that Nick Comford and Hank's brother, Bill, became Hank's deputies right after the election. It was during his first term that Hank Tuttle prohibited the wearing of revolvers in Glendive proper. "Sufficient time will be given to all men to put their revolvers away, and all are requested to do so and avoid trouble, as the above will be strictly enforced after this date." [GT, 25 September 1885.] Wilbur Tuttle later wrote: "Things had become so bad that it wasn't safe for anyone to be out on the street. Disarmament was the only solution. The two deputies were my Uncle Bill [Tuttle] who was a two-gun man, and Nick Comfort [sic]...." According to Wilbur, the three men had to gun down "a quartet" but "it worked pretty good" and things calmed down after that. [MTMN, p. 14.] Henry Tuttle ran for sheriff again in the election of 2 November 1886. He won and served his term through the end of 1888. [HYV, p. 378. OTOL, p. 2.]

In 1889 Henry accepted a position in law enforcement as a Missoula County deputy sheriff. He was based in Grantsdale, a small, recently platted (1885) community (now in Ravalli County) in the Bitter Root Valley south of Missoula. His territory was the south end of the Bitter Root Valley. This move placed Hank and his family back among the huge clan his sister (Carrie, Mrs. Frank Johnson) had married into: the Scribner, Johnson, Perry, Van Blaricom, and Woods families. In 1899, Henry Tuttle (then about age fifty-two) became one of the first forest rangers in the U.S. Forest Service. In that same year, Hank and an associate, Nathaniel E. ("Than") Wilkerson (age thirty-two), built the first ranger station (the Alta

Station) in the United States on the edge of the Bitter Root Valley in western Montana. [BTrls, pp. 166–168.]

In 1885, Henry Tuttle's parents, William W. and Elizabeth Tuttle, had followed their sons Hank and Bill to Glendive. [WN, 13 March 1958.] Born 8 January 1816, William was sixty-nine years old when he and Elizabeth made the move. Three years later, in the summer of 1888, William and Elizabeth accompanied Henry's family when they made the move from Glendive to the Bitter Root. There they joined their daughter, Carrie (Tuttle) Johnson, and her extended Scribner family. Hank finished his term as sheriff of Dawson County and then joined them in Grantsdale in February of 1889. William died on 23 December 1896. [WN article written sometime in the 1950s. The clipping is in the possession of Mrs. Jack (Ada) Powell of Hamilton, Montana.]

The *Western News* dated 23 December 1896 reported William's obituary:

> William W. Tuttle passed over to the silent majority at the home of his son, H. C. Tuttle, Grantsdale, at 9 o'clock this morning. The gradual breaking up from old age was the cause of his death. Up to a few days ago Mr. Tuttle had been around, hale and hearty for one of his years. Mr. Tuttle's relatives in this section are H. C. Tuttle and family of Grantsdale and Mrs. D. A. Bishop of this city [Hamilton], a granddaughter. Mr. Tuttle was born at Helbron, Tallon Co., Conn., Jan. 8, 1816, and lacked but a few days of being 81 years of age. He removed to the territory of Minnesota in 1851, came to Glendive, Mont. in 1885, and to Grantsdale in 1888. Mr. Tuttle enjoyed the distinction of being the oldest Odd Fellow in the state, having been a member of the order continuously for 52 years. The funeral will take place in the residence tomorrow. The remains will be interred in the Grantsdale cemetery.

Henry C. Tuttle and his family and his mother were shown living in dwelling number 112 in the 1900 census of Ward Township, Ravalli County, Montana:

> Henry C. Tuttle, born 18 July 1847, age 52, married 27 years, born Connecticut, Forest Ranger

Anna (Dineen), wife, born March 1854, age 46, married 27 years, mother of 8 children of whom 6 are still living, born in Germany, immigrated to the United States in 1865, can read, write and speak English

Wilbur, son, age 16, born November 1883 in Montana, attended school the last nine mos.

Austa, daughter, age 10, born September 1889 in Montana, in school the last seven mos.

Gordon, son, age 9, born September 1892 in Montana

Alice C., daughter, age 2, born April 1898 in Montana

Elizabeth, mother, age 73, born September 1826 in Connecticut

Elizabeth Tuttle, Henry's mother, died in 1905. Her obituary was published in the *Ravalli Republican* on 11 August 1905:

Grandma Tuttle Died in Grantsdale at the Advanced Age of Seventy-Nine Years. Mrs. Elizabeth A. Tuttle, familiarly known as Grandma Tuttle, died at Grantsdale Saturday. She was nearly 79 years of age, being born September 17, 1826. At an early age she was married to William W. Tuttle, who died December 24, 1896. She was the mother of seven children, all of whom are living except one daughter. The funeral was held Monday afternoon by Rev. L. L. Kneeland, pastor of the Baptist church, and the body was interred in the Grantsdale cemetery.

She leaves a son, Assistant Land Agent H. C. Tuttle, and a daughter, Mrs. George R. King, who reside at Grantsdale. The former was away at the time of his mother's death and all efforts to locate him were futile. His official work takes him to all portions of the western part of the state and frequently he is away from the railroads and communication.

Both William and Elizabeth Tuttle's graves in the cemetery by the old Grantsdale bridge are unmarked.

Some time after 1905, both Henry and Anna (Dineen) Tuttle moved from Grantsdale to the vicinity of Portland, Oregon. Their fate remains unknown.

Wilbur Tuttle was one of Henry and Anna Tuttle's children. Born in Glendive on 11 November 1883, Wilbur grew up in Glendive (1883–1888) and Grantsdale (1888–1907). In 1907, he became a cartoonist for the *Spokane Chronicle,* a job he held for ten years. At the age of thirty-four, Wilbur moved to Hollywood and, in 1918, began writing motion picture scripts. He became friends with many of the major movie stars, producers, and directors (especially those associated with westerns). Over the next thirty-eight years he published more than one-thousand magazine articles in addition to several movie scripts and, according to *Who's Who, 1961–1970,* he wrote some fifty-five books on western subjects. In one of his last books, *Montana Man,* Wilbur recalled his childhood living in the sheriff's quarters above the Glendive (Dawson County) jail. He was a lifelong fan and self-described "ardent supporter" of the sport of baseball. Elected in 1935, he served as president of the Pacific Baseball League until 1943. During the 1950s he lived in Van Nuys, California. Sometime during the late 1950s or early 1960s, Wilbur wrote and narrated "The Hashknife," a radio show broadcast from a station in the Los Angeles area. Wilbur C. Tuttle died in California on 9 June 1969 at the age of eighty-five. [WN, 14 August 1961. OTOL, p. 307. MTMN, p. 187.]

[Special thanks to Mrs. Jack (Ada) Powell of Hamilton, Montana, for her assistance in researching the Tuttle family. Mrs. Powell is a descendant of Henry C. Tuttle and Anna (Dineen) Tuttle.]

Who's on first? An article in *Our Times, Our Lives* reported that "Mr. Snyder [the brother-in-law of Margaret Dion, Henry Dion's wife] operated the first butcher shop in Glendive." [OTOL, p. 89.] Hoopes, however, pointed out that R. W. Snyder came to Miles City from the Black Hills late in 1881. Later, in March of 1882, he and Benjamin A. Savignac "partnered up and bought out the N. W. Comford Meat Market" (a.k.a. "The Glendive Meat Market") in Glendive. [TLW, p. 309. See Chapter 24, "Some Oldtimers," for biographical details on B. A. Savignac (frequently spelled as "Savinack" or "Savanack") and R. W. Snyder. See Chapter 14, "Mickey Farrell and the Irish Contingent," for the biography of Nicholas W. Comford.]

The Grand Army of the Republic (GAR) was a patriotic society of Civil War veterans organized in 1866 at Decatur, Illinois. [CEnc, 1945, Vol. 6, p. 405.] Following the Civil War, a number of veteran and patriotic organizations were formed. Primary among them were the GAR, the United Confederate Veterans, the Sons of Veterans, the Daughters of the GAR, and the Daughters of the Confederacy. The GAR, composed exclusively of veterans of the Union forces, was by far the largest and most important. In 1890, the organization had 404,489 members. Also affiliated with the GAR was the Woman's Relief Corps, founded in Denver in 1883. The mission of this group was to perpetuate the memory of dead Union soldiers (tombstones and other memorials) and to care for their dependents. [CEnc, 1945, Vol. 11, p. 89.] In existence for eighty-three years, the last GAR post was disbanded in 1949.

The records of the Glendive GAR were reportedly destroyed in one of Glendive's many fires. Consequently, the only Dawson County GAR information discovered has been through tidbits reported in the Glendive newspapers and the "Descriptive Book of the Thomas L. Kane Post No. 12, Department of Montana, Grand Army of the Republic" (hereinafter GARDB), which are the "muster in" and "muster out" records of the Glendive chapter. The first mention of the GAR in Glendive occurred on 1 December 1883 when the *Glendive Times* enquired simply: "Are there enough to start a branch of the Grand Army of the Republic?" The chapter was apparently organized in Glendive on January 21, 1885, since that is the earliest "muster" date shown on the membership rolls.

The Glendive post of the GAR was originally constituted as Post No. 21 of the Department of Utah on date unknown. The Montana Department was organized on 10 March 1885. Attending that organizational meeting were representatives of the following posts which existed in Montana Territory at that time (all bearing their Department of Utah GAR post numbers): Post No. 2, Fort Custer; Post No. 6, Butte; Post No. 8, Helena; Post No. 9, Deer Lodge; Post No. 10, Virginia City; Post No. 13, Livingston; Post No. 17, Billings; Post No. 18, Bozeman; Post No. 19, Missoula; and Post No. 21, Glendive. It was announced that the posts would be renumbered "in due time" as the Department of Montana organized. Since the first "musters" recorded in the "Descriptive Book of the Thomas L. Kane Post No. 12, Department of Montana, Grand Army of the Republic" all bear the date of 21 January 1885, the Glendive post was organized in time to send delegates to the statewide encampment that occurred just six weeks later. (Do not confuse the post name of "Thomas L. Kane" with Thomas B. Kean, the early Glendive settler who filed the first land claim on the Glendive townsite in Helena in 1872. In that year, Kean was a bugler in the Stanley military expedition that escorted the NPRR survey teams to the Powder River. See the biography of Thomas B. Kean in "Old Dawson.")

In attendance representing Glendive at the formative Montana meeting in March of 1885 were Pierce Hoopes, C. E. Waters, and M. P. Wyman. Hoopes was elected as an "Aide-de-Camp" to the territorial organization, while Wyman was elected to the territorial "Council of Administration." C. E. Waters was selected to represent the Montana organization at the forthcoming "National Encampment" scheduled to be held in Portland, Maine. [HML, pp. 387–388.]

Dr. Lorman Hoopes reported that Ela C. Waters (see C. E. Waters above) was born in 1849 in Martinsburg, Lewis County, New York. He was raised in Fond du Lac, Wisconsin, attended Ripon College and enlisted in "A" Company, 38th Wisconsin, in 1864. Following the Civil War, he was a "drummer" (a traveling salesman) for a New York firm until 1882. He married Ms. Martha B. Armory in Fond du Lac on 4 March 1877. In 1882 he and Anton Klaus opened Merrill House, a hotel in Glendive. In 1885, Klaus dropped out of the partnership. Ela Waters also got into the cattle business with R. H. Moore in 1885. The ranch, known as "Waters and Moore," grazed the Smith Creek and Shadwell Creek drainages on the east side of the Yellowstone. They were still in business in 1886. [TLW, p. 362]

"M. P. Wyman" was apparently the honorary "Major" Moses P. Wyman, who, in 1883, was the road master for the Yellowstone Division of the NPRR. He was reported by the YJ in January of 1886 as doing the same work and still residing in Glendive. [TLW, p. 376.] (Since Wyman was the only member of the Glendive chapter of the GAR who served with the U.S. Navy during the Civil War and he was an enlisted man, a Fireman 1st Class, the honorific "Major" must have been the result of his employment.)

On 9 August 1885, the *Glendive Times* reported: "The Thomas L. Kane Post No. 12, Montana, received GAR badges today. They are very nice."

Levi Van Blaricom reportedly served as the Quartermaster for the Glendive post of the GAR for about three years (ca. 1885 through ca. 1887). There were occasional notices in the Glendive newspapers acknowledging his role.

The roster of the Glendive GAR post, written in the recognizable script of James McCormick, the Irish-born Dawson County court recorder, included the following fourteen men who are discussed elsewhere in this book:

Name	Rank	Civil War Unit	Dates Served
Bamber, John	Private	20th Connecticut Infantry	1864–1865
Bendon, Nathaniel	Private	11th Pennsylvania Infantry	1861–1865
Burns, John L.	Private	142nd New York Infantry	1862–1865
Bonham, Phillip	Private	1st Nevada Cavalry	1863–1866
Hoopes, Pierce J.	Private	1st Tennessee Infantry (USA)	1861–1864
McCormick, James	Corporal	19th Connecticut Infantry	1862–1865
Newlon, William	Private	156th Illinois Infantry	1862–1865
Slawson, Eben	Private	2nd New York Heavy Artillery	1864–1865
Tuttle, Henry C.	Private	Hatch's Battalion of Cavalry (Minnesota)	1864–1865
Van Blaricom, Levi	Private	4th Minnesota Infantry	1861–1865
Wyman, Moses P.	Fireman 1st Clas	The Frigate Minnesota	1861–1864
Waters, Ela C.	Musician	38th Wisconsin Infantry	1864–1865

When one considers that there were forty-four enrolled members of the GAR in Glendive and then add to that the number of men known to have served in or with the military between the Civil War and the beginning of "settlement" in 1880 (Jimmy Crain, Bill Cheney, Morris Cain, Johnny O'Brien from Newlon, John O'Brien, the iceman from Glendive, Charlie Stierle, William Sartin, Charlie Adams, Mickey Farrell, and Andrew Smith, to name a few), it quickly becomes apparent that the early settlers of the lower Yellowstone were not a defenseless lot. There were also men like U.S. Deputy Marshal Alex Ayotte (wounded during his service) and local attorney Henri Haskell (wounded at Gettysburg) who had served in the Union Army during the Civil War but who, for whatever reason, chose to not join the GAR. Additionally, there were hundreds of ex-Confederate soldiers who had located in Montana who never talked much and who never got on anybody's list. There were also men like Pierre Wibaux and the Marquis de Mores, both of whom had served as officers in the French cavalry. These were all men not only trained in the art of war, but who had actively soldiered. This widespread background of military training and experience helps explain the sudden rise and then immediate disappearance of clandestine and unidentified vigilante groups such as the Montana Stranglers. There was a huge inventory of men who knew how to act and fight as a unit, who could create and/or follow orders, and who had absolutely no reason to "crow" or otherwise brag about their deeds. If the law couldn't or wouldn't handle a situation, they knew how to eradicate a perceived problem in short order—and they frequently did.

Fort Buford: the Indian reservation that never was: *Gros Ventre* was originally a French term meaning "big belly." [JLC, p. 54, footnote 14.] Pronounced "Gro-von," this name was unfortunately applied to two separate, unrelated tribes and can cause no end of confusion. The group Norton referenced here were the "Gros Ventre of the Missouri," a group closely related to the Crow tribe. Also known as the Hidatsas (or Minnetarees*) (JLC, p. 54, footnote 14), they were ultimately located in western North Dakota at Fort Berthold with the Arikaras and the remnant of the Mandans. [CE, p. 345.] Their primary villages were on the Knife River where it intersected the Missouri, somewhat upstream from the Mandan villages when Lewis and Clark stayed at Fort Mandan during the winter of 1804–1805. [JLC, pp. 57–58.] Of ancient Crow origin or vice versa (it may be more appropriate to say the Crow are of ancient Hidatsa origin—see DFIT, pp. 137–139, footnotes 1–4)—the Hidatsas were known to travel far into western Montana, raiding and trading. [JLC, p. 77, footnote 2 and pp. 88, 114, and 146.] It was Missouri River Gros Ventres (Hidatsas) who had captured Sacajawea, a Shoshone, in the vicinity of Three Forks at the eastern base of the Rockies, and it was Hidatsas who gambled her off to Charbonneau to become another in his long succession of Indian wives. [JLC, p. 64 and footnote 7.] Long friendly to the whites, the Hidatsas were not confined to their own reservation at Fort Berthold until 1894. It is of some interest to note that the famed Hagen [sic] Site, the prehistoric earth lodge discovered on the west side of the Yellowstone River near Glendive on the old Tom Hagan property, is considered to date back to the transitional period or "split" between the more horticultural Hidatsas and the hunter-gatherer Absarokas

("Ap sar roo kai") or Crow culture. [DFIT, pp. 137–139 and footnotes 1, 2, 3, and 4.]

*No one can seem to agree on the spelling of "Minnetaree," the Mandan name for the Hidatsa, except the spelling used herein appears to be the most common. (Father DeSmet, cited in POY, p. 125; Edwin Thompson Denig in DFIT, p. 137; and Bernard DeVoto in JLC, p. 84), Footnote 6.) However, see "Minnetarees" (Mark Brown, POY, p. 127), "Minetarees" (Meriwether Lewis cited by Bernard DeVoto in JLC, p. 120), "Minitarees" (Clark cited by DeVoto in JLC, p. 136), and "Minitari" (Carl Waldman in ANAI, p., 227).

The "Gros Ventre of the North" (or "Gros Ventre of the Prairies") was a tribe of Canadian origin related linguistically to the Algonkian-speaking Cree, Arapaho, Cheyenne and the three Blackfeet tribes. [MWP, p. 14.] Originally living between the forks of the Saskatchewan River, the Blackfeet called them "Atsina" ("gut people") and that, unfortunately, like the Indian sign language for "Hidatsa," also translated to "Gros Ventre" in French. Relative latecomers in moving to the plains of Montana, the Atsina tended to stay north of the Missouri River and, loosely confederated with the Blackfeet, they were, more or less, in a continual state of war with the Assiniboine. [MWP, p. 14.] About 1867, "after a major falling out and defeat at the hands of the Blackfeet, the Gros Ventre (Atsina) formed a coalition with the Assiniboine. These two tribes [thereafter] shared the Milk River Valley." [FIV, Vol. .2, p. 658.]

Norton was understandably mistaken in his belief that the "reservation" near Fort Buford was "Gros Ventre." Up until 1894, if one traveled down the Yellowstone River from Glendive to Fort Buford, at least one encampment of Gros Ventres (Hidatsas/ Minnetarees) could be found on the west side of the river (see FVBM, see the George McCone biography in the Glendive Library and see also contemporary maps indicating the Indian encampment on the lower Yellowstone River) with another near Fort Buford itself. The military reserve was in the shape of a square measuring thirty miles on each side, with Fort Buford located in the center, about two miles inside Dakota Territory. It thus encompassed land on both sides of the Yellowstone as well as both sides of the Missouri River. To confuse matters a little more, the thirty-mile dimension of the Fort Buford Military Reservation meant the "line" for Fort Buford was fifteen miles to the north, south, east, and west of the fort itself. That placed the westernmost boundary of the fort's "preserve" some twelve miles or so inside Montana Territory, and, at one time, it abutted the Fort Peck Indian Reservation. Built in 1869, Fort Buford was never intended to be an Indian reservation, but Gros Ventres (Hidatsas) were allowed to stay there near the fort as protection from the Sioux, until their forced removal in 1894. (See below.) Norton simply believed what he saw: tepees, Indians, and Gros Ventres. That all summed up to him as a Gros Ventre reservation, but it wasn't. (For a more complete discussion of Fort Buford and the Fort Buford Military Reservation, see that subject in "Old Dawson.")

The real "Indian reservation" lay immediately west and north of the Fort Buford reserve. As a result of the treaties of 1851 and 1855 and up until 1888, all of the land north of the Missouri River extending west from the Montana territorial border with Dakota Territory to the crest of the Rocky Mountains was one vast reservation containing the Blackfeet on the west, the Assiniboine and Gros Ventre of the Prairies (the Atsina) in the center, and the Assiniboine and Yanktonai Sioux in the east. Early on, the various agencies were located at Fort Benton, the Blackfeet Agency, Milk River, and Fort Belknap. Later, to include the Lower Assiniboine (meaning that portion of the tribe living around the Missouri River in eastern Montana Territory) and the Yanktonai Sioux, who were then using the traditional Assiniboine hunting grounds in that area, the Fort Peck agency was established in 1871. The agency was originally sited at the Fort Peck trading post established by Durfee and Peck in 1869. In 1879, separate facilities were built and the agency (while the reservation itself retained the name of "Fort Peck") relocated to Poplar River, with a sub-agency at Wolf Point. [FIV, Vol. 2, pp. 658–659.]

In 1888, Congress removed some 17,500,000 acres from the Indian lands north of the Missouri and established the boundaries for the three remaining reservations. The Blackfeet were located at Browning. Assiniboine and the Atsina ("Gros Ventre of the Prairie") were settled farther to the east at the Fort Belknap Reservation in north-central Montana. Finally, Sioux and Assiniboine were located on the Fort Peck Reservation just east and north of Fort Buford. [FIV, Vol. 2, p. 659 and p. 662. See HAST for a more complete history of the Fort Peck Reservation.]

As a result of the Fort Laramie Treaty of 1851, the Mandans, Arikaras, and Hidatsas ("Minnetarees / Gros Ventres of the Missouri") had been placed on the reservation at Fort Berthold, Dakota Territory (now North Dakota). (Note that most contemporary literature of the 1880s and earlier used the term "Gros Ventre" to describe the Hidatsa.) By subsequent treaty modification in 1866 and an Executive Order of 1870, that reservation extended west to the Yellowstone River until 13 July 1880. On that date, President Rutherford B. Hayes moved the western boundary of the reservation some seventy-five miles or so to the east, away from the Yellowstone. The result was, more or less, the size and shape of the existing reservation of the "Three Confederated Tribes" now known as the Fort Berthold Indian Reservation. There were two bands of Hidatsas, however, who were allowed to remain on the Yellowstone and in the vicinity of Fort Buford for a number of years. In 1891 elements of the 25th U.S. Infantry Regiment and some men from the 10th U.S. Cavalry arrived at Fort Buford. It was one of the unpleasant duties of these "Buffalo Soldiers" to forcibly gather up the remaining groups of Hidatsas in 1894 and remove them from Fort Buford and the lower Yellowstone to Fort Berthold. It was reported that "their lamentations and cries could be heard a long way." [CE, p. 345.]

Wounded Knee, the last gasp of the plains Indians: On 1 January 1889, Wovoka, a Paiute mystic from Nevada, claimed a vision "came in the time when the sun had died." Prophetically, the vision had occurred to him during an eclipse of the sun. He saw the Earth perish and it was then reborn in an aboriginal state inhabited only by the Indians. The land would be bountiful with lush grass and unending herds of buffalo as before the coming of the white man. All of the believers and the ancestors of the believers would be reborn and there would be an eternal existence free from any suffering or want. In order to achieve this "new world," the Indians must cease to war against each other and they must shun the ways of the whites, especially alcohol, which Wovoka termed "the destroyer." He advocated prayer and meditation and he created the "Ghost Dance" through which the participant might temporarily glimpse the paradise soon to be realized.

A Minneconjou Sioux named Kicking Bear and several other Sioux traveled first to Pyramid Lake in Nevada. There they were told the Messiah had returned and Christ must have sent for them to come there. They were told to travel farther south to Walker Lake, Nevada, where Jesus Christ would next reappear. They did so and along with hundreds of other Indians they waited for the return of the Messiah. At sunset, Jesus appeared and told them how he, too, had been poorly treated by the white man and that he had returned to make everything as it used to be and make it better. Jesus stayed with them and taught them the Ghost Dance and he flew above them and taught them new songs to accompany the dance.

According to some versions of the story, Kicking Bear and his disciples, upon their return to the Dakotas, added a couple of new twists to the gospel of Wovoka. They disregarded the principles of non-violence espoused by Wovoka and, instead of biding their time awaiting the disappearance of the white man as Wovoka advocated, they preached for the active elimination of the whites. They also added the idea that their Ghost Dance shirts provided invincibility to the white man's bullets. "White officials became concerned about this new religious fervor tinged with activism and, in November of 1890, banned the Ghost Dance on Sioux reservations." [ANAI, p. 158.] When the Ghost Dance rites continued, the troops were called in. General Nelson Miles moved his headquarters to Rapid City and, on 12 December 1890, ordered the arrest of Sitting Bull at Standing Rock. During the arrest, which occurred just before dawn on 15 December, a melee ensued and Sitting Bull, along with seven of his warriors and six of the forty Indian police sent to arrest him, were slain.

On 28 December 1890, elements of the 7th U.S. Cavalry under the command of Colonel James W. Forsyth surrounded a group of Sioux and moved them to a camp on Wounded Knee Creek. This is the same James W. Forsyth who had, along with steamboat Captain Grant Prince Marsh, directed the waterborne military exploration to determine the head of navigation of the Yellowstone River in 1875 and for whom the Montana town of Forsyth was named. There were about five-hundred cavalrymen present as well as four rapid-firing Hotchkiss artillery pieces placed to cover all four corners of the camp. The Sioux camp numbered about one-hundred-and-twenty men and two-hundred-and-thirty women and children. On the morning of the 29th, the troopers entered the encampment to gather up all of the firearms. A single shot was fired (most witnesses believe the shot was accidental, the product of a scuffle) and the place exploded. Twenty-five soldiers were killed, and thirty-nine were wounded. At least one-hundred-and-fifty Indians were killed and fifty more were wounded. The scene became that of a charnel house as the artillery was loosed on those Indians trying to flee the slaughter. Forsyth was later charged with "the killing of innocents" but was exonerated.

With Sitting Bull's death and the slaughter at Wounded Knee, the Ghost Dance rituals subsided and, for all practical purposes, the Indian wars of the plains were over. Wovoka, the Paiute mystic who started the Ghost Dance movement, died in obscurity at about the age of seventy-six in 1932 in Schurz, Nevada. [AWY, p. 113.] [To read some of the many conflicting versions of the Ghost Dancers, Sitting Bull's death, and the story of Wounded Knee, see MWP, p. 589; ANAI, pp. 158–159; LOD, pp. 220–233; BHND, pp. 149–153; and BMH, pp. 415–445. Also see these same subjects in HAST.]

The military "laid claim" to the Yellowstone during the Great Sioux War. Bozeman interests commissioned the construction of the paddle wheeler *Yellowstone* (the third boat of that name) in 1875, intending to shorten the long haul to Fort Benton and then overland to Bozeman. Coming up the Missouri just before the Custer massacre in 1876, the captain of the *Yellowstone*, John Massie, got a stern warning from the military at Fort Buford to "stay off our river." The army was having a tough enough time with civilian casualties on the upper Missouri and they wanted no more civilians on "our river" (the Yellowstone) to become "Sioux targets." The boat diverted to Fort Benton, arriving on 24 June. Ironically, on the way back down, the *Yellowstone* got "drafted" by the army at Fort Buford and spent some time on the Yellowstone ferrying Terry's troops around. [FBWIP, p. 155.] In 1877, the river was fairly alive with steamboat traffic, almost all of it related to troop movements, logistics, and the construction of Fort Keogh and Fort Custer. Beginning with the season of 1878, however, the river was essentially open to any and all comers.

"Grasshoppering": "Missouri [and Yellowstone River] boats were not rigid craft; often the timbers of a steamer would bend and yield as much as two feet in crawling over a bar." [LOD, p. 102.] If the boat became stranded on a sandbar, the crew would set the two spars, one located on each side of the bow, on the bottom. The

**THE *FAR WEST* DISPLAYING "GRASSHOPPER" SPARS
(BUILT IN 1870)**
ILLUSTRATION BY ALEX AMEZCUA

spars were set at an angle so the tops were ahead or forward of the bottoms. A manila cable was secured to the gunwale of the boat, passed through a tackle-block on the spar, and then attached to a capstan. As the capstan turned, the boat was lifted ahead and the paddle wheel would help push the boat forward. The spars would then be raised and re-set farther forward and the process was repeated until the boat was completely lifted over the bar. "From the grotesque resemblance to a grasshopper which the craft bore when her spars were set, and from the fact that she might be said to move forward in a series of hops, the practice came to be called 'grasshoppering.'" [COM, pp. 86–87.]

The Missouri River boats rarely traveled at night: While not the leviathans that traversed the Mississippi River, the Missouri River boats were still substantial. "The average boat measured about two-hundred-and-twenty feet in length, thirty-five feet in width, and carried five-hundred tons of freight. She was built with a flat bottom and was of shallow draft, drawing about three feet of water empty and about four feet when laden. And sometimes even that was too much, for the tricky Missouri, filled with shifting sandbars, kept the boat walking on her stilts half the time." [LOD, p. 100.] As the Missouri River traffic moved on up the river beyond Fort Buford, the steamboat companies started building even shallower draught boats that drew only three feet of water fully loaded. By 1875, the *Josephine* set the precedent for boats designed specifically to navigate the Yellowstone and the upper reaches of the Missouri in periods of low water. With a capacity of about two-hundred-and-fifty tons, the *Josephine* drew only twenty-two inches of water fully loaded. [FBWIP, p. 154.] "Captain Marsh had named her *Josephine* after the little daughter of General [David Sloane] Stanley, whose home was then at Fort Sully, the headquarters of the 22nd Infantry" and who, in 1873, had ordered and supervised the construction of Stanley's Stockade near Glendive. [COM, p. 184.] It had been the *Josephine* that had carried Colonel James W. Forsyth and Captain Grant P. Marsh to the head of navigation on the Yellowstone in 1875. They crossed "Hell Roaring Rapids" west of Pryor Fork and reached a point estimated to be forty-six miles west of Pompey's Pillar or some four-hundred-and-thirty-eight miles above the mouth of the Yellowstone. As the crow flies, they were less than sixty miles east of the present corner of Yellowstone National Park. [COM, pp. 219–220.]

A quick reading of various steamboat logs confirms the ban on traveling at night. Almost every entry starts with "Weighed anchor at daylight" and ends with "Anchored at 9:30 PM" or "Anchored in midstream on a bar." Additionally, if the boat stopped in a wooded area and needed fuel—and if the locale was deemed safe enough—the crew would use the anchorage to gather sufficient logs or debris to get them to the next woodhawk site. Jerome Greene reported on the trip of the *Durfee* going up the Yellowstone late in July of 1876: "The trip was slow, the steamboat able to ascend the river only from daybreak, about 3 A.M., to 6 P.M., when the crew moored the vessel and collected wood along the bank." [YComm, p. 24.]

Captain Grant Prince Marsh was one of the very few boatmen who did not adhere strictly to the "no-sailing-at-night" rule. Marsh, however, had been navigating the upper Missouri from St. Louis to Fort Benton from 1866 and had been on the Yellowstone since 1873. Probably the most experienced captain on either of the rivers,

Marsh never suffered any serious accidents from his occasional night runs. His run carrying the wounded from the battle at Little Big Horn to Bismarck set a record that was never bested. [TLW, pp. 215–217.] At the helm of the *Far West*, Captain Marsh covered the seven-hundred-and-ten miles in fifty-two hours. [COM, p. 306.]

CHAPTER TWELVE

1884:
The Army Payroll Robbery

AS FAST AS THE BUFFALO WERE ELIMINATED from the range, people saw the opportunity to stock it with cattle. In the spring of 1884 there was a decided cattle boom all over eastern Montana. The ranges were free, and taxes were nil or next to nothing. While the preceding winters had been cold, there was always plenty of feed on the range and the cattle had been coming through with very few losses. The country was truly beginning to look like a livestock gold mine with free range and very little feeding to do. Men were actually wondering what they would do with all their money in a few more years.[160]

It wasn't all a bed of roses during the cattle boom of 1884, however. I was still working for the **101** ranch on the east side of the Yellowstone.[161] There was a stage road on the opposite side of the river, but the river was not fordable and we had no boats. With no means of crossing the Yellowstone, we had no knowledge of happenings on the other side. The **101** had just taken possession of Smith Creek as part of his range that spring. It was the 14th of May 1884 and my job for the day was to see if any of our cattle had drifted south along the river past Devil's Canyon and on into the large flat just beyond (now called "Valentine Flat"). I was just working my way up the steep country that led south to Devil's Canyon when, suddenly, I heard the sound of gunfire coming from across the Yellowstone. I stopped my horse so I could better hear. It wasn't just a shot or two, it was a regular fusillade and it continued for a full minute or two.

---

[160] SNVB manuscript, pp. 31–32.

[161] See *"Griffin and Ward and the* **101** *ranch"* in Author's Notes following this chapter.

From my elevated position I could see a small cluster of seven riders making tracks toward the Yellowstone. They were obviously in a hurry since they didn't take the time to find a ford. Instead, they forced their horses to plunge into the river and swim across. The current swept them past me, and they came out below the **101** shack less than a mile from my position up on the hill. I was never close enough to identify the men, but I could clearly see their activities. When they got to my side, one of the group was lagging a little behind. There was something wrong with one of his legs, I have forgotten what. Just before he got to the bank of the river, I saw two of his companions turn around and shoot him dead. For whatever reason, they must have considered him a marked man.[162] As his body floated off with the current, one of the men grabbed the reins of the victim's horse and, with the horse in tow, the six men rode away in an easterly direction.[163]

A few days earlier, a $10,000 cash payroll, intended for the soldiers garrisoned at Fort Buford (among them one or two companies of the famed 7th Cavalry), had arrived in Glendive on the Northern Pacific under heavy guard. At that time, the post was under the command of Lieutenant Colonel Joseph Whistler, one of the true "old hands" who had served many of his years with the Army in Montana.[164] Traveling in two wagons, one a military ambulance, the other an escort wagon (which may also have been an ambulance), Major Charles Whipple, the paymaster, was escorted by Mr. Such, the payroll clerk, the two wagon drivers, and six soldiers under the command of Sergeant Aquilla Coonrod. Whipple had divided the money into two $5,000 lots and had secured the funds in two strongboxes, one in each wagon. This small company departed Glendive bound for Fort Buford early in the morning of 13 May 1884. They expected to cover the eighty miles in two days.

Major Whipple and his men crossed the Glendive ferry to the west (north) side of the Yellowstone and proceeded to follow the old military road downstream. They went by Bamber Springs and passed through the Slawson ranch and stagecoach station. By

[162] See *"The 1942 letter to Gene Autry"* in Author's Notes following this chapter.

[163] See *"Don McArthur: killer, victim, or both?"* in Author's Notes following this chapter.

[164] See *"Lieutenant Colonel Joseph Nelson Garland Whistler"* in Author's Notes following this chapter.

sunset of the 13th, some forty miles out of Glendive, they had reached the Burns ranch and roadhouse and the party camped that night on Burns Creek. They were then about halfway to Fort Buford. Major Whipple apparently realized that the next day they would be passing through some country where the firepower advantage of the two wagons traveling one in front of the other would be lost. In one area in particular, about four miles downstream from the Burns ranch, the road took a very sharp turn around the point of a bluff and then immediately headed up a narrow ravine that would take them from the river bottom up to the flat on top. It would be impossible for the two wagons to support each other at that point without the soldiers temporarily abandoning one wagon or the other.

While there is no record indicating the existence of any rumor concerning a sizable outlaw band, this part of the country had long since earned its reputation as one geographically favorable to unlawful acts. In addition to being forty miles from the law in either direction, its long draws and steep hills provided an ideal location for the lawless to carry out their plots. John Burns had long since adopted the habit of chaining and padlocking his horse barns every night. No one will ever know, of course, whether it was the result of overheard gossip, smart planning, or just plain old premonition, but just before daybreak on the day of the robbery attempt, Major Whipple quietly got up without arousing anyone. He took the $5,000 in cash from the strongbox in the rear wagon (the "escort wagon") where it was normally kept and placed it in the strongbox of the lead wagon (the "ambulance") along with the rest of the payroll. He told no one of this switch and, after breakfast on the 14th of May, the two wagons proceeded on toward Fort Buford.

About four miles north of the Burns place, the road went from the river bottom down by the Yellowstone up through a ravine that led up to the elevated flat known as "Grant's Prairie" (on which the town of Savage is now situated). As the first wagon cleared a particularly sharp bend just below the top of the grade, the seven outlaws attacked. With no warning they opened fire. The men in the first wagon attempted to return the fire. Sergeant Coonrod was killed[165] and the driver, Private Arthur Beard,

---

[165] See *"Sergeant Aquilla Coonrod"* in Author's Notes following this chapter.

was slightly wounded. With a second volley by the outlaws, the remaining men jumped out of the wagons to assume safer positions on the ground and it was then that Private James Birch was severely wounded in the shoulder.[166] Simultaneously, the lead team of mules panicked and ran away with the driver, Beard, and with Sergeant Coonrod's body still in the ambulance. Major Whipple, the paymaster, knowing the payroll was in that wagon, spurred his horse in pursuit. The outlaws, believing the payroll to be in the second wagon (where it normally would have been) let Whipple and the first wagon go and concentrated their attentions on the second or "escort" wagon. Thus, Whipple and the first wagon got to the safety of Scott's Ranch up on Grant's Prairie about four or five miles farther north (about where the settlement of Savage is now located).

In the meantime, the outlaws concentrated on the second wagon, believing that it carried the payroll. In their first volley, to ensure their prey couldn't escape, they shot and wounded or killed one of the mules in the team pulling the second wagon. They soon neutralized the five remaining soldiers, the driver and Mr. Such, the payroll clerk, and rifled the wagon in search of the payroll. Not finding anything, and after bending the rifles of the troopers and confiscating whatever side-arms there were, they ordered everybody, including the severely wounded Private Birch, into the wagon and sent it off back down the road toward Johnny Burns' place, some four miles distant.

Realizing they wouldn't be able to catch up with Whipple and the wagon containing the payroll before they reached Scott's Ranch, the seven men cut the telegraph line and fled across the Yellowstone into the remote **101** country. From there they probably dispersed and fled the country or melted back into the local scenery.

When Whipple and the ambulance containing the payroll and Sergeant Coonrod's body arrived at Scott's place,[167] the only military escort remaining consisted of Major Whipple and the wounded driver, Beard. Whipple had no idea what had transpired back at the Burns ranch and had no way of knowing where the

---

[166] See *"Died. James Birch-Private..."* in Author's Notes following this chapter.

[167] See *"Scott's Ranch"* in Author's Notes following this chapter.

would-be robbers had gone. For all Whipple knew, they might still be in pursuit of him and the payroll. Thus Whipple organized himself, Beard, and the two civilians who worked at Scott's (Heffernan and Austill) and "holed up" in a defensive stance for the remainder of the day.

After spending the night of the 14th barricaded and on the defensive, Private Beard was sent from Scott's Ranch to Fort Buford late the next morning. Beard didn't reach Fort Buford until sometime late in the evening on the 15th of May. (It was about thirty-five miles from Scott's place to the Missouri, then across on the ferry, and then another three miles to the fort.) After a forced march through the night of the 15th, a troop of the 7th Cavalry arrived at Scott's from Fort Buford at daylight on the 16th.

Once the payroll had been delivered to Fort Buford, most of the post was ordered out in search of the perpetrators. Evidence of the killers' presence was found on the right bank of Box Elder Creek, but that was it.[168] They never found a soul. Some years later some badmen were taken in connection with some other robberies. They confessed their part in the famous Fort Buford payroll job but it was never proved one way or the other.[169]

---

[168] See second paragraph of "Scott's Ranch" in Author's Notes following this chapter.

[169] See Map 6, "The U.S. Army payroll robbery of May 14, 1884," to locate the scene of the robbery and the escape route of the bandits.

CHAPTER 12–AUTHOR'S NOTES

The events surrounding the robbery attempt: As might be expected, there are many versions of the story of the attempted robbery of the Fort Buford payroll and the murders associated with it. [See the telegram sent by Lt. Col. Joseph Nelson Garland Whistler, the commanding officer at Fort Buford, to General Alfred H. Terry at Snelling, Minnesota, on 16 May 1884 reprinted in CE, p. 708. Letter written by Stephen Norton Van Blaricom to Gene Autry on 22 February, 1942 (cited below). "Savage," article by Vera Brown Darnall and Arthur S. Hall in CE, pp. 705–708. *The Champion Buffalo Hunter* (VS, pp. 98 and 99). "Fort Buford," article by Mary Mercer (utilizing the research of Ben Innis) in CE, pp. 342–346.] The version recounted in the text presents the most plausible scenario.

Griffin and Ward and the 101 ranch: The "Griffin Brothers" were M. A. and Arnold Griffin, and Henry Ward was the third partner and the foreman. The partnership used the **101** brand. [TLW, p. 361. Also see MSD, p. 164.] The Ward brothers, William O. ("Oscar"), Asa, and Henry, were known to be ranching on the east side of the Yellowstone River north of Glendive by 1880 (or earlier) using a cursive **W** brand (not to be confused with the **W** later used by Pierre Wibaux) on the right hip with the **101** on the right rib. [MSD p. 165.] Oscar Ward used the cursive **W** on the left hip with the **101** still on the right rib. [MSD, p. 165.] The Griffin Brothers also ran cattle, utilizing the same cursive **W** turned over into a cursive **M** preceded by a capital **G**, thus **GM** on the left side with the **101** on the right side. [MSD, p. 155.] These four entities (the Griffin brothers; Oscar Ward; the Griffin brothers and Henry Ward; and, finally, the Ward brothers) operated in concert and were commonly called the **101** ranch. The **101** was probably "the ranches" noted by the editor of the *Yellowstone Journal* to have been "established [and trespassing] on the Gros Ventre-Mandan-Arikara Reservation at the mouth of Glendive Creek or close thereby" in 1877. [Cited in TLW, p. 136.] On the west side of the Yellowstone, young Ed Marron was claimed to have been operating "a ranch" along Sevenmile Creek in 1877. Phillip Bonham and Thomas John ("Jack") Gorman were also believed to have been grazing a few cows on the west bank of Yellowstone in 1877, but they were located farther north near the Fort Buford reservation boundary. In any case, Marron, Bonham, and Gorman were very minor operators and they were on the wrong side of the river to have been the subjects of the *Yellowstone Journal* article.

The Griffins and the Ward brothers, however, were a commercial operation and, given the four locations of the **101** brand in conjunction with the cursive **W** and the cursive **M**, they would have had the appearance of being more than one ranch. The Griffin and Ward brothers were the certainly the first cattlemen known to be grazing in the area east of the Yellowstone. One occasionally finds references to "101 Creek" in memoirs written by early Wibaux area cowboys. [WTW–TM, p. 111.] "One-O-One Creek" is now a remote tributary to Bennie Peer Creek that joins Bennie Peer at a point just inside the Dakota border in the Little Missouri National Grassland. Bennie Peer Creek, in turn, joins the Yellowstone opposite Sidney. Since Bennie Peer didn't show up in the Yellowstone country until the 1880s, one suspects that "101 Creek" referenced all of what is now "Bennie Peer Creek," not simply the upper drainage as is now indicated. In any case, from 1877 until Pierre Wibaux's appearance in 1883 and his subsequent expansion in 1884, the **101** was grazing all over that country east of the Yellowstone from Glendive Creek as far north as the Missouri River.

In 1877, the **101** wasn't a "ranch" in the traditional sense of having a headquarters with corrals and buildings at some central location with "line shacks" out in the periphery. Until at least 1880 or 1881, they were "high-graders" moving from location to location following the best grass and water. The **101** simply operated from cow camps that were continually moved as the cattle migrated. If they built anything at all, it would have been dugouts or dirt-roofed log shacks to use as temporary winter quarters. Sometime in 1881, Hank Ward may have established a sort of headquarters on 101 Creek and converted some of his dugouts and shacks into line camps for the use of his cowboys.

In 1877, there had to have been some sort of arrangement with the Hidatsa (they were the "Gros Ventre" to the white locals of the Yellowstone River area) that allowed the Wards and Griffins and their **101** brands to be grazing cattle on the reservation. The Hidatsa were well aware that the east side of the Yellowstone was their land and they weren't shy about shooing away settlers or trespassers. In one well-known incident that took place in December of 1879, railroad surveyors Winston and Shaw tried to jump ahead of the Northern Pacific construction and claim land at the junction of Glendive Creek and the Yellowstone. Chief Crow-That-Flies-High and his band of Gros Ventres (Hidatsas) camped in the middle of the Winston and Shaw site and refused to let them build. [TLW, p. 136.]

It was not until the Executive Order of President Rutherford B. Hayes dated 13 July 1880 that the lands east of the Yellowstone were removed from the Hidatsa-Mandan-Arikara reservation and placed in the public domain. It was only after that date that any type of permanent structure was allowed. On the west side of the Yellowstone, however, it had been a different story. Frank Muzzy and Fred Rounserville set themselves up on Crittenden Island to sell wood to the paddle wheelers in 1876. Woodhawks like Jimmy Crain at Crain Creek (now misspelled as "Crane" Creek), Bill Cheney at Lone Tree Creek, Coykendall at Thirteenmile Creek, and young twenty-year-old Ed Marron at Sevenmile Creek had established themselves on the west bank of the Yellowstone by 1877. French Joe Seymour at Fox Creek and George Morgan and John O'Brien at Ninemile Creek (now Morgan Creek) also had their trading establishments up and going on the west bank in 1877. Cattlemen Phillip Bonham and Jack Gorman were there in that same year. John Burns moved his family out to Evan's Creek (now Burns Creek) in 1878. George Grant on Grant's Prairie (at what is now Dunlap Creek) and Eben Slawson at Slawson Creek (now Linden Creek) and their families were established on the west bank of the Yellowstone in 1879. Both George Grant and Vic Smith were known to have been hunting buffalo in eastern Montana Territory by 1873. Mrs. Grant, however, didn't show up until 1879. That may have been the same year when Smith's consort, Fanny, who appeared on the 1880 census, accompanied him from Bismarck to the lower Yellowstone country. [VS, pp. 24–25. See "Vic Smith" in "Old Dawson." Also see *"The Slawson and Grant families"* in Author's Notes following Chapter 21.] On the east side, however, Nathan "Squaw" Brown and his family were the only whites known to be "in residence" (on Belle Prairie) in 1879 and 1880. [See the subject of early settlers in "The Census of 1880" in "Old Dawson."] It was only after July 13, 1880, that graziers started to "lay claim" to various tracts of the open range east of the Yellowstone River to be their exclusive grazing territory.

The "R. H." Ward of Griffin and Ward noted in Dickinson, North

Dakota, history is certainly the same man as Henry Ward of the Ward brothers. [DJ, p. 474.] Dr. Lorman Hoopes noted that Griffin and Ward brought 3,000 head of cattle onto Cottonwood Creek and the Yellowstone River, some twenty-five miles northeast of Glendive, "in the early 1880s." [TLW, p. 144.] Hoopes also noted that "H. R." Ward was the foreman of Griffin and Ward. [TLW, p. 361.] William Mabee wrote that "H. R. Ward, the Cottonwood Creek stockman was in town." [GT, 22 November 1885.] A month later, just two days after Christmas, Mabee took note that "Mrs. H. R. Ward died." [GT, 27 Dec. 1885.] That was the same day that Mabee reported on the passing of "old man Comford," Nick Comford's father. The **101** lasted through the winter of 1886–1887, but, sometime in 1887, Pierre Wibaux bought all of the **101** cattle that survived the "killer winter" and incorporated their range into his rapidly expanding **W**. [See Chapter 15.]

The 1942 letter to Gene Autry: "While I didn't see the robbery itself," Stephen Norton Van Blaricom wrote in a letter to his brother, Fred," I did witness a subsequent murder related to it and that event was never reported in any newspaper, then or since." Almost fifty-eight years after the robbery attempt, on the evening of 12 February 1942, Gene Autry, Hollywood's original singing cowboy, did a national radio broadcast telling of the events surrounding the attempted Fort Buford payroll hold-up. Upon hearing the program, Stephen Norton Van Blaricom wrote immediately to Gene Autry. An excerpt from the letter follows:

February 22, 1942

Salem, Ohio

Dear Mr. Autry:

I was very much interested in your broadcast of last evening. You will no doubt be surprised to hear from a person who was a near eye witness to the holdup you used for your story concerning the government paymaster near Fort Buford in the summer of 1884.

I was a fifteen-year-old boy living at the time on a ranch directly across the Yellowstone River from where the incident occurred. I heard the shooting while it was going on, but I had no idea as to what was taking place. Whatever news we got came to us from Glendive, some forty miles up the river. It was thus several days before we learned what had happened. It was then that we got the complete story.

The would-be robbers killed an Army sergeant who was part of the guard.

When they went to look for their loot…it wasn't there.

What happened next, however, has never been publicized. To make their escape they went directly to the Yellowstone and crossed over to our side, swimming their horses all the way. The current carried them downstream and they came out about a mile below our ranch house. It was here that they perpetrated another tragedy. There was one of their crowd that had something wrong with one of his legs, I have forgotten what. I don't remember whether he was shot or if he had hurt it swimming his horse across the river. There were six or seven of them and had they been robbing a train or a bank, they would not have been so cautious. They had just attempted to rob Uncle Sam's paymaster, however, and had committed a murder in the attempt. Now that was something else again. Whatever the case, they must have figured this fellow would somehow be a marked man. They left him right where they came out from the water with a bullet in his heart.

S. N. Van Blaricom

Salem, Ohio

[The original of this typewritten letter is in the possession of Fred Van Blaricom's daughter, Emma Freeze, of Hamilton, Montana. Written in hand on the bottom of the letter: "Autry used this story about three months ago. I remembered all about it. This is the first draft of the letter I wrote him." Norton sent his brother, Fred, this "first draft" about three months after Autry used Norton's information for a follow-up story on the holdup.]

Don McArthur: killer, victim, or both? Vic Smith, in his memoir written some twenty-five years after the robbery attempt, implicated one of his erstwhile hired men, Don McArthur, as one of the robber gang. Smith described how McArthur had been working for him in the spring of 1881 at his ranch on Beef Slough, a tributary of the Yellowstone about four miles south of Dunlap Creek. McArthur got bucked off a horse and, in the process, crushed his ankle. Smith took him to the Army hospital and doctor at Fort Buford where they amputated his leg just below the knee. According to Smith, it was the bandit "with a peg-leg who demanded the safe." Smith also said it was "the robber with the wooden stump" who did all the shooting during the hold-up. Smith wrapped up his case by stating: "As everyone recognized the wooden stump of the killer, he was arrested and tried at Glendive...McArthur was handed the Scotch verdict: guilty but not proven." [VS, p. x and pp. 98–99.]

No record of the arrest of Don McArthur in Glendive has been found. No record of a trial "Territory of Montana vs. McArthur" has been discovered nor does any other record yet found indicate that anyone was ever tried for the crime.

It may well be that Norton witnessed the murder of Don McArthur. Although he was a relatively well-known figure (it was McArthur who operated the "River House" saloon for some time at the ferry site opposite Glendive), no evidence of the presence of Don McArthur in Glendive or anywhere else after the date of the hold-up has been found.

Lieutenant Colonel Joseph Nelson Garland Whistler: Born in Wisconsin, Whistler had been appointed to West Point from Florida in 1842. He later served as an officer in the Union Army throughout the Civil War. In 1871, Whistler was in charge of the military escort for the first NPRR survey party to venture out to the Yellowstone River and Glendive Creek. [See this subject in "Old Dawson."] He served as commanding officer at the Tongue River post in 1876 while Miles was out in pursuit of the Sioux. In 1882, Whistler became the post commander at Fort Buford. [CE, p. 345.] The *Bismarck Times* reported on 16 May 1884 that he was still the commanding officer at Fort Buford. Lieutenant Colonel Whistler retired from active military service at Fort Buford on 19 October 1886. He spent the rest of his life in St. Paul, Minnesota. [TLW, p. 366.]

Sergeant Aquilla Coonrod, a recipient of the Congressional Medal of Honor, was one of the heroes of the 5th U.S. Infantry Regiment from the "Indian Campaigns" of 1876–1877. He received the Medal of Honor from General William Tecumseh Sherman when Sherman visited the Tongue River Cantonment on 18 July 1877. [TLW, p. 74.] Coonrod was awarded the medal for "Gallantry in action" while serving as a Sergeant with Company "C", 5th U.S. Infantry, at "Cedar Creek, [and Wolf Mountain], etc., Montana Territory, October 1876 to January 1877." [USMHR, p. 732.] Having served in the Union Army during the Civil War (1861–1865), Coonrod was an experienced veteran who had also served with Custer and the 7th U.S. Cavalry prior to 1876. During the Great Sioux War, he was the First Sergeant of "C" Company (Captain Edmond Butler) of the 5th Infantry at the battles of Cedar Creek and Wolf Mountain. [See BSGSW, Chapter 10 and Chapter 14, for Captain Edmond Butler and detailed descriptions of the battles at Cedar Creek and Wolf Mountain.] Prior to his transfer back to the 7th Cavalry, he had been a sergeant in the 2nd U.S. Cavalry in the troop under the command of Captain Hill. [TLW, p. 74.] In 1884, Sergeant Coonrod was in Troop F of the 7th U.S. Cavalry stationed at Fort Buford. On the date of his death, he was the senior NCO in the security detail charged with guarding the Fort Buford payroll. [TLW, p. 74 and p. 366.]

The report of the Assistant Surgeon at Fort Buford, R. W. Johnson, adds some information regarding the events which occurred during the payroll robbery: "...Major Whipple and escort were attacked by road agents about 46 miles from the post. Seven masked road agents sprung up out of a hole and commenced firing into party. Only two shots were fired in return, one highwayman being wounded. Sgt. A. Coonrod, [Troop] F, 7th Cavalry, was killed by two shots (abdominal). Road agents driven off." [CRYC, p. 32.]

Sergeant Aquilla Coonrod was buried in grave #G-233 in the cemetery at Fort Buford. The entry in the cemetery record reads: "Aquilla Coonrod–Sergt. Company F, 7th Cavalry–May 14, 1884–Murdered by Road Agents." Sergeant Coonrod's body was among those one hundred-and-fifty-two transferred from the Fort Buford Cemetery to the Custer Battlefield National Cemetery (near Hardin, Montana) in April of 1896. [CYRC, p. 34.] A military tombstone indicating he was awarded the Congressional Medal of Honor now marks his grave.

"Died. James Birch–Private, Company I, 7th Cavalry–August 13, 1884–Abcess [sic] **of Brain":** While this "cause of death" report of the medical officer at Fort Buford makes no mention that the abscess was a result of the attack on the 14th of May, that event occurred only ninety days prior to Private Birch's death. Whistler's telegram states that Private Birch "was severely wounded in the arm" and he also stated that the wound was received while the private was "in the act of discharging his weapon." Private James Birch was buried in the Fort Buford Cemetery in an unnumbered grave. [CRYC, p. 32.] It is unknown if Private Birch's body was among those transferred from the Fort Buford Cemetery to the Custer Battlefield National Cemetery in April of 1896. The record is not at all clear on this point. [CRYC, p. 34.] It does appear, however, that there was not one soldier but two: Sergeant Acquilla Coonrod and Private James Birch, who died as a result of the Fort Buford payroll robbery of May 1884.

Scott's Ranch: According to Vic Smith (VS, p. 99), Scott's place (a.k.a. the "Halfway House") was a road ranch and stagecoach station under the management of Fred Rounserville (who, along with Frank Muzzy, established the first Yellowstone River woodhawk site in 1876). [See Muzzy and Rounserville in "Old Dawson."] John Heffernan had moved out of Fort Buford in April of 1883 and he had been working at Scott's ranch since that date. Heffernan and a man by the name of A. A. Austill were both at Scott's when Major Whipple, Private Beard, and the ambulance showed up on the 14th of May. Heffernan reported that he, Austill, and Whipple then guarded the payroll until a company of the 7th Cavalry showed up at daylight on the 16th and relieved them.

In 1885, Leeson added further information regarding the robbery: "Three days later [after the robbery attempt] Major Bell, in command of Troop 'F', 7th U.S. Cavalry, found a deserted shack in the woods near the scene, and evidence of recent occupation. The signs discovered gave it the appearance of a regular resort. Ranchmen, while rounding up their cattle, [also] discovered a deserted tent supplied with a new stove, provisions, etc. The tent was pitched on the right bank of the Box Alder [*sic:* Box Elder Creek, on the east side of the Yellowstone not far from the location where Stephen was working]. Alexander McCannon, a horse dealer, was arrested for being an accomplice of the agents." [HML, p. 315.] No record of the arrest or trial of Alexander McCannon has been discovered.

A few years later there were unsubstantiated reports that one or two convicts at the Montana State Prison at Deer Lodge privately confessed their participation in the robbery attempt. It may have been these "confessions" to which Stephen Norton Van Blaricom referred.

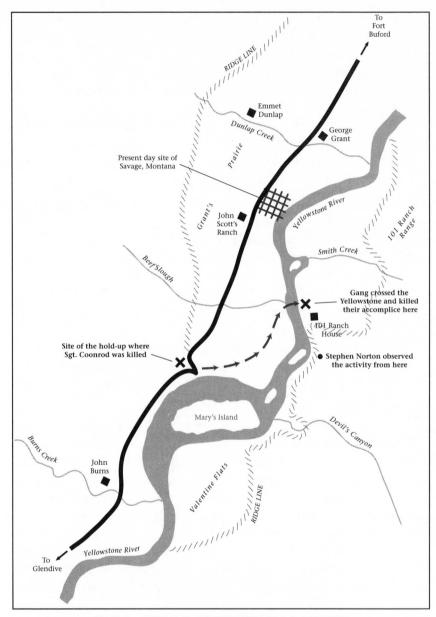

**MAP 6—THE U.S. ARMY PAYROLL ROBBERY
OF MAY 14, 1884**

[NOT TO SCALE]

CHAPTER THIRTEEN

The Stranglers
and Redwater Gold

1884 WAS ALSO THE YEAR THE STRANGLERS showed up. Horse and cattle theft had become so rampant and costly that the livestock growers organized a posse to clean up central and eastern Montana and western Dakota Territory. This vigilante group, about twenty strong and led by "Floppin' Bill" Cantrell, soon became known as the Montana Stranglers. They hanged somewhere between sixty and one-hundred men. Just as their victims were never all accounted for, neither were the actual numbers nor identities of the Stranglers themselves. Depending on who got hanged, the Stranglers were variously regarded as heroes or murderers.[170]

It was claimed that Granville Stuart[171] organized the Stranglers, but nobody could ever prove it. It was also claimed that Teddy Roosevelt[172] volunteered his services for the manhunt but Stuart turned him down, thinking that he would draw too much publicity. The only man I ever knew for sure who had any involvement with the Stranglers was Johnny Goodall[173] from over at Medora. Johnny had a first-class horse named "Snowball" and he delivered Snowball and a dozen more good horses to the

---

[170] See *"'Floppin' Bill' Cantrell and the Montana Stranglers"* in Author's Notes following this chapter for the biography of "Floppin' Bill" Cantrell and a more detailed discussion of the Montana Stranglers.

[171] See *"Granville Stuart"* in Author's Notes following this chapter.

[172] Teddy Roosevelt's ranches, the Maltese Cross, the Elkhorn, and the smaller Triangle, were located on the Little Missouri in Dakota Territory. [TLW, p. 302.] He was, however, a member of the Eastern Montana Live Stock Association (merged with the Montana Stock Grower's Association in 1885) and he made occasional trips to Glendive in that regard. It was through the cattlemen's association that Roosevelt and Stewart became acquaintants.

[173] See *"Johnny Goodall"* in Author's Notes following this chapter.

corrals at Mingusville for the vigilantes to use while they were scouring out that part of the country east of the Yellowstone. Goodall never claimed to have been a part of the Stranglers, but he didn't hide the fact that he supplied them horses.

About fifteen years after the Stranglers came and went, old Charlie Krug[174] told me that the NP had, on one occasion, furnished the Stranglers with two boxcars for their mounts, a good coach for them to ride in, and an engine and a tender. This was long before my time with the NP and I never heard one word of this during my subsequent years with them. But, then, after the event, everyone really clammed up about the Stranglers because no one wanted any of the victims' friends seeking revenge on the participants or their families. Anyway, Charlie said the Stranglers boarded this special train at the first siding east of Billings. As the train moved east, it would be directed to stop here and there and then it would wait at the next siding down the line. After the Stranglers had completed their bloody work, they would return and reboard their little train. This continued all the way down the line to Mingusville and Medora.[175] In addition to both sides of the NP track, the Stranglers also cleaned out the Missouri Breaks. They hit both sides of the Missouri almost from Fort Benton clear down to below the confluence of the Little Missouri in Dakota Territory.

Their deeds done, the Stranglers disappeared as quickly as they arrived, their identities forever shrouded in secrecy. Their work, however, accomplished the desired result, and livestock theft[176] all but disappeared for a number of years.

The other big excitement for the year of 1884 was the gold strike up at the head of the Redwater. Located about sixty miles north and east of Glendive, Redwater Creek was on the north side of the divide that separated the drainage between the Yellowstone and the Missouri rivers. It eventually flowed into Redwater River

---

[174] See *"Charlie Krug"* in Author's Notes following this chapter.

[175] M/M, p. 163. YC, p. 65.

[176] Notice that Stephen Norton Van Blaricom did not use the word "rustler" for any of the Strangler's victims. Although the term was occasionally used to describe a cattle thief or a horse thief, "rustler" more often described "an alert, energetic driving person...a hustler." [TID, p. 1992.] Thus, if Bob was called a "rustler" in the press—and it was a very common term used by newspapers in the West—he was being portrayed as an energetic person who went out, dove into his work, and got things done.

and finally into the Missouri. Jimmy Seeds[177] was one of those early settlers of Dawson County who had arrived about 1880. He was out scouting around the Redwater country when he pulled up some grass not far from the creek and the roots were holding a strong color of gold. It was also evident from some old diggings in the area that someone, years before, had prospected the immediate area. Not being a man of restraint or cool thinking, Jim immediately set out for Glendive. Once there, he rushed around town announcing his "strike." The dust was shaken out of the grass roots and was assayed...and it was, in fact, gold!

Well, to say that the news started a stampede would be understatement. Every old-timer and everybody else who had any means of transport lit out in a cloud of dust. They crossed the Redwater divide on the second day, and by the third day they had the whole length of the Redwater staked out, and that included claims in the creekbed itself. I can remember some of those who shot out of town like bolts of greased lightning: Harry Helms[178] and Henry Dion[179] were in the lead pack. Henry just up and left his wife, Margaret, and Lewis and Harry, their three-year-old and one-year-old sons, in town to mind the store. George Tingle,[180] our Dawson County representative to the Montana Territorial Legislature, was hot on their heels. Even our Dawson County Justice Court Judge John Walton laid down his gavel in a hurry and headed for the Redwater. I'm not so sure, however, that Jim Seeds, who started the whole thing, ever even tried to beat any of them back up there. I believe that old Jimmy just stayed in Glendive and relaxed and had a beer or two while the town emptied out.

Well, word spread far and wide about the Redwater Creek gold strike. It went as far as the Gallatin Valley, because within a week or so Major W. W. Anderson of Bozeman showed up at the "gold fields" to investigate. To make a long story short, nobody ever found a thing. The working men had to make a choice when the gold fever struck: abandon their jobs and not get them back (for

177 See *"James T. Seeds"* in Author's Notes following this chapter.

178 See *"Harry Helms"* in Author's Notes following this chapter.

179 See *"Henry Dion"* in Author's Notes following this chapter.

180 See *"George Tingle"* in Author's Notes following this chapter.

there were men a-plenty looking for work) or stick it out and watch the rich get richer. Jimmy Seeds ultimately turned out to have provided quite a laugh for those who decided not to "fly off in a cloud of (gold) dust," so to speak, but he certainly didn't endear himself to that element of the upper crust who chose to lead the "charge at the Redwater." The story going around town was that Custer himself wouldn't have stood a chance against them. And so ended, in a week or two, the first and last incident of "gold fever" in Dawson County.[181]

Between the middle of November and the first of December, the Yellowstone would begin to ice up. Once that process started, it continued fairly rapidly until it was possible to take horses and wagons across it.[182] During the interim, communications with the west bank were broken since it was impossible to cross the Yellowstone. The reverse happened in the spring. Thus it was that for a couple of months every year, since there was no road on the east side of the Yellowstone (or "south side," if you prefer), there was no movement between Glendive and Miles City except on foot, by horseback, or by train. The only wagon or stagecoach traffic from Glendive was east to Dickinson and Bismarck. Between Glendive and Fort Buford, things could get even worse since the only road north was on the west side of the river. Transportation to Buford would be totally shut down until the river froze sufficiently to allow traffic to cross.

Some mention should be made regarding the Fort Buford ferry. Many people today mistakenly believe it was located at the fort. It wasn't. The site of the Fort Buford ferry was about three miles up the Missouri from the fort, about where the old fur trading post of Fort Union had been located. That's where the names of Fourmile Creek and Twomile Creek on the south side of the Missouri came from. That was the distance on the road to those creeks from where the ferry crossed the Missouri to get you to the Fort Buford side. The ferry was located far enough upstream from the confluence of the Yellowstone and the Missouri so that the continually changing river course at the confluence and below

---

181 W.P.A. files on Dawson County history, Glendive Public Library. Also see OTOL, pp. 962–963.

182 "The river froze over today (Thursday). Foot traffic and teams will be able to cross on Monday if the cold snap continues." [17 November 1900.]

would not affect the landing locations or the cable bracing and anchoring systems necessary at either end of the cable.[183]

Before the ice commenced to form in the fall, the Glendive ferry had to be pulled out of the river and dragged up some distance on the east bank.[184] A number of teams had to be utilized for this task due to the great weight of the ferry. If this had not been done, the massive chunks of ice released by the spring thaw would have crushed the boat into kindling.[185] This scene was repeated every year at all of the ferry sites both up and down the river, Fort Buford, Glendive, Terry, Miles City, and Forsyth.[186]

I cannot leave the year of 1884 without telling you about the miracle of "Jerry the Bum." I never knew his last name and I don't think anybody else did either. He had just shown up in Glendive shortly after my mother died in the early fall of 1882. No one ever saw him work or buy a drink, yet he was always drunk and eating the free sandwiches and soup that the saloons put out for their paying customers. He only had half his teeth and never took a bath or washed his clothes or combed his hair. By the spring of 1883, never having paid for a thing in some six months, he wasn't a popular moocher. He hung around through the spring and summer of 1883 when, to everyone's amazement, he actually cleaned out a few stalls at the local livery and swamped out a saloon or two. It didn't help his sanitation or appearance any, but at least he could pay for his own booze.

It was soon after, early in September, that Jerry got drunk, staggered out of the saloon, and flopped himself down under some sagebrush on the outskirts of town to sleep it off so he could have another run at it tomorrow. Well, this time it was a little different

---

[183] See *"The Fort Buford ferry"* in Author's Notes following this chapter.

[184] See *"The ferry at Glendive"* in Author's Notes following this chapter.

[185] GI, Saturday, 22 November 1884: "The ferryboat was yesterday taken out of the river for the Winter." In later years, not everyone believed in the necessity of pulling the boats out of the river. The result could be disastrous: "In the fall of 1902 or 1903, the (steam-powered ferry boat) *Sam Lilly* was not removed from the (Missouri) River before it froze and when the ice broke up the following spring, the Sam Lilly floated along with the ice and sank (while the owner helplessly watched)." [CE, photo caption, bottom of p. 351.]

[186] Leeson wrote: "(In 1883) the ferry at that point (Terry) is the only means of crossing the Yellowstone between Glendive and Miles City." [HML, p. 536] However, Will Mabee, the editor of the *Glendive Times*, noted that the "Bradford" *[sic]* (the Blatchford) ferry located between Miles City and Terry was operating in 1883, perhaps earlier. [GT, 28 April 1883.] Apparently, "Blatchford" and "Terry" were references to the same ferry at or near Powder River.

because he flopped himself down right on top of a rattlesnake. Come morning, when somebody found him, he wasn't dead but he was puffed up pretty good and he really looked like he was on his way to checking out soon.

Jerry the Bum didn't have any money for a hospital or a doctor anyway, so that put "Doctor" Jim Taylor, our saloon-owning sheriff, in charge. Well, Sheriff Jim had owned the Star Saloon, and that was one of Jerry's hangouts (along with the other ten saloons in town). Sheriff Jim prescribed Jerry's usual, whiskey, and said it would either cure him or kill him, and well or dead, he would either stay with us or go out happy. And in these circumstances, instead of his usual free-loading, the county would pay for Jerry the Bum's booze.

Somebody sent a wire to Father Lindesmith, the Catholic priest at Fort Keogh and Miles City, to come to the Glendive jail and give last rites to his stricken acolyte. How Jerry the Bum had ever communicated to anyone that he was a Catholic or if he really was one will never be known. It could be that he made that decision right after he woke up snake-bit and somehow mumbled it out.[187] In any case, Father Lindesmith came to the Glendive jail to minister to Jerry, who was clearly on his last legs. Well, the next morning the swelling began to subside and some of his normal coloration was starting to return. Within a week the swelling was gone, and Sheriff Taylor had to start reducing the whiskey allotment so that maybe Jerry the Bum would be able to walk out of the jail if he recovered. And recover he did. Father Lindesmith remarked that he was impressed by "the faith and charity" displayed by Jerry, his cellmates, and the sheriff. Believe me when I say that the sheriff, the cellmates, and everyone else in town were a lot more impressed by the results of Father Lindesmith's ministrations of "faith and charity" than their own. Two weeks after Father Lindesmith visited him, Jerry the Bum walked out of the Glendive jail a recovered man (from the snake-bite, that is) and went right back to his slovenly ways.

It was the early summer of 1884 that Jerry finally wore out his welcome. His body odor and the stench from his clothing and his

---

[187] There's little mystery here. Sheriff Jim Taylor and his wife, Ellizabeth ("Lizzie") Gloster, were Catholics. Father Lindesmith had married them near Glendive on 1 June 1882 at the house of the bride's brother, James Gloster. [TLW, p. 338.] In any case, Father Lindesmith was well known for ministering to Catholics and non-Catholics alike.

breath was such that you couldn't get within twenty feet of him. And he was one of those half-obnoxious devils, always wanting to get up close and put his arm around your shoulder to let you know what good friends you were. Once he had you in his grasp, he would then give you a big wink just to let you know that the world was right between the two of you. He would then hang on like a suction cup until you bought him a drink or gave him a coin or two or some other reward to get him unlatched. If the stench didn't put you down, you knew that your life would go well until the next time you ran into him. Finally, even the press started to campaign against his continued tenure in Glendive: "Jerry the Bum must go!" I doubt that Jerry could focus enough to read but that probably wouldn't have made much difference anyway. One day his smelly and beleaguered countenance was just gone. He didn't appear in Miles City so he must have gone on to some bigger venue like Seattle, Minneapolis, Chicago, or St. Louis, where he could simply lose himself in the numbers. All in all, it was a tragedy. Truly, Jerry the Bum's life had been spared by a miracle, yet he could bring himself to change nothing.[188]

---

[188] TLW, "Jerry the Bum," p. 177. "Jerry the Bum must go!" GT, 31 May 1884.

CHAPTER 13–AUTHOR'S NOTES

"Floppin' Bill" Cantrell and the Montana Stranglers:
Formed in 1884 in response to the epidemic of cattle and horse stealing, the "Montana Stranglers" was a vigilante group directly led by William ("Floppin' Bill") Cantrell. With the formation of this group commonly attributed to Granville Stuart of the **DHS** ranch in the Judith Basin, they were also frequently referenced as "Stuart's Stranglers." Estimates put the Stranglers at somewhere between seventeen and forty participants depending on the day and location. [CE, p. 345.] In June and July of 1884, the group (or, perhaps, groups) rode through the Missouri Breaks, central-eastern, and northeastern Montana Territory and continued on into western Dakota Territory. It has been variously estimated that they hanged, shot, or otherwise disposed of between sixty and eighty-seven suspected horse and cattle thieves. Some writers have put the death toll at one-hundred or more. Whatever the body count, not all of their victims were proven thieves or even "wanted" bad men. As a result, many people, the famed buffalo hunter Vic Smith among them, regarded Cantrell and the Stranglers as a brigade of murderers.

Floppin' Bill Cantrell has been frequently identified as the nephew of the infamous Civil War raider William Clarke Quantrill (of "Quantrill's Raiders" who torched Lawrence, Kansas, in 1863). Born in Arkansas about 1849, Cantrell was known to have been a woodcutter on the upper Missouri River in the Dakota Territory by 1869. A large man even at twenty, his friends at the Toughtimber wood yard initially called him "Big Bill." [KL, pp. 273–276.]

Bill was an experienced woodcutter with an unusual, almost artistic way of handling an ax. In his "droll native Arkansas twang" he described his style as "floppin' the ax." His friends applied the term as a sobriquet and thereafter he became known on the upper Missouri River as "Floppin' Bill" Cantrell. In 1870, he worked a short time as a laborer at the Fort Berthold agency and later was one of the witnesses who testified at the Reeder murder trial in Yankton. By 1872, he had located a claim on property adjoining the village of Burleigh (south and east of the present Bismarck). When the railroad did arrive, the route took it farther north and Burleigh dried up and blew away. Along with Bismarck's success went Bill's hope for making a fast fortune in the real estate business. [KL, pp. 273–276.]

Cantrell sold out for a few dollars in 1873 and worked his way up the river to Fort Peck. While watering a few head of the trading post's cattle outside the post compound, Bill and his companion were ambushed by five Sioux. Before the affair was over, Cantrell had been shot through the groin. "For several months...Cantrell lay in the surgeon's care at the Fort Buford military hospital. His case was a critical one, but a robust physique pulled him through." A few months later, he showed up in the Fort Peck country again, this time operating his own woodhawk site. "Matrimonially inclined he had 'spliced up' with a fair daughter of the Assinaboine [sic] tribe, and with a good team of ponies and ready wood sales to passing steamers, the Cantrell establishment seemed in a prosperous way." [KL, pp. 273–276.]

Around 1875, as the Canadian Mounties started closing down the forty or so establishments that comprised the "Fort Whoop Up" (Fort Hamilton) whiskey trade up north in the Cypress Hills country, many of the really rough elements of that crowd relocated themselves in the Missouri River Breaks. "A regular line [of thieves, murderers, whiskey traders, and river pirates] was established along the Missouri as far as Bismarck. They established themselves at some wood yards by either buying out or running out the owner if they could not trust him. One of the first that was tabooed by these gentry was Floppin' Bill." [KL, pp. 273–276.] First they stole his team. He replaced them. The outlaws returned and set him afoot again. This time Cantrell thought his horses had only strayed so he went out on foot to search for them. When he returned, his "South Assinnaboine [sic] bride did not come out to greet him as was her usual way." Bill never saw her again nor did he ever discover her fate. When Cantrell discovered the kidnapping of his wife, Joseph Henry Taylor wrote "[he] could only seat himself down on his deserted door step and cry. And yet—short as that time was—while he sat down a Dr. Jekyll, he arose a Mr. Hyde." [KL, pp. 273–276.] Thus, when Granville Stuart decided to assemble his vigilante group in 1884, he found a willing, vengeful, and merciless leader in the person of Floppin' Bill Cantrell.

It has long been assumed that Cantrell and his vigilante group were covertly aided and abetted by various members of the Eastern Montana Live Stock Association and that included a number of prominent Dawson County and Glendive cattlemen. Reece

Anderson, a foreman at one of Granville Stuart's ranches, was identified as a leading participant by Vic Smith and Dr. Lorman Hoopes. [VS, p. 137 and p. 139. TLW, p. 6.] (This is the same Reece Anderson who, along with brothers James and Granville Stuart, made the first recorded discovery of gold in Montana at Gold Creek in 1858. [M/M, p. 64.] It is doubtful that Anderson himself ever actually rode with the Stranglers; it appears that he was simply the "contact man" between Granville Stuart and Cantrell.) Hermann Hagedorn reported that Louis La Pache, a French-Canadian horse thief awaiting trial in Miles City, was bailed out of jail and engaged as Cantrell's guide. [RBL, p. 195.] Dr. Lorman Hoopes wrote that A. W. "Gus" Adams, the Miles City–based stock inspector and range detective was "the only outsider to go along with the vigilantes as they cleaned out eastern Montana Territory." [TLW, p. 1.]

The Gus Adams named by Dr. Hoopes is the same Gus Adams of "Adams and Christie, the new blacksmiths in Glendive," who were announced in the GT on 13 April 1882. In 1884, Adams was working out of Miles City as "a stock detective and range detective" for various ranchers of eastern Montana Territory. [TLW, p. 1.] He may have been an employee of the Eastern Montana Stockgrowers Association (a.k.a. the Eastern Montana Livestock Association), the organization formed by Granville Stuart and others in Miles City on 12 October 1883. [TLW, p. 101.] (A substantially older organization, the Eastern Montana Protective Association had merged with the Montana Stock Grower's Association concurrent with the latter's first meeting on 15 August 1882. [TLW, p. 256.]) In such a role, Adams would have been familiar with the prime suspects and their locations, especially in the Miles City, Missouri River Breaks, and Glendive areas.

While a few of the ranchers who provided horses and supplies to the Stranglers let their names be known, none of the actual participants of the vigilante group (aside from Floppin' Bill Cantrell, Reece Anderson, Louis La Pache, and Gus Adams) were ever positively identified. Johnny Goodall, the Marquis de Mores' young ranch foreman, openly admitted to providing horses to the group when they stopped in Mingusville (TLW, p. 139) and Bill Conley, who later ranched around Dickinson, told John Leakey that he was a "horse wrangler" for the Stranglers but "didn't know what they were up to until later." [WTW–TM, p. 137. TLW, p. 71.]

WILLIAM "FLOPPIN' BILL" CANTRELL, CIRCA 1886
PHOTO COURTESY OF THE MONTANA HISTORICAL SOCIETY RESEARCH CENTER PHOTOGRAPH ARCHIVES, HELENA

Hermann Hagedorn wrote that both Theodore Roosevelt and the Marquis de Mores met Granville Stuart in Glendive in June of 1884 and attempted to enlist in the active pursuit of the rustlers. Stuart reportedly turned them down, fearing both the publicity they would bring as well as what he perceived to be their potential for being "loose cannons." Hagedorn also speculated, as many contemporaries believed, that the Stranglers were not a single group of men under Cantrell's leadership at all, but that Stuart had established and directed additional groups who quickly assembled themselves in various locations and followed the precedent set by Floppin' Bill and his cohorts up on the Missouri River and elsewhere. There were also rumored to be renegade "copy cat" groups who used the opportunity to settle old scores or to take care of "nester" problems created by small settlers who built by water holes or in the more lush pasture areas or otherwise simply interfered with the established concept of an "open" range. [RBL, pp. 146–147.] Finally, there were the rumored "Texas Cowboy Stranglers," a group of twenty-eight Texans supposedly "hired by the stockmen of Montana" who worked the Yellowstone River country from the area of modern Livingston to somewhere between Miles City and Glendive. After hanging their first victim, the Texans reportedly split up into seven groups of four, each group led by a Montanan familiar with the lay of the land, and they set out to "earn their 'bonus,'" ultimately shooting or hanging six men. [HABS, p. 596.]

The Stranglers started their activities with a bang in June of 1884. Cantrell and his men swept into the notorious nest of reprobates and cattle thieves located at Bates Point in the Missouri River Breaks led by "Stringer Jack" (John Stringer). Several of the eleven outlaws were shot dead, and the rest were taken from the deputy sheriff into whose custody they had fled for "protection" and were hanged. The group continued on down the Missouri, disposing of victims as they went. Soon there were hangings and shootings in the Powder River country, the lower Yellowstone, and on into Dakota Territory, especially along the Little Missouri. Some claimed that Stuart himself joined another group of vigilantes on the lower Yellowstone. "That band, whose activities have been lastingly veiled in secrecy, ran a special train down the Northern Pacific tracks, stopping periodically to deal with rustlers." [M/M, p. 163.]

Vic Smith claimed there were eighty-three known victims, not all of them guilty. Among them were seven men "arrested" at Poplar who claimed to be miners but who were turned over to Cantrell by Captain Rhode, the Army officer in charge at Poplar. Smith also named as victims Evan ("Eddie") Bronson (the son of Lieutenant Nelson Bronson, an officer at Fort Buford), Jack Williamson, a former scout for Colonel John Gibbon during the pursuit of the Nez Perce in 1877, and Bill Close, an associate of Williamson. [VS, p. 138.]

Jack Williamson had a record of being a man with cool nerve. In addition to the Nez Perce campaign, Williamson had served as a courier and dispatch rider for both Gibbon and Terry prior to and during the Sioux wars of 1876 and 1877. He had accompanied the Gibbon column that departed Fort Shaw (in the Sun River country) in search of the Sioux in spring of 1876. While they were on the Yellowstone in May, they attempted to hook up with General Terry, who was presumed to be in the vicinity of Glendive Creek or Powder River. Near the Rosebud on 27 May 1876, "a skiff was put in good order, supplied with extra oars and with padded oarlocks, and this evening, just after dark, sailed on its venturesome voyage, the crew consisting of citizen Williamson and two soldiers of Captain Clifford's company, Bell and Stewart, who had volunteered for the service." The dispatches were safely delivered. [MMC, p. 126 and p. 138.]

Vic Smith wrote that Jack Williamson and Bill Close were riding together in the same wagon somewhere between Fort Buford and Poplar and both were "shot dead on their wagon seat and their horses appropriated." [VS, p. 138.]

Smith also told of another victim, a "perfect gentleman…named Downs, a recluse of probably sixty years of age," who lived alone with his "well stocked library of choice books" in his "neat cabin" along the Missouri River near that stream's confluence with the Musselshell. [VS, pp. 138–139.] Tom Donovan recounted that William "Billy" Downs was hanged along with Charley Owens on 4 July 1884, both charged with: "Aiding and abetting horse thieves and for being in possession of stolen horses, cattle and hides." [HABS, p. 594.]

The oral history of Glendive also recounts the hanging of John F. Butler: "John Butler was hanged by the Stranglers on the west side of the Yellowstone. It occurred right near the ferry and he was left for dead. Lucky for him, his wife had seen the whole thing, followed them and cut him down right after the Stranglers left. He always wore a neckerchief, a scarf or a high collar to hide the scars." [Elmond Anderson to correspondent John Steffen.] Following his narrow escape, John F. Butler worked many years for the various owners of the water delivery company that hauled water from the Yellowstone to the houses and businesses of the town. John Butler was born in Rice County, Minnesota, on 23 September 1859. He worked on farms in Minnesota until he married Theresa Kehoe. Hoping to find work, they arrived in Glendive on 9 May 1881, just before the railroad arrived. Known locally as "Water John," he could be seen with his team tugging either a stoneboat or a small wagon full of fifty-gallon barrels around Glendive. [PA, p. 34.] He finally bought the company around 1899. In an ironic twist of fate, John Butler bought the water wagon of Joe Hurst while Hurst was being tried for the murder of the Dawson County Sheriff Dominic Cavanaugh. [GI, 25 March 1899.] Hurst was later convicted and hanged in front of the Dawson County Jail in Glendive. [See the story of Dominic Cavanaugh and Joe Hurst in THWT.] John F. Butler was appointed to be the postmaster of Glendive on 11 January 1916 and he served until he retired from that position in 1919. Mr. Butler died in Glendive in 1922 at about the age of sixty-three. [PA, p. 34. Also see OTOL, p. 62.]

Along with many others, Vic Smith found Cantrell's and the Stranglers' activities totally reprehensible. Smith sent out word that he would kill Cantrell "on sight." The two men apparently never met since Vic Smith claimed that Cantrell was gored to death by a steer in the Kansas City stockyards "some fifteen years later" (or about 1899). Other sources state Cantrell was hit and killed by a train in Kansas City in 1901. [VS, pp. 137–139 and pp. 233–234.]

There are almost as many versions of the Stranglers and their victims as there have been men who told the tale. Unlike their more famous and earlier Virginia City counterparts, none of the secretive vigilantes of 1884 ever admitted their participation to anyone, and they carried the names of their accomplices, and many of their victims, to their graves. The lifelong silence of the participants, the likelihood of splinter groups not authorized by nor under the control of Granville Stuart, Reece Anderson, or Floppin' Bill Cantrell, and the very real prospect of the presence of "copy cat" groups carrying out their own agendas will make it forever impossible for historians to identify the Montana Stranglers or to accurately recount the scope of their deeds.

Granville Stuart was born 27 August 1834 in Clarksburg, Virginia (later West Virginia). The family moved to Iowa in 1837. His father was one of the "49ers" who went to California during the gold rush. The father returned in 1851, picked up Granville, Granville's brother, James, and returned to California. Reece Anderson, Granville Stuart, and his brother, James, left California and headed to Montana in 1857 and spent that winter (1857–1858) in the Beaverhead Valley. They struck gold at Gold Creek in 1860, and that is believed to be the first real evidence of gold in Montana. In 1879, Stuart got into the cattle business with the Davis Brothers and S. T. Hauser. They named their ranch the **DHS** (Davis, Hauser, and Stuart). In the company of Tom Irvine (the sheriff of Custer County), Stuart scoured central Montana for a ranch site. He finally selected one in the Judith country. (The army established Fort Maginnis at the upper end of the **DHS** hay meadows later that same year.) In 1883,

Conrad Kohrs bought out the Davis brothers and Hauser. While Kohrs kept the **DHS** brand, he changed the name of the ranch to the Pioneer Cattle Company. Stuart stayed on as one-third owner and manager. In June and July of 1884, according to Dr. Lorman Hoopes, Stuart was the "active head of the vigilantes secretly approved by the eastern Montana Territory ranchers plus those of western Dakota Territory, who contributed riders, horses, supplies and money to rid the countryside [meaning central and eastern Montana Territory and western Dakota Territory] of horsethieves, in particular, and rustlers in general." [TLW, p. 334.] The **DHS** was running about 40,000 head of cattle in 1886. When spring came, following the disastrous winter of 1886–1887, the **DHS** cowboys could only find some 7,000 alive. Stuart got out of the cattle business shortly thereafter. [See ABTW for the complete biography of Granville Stuart.]

Johnny Goodall: John W. ("Johnny") Goodall was born 30 September 1857 in Portland, Oregon. He returned with his family to Missouri in 1868. The family moved to the Snake River country in Idaho in 1871, then, in 1872, to Baker County, Oregon, where his father got into the freighting business. He farmed with his father until 1876, when he hooked up as a rider for Tyler, Tennen, and Armstrong, a Texas cow outfit. In 1880, he hired on with Mason and Lovell at their ranch located on the Big Horn River in Montana Territory. In August of 1883, Lovell sold three-thousand head to Haupt, a buyer for the Marquis de Mores. Lovell then recommended Goodall to de Mores as a young man capable of running the ranch the Marquis was assembling. Goodall got the job and became the ranch's foreman at the relatively young age of twenty-six.

In the summer of 1884, John Goodall personally delivered fifteen of the top horses from the Marquis de Mores' ranch to the Montana Stranglers at Pierre Wibaux's corrals in Mingusville. In 1885, Billings County, Dakota Territory, was formed and John Goodall became one of the county's first three commissioners. In 1886, he was named foreman of the Little Missouri roundup. That same year, he married Mary Coleman. During the winter of 1886–1887, his "savvy" pulled the herd of the Marquis de Mores through without the great losses suffered by most of the other ranches. In 1887, after the Marquis permanently left his Medora property, Goodall opened a livery stable in Dickinson, Dakota Territory. [TLW, pp. 138–139.]

John Leakey reported that Johnny Goodall was the foreman at "old man" Lovell's ranch, the **ML** in western Dakota, in 1893. [WTW–TM, p. 92.] (This was probably the same "Lovell" of "Mason and Lovell," the very early Custer County cow outfit Goodall worked for on the Big Horn River in 1880.) Goodall was also known to have worked as foreman for the **7–7** (7-Bar-7), another Dakota ranch. [WTW–TM, p. 174.] Leakey also mentioned that John Goodall had been among the "sheriffs and deputies" who showed up at Leakey's ranch in 1901 on the search for one Bill Clark, a known rustler. [WTW–TM, p. 152.]

Charlie Krug was born in Ohio on 1 November 1846. He went to work in railroad construction in 1868. His sister, Emma, was a severe asthmatic and he moved around trying to find her some relief: Colorado, Arizona, New Mexico, and Utah. In 1877, Krug and a companion made the hazardous journey through Indian country from Red Rock, Utah, to the Tongue River Cantonment, Montana Territory (the post which preceded Fort Keogh), and then on to Mandan, Dakota Territory. There he went to work for the NP. Charlie came into Glendive as the train conductor on the first train to arrive on 5 July 1881. In that same year, he bought one of the first cottages built in Glendive and sent for his sister. In addition to working for the railroad, Krug started raising cattle and, over the next few years, increased his herd substantially.

George McCone mentioned that "Mr. Charles Krug, of Glendive, was employed" at a Northern Pacific surveying camp in eastern Dakota Territory in July 1879, when McCone arrived carrying two wounded mail carriers in his Bismarck–Miles City mail service buckboard. The two men, Green and Donovan, had been shot by a small group of Sioux some thirty-five miles southeast of Krug's survey crew. McCone, who found the men the day after they were attacked, knew that Krug and his men were the nearest to assist them. Green "suffered intense agony" and died within an hour of his arrival at the NP camp. Donovan, however, recovered fully from his wounds. McCone noted that he and Charlie Krug would frequently get together in later years and recount the stories of those early days. [From "Green River to Little Beaver," p. 4 as compiled in SGJC.]

Krug reportedly spoke fluent German. Richard R. Hein, who

descended from German immigrants, wrote: "Some of this [stories of the early days in eastern Montana and western Dakota Territory] was in German as Mr. Krug spoke German well." [YC, p. 57.]

The winter of 1886–1887 wiped out his hard-earned cattle operation, so the following years he switched primarily to sheep. By 1900, Krug was one of the biggest ranchers in Montana Territory, running 25,000 head of sheep, 1,000 head of cattle, and 250 horses. He once owned some fifty-four sections (34,560 acres) of land and became, by reputation at least, Glendive's first millionaire.

Charlie was well known and respected for his charitable spirit. Many neighbors told how "Mr. Krug" had given them loads of hay or otherwise helped them out—or, in some cases, literally saved them, during some of the "tough winters and tough times." All of them agreed that Charlie Krug never asked for nor received one penny for his benevolence. [YC, pp. 53–54.] Marie MacDonald speculated that it was Charlie Krug's attitude that saved the Glendive banks during the banking panic of 1919. Charlie was the president of the Merchants National Bank. "A reputed millionaire, Mr. Krug publicly declared that if necessary he would use every penny he had to keep his bank solvent and [he was prepared to] go out of Glendive [just] as broke as he had entered." [GHMT, p. 56.]

It wasn't that Charlie didn't know how to save a penny here and there. Before he built his home in Glendive, Charlie lived on his ranch, the .K (Dot K), not far from Marsh (south of Glendive). [MSD, p. 157.] He would frequently flag down the train at his ranch and ride into either Marsh or Glendive. There he invariably visited with some of the old timers, and they would tell of their Indian adventures, mutually lament the extinction of the buffalo, and rue the coming of the "honyockers" (slang for homesteaders who were farmers rather than livestock grazers). Either through his past service to the railroad or because of his acquaintance with so many of the employees of the Northern Pacific, it was noticed by many, especially the children, that Charlie never had to purchase a ticket. "We heard that Mr. Krug could flag down any train [bound for any destination] and not need a ticket." Krug was by local reputation a very wealthy man "and listening to all that talk made us kids think that he owned the railroad." Well, it turned out (much to the chagrin of Glendive's younger set) that Charlie Krug didn't own the Northern Pacific, but to everyone "he was one nice old man." [Richard Hein in YC, p. 56.]

In 1900, at age fifty-four, Charlie Krug married his thirty-two-year-old housekeeper, Mrs. Annie (Hackney) Ketchum, a recently divorced lady with two daughters. ["Decree of divorce to Annie Ketchum on grounds of willful neglect." GI, 20 May 1899.] They then had five children (three boys and two girls), born between 1901 and 1909. In 1907, he built a twenty-five-room brick home in Glendive on the corner of Bell and Douglas. Herbert C. Chivers, a well-known architect from St. Louis, designed the neoclassical-style mansion. (The home, now a bed-and-breakfast, still stands at 103 North Douglas Street.) After moving into town, Charlie served as the president of Merchant's National Bank in Glendive and was active in milling and other economic activities. He was known to have invested in Seattle real estate during the Alaska gold rush.

Charlie Krug suffered a stroke in 1926. After living three years almost totally paralyzed and partially blind, he died on 6 December 1929 at the age of eighty-three. He was buried in the Glendive (Dawson County) cemetery. Annie Krug, Charlie's wife, lived until 20 November 1950, when she died in Glendive at the age of eighty-two. [OTOL, pp. 179–181. TLW, p. 192. GTHG, pp. 40–41.]

James T. Seeds came to Montana in the 1870s. According to his niece Lavilla (Seeds) Rapp, Jim, born about 1853, was once a scout and interpreter for the 7th Cavalry and Colonel George Armstrong Custer. [OTOL, p. 254.] Seeds is found on the 1880 U.S. Census for Dawson County as "Seeds, James T., age 27, born Missouri." He was shown as a laborer (woodcutter) boarding with "Henry J. Blount, age 39," a "woodyard operator" on the Yellowstone. Hoopes reported that Seeds became a stockman in Dawson County around 1881. [TLW, p. 314.] Around 1940, a W.P.A compiler wrote: "Mr. Seeds was one of the first white men to locate in eastern Montana in 1880. Being an ex-soldier he was fond of scouting around and one day [in 1884] he found gold in the shape of colors which were at the grass roots [on the bank of the Redwater]." [OTOL, p. 962. Also see the "Works Progress Administration files of Dawson County History" received from "Professor Burlingame of Bozeman, Montana," located in the Glendive Public Library.]

Seeds didn't go through life trouble free. In December of 1885 Jimmy

Seeds cut his foot severely while chopping wood. [GT, 6 December 1885.] Two years later "J. T. Seeds had a dispute with the [Northern Pacific Railroad] Superintendent's colored porter, who finally pulled a revolver. Seeds hit him over the head with an iron bar. Seeds has been charged and will stand trial." [GI, 20 August 1887.]

Regardless of the outcome of the trial (unknown), Seeds apparently maintained a gift for hyperbole. Marie MacDonald quoted James T. Seeds' description of the effects of immigration in the early 1900s: "He said that one day he crossed the flat between Deer Creek and Lower Seven Mile that was entirely vacant and on his return within six hours he saw one man erecting a new building, another on an adjoining claim unloading lumber, while a third on another claim was plowing." [GHMT, p. 42.]

Harry Helms was born 8 October 1840 in Cincinnati, Ohio. When he was age nine, his family moved to Indianapolis. At the age of eighteen, around 1858, Harry became a ship's carpenter. He then worked for a number of years on various paddle wheelers plying the Mississippi and its tributaries. In 1876, he was the carpenter on the *E. H. Durfee* (Captain Robert Mason) that came up the Yellowstone to the Big Horn and returned the remnants of Reno's troops (Morris Cain among them) to Fort Lincoln.

In 1880, after twenty-one years of working as a carpenter on the steamboats and after many trips on the Missouri and the Yellowstone, Harry selected the new townsite of Glendive in which to open his restaurant (The Bon-Ton Restaurant) and his landmark saloon (The Bon-Ton Saloon). For a period of time, at least through January of 1882, the proprietorship of the saloon was shown as "Helms & Shortsleeves." No one could ever identify who "Shortsleeves" was. Many suspected it was Harry himself. Not known as an idle man, Harry was willing to "roll up his sleeves" and tackle any job that needed to be done. Helms reveled in the "Shortsleeves" mystery. "You'll meet him one day," was Harry's typical comment.

Harry married Lizzie May of Minneapolis in Glendive in 1883. Their only child, Gertrude, was born in Glendive in April of 1892. [Dawson County Marriage Licenses, OTOL, p. 509.]

Helms lost his wood-frame building during the huge fire of March 1886 that destroyed much of downtown Glendive. Helms and Mickey Farrell teamed up to rebuild and decided to build a

HARRY HELMS, 1896
ILLUSTRATION BY ANGEL CERVANTES

new frame building for Farrell on "Farrell's old corner." Harry, an experienced carpenter, built the framing and interior for the new building himself. Harry also decided to locate a new brick building on his old property. Although it was common knowledge that he and Henry Dion got into a race to see which of them would open Glendive's first brick structure (Harry Helms laid the first brick on 27 June 1886; Henry Dion started the next day), "history does not record how the race between Helms and Dion turned out."

When Harry rebuilt, he put both his restaurant and saloon in the same building. Despite the fact that the restaurant and saloon operations had separate doors, once inside, patrons discovered they shared common floor space. (This was a fairly common setup. Mickey Farrell's had the same floor plan.) His new ad read: "Go to Harry's Bonton Restaurant for meals, wines, liquors, and cigars." Grace Marron Gilmore recalled: "The proprietor of the Bonton was Harry Helms, a little short fat man, whose main pastime was passing drinks over the bar and sunning himself in front of his place of business. I can see him yet, sitting in his armchair with his white apron on, greeting his many friends as they passed." Wilbur Tuttle, who was six years old when he left Glendive in 1889, also remembered Harry Helms, but more especially his parrot: "A man named Harry Helms owned a famous saloon on main street. Out in front of the place hung a caged parrot, which was a novel attraction at that time. If you walked past the swinging doors at the front of the saloon and didn't go in, the parrot would yell out: 'If you don't like Harry's whiskey, you can go to Hell!'" Tuttle also recalled that things could get exciting pretty fast there on the main drag by Harry's place: "We had a hired girl. I was about six years old and she was leading me by the hand up the main street. [Suddenly] the street was filled with wild cattle [and] wild cowboys...shooting wild. My dad [Hank Tuttle, the Dawson county sheriff] was normally a mild, cool-blooded man, but he yelled: 'Katy, get that damned kid off the street before some cowboy shoots him!' Katy could take a hint. She had hold of my left hand, and I'll swear that no part of my body ever touched the ground on the way home. I swayed out behind her like the tail of a kite."

In addition to his social acumen, Harry was well known for his stable of fine-blooded stock, particularly harness horses and trotters. Hoopes noted that Helms was "a great hand at harness horse breeding."

One cannot write about Harry Helms without mention of his great friend and partner, Fred Volkert. Born in Germany 10 December 1857, Volkert had immigrated to Baltimore with his parents, four brothers, and two sisters in 1872. His father died in 1877 and his mother died in 1878. Young Fred ended up in Chicago, where he worked for a year or so in a picture-framing factory. He found his way to Minneapolis in 1880 and then went on to Bismarck in March of 1881. He worked for his passage on a steamboat up the Missouri and the Yellowstone in the summer of 1882, got off in Glendive, and took work that fall as the janitor at the temporary courthouse. (Dawson County was organized in September of 1882. In June of 1883, the county commissioners let the contract to W. S. Hurst to build the first "proper" courthouse. Hurst was to have the work completed by 1 October 1883. [GT, 30 June 1883.] The *Glendive Times* then reported on 27 October 1883 that Mr. Hurst was nearing the completion of his work on the courthouse. In the meantime, between September of 1882 and November of 1883, the Dawson County Courthouse functioned in an informal temporary location.)

Fred took out a claim on Cracker Box Creek and accumulated two-and-a-half sections of deeded land. He also got into the saloon business on Bell Street in Glendive and, according to acquaintances, Fred ran the saloon like a private business and professional men's club. Around 1890, Harry Helms and Fred Volkert became partners in the wholesale liquor business. During this partnership they built a fine brick structure from which to conduct their business on Bell Street. A staunch Democrat, Harry was elected Dawson County Commissioner in 1892. He, Lizzie, and Gertrude were still living in Glendive at the turn of the century. Sometime after 1900, Harry Helms died and, in 1920, Fred Volkert donated their partnership's "splendid property" on Bell Street to the Elks Club (as it was known during the 1930s and later as "the Elk's Home"). Fred never married and he retained a life estate in an apartment in the Elk's building. He lived the last five years of his life in Florida and California. Mr. Volkert died in California on 18 November 1928 at the age of seventy. At his request, he was brought back to Glendive for burial.

Grace Gilmore recalled that Fred Volkert "remembered the undernourished school children of our city with a milk fund that will provide milk for our 'kiddies' for all time." In fact, Mr. Volkert left quite a substantial trust fund to Glendive School District No. 1 and gave the district quite a bit of latitude in their use of the funds as long as the money was used to assist needy children. In addition to milk and hot lunches, the Volkert Trust has paid for a wide range of services and products through the years. Among them have been orthopedic braces, dental work, eyeglasses, surgical removal of tonsils and adenoids, cod liver oil, orange juice, and ovaltine. Even following those expenditures over a period of fifty-seven years, the trust had grown to a balance of $115,000 in 1987.

[OTOL, p. 132, pp. 312–313 and "Dawson County Marriage Licenses," p. 509. TLW, p. 158 and p. 317. USC, Dawson County, 1900. Wilbur Tuttle in MTMN, pp. 8–9. Grace Marron Gilmore in IVEM, Thursday, 19 December 1935.]

Henry Dion was born 7 September 1846 in Quebec, Canada, the sixth of eleven children. He came to the United States in 1867 and began contracting and building water tanks for the Union Pacific Railroad as far west as Cheyenne. In 1872, he went to Dakota

Territory to help build Fort Abraham Lincoln. In 1875 he joined the first wagon train into the Black Hills to search for gold. In 1877, he returned to Quebec to visit his family after an absence of ten years.

Returning to the United States in March of 1878, Dion ended up in Miles City, where he stayed a year. In the spring of 1879, he returned to Bismarck, where he set himself up in the saloon business. He took his tent and then followed the railroad construction crews until 9 December 1881, when he opened a combination billiard hall, liquor "sampling" room, and general store in Glendive. In a service performed by Father Lindesmith in Miles City, Henry, age thirty-six, married Mrs. Margaret (O'Connor) Elliot, age nineteen, on 7 September 1882. Previously married, Margaret already had a son, Louis, born in February of 1881. Through the years, Henry and Margaret had four children, three boys and a girl. Appointed by Governor Potts in September of 1882, Henry Dion was Dawson County's first sheriff, a position he held for three months. (James Taylor, elected sheriff in the county's first elections, held in November of 1882, took office in January, 1883.) Dion was one of Glendive's most active promoters and investors during the early years of the town. Always very active in politics, he was the county treasurer (1895 only) and a county commissioner (1909–1913). Henry died in Glendive on 1 November 1920 at the age of seventy-four. [OTOL, p. 2 and pp. 88–89. MISB, pp. 1,144–1,145. TLW, p. 94. USC, Dawson County, 1900.]

George Tingle came to Glendive to replace Nelson E. Lawrence as the land agent for both the NPRR and Lewis Merrill's Yellowstone Land and Colonization Company. Although Tingle was a "short-timer" in Glendive, he had a most varied and interesting career. He and his family arrived in Glendive in the last week of June 1882. Obviously a close associate with Lewis Merrill, the GT reported on 6 July 1882: "Mr. Tingle secured Gen. Merrill's cottage into which he at once moved." The same article also pointed out that Mr. Tingle was once the sheriff of Wheeling, West Virginia. He was appointed Dawson County's first clerk and recorder in September of 1882. With the election of November 1882, he became Dawson County's first representative to the Montana Territorial Legislature. He was a charter member of the Protestant Episcopal Society of Glendive, organized in the fall of 1882. On 10 September 1883, he represented the Territory of Montana at the World's Exposition. In November of 1884, Tingle was re-elected to the Montana Territorial House of Representatives from Dawson County.

On 9 May 1885, the *Glendive Times* reported: "The Hon. George R. Tingle, who received the appointment of Chief Seal Agent of Alaska, left in company with his family Sunday evening for San Francisco...." [OTOL, p. 304.]

The Fort Buford ferry: Early in the Sioux campaign of 1876, the steamboats conveying troops, horses, and supplies simply chugged past Fort Buford and went on up the Yellowstone as far as the Tongue River Cantonment. ("Tongue River Cantonment" wasn't renamed "Fort Keogh" until after General W. T. Sherman's insistence on a name change in official correspondence dated 25 July 1877. [Sherman to McCrary letter cited in YComm, p. 224 and YComm, Footnote 12, p. 297.]) Recognizing the forthcoming dilemma of maintaining his supply lines as the water level in the Yellowstone receded, it was on 5 September 1876 that General Terry ordered the construction of the Glendive Cantonment on the west side of the Yellowstone. "All the time [during the late fall and winter of 1876 and the spring of 1877], wagon trains from the Glendive Cantonment made frequent trips to and from Fort Buford to get goods and foodstuffs to sustain the garrisons upstream." [YComm, p. 81.] In addition to large and frequent military wagon trains, a civilian outfit, the Diamond R Freight Company, was using the Fort Buford–Glendive Cantonment–Tongue River Cantonment route for ox trains by the fall of 1876. [YComm, p. 73.] Prior to the Sioux campaign of 1876–1877, there was no road up the Yellowstone. Since there were no settlements in eastern Montana Territory except for distant Bozeman, there had been no need for a ferry across the Missouri.

Initially, steamboats provided the ferry service across the Missouri River for the military, men, horses, equipment, and supplies moving between Fort Buford and the Yellowstone River trail leading to the Glendive Cantonment and the upriver posts at Tongue River (Fort Keogh) and the Little Big Horn (Fort Custer). Sometime during the Sioux campaign or immediately thereafter, a cable ferry was installed across the Missouri River near the old site of Fort Union. Known as the Fort Buford ferry, that underwater cable-operated system lasted for a number of years. (The underwater cable allowed the paddle wheelers to pass over it and not interfere with the river's traffic. What is not known is whether the Fort Buford ferry was a horse-drawn or steam-powered arrangement or whether, like the Yellowstone River ferries, it simply relied on the river's current to propel it across.) Young Tom Jarvis, age twenty-eight, and several helpers were operating the Fort Buford ferry when John Burns took the Dawson County census in June of 1880. [USC, Dawson County, 1880.] Since Tom Courchene (a.k.a. Tom Cushing) and Alex Ayotte were known to have been the owners of the Fort Buford ferry about 1880, it is likely that Jarvis and his assistants were employees of Cushing and Ayotte.

On some unknown date, but sometime around 1890, the steam-powered ferry *Sam Lilly* was put into use. As well as transporting civilians and freight, the *Sam Lilly* was known to have been used "for a number of years" to transport civilian traffic in general and soldiers from Fort Buford back and forth across the Missouri. [CE, p. 351.] Fort Buford was closed and abandoned as a military post on 1 October 1895 [CE, p. 345] and the *Sam Lilly* sank, crushed by ice, during the spring break-up in 1903 or 1904. [CE, p. 351.]

The early ferries utilized various mean of propulsion. Underwater cables allowed the steamboats to pass over them; above-water cables were used where there was no steamboat traffic. Both relied on the river's current for power. In some instances, however, horses provided the motive power by pulling the ferry across using the cable simply as a stabilizer (the Fairview ferry at the turn of the century). [See the Steve Douglass interview with Gladys Kauffman in AIR, Vol. 1, p. 96.] Things really went big-time when steam engines were placed on some of the ferries, or steam-driven tugs were used to push the ferry barge.

The ferry at Glendive was not installed until after the ice broke up in the spring of 1882. "Don McArthur has secured the ferry permit and has taken out his licence *[sic]*." [GT, 23 February 1882.] (This is the same Don McArthur mentioned by Vic Smith as a participant in the attempted robbery of the army paymaster. See Author's Notes–Chapter 12.) The McArthur ferry operated with an underwater cable set about four feet underwater to allow the paddle wheelers to cross it. The result, however, was a very slow ferryboat since, in addition to crossing the river with the power of the current, it had the additional burden of having to lift the cable as it went. McArthur was not slow to pick up on the fact that men would be waiting for some time for the ferry on the west side of the river. The advertisement for his saloon read: "River House is located at the Ferry landing opposite [Glendive]. Don McArthur, Prop." [GT, 4 May 1882.] Whatever cable he initially put across the river, McArthur discovered it was too light: "A new 1-and-⅛-inch cable has been installed on the Glendive Ferry." [GT, 7 September 1882.]

By 1883, the Yellowstone River traffic above Glendive was finished. With the coming of the railroad in 1881, there was no commercial river traffic between Glendive and Miles City after the navigating season of 1882. [TLW, p. 380.] Thus, the necessity of steamboats crossing the cable at the Glendive ferry was gone by 1883. When the steamboat traffic ended, the cables were set above the water line. "The Ferry's elevated cable has been put to good use these last two weeks. People and mails are going over by the basket!" [GT, 7 April 1883.] It seems curious today to realize just what the mark of a western boomtown was: "Glendive is Booming! The Ferry [across the Yellowstone]...plys across [each way] twice a day!" [GT, 4 April 1883.]

"Last year [1882]," editor Will Mabee wrote, "the [Glendive] ferry company gave us a ferry with an underwater cable and lost money the whole season through. This season [1883] they have repaired their boat, raised the cable and are now operating the best ferry on the Yellowstone. This has not been done without considerable expense and we think they are justly deserving of credit for their efforts...in the face of continued loss and expenditure. At Bradford* [sic], the distance is but 500 feet and the charge is $2.50 per team. Miles City's cable is but 800 feet and they charge $1.00 a team. At Glendive the river is 1,000 feet and we charge the same as Miles City. The settlers of Glendive can also buy tickets, fifty rides for $6.25, which we think is quite reasonable." [GT, 28 April 1883.]

* "Bradford" is presumably a spelling error resulting from the mispronunciation of "Blatchford." Blatchford was the site of the ferry crossing of the Yellowstone near the Powder River, immediately south and west of Terry. It was also the point where the Fort Keogh–Bismarck stagecoach

route (1878–1882) turned east and headed for Bismarck. [See "stage mail route" in TLW in map and photo section following p. 211.] This was the same location where Frank ("Doc") Zahl, the famed buffalo hunter of "The Big Open," located his road ranch in the summer of 1879. [TLW, p. 386.] About 1885, Blatchford was recognized as a "new town." [TLW, p. 26 citing YJ, 30 May 1885.]

The Glendive ferry operated from 1882 through most of the season of 1895 under various guises of ownership: Don McArthur (1882–ca. 1884), Douglas and Mead (ca. 1884–1890), and, finally, Frank Kinney (1890–1895 and, when the Glendive bridge was destroyed by the ice break-up, April 1899 through freeze-up in 1901). [GT, 23 Feb 1882. OTOL, p. 14. OTOL, p. 12.]

The first bridge to cross the Yellowstone was built at Glendive in 1895 at a cost of $3,600. It was 1,750 feet long and, to allow steamboat traffic, had a central span of three-hundred-and-thirty-six feet that turned on a pivot located in the river. Ice destroyed the bridge on 7 April 1899. The *Glendive Independent* reported that one of the spans floated six miles downstream on the ice. [GI, 29 April 1899.] The Glendive ferry was put back into service until a second bridge was completed in 1902. [GTHG, p. 58. IVEM, 20 November 1935. GI, 17 November 1899 and 23 March 1901.]

CHAPTER FOURTEEN

Mickey Farrell and the Irish Contingent

WHEN WE ARRIVED IN GLENDIVE in April of 1882, Mickey Farrell's place was located on the corner of Merrill Avenue and Valentine Street.[189] This was one of the most popular properties in early-day Glendive. He was open twenty-four hours a day, three-hundred-and-sixty-five days a year. Modern movies have called places like Mickey's a "saloon." If that was a saloon, then we had better cover that ground a little bit. It was a single-story building that, in the front (streetside), contained a large single room that was a restaurant on the right side and a stand-up bar on the left. The bar side had a piano, a table for dice, another for keno, and three or four card tables. The half-dozen or so restaurant tables were also available for use by card players whenever necessary, and that was usually later in the evening. To the rear of the building, behind the kitchen, was a large sleeping room where the dozen or so bunk beds were separated by curtains. A soup kettle was always going, and the sandwiches in the bar were free. You could buy beer or sarsaparilla by the glass or pitcher, but whiskey was sold by the bottle only. That was the practice in the Montana "saloons" of the day. If you wanted whiskey by

---

[189] Advertisement in the GT, Thursday, 2 August 1884:

M. FARRELL
DEALER IN FINE
WINES, LIQUORS & CIGARS
MILWAUKEE BEER
also a first class
RESTAURANT
in connection
CALL AND BE CONVINCED
CORNER OF MERRILL AVENUE
&
VALENTINE STREET

the drink you had to go to a "sample room" like Henry Dion's. The big treat at Mickey's, if you could afford them, was to have fresh canned oysters cooked any way you wanted. The same was true with fresh canned fruit. The airtight peaches were by far the most popular.[190]

The patrons of the Glendive saloons were always a mix of train crews, track maintenance crews, men from the train sheds and roundhouse, cowboys, travelers, a few soldiers from time to time, and locals. In general, the men frequenting these places were there to relax and have a good time. If things did "heat up," however, they could become as rough a crowd as you might ever want to meet. Up until 1884 or 1885, when Sheriff Tuttle made everybody stop wearing concealed weapons and side arms, things could become touch and go pretty fast, especially after dark.[191] After the guns went, it could still get a little rowdy sometimes but the immediate threat to life and limb slowed down a lot.

It may be of interest to some of the younger people today to know what Mickey charged for his offerings during the years between 1880 and 1885. Soda pops and sarsaparillas were six for a quarter or seventy-five cents per twenty-four-bottle case if you bought it in a store. It was three for a quarter at Mickey's—but his sarsaparilla came with entertainment. Keg beer sold at two bits for two schooners. If you wanted bottled beer, it was two bits a bottle. If you went to a sample room that sold whiskey by the shot, it was two shots for two bits. Mickey, like almost all of the saloons in eastern Montana and western Dakota territories, only sold his whiskey by the bottle. Depending on the quality, he paid $3.00 to $8.00 per gallon for it. He poured it into his own bottles, "fifths," which equaled one-fifth of a gallon or four-fifths of a quart, and sold it for $2.00 to $6.00 a bottle. I remember Mickey paid twenty-five cents to fifty cents for a can with a dozen oysters in it and I think he charged $1.50 for that same dozen cooked up however you liked them and served on a plate with a knife

---

[190] Norton's interpretation of "fresh" apparently meant the oysters (or peaches or whatever) were "fresh" when they were placed in the can. Such canned goods were commonly called "airtights." Many of Mickey Farrell's ads read: "Oysters served in every style." [See the advertisement in the GI, 20 December 1884.]

[191] See *"The disarming of Glendive"* in Author's Notes following this chapter regarding the prohibition of concealed weapons and sidearms in the town of Glendive.

and a fork. A typical restaurant breakfast of a fried beef, buffalo, or mutton steak, with canned tomatoes, biscuits, and coffee was $1.00. A side serving of breakfast eggs was extra at $1.00 to $1.50 per dozen or fifteen cents each if you wanted less than six. Fresh canned fruit in a restaurant was fifty cents for a one-pound can. If you were more conservative, however, you could go to a regular store and buy dried apples, peaches, prunes, and apricots for ten pounds to the dollar.[192]

Mickey Farrell was the best of friends to our family in our first years in Glendive. Mickey was in his mid-thirties and, in addition to being a big man anyway, was also somewhat overweight, coming in somewhere around two-hundred-and-fifty pounds. Born in Ireland, he came to America with his parents when he was about ten years old. As a young man, he had served some time in the military, in Kansas and Texas as I recall. Following the Custer massacre he came out to Montana Territory, where he was involved in the construction of both Fort Keogh and Fort Custer in 1876 and 1877. He then worked in and around Miles City until he paired up with Jim Butler.[193] I know Butler owned a saloon there in Miles City. Mickey told me that he and Butler opened up "Jim's Opera House" on Merrill Avenue in Glendive in November of 1880. During the winter of 1880–1881, Louie Mixter brought in his "Music Hall" from Cedar Creek[194] and plunked it down just a few doors away from the "Opera House." That was the beginning of Glendive's "saloon row." In the summer of 1881, Mickey bought out Jim Butler and moved the place to the corner of Merrill and Valentine Street. From then on, his place was just called "Farrell's."[195]

Mickey was certainly one of the first men, if not the first, to have situated himself in the platted town of Glendive. That's not to be confused with "Old" Glendive, the first settlement located on the flat overlooking the south bank of Glendive Creek.[196]

---

[192] The prices quoted are close equivalents to those cited by Dr. Lorman Hoopes in TLW, pp. 400–401.

[193] See *"James Butler"* in Author's Notes following this chapter for his biography.

[194] See *"Louis B. Mixter"* in Author's Notes following this chapter.

[195] See *"Mickey Farrell"* in Author's Notes following this chapter.

[196] See *"'Old' Glendive, 'New' Glendive"* in Author's Notes following this chapter.

Those early and primitive structures in the original settlement had been built in the late summer of 1880 and were mostly made of walls or half-walls of chinked cottonwood logs with canvas sides, and canvas or mud roofs. Some of them were just wooden frames covered with canvas. There wasn't a wooden floor among the dozen or so buildings.

Once it had been decided exactly where the NPRR track would turn off of the Glendive Creek route and head up the Yellowstone toward Miles City, Merrill and others platted the permanent Glendive townsite. That was, I believe, around November of 1880. Over the rest of that winter of 1880–1881 old Glendive was slowly abandoned and the merchants all moved a couple of miles south and started to build more permanent structures in New Glendive.[197] That was when Mickey and Jim Butler came in to take care of the grading crews for the Northern Pacific, many of whom were then employed by the Harpsters[198] in this part of the country. Their saloon and restaurant was originally called "Jim's Opera House" because the place had live music every night.

Mickey lived on the east side of the railroad tracks between my father's place and downtown. When our mother died in September of 1882, Mickey helped out immediately, not by giving us things but by offering all of us older boys and my father part-time jobs whenever we were around. He was constantly adding on or remodeling, and father helped with carpentry tasks.[199] We boys could always go into Mickey's and help do dishes or mop the floors or clean up tables or whatever. His restaurant ran twenty-four hours a day and the soup kettle was always full, hot, and free. He had a very pleasant older Negro woman, Lou by name, who kept house for him and worked as a cook in Mickey's saloon and restaurant. Lou took to my younger brother, Fred, and for all of the time we lived there she would mend his clothes and look out for his personal hygiene and health in general. She was

---

[197] TLW, p. 136.

[198] See *"The Harpster family"* in Author's Notes following this chapter.

[199] GT, 27 April 1882: "M. Farrell is building an addition to his restaurant." GT, 11 May 1882: "Farrell has added a lodging department to his restaurant." GT, 11 May 1882: "M. Farrell is entirely reconstructing his saloon and restaurant. A new front being the chief improvements."

equally kind to us three older boys, but after the first few weeks following my mother's death, we were rarely around.[200]

Mickey was part of that Irish contingent who inhabited so much of early eastern Montana Territory. A few had been miners in the Bannack, Virginia City, and Helena areas and then moved eastward after the Custer affair in the summer of 1876. A lot of them were like Johnny O'Brien, Charlie Stierle, William Sartin, Charlie Adams, Morris Cain, and Tom Kean, who had all come west with the army and later, following their discharges, had simply stayed on. A surprising number were civilian mechanics like Mickey, employed in the construction of Fort Keogh and Fort Custer and other military outposts and Indian reservation buildings in eastern Montana, and who then became the first inhabitants of the Yellowstone from Bozeman to Fort Buford and points in between. Still others, like the Tuttle boys and the Harpsters, were part of the railroad construction gangs, the graders and the tracklayers, while others like David Mead and Jim Taylor and Henry Dion followed the tracks, providing supplies and services.

The Irishmen, however, were unique in the sense that they had a common background, a common accent, and a common religion, and so they tended to migrate toward each other. Glendive was no exception. Mickey Farrell was originally a partner with old James Butler. Butler was as Irish as they came and he was the father-in-law to both Nick Comford and John J. O'Brien,[201] the Glendive iceman. John J. should not be confused with Johnny (John W.) O'Brien,[202] another Irishman from down in the Newlon area who was one of the really early settlers of the lower Yellowstone. Comford, Butler's other son-in-law, was a cattleman from the Fort Benton area. He came into town in June of 1881, started the Glendive meat market, and took over what was left of a 200-acre patch of cottonwoods located just north of town along the river. The locals called that pile of poplars "timber," and, except for the stumps, all the big stuff was mostly gone when we arrived in the spring of 1882, consumed by the building of the

---

[200] FVBM.

[201] See *"John J. O'Brien"* in Author's Notes following this chapter.

[202] See *"John W. ('Johnny') O'Brien"* in Author's Notes following this chapter.

two towns.[203] Comford then partnered up with Will Raymond and built and operated Glendive's "Livery, Feed and Sales Stable."[204] It was at this stable that a Catholic priest held the first public mass in Glendive in 1882, not long after we arrived.[205] The Glendive Livery, Feed and Sales Stable was also, interestingly enough, the first place where I ever saw a real musical performed, "The Magic Doll."[206] It was a small production but it drew good crowds. I never forgot that event, and to this day I can still hum one of the main tunes from it. When Dawson County's first elections were held in November of 1882, Nick Comford became one of our first three elected county commissioners, and his partner, Will Raymond, became our first elected county clerk and recorder.[207]

James Butler's other daughter, Addie, married John J. O'Brien in 1882. Although an army veteran, O'Brien was a young man, under thirty I suppose, who had located in Glendive just a year ahead of our arrival in April of 1882. He was a drayman and, from the winter of 1881 forward, the iceman for the community. Father Lindesmith married Addie Butler to John J. O'Brien at 3:00 A.M. at James Gloster's[208] house on the west side of the Yellowstone on June 1, 1882. In the county elections of November 1882, John J. O'Brien became the county assessor for Dawson County.[209]

Also married at the famous 3:00 A.M. ceremony[210] by Father Lindesmith were James Taylor and Elizabeth Gloster, James Gloster's sister. Now, Jim Taylor really was a Glendive old-timer. He ran the

---

[203] The "two towns" Stephen Norton Van Blaricom was referring to were "Old" Glendive on the flat above Glendive Creek and "New" Glendive located a couple of miles to the south alongside the Yellowstone River.

[204] See "Nicholas W. ('Nick') Comford" in Author's Notes following this chapter.

[205] The GT, on 20 July 1882, reported that the Rev. J. G. Venneman of Helena held mass at the Comford and Raymond livery stable. Despite the earlier presence of Father Lindesmith, who Dr. Hoopes recorded as "ministering to the Catholics and non-Catholics of eastern Montana since 10 August 1880" (TLW, p. 204), Venneman's may have been the first public mass held in Glendive.

[206] "On 22 July 1882, The Magic Doll, a musical extravaganza, was performed at the Comford and Raymond Livery Stable." Also in 1882, the livery stable was the location for a production of The Boston Comic Opera. [TLW, p. 70.]

[207] See "William H. Raymond" in Author's Notes following this chapter.

[208] See "James Gloster" in Author's Notes following this chapter.

[209] It is debatable whether or not John J. O'Brien actually became the county assessor for Dawson County. See Author's Notes regarding John J. O'Brien.

[210] See "The 'famous' 3:00 A.M. double wedding" in Author's Notes following this chapter.

store and saloon for Winston Brothers and Shaw up on the flat above Glendive Creek in the mid-summer of 1880. By the time he was married by Father Lindesmith in June of 1882, he was deputy sheriff to the famous Tom Irvine, the Sheriff of Custer County[211] who provided the law here until Dawson County was formed in September of 1882. With the election of November of 1882, Jim Taylor became the first elected Sheriff of Dawson County.[212]

Robert Pontet and Peter Gallagher showed up in Old Glendive in September of 1880. Just before Christmas of 1880 they opened their ready-made clothing store on Kendrick and Valentine, across the alley from Mickey Farrell's place in New Glendive. That was only a month behind Mickey Farrell and Jim Butler. Despite their energy, the clothing deal didn't go over too well. Pontet and Gallagher soon trimmed the clothing store down to those items that were selling well in Glendive in 1881, namely liquor and cigars. In 1882, Peter's brother, Charles Gallagher, appeared in Glendive. He came direct from Ireland. He partnered up with Peter and they gave the clothing and tailoring business another whirl.

It was about that time that Robert Pontet and Peter Gallagher both went into politics. Robert was appointed one of the first three Dawson County Commissioners and he was liked well enough that he hung onto office even after the November elections. Peter Gallagher secured himself a position as the deputy clerk of the Dawson County Court. Like his new partnership with his brother, that only lasted a few months—Peter soon tired of the tailoring business again. About 1884, maybe 1885, Peter left town and went to Butte, where he joined the police department, married, and never returned to Glendive.

When Peter left, Charlie went to work for the Northern Pacific at the roundhouse. That's about when Michael Kelly showed up, also direct from Ireland. First he partnered with Charlie in the tailoring shop and then he "partnered up" with Charlie's sister-in-law. Both of Kelly's partnerships "took." Kelly got a wife, Charlie Gallagher got an active partner (and kept his job with the railroad),

---

[211] See the biography of Sheriff Tom Irvine in "Old Dawson." Irvine was one of the more colorful characters in the early days of settlement of eastern Montana. Among other things, Irvine was instrumental in helping Granville Stuart find and locate his **DHS** ranch in the Judith Basin. [TLW, p. 334.]

[212] See *"James Taylor"* in Author's Notes following this chapter.

and Glendive had the ready-made clothing and tailoring shop back in business, for the third time. The "Gallagher and Kelly" store was located right beside Mickey Farrell's place on Merrill Avenue until their partnership broke up in 1887 and Mike Kelly moved his family down to Fort Buford. Another clothing store later came into town, but that was the last attempt at providing the citizens of Glendive with a tailor for a number of years.[213]

While these men—Comford, Taylor, J. J. O'Brien, Pontet, and Peter Gallagher—didn't occupy all of the seats of government, you can see that the Irish contingent was well represented in the early day governance of Dawson County. And Mickey Farrell was in "pretty tight," as the saying goes, with his fellow countrymen. They were a gregarious lot who conformed quite well to the Irish stereotype: drinkers, talkers, and not shy in their opinions. All in all, they fit in quite well with the larger community and did many things to promote the growth of Glendive. But, it was Mickey who, for whatever reason, established an affinity with our father and me and with my brother, Fred, in particular.

Just after the first of the year in 1883, Mickey had saved enough money to take a little time off. He was in his mid-thirties and he was starting to get a little cabin fever. He put Jim McCormick,[214] one of the most pleasant and gracious men in Glendive, in charge of his establishment and announced he was going to travel in the East for a few months.[215] He hadn't been gone too long when word was going around that he had married. That was confirmed when he returned. Although he returned alone, he said he would be bringing his wife out later that spring.[216]

It was just before Christmas of 1884 that Mickey Farrell's original place burned to the ground.[217] It was a total loss and Mickey quickly relocated himself into the old Senate Building. He

[213] See "A Tale of Four Irish Tailors" in Author's Notes following this chapter.

[214] See "The quiet Mr. James McCormick" in Author's Notes following this chapter.

[215] GT, 20 January 1883: "Michael Farrell has gone east on a trip for a few months. He will go as far as Arkansas before he returns. James McCormick will manage the business during his absence."

[216] GT, ____ 1883: "Michael Farrell returned from his eastern trip last Thursday. During his absence he repented the folly of living in single blessedness and secured a partner for the doubles act. He will bring his better half to the Metropolis in the spring."

[217] GI, Saturday, 20 December 1884: "At nine o'clock last Wednesday night, Farrell's restaurant burned." Also see FVBM.

was open again in less than a week, this time under the moniker of "The Senate Saloon."[218] "The Senate" was the result of some sort of association with Harry Helms, the owner of the venerable "Bon-Ton Saloon." Harry built Mickey a new building following the conflagration of March 1886 when all of the downtown business area containing some thirteen buildings burned.[219] Mickey stayed in business in Glendive for a number of years. He was still there when the family left in the spring of 1887. As I grew up and, especially after I went to work for the railroad and traveled more, I lost track of Mickey. One day he was gone. Where he went and what became of him, I don't know, but his role in helping out our family when we were in serious trouble following the death of our mother will always be remembered and greatly appreciated.[220]

---

[218] GT, 27 December 1884: "Mickey Farrell reopened Christmas Eve in the Senate Saloon and is enjoying a good trade." GT, 7 June 1885: "Mickey Farrell's business house is undergoing repairs. It is being clothed and papered and a fresh supply of paint is being added. These improvements will make the Senate of very pleasing appearance." GT, 14 June 1885: "Mickey Farrell has completed his improvements and now his place is nicely grained and the walls papered. It presents a better appearance than ever before and reflects credit on the enterprise of the proprietor." GT, 21 June 1885: "Mickey Farrell has opened his keno game." Also see FVBM.

[219] See "Mickey Farrell, Harry Helms, and the Glendive fire of 1886" in Author's Notes following this chapter.

[220] Interview with Emma (Van Blaricom) Freeze, August, 1992. Emma did not know Mickey Farrell's name. She simply said that there was a saloonkeeper in Glendive who "really helped the family out just after my grandmother died. He gave Uncle Norton and my dad [Fred] work whenever he could. I think Grandpa Levi worked there once in a while, too." Mickey Farrell and his black housekeeper, Lou, were both mentioned by Fred Van Blaricom in his memoir.

CHAPTER 14–AUTHOR'S NOTES

The disarming of Glendive came in two steps: First, concealed weapons were banned in 1884. Second, in 1885, revolvers were prohibited. The following editorial appeared in the *Glendive Independent* on 5 July 1884:

> We are pleased to see that Sheriff [Jim] Taylor [Hank Tuttle's predecessor] has posted notices around town containing a reprint of the law against carrying concealed weapons. If this law were rigidly enforced we should hear less of murders committed in drunken brawls. It is perhaps natural in men spending so much of their time on the prairie to indulge in an excess of jollity when they reach town. Then, they easily become involved in affrays and the first impulse is to "pull a gun." When all are compelled to remove their weapons on coming to town, their own safety as well as that of other citizens will be assured.

A year later, on 27 September 1885, the following advertisement was printed in the *Glendive Times*:

> Notice: All parties are hereby given notice that the carrying of revolvers in the town of Glendive is now strictly forbidden as it is a misdemeanor punishable by a fine or imprisonment. Sufficient time will be given to all men coming to town to put their revolvers away, and all are requested to do so and avoid trouble, as the above will be strictly enforced after this date. Dated September 25, 1885. Henry C. Tuttle, Sheriff.

Both of these regulations came from Dawson County, not from the territory of Montana or from the city of Glendive. The city of Glendive didn't incorporate until 6 October 1902.

James Butler was born in Ireland in 1811. It is unknown when or where he entered the United States, but he resided in Minnesota from at least 1852 until his move to Miles City. He was likely in eastern Montana early (1879 or earlier), since he and George Troeschman, a German immigrant, opened a saloon ("Trishman & Butler") in Miles City in March of 1880. [TLW, p. 350.] Troeschman is listed among the civilian personnel attached to the Dakota Column of General Terry in 1876 and he was at the Powder River supply depot in June of 1876. Troeschman was also known to have been a lead carpenter at Fort Keogh in 1880. [TLW, p. 350.] In mid-July of 1880, when he was sixty-nine years old, Jim Butler opened his own saloon ("Butler's Saloon") in Miles City "in grand style, amid the braying of brass." [TLW, p. 46.]

On 7 November 1880, Butler and Farrell opened their restaurant-saloon, the "Opera House" (a.k.a. "Jim's Opera House") in "new" Glendive with Mickey Farrell as the manager. It was the first business opened in the new townsite platted by Merrill.

Jim Butler continued to personally operate his Miles City saloon until he retired in 1881 at the age of seventy. He soon moved to the Glendive area, where he first lived on the west side of the Yellowstone with his youngest daughter, Addie. When he moved into Glendive proper later in 1881, Butler was already the father-in-law to Nicholas W. Comford, the Glendive cattleman, meat shop, and livery stable owner. In June of 1882, John J. O'Brien, the Glendive drayman and ice storage operator, married Jim's daughter, Addie.

James Butler died at the home of John J. O'Brien in Glendive on 8 April 1886 at about the age of seventy-five. His funeral, the first such ceremony held in the Catholic Church in Glendive, took place on 10 April 1886. Father Lindesmith, the Catholic priest of Fort Keogh and Miles City, officiated. James Butler, "a good son of Ireland," was buried in the Dawson County Cemetery. [TLW, p. 46.]

Louis B. Mixter made a brief career between 1878 and 1881 out of following the railroad construction crews with his saloon and whorehouse all the way from Bismarck to the Cedar Creek railroad construction "settlement" south of Glendive. By February of 1881, he had pulled out of Cedar Creek and erected a building on Merrill Avenue in Glendive, operating under the name of "Mixter's Music Hall." It was Mixter's building that became the centerpiece of the oldest known photograph of Glendive. [See OTOL, p. 11.] Mixter has the unique claim of being counted three times in the 1880 census. He is shown late in June on the Billings County census (undated) out on the railroad construction line in eastern Dakota Territory as "Louis Mixter, 35, unmarried, Saloon Keeper." On the 26th of June he was enumerated again in Billings County as "Louis B. Mixter, 35, single, Saloonkeeper." [USC, 1880, Billings County, Dakota Territory.] Only nine days earlier, however, he was picked up in the Bismarck census as "Louis Mexter *[sic]*, 35, residing with his wife, Eleanor, age 34," and two boarders, "Tom McNair, a single

GLENDIVE, 1881
ILLUSTRATION BY ALEX AMEZCUA

28-year-old laborer," and "Mary Bell, a married 21-year-old Prostitute." [USC, 1880, Bismarck, Dakota Territory.] It is noteworthy that
the enumerator of the NPRR construction crews in Billings County
was so much more discreet than his counterpart in Bismarck. There
were no prostitutes enumerated among the railroad workers. There
did happen to be, however, a few women who described themselves
as "actress" or "hatmaker," both activities being absolutely essential
to the building of a railroad. Unfortunately, Louis wasn't long for
this world. On 20 May 1882, the *Yellowstone Journal* reported his
death: "Louis B. Mixter, a prominent businessman of Glendive died
this week of small pox after only a few days sickness." He was about
thirty-seven years old at the time of his death.

Michael ("Mickey") Farrell was born in 1848 in County
Longford, Ireland. The family moved to Brooklyn in 1857. Farrell

was in Kansas 1866–1869 and then Texas and the Indian Territories (now Oklahoma) from 1869 through 1876. Although no military record has been discovered, there is evidence that Farrell served in the military, since on 21 January 1886 he paid $1.00 to James McCormick, Clerk of the Court, to "Certificate and Seal on Pension Papers." [See Receipts of the Clerk of the Court, 21 January 1886.] He worked as a laborer during the construction of the Tongue River Cantonment (which later became Fort Keogh) in 1876 and at Fort Custer in 1877. Hoopes stated that Farrell was a resident of Miles City from 1876–1880. [TLW, p. 109.] He shows on the 1880 Census in Miles City as a "Laborer, Age 32." [USC, 1880, Custer County, Miles City, Montana Territory.]

In 1880, Farrell was living next door to Frederick and Mary Jane Miller and their two children. Shortly thereafter Mary Jane divorced Miller, moved to the Powder River country, and married "Doc" Zahl, the famed buffalo hunter. Over the next few years, she divorced Zahl, changed her name to "May," and married Bill Jordan, a Texas cowman who got into the hotel business. In 1897, they moved to Glendive and purchased the old Yellowstone Hotel. They opened their new landmark Jordan Hotel complete with "electric and gas lights, steam heat and electric call bells" in Glendive in 1902. [See the complete story of Bill and May Jordan in "Old Dawson."]

It was probably at Miles City where James Butler and Mickey Farrell became acquainted. It is possible that Farrell, a big-framed and somewhat overweight man, was a "suds slinger" or a barman and/or a "bouncer" (or both) at the "Trishman and Butler" saloon or at "Butler's Saloon" (both in Miles City). Hoopes stated that James Butler and Michael Farrell opened "['New'] Glendive's first business place" on 7 November 1880 (TLW, p. 46) and that Farrell bought Butler out of the Glendive store in July of 1881. [TLW, p. 109.] First known as "Jim's Opera House," the operation went through a number of name changes and locations: "Butler and Farrell's," then "M. Farrell's Restaurant and Lodging House–Fine Wines, Liquors and Cigars," and later "The Senate Saloon." Most references, however, describe "Farrell's place" or "Farrell's saloon" or simply "Mickey Farrell's." [TLW, p. 136. FVBM.] Farrell reportedly married early in 1883 while on a trip to the east. He returned to Glendive and was still there in 1887. [See THWT for more details regarding this colorful character.]

"Old" Glendive, "New" Glendive: The first structures in "Old" Glendive, located on the flat immediately south of and above Glendive Creek, were temporary locations built by sutlers, saloonkeepers, and others catering to the railroad grading contractors and track-laying crews. These buildings started showing up almost immediately after 13 July 1880—the date on which President Rutherford B. Hayes withdrew some 60,000 square miles of land from various Indian reservations in the United States and its territories. Much of the land on the east side of the Yellowstone River, including all of Glendive Creek, was, until that date, part of the Arikara-Mandan-Gros Ventre (Hidatsa) Fort Berthold Reservation.

When the Northern Pacific construction actually arrived, however, the track curved south from Glendive Creek before it ever reached the original "settlement" (of "Old" Glendive). The NP started paralleling the Yellowstone about two miles south of "Old" Glendive. Thus it was that in October 1880 Lewis Merrill and his Yellowstone Land and Colonization Company completed their survey and platted the townsite of "New" Glendive on both sides of the railroad tracks some two miles south of the squatter settlement. The plat wasn't approved and returned until December 1880, but some construction was already being done at the new site, e.g., Butler and Farrell's saloon was reportedly opened on 7 November 1880.

During the winter of 1880–1881, the original squatter settlement of "Old" Glendive started dying off as the businesses migrated to the newly platted town situated by the tracks. The "boom" occurred when the weather broke in the spring of 1881, but there were eighteen businesses, half of which were saloons, already in operation in "New" Glendive by May of 1881. By that same date, the "Old" Glendive site was completely abandoned. To confuse matters even more, the Glendive Cantonment site (1876–1879) on the west side of the Yellowstone River was also occasionally referenced as "old Glendive." [Father Lindesmith diary, 21 July 1881.] Other sites through the years, in addition to those three just named, have also been referenced simply as "Glendive." [This subject is discussed at greater length in "Old Dawson."]

The Harpster family: George Harpster and three of his sons, Enoch, John Z., and Elmer, worked as grading contractors for the NPRR from the time construction started in Mandan in 1877 until work was completed to Miles City on 28 November 1881. They had a large operation consisting of some two-hundred horses and about one-hundred employees. The family home was in Diamond Bluff, Wisconsin, where Mrs. Harpster and the rest of the Harpster children lived and to which George and his three sons returned each winter.

During the winter of 1879–1880, the Harpsters wintered their two-hundred or so horses north of Glendive Creek on Belle Prairie, apparently under the care of Nathan R. "Squaw" Brown and his family. After building their own housing out on Belle Prairie sometime in 1880, the Harpster boys and their sister, Hettie, stayed and tended their horses there during the winters of 1880–1881 and 1881–1882.

George Harpster became ill in or around Miles City in 1881 and returned home to Diamond Bluff, where he died in April of 1882. Upon their father's death, the boys and their sister, Hettie, immediately sold the grading operation and went into the cattle business based out of their Belle Prairie ranch near Glendive. Thus, what had been the winter headquarters at Belle Prairie became the permanent homesite for the Harpster clan. [OTOL, p. 370. HBM. THWT.]

John J. O'Brien was born in 1854 in Massachusetts. He served in the U.S. Army from about 1872 until 1877 or 1878. O'Brien was a soldier with Stanley and Custer attached to the Rosser surveying party on the Yellowstone in 1873. He was later with the army in Texas. By 1880, however, he was working as a grader on the construction of the NPRR. O'Brien located at Glendive in July of 1881 where he was a drayman and where he later (following the winter of 1881–1882) was self-employed in the ice business. On 1 June 1882, he married Addie Butler, the daughter of James Butler (and the sister of Mrs. Nick Comford) at the home of James Gloster with Father Lindesmith officiating. (This was half of the famous 3:00 A.M. ceremony in which Lindesmith married Addie Butler to John J. O'Brien and Elizabeth Gloster to James Taylor. See below.) John J. O'Brien was elected Dawson County Assessor in November of 1882. [TLW, p. 272.] (Note that OTOL, p. 2, shows D. S. Prescott as being the county assessor effective November of 1882. The election returns, however, clearly show the election going in favor of John J. O'Brien by a substantial majority. Grace Marron Gilmore, in an article in IVEM, 10 October 1935, confused John J. O'Brien and John W. O'Brien with each other when she erroneously reported that John W. O'Brien, see below, had been "the first elected Assessor of Dawson county.") John J. O'Brien was still the ice dealer in Glendive in 1885, 1886, and 1887. [TLW, p. 272. GI. 8 January 1887.] Jim Butler, John O'Brien's father-in-law, died in O'Brien's home in Glendive in April of 1886. [TLW, p. 46.]

John W. ("Johnny") O'Brien was a second generation Irish American. He was born in Covington, Kentucky, on 12 March 1850. His father, John Harry O'Brien, was born in Ireland in 1826 and emigrated to the United States in 1845. John W. ("Johnny") O'Brien was one of the very earliest of the "old hands" to settle on the Yellowstone. Discharged from the U.S. Army at Fort Buford in 1870, he had been in the woodyard business at various locations on the Missouri River from that date. He and George Morgan established a trading post and woodyard at Ninemile Creek (now Morgan Creek) on the Yellowstone in 1877. [CE, p. 987.] They bought out "French Joe" Seymour's store and trading post on Fox Creek in 1881. [IVEM, 10 October 1935.] Morgan soon sold John his interest in the Seymour business. Johnny O'Brien married Eleanor Kennedy at Fort Buford on 21 August 1881. A native Pennsylvanian born 26 December 1846, Eleanor was three years older than John on the date of their marriage. They moved into the former Seymour property and settled near what became the Newlon settlement. They had three children, George, James, and Frances Mary (who died in Newlon at age twelve). Johnny and Ellen O'Brien lived out their lives near Newlon. Their tidy, whitewashed store, stable, and hotel became one of the best-known properties on the Yellowstone between Glendive and Fort Buford. Eleanor O'Brien died in Newlon on 27 May 1904 at the age of fifty-seven. The newspaper stated that Mrs. O'Brien's funeral was "the largest ever held in the [lower Yellowstone] Valley [with] over two-hundred gathering to pay the last sad tokens of respect...." [Unidentified 1904 newspaper clipping from the Gateway Museum.] Johnny O'Brien died at Newlon in 1915. [IVEM, 10 October 1935.] Both are buried in the Newlon Cemetery.

Nicholas W. ("Nick") Comford was born in Canada in 1844 to Richard Comford and Julia (Purcell) Comford, one of thirteen children. In 1850, he moved with his family to Chilton, Wisconsin, where they lived until 1858. From 1858 through 1867, they farmed in Minnesota. In 1868, Nick went by himself to Elk Point, Dakota Territory, where he farmed and raised livestock through 1871. In 1872 he reportedly built the first house in Bismarck, Dakota Territory. Comford subsequently freighted from Sioux City throughout the Dakota Territory. He then raised cattle in the Fort Benton area from 1875 until 1881, when he moved from Fort Benton to Glendive in June of that year. There he invested in and developed real estate, including the Glendive Meat Market, the Glendive Livery (in partnership with William H. Raymond), and "200 acres of timber next to town" (meaning the huge poplar grove that then extended north from the mouth of Glendive Creek).

In March of 1882, he sold his Glendive meat shop to R. W. Snyder and Ben Savignac. Sometime before his move to Glendive in 1881, Nick Comford had married a daughter of James Butler so, on 1 June 1882, Nick and John J. O'Brien became brothers-in-law. (See "The famous 3:00 A.M. double wedding" below.) Active politically, Comford was one of the three original Dawson County Commissioners elected in Dawson County's first election held in November of 1882. He sold his Glendive livery to Frank Muzzy and James Costello in October of 1883. Wilbur Tuttle reported that Nick Comford had become a Dawson County Deputy Sheriff by 1885: "The two deputies [to my father, Hank Tuttle,] were my Uncle Bill [Tuttle]...and Nick Comfort [sic], who would rather shoot than eat." [MTMN, p. 14.]

Nick Comford's parents arrived in Glendive from Minnesota in 1882 to live with their son. Julia (Purcell) Comford, Nick's mother, was a "close relative" (sister?) to Archbishop Purcell of Cincinnati, Ohio. Given last rites by Father Lindesmith, she died in Glendive on 21 May 1883. [TLW, p. 70.] Two years later, just two days after Christmas, the Glendive newspaper, in its own inimitable way, delicately reported the death of Nick Comford's father: "Old man Comford died." [GT, 27 December 1885.] Nick was appointed to the post of Deputy U.S. Marshal in October of 1886. [GI, 30 October 1886.] It is unknown when Nick Comford and his wife left Glendive but it is likely that the move was prompted by the federal appointment. (His predecessor, Aleck Ayotte, worked out of the federal installation at Fort Buford.)

William H. Raymond was born in 1848 in Marengo, Illinois.

By 1872, he was in the grocery business in Charles City, Iowa. In 1880, he was in the mercantile business in Fergus Falls, Minnesota. Will Raymond went to Glendive in 1881, where he soon became a partner with Nicholas Comford in the Glendive Livery. He was elected Dawson County clerk and recorder in November 1882, 1884, and 1886. [TLW, p. 293.] Raymond was neither born in Ireland nor was he Catholic. He just happened to be Nick Comford's partner. [See OTOL, p. 19, wherein W. H. Raymond is listed as one of the first group of trustees of the Methodist Episcopalian Church incorporated in Glendive on 4 February 1884.]

"Jim Gloster is one of Glendive's oldest settlers." [GT, 8 June 1882.] "[In November of 1881,] Miss Elizabeth [Lizzie] Gloster, of Irish descent, came from Toronto, Canada, to Glendive to be with her brother, James Gloster." [FLP, p. 22.] Sometime before that date, James Gloster had married Margaret Talby. Hoopes noted that Father Lindesmith's diary on 1 June 1882 recorded Lindesmith "did, at James Gloster's house, marry James Taylor and Elizabeth Gloster." Later, on 22 October 1882, a son, Richard Ignatius Michael Gloster, was born to James Gloster and Margaret (Talby) Gloster. Father Lindesmith then baptized the baby on 9 April 1883 at the home of Mr. and Mrs. James Taylor. The sponsor was Jim Gloster's sister, Elizabeth Taylor. [TLW, p. 137.]

The "famous" 3:00 A.M. double wedding: The weddings were to take place at the home of James and Margaret (Talby) Gloster, about five miles north of the Glendive ferry in the vicinity of Deer Creek (on the west side of the Yellowstone). On 1 June 1882, Lindesmith's train from Miles City arrived quite late and the ferry was shut down for the night. Since the double wedding had long been scheduled, the parties had arranged for a dory to carry the priest across the Yellowstone. There he was met by a wagon and transported the five miles to the Gloster's home. By the time Lindesmith arrived and got the preliminaries out of the way, it was 3 A.M. At that hour, Lindesmith married John J. O'Brien, the Glendive iceman, to Addie, Jim Butler's daughter (which made O'Brien and Nick Comford brothers-in-law) and married local saloon owner and Custer County Deputy Sheriff James Taylor to Elizabeth Gloster (Jim Gloster's sister).

The O'Brien and Taylor marriages completed, Lindesmith then announced that he was unable to stay at the Gloster ranch since he had other obligations in Miles City later that afternoon. Around 4 A.M. Lindesmith was hustled off on the five-mile ride in the wagon back to the ferry landing across from Glendive. The ferry still wasn't running at that hour so he got back in the rowboat, rowed himself the thousand feet or so across the Yellowstone and then walked from the river to the train station. There he caught the 7:30 A.M. train and arrived in Miles City in time to attend to his duties that afternoon. [FLP, pp. 22–23.]

James Taylor was born in New Bedford, Massachusetts, in 1844. At the age of eight, he moved with his parents to Canada where they resided for the next ten years. In 1862, he returned to Houghton, Massachusetts, where he stayed until 1869, when he went to Minnesota to work on the construction of the NPRR between Duluth and Brainerd. In 1870, at the young age of twenty-six, Taylor was elected as the chairman of the Cass County Board of Commissioners. He operated the Brainerd ferry until 1877, when he departed for Bismarck. There he went to work for Winston Brothers and Shaw, a general trading company. He was still working for this outfit in 1878 and 1879 as they followed the NPRR construction across western Dakota and eastern Montana territories.

James Taylor set up the Winston Brothers and Shaw general store and saloon in "Old" Glendive on the flat above Glendive Creek in July or early in August of 1880. [FLP, p. 22.] This was probably the first business establishment located in "Old" Glendive, although a number of others (among them the J. J. Graham store, the Douglas and Mead general store with manager David R. Mead, and the M. J. Quinn grocery store under the management of blacksmith Morris Cain) arrived in the same cloud of dust.

On 14 August 1880, Joseph "Wolf" Allen succeeded in having the Custer County Commissioners appoint Allen the justice of the peace for the dubious "Glendive Township of Custer County" and he then named James Taylor as the township's "Constable." In February of 1881, coincidental with the moving of his store and saloon to "New" Glendive (the townsite platted by Merrill and the Yellowstone Land and Colonization Company), Taylor was then appointed deputy sheriff to assist the sheriff of Custer County with the administration of law and order in Glendive Township. Taylor's territory covered all of that country north of O'Fallon Creek to the

Missouri River and east from the Yellowstone River to the Dakota border. In the meantime, Jim continued to manage the Winston Brothers and Shaw general store and saloon. Feeling a little overextended, Taylor recruited Morris Cain, the blacksmith who was also operating the M. J. Quinn grocery store in "Old" Glendive, and got Cain deputized to help him out.

On 1 June 1882, James Taylor married Elizabeth Gloster, the sister of James Gloster, at Gloster's home on the west side of the Yellowstone. Two months later, on 3 August 1882, the Montana Territorial Apportionment Board approved the organization of Dawson County, and Territorial Governor Benjamn F. Potts (1870–1883) appointed Henry Dion as sheriff. Dion immediately swore in James Taylor as his deputy. Somewhere along the line between February of 1881 and August of 1882, Taylor had severed his connection with Winston Brothers and Shaw and had opened his own "Star Saloon" in Glendive. (The Star may have been the old Winston Brothers and Shaw set-up with the "general store" part of the operation gone.)

The first election in Dawson County was held in November of 1882 and, still operating the Star Saloon, James Taylor became the first elected sheriff of Dawson County. ["Sheriff Taylor is operating the Star Saloon." GT, 23 June 1883.] Taylor apparently attempted to get out of the saloon business early in 1883. Curiously, there were two announcements of the sale. The first announcement was made in February: "Joe Bernard has bought out James Taylor's saloon." [GI, 10 February 1883.] The second notice came two months later: "James Taylor, Sheriff, has sold...the Star Saloon to Joe Bernard." [GI, 7 April 1883.] The deal with Bernard apparently didn't take, because in August of 1883 Taylor sold the Star to Harry Burgard of Miles City. (This is the same Henry Burgard who once owned and operated the Commercial Hotel, the big Northern Pacific train crew hangout, in Miles City. See "The Commercial Hotel" in Author's Notes following Chapter 23.) Burgard apparently didn't have a lot of fun at the Star either, since the *Glendive Times* reported on 15 March 1884 "the Star Saloon will be opened by Becker and Campbell." Taylor continued on as the sheriff of Dawson County until Henry Tuttle, one of the deputies Taylor had hired in 1882, was chosen as sheriff in the elections of November 1884. The Star Saloon, however, was like the proverbial bad penny—Jim Taylor just couldn't get rid of it. It was a terse advertisement in the *Glendive Times* on 10 May 1885 that announced that the Star had come back into Jim Taylor's ownership: "Star Saloon. James Taylor, Prop." Jim and Elizabeth (Gloster) Taylor were still living in Glendive and Jim was still operating the Star Saloon in 1886. [TLW, p. 338. OTOL, p. 2. CE, p. 1042.]

A Tale of Four Irish Tailors–Robert Pontet, Peter Gallagher, Charles Gallagher, and Michael Kelly: Robert Pontet was born on Christmas Day, 1843, in Dublin, Ireland. Pontet led a rather eventful young life. In 1856, at the age of thirteen, he left home and went to sea. He served on ships that sailed the Mediterranean, the North Sea, the North Atlantic, and down the west coast of Africa. In 1861, at the age of eighteen, he served as a cabin boy on a voyage to Australia. Once he arrived in Australia, he went ashore and spent the next three years (1861–1864) unsuccessfully trying to make a stake as an Australian resident. In 1864, he went back to sea in the merchant service and ended up, from 1864 through 1868, sailing between various South American ports in Panama, Cartagena, Maracaibo, Belem, Rio de Janeiro, Buenos Aires, Valparaiso, Callao, and Guayaquil.

In 1868, Pontet immigrated to the United States at Baltimore. He then engaged in railroading and mining in the American West from 1869–1871. In 1871 or 1872, he went to Fargo in Dakota Territory, where he resided until 1878. In that year, he went farther west and started freighting in and out of the Black Hills. He stayed in the freighting business until he went to Glendive around September of 1880.

Peter Gallagher was born in Bunbeg (An Bun Beag), County Donegal, Ireland, in 1856. By 1878 he was a night watchman in Bismarck, Dakota Territory. After clerking for two general store contractors to the Black Hills Railway Company and the NPRR, he arrived in Glendive in September of 1880 and soon partnered up with Robert Pontet.

By 20 December 1880 Pontet and Peter Gallagher had opened a "ready-made clothing" store in "New Glendive," one of the new town's earliest stores. By the middle of 1881, however, they had "tailored down" their unsuccessful business to selling cigars and spirits, two items in which they noticed the residents of Glendive "took a more active interest." Peter Gallagher, however, rented a small storefront on Merrill Avenue right by Mickey Farrell's saloon and he continued to do tailoring on his own.

Charles Gallagher was Peter Gallagher's brother. He married

Catherine Dougherty in Bunbeg, County Donegal, Ireland, in 1880. (Charles and Peter had four other brothers and a sister. Their parents had a small hotel in the village of Bunbeg.) In the spring of 1881, Charles and Catherine immigrated to Philadelphia and, in 1882, headed to Glendive where, after he and his wife set themselves up in the boardinghouse business, Charles joined Peter in the tailor's shop. This partnership didn't last long. When they closed the doors to the tailor shop in the summer of 1882, Peter explained: "The town is too small to support a business of that kind, besides, this being cattle country most men are satisfied with blue jeans, red shirts and ten-gallon Stetson hats."

In August of 1882, Robert Pontet (at the age of thirty-eight) was appointed by Governor Potts to be one of the three original Dawson County commissioners. In November of 1882, he was elected to that office and remained a county commissioner through 1884. [TLW, p. 285. OTOL, p. 2.] Through all of this, Pontet and Peter Gallagher remained partners in their liquor and cigar business. (Peter Gallagher was the self-proclaimed "junior partner.") Peter Gallagher also held the position of deputy clerk of the court. (The clerk of the court was James McCormick, another Irishman. See below.)

After Peter and Charles Gallagher closed out the tailor shop in 1882, Charles went to work for the Northern Pacific. Charles and Catherine continued to run the Gallagher Boarding House in Glendive, that location said to have later become the site of the Jordan Hotel. Shortly thereafter, Peter Gallagher moved to Butte, where he became a member of the police force. He later married Brigid Peoples, an Irish girl from his hometown of Bunbeg. The partnership of Robert Pontet and Peter Gallagher in the liquor and cigar business continued until 7 April 1887. The *Glendive Times* reported a few days later: "The partnership of Pontet and Gallagher has been dissolved." [GT, 23 April 1887.] It is unknown what became of Glendive's world traveler, Robert Pontet, after 1887.

Michael M. Kelly was born in County Kerry, Ireland, on 10 May 1851 and immigrated to America in 1880. The *Glendive Times*, on 23 July 1883, announced his arrival in Glendive, stating he was a "merchant tailor from Chicago." (Family records indicate he emigrated from Ireland and then trained as a tailor in Boston and Denver.) Charles Gallagher and Kelly met in Glendive and, sometime in late 1883 or early 1884, decided to be partners in the clothing and tailoring business.

Michael Kelly soon met Charles Gallagher's sister-in-law, Brigid Dougherty, a young woman born in Letterkenny, County Donegal, Ireland, on 21 February 1861. They were married in Glendive on 17 May 1884. Patrick Michael Kelly, the first of their eight children, was born in Glendive on 6 April 1885. The child was baptized in the Kelly's home on 21 April 1885 by Father Lindesmith of Fort Keogh. The sponsors were Charles and Catherine (Dougherty) Gallagher.

Dr. Hoopes, deferring to contemporary newspaper accounts, spelled the name as "Dagherty." [TLW, p. 185.] Gallagher family correspondent Irene Stingley spelled the name as "Doherty." [OTOL, p. 106.] The marriage certificate of Michael Kelly and Brigid spelled her name as "Dougherty" (OTOL, p. 509) as did Kelly family correspondent Alice Kelly MacGrady. [CE, pp. 939–941.] The MacGrady articles in *Courage Enough* spell "Brigid" (marriage certificate) as "Bridget." The spellings as signed on the marriage certificate by the parties themselves were used herein.

The Michael Kelly and Charles Gallagher clothing and tailor shop lasted until 1887. Around the first of August in that year, the Kellys moved to Fort Buford, "where Mr. Kelly was the fort tailor, employed by the government" for the next eight years. Fort Buford was officially closed by the U.S. Army on 1 October 1895. About 1896, Michael and Brigid (Dougherty) Kelly moved themselves and their children to the old T. A. Kemmis homestead near Sidney. Michael Kelly died there on 11 July 1918 at the age of sixty-seven. He was buried in the Sidney cemetery. Brigid (Dougherty) Kelly moved into Sidney in 1921. She lived in the town until her death on 24 February 1945 at the age of eighty-four. [TLW, p. 185. OTOL, p. 106. CE, pp. 939–940.]

When Michael Kelly left Glendive in 1887, the clothing and tailor shop, operated by four successive Irishmen (or combination thereof), closed for the second and final time. In the seven years the tailor shop had struggled along, it had gone through five metamorphoses: first, the partnership of Robert Pontet and Peter Gallagher; then Peter Gallagher by himself; then Peter Gallagher and his brother, Charles; then closure; and, finally, Charles Gallagher and Michael Kelly.

After Michael Kelly moved to Fort Buford, Charles Gallagher stayed in Glendive and continued to work for the railroad. He and Catherine had one son, Patrick, born in Philadelphia in April of 1882, and five more children, all born in Glendive between 1883 and 1891. In 1892, a young German immigrant girl, Charlotte Traumann (born 1875 in Boken, Germany), started working in the boarding house for Charles and Catherine. Catherine died in 1893, leaving Charles Gallagher with their six children. In 1899, Charles, then about forty, married Charlotte Traumann (about age twenty-four). They then proceeded to have eight more children between 1900 and 1913, the first five born in Glendive between 1900 and 1907. Around 1908, Charles and Charlotte Gallagher moved from Glendive to a farm near Richardton, North Dakota, where their last three children were born. Both Charlotte and Charles Gallagher lived out their lives near Richardton and both are buried there. [OTOL, pp. 106–107.]

Little is known of the quiet Mr. James McCormick. Born in Ireland around 1836, James McCormick acted as secretary to the group of ten men headed by Judge Joseph "Wolf" Allen who, on 9 September 1881, met to draft the petition to Governor Potts of the territory of Montana to organize Dawson County and thus separate it from the administration of Custer County. Once the county was organized and the court established, McCormick was appointed clerk of the court, a job he held for many years. Most of the early court documents for Dawson County are written in Mr. McCormick's handsome script.

Grace Gilmore remembered Mr. McCormick in her column, "Pages from the Past," in *The Independent Voice of Eastern Montana* on Thursday, 30 October 1935: "James McCormick, who so ably helped in framing our county's destiny, was a man of deeds more than words. Unfortunately, little can be written of him as he never talked about himself or his kin. As I recall him he was a kind and thoughtful man, a true Irish gentleman of the old stock. His square-dealing and his unswerving judgement could always be relied on. McCormick lived alone in a little shack on the road to what is now the fairgrounds, but his shack was demolished by high water years ago."

Listing his profession as "Electro Plater," James McCormick mustered into the Glendive post of the Grand Army of the Republic on 21

January 1885. He stated that he was born in Ireland and he gave his age as forty-nine. He had served in the Union Army for a period of "35 months and 3 days." He entered the military as a Corporal in the 19th Connecticut Infantry on 4 August 1862 and ended his service on 7 July 1865 as a First Sergeant with the 2nd Connecticut Heavy Artillery.

James McCormick was mentioned from time to time as being responsible for various businesses in the absence of their owners. He was apparently one of those rare, well-liked, and trusted individuals, a small town functionary known by everyone but about whom almost nothing was written. His death in Glendive at about age sixty-four was reported in the *Glendive Independent* on 14 July 1900.

Mickey Farrell, Harry Helms, and the Glendive fire of 1886: Mickey Farrell's relationship with Harry Helms was probably that of friend, competitor, tenant, and landlord. There was never any mention of Helms and Farrell being partners. Harry Helms was an experienced carpenter known to have built more than one building in Glendive. Harry may have owned the old "Senate Saloon" building that Mickey moved into immediately following the loss of his building in the 1884 fire. Following the fire of March 1886, Harry, as Mickey Farrell's landlord, built a new wood-frame saloon for Mickey. A couple of months later, immediately next door to Mickey's new place, Harry replaced his own saloon, the Bon Ton, but this time he built the structure completely of brick. 1886 was not a good year for Glendive when it came to fires. The *Glendive Times* headline on 10 January 1886 read "Disastrous Fire" and the article explained how the Hope Davis drug store and Henry Dion's store had gone up in flames. On 28 March 1886, under the banner of "Devouring Flames," the same newspaper reported: "Block Eight wiped from the face of the earth, but the Phoenix will rise again. Where Tuesday thirteen business houses were, nothing but debris and ashes remain." Just two weeks later, on 11 April 1886, the *Glendive Times* reported: "Glendive Roller Rink Destroyed [by Fire]." It was never proved regarding the fires of January, March, and April of 1886, but arson was a fairly common phenomenon in Glendive. It was repeatedly reported in the newspapers of the day. The loss of at least fifteen buildings over a four-month period appears more than coincidental.

CHAPTER FIFTEEN

1885:
Working the Roundup

T HE CATTLE RANCHERS OF EASTERN MONTANA, from the Rocky Mountains on the west to the Dakotas on the east, were formed into a Livestock Grower's Association. They held their annual meeting in late March and would district the country for the annual roundups. A manager was appointed for each district, usually a foreman from one of the larger outfits. Our district, which contained Pierre Wibaux's original **W** range, was from the east side of the Yellowstone to the west side of the Little Missouri, and from a southern line created by Glendive Creek, Mingusville, and Medora, then bounded by the Missouri River on the north. This territory was roughly forty miles wide by eighty miles long.[221]

The spring roundup would start about the middle of May. One of the larger outfits supplied a wagon and a four-horse hitch[222] to pull it. This wagon had a mess box that was the width of the wagon box, and four shelves high. The door to the mess box was fastened with hinges at the bottom, and, at the top, a couple of hinged legs were fastened so that when the back door was let down it formed a sort of table for the convenience of the cook. We were never allowed to use it for eating purposes. A dry cowhide was slung underneath the wagon in which the heavier cooking

---

[221] Unless otherwise noted, the source for Chapter 15 is the SNVB manuscript, pp. 33–36 and p. 38.

[222] A "four-horse hitch" consisted of two two-horse teams, one team behind the other, hitched to a common pulling point such as the tongue of a wagon or stagecoach. One could occasionally see six-horse or eight-horse hitches and greater (remember "Twenty Mule Team Borax"), but they were usually used only when two or more wagons were linked together. It took very skilled and experienced teamsters to handle the six-horse, eight-horse, and larger hitches.

utensils were stored when moving camp. The rest of the wagon box was used for hauling food, the bedrolls, and clothing changes for the punchers and other necessary equipment such as a tent or two in case it rained. Some of the bigger outfits would have a wagon just for the bedrolls, clothes, and tents. Sometimes, in a really big outfit like the **XIT**,[223] there would be a chuck wagon and two bed wagons.[224]

One of my first jobs was to keep the cook supplied with wood and to keep the fires stoked and going. That job was almost always assigned to the youngest member of the crew. You ran some risk of being saddled with the nickname of "Hoodie," as in "Cookie" (the cook) and "Hoodie" (his young "hoodlum" that did all of the menial tasks). I was fortunate in that I never got stuck with that "Hoodie" monicker. I knew some men who went through their entire lives as "Hoodie" Jones or "Hoodie" Smith because they had started out pretty young and the name stuck.[225]

Both years I was with this roundup we had the same cook. He has long since gathered to his forefathers, but I must pay him his just tribute. He showed me the ropes, and, despite my mistakes, he never once raised his voice to me. When I erred, he quietly instructed. When I did well, he gave me praise. Old Dad Smith[226] was absolutely one of the finest and kindest old men I have ever known.

I harken back to these roundup days every time I am in my wife's kitchen. The comparison that arises will undoubtedly get me into serious trouble with my housewife friends. I could back up a good-size truck to our kitchen door and fill it with the

---

[223] The story of the XIT is recounted in Author's Notes following Chapter 16.

[224] HYCW, Fall/Winter 1992, Vol. 22, No. 2, photographs, p. 9 and p. 12.

[225] The chuck wagon cook's helper, who cut the firewood, peeled the "spuds," washed the dishes, and otherwise did menial tasks, was usually the youngest member of the trail or roundup crew. The older cowboys jokingly called them "hoodlums" or "hoodies" because of their young age. Occasionally the nickname would stick with a cowboy for the rest of his life. Older cowboys called "Hoodie" were proud of the monicker because it meant that their peers knew they had been out on the range working roundups since childhood.

[226] This is probably the same "Smith" of the Mingusville area who, along with his wife and family, attended the funeral of Pierre Wibaux's personal servant, Marcel Lebrun. Father Lindesmith performed the service. Lindesmith wrote in his diary: "[After the service,] I again made a few remarks, and dismissed the people. They seemed reluctant to go. I went to several and spoke to them (individually) especially a Mrs. Smith and family, who has eight boys and two girls; and a squad of cowboys...Nearly all of the men carried cartridge belts and revolvers openly on their hips." [FLP, p. 21.]

utensils my wife thinks she must have to cook for three or four people. A roundup cook had to cook for twenty to twenty-five husky men with appetites like wolves and he had to move camp at least once, often twice, each day. And all he had were three Dutch ovens, two skillets, a coffeepot, and a stew pan or two. He got these meals for twenty-five men going over two or three campfires and I am here to state with no reservation that I never had better meals anywhere than he used to give us.

Well, the date would be set for the roundup and the meeting place appointed. All the affected ranches would send their quota of men and horses ready to go to work. We usually had from twenty to twenty-five men in our outfit. Each man was allocated six "circle" or "day" horses and one "night" horse on which he would stand his night trick on the remuda.[227] The roundup would start at one end of the district and move toward the opposite end, working up and down all the small streams that fed the bigger rivers. Each day the foreman would call all the men together well before dawn and direct them as to what country they were supposed to cover that day. They would, in effect, make a large "sweep" and bring everything they found into camp. This was usually accomplished in the forenoon. The afternoon would then be devoted to sorting the assembled herd. All of the cattle found on that range that were too far from home would be held aside and then driven back to their home range, whether it be inside or outside of our district. Following this sort, all the calves would then be branded and the males castrated.

Branding the calves was one of the major operations. Often we would have as many as two-hundred or more to brand in an afternoon. With this much volume, all humane principles are abandoned, thrown to the gods. The puncher will ride into the herd and spot a calf. He will note the brand on the dam, for even in large, milling groups of cattle, mother and baby will always "pair" and the smaller the calf the surer the pairing. Noting the brand on the mother cow, the puncher will maneuver until he can drop the loop of his lariat under the calf's belly in front of the calf's feet (hind feet are preferable, but front ones will do). As the

---

[227] A "remuda" was the group of saddle horses from which was chosen those to be used for the day's work. [TID, p. 1,921.]

calf steps into the loop, the cowboy jerks the loop tight, takes a turn around the pommel of his saddle, and the horse knows the rest. He starts for the fire at a fast trot, maybe even a lope, with the calf bouncing along behind, bawling out his protest.

At the fire the mounted cowboy will call out the mother's brand, and two men will grab the bawling baby bovine. They will put him on his side before he ever gets a chance to regain his feet from the rope and, with a hold learned of long practice, he will be made absolutely helpless. Almost immediately a third man will step up with the right iron, red-hot from the iron fire. There is the smell of burning hair accompanied by a plaintive wail of distress, and the little critter is marked for life. If the calf is a male then only another brief minute will be required to dispatch any future claim to posterity. Up the calf will hop, looking furtively for its mother. Once paired, momma and baby will be eased off into the "worked" bunch, and the mounted cowboy is immediately off in search of his next victim.

It was here that I learned of the term "dogie."[228] One day I asked one of the Texans what they meant when they used the term. I often heard them say at roundup, "I'll go out and get another dogie." Soon that rider would return, dragging a calf behind his horse, the mother bawling her head off in the herd. I asked, "What do you boys mean when you talk about a calf as a doggie?" An older Texan quickly explained, "Wuhl, first of all, son, we ain't a-sayin' 'doggie.' That there's a small dog. We're a-sayin' 'dogie,' and that there's a little baby calf who's lost from its mammy and whose daddy's done run off with another cow." Well, I never have really believed that daddy part, but I do believe it came down to mean a baby calf separated from its mother.[229]

It is difficult for me to explain the glamour we now find associated with the earlier western pioneer life, especially the cattle business. A lot of it, of course, is attributable to the romance of the modern public with the motion picture screen. Why would the romanticized imagery of the past hold more interest than

---

[228] Pronounced DOE-gee ("g" as in go). TID (p. 668) defines "dogie" as "a motherless calf in a range herd."

[229] This version of "dogie" is also preserved on a sign placed at a freeway rest stop outside of Miles City.

the actual lives of today? The dude ranch of the present time is simply an attempt at re-creating the old life. Its only appeal can be to those who never had the privilege of taking part in the real thing. The problem is that the old stage settings are gone forever and they are essential to the play. They cannot ever return to our America. The wild, free expanses, so necessary to unrestricted activity, have permanently departed and so, consequently, are the times when a man could saddle his horse and ride to his heart's content with no restrictions, no boundaries, no fences, no roads. Every mile covered brought a new discovery. A man was an explorer, then, in the companionship of his horse alone, and that companionship could only be described as a mutually accepted dependency between two free, but willing servants.

In addition to packing wood for the cook fires, it was my job to take care of the horse cavy[230] in which there were about one-hundred-and-fifty head. The riders would all change their mounts at noon, not riding one horse more than half a day, for they rode them hard. Each horse then had a two-day rest, not being ridden over half a day every three days. We had a sort of corral, made out of rope, strung out in a circular fashion with both ends tied to the chuck wagon. It was into this corral that we put the next day's horses every night. Each man had to go out to the cavy and catch his own two horses for the next day and put them in the corral. This was done around dusk, the last task of each day, accomplished with the cowboy's lariat. The horses, however, soon learned to know when their number was up. They would put their noses right down on the ground so it would be difficult to get a rope on them. Some of them quickly learned another trick and that was to put their heads tight up under the bellies of their more willing friends. The cowboys, though, were pretty crafty themselves and, eventually, through patience, perseverance, and just plain treachery, they always got their two horses for the evening. I never tired of watching this ritual of sly horse versus crafty cowboy.

Horses are very much like men, some good, some bad, with

---

[230] "Cavy" is the shortened, Americanized form of the English word "cavayard" or "cavyyard," which, in turn, derived from the Spanish word *caballada* (a gathered herd of horses). [TID, p. 357.]

the latter packing varying degrees of badness. We had some that were designated as outlaws, truly bad enough to be dangerous. It was understood that no foreman could require any rider to take such a horse as one of his regular string. They were free lances, however, and any rider who wanted could take one of these as an extra mount, riding him when and as he pleased. The **W** had two such horses, a black and a cream. The black was an absolute killer. He would throw his rider and then stomp on him if he could. He had, in fact, killed one man. The cream was not so vicious but seemed to just want to try his rider's mettle in the most extreme way, by bucking himself up high and then coming back to earth on his side. It was tough on him but it had the potential of being a lot tougher on the rider. He was a rough customer and none of the regular **W** ranch hands would tackle him. Between the two of them, however, I believe they were the most beautiful specimens of horseflesh I have ever seen.

We had a Mexican in the roundup outfit, Don Diego by name, who had come up over the trail from Texas. Which ranch he worked for I don't remember but they had themselves one tremendous horseman on their hands. This fellow had done nothing else in his life but punch cows and ride horses and he could ride anything that wore hair. The Mexicans were great for decorating their outfits with everything the market could afford and his rigging was complete. A little bit of a loner, Diego cut quite a figure himself, maybe thirty years old, about five-foot-ten, naturally tan and well built. He sported a dark handlebar mustache and wore those big Spanish rowels, not the normal spur. He wore a black, flat-brimmed hat, and I remember he always kept his shirt tidily buttoned up regardless of the temperature. Well, he claimed both the black and the cream and he would ride them any time he felt like it. The odd part of it was that these horses knew him as their master the instant he touched either of them. No one ever saw him have much trouble with either of the pair. When this man got his saddle on one of these beautiful, spirited horses and climbed onto his hurricane deck, it truly was a thing to behold. It was an inspirational sight to any young man of high resolve and it was one of the most impressive things I have ever seen.

We had three or four other Mexicans in our district's roundup outfit. They were all excellent stockmen and they were masters of their long rawhide lariats. One of them, however, wasn't as socially well adjusted as a lot of us might look for. During the roundup in the fall of '85, we had come into the neighborhood of the small village of Little Missouri,[231] Theodore Roosevelt's old post office when he was a ranchman in that country. The boys got going early in the morning that day and hustled so they could go to town in the afternoon. They all ended up in one saloon. The room was small and it was crowded. They had just got going good when old Mex came in, drew his gun, thumbed the hammer, and let one off into the ceiling, yelling at the same time, "Put 'em up!" What he really meant was "Set 'em up!" but something got lost in the translation, and in the excitement of the moment everybody thought it was some kind of a hold-up. Guns were coming out of holsters everywhere until our boys recognized Mex. There was a fellow there, however, who was not of our party. He was leaning against the bar and he was putting his thumb and forefinger in his vest pocket, reaching in to get a match to light his cigar. Mex mistakenly thought he was going for his gun. Well, Mex's next bullet passed between the man's thumb and forefinger, grazing both, then proceeded in and out of about three inches of his side. Well, that settled the frivolity in Little Missouri and apparently the fellow who was mistakenly shot by Mex did have some friends.

I was in camp, left there as camp tender, when I saw Mex coming alone. It was kind of like being approached by a fast-moving dust devil with Mex and his horse right in the middle of it. He was totally breathless and as white as his tawny skin would ever permit him to be. He was trying to tell me something but, in his excited state, it was all coming out in Spanish with a "Put-em-up! Set-em-up! Set-em-up! Put-em-up! I dunno!" thrown in every once in a while. This would be followed by an occasional "Bang!" and another "I dunno!" maybe just for good measure. I never could make heads or tails out of what Mex was trying to tell me until one the boys related the whole thing the next day.

---

[231] See *"Little Misery and Little Sin City"* in Author's Notes following this chapter for a more detailed description of the towns of Little Missouri and Medora.

That's when I figured out that "Put 'em up! Set 'em up! I dunno!" translated into "I didn't know there was any difference between 'Set 'em up' and 'Put 'em up!' " and "Bang! I dunno!" meant "I don't know why they all started drawing their guns!" In any case, it seems that our boys got a doctor and had the fellow fixed up. They also finally cleared old Mex of the robbery attempt he never meant to attempt. Mex paid the bill and nothing more ever came of it. Except I think it scared him out of a full year's growth!

While I was working for the **W**, the county commissioners decided it was time to slow things down in Glendive a little bit. A year earlier, in 1884, they had passed a law prohibiting the carrying of concealed weapons, derringers, pepperboxes, and the like. In 1885, they decided to prohibit the wearing of revolvers or sidearms of any kind. There had just been too many shootings, and every time somebody wanted to raise a little whoopee or got into an argument, out would come the guns. Well, it fell to Sheriff Hank Tuttle to enforce this new rule. His deputies at that time were his brother, Bill Tuttle, and Nick Comford, a cattleman who had come to Glendive from Fort Benton in 1881. The three men posted signs regarding the disarmament requirement at the livery stable, many of the stores, and all of the saloons in town. I wasn't there but the story goes that four cowboys rode into town, stabled their horses at the livery, and went over to Coleman's General Store. They made no move to rid themselves of their sidearms. They then wandered over to a nearby saloon where they stood having their drinks while looking right at one of the warning signs. Still no action. The bartender warned them about the new policy, and they laughed and snorted and made some comments like "The Hell they say!" At that time Sheriff Tuttle entered the saloon from the back door and Bill and Nick came in the swinging doors at the front. There was some polite conversation and then some not-so-polite conversation and a few moments later the town's hardware man and undertaker, William Lowe, had a new quartet on his hands.[232]

I had occasion some years later to ask Wilbur Tuttle, Hank's son, about the gunfight that day. He told me that he had asked

---

[232] MTMN, pp. 14–15. Also see *"The many biographies of William Lowe"* in Author's Notes following Chapter 24.

his father about the circumstances: "Well," replied Hank, "we was a-wonderin' if them four ranahans[233] could read. That's when Bill Coleman from the general store came up to me and said, 'They stood right there in my store and read the sign out loud.' That was all we needed. There wasn't much to say after that."[234] That pretty much stopped the rowdies from carrying their weapons around in Glendive. Sheriff Hank Tuttle and his deputies had gained the respect of the entire community. Things got better after that and Glendive started to look a bit more like a respectable place.

---

[233] There can be little doubt that Hank Tuttle's use of the word "ranahans" was meant to describe a group of cowboys "out on a spree" looking for trouble. See *"The term 'ranahan'"* in Author's Notes following this chapter for the interesting (and speculative) etymology of this word.

[234] MTMN, p. 15.

CHAPTER 15–AUTHOR'S NOTES

Little Misery and Little Sin City–The turbulent twins of the Little Missouri: By the fall of 1883, Little Missouri and Medora were located side-by-side on the Northern Pacific track, with the Little Missouri River separating them. Little Missouri, located on the west bank, was the former Bad Lands Cantonment. It had been maintained as a small military post from 1879 until the spring of 1883. The post office, established there in 1880, was originally called "Comba," named after Major Richard Comba, the commanding officer of the units of the 7th Infantry Regiment stationed there to protect the NPRR construction workers and supplies. [TLW, p. 52.] The post and the little civilian village attached to it quickly gained the sobriquet "Little Misery."

In 1883 the army abandoned the Bad Lands Cantonment and the buildings were purchased by Lieutenant Commander Gorringe of the United States Navy. The place was guarded and managed by Frank Moore, who rented it out to hunters. Under Gorringe's ownership, the old barracks became the "Pyramid Park Hotel," while the saloon next door was called "Big Mouth Bob's Bug Juice Dispensary." Directly across the NP tracks from the cantonment were four or five shanties, a livery, a boarding house ($1.50 per night or $6.00 a week), and six more saloons. Among them were "The Elk," which housed the local barbershop, and "Little Tom's," which offered "Cowboy Bitters, Dude Soda and rest for the weary." [TLW, p.206.] Little Misery gained somewhat of a reputation as a hangout for young and besotted remittance men who were out for their year or so of unfettered "fun" in America's wild west. ("Remittance: an instrument which effectuated the transmittal of money...as to a distant place. Remittance man: one living away from the British Isles but subsisting chiefly on remittances from home." TID, p. 1,920.)

In an article dated 26 January 1884, the *Glendive Times* noted: "Little Missouri is fast gaining a very unenviable reputation. It seems as though what law does exist in the place cannot be enforced. There are so few of the better class of citizens [that]...[the formation of] a committee of safety ["vigilantes"] is out of the question."

The Marquis de Mores entered the scene in 1883 and, directly across the river from "Little Misery," started his own town of Medora (which he named after his wife). Medora, with its beef processing and shipping facilities, quickly outgrew Little Missouri, and it soon came to be known as "the little sin city of the bad lands." It came complete with its own newspaper, the Bad Lands Cowboy, and, by 1885, "a dozen or more" saloons. [RBL, p. 260.]

While the Pyramid Park Hotel remained in business, by 1885 the tiny village of Little Missouri was fading from existence. For all practical purposes, both places, Little Missouri and Medora, nearly vanished soon after the Marquis de Mores shut down the abattoir and left the country in the autumn of 1887.

Between 1879 and 1887, neither Little Misery nor its counterpart across the river, the "little sin city" of Medora, could be considered a safe haven for the faint of heart. Their nicknames gave a fair indication of the type of reception one might expect there. Before Billings County, Dakota Territory, was organized, Little Missouri had the only semblance of a jail. A ten-foot-by-ten-foot structure left over from the cantonment, it was sturdily built and dubbed "The Bastille" by some local history buff. The structure really served as a place in which to let the rowdier local inebriates "dry out" until the next day. One night one of the railroad crew, a popular fellow among the railroaders by the name of "Black Jack," was placed in the Bastille for the night. His compatriots, unable to bust him out of the solidly built structure with conventional tools, drove a train up, derricked the building onto a flat car, and hauled it a mile or two down the tracks where they could work it over at their leisure with axes and crowbars. They succeeded in dismantling the Bastille board-by-board and beam-by-beam while Black Jack slept through the whole event. That was the end of incarceration in either Little Sin City or Little Misery for some time. [RBL, p. 135.]

The term "ranahan" is not to be found in a standard dictionary. It was pure slang that may have worked its way north with the Texas cowboys. In the nineteenth century the term was commonly used as a derogative to describe someone of rank incompetence. The etymology of "ranahan" is debatable, but a most likely suspect is "ranny" + "hand" (as in "cowhand"). The term "ranny" is an archaic English term describing "an inferior calf of mongrel breeding." [TID, p. 1881.] Thus used, "ranahan" could have described a drover of such little experience or skill that he was fit only to herd the scrubs. It was also used to describe a person who was attempting to act like or pass himself off as a cowboy but who had absolutely no skills or experience in that profession. Others have speculated that the words "ranahan" and "rantan" were close enough that the definitions merged. TID (p. 1,882) defines "rantan" as: "1. a knocking, banging or pounding noise" or "2. riotous conduct; a spree." "Rantan" is related to the archaic English word "rant" which described "a rousing good time; a spree." [TID, p. 1,882.] "Spree" is defined as "a bout of reckless merrymaking usually accompanied by heavy drinking." [TID, p. 2,229.] Thus defined, a "ranahan" could be taken to be a cowboy in town looking to have "a rousing good time" or "out on a spree" looking for trouble. There seems to be general agreement that the term "ranahan" evolved into a generic word meaning "cowboy" by the early twentieth century and, by the 1930s, frequently shortened to "ranny," came to mean a "top hand" or an experienced cowboy. [Cowboy Lingo, p. 22.] Thus it was that, over a period of fifty or sixty years, the word "ranahan" transitioned from an extreme derogatory to a descriptive of high esteem and praise. Today, at least in the Pacific Northwest, the slang terms of "ranahan" and "ranny" are infrequently heard or seen in print.

CHAPTER SIXTEEN

The Cowboys of Montana

MOST PEOPLE DON'T REALLY KNOW a lot about the Montana cowboys of the 1880s. They were composed primarily of "old-time" Montanans, followed by Texans, and then Mexicans and Texians in about that order. The "old-timers" were the boys who made up and cowboyed the first outfits in western and central Montana. Of course, old Johnny Grant was the first of them. He and his dad and brother came into the Beaverhead country in 1850. By the 1860s they were running thousands of head in the Deer Lodge. Con Kohrs and Bob Ford in the Sun River and Bill Gordon and the Moore boys in the Smith River and the Upper Musselshell developed their outfits in the early 1870s. Bob Coburn had his **Circle C** on Flatwillow Creek, T. C. Power started the Judith Basin Cattle Company, and Jim Fergus was chasing his cattle all over Armell's Creek. Finally, about 1880, Granville Stuart located the **DHS,** the huge Davis-Hauser-Stuart outfit, up around Fort Maginnis.[235] These early ranchers all basically raised conventional cattle based on the English Shorthorn[236] that had been brought in from the East or from Oregon. In those early days a stray herd of Texas Longhorns would show up once in a while, but they were basically a curiosity until the cattle boom of the 1880s.[237]

---

235 M/M, pp. 146–150.

236 Reference to the preponderance of Shorthorn and Shorthorn-cross cattle on the early Montana ranches can be found in M/M, p. 156. The shorthorn was developed in England as a dual-purpose, moderately-sized breed used for both dairy and beef production. Through the years, the beef characteristics were emphasized and they became generally recognized as a beef breed. Their coloration varies from a dark, solid red to roan. Shorthorns were naturally horned (today there is a "polled" or hornless variety) and, with a fairly heavy coat, they are quite tolerant of cold weather. Also see M/M, Chapter 7, "Stockmen and the Open Range," (pp. 145–171) for a discussion regarding early-day Montana livestock growers in general.

237 Nelson Story is generally credited with driving the first set of Texas Longhorns into Montana's Gallatin Valley in 1866. [M/M, p. 148.]

Most of the original Montana cowboys were men from the central frontier states and territories, especially Minnesota and Wisconsin, who had followed the mining boom into Montana Territory. Some of the early herds had come in from Oregon and, as a result, a few of the top cowboys were Oregonians. There were also a fair number of first-generation Irish immigrants among them. The Montana men could sometimes be a tough lot for drinking and fighting in town, but on the ranches liquor was strictly forbidden and, in general, everybody but stock thieves got along pretty well out in the country.

The noteworthy trait that set the Montana boys apart from their Texan peers (both parties would argue vehemently that they had no "peers") was that the Montanans spent some of their money on equipment (saddles, rifles, ropes, tarps, and other gear) and on their clothes (colorful bandannas, Angora wool chaps, good pants, coats, boots, and shirts, and long-handled woolen underwear and woolen socks). I always believed that the cause of this phenomenon, that of always spending a little money on clothing and gear before it went anywhere else in town in pursuit of liquor or women, came from their previous experience with the cold Montana winters.

It was the spring of 1883 when the invasion of eastern Montana by the Longhorn outfits from Texas began in earnest. I believe the Hash Knife, which by the end of 1883 covered a lot of what is now the Montana–Dakota state line country south of Glendive, was the first Texas ranch to move cattle north of the Black Hills and into Dawson and Custer counties. The **777** showed up later in the same year. The **OX** was another early outfit that pushed a lot of Longhorns in from Texas. The **XIT** followed a few years later.[238]

The locals regarded the first Longhorns that showed up as real oddities. Some described them as a pair of horns walking on four stilts being followed around by a bushy tail.[239] The Texans were primarily "steer men" looking for cheap feed. Their Longhorn

---

[238] See *"Texas ranches in Montana"* in Author's Notes following this chapter for a description of some of the larger Texas ranches that operated in Montana from the 1880s through the turn of the century.

[239] "Robert Coburn reported the Longhorns as being nothing but 'all horn and bushy tails.'" [M/M, p. 156.] Modern Longhorns are noted for their ease in calving, their lean red meat, and for being naturally disease resistant and hardy.

steers were looked upon with some disdain by the "old-timers," who tended to be Shorthorn cow-and-calf operators. The Texans essentially trailed long yearlings or two-year-olds north, following the old Chisholm Trail.[240] They would winter them over for a year or two and then sell them as grass-fed three, four, or even five-year-olds. With these herds, of course, came their trail bosses and their chuck wagons and their cooks, their remudas, and their Mexican and Texan drovers.

It wasn't only the Texas Longhorns that were oddities. We expanded our Montana vocabulary to describe the men who accompanied those herds. First, there was the generic "Texan," but we also learned about "Texicans" and "Texians." "Texian" was used to describe the bosses or managers of the cattle drives. Calling a man a "Texian" implied that he was a man of long experience and that he was an expert in handling and caring for livestock. The term "Texican" referred to the Spanish-speaking boys who came with the herds. "Texican" didn't necessarily mean that they were born in Texas. It simply meant that they had come north with a herd from Texas. Through the years, I met a number of them who had come from south of the border, especially the Mexican states of Chihuahua, Coahuila, and Nuevo Leon. I guess "Texican" was accurately used to describe a man of Spanish-speaking ancestry who was born and raised in Texas, but in Montana we used the term interchangeably with "Mexican." We couldn't tell and we didn't care who was born where.

The Texicans and Mexicans who came north with the Texas herds were absolute masters of the long rope. Made from rawhide, their ropes were longer and lighter-weight than the standard hemp affairs that either the Montanans or the Texans used, although many of the Texans had adapted to the rawhide. The Mexicans usually weighted the hondo, or the leather-bound loop through which the circle of the lariat or "la riata" was formed, with a fair

---

240 Not all of the cattle were trailed from Texas into Dawson County. In 1884, it was estimated that it cost about $1.00 per head to trail cattle from Texas to Nebraska, a journey of about 1,000 miles. The same distance on railroad cattle cars cost about $3.00 per head. The price differential seemed to provide no deterrent to shipping by rail. In April of 1884, the *Glendive Times* grabbed the title "Queen City of the Cow Land" for Glendive after reporting that the NP had "delivered 98,219 'pilgrims' to Glendive this year." In one week alone, 12,800 head were reported unloaded at the NP's Glendive livestock shipping yard. [GT, 14 April 1884. TLW, p. 60.]

amount of lead. They were deadly accurate with these rawhide ropes up to some amazing distances. Forty-foot ropes for them were quite common, but many of them sported sixty-footers.

Another trait the Mexicans and Texans shared was the habit of tying off their ropes on their saddle horns. The Montana boys didn't do that. They would rope the calf or cow or steer first and then dally the rope around the saddle horn. The southerners called a cowboy who followed that practice a "dally welter."[241] There were plusses and minuses both ways. The Montanans could get rid of that rope real fast if the animal they roped somehow got behind them or, if they got in trouble some other way, they could avoid having a real wreck. On the other hand, the Texans and the Mexicans never lost a rope or a critter. Another real benefit was that they kept all of their thumbs and fingers.[242]

The Mexican boys always rode what we referred to as a Mexican saddle, a flat-pommel rig designed for tying down the rope on the saddle horn before an animal was roped. That Mexican saddle was usually double-cinched or "double-rigged" with one cinch strap immediately behind the front legs and another at the rear of the horse's rib cage. Almost always those Mexican saddles were fitted with fine leather "taps" or tapaderos that were formed around the stirrups so the rider's feet couldn't get knocked out by any brush or, for that matter, cattle. The taps also precluded a man from getting his foot through a stirrup and he avoided being "hung up" in his saddle if he ever lost his seat.

The Mexicans loved adornment, and they decorated their saddles with "conchos," bright silver medallions that separated the leather thong "tie-ties" or tie-down straps located at the four corners of the saddles, one on each side in front of the cantle and one on each side behind the seat. Their bridles and martingales would also

---

[241] Helena Huntington Smith described a "dally welter" as a "roper who wraps the end of his rope around the saddle horn, Oregon style, instead of tying it fast the way the Texans do. The term came from the Spanish de la vuelta (literally, "of the turn"). [WPTN, Footnote 1, p. 38.]

[242] "The Oregon style of dally welting seems to have prevailed on the Northern range. But Southern opinion of it was summed up in the disgusted remark of Rafael...'Montana territory cowboys no too much account. T'row a big loop, all-a-time dally welt, cut of a t'umb, no tie like a Tex.' The charge about cutting off thumbs when the rope is not made fast is all too true. Montana and Wyoming are still (1939) full of cowboys with thumbs and fingers missing." [WPTN, Footnote 2, p. 137.]

have silver ornaments and they almost invariably used those long extended Spanish bits to which their reins were attached.

The Mexicans were absolutely superior horsemen. There were no finer riders anywhere in the world. Where they developed this affinity for their mounts, I have no idea, but they had a "horse-sense" that few others possessed. It was almost always a foregone conclusion that the top buckaroo at any of the horse outfits was a Mexican "vaquero." They always said that calling them vaqueros was wrong. They said that meant "cow-boy." They were "caballeros," "horsemen" they said, and that we were the "vaqueros." We would respond that that was what we meant...that they were the best "cowboys" around and so we called them vaqueros, just like their Texan counterparts did. We never did get that straightened out, but we meant it as a compliment and they took it as such.

Perhaps even more than their Montana counterparts, the Mexican boys were fine dressers. They always wore fine leather vests and the best boots with long leather decorative straps hanging down each side. They used what we called a Spanish rowel with small "clangers" on the side that would make a little jingle when they either rode or walked. Many of them wore no chaps at all, but instead wore leather pants. They invariably carried a razor-sharp six-inch or seven-inch hunting knife on their persons. Excellent shots, the Mexicans always carried the best in rifles, usually packing a short saddle carbine on their saddle in a leather scabbard. For some reason, however, they loved the old U.S. Navy Colt as a sidearm. While a little outmoded, that old Navy still packed a lot of wallop and it looked like a small cannon when it came out of its holster. Just the appearance of one in certain situations could calm down a big man or a small crowd.

The only problem the Mexicans had in Montana was that they wintered hard. When winter came we always joked that you couldn't tell a Mexican from a wolfer because of the buffalo coats and robes they would pile on. Very few of the Mexicans stayed on once the herds they came in with had been sold. For the most part they would return to Texas in the fall, pick up a new herd the next spring and ride north again, and so the cycle would go. Those few who did stay on in a permanent capacity tended, with good reason, to migrate to the big horse outfits where their outstanding skills as horsemen could be put to good use.

The Texan drovers, on the other hand, were another story. In general, they were very young and had no money. For most of them it was their first time away from home and many were from the most remote parts of Texas. They tended to be pretty drab dressers. Their hats were usually sweaty and dusty and beat up. Only a few of them had chaps. They wore those light Texas cotton long-handles all year 'round for underwear and they never packed anything more than a henskin[243] for a blanket. They rode pancake saddles,[244] had worn out equipment in general, and usually packed some old large-bore rifle and a skinning knife. If they had a handgun at all it was usually just some old derelict. They cussed and fought amongst themselves, and with anybody else if the opportunity came along. Once they were paid, they were the first into town, spending all their money on whiskey and women and let the devil take the hindmost.

It was left up to the Texans whether to return south after a herd sold or stay around this country. There was a trick to it, however, since almost all of the cowboys of that era rode ranch-owned horses and, in the case of the Texans, used ranch-owned tack. If the Texans didn't go back south with their boss, they were left afoot, and they were one long way from home. Every year there were a certain number of them who, having been paid off by their Texas employer, went out and whoopied and got left behind. For the most part, this class of Texans worked cheap and never improved their status. Most of these stragglers spent a lot of their time riding the grub line[245] and then, after a year

---

[243] "...they didn't have any warm blankets. Them henskins they brought up from Texas wouldn't cast a shadow on the ground if you'd hang 'em up." [E. C. "Teddy Blue" Abbott in WPTN, p. 98.]

[244] "Pancake saddles," usually called "pancakes," referred to a worn-out or broken-down saddle. In a direct slap at the Texans, "pancakes" were often called "kaks" with the "a" pronounced as in "yaks" to mimic or otherwise affect a southern "accent" as in "pan-kaks." Some Texas cowpokes even got the nickname of "Kak" attached to them: "Kak" Jones or "Kak" Smith, for example. [WTW, Book II, p. 134.] The pronunciation of vowels by the Texans provided a never-ending source of bunkhouse humor (and a fistfight or two). "There never was a southerner who ever farmed with horses," one commentator once snidely observed. "They always formed with harses." [HH tapes.]

[245] A cowboy who was "riding the grub line" was typically out of work and moved from ranch to ranch, taking whatever temporary odd jobs he could find in exchange for the lowest wages paid, some feed for his horse (if he had one), a few nights in the bunkhouse (if there was one), and two or three meals a day. Unless they got lucky, they were never considered part of the permanent ranch crew.

or two, they would meander back south on the cheapest horses they could find. Some of the Texans who stayed deliberately, however, had made connections, settled in on a year-round basis and got permanent jobs, especially with the big Texas outfits like the Mill Iron, the Hash Knife, the **777**, the **OX**, and, later, the **XIT**.[246] A few more of them took full-time jobs with the Montana outfits and the foreign-owned ranches like Pierre Wibaux's setup, the Scottish-owned Matador, or Moreton Frewen's enormous Powder River Cattle Company down on the Montana–Wyoming border.[247]

There was another class of Texas cowboys. These were the professional drovers, wranglers, and the trail bosses. These men, after their herd sold, immediately headed south again, intending to pick up another herd. They tended to stay with one outfit until it sold out or until they were needed to bring another herd north. You never really saw these men unless you went to work for one of the Longhorn steer outfits or unless you happened to be in town the day when one of their herds was sold and shipped east. These men were always well mounted and outfitted, and well armed with a good revolver, a first-class rifle, and a Bowie knife. They always wore good clothes and boots, good leather chaps, and a neckerchief. About the only thing they had in common with the average Texas drover were their accents and those lightweight cotton longhandles. These "Texians"[248] were generally the outriders, the horse wranglers, and the Texas trail bosses who, along with many of the Mexicans, were the professional "long riders"[249] of the famed Texas cattle drives. Some of these men would stay in Montana, and they became the managers or foremen of some of the major ranches in the country. A few of them started their own herds with varying degrees of success.

The Texans rode their horses a little different. They roped a little different and they talked a lot different. We believed they

---

246 The **777** and the **OX** both drove in a lot of Texas Longhorns with a lot of Texan drovers. As a consequence the locals incorrectly assumed they were Texas outfits. The **777** owners were from Kansas, while the **OX** owners lived in Kansas and Missouri.

247 See *"The Texas cowboys"* in Author's Notes following this chapter.

248 See *"The Texians"* in Author's Notes following this chapter.

249 See *"Long riders"* in Author's Notes following this chapter.

even walked different, although they were so rarely off their horses that would have been difficult for anyone to prove. All in all, the Texas cowboy we saw in eastern Montana was a different breed of cowhand from his Montana counterpart.[250]

There was one common denominator, however. Regardless of where a cowboy came from and regardless of which ranch he worked for, when there was work to be done or cattle to be moved, each and every one of them rode for the brand.[251] No owner, no manager, and no cowboy ever expected less.

---

[250] For a brief discussion of Texas cowboys on the plains of eastern Montana, see M/M, pp. 154–157

[251] See *"They 'rode for the brand'"* in Author's Notes following this chapter.

CHAPTER 16–AUTHOR'S NOTES

Chapter 16 was written from notes left by Fred Van Blaricom and from notes taken during Van Blaricom family interviews, especially Alice (Van Blaricom) Hyatt and Emma (Van Blaricom) Freeze. Additional observations were derived from the sources footnoted and from descriptions rendered by many individuals interested in "cowboy" history. Holly Hyatt, whose love of the west and extensive knowledge of horses and equipment went back to the turn of the twentieth century, described the various types of gear and tack.

Texas ranches in Montana: The Hash Knife, the Mill Iron, and the **XIT** were, indeed, Texas-based companies. The Mill Iron and the Hash Knife, however, were simply two different brands for the same outfit: the Continental Land and Cattle Company. The operation was headquartered in Dallas, Texas, and owned by Col. John M. Simpson and W. E. Hughes. According to Dr. Hoopes, the Hash Knife had scouted the territory in 1879 and had moved their first herds from Texas into Custer County in 1880. "They established their main ranch on Box Elder Creek, [about twenty miles] due east of Ekalaka." [TLW, p. 153.] Others, while recognizing the Hash Knife as "possibly the first Texas enterprise north of the Black Hills," put them into Montana Territory a bit later: "By late 1883 the Hash Knife had moved northward to the Montana-Dakota border area." [M/M, p. 155.] The Continental Land and Cattle Company used the Mill Iron brand in Texas and the Hash Knife brand in Dakota and Montana. Consequently, a lot of the cattle (all of those trailed in from Texas) carried the Mill Iron brand. Sometimes they packed both the Mill Iron and the Hash Knife marks. Finally, in 1897, the company did away with the Hash Knife brand and converted their entire operation to the Mill Iron. [TLW, p. 153 and p. 252.]

The **777** was a Kansas outfit that trailed a herd of Texas Longhorns into eastern Dawson County in 1883. The **777** and Pierre Wibaux of the **W** used adjoining ranges. Between them, they extended fifty miles on either side of the Northern Pacific right-of-way from a point about halfway between Glendive and Mingusville almost to Dickinson, Dakota Territory. [TABC, p. 18.] Wibaux grazed primarily in the country north of the railroad while the **777** was often described as operating "in the Little Missouri country south of Mingusville." Although the **777** brought thousands of Texas cattle into the country, it was financed and owned by D. B. Berry of Strong City, Kansas. Berry's partner (and ranch manager) was Henry S. Boice, P.O. Mingusville. Bill Follis was the livestock boss of the **777** from 1885 until the company closed out in 1897. [TLW, pp. 20–21. TABC, pp. 17–19.] John Leakey reported Follis was among the sheriffs and deputies who came to his place in western Dakota in 1901 in search of a known rustler, Bill Clark. Johnny Goodall (see below) was also in the group. [WTW–TM, p. 152.]

The **OX** ranch of John Smart, W. A. and John R. Towers (all three of Kansas City) and James R. and Thomas Gudgell (both of Independence, Missouri) was headquartered in southwest Dakota Territory near Marmarth. Their huge 75,000-head operation, however, grazed into Montana Territory on the Little Beaver Creek country south and east of modern Baker. Some claim the ranch to have been operating in the area since 1870 [TABC, p. 19] but no evidence supports that statement. Hoopes (among others) states the **OX** came into the Dakota–Montana country in 1883 and brought Texas Longhorns with them. Like the **777**, locals assumed they were a Texas outfit because they brought in so many Longhorns and Texan drovers. George Towers, a nephew of two of the owners, was the ranch manager. Hoopes described their headquarters as located "at the mouth of Little Beaver Creek just above present day Marmarth. It was about fifty miles or three day's ride to the NPRR at the nearest village of Medora. The **OX** ranchhouse was built by Fred LeBrech, an old-time buff hunter. It was a log cabin, notched at the ears, plastered inside and out with alkali mud; pole roof, covered with brush, and on top of that, a layer of mud mortar, three inches thick, covered with soil, about one foot deep; and a huge fireplace." [TLW, pp. 348–349.]

Although the **XIT** brand stood for "Ten in Texas," the legal name of the corporation was the Capitol Freehold Land and Investment Company. When the Texas legislature decided to build their capitol in Austin, they discovered they didn't have enough money to get the job done. Their answer was to offer what they had plenty of— and that was land. John Farwell made the bid, representing a group of English and American investors out of Chicago. Farwell was successful, and his group "was given 3,050,000 acres [4,786 square miles]…in the Texas panhandle to fulfill the contract. Farwell's land encompassed ten entire counties and this became the **XIT** Ranch.

Those ten counties in Texas became the largest ranch under fence in this nation." [TABC, p. 19.] The Texas-based **XIT** was a latecomer to eastern Montana. In 1889, Farwell leased two-million acres and established the ranch headquarters on Cedar Creek between Fallon and Glendive. Their early range extended from Custer County up into the southeastern part of Dawson County and approximated a rectangle some eighty miles north to south and two-hundred miles east to west. [TABC, pp. 19–20.] The first 10,000 head of **XIT** cattle started for Montana in the spring of 1890. They arrived about the first of August. O. C. Cato was the **XIT** foreman in Montana for several years. Even though the **XIT** arrived in Dawson County a little late, the ranch stayed in business nearly twenty years and grew into a huge operation controlling some two-million acres of rangeland in Dawson County alone. Marie MacDonald wrote: "No outfit ever dominated the range country as the **XIT** did." The ranch trailed in cattle from Texas until 1896, long after most of the other Longhorn-based ranches were out of business. MacDonald reported that the ranch shut down its Montana properties around 1909. [GHMT, p. 22.]

The Texas cowboys: The northern cowboys often referred to their Texan counterparts as "rawhides." This derisive term referred to "the Texan's habit of mending whatever broke down or fell apart...from a bridle to a wagon tongue, by tying it up with strips of rawhide." Of course, the Texan cowboys could hold their own in the name-calling department. Raised on horses, the Texans referred to the "northern cowpunchers [as] God-damn knock-kneed Oregonians," thus implying that the northerners had never spent enough time in the saddle to become bow-legged—hence not worthy of recognition as expert horsemen. [WPTN, Footnote 2, p. 137.]

Hermann Hagedorn took note of the "wild side" of the Texas cowboys who showed up at the stockyards in Mingusville: "The men were Texans, most of them, extraordinary riders, born to the saddle, but reckless, given to heavy drinking, and utterly wild and irresponsible when drunk." By late evening they would "drift over to the board shack that was the railroad station, and shoot it full of holes." Hagedorn observed that there was no particular reason for doing this: "...they had no grudge against either the railroad or the particular operator who happened to be in charge. They were children, and it was fun to hear the bullets pop, and excruciating fun to see the operator run out of the shack with a yell and go scampering off into the darkness." [RBL, pp. 243–244.]

Most of the native Montana cowboys, the Mexicans, and the professional Texas trail drovers (those men who made a career out of trailing herds north) owned their own saddles, bridles, lariats, and other paraphernalia. The typical drover, however, was provided everything except his bedroll and clothes. This practice evolved because the normal drovers were so young and so poor they came to the ranch with nothing. Most of the men who "settled in" and worked at permanent ranch locations usually accumulated their own gear or "tack." A few eventually owned a horse or two they used for their personal transportation. This invariably required the ranch manager's permission, however, since their personal horses would be grazing with the ranch's horse herd. The ranch always owned all of the horses it took to operate the property. It took about five horses per week per cowboy just to run the place. It required seven horses or more per week for every man who was working a roundup or a trail drive. The roundup horses were only used for a half-day every third day. Few, if any, of these ranch horses were grain fed, as is the modern practice, so it took the horses a full week to recover from a hard day's use and eat enough grass to maintain their body weight and condition. [HH tapes. AVBH. FVBM. SNVB. Ann Falor.]

The Texians: Fred Van Blaricom and Alice (Van Blaricom) Hyatt (Fred's sister and Holly's mother) both used the term "Texian" to describe any southern stockman of European ancestry who was well-dressed and/or well-mounted. That presumably distinguished him from other white southerners whose general image (held by many northerners for a number of years following the Civil War) was that of "a shabbily-dressed, tobacco-spitting, slow-speaking drawler—unkempt, illiterate and, if he wasn't walking, riding a mule." [HH tapes.] "But," Alice said (after many years of being a laundress), "they all still wore those light cotton long-johns." Alice's knowledge that southerners wore light cotton "long-handles" in both summer and winter (as opposed to the "winter woolies" worn by the Minnesotans and Montanans) was almost certainly supplemented by the fact that her own husband, Nathan Lee Hyatt, born in 1858, came to the Pacific Northwest via the Oregon Trail in 1875 from the Blue Ridge Mountains of North Carolina. Her husband's background and personal habits may also have contributed to her and their children's generalized assessment of the clothing and linguistic traits of many southern males of that era.

The word "Texian" is supposed by many to have originally been used to describe American residents who migrated to Texas when it was still part of the Mexican province of Texas y Coahuila and later fomented the revolution that resulted in the Republic of Texas. [See Dale Walker in *Legends and Lies,* footnote on p. 25.] The term "Texian" was apparently expanded (on the northern plains, at least) to mean a ranch manager, a herd boss, a "long rider," or any other Anglo-American Texan who was a knowledgeable, well-mounted, experienced stockman.

Long riders: Men who could come off the long cattle drives, Texas to Montana or Nebraska, for example, with their cattle and horses in good condition were respectfully called "long riders" by their peers. Very few could qualify. These thousand-mile-plus cattle drives went across rugged and dry country where there wasn't always a lot of feed. They covered between ten and twenty miles every day. The trail herds usually contained between one-thousand- and five-thousand head of cattle and fifty to two-hundred head of horses. A cowboy's horse could easily be ridden fifteen miles in a normal half-day of hazing a trail herd. In the longer cattle drives, a drover would ride two horses every day, normally swapping them at noon. After a hard day's use, the horse would be placed back in the remuda. The very next day—and the next and the next—the remuda would be moved ten miles or more just to keep up with the herd they were trailing or rounding up. It took an extremely knowledgeable and experienced "trail boss" to move a herd from Texas to Montana and not have his horses worn out and thin by the end of the drive. Many of the remudas would require a full season of rest and grazing to recover from a long trail drive. Only the most masterful herd bosses and drovers were ever afforded the honor of being called a "long rider." [HH. AVBH.]

They "rode for the brand": Many of the cattle outfits were the investments of non-resident owners. As Marie MacDonald observed: "The old-time cowboys, also called 'hands' or 'peelers,' often did not know the name of the man [nor, in the case of corporations, the names of any of the stockholders] they worked for. The brand owner might have been a corporation, [an individual capitalist or a partnership] in Chicago or New York or London. Or the owner might change. It was to the brand that the men gave their loyalty." [GHMT, p. 22.] Thus it came to be that a cowboy employed for any length of time by one ranch was said to "ride for the brand." Over time another nuance was added. The highest compliment that could be given a cowboy was that, regardless of the ranch or manager he worked for, the unpleasantness of the task or the condition of the weather, if he performed his work routinely and well, it was said of him that "he rode for the brand." [HH and others.]

CHAPTER SEVENTEEN

The Fall and Winter of 1885:
Louis Riel, Coyotes, and Astronomy

I T WAS A LITTLE AFTER THE FALL ROUNDUP of 1885 when the Canadians hanged Louis Riel. Everybody remembers Custer and Sitting Bull at the Little Big Horn in 1876. That was only six years before we came to Glendive in 1882. Almost everybody remembers Chief Joseph and his surrender in October of 1877 after the siege at Bear's Paw, only forty miles from safety in Canada. A few remember Sitting Bull's surrender at Fort Buford in July of 1881, a scant nine months before we arrived in Glendive. But practically nobody remembers Louis Riel and the Métis[252] Rebellion up in Canada.[253] I always thought it was a little odd that the Canadians hanged an American citizen and nobody on this side of the border made a big fuss about it.[254]

Louis Riel introduced himself to Montana Territory right here in Dawson County in 1879, up on Beaver Creek near its confluence with the Milk River.[255] In 1879, that area was in the very heart of Indian country and well away from any white settlements. That's probably why people in Dawson County never think of him. They should, however, because he was a part of the county's

---

[252] "Métis: a French word denoting a person of 'mixed blood' or 'half-breed'; especially one of French and Indian ancestry." [TID, p. 1,424.]

[253] The "Métis Rebellion" to which Stephen is referring is more commonly known today as the Northwest Rebellion. There were three rebellions in Canada involving the Métis and the Riel family. [See SE and RLR.]

[254] On 16 March 1883, Louis Riel was granted United States citizenship in Helena, Montana Territory. [SE, p. 349.]

[255] See *"Beaver Creek"* in Author's Notes following this chapter.

history. After wintering in the Milk River country, the large group of Métis he was living with crossed the Missouri, went up the Musselshell, and ended up on Flat Willow Creek, about forty miles southeast of Lewistown. After marrying a girl whose family lived just south of the Little Rockies, Riel moved into the vicinity of Carroll Landing for a couple of years.[256] In 1883 he went from Carroll Landing up to St. Peter's Mission by Sun River and from there, in 1884, he went back to Canada.[257]

I once met Louis Riel at Mrs. Nolan's boarding house in Keith (now Wibaux).[258] That was in the summer of 1883. I had been sent into Keith to pick up some supplies for the ranch I was working for that were being sent in by train. My boss told me to stay at Mrs. Nolan's since it was the only decent place in town. She and her daughters were friendly, the place was spotless, and the food was good. Mrs. Nolan introduced us at her breakfast table but Riel's name meant little to me at the time. I was only fourteen and we spoke of nothing of substance during our chance encounter. I immediately heard the French accent, however, and he inquired of Mrs. Nolan about a friend of his, also French in name, another Métis I supposed. I never put two and two together until 1885 when the newspapers told of his being hanged up in Canada in November. That's when I realized that was the man I had met while he was waiting to catch the train in Keith in the early summer of 1883. It never occurred to me until years later that two famous and wealthy Frenchmen, both adventurers to the core, lived in Medora and Keith. Pierre Wibaux[259] had his headquarters in Keith, and the French Count[260] was busy building Medora[261] at that time. Whether these men ever met Riel or whether he ever solicited them for funds for his

---

[256] See *"Riel's marriage in Montana"* in Author's Notes following this chapter.

[257] See SE, pp. 337–362, regarding Riel's Montana days. See *"Louis Riel's Montana homesites"* in Author's Notes following this chapter.

[258] See *"Beaver–Keith–Mingusville–Wibaux"* in Author's Notes following this chapter.

[259] Wibaux is pronounced WEE-bo. See Chapter 21 for more details on the life of Pierre Wibaux.

[260] The "French Count" Norton referred to was the Marquis de Mores, Antoine Marie Vincent Manca de Vallambrosa. See Author's Notes following Chapter 9 and following Chapter 21 for more information regarding this colorful and controversial character.

[261] The town was named after Medora von Hoffman, the wife of the Marquis de Mores.

LOUIS RIEL, 1869
PHOTO COURTESY OF SASKATCHEWAN ARCHIVES BOARD, R-A533 (DETAIL)

attempt to establish a Métis state free from Canadian authority will never be known.[262]

Anyway, in 1884, the Métis were ready to make another run at throwing out the Canadians and they sent Riel's friend, Gabriel Dumont, down to Montana to find Riel. When Dumont found him, Riel was teaching school up at St. Peter's Mission near Sun River and Fort Shaw. It took little effort for Dumont to convince him to return, and, by the end of the year, Riel was back up in Canada trying to fulfill his dream of establishing an independent Métis state. His big mistake was to take on the Mounties during the spring of 1885. The Mounties were Canada's version of the Texas Rangers. These were hardy and determined men, dedicated to their duty, and totally unlike the rag-tag militia Riel had encountered during his first attempt at revolution back in

---

[262] It is most unlikely that Riel was in the village of Keith to contact either Pierre Wibaux or the Marquis de Mores in the late summer or early fall of 1883. See *"Norton's chance meeting with Louis Riel"* in Author's Notes following this chapter.

1869. In any case, Ottawa soon sent out a huge army of several thousand men, and it was over in weeks. This time the Canadians showed Louis Riel no mercy. Despite a well-coordinated attempt by the Métis to rescue him, Riel was hanged in Regina on the morning of November 16, 1885. His friend, Gabriel Dumont, who was also the general of his army, somehow escaped to the United States, where he became part of Buffalo Bill's Wild West Show for some time.[263]

Whatever became of the substantial Métis settlements in Montana and the United States, I have no idea.[264]

Earlier in the fall of '85, some months before the execution of Louis Riel, I had hired out to a small outfit gathering beef cattle.[265] It was only to be for five or six weeks, but I think that those weeks stand out as the most pleasurable and interesting of my career. I was to be the night wrangler for the horses of the outfit. They had about twenty-five head with them and my job was to take them out after supper to the best feed I could find and let them graze. I would then stay up with them all night to make sure none of them wandered away. Most of the nights were clear and beautiful, and the weather warm. I would take the horses out to a good location, often more than a mile from camp. They were hardly any trouble if the feed was good, and that left me time to amuse myself as I could.

The coyotes were the most interesting company. They would range themselves about me on the hills and keep up their querulous gibberish for hours at a time. To me it was one of the most interesting sounds I have ever heard. It absolutely defied analysis, understanding, or imitation. I have often wondered why some enterprising phonograph company has never produced a record of the coyote's call. It could be done, for their captivity doesn't impinge at all on their ability or willingness to serenade.

---

[263] See *"Gabriel Dumont"* in Author's Notes following this chapter. For information regarding the imprisonment, trial, and execution of Louis Riel, see SE, pp. 558–559. For biographical details regarding Gabriel Dumont, see SE, pp. 307–310.

[264] See "Old Dawson" for a discussion of the Métis, the Riel rebellions, details concerning the life of Louis Riel in Montana, and the fate of the Montana Métis.

[265] This may have been E. P. Lovejoy's **Diamond L** ranch. Fred Van Blaricom, Norton's brother, noted in his memoir that Norton worked for Lovejoy from time to time. Dr. Hoopes mentioned the Lovejoy ranch as being located on Sevenmile Creek. [TLW, p. 208] The ranch's brand was recorded. [MSD, p. 158.]

They would come soon after dark, start their music, and keep it up until about ten o'clock. My interpretation of their harangue always was: "What's that guy doing out here with all those horses? He's got his nerve. We can't catch any rabbits with him around. Let's run him off!" Sometime around four o'clock in the morning, just before dawn, they would be back again, I suppose just to see if I had had the nerve to stick around. A coyote is just about as dangerous to a human as a red fox, and that isn't dangerous at all. There are many naturalists, however, who consider him to be the most intelligent four-footed animal that lives.

Next in my line of interest were the skies. In the clear atmosphere of eastern Montana, where there is no smoke and much less humidity than in the East, the sky is much more attractive. I would lie on my back on the warm ground and dream wakeful dreams while tending to my horses. I had no knowledge whatsoever of the science of astronomy but I did know of the Big Dipper, the Little Dipper, and the North Star, and I could identify those bodies. By observing them through the night I found that I could tell the time by it as accurately as by the sun in the daytime. From that day my interest in the stars has never ceased, but for years it lay dormant for the simple reason that I was never fortunate enough to meet any sky-minded people. About 1912, I had a friend who visited me at my home in Ohio. He stayed for two or three weeks and he knew his astronomy very well. From him I got the start I had wanted for years. While I lay no claim to being an astronomer in a mathematical sense, I am not ashamed of my knowledge of the geography of the heavens. My general knowledge has become sufficient that when I read what the scientists have to say I know what they are talking about.[266]

---

[266] See *"Astronomy"* in Author's Notes following this chapter.

CHAPTER 17–AUTHOR'S NOTES

Chapter 17 is based on an interview with Fred Van Blaricom's oldest child, Emma (Van Blaricom) Freeze, in the summer of 1992 and interviews with Stephen Norton Van Blaricom's youngest daughter, Ann (Van Blaricom) Falor, in 1993 and 1994. There have been a number of biographies written about Louis Riel and the rebellions led by the Riel family. Probably the most authoritative book containing details regarding Louis Riel's stay in Montana from the summer of 1879 through 10 June 1884 is *Strange Empire*, written by Joseph Kinsey Howard in 1952. A more recent source is *Riel, A Life of Revolution*, written by Maggie Siggins in 1994. The last three paragraphs of the chapter are based on SNVB, pp. 36–37. There is an essay on Louis Riel and the Riel Rebellions in "Old Dawson."

Beaver Creek: The "Beaver Creek" that is a tributary to the Milk River should not be confused with the other Dawson County "Beaver Creek" that flows through modern Wibaux near the North Dakota border and is a tributary to the Little Missouri River. According to Maggie Siggins, "The band that Louis latched onto was located a little south of the Frenchman River, on Beaver Creek, not far from Wolf Point about seventy miles north of the Missouri River." [RLR, p. 290.] Siggins was apparently describing a location on Beaver Creek about seventy miles north of Wolf Point (which is located on the Missouri River) and "a little south of" today's Frenchman Creek. That more or less describes the modern area of Saco–Beaverton, about midway between Malta and Glasgow, Montana, on the common boundary of today's Valley and Phillips counties. [See MAG, p. 91 and pp. 74–75.]

Riel's marriage in Montana: "During one of the [Métis] hunting expeditions Louis met the family of Jean Monette *dit* Bellehumeur ['called Good-tempered'], who had followed the buffalo south from his old home at Fort Ellice, on the western boundary of Manitoba. He had settled between Carroll and the Little Rockies... and Louis became a frequent visitor because Monette had a daughter, Marguerite." [SE, p. 345.] Louis Riel (born about 1844) and Marguerite "Monet" (born about 1861) were married on 27 April 1881 after the Métis group had moved to Flat Willow Creek in Montana Territory (in modern Petroleum County about thirty miles west of the Musselshell River and some twenty miles southwest of the present-day town of Winnett). [RLR, p. 300.]

Louis Riel's Montana homesites: Despite his relative notoriety, Louis Riel lived quite openly for five years in various Montana locales: on Beaver Creek (east and south of today's Malta), Flat Willow Creek (some distance southeast of modern Lewistown), near Carroll Landing on the Missouri River, and, finally, at St. Peter's Mission near Sun River. These could all be described as isolated locations. Dawson County historians have never made mention of the fact that Riel spent the summer and fall of 1879 and the winter of 1879–1880 on Beaver Creek in that remote northwest area of the county. Additionally, if one placed the old site of Carroll Landing inside the western boundary of Dawson County (a most Montanans did), then Riel could also be said to have resided in Dawson County from the fall of 1881 until April of 1883.

Beaver–Keith–Mingusville–Wibaux: The town now called Wibaux is located on Beaver Creek about twenty-eight miles southeast of Glendive. The site was initially called "Beaver" or "Beaver Creek" during the railroad construction period of 1880 and 1881 (and not to be confused with "Beaver Hill Siding" located a few miles to the west). Keith Post Office was established there in 1882 with William Fountain as the first postmaster.* [NFM, p. 153.] To ensure the immortality of Minnie Grisy and the fame (or infamy) of her husband, Gustave "Gus" Grisy, the Grisys succeeded in getting the name changed to "Mingusville" in July of 1884. Gus Grisy, Pierre Wibaux's first partner, became the postmaster. In the fall of 1894, Pierre Wibaux secured enough signatures to effectuate the final name change to "Wibaux." The name change took effect in 1895, with Luther Allen as postmaster. [NFM, p. 186 and p. 289.] According to John Leakey "There weren't actually a dozen houses in the whole place...when old Pierre petitioned to change the town's name." [WTW–TM, p. 104.] Curiously, "old Pierre" (born 12 January 1858) was all of thirty-six years old when he petitioned to change the town's name. (It may be that what made "old Pierre" old was that Leakey was eighty-two years "old" himself when he wrote his memoir. Leakey was born near Uvalde, Texas, on 27 September 1873, so he was fifteen years younger than "old Pierre.")

> John Leakey, in his memoir *The West That Was,* remembered the name of a place in that area called "Heath" as being "a little hide-buying station" back in "buffalo times." [WTW–TM, p. 172.] "Heath" and "Keith" were undoubtedly

the same place. Leakey's memoir was penned between 1955 and 1956. He was recalling pure hearsay since he didn't show up in eastern Montana from Texas until 1893, some nine years after people stopped calling the place "Keith." [WTW–TM, pp. vii–viii.]

From the perspective of the greater Scribner–Van Blaricom–Tuttle clan, the place was called Beaver or "Beaver Creek" when Hank Tuttle and his younger brother, Bill, worked their way through on the Northern Pacific construction crews in 1880 and 1881. It was "Keith" when Sarah Susan Van Blaricom died in August of 1882. It was still "Keith" in 1883 when Norton was working for the **101** (the ranch then extended from Cottonwood Creek on the east side of the Yellowstone up through One-O-One Creek in Dakota Territory) and when he met Riel in the summer of that year. The place became "Mingusville" in 1884 and so it was known when Freddie Van Blaricom rode through on his way to Dickinson in the fall of 1885. The place continued as "Mingusville" during Hank Tuttle's four-year tenure as Dawson County Sheriff (1885 through 1888). It kept that name until 1895, fully eight years after the Scribners and Van Blaricoms left for the Bitter Root. Thus, only Norton (who stayed in Glendive until 1900) ever knew the village as "Wibaux."

Norton's chance meeting with Louis Riel: Stephen Norton Van Blaricom recorded nothing about Louis Riel or Gabriel Dumont in his memoir. It is only through the oral history of the Van Blaricom family, as related by Fred Van Blaricom's oldest daughter, Emma Freeze, that there is record of Norton's purported encounter with Louis Riel. Emma, in a 1992 interview, recalled that her father once told her that his brother, Norton, "had met Louis Riel in a boarding house in some little town out in the country about a year after the family's arrival in Glendive." This time frame and location coincides with Riel's trip from Sun River, Montana, back to Manitoba via Pembina, Dakota Territory, and return—from about June 4 through 15 Aug. 1883 (RLR, pp. 311–319)—and it fits with Stephen Norton Van Blaricom's ranch employment on the east side of the Yellowstone. [See chapters 10 and 11]. "Riel," Emma continued, "was the leader of that French rebellion up in Canada and the Mounties ended up hanging him. Uncle Norton met him a couple of years before that." In an obvious (but totally erroneous) reference to the Marquis de Mores and Pierre Wibaux, Fred also stated that Norton told him "Riel hid out in Montana for a number of years. He probably got support from those French counts who lived in Medora and Mingusville."

Fred's statement that Riel "hid out" in Montana is simply in error, unless he perceived Riel to have been hiding out from Canadian authorities. His residencies at Beaver Creek (the Beaver Creek tributary to Milk River), Carroll Landing, the Judith Basin, and St. Peter's Mission were, in fact, all well known to American officials. Just as he had been in Manitoba, Riel was politically active in Montana. He wrote frequently about the plight of the thousand or so Métis located in central Montana. In May of 1880 Riel had traveled from Carroll to Fort Benton and applied for United States citizenship. [RLR, p. 297.] In August of 1880, he communicated directly with Colonel Nelson A. Miles advocating the establishment of a Métis reservation and offering the use of Métis "influence, such as it is, among the Indians." [SE, p. 343.] In September of 1882, he had been deputized by U.S. Marshal Alexander Botkin to gather incriminating evidence against Simon Pepin, the Diamond R's trader at Carroll and the Fort Belknap Indian Reservation. [RLR, p. 305.] On 16 March 1883, he was granted United States citizenship in Helena. [SE, p. 349.] Recently released from jail in Fort Benton, he was, at the time of his trip to Canada in the summer of 1883, the defendant in a voter fraud case at Fort Benton (RLR, p. 311) and he was a fairly frequent subject in western Montana newspapers. [SE, p. 349.] (The voter fraud case against Riel was dismissed in April of 1884.) Clearly, Louis Riel was a relatively well-known person in Montana Territory.

The likelihood that Pierre Wibaux or the Marquis de Mores had anything in common with or supported Louis Riel in any way is most improbable. There is certainly no reference made to Riel in any of the Wibaux or de Mores biographies nor vice versa. The only thing they would have had in common was their ability to speak French. The possibility that either the Marquis de Mores or Pierre Wibaux would have had any interest in the plight of the Métis in Canada (or the United States) would have been most remote. Their presence in the American West was apolitical. They had located themselves in Montana and Dakota territories solely for the purpose of making their fortunes in the cattle business.

The possible dates of the chance meeting of Stephen Norton Van Blaricom and Louis Riel, either early in June (on Riel's way east) or in mid-August of 1883 (on his return trip), make it highly improbable that Riel was in either Keith (Mingusville) or Medora for the express purpose of seeing Wibaux or the Marquis de Mores. Wibaux had accompanied the Marquis to Montana in March of 1883. He had picked the Beaver Creek / Keith location for his ranch only in June of 1883. [TLW, pp. 368–369.] The Marquis de Mores didn't undertake the construction of Medora until after 1 April 1883. [TLW, p. 233. RBL, p. 59 and p. 61.] It wouldn't have been likely that Riel even knew of either of these men when he left St. Peter's Mission (some twenty-five miles southwest of Sun River and Fort Shaw) the first week in June of 1883. On the other hand, the presence of both of these wealthy Frenchmen was certainly well known locally, and Riel, not shy about soliciting funds for his cause of Métis independence, may simply have stepped off the train in Keith to "take his chances" and ask for financial support from Pierre Wibaux and/or Gus Grisy. He was notorious for meeting with anybody who could possibly help his cause. He met with President Ulysses S. Grant in Washington City in 1875 (SE, p. 321), Chief Sitting Bull of the Sioux at Wood Mountain, Canada, in 1880 (RLR, p. 294), and, in 1883, at Fort Benton with Montana territorial legislator J. J. Donnelly, the last of the Irish Fenians who had long dreamed of fomenting revolt in Canada (SE, pp. 353–354).

The more likely scenario was that Riel was in Keith simply looking for another Métis for either a deposition or a signature. When he departed St. Peter's Mission near Sun River during the first week in June of 1883, he was carrying legal documents relating to land claims in Manitoba for some twenty Métis families residing in Montana, and he was looking for witnesses for his own voter fraud trial that was pending in Fort Benton. [RLR, p. 311.]

According to Hermann Hagedorn, Mingusville "was a lurid little place [but it] was becoming an important cattle [shipping] center." The **W**, the Hash Knife, the **OX**, and the **777** shipped cattle to the east from Mingusville via the Northern Pacific. "Civilization had not kept pace with commerce. Medora [which was considered to be a 'wild and woolly' venue]...might have appeared almost sober and New Englandish [in comparison to Mingusville]." [RBL, p. 242–243.] The village consisted of nothing more than a boarding house, the stockyards, the railroad depot and telegraph office, a section house for use by the track maintenance crew, a saloon, and Gus Grisy's saloon/post office, which had a loft "where you might sleep if you had the courage." It was Grisy's saloon/hotel where Roosevelt had his well-known encounter with the drunken bully in 1884. The whole town had a resident population of about a dozen. There were the two saloonkeepers and Gus Grisy's wife, Minnie, a half-dozen railroad employees, and Mrs. Nolan and her daughters who ran the boarding house. [RBL, p. 151 and pp. 242–243.]

Gabriel Dumont was a close associate of Louis Riel and he became the military commander of the Métis militia in Canada. In the closing moments of the 1885 rebellion, Dumont somehow escaped capture by Canadian authorities and, by 1 June 1885, he had crossed into Montana Territory. Utilizing Métis communities and Indian and Métis camps, Dumont organized an escape route for Riel complete with armed men, food, and fresh horses stationed every ten to twenty miles over the entire four-hundred-and-fifty-mile distance from Regina, Saskatchewan, to Lewistown, Montana. Canadian authorities, however, learned of the escape scheme and turned the Regina prison into a veritable fortress. The escape plot failed. [SE, pp. 555–556.]

In an apparent reference to Gabriel Dumont, Fred told his daughter, Emma, "[George Grant] knew the man they sent from Canada to find Louis Riel in Montana Territory. I don't remember his name, but he was quite a famous horseman and, after the rebellion, he escaped to the United States and ended up in Buffalo Bill Cody's Wild West Show."

Emma did not remember George Grant's name. She remembered only "that old buffalo hunter who was the son-in-law to the people at the stagecoach station [Eben and Louisa Slawson] who sometimes took care of my father." Fred would show up there occasionally and stay for short periods of time. [See THWT.] George Grant was married to Imogene, the Slawson's oldest child (1853–1897). Owen Lovering, who had also been a professional buffalo hunter, was the other son-in-law of the Slawsons. He married Elsie Slawson on 1 January 1883. Grant was known to have come into Montana to hunt buffalo as early as 1873. Owen Lovering, however, only showed up from Deadwood in 1880. [CE, pp. 955–957.] Lovering, therefore, would have had only one full season in which to have met Dumont, while George Grant had been out on the prairie hunting for some seven years before the Loverings arrived.

There is too much coincidence in Emma Freeze's narrative to believe that the man George Grant purportedly knew was any other than Gabriel Dumont. Dumont commanded Riel's "army" on two occasions (the Riel Rebellion of 1869 and the Riel Rebellion of 1885). Dumont survived the second rebellion, fled Canada, and did, in fact, end up in William F. Cody's Wild West Show. Louis Riel resided in Montana Territory from the late summer of 1879 through June of 1884. Dumont almost certainly hunted buffalo in Montana during Riel's tenure and probably hunted with other Métis in Montana even prior to Riel's arrival. It is also known that Dumont returned to Montana for a period of time after the failure of the Métis uprising in 1885 and did hook up with Buffalo Bill and his Wild West Show for a period of time. (Although it is historical fiction, the well-researched *Lord of the Plains* by Alfred Silver takes note of Dumont's time with the Wild West Show in Chapter 57, pp. 407–412.)

Astronomy: Sometime around 1912, Stephen Norton Van Blaricom befriended an (amateur?) astronomer who was somehow affiliated with Carnegie Tech in Pittsburgh. Norton's daughter, Ann (Van Blaricom) Falor, reported that her father would travel to the school four or five times a year to "observe the heavens" generally or to watch some special event his astronomer friend knew would occur on certain dates. It was unclear to his daughter whether Norton was allowed access to a large institutional telescope in Pittsburgh (if there was one) or if the observations were occurring from a privately owned telescope located at the astronomer's home. In any case, Norton was an avid amateur astronomer for the last thirty-three years of his life. [Interview with Ann (Van Blaricom) Falor, 6 February 1994.] The astronomy enthusiast may have been a fellow named Harry Brown. Norton wrote in his diary on 20 October 1939: "Harry Brown spent two weeks with us around the first of the month. I then visited with him the 16th–19th and saw the new planetarium."

CHAPTER EIGHTEEN

1886:
Hay, Skunks, Cats, and Cows

AFTER THE SPRING ROUNDUP OF '86, I was working for a rancher on the west side of the Yellowstone helping to make hay. We would take two teams with us and a hay wagon, a mower, and a rake. The machines were made especially for that country as the grass was so short everything had to be close together, that is, the mower guards, the sickles on the cutter bar, and the tines in the rake. We might go ten or twelve miles to some patch of grass we knew about and work all day. If we got one full load on the wagon it was considered a good day's work.[267]

This rancher owned an especially good team of horses that came from Oregon, and they had strayed—as imported horses almost always will. He needed the team badly and had looked everywhere for them. One morning he said to me, "Van, if you can find those horses I will give you a ten dollar bonus on your wages."

"All right," I said, "if that's your wish, I'll give it a try. Give me a saddle horse and two or three days grub. I think I know where they are. At least I know where I'll look."

There was a piece of high country about sixty miles to the southwest that I had in mind. A fellow we all called Cracker Box Dan was an old character who made a business of hunting down lost or strayed stock. He had once told me that he found most of the stray horses up in that country, a district known as the **NY** range.[268]

---

[267] Unless otherwise noted, the source for Chapter 18 is the SNVB manuscript, pp. 22–25.

[268] The **NY** brand was registered to "Pearson, Estabrook and Clark, Glendive." [MSD, p. 161.] While little is known about Pearson or Clark, Estabrook was relatively well known in early Dawson County. See the biography of *"Barney Estabrook"* in Author's Notes following this chapter.

I reached there late in the afternoon. Just about sunset I found the horses, so I drove them to a shack right there on the **NY** that wasn't too far from where I was. There was a small corral next to it and I put the horses in it for the night. It was well after dark when I got there and I let myself into the line shack to spend the night.

Having no lantern of any kind, I crawled up into an upper bunk so I wouldn't have to befriend any critters of the lower variety that might have wanted to make my acquaintance during my sleeping hours before dawn. It was so hot I didn't shut the door—that cool night air felt pretty good. A couple of hours later I was awakened by the darnedest commotion! It sounded just like a dance was being held on the cabin floor, complete with footsteps, shuffling, and tiny little voices! I lit a match and peeked out over the side of the bunk. If there was one there were fifteen little baby skunks playing all over the floor, tussling and running and, all in all, putting on quite a show. The party also came complete with two adult chaperones, both of which stiffened their tails right up at the appearance of my light. Needless to say I quickly put out the match and, very quietly, went back to sleep. In the morning they were gone.

The day I got back to the ranch with that Oregon team was the hottest day I have ever known. The thermometer registered one-hundred-and-twelve degrees.

This rancher's wife had a maiden aunt living with them. She was a very nice person, but the petals of the flower of her maidenhood had long since withered and fallen and the brown seedpods of older age had taken their place. She had a tabby cat of the male variety on which she lavished the love and affection nature had endowed her with for the care of her own babies. Circumstances having denied her this, I have to tell you that this cat was in clover. In his own haughty way, however, this tom wanted nothing to do with any person of the male variety. Any attempt to stroke him or pick him up only resulted in a quick claw mark deeply scratched in your hand. It was almost like a set-up, for he would let you approach him all right. You could even touch him. After that you were on your own and he, being related to the owners, was completely immune from any punishment for his treacherous actions.[269]

One day the whole family went off to town. They were to be gone until the next day, and right here and now I deny being the originator of the devilish plot that unfolded. "But, Van," said my chum, "this cat should be taught that life is not all honey and skittles. He should have some lessons in humility and he should learn to show appreciation for others who care for him. By the way, are you at all versed in surgery?"

I confessed that I had drawn blood for a cause.

"Well, you're on. See that your scalpel is in order, sir!"

He found a boot with plenty of leg and slipped on his leather gloves. A minor caterwauling could be heard as he eased old Tommy in headfirst. He then proceeded to stick the cat-filled boot between his legs and any wrestler will tell you that is a fatal hold. In less than a minute, Tommy was reduced to the physical status of a mule, without hope of posterity. When the family came back they all puzzled over Tommy's shyness. Within a week, however, he was back in the arms of his mistress but with the remarkable difference that he would let everybody pet him, including us. I don't think she ever discovered the reason. Tommy certainly never told and neither did we!

In the fall of '86 I was out of a job. I learned that the **HS** outfit managed by Ed Marron proposed to drive eleven-hundred head of beef steers from their range on the Redwater to Rapid City, Dakota Territory.[270] At that time that was the end of the Elk Horn and Missouri River Railroad. The plan was to ship the steers by rail down into Nebraska and winter them there for the spring market. The distance we would drive the cattle was two-hundred-and-fifty miles straight across country. We would not cross a public road or see a fence in the whole distance.[271]

---

269 The ranch described by Stephen in this section belonged to John L. Burns. In addition to being a well-known horse breeder, Burns ran a stage stop and road ranch near the mouth of Burns Creek. His sister, Mrs. C. A. Backus, arrived by herself from Iowa early in 1883 and lived with the Burns family for a number of years. [CE, p. 1,042.] Mrs. Backus worked primarily as the cook and housekeeper for the Burns' roadhouse guests. The ranch operated under the **JB** brand. [MSD, p. 150. See THWT for the biography of John L. Burns and his family.]

270 See *"The HS ranch"* in Author's Notes following this chapter for the story of the **HS** and the biographies of the ranch's foreman, Ed Marron, and his wife, Grace (Bendon) Marron.

271 The country wasn't perfectly trackless in 1886. To get from the Redwater country to O'Fallon Station on the south side of the Yellowstone, the drovers would have crossed the Fort Buford–Fort Keogh road.

The cattle were divided into two groups of five-hundred-and-fifty each. Each herd had its own mess wagon and a cook and six men with some thirty-five saddle horses and a wrangler. That arrangement gave us a lead man who was also the herd boss, two point men and two flankers on each side of the herd, and one man for the drag.[272] We would switch positions every three hours so nobody got stuck in the dust for too long. We crossed the Yellowstone River at O'Fallon Station of the Northern Pacific Railroad and continued on up O'Fallon Creek. The length of a day's drive would always be from water to water, the cattle grazing all the way. Thus some days we would have rather long drives, while on others they would be comparatively short. The water proved scarce but we reached the headwaters of the Little Missouri without adventure.

The morning after we reached the Little Missouri we knew we were going to have a short drive that day, so the foreman ordered the herd held until after dinner.[273] It was a beautiful day, the sun warm and the skies clear, so we all left camp. Even the cook took a stroll up the creek. Preparing to set up for dinner, the cook and two of the riders came back to camp about 11 o'clock. And did they ever get a surprise! Crawling in and around the pots and pans and our bedrolls was a swarm of rattlesnakes. We killed eleven. We had camped right over their den and they had come out for a final airing on this warm sunshiny day. I might add that this experience caused none of us to suffer from nervous shock. The country was liberally infested with rattlesnakes and we were so accustomed to them that we felt as little concern about them as the ordinary housewife does over a common spider. Unless a rattler was right in our camp or in town or snuggled up against

---

[272] Had the herd been larger, an additional pair of riders would have been added, one on each side, riding between the point men and the flankers. These men were called "wheelers." There could also have been a bed wagon pulled by a team of four that would have carried the men's personal bedding, clothing, and toiletry. [HYCW, Fall-Winter 1992, Vol. 22, No. 2, p. 15.] On short drives like the one described by Norton, the five cowboys and the wrangler would have provided their own night watch, two at a time, on three-hour shifts. On longer drives, full-time night crews were added.

[273] In Norton's time and place, the three daily meals were called breakfast, dinner, and supper. When the term "lunch" was used, it implied a snack. For example: "Lunch was served at midnight following the dance." or "During harvest we were served a small lunch between dinner and supper." Thus, when Norton wrote that the herd was "held until after dinner," that meant the herd was held until approximately one o'clock in the afternoon.

or inside a line shack or a ranch house, we normally paid them no attention.

A few days after this we had our only spell of weather. The wind came up in the morning and soon was blowing a regular gale. In the afternoon it started to snow and by dark it was coming down like a regular avalanche. It wasn't so cold, but the snow was wet and heavy and the wind was blowing it horizontally. The cattle refused to bed down, leaving us with the risk that they would disperse in the storm and scatter in every possible downwind direction. Consequently we stayed on the job all that night during the storm and kept them moving in a circle. We arrived at Rapid City about a week later and without further incident.

Once the steers had been loaded into the railroad cars, our duties were done and we were all out of a job. The wagons and horses, along with the regular men, would return to the Redwater and any of the rest of us who wished to do so could go back with the outfit free of charge. Only two or three of the boys returned with the regular outfit. The rest of them went out on a bust and that was that.

CHAPTER 18–AUTHOR'S NOTES

Barney Estabrook was rarely mentioned in either of the Glendive newspapers. For whatever reason, the *Yellowstone Journal* out of Miles City seemed to have more interest in his activities. While the newspaper consistently spelled his name as "Esterbrook," both his brand registration and his marriage license in Glendive was made out to "Barnard Estabrook" so the latter spelling has been used herein. A. B. Estabrook was reported to be running cattle in "the Yellowstone Valley" in July of 1884. [YJ, 5 July 1884.] "Barney Esterbrook *[sic]* was appointed Deputy U.S. Marshal in Glendive." [YJ, 15 August 1885.] On 1 November 1885, Barnard Estabrook married Minnie Ray, the daughter of Col. Josiah H. Ray (the Glendive hotelier who was elected Dawson County's Superintendent of Schools in the elections of 1882). [TLW, p. 293. Also see "Marriage Licenses, 1882–1887" in OTOL, p. 509.] The cattle operation of "Pierson, Esterbrook *[sic]* and Clark" had "range on the north side of the Yellowstone River; p. o. Glendive; range is Bad Route Creek." [YJ, 7 November 1885. Also see TLW, p. 283.] It was almost exactly sixty cross-country miles to the southwest from John Burn's **JB** ranch, where Norton was working, to the high country headwaters of Bad Route Creek, where the **NY** range was located. "Cracker Box" Dan, to whom Norton referred, was probably an old denizen of Cracker Box Creek (named after the wooden U.S. Army cracker boxes used to develop the springs at the creek's headwaters) and was thus familiar with that part of the country. Cracker Box Creek was about six miles north of Bad Route Creek; Timber Creek was located between the two. From Glendive to Bad Route Creek was about forty miles southwest as the crow flies.

The HS ranch, foreman Ed Marron, and his wife, Grace: Thomas Hubbard and Henry Sampson, the owners of the **HS**, were New York City millionaires. In an interesting twist, the ranch had an address of "p. o. Glendive, Montana Territory," but all business mail was directed to "HS Ranch, New York City."

An unqualified reference to "the **HS**" can lead to some confusion since the Hash Knife outfit (the Continental Land and Cattle Company out of Texas), located on the headwaters of the Little Missouri in Custer County, also used the **HS** brand. (The Hash Knife was owned by W. E. Hughes and John M. Simpson of Dallas, Texas, hence the initials "**HS**".) The Hash Knife, at one-hundred-thousand head of cattle plus a three-hundred-head horse-breeding unit, dwarfed even the big Hubbard and Sampson operation. [TLW, p. 153.] While one of the Hubbard and Sampson brands was registered for the animal's right shoulder, another Hubbard and Sampson brand and the Hash Knife brand were both registered to be placed at one of two different locations: the right rib and/or the right hip. [MSD, p. 122 and p. 156.] Fortunately, the brands of the two ranches did not look alike. The Hash Knife used the letters "**HS**" while at the **HS** ranch the brand was a wide "H" with the "S" placed in the center of the "H." [MSD, p. 156] The Hubbard and Sampson cattle also wore a "lazy 6" or "lazy 9" (depending on how you read it) on the right jaw. The biggest plus was that the Hughes and Simpson Hash Knife operation was centered in southeastern Custer County while Hubbard and Sampson were in central Dawson County. Consequently, the Yellowstone River flowed between the two ranches and their headquarters were separated by nearly one-hundred miles.

Tom Hubbard and Henry Sampson, the New York millionaires who owned the **HS** ranch, should not be confused with the "cattle kings of the Rosebud," R. J. Hubbard of Mankato, Minnesota, and J. J. Thompson of Muddy, Custer County, Montana. Fortunately, the Hubbard and Thompson brands were the **OD**, the **T**, the **N**, and the **Z**. [MSD, pp. 123–125.] There was another Glendive-based cattle operation (which, like the **HS**, had a New York mailing address) named Sampson and Fahnestock. Its manager was Charles A. Doyle and its brand was an **X** with a bar above it (commonly called the "**Bar X**"). [TLW, p. 307. MSD, p. 163.] This short-lived outfit, which started in 1886, grazed on Spring Creek, just to the south of the Hubbard and Sampson range on Sevenmile Creek. (It was, fortunately, far to the west of the Hashknife range on the Little Missouri.) The mailing address of Sampson and Fahnestock was New York City so it is possible that the Sampson of Sampson and Fahnestock was the same Henry Sampson who was involved in the Hubbard and Sampson operation. Additionally, there was a Sampson and Dale outfit with a Glendive address. [MSD, p. 163.] In any case, in 1886, one could find the **HS** ranch of Tom Hubbard and Henry Sampson (of New York City) on the Redwater and Sevenmile; the **HS** ("Hash Knife") ranch of W. E. Hughes and John M. Simpson (of Dallas, Texas) in the Little Missouri–Mingusville–

O'Fallon Creek triangle; the Rosebud operation of R. J. Hubbard and J. J. Thompson (of Mankato, Minnesota); the Spring Creek ranch of Sampson and Fahnestock (of New York City); and the Glendive-based Sampson and Dale—five separate organizations—all operating at the same time in the same general area.

No mention can be found of either the 10,000-head Hubbard and Thompson, or the Sampson and Dale outfits after the killer winter of 1886–1887. In 1887, Sampson and Fahnestock sold the **Bar X** to their manager, Charlie Doyle, who ran it successfully for many years. [GHMT, p. 22.] As a single-owner entity, the vast Hash Knife outfit owned by Hughes and Simpson outlasted them all. By 1897, however, there were too many **HS** brands in Montana and Dakota to suit Hughes and Simpson, so they converted everything at the Hash Knife to their Texas Mill Iron brand. The famed Hash Knife–Mill Iron operation stayed in the cattle business for many more years after 1900.

As manager of Hubbard and Sampson's **HS**, Ed Marron became one of the best-known cattlemen in eastern Montana. Born 12 September 1856 in Utica, New York, the Marron family moved to Assumption, Christian County, Illinois in 1861. Marron had first appeared in the lower Yellowstone country and "the Big Open" in the fall of 1873 where, having just turned seventeen, he was possibly working as a skinner for buffalo hunter George Grant. The next two seasons, 1874 and 1875, young Marron was employed as the guide to two New York millionaires, Thomas Hubbard and Henry Sampson, when they came to Montana Territory to hunt buffalo. Hubbard and Sampson fell in love with the country and decided to put together a ranch someday. In 1876, Marron's parents moved from Illinois to Dakota Territory. He then set himself up in the woodyard business on Sevenmile Creek during the 1877 Yellowstone navigating season, while the Sioux campaign was on. Hoopes noted that while Marron had established his own small cattle ranch on the Sevenmile by the fall of 1877, he continued to hunt buffalo and trap out of that location. (That early date certainly places Ed Marron as the first cattleman to establish a ranch on the west side of the lower Yellowstone Valley.) Ed Marron partnered with another young man, Andrew ("Glendive") Smith (born in New York City in 1855), to "hunt buff" for the NPRR construction crews in 1880, 1881, and 1882. (Recall that it was Andrew Smith

EDWARD MARRON, 1896
ILLUSTRATION BY JUAN MORA

who had accompanied Bill Cheney on his famed "ride for life" in the fall of 1877. See Author's Notes following Chapter 7.)

In 1882, Hubbard and Sampson contacted Marron to run the ranch they wanted to assemble. The two millionaires came out and the three men collectively decided to locate the new undertaking on the Redwater. Marron pulled out of his Sevenmile digs and selected a headquarters on the Redwater, about twelve miles below the present-day site of Richey, Montana. The Redwater flowed to the northeast and paralleled the north side of the divide that separated the Missouri and Yellowstone river drainages. It dumped into the Missouri opposite Poplar, centered about equidistant from the Hardscrabble drainage to the east and Wolf Point to the west. On the opposite side of the divide were Threemile, Sevenmile, Morgan (previously called "Ninemile"), Thirteenmile, and Burns creeks, all of which drained into the Yellowstone. In 1883, the cattle started pouring into the **HS**. By crossing the divide and expanding their range to include Sevenmile Creek, in addition to the Redwater drainage, the ranch quickly grew into an outfit that grazed around twenty-five-thousand head. As part of the deal with Hubbard and

272 • An Uncommon Journey

Sampson, Marron was allowed to have his own herd of cattle as well. It was possibly this arrangement that led to the **HS** incorporating the Sevenmile country into their operation. That had been Marron's grazing area prior to his involvement with Hubbard and Sampson. [TLW, p. 167 and p. 215. GHMT, p. 22. OTOL, p. 14. MSD, p. 156.]

Ed, who was then twenty-eight, married fifteen-year-old Grace Bendon on 24 December 1884 at her father's home, about one mile west of Glendive. Grace described her welcome to the ranch:

> The first week was spent at the hotel in Glendive waiting for the weather man to get over his New Year's celebration. Then we started for our home, 60 miles away. We had a sled and 2 prancing bronchos *[sic]*, but as the snow was very deep and the weather very severe, it took us three days to make the trip. There was no road, no fences...just snow and wind-swept prairie. Finally, we arrived at our journey's end and found 6 cowboys and a Mexican cook anxiously waiting for us. Dinner was on the table. It consisted of baked beans, raw tomatoes served in the can, back bacon, sour dough bread and what the cowboys called "spotted dog," which was rice boiled with raisins in it...and, Oh! I have never seen such big raisins. I will never forget that reception.

Grace also described her life as the only woman on a frontier cattle ranch:

> To the cowboys I was a real curiousity as I was the only white woman on the Red Water *[sic]* and that stream was 90 miles long. It was six months before I had the opportunity to speak to another woman. Cowboys would come for miles to see the bride but when they arrived they were half-starved and partly frozen and too shy to even speak to me. These were free and happy days, but they were lonely at times. Sometimes I would find myself screaming at the top of my voice when I was alone. I would ask myself what I was crying about but I could not answer. Today I know it was only loneliness...and my woman heart longed for the companionship of one of my own sex. It is good for us to be alone at times...it gives us a chance to explore our own minds, but too much of it is terrible. [Grace Marron

Gilmore, draft letter or speech notes dated 9 January 1923, p. 19–20 and p. 22. Frontier Gateway Museum collection.]

In one of life's odd coincidences, Grace (Bendon) Marron was born to Nathaniel Bendon and Mary C. (McCoy) Bendon in Alliance, Stark County, Ohio in 1869. At that time Alliance, Ohio, was the parish of Father Eli Lindesmith. In 1880, Lindesmith became the priest at Fort Keogh near Miles City. The Bendon family then moved to Glendive in October of 1881 when Grace was twelve years old. When Grace married Ed Marron three years later, it was Father Lindesmith who performed the marriage ceremony at her parents' home. [TLW, p. 19.] Lindesmith remembered the couple's mid-winter departure for the ranch on the Redwater: "Ed Marron prepared a large sled box three feet high, filled it with soft oats straw, covered it with bows and a tarpaulin. He then threw in plenty of blankets and buffalo robes and in the midst of these he placed his wife. He then hitched four strong horses to the sled and carried her home." [Quoted in TLW, p. 215.]

Ed Marron and Grace made their home at the **HS** ranch headquarters on the Redwater for the next thirteen years until Ed's sudden and unexpected death from a heart attack on 8 June 1898 at the age of forty-one. He was buried in Glendive.

In 1904, Hubbard and Sampson sold their **HS** operation and brand to Henry Douglas and David Mead, the two brothers-in-law who were long-time Glendive entrepreneurs. [EBDC, p. 62. GHMT, p. 22.] Douglas and Mead downsized the operation somewhat, but continued to operate the ranch for a number of years.

Following Marron's death, Grace left the **HS** and moved into Glendive. Five years later, on Christmas Day, 1903, Grace (Bendon) Marron, who was then thirty-four, married James W. Gilmore, a sixty-seven-year-old retired sheep rancher. Jim Gilmore died in Glendive on 23 February 1912 at the age of seventy-six. That left Grace, then forty-three years old, a widow for the second time. She never remarried. Instead, she devoted a great deal of time to civic activities. She started the Women's Club of Glendive. She was active in the Women's Christian Temperance Union and in the women's suffrage movement in Montana. During World War I, she worked for some time in Washington, D. C. Always active in her church, she went to Europe in 1919 with Catholic Welfare.

When she married Jim Gilmore in 1903, they moved into the first frame house erected in Glendive. Grace's father, Nathaniel Bendon, had built the house in 1881 just after he arrived in Glendive, employed as a carpenter by the Yellowstone Land and Colonization Company. One of the more picturesque residences in Glendive, it was known for many years as "the Gilmore House." Unfortunately, Grace lost her home during the Great Depression. She lived in an apartment in Glendive for a few years and "her last ten years were spent in poverty in Marsh."[OTOL, p. 110.]

Grace (Bendon) (Marron) Gilmore died 5 May 1950 at the age of eighty-one. Fortunately, Grace had been a great recorder all of her life and she had written numerous articles concerning early Glendive which local newspapers (especially *The Independent Voice of Eastern Montana* in the 1930s) had printed. She had also written a host of letters to friends and acquaintances, some of which found their way into print. She was an occasional speaker at different events and many of the notes to her speeches have also survived. [TLW, p. 19, p. 167, p. 215, and p. 307. GHMT, pp. 21–22. OTOL, pp. 109–110 and p. 960. MISB, p. 1,112.]

Christmas of 1886 and My New Year's Celebration of 1887:

A Cold and Lonely Ride Across O'Fallon Divide

APID CITY WAS THE END OF THE RAILROAD. All the freight from there into Dead Wood and a number of the surrounding smaller towns was handled by bull teams and Tallaho coaches.[274] It was a colorful sight to see those Mexican teamsters with twelve teams of oxen[275] and three wagons hooked together toiling along the roads. It was even more interesting to watch them in-span or out-span. They would stop and unyoke the oxen, leaving the yoke in place. The unfettered oxen were then free to wander off and graze. After the oxen had grazed for the allotted time, the driver would call out a command to them and every ox would come in and take his place by his own yoke. The Mexican bullwhackers were first rate.[276]

Rapid City was larger, better organized, and more cosmopolitan than any of the towns along the Yellowstone. Nevertheless, it was still very much a frontier town. The place reeked of every form of dissipation known to man, and our boys were real suckers for the set-up they found there. In three to four days not one of them had a red cent to his name, and some of them had not even taken the precaution to get their winter clothes. They were a sorry-looking lot when they sobered up.

---

[274] See *"Yoicks! There's the Tallyho coach plodding along!"* in Author's Notes following this chapter for a discussion of the frontier's "Tallaho" coaches.

[275] "Twelve teams" meant there were twenty-four oxen.

[276] See *"The bullwhackers"* in Author's Notes following this chapter.

I was a boy of seventeen, a few years younger than the rest of the crew, and had taken no part in the debauch. I had given my money to the hotelkeeper to keep for me. I should have gone back with the outfit, but I had found one of my younger brothers, David,[277] working for different freighting outfits there in Rapid City. Born in April of 1870, almost exactly a year younger than me, he had turned sixteen since I had seen him last. The two of us decided I might as well spend the winter there, since, like him, I had nothing in particular to go back to. I learned, however, that my foresight was much at fault. The boys from the drive were now facing the problem of getting through the winter. They suffered under the handicap of not knowing anything but ranch work, and there would be none of that forthcoming until spring. But, truly, the Lord provides (sometimes).

Into this picture came a tie contractor. This man had a railroad tie contract, owned a piece of timber with a cabin, and was looking for a crew of men to work the timber into ties. The hotelkeeper had told him about our small crowd of young drovers and he had arranged a meeting. I still remember the remark he made: "Heaven must have sent you boys."

Well, I personally never thought Heaven had much to do with it. If Heaven had sent that crowd of rowdies, then Heaven just wasn't working according to Hoyle on that day. There was not one of those fellows who could handle an ax any better than an old woman. Of course, their new employer didn't know that. They had seen me using an ax around camp, and they knew I was much more proficient than any of them. I had learned to use an ax when I was a small boy back in Minnesota. Well, they insisted that I go with them, feeling sure that without me they would be able to cut no more ties than enough to pay their expenses.

I agreed to go along. We all got along very well together and we managed to cut just about enough ties to keep our grocery bills paid. With me spending about half my time being the "tutor of the ax," this was accomplished without any of them losing a finger, a toe, or a foot. I witnessed some of the most bizarre

---

[277] David Cass Van Blaricom was the second son and second child of the nine children of Levi Van Blaricom and Sarah Susan (Johnson) Van Blaricom. David was twelve years old when his mother died in Glendive on 25 September 1882. For his brief biography, see Appendix 8, "David Cass Van Blaricom, Brother of Stephen Norton."

methods of wielding an ax ever conceived by man, and oftentimes the old wood chips flew off into space at totally unpredictable angles. In about three weeks, though, the boys were getting real itchy to go into town. None of them had a cent, however, and they all knew that I had salted away my pay from the cattle drive somewhere. I soon saw that my pay and I would likely be parted before winter's end. So it was that one morning I told them I was going to walk down to our supply depot for some things. I didn't say I was leaving, but that's what I did.

I went on down to Rapid City and collected the rest of my money from the hotelkeeper. I looked up my brother, David, and said good-bye. I then went to the livery stable and bought a horse for $35.00. I had decided to return to the Yellowstone alone. It was a few days before Christmas, 1886, and the weather was fine. I remember thinking if it held for ten days that I could make the two-hundred-and-fifty-mile trip and be back in Glendive in time for New Year's Day of 1887. It was a groundless judgment and it might have—and nearly did—cost me my life.

I have not been able to accurately recall the date, but I left Rapid City sometime between December 15 and 20. For the purposes of this story, let's say I left on December 17. Luckily I had taken the precaution to dress warmly, and I had two blankets with me. My second day out of Rapid City the winter came in with a blast and it proved to be the worst winter Montana has ever known. I am sure it still stands today as some sort of a record. The Hash Knife outfit on Box Elder Creek, a tributary of the Little Missouri, had driven in twenty-five-thousand head of young stuff that fall. They never found a live one come spring.

I made connections with ranches every day. I was obliged to stay at each place two to three days waiting for storms to pass. The night of the day I left the Hash Knife Ranch[278] I spent with a sheep man on the east side of the divide between the Little Missouri and the Yellowstone rivers. As I was setting out to leave the next morning, this man said to me, "Kid, you may have some trouble getting across the divide. You'll find the snow deeper on

---

[278] The Hash Knife (the Continental Land and Cattle Company) changed its Montana name and brand to the Mill Iron (the same company's Texas entity) in 1897. The old Mill Iron (Hash Knife) headquarters site shows on modern maps some twenty miles to the east and slightly south of Ekalaka, Carter County, Montana.

top than it is down here. I'll give you a little lunch to take along. You may need it." His observation proved to be all too true.

It was quite cold the morning I left the sheep camp, and, as the herder had predicted, the snow kept getting deeper. My horse was not in the best of condition, and it had been up grade and uphill all that day. I got off and led him wherever I could, but the best we could do was to reach the summit of the divide when darkness came. My horse was done in for the day, so I simply had to make the best of a very bad situation. There was absolutely nothing out of which I could build a fire. The snow was deep, and it was blowing pretty hard. The temperature was well below freezing. There was no possibility of reaching any shelter. And it wasn't a case of being sent to bed without my supper. There wasn't any bed, just like there wasn't any supper.

I unsaddled my horse and pinned him. It looked fully as hopeless for him as it did for myself. The snow was deep and he would have to paw for what he could get, and I knew that wouldn't be much. There wasn't anything I could do about either of our situations, however, so I looked around to see how I was going to spend the night and survive. I found a little gully about two feet deep that fit me nicely. I kicked the snow out of it for the length I would need. I put one of my blankets under me and the other blanket over me, and I went to sleep. In a short time the snow had drifted over me and, believe it or not, I was snug as a bug in a rug. I slept as sound as a monk in a monastery, sans pajamas.

The stage, of course, was set here for a thrilling story. The headlines would have read: "Young man found frozen to death at the head of O'Fallon Creek!" All that prevented it was that I did not get frightened over my predicament. Fear has always been the cause of more death than bullets. When fear takes possession, reason and judgment take their leave. The subject is then at the mercy of whatever danger besets him.

I have personally witnessed several cases of this "fear" phenomenon. One young fellow from the East left Glendive and went out hunting on foot. He crossed the Yellowstone on the ferry and headed north. He then went up a nearby creek that led him to the northwest for several miles and, still in the Yellowstone drainage, he wandered over a divide or two to the north. He then found himself in strange surroundings. Fear got the best of him and he went totally berserk. It was two more days before we found him. He had lost his gun and his hat and he was as mad as a March hare. This boy's problem would have been very simple if he had kept his wits about him. But we must remember that there are many individuals who just cannot control their fears. If this boy, when he found himself confused, would have sat down and composed himself and thought about it, he would have known that water must run downhill. He could have easily understood that the water in the nearest creek must inevitably flow to the nearest river (which in this case was the Yellowstone) and by the Yellowstone there was a stage road he could have followed. He need not have been lost but for a few hours, not for a few days. He had expected to see a wolf or a bear or some other predatory wild animal coming at him from behind every rock he passed. It is true that there were then plenty of wolves in those hills, but no wolf will bother a human being if, instead, he can dine on a weak yearling steer or a sheep. This young man, however, was convinced otherwise, and when we found him after three days he was completely, if temporarily, out of his mind with fear.

Well, morning came as it will and I had slept. I was beginning to feel the necessity of finding some place I could get something to eat. I pushed up my counterpane of snow and looked about. Things were very much as the day before—windy and the temperature well below zero. My tonsorial requirements were really pretty evident but I had nothing with which to accomplish them. It was probably just as well that I didn't have the wherewithal to wash my face for if I had it would have been instantly frozen.

My horse had made it through the night okay, so I put the saddle back on him and we were on our way. I knew there was a horse ranch on the creek I was going down, but I had little feel for the distance I might be from it. I had gone no more than two or three miles when, rounding a bend in the creek, I suddenly came upon a tent sitting there in the snow. I could see smoke coming up from the stovepipe so I felt sure of temporary haven.

I rode up to the tent and a man stuck his head out of the opening, fully as surprised as I was at the sight of a visitor. You can understand our mutual enjoyment when we discovered that we were old friends. This young fellow had been our night horse wrangler on the trip over to Rapid City with the cattle. He had seen beaver sign along this creek and had decided that he would outfit himself and spend the winter trapping. He had come this far with the outfit on their way back to the Redwater. At his invitation I stayed on with him for two days. It was already 1887 and I cannot tell you today where I had passed either Christmas or New Year's.

For the benefit of anyone who might believe that young people must see the bright lights of "civilization" and hear the now "avant-garde" music of jazz to be content, I want to tell you what this boy's plans were for the winter. Although I never knew his real age, he was not over twenty-five years old. He had got himself a tent, a sheet iron stove, some flour, bacon, and potatoes, a few cans of tomatoes, and some tinned fruit. He had made his winter camp there by a small pool of water where he did not expect to see another human soul until the following spring, sometime in March (maybe) or April (maybe) or May. For all of at least four months, perhaps five, he would be absolutely alone.

You've got to understand that the farthest thing from his mind was any doubt as to why his presence there should even be questioned, let alone be expected to elicit some feeling of sympathy. And boredom would certainly not be among any of the issues. He would see and hear things every day that would be vastly more satisfactory to the untarnished muse than bright lights and jazz. He would, after all, be watching his beavers, studying their habits and regretting that he must take some of them for their pelts so that he might trade them for the things that he, in turn, would require for his own survival. He would hear the silence of a snowfall—that total lack of sound few among modern men are fortunate enough to ever experience. Often the wolf and the coyote would sing to him at night, a symphony sure to put terror in the heart of the uninitiated, but he would know his company and be unafraid. He had learned to distinguish some of their cries and one of the wolves he had named "Old Pete." Wolves have a home range they will not leave unless they are crowded pretty hard. Conversely, Old Pete knew that, in order to avoid a severe dose of lead colic, he shouldn't get too chummy with his uninvited guest.

My friend spent many of his isolated winter hours observing the deer and antelope, many of which will stay in certain areas for months on end. He learned of their traveling patterns and he came to understand that a kind of family organization or social structure existed among them. He watched the prairie hens come home at night to roost and saw them fly plop into the snowdrifts, leaving no track with which to betray their presence to an enemy. He saw a night sky that is a thing of ethereal beauty, a sight never seen in a city or in the industrial East with all its smoke and humidity.

This boy had his feet on the ground. His pleasure was in the Truth and Beauty of Nature as it was created. Much of mankind views life only through rose-colored glasses and, consequently, must live in an atmosphere of sham and artificiality. It is much the same difference we find between a beautiful rose with its alluring fragrance and a copy in tinsel. The one lives, propagates, dies, and lives again. The other is never imbued with Life.

I left the welcome company of my introspective and observant friend on the morning of the third day. I never saw him again.

I reached the horse ranch before nightfall and I was storm-stayed one day there. The following day I reached the Yellowstone River at the confluence with O'Fallon Creek. With no downstream trail at all on the east side, I had to cross. The Yellowstone had frozen over with drifting ice and that fact made it difficult to find a crossing where I could get my horse across. I finally made it, however, and by nightfall of January 10, 1887, I had reached the home of some friends. My long and eventful trip from Rapid City was finished. My horse and I had been on the trail for some twenty-three days. Except for the first day out of Rapid City, the temperature had remained below zero the entire trip.

It was shortly after I returned to Glendive that the thermometer really plummeted. It went down to minus sixty degrees Fahrenheit later in January and February. The killer winter of the Northern Plains had arrived.

CHAPTER 19–AUTHOR'S NOTES

Chapter 19, unless otherwise noted, is based on pp. 25–30 of the Stephen Norton Van Blaricom memoir. He did not specify the actual date of his arrival in Glendive nor did he enumerate the number of days the journey had taken. Both the date and the number of days stated were estimated by the author from the description of the trip provided in the manuscript. [To follow the approximate route taken by Norton on his wintry trek from Rapid City to Glendive, see Map 7 *"Cold and Lonely Ride."*]

Yoicks! There's the Tallyho coach plodding along! The western American descriptive of a "Tallyho coach" or "Tallaho coach" had nothing to do with the phrase of "Yoicks and tally ho!" so famously shouted by mounted English hunters when the fox suddenly appeared from its hiding place. "Yoicks" was an archaic English term of encouragement given to hunting dogs. It was also a British exclamation of excitement. [TID, p. 2,653.] "Tally" meant "mark" or "target," and "ho," usually accompanied by vigorous pointing, was meant as "I see him over there!" Thus, "Yoicks and tally ho!" translated into "Good job, hounds! I see our fox over there!"

In England, a "Tallyho" was a rather elegant four-horse carriage. The name derived from a famed commercial coach, the *Tally Ho,* which traveled regularly between London and Birmingham. [TID, p. 2,335.] One can easily envision the first-class English coach speeding along through the countryside, carrying its wigged and powdered passengers, with the liveried coachman cracking his long whip above the racing four-in-hand of dappled grays and yelling out, "Tally ho!" It was a warning meant to clear the road ahead: "The *Tally Ho* is coming!"

In America, especially in the West, the phrase "Tallyho coach" or "Tallaho coach" was a euphuism used to describe two or three freight wagons linked together, being pulled slowly and laboriously by multiple yokes of oxen, while the bullwhacker trudged beside his bovine charges cracking his enormous whip. The whip was the only similarity with the famed Tally Ho.

The whip rarely, if ever, touched any oxen. The bullwhackers were experts at placing the "working end" of the whip (two tapered leather strips about one inch wide and six inches long called "clappers" or

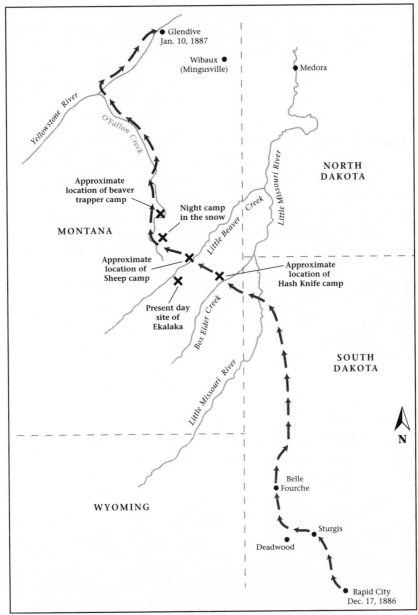

MAP 7—STEPHEN NORTON VAN BLARICOM'S "COLD AND LONELY RIDE" FROM RAPID CITY TO GLENDIVE DECEMBER 17, 1886 - JANUARY 10, 1887

[ABOUT 260 MILES. MAP NOT TO SCALE]

"flappers") just behind the ears of the teams. It was the explosive "cr-r-a-a-ack" of the flappers on the end of the whip that urged the animals forward. The same was true with the whips used in conjunction with the teams of horses used to pull stagecoaches, freight wagons, and so on. The bull whips and carriage whips varied widely in length according to the skill of the user; in experienced hands, they could reach out some astounding lengths.

The bullwhackers: Although Norton mentioned "those Mexican bullwhackers" and reported them as being "first rate," bullwhacking was not the exclusive province of Mexicans. Photographs of the great ox teams and their handlers show men of every race and color involved. Women got into the act occasionally as well. A list of Calamity Jane's (Martha Canary) activities was reported by the *Glendive Times* on 9 February 1882: "Calamity Jane, ex-female scout, bullwhacker and a hard citizen of the Black Hills passed through Glendive one day last week on her way to Miles City."

CHAPTER TWENTY

The Winter of 1886–1887

AS FAST AS THE BUFFALO WERE ELIMINATED from the range, people saw the opportunity to stock it with more and more cattle. In the spring of 1884 there was a decided and noticeable cattle boom. The ranges were free, and the taxes were almost nil. While the previous winters had been cold, there was plenty of feed on the range, and the cattle had been coming through with very few losses. Eastern Montana truly was beginning to look like a livestock gold mine with free range and no winter feeding to do. Men were actually wondering what they were going to do with all their money in a few more years.[279]

But alack and alas! Something dreadful always happens to these soft, sure things. The summer of '86 had been unusually hot and dry, and the grasshoppers had taken more than their normal share of the feed. More important, even to an eye as young as mine, there were far too many cattle on the range. In addition to the thousands and thousands of cattle brought in by the large investor ranches, there was now an abundance of small ranchers who had appeared, each with two or three-hundred head of cattle, drifting along on credit, selling just enough in the fall to pay their expenses. Everyone knew in the fall of 1886 that the situation was bad, with feed being so short, but little did they dream of what was about to happen.

Up until about the middle of December the temperature had been fairly moderate, but the snowfall had been heavy and totally covered whatever grass there was. The cattle were getting hungry because they wouldn't burrow their muzzles underneath that

---

[279] Unless otherwise noted, the source for Chapter 20 is SNVB, pp. 31–32.

snow in order to graze. About the 15th, a chinook[280] came in and the snow started to melt. It looked like some relief was in sight. In that week before the Christmas holiday, however, the devil himself must have opened up the gates from the North Pole. And, believe me, he left them open! The thermometers plummeted and that slushed snow left by the chinook crusted up and set itself as hard as concrete.[281]

Already hungry when that blizzard came in out of Canada late in December, the livestock quickly became desperate for feed. The horses and sheep would paw at the crust, sometimes getting through to find a bite or two. The cattle, however, didn't know how to paw and, with no upper teeth like a horse or a sheep, they were at a real disadvantage. Within a couple of weeks they began to wander up to buildings or into settlements and eat the tarpaper or newspaper or whatever they could find right off the buildings.[282] They would gnaw at the buildings and then shelter against them and die. Water also became a serious problem. The big rivers, like the Missouri and the Yellowstone, would get air holes, and the cattle tried to get to them to drink. Instead, they would crowd, fall through, and drown.[283] The smaller streams, like Beaver Creek and the Little Missouri, froze solid. The cattle would go down into draws looking for water and shelter. A snowstorm would blow in and simply cover them up, all huddled together, and suffocate or freeze them to death—sometimes a few, sometimes hundreds at a time.[284] The young Texas stuff that had been driven up that summer all died first. They didn't have any winter hair, they weren't used to the climate at all, and they didn't

---

[280] In eastern Montana, the term "chinook" is used to describe a warm, dry, westerly wind that originates on the eastern slopes of the Rocky Mountains and descends out over the plains. [TID, p. 391 and p. 881.]

[281] See *"The killer winter"* in Author's Notes following this chapter.

[282] "Starving cattle staggered through village streets, collapsed and died in dooryards. Five-thousand head invaded the outskirts of the newborn city of Billings, bawling for food. They snatched up the saplings the proud city had just planted [and] gorged themselves upon garbage." [Joseph Kinsey Howard as quoted in M/M, p. 165.]

[283] E. C. "Teddy Blue" Abbott described how hard the cowboys worked trying to get the desperate cattle watered at temperatures of fifty and sixty below zero. He told how the legs of the cow ponies were cut and bleeding and how "the cattle had the hide and hair wore off their legs" from the icy crust. The raw flesh on their legs was exposed. "It was surely hell," Abbott wrote, "to see big four-year-old steers just able to stagger along." [WPTN, p. 176.]

[284] RBL, p. 435.

know how to eat the bark off the cottonwoods. They all died. The older, shaggy, native Montana cows went last. They knew to eat the small cottonwood limbs and bark and they knew the country, but even they were dying.[285]

No one will ever know an accurate tally of the livestock losses suffered that winter. The horses and sheep fared better than the cattle. I would personally reckon the cattle deaths at eighty percent or more. They died not by the hundreds or thousands, but by the hundreds of thousands.[286]

The winter of 1886–1887 wasn't that easy on people either. It was so bad that it was a real risk for people to leave their cabins.[287] Cowboys would go out to try to help their cattle at least get access to water, and they were never seen again. They would wander in circles, lost in those storms until they succumbed to the cold. Disoriented children died less than a hundred feet from the doors of their homes after they had simply gone to the stable to milk the cow or do their chores.

The people who died out on the prairie and were found, or the people who died in their homes or their dugouts or in the line shacks, couldn't be buried. The ground was frozen so hard a pick wouldn't touch it. Once they were froze up so the wolves couldn't take them, the dead were simply laid outside at the end of the cabin and left there, covered by a blanket of snow and ice until spring thaw.[288]

Not a few people lost their minds to cabin fever that winter, and one or two were known to have committed suicide. That included Emma, the young woman who was the maid and cook at the Wibaux ranch headquarters near Mingusville.[289]

---

[285] See *"Cowboy artist Charles M. Russell"* in Author's Notes following this chapter.

[286] RBL, p, 435 and pp. 438–439.

[287] "With a wind chill index likely hovering around minus 80 degrees Fahrenheit, stockmen were forced to keep to their houses for weeks as this terrible blizzard decimated the livestock." [RL, pp. 5–6.]

[288] "The partner of Jack Snyder...died and could not be buried, for no pick could break through that iron soil; and Snyder laid him outside the cabin they had shared, to remain there till spring came, covered by the unremitting snow." [RBL, p. 436.]

[289] During the winter of 1886–1887, Pierre Wibaux had gone off to France to raise money and had left his wife, Nellie, at the ranch in Montana. Henry Jackson wrote a brief but macabre letter to Pierre to let him know that, except for a couple of items, things were all right at home. *(Footnote 289 continued on next page.)*

I had worked both the spring and fall roundups of 1885 as a part of the **W** crew, and I was with them again in the spring of '86. Putting that on top of my experience with the Ward boys, I had come to know that country between the Yellowstone, Little Missouri, and Beaver Creek pretty well. I had heard that Pierre Wibaux was planning to buy cattle that spring of '87, so I went out to the **W** and asked Sid Tarbell, the foreman, for a job. Sid and old Dad Smith and the rest of the crew remembered me and so sometime late in February I got put on full-time.

I hadn't been at the **W** but a couple of weeks when the weather started to let up. Sometime during the first week or two of March, a warm chinook came through. There were a few brief storms here and there after that, but the first of March was really the end of it.[290] And that's when the cattle started floating.

I have been told that the ice break-up in the spring of 1887 on the Yellowstone River at Glendive was pretty smooth and didn't cause much damage.[291] That sure wasn't the case on the Little Missouri. You could hardly describe it. We were working some cattle over on the east side of the **W** range not far from the Little Missouri when we became aware of this distant but immense roar. We went over to investigate and discovered the river was clear out of its banks. Normally, the break-up on the Little Missouri was not a real tourist draw. It would jam up in a few places, but usually it was not an exceptional event and, in a few days, it was done. This time, however, the river was completely full of huge ice-cakes that were tumbling over each other and tearing up everything in their course, and that included the cottonwoods that lined the banks. The sound of this destruction carried for miles. Mixed in with the water, the ice-cakes, and the trees were all of those thousands of cattle that had frozen to death in the innumerable draws and tributaries

---

[289] (continued) "Dear Pierre, No news except that Dave Brown killed Dick Smith and your wife's hired girl blew her brains out in the kitchen. Everything O. K. here. Yours truly, Henry Jackson" [Jackson's letter cited in RBL, p. 436. The "hired girl" was Emma D'Hellin, age thirty-four. See FLP, p. 22.]

[290] On 5 March 1887 the *Dickinson Press* reported: "...a welcome Chinook wind paid us a visit...."

[291] "The ice broke at 7:45 P.M. Thursday evening and passed out quietly without damage." [GI, 12 March 1887.] The same newspaper, however, reported: "Bridges on the Northern Pacific have washed out both east and west of town."

of the Little Missouri and they were moving downstream. This same phenomenon was happening over on the Yellowstone. Of course, both the Yellowstone and the Little Missouri dumped into the Missouri River, so I can't even imagine what it must have been like down at Bismarck. The cattle sometimes floated with their heads up, sometimes partially submerged with only their backs showing and sometimes with all four legs sticking straight up into the air—thousands upon thousands of them mixed in with the chunks of ice of the thawing rivers. It was a memorable and ghoulish site, unforgettable to those who saw it and, fortunately, not one likely to be witnessed again.[292] Later, the stench of those thousands of cattle that didn't float away cast a pall on the whole country for another month or two.

By the end of March in the spring of 1887, the whole country knew it was busted. It was estimated that fully eighty percent of all the cattle in Dawson County, Custer County, and eastern Dakota Territory were dead.[293] People could see what had happened and they were dazed. They couldn't go on. They had nothing to go on with.[294]

Pierre Wibaux was a Frenchman who had substantial monetary reserves in his homeland. He was optimistic enough in the future of the cattle business to venture again. He went around to some of the small and large ranchers, and the conversation would be: "Well, what do you think you have left?" Invariably the answer would be, "I don't know." "Well, let's ride your range for a day or two and we'll see what we can find." This they would do and from that they would form an estimate as a basis for the sale.

---

[292] Lincoln Lang told a similar story to Hermann Hagedorn. Lang is quoted in RBL, pp. 437–438.

[293] Norton was estimating losses in the lower Yellowstone country. "West-central [Montana] ranchers fared much better than the reckless newcomers to the east. From loss rates of less than 40 percent in the valleys of the Sun, Teton and Marias rivers, the curve reached up to 90 percent kills on some lower Yellowstone ranches." [M/M, p. 166.] Some sources estimated a sixty percent death loss across the board among Montana Territory's beef herds. That would have represented around 360,000 head lost from an estimated inventory of some 600,000.

[294] Mark Brown cited John Clay to point out the magnitude of the disaster: "John Clay, the astute Scotsman who was the economic historian of the range business, made this summary of the effects of the winter of 1886–1887: 'From the inception of the open range business in the West and Northwest, from say 1870–1888, it is doubtful if a single cent was made if you average up the business as a whole.' " [POY, p. 394.]

Wibaux bought a large number of brands in this fashion and he ended up making quite a fortune.[295] He was also among the very first to start putting away enough feed to avoid starvation during the next winter. The ranch management practice of storing feed really took hold after the winter of 1886–1887, and those who stayed on and were successful in the livestock business never left themselves open like that again.[296]

As so often happens in nature, the times following such a bleak period were glorious indeed! The heavy snowpack, responsible for the deaths of so many cattle, paradoxically became the source of sufficient soil moisture to produce excellent stands of grass in 1887 for those animals that survived. The following year, 1888, was also favorable, since the livestock numbers were still so short it was impossible to overgraze the country. The cattle market rebounded in 1888, the grass was plentiful, and Pierre Wibaux became a very rich man, one of the largest cattle ranchers in the United States.[297]

The winter of 1886–1887 signaled the beginning of the end of the open-range livestock business. Britain was then the financial center of the world, and English and Scottish investors had freely disbursed huge sums of capital into large cattle companies in North America. All of a sudden, stockmen and investors alike discovered that all of that "free" open-range grass wasn't as cheap as it had all sounded in the first place. Now, well aware of the tremendous risk inherent in operating on uncontrolled and overgrazed rangeland, and realizing the huge investments that would be required to develop winter feed reserves, the sources of outside investment, especially from the east and the British Isles, all but dried up. While the open range didn't immediately disappear, the winter of 1886–1887 clearly provided the starting point for the beginning of a new era.[298]

---

[295] "Pierre Wibaux...returned to France, secured further credit, and steadily expanded his eastern Montana herds until he ranked as one of the largest individual cattle owners in the United States." [M/M, p. 166.] Marie MacDonald wrote that Wibaux "acquired the surviving cattle of many small operators and of several large herds, a total of 146 brands and some 40,000 cows." [GHMT, p. 22.]

[296] See *"Had anyone bothered"* in Author's Notes following this chapter.

[297] M/M, p. 166–167.

[298] "The old careless days of the range were gone. No longer did a rancher dare turn a herd loose on the open range without provision for winter...and the whole business of ranching underwent a slow but definite and permanent change." [POY, p. 392.]

CHAPTER 20–AUTHOR'S NOTES

Those writing about the "killer winter" of 1886–1887 have differed in their descriptions of the storms. There is agreement, however, that an Arctic front covered the entire plains area in mid-November of 1886. Six inches of snow later drifted in, accompanied by sub-zero winds. By Christmas, both the Missouri and the Yellowstone rivers had frozen over. A chinook occurred early in January and was followed by a few days of drizzle. The thermometer plunged again (Fort Keogh reported a temperature of sixty degrees below zero on January 14) and it had the effect of forming an impermeable crust of ice. The Laramie *Daily Boomerang* of 10 February 1887 reported: "The snow on the Lost Soldier division of the Lander and Rawlins stage route is four feet deep, and frozen so hard that the stages drive over it like a turnpike." [RL, February 1987, pp. 5–6.]

Cowboy artist Charles M. Russell portrayed the story of the disastrous winter of 1886–1887 most eloquently in his watercolor sketch entitled "Waiting for a chinook–The last of 5,000." Charlie worked for two stockmen living in Helena who ran some five-thousand head in the Judith Basin. Their foreman, Jesse Phelps, also operated his own small ranch, the **OH**. Russell was at the **OH** late that winter when one of the owners, L. E. Kaufman, wrote Phelps inquiring about the condition of their herd. To show how bad things were, Charlie painted his sketch on a piece of pasteboard to go with the letter Phelps was to write. Upon seeing the painting, Phelps remarked, "Hell, Louie don't need a letter," and he mailed Charlie Russell's drawing instead. When Kaufman received it, he reportedly just went out and got drunk. [NG, pp. 60–95.]

Granville Stuart was so heartsick at the devastation that he wrote: "A business that had been fascinating to me before suddenly became distasteful. I wanted no more of it. I never wanted to own again an animal that I could not feed and shelter." [Stuart is quoted in M/M, p. 165. According to Dr. Lorman Hoopes, Stuart got out of the cattle business "shortly thereafter." TLW, p. 334.]

Had anyone bothered to refer to the practices of the old fur traders, the necessity of storing winter feed would have been obvious. Edward Harris had accompanied Audubon to the upper Missouri and Fort Union in 1843. He reported that "The provision of winter feed for the horses and other stock was...a difficult problem." He noted that there were "two- or three-hundred acres of big bluestem that were suitable for mowing." Edwin Denig, then the chief factor at Fort Union, told Harris that two-hundred-and-fifty cartloads of hay were cut every July and "stacked up... for winter use of horses and cattle, the winter being so severe and long, and snow so deep that little food is to be found for them on the prairies at that season." [UMA, p. 143, and AHJ, pp. 187–188, cited as footnotes 62 and 63 in FTAW, p. 101.] The vast majority of livestock growers of the early and middle years of the 1880s naively chose to believe in the propaganda of the Northern Pacific Railroad.

CHAPTER TWENTY-ONE

1887

THROUGH THE YEAR OF 1887, I spent most of my time working for Pierre Wibaux at the **W** ranch. Headquartered at Mingusville, he spent the year buying out most of the surviving groups of cattle in the country. That included the remnant of the herd of my first employer, the Griffin Brothers and Hank Ward, owners of the **101**. Their ranch was in the Cottonwood Creek country just west of the **W**. Hank's brothers, Oscar (William O.) and Asa, sold out to Pierre at the same time. Wibaux's theory was that if cattle had managed to survive the winter of 1886–87 then they were the right kind of stock to breed for this part of the world.[299]

Mr. Wibaux was one of the real success stories of Dawson County. He was only about twenty-five years old when he arrived in 1883. He had made the acquaintance of the Count of Medora[300] in Chicago and it was that meeting which led him to Dawson County.

He first partnered up with Gus Grisy out on Beaver Creek, near what was then Keith. Their outfit was called the **G Anchor W,** but that deal only lasted maybe a year. Gus and his English bride, Minnie, were married in the winter of 1883. Early in 1884, Pierre Wibaux left Montana and went back to Europe for a short while. He married a delightful English woman, Mary Ellen ("Nellie") Cooper, and he brought her back to this country with him that same year. It was only a few months later that Wibaux and Grisy split up.[301] Grisy and his wife started the post office and saloon and changed the name of "Keith" to "Mingusville," combining their two names, Minnie and Gus, to gave the town its new name.

---

[299] SNVB, p. 32. Marie MacDonald noted that Wibaux "reasoned that these would be the hardiest of cattle and so they proved. Through the Nineties, Wibaux prospered greatly...." [GHMT, p. 22.]

[300] "The Count of Medora" referenced by Norton was the Marquis de Mores, founder of the village of Medora on the east side of the Little Missouri River in Dakota Territory.

[301] See *"Pierre Wibaux"* in Author's Notes following this chapter.

Some said it was the two women who caused the men to decide to go their own ways, but I never thought that was necessarily true. Gus was much more into "the good life" than Pierre. The prospect of living an unfettered life in Montana Territory really appealed to Grisy. Pierre, on the other hand, was seriously into his work and fully intended to have a cattle operation of real consequence. With Gus it was play, play, play.[302]

The word was, that when Wibaux left the partnership, he took all of the cattle and all of the debts with him. Ole Berg was Wibaux's first foreman until Sid Tarbell showed up in 1885. Tarbell was the **W** boss when I worked there in 1887 and he was still there at least through 1888.[303] I heard that when Sid died he was buried in what came to be known as "the Poker Jim cemetery" out near the old Wibaux headquarters north of town.[304]

Pierre Wibaux was a very bright man. An ex-cavalry officer with the French army, he was also an excellent horseman. Up through the winter of 1886–1887, however, he wasn't a particularly large cattleman. He and Grisy only owned a few hundred head, and, after they split up, Wibaux continued on with about 800 head of his own. Immediately after the killer winter, he returned to France and assembled a half-million dollars with the promise that he would pay back the lenders with a million dollars in ten years or less. He soon purchased what was left of the **101** cattle from the Griffin and Ward boys, and, since it was right next to him, he glommed right on to their range as well.[305] Mixed in with all of his many smaller purchases in 1887, he also bought up the remnants of some of the bigger outfits: the **FUF** up in Forsyth and the **3 Bars** herd from Hunter and Evans up north in the Big Dry Creek[306] country. In the spring of 1889, Wibaux purchased the remnant of Moreton Frewen's huge Powder River

---

[302] The site was originally named Beaver during the survey and construction of the Northern Pacific (from 1879 or earlier). The name was then changed to Keith (1882), then Mingusville (1884), and finally Wibaux (1894). For details regarding the name changes of the village and the biography of Gus Grisy, see *"Gustave Grisy"* in Author's Notes following this chapter.

[303] TLW, p. 337 and pp. 368–369.

[304] WTW–TM, p. 119.

[305] See *"Griffin and Ward and the 101 ranch"* in Author's Notes following Chapter 12.

[306] PW, p. 10. Also see *"Robert Hunter and Capt. A. G. Evans"* in Author's Notes following this chapter.

herd from down south on the headwaters of the Powder River in Wyoming.[307]

While the winter of 1886–1887 really marked the starting point of Pierre Wibaux's fantastic career in the cattle business, it proved the end of the line for the other wealthy Frenchman in the area, the Count over at Medora. Although the Count's cattle got through the winter okay thanks to the hard work and good management skills of his young foreman, Johnny Goodall, the business side of his empire collapsed. After the disastrous winter was over, he publicly stated that he wasn't going anywhere, that he had "come to Dakota Territory to stay."[308] Not long after that he announced his scheme to sell the French army all it could eat of Montana Longhorn beef soup. That idea fizzled. Then came his "discovery" of gold somewhere in western Montana. Finally, he announced that he and his wife were taking the rest of the year off to hunt tigers in India and that was the last we ever saw of him. It wasn't long after that the town of Medora died, too. Many of the buildings were eventually carted off to other locations, mostly to Dickinson, and that was, more or less, the end of it.[309] It wasn't but a few years later that I read in a newspaper where the Count had died—murdered somewhere out in Africa on the north end of the Sahara Desert.[310]

I should mention two other significant events that occurred in 1887. The first was the departure of my greater family. The winter of '86–'87 treated us no better than the rest of the people in the country. Everybody in any way related to the livestock industry came out of that winter nearly destitute. Most of my family decided

---

[307] PW, p. 10. The substantial remnant of this herd, the Powder River Cattle Company, was said to have been ten-thousand head of cattle with four-hundred horses "thrown in" the deal. [POY, p. 392.] Moreton Frewen was twenty-five years old when he and his brother, Richard, first saw the upper reaches of the Powder River in December of 1878. He was one of the earliest of the large cattle investors to come into the high plains of northeastern Wyoming and southeastern Montana. His range extended for many miles along the Powder River. He also grazed some of the country up around Forsyth. By his 1881 marriage to Clara Jerome, Frewen became the uncle of Winston Churchill. [TLW, p. 127.] See "Moreton Frewen" in Author's Notes following this chapter for biographical details regarding this colorful character.

[308] RBL, p. 450.

[309] RBL, p. 449 and pp. 451–452. TLW, p. 233 and p. 277.

[310] For a description of his adventures and circumstances following the departure of the Marquis de Mores from Medora and his death in North Africa, see "The fate of the Marquis de Mores" in Author's Notes following this chapter.

to pull out and so they did.[311] They originally intended to go to Washington Territory, but during the wagon trip across Montana they diverted into Victor and the Bitter Root Valley just south of Missoula. They settled and stayed there until after the turn of the century, and many of them, including my brother, Fred, and his family, live there to this day.[312] Hank Tuttle, who was still sheriff, and his brother, Bill, who was his deputy, stayed until his term as sheriff expired in 1889.[313] My father, my next younger brother, David, my eldest sister, Mary, and I were the only ones of my immediate family who decided to stay on in Dawson County.

My father, while intending to catch up with the larger family group later, was unable to travel overland with them. His old Civil War wound, his hip, would not stand the continual jolting of traveling in a wagon for the three months they estimated it would take them to get to Washington. Father hung around town, still living in his cottage and doing whatever odd jobs he could find to support himself: grave-digging, chopping firewood, nursing wounded prisoners at the jail, cleaning chimney flues, escorting prisoners to Miles City, and cleaning up at Mickey Farrell's saloon and other businesses in town. My brother David had returned from Dakota and was living with our father. Like Father, he did whatever kind of work he could find around town. I was fortunate in that I had a decent job at the **W** ranch.

As to the other event of 1887, I have some misgivings about mentioning it at all. Normally, one would not relate the events of a scandal, but this was not merely a case of social injustice. This was a criminal act. The two victims themselves survived the event and

---

[311] GDI, 21 May 1887: "F. L. Johnson and family and Z. Scribner and family crossed the river to-day. They intend to go overland to Washington Territory. F. L. Perry and family will start Monday for the same destination. We trust these families will find the land of promise all they picture it. Bon voyage." [The details of the trek across Montana are recounted by Fred Van Blaricom in THWT.]

[312] Five of Norton's eight brothers and sisters—David, Jim, Fred, Dora May, and Effie—all married and lived out their lives in the Bitter Root Valley. Levi Van Blaricom and Zachariah Scribner both died in Victor (Zachariah in 1901 and Levi in 1902) and are buried there. After the turn of the century, Mariah (Beardsley) (Johnson) Scribner and all of her children moved from the Bitter Root to the Okanogan country of Washington state and lived there the rest of their lives. For the complete story of what became of the greater family see THWT. The story is also recounted in *Bitter Root Trails IV*, pp. 572–578 and pp. 650–662.

[313] Henry Tuttle moved his wife and children to Grantsdale (today a small community near Hamilton in the Bitter Root Valley south of Missoula) in 1888. Henry and Bill both stayed on in Glendive through January of 1889 until Henry completed his term as sheriff. Henry then joined his family in Grantsdale, and Bill moved on with him. [HVBG, pp. 187–191.]

grew to be greater people because of it. In any case, our immediate family members were all well aware of the details, and now that more than fifty years have passed it is time that the despicable deeds of the heretofore unidentified villain of the story be told.

My sister Mary was three years younger than I. She was born March 7, 1872, the last of the three children born near Waterville, Minnesota. Following our mother's death in 1882, our grandparents, Grandma and Grandpa Scribner, had taken in Mary. Shortly thereafter, she moved in with our uncle and aunt, Frank and Carrie Johnson. Uncle Frank, and Hank and Bill Tuttle,[314] Aunt Carrie's brothers, were, at that time, deputy sheriffs for the county.

Following the end of the school term in June of 1885, after Mary had turned thirteen, a deal was worked out that she would live down at Slawson's road ranch, working at housekeeping and kitchen chores in exchange for her room and board. The ranch was about eighteen miles north of Glendive, located on the west side of the Yellowstone at what was Slawson Creek.[315] Like the Burns Ranch, it was a stage stop on the Glendive–Fort Buford road, and the Slawsons frequently fed and sometimes overnighted travelers. Stagecoach horses were kept at the road ranch, and Eben and his son, Willard, would provide fresh horses while the stage's passengers ate a meal. Teddy Roosevelt was known to have stayed there on occasion, and it was reported that he especially liked Mrs. Slawson's dried apple pie.[316]

My father and my grandparents had known Eben and Louisa Slawson for some three years. The Slawsons were about my father's age. Eben was a Union Army veteran from a New York artillery regiment, I believe, and, the few times I was around him, he always presented himself well and was quite cordial. He had been appointed one of Dawson County's first three county commissioners. Louisa was a pleasant lady with a reputation

---

[314] In the election of November 1884, Henry ("Hank") Tuttle was elected sheriff of Dawson County. He served two consecutive two-year terms: 1885 through 1886 and 1887 through 1888.

[315] Slawson Creek is now called Linden Creek. Ebenezer Slawson sold his road ranch to Henry Linton in 1888. The name Linden Creek was the result of the mispronunciation and misspelling of Henry Linton's name. (The same thing happened at Crane Creek, which was named for early settler Jimmy Crain.)

[316] FVBM. Teddy Roosevelt's fondness for Louisa Slawson's dried apple pie is recounted in THWT.

as an excellent cook. Three of their four children were married with families of their own, and they were located on different ranches right there on the lower Yellowstone. All of these people were substantial and well regarded by their neighbors. All things considered, it looked like a good situation for Mary.[317]

There doesn't have to be a black sheep in every family, but Willard Slawson, the son still at home, was the bane of his parents. When our greater family left Glendive in April of 1887, he was about twenty-one, six or seven years older than Mary. At that time she had opted to stay on with the Slawsons. In late September of that year we found out why. She showed up one day at my father's place. Both my father and David were there. She said that she was five or six months pregnant, that Willard Slawson was the father, and that he was now telling her he wanted nothing to do with her except for her to get out of his life. These conditions obviously made it impossible for her to continue to live at the road ranch.

Mary was only fifteen when she came walking those eighteen miles into town. Whether she had been enamored with Willard when the family left—and hence her decision to stay behind—or whether her circumstance related to Willard Slawson was more sinister, only Mary and Willard will ever know. In any case, my father and Mary and brother David headed for the sheriff's office. Henri Haskell,[318] then Dawson County's prosecuting attorney, was not a man to trifle with. John Trumbull, Slawson's attorney, soon explained to him the two choices he had for being responsible for his actions: marry the girl or get sent to the Montana Territorial Prison in Deer Lodge for his ruthless exploitation of a minor child. He quickly accepted the marriage option, and then, within days, he abandoned her. He was never seen in that country again.[319]

---

[317] For the brief biographies of Ebenezer and Louisa Slawson and their son-in-law and daughter, George and Imogene Grant, and their respective families, see *"Ebenezer and Louisa Slawson and their children"* in Author's Notes following this chapter.

[318] See Chapter 22 for the biography of Henri Haskell.

[319] Stephen Norton Van Blaricom recorded nothing about Mary Van Blaricom's relationship with Willard Slawson. As Emma Maud (Van Blaricom) Freeze (Fred's daughter born 10 October 1904) pointed out in a 1992 interview: "We all knew Aunt Mary had a daughter. We didn't know who the father was, but we would never have asked or said anything. That just wasn't done in those days." The identity of Willard Slawson and the story of the affair were only discovered by the author from the Mary Van Blaricom marriage certificate in Glendive and pre-1900 court records in Dawson, Missoula, and Ravalli counties. Norton Van Blaricom's reaction and his comments were reported by his niece, Emma (Van Blaricom) Freeze, in 1992.

During the winter of 1887–1888, Mary became the mother of a beautiful baby girl.[320] The marriage to Willard Slawson, however, cost her dearly. In the spring of 1888, she and her baby, Emma, and our father followed the rest of the family to the Bitter Root. A few years later, she met a gentleman there and fell in love. The laws of Montana, however, would not let her claim abandonment without finding and serving papers on Slawson. The court reasoned that this blackguard might re-appear sometime in the future and do her the courtesy of taking her back as his wife. He was finally found living in the vicinity of his parents in the small settlement of Old Mission, Washington,[321] and he was served there by the sheriff of Kittitas County. Even then the court in the Bitter Root was not prepared to grant her divorce request on the strength of her own testimony or on the strength-of-character witnesses stating that she was a good and industrious woman. The only thing that finally worked in her favor was Willard Slawson's repeated failures to obey the Montana court's orders to appear at the hearings. Fully seven years after his abandonment of her and their child in Glendive, the Ravalli County Court finally granted her a divorce.[322]

In addition to the crimes perpetrated against this girl at the Slawson ranch when she was only fourteen, Willard Slawson's careless inactivity forced her into seven years of legal bondage while she tried to divorce him. Having successfully used the marriage as a ploy to avoid prison, he fled into a shameful hiding hundreds of miles away. Once found, he then refused for years

---

[320] Emma Mabel Van Blaricom was born in Glendive, Dawson County, Montana Territory, on 16 December 1887. [HVBG, pp. 189–190.]

[321] Eben and Louisa Slawson sold their road ranch in 1888 and moved to Old Mission, Washington Territory. The village, then known as "Old Mission, Kittitas County, Washington Territory," is now Cashmere, Chelan County, Washington.

[322] After initially filing for her divorce from Willard Slawson on 7 October 1890 on the grounds of abandonment and desertion, Mary Van Blaricom was finally granted her decree four years later on 10 October 1894 while residing in Victor, Ravalli County, Montana. The date of the decree was seven years to the day from the date of her marriage to Slawson. The divorce decree was allegedly awarded solely because of the repeated failure of Willard Slawson to appear at any of the hearings or to respond to any of the pleadings. Whether there was any significance relative to the seven years of abandonment and some statute of limitations in Montana territorial or state law is unknown. There was no statement to that effect in the decree. For the 1887 court records of the Territory of Montana vs. Willard Slawson, Mary's marriage to Willard Slawson and other legal documents pertaining to their relationship, see *"Mary Van Blaricom vs. Willard Slawson"* in Author's Notes following this chapter.

to even respond to the divorce action that would have allowed her to return to a normal life. In a further demonstration of his squalid demeanor, he cared not one whit about his own daughter. It says much about a man's character when, not once in his entire life, did he ever see or even attempt to communicate with his own child.

Fortunately, this story has a happy ending. Mary met a young, industrious fellow in Victor who, by coincidence, had also been raised in Glendive. They hit it off immediately and were wed in Victor in 1895. Forty-five years later, Mary is still happily married to Herbert Eddy[323] and they have enjoyed a wonderful relationship throughout their years together. Young Emma grew into a beautiful woman. She has long been married, has her own family, and is leading a satisfying and productive life. The Eddys and their four children and Emma have lived north of Edmonton in Alberta, Canada, since about 1915.[324]

---

[323] See *"Herbert Eddy"* in Author's Notes following this chapter for additional information regarding Herbert and Mary (Van Blaricom) Eddy.

[324] Emma Mabel (Van Blaricom) (Eddy) (Travis) Rutherford died near Edmonton, Alberta, Canada, on 2 November 1959 at the age of seventy-one.

CHAPTER 21–AUTHOR'S NOTES

Pierre Wibaux was born 12 January 1858 in Roubaix, France. His family had owned and operated cotton and woolen mills and dye works in the area since 1810. Given a good education, he spent his eighteenth year serving in the French Dragoons. He spent the next three years traveling on the continent, finally moving to England in 1880. He studied the textile industry in Great Britain, and during that time he met his future wife, Mary Ellen ("Nellie") Cooper. Enamored with tales of the American West he had heard from his English friends, Pierre decided to abandon his future in the family businesses and go it alone in America. Learning of his decision, his disappointed father handed him $10,000 as a sort of cash-out for his future inheritance and bid him adieu.

Wibaux arrived in America in 1883 and went straight to Chicago to study the meat packing industry. There he met the Marquis de Mores, another young Frenchman, who encouraged him to head for the plains and get in the cattle business. Wibaux accompanied de Mores to the whistle-stop of Little Missouri where, within weeks, he selected for his headquarters a site on Beaver Creek near Keith, Montana Territory. He then entered into a short-lived partnership with Gustave Grisy, a countryman, under the brand of

PIERRE WIBAUX, SEPTEMBER 27, 1900
PHOTO COURTESY OF THE MONTANA HISTORICAL SOCIETY RESEARCH CENTER PHOTOGRAPH ARCHIVES, HELENA

G Anchor W: Wibaux spent the winter of 1883–1884 in Europe. On 13 March 1884 he married Mary Ellen Cooper in Dover, England, and, following their honeymoon, they returned together to Montana. By November of 1884, Wibaux had bought Grisy out of their cattle partnership and continued his ranching enterprise under the name "The Royal Chambord Ranch," utilizing the **W** (W Bar) brand.

Wibaux was not a particularly large operator until he returned to France in the winter of 1886–1887. There he borrowed half a million dollars from associates and returned to Montana, where he bought out a multitude of outfits at bargain prices. At its peak in the 1890s, it has been estimated the **W** owned about 65,000 cattle and 300 saddle horses. No one but Pierre ever knew the exact number of cattle he owned. Estimates ran from a low of 40,000 to a high of 200,000. [PW, p. 15.] In 1901, he sold his Wibaux-based ranches and moved west across the Yellowstone River. He grazed his cattle in the Redwater River country northwest of Glendive, and, from that point on, he headquartered at Circle. A few years later, he closed out his cattle business completely and concentrated on his banking interests in Miles City. Wibaux also became one of the largest stockholders of the American Bankers Insurance Company in Chicago.

Around 1912, Pierre was diagnosed with cancer of the liver. He went to Chicago for treatment and died there on 21 March 1913 at the age of fifty-five. He bequeathed $10,000 to Miles City for a public park. His substantial estate went primarily to his son, Cyril Wibaux (then a lieutenant in the French Army), with remainders to his widow and two nephews in France. His will directed that his remains be cremated without religious ceremony and that his ashes be placed in an urn. It also directed his son to commission a bronze statue of Pierre, to place his ashes in the ground at Wibaux, and to then position the statue over his final resting place. That rather remarkable memorial still stands in the town of Wibaux. [DJ, pp. 484–486. HYCW, Fall–Winter, 1993, Vol. 23, No. 2, pp. 3–15. TABC, pp. 39–41.]

Gustave Grisy, like Pierre Wibaux, had been raised in Roubaix, France. The two men had been friends since they were children. In the middle of 1883, Wibaux and Grisy became partners in a ranch, the **G Anchor W,** located in the Beaver Valley near Keith. [TABC,

p. 31.] (The site was known as "Beaver" during the railroad survey and construction period for the simple reason that the railroad intended to cross Beaver Creek there. Once the track was laid in 1881, the railroad named their station/telegraph office in that location "Keith." The post office accepted that name in 1882.) Grisy went by the nicknames of "Gus" or "Gust." Most of the ranch hands called him "Gus," but Father Lindesmith, who was a great admirer of both Wibaux and Grisy, called him "Gust." [See FLP, p. 21.] Gus Grisy married Miss Minnie Allen of Thrapston, England, in New York City on 12 December 1883. Only three months later, on 13 March 1884, Pierre Wibaux also married an Englishwoman, Mary Ellen ("Nellie") Cooper, in Dover, England. The two English brides had been classmates in France. After recording in his diary that "Wibaux was married six months ago," Father Lindesmith described the two families around September of 1884:

> The two men are Frenchmen two years in America, eighteen months on their ranches. They are college-educated men. They speak good English. Their wives are English ladies who were educated in a convent in France and speak French to perfection. I am delighted with these people. I love them. They are people who come up to my idea of men and women...they firmly believe that religion is the first and greatest ornament of a gentleman or a lady. God Bless them forever. [FLP, p. 21.]

Grisy, however, seems to have strayed from living his life exactly on the lines of the "Golden Rule" some time before Father Lindesmith penned his laudatory. In a play off their two names—and with the encouragement of Minnie and Gus—people had taken to calling the whistle-stop "Mingusville." [TLW, p. 164.] Early in 1884, Grisy had started his own saloon / hotel in the small settlement. On 9 May 1884, the *Yellowstone Journal* wrote a "tongue-in-cheek" article describing their little village and the opening of Gus's new enterprise:

> Mingusville is a model town. It consists of a [railroad] section house, Mrs. Nolan's boarding house, a general store, and [now] two saloons. Its population numbers twenty-five. Five barrels of whiskey have been secured for the opening of a [second] saloon this A.M.

By July of 1884, Grisy had succeeded in getting the town's name officially changed from "Keith" to "Mingusville." As the new postmaster in town, Gus also had the foresight to consolidate his businesses and moved the post office inside the saloon–hotel. These activities left him little time for the Wibaux–Grisy cattle enterprise.

By November of 1884, the partnership between Wibaux and Grisy was dissolved and the two men went their separate ways. While Grisy called his small remnant holding "The Fleur de Lis" (FLP, p. 22), when he and Wibaux split he quickly got out of the cattle business. Gus then threw himself wholeheartedly into the day-to-day and night-by-night operation of his saloon, his rough-and-tumble hotel loft, and his erstwhile post office. It didn't take long for the residents of the area to corrupt the name of "Mingusville" to more aptly reflect their perception of Grisy's behavior. They called the place "Dingusville." [TABC, p. 77.]

Grisy's combined activities (or inactivities) as postmaster and saloonkeeper infuriated the local women who didn't want to go into a saloon to pick up their mail. [TLW, p. 146.] The locals soon came to hold an opinion of Gus Grisy quite different from that expressed by Father Lindesmith only three or four months earlier. The frustrated female patrons of Beaver Valley vented by writing a letter to the editor of the *Glendive Independent:*

> Mingusville, M.T., Dec. 17, 1884. Dear Sir: Our Mingusville post office saloon is a concern...We have long enough... endured in silence the outrageous mismanagement of the office under the regime of Mr. Grisy. We do not like to send our children into the saloon, nor do we like to go there ourselves [and be forced] to find the assistant postmaster and ask him to leave his [precious] bar business for a moment and serve us in mail matters. [He] takes his sleep by day, where he sleeps it matters not, the concern is locked, and the unfortunate [patron]...must find him if he can. We want better...than this. We [resent] all of the insolence and indignities heaped upon us by Mr. Grisy. No doubt there's good timber in him, but...we think him too fresh. [Before] he tries to serve us...he should season for about ten years and, in the meantime, study the ways of American people.

> We want the post office distinct from a saloon, want our
> mail when called for, and want the office open during lawful
> hours. If this is asking too much of Mr. Grisy, we shall ask it
> of the United States Post Office Department.

Life in the Wild West just didn't live up to Gus Grisy's expectations.
Not being front-runners in the Beaver Valley popularity contest,
Gus and his bride departed Mingusville in 1886 and returned to
France. (It was eight years after Gus and Minnie departed that Pierre
Wibaux, in 1894, got the name of the town changed to "Wibaux.")
Minnie (Allen) Grisy died in 1929. Gus died in 1931. They were
both buried at Bath, England. [TABC, p. 31.]

Robert Hunter and Capt. A. G. Evans: Robert Hunter was a
Scotsman who started out in Texas quite young. He had cattle-
bossed at least four, maybe five trail herds of Texas cattle up to
the Kansas country before he got in the commission business with
Captain A. G. Evans. Eventually, Hunter became the president of the
National Cattlemen's Convention in St. Louis. It was he and Evans
who, in 1876 or 1877, bought out the livestock and ranches of John
S. Chisum in the Pecos River country of New Mexico. [John Chisum
of the Pecos River should not be confused with Jesse Chisholm for
whom the famed Chisholm Trail was named. See "The Chisholm
Trail," by John Rossel, in the *Kansas Historical Quarterly,* February
1936 (Vol. 5, No. 1), pp. 3–14.]

At the time the Hunter–Evans partnership was formed, Captain
Evans was a man of about fifty years of age. He had been an officer
in Wahl's Texas Legion and had fought for the Confederates at
Vicksburg and Holly Springs, among other battles. Like Hunter,
Evans had been a Texas trail boss moving cattle up to Abilene.
Hunter and Evans partnered up about 1874 and headed up into the
Niobrara River country of northern Nebraska. Finally, in 1883, with
too many settlers and too much drought in Nebraska and Kansas,
they moved their outfit into the Big Dry country of Dawson County.
Wibaux closed them out in 1887 and in so doing he picked up some
cattle that were direct descendants of John Chisum's original herd.
[TLW, p. 107 and p. 170.]

Moreton Frewen (whose surname was frequently spelled "Freuen")
was, by marriage, the uncle of Winston Churchill. Frewen was
married to Clara Jerome, the first daughter of Leonard Walter Jerome,

MORETON FREWEN
PHOTO COURTESY OF THE MONTANA HISTORICAL SOCIETY-LIBRARY, HELENA

a wealthy American Wall Street trader, and his wife, Clarissa (Clara) (Hall) Jerome. Married on 5 April 1849, Leonard and Clara Jerome had four daughters: Clarita (Clara), born April of 1851; Jeanette (Jennie), born January of 1854; Camille, born November of 1855; and Leonie, born in 1858. The first three girls were born in New York City. Leonie was born in Paris. In 1863, Camille died of a sudden fever at the age of seven. [JEN, Volume I, pp. 14–25 and p. 254.]

Jennie, the second Jerome daughter, married Lord Randolph Henry Spencer Churchill, the second son of the seventh Duke and Duchess of Marlborough in Paris on 15 April 1874. [JEN, Vol. I, pp. 61–70 and pp. 93–95]. Winston Spencer Churchill was born to this marriage (an unlikely "two months premature" according to all contemporary sources) at the home (the 320-room Blenheim Palace) of his grandparents on 30 November 1874. [See next-to-last plate, JEN, Vol. I between pp. 128–129.] Some seven years later, in 1881, Jennie's older sister, Clara, married Moreton Frewen in New York's Grace Church. [JEN, Vol. I, p. 151.] Frewen was twenty-eight years old and Clara thirty when they wed. Leonie, the youngest child, married Lieutenant John Leslie, of the British Grenadier Guards, in New York's Grace Church on 2 October 1884. [JEN, Vol. I, p. 176. JEN, Vol. I, Chapter 10, Footnote 17, p. 342.]

Jennie (Jerome) Churchill strongly opposed her sister Clara's marriage to Moreton Frewen. She viewed Frewen as an irresponsible and incompetent vagabond who would doom her sister to a life of poverty. [JEN, Vol. I, p. 150.] Jennie was not far wrong.

Moreton Frewen descended from an old Sussex family. He was born on 8 May 1853, the third son of a wealthy Sussex squire, Thomas Frewen, and his second wife, Helen Louisa Homan of County Kildare, Ireland. [SP, p. 15 and p. 69.] A well-known sportsman, he was considered one of the best "gentleman riders" in all of England. He had ventured off to the American West in 1878 (TLW, p. 127) where he had reportedly "known everyone there from Buffalo Bill to Sitting Bull." He wandered around Texas for a while and spent nearly a year working as a drover in Colorado. [JEN, Vol. I, p. 150.] Much like Teddy Roosevelt, Frewen became totally enamored with the West and convinced himself he could make a vast fortune on the western plains in the cattle business. In 1879, at the age of twenty-five or twenty-six, he built his log "Castle," the ranch headquarters just below the north and middle forks of the Powder River. [TLW, p. 127.] In that same year, he bought the **76** brand and his first two-thousand head of Shorthorn cattle from Tim Foley. [TLW, p. 286.]

Following her New York City marriage to Frewen on 2 June 1881, Clara (and her French maid) spent her honeymoon in Moreton's large log cabin ("The Castle" or "Frewen Castle" at "the Home Ranche") perched atop a bluff alongside the Powder River in northern Wyoming. [SP, pp. 59–65.] Moreton had established his own store and trading post some twenty-five miles south of the ranch headquarters, and had installed a telephone line between the two points. He reveled in watching "the Redskins...more naked than ashamed...talking to one another through it." [JEN, Vol. I, p. 151.] Clara soon believed she was pregnant. While off on a hunting trip with a large group of British guests, she became ill. [SP, p. 66.] With the nearest doctor some two-hundred miles or four days away in Cheyenne, Clara miscarried at the Wyoming ranch. She took the baby's body to New York for burial and never returned. [JEN, Vol. I, p. 176.]

Moreton, in the meantime, assembled a huge cattle operation using investor money from England. At one time the ranch grazed some forty-five-thousand head...maybe. As wise as he supposedly was to the ways of the American West, one long-circulated story claimed that he once sat on his horse facing a hill while some twenty-one thousand head of cattle he was purchasing were driven between him and the hill so he could inspect them. There was just one small problem. It was really one herd of seven-thousand head driven around the hill three times and Moreton, so the story goes, bought them each time they came past. [JEN, Vol. I, p. 176.] Moreton denied this story to his dying day.

In 1885, Moreton and his board of directors had a huge falling out over the lack of profits. [TLW, p. 127.] On 24 June 1885, Frewen left the Powder River country and never returned. Although Frewen continued to own a large percentage of the company, Sir Horace Plunkett, another English cattleman on the Powder River, assumed management of the ranch. The winter of 1886–1887 put an end to Moreton Frewen's dreams of a cattle empire on the upper reaches of the Powder River. [JEN, Vol. I, p. 181.] Sir Horace sold the cattle, reportedly some forty-thousand head, to Pierre Wibaux and shut down the ranch, the store, and the telephone line. Undeterred, Moreton Frewen took off in pursuit of his next global enterprise.

While some financial acquaintances waggingly played off his name, "Moreton Frewen," and called him "Mortal Ruin," many investors continued to support him in some grandiose schemes. Jennie Churchill's biographer, Ralph G. Martin, described his abilities: "Never was there a more brilliant, eloquent man who failed so magnificently in so many schemes in so many places...." [JEN, Vol. II, p. 33.] Randolph Churchill recommended Frewen and his financial advisory skills to Sir Salar Jung, prime minister of the Indian state of Hyderabad. It turned out that Sir Salar had been banished from Hyderabad, and, in the end, the only thing Moreton accomplished was to strike a bargain in a Turkish harem for a bride for Sir Salar while Salar was in exile in Cairo. [JEN, Vol. I, p. 253.]

Frewen went straight from Turkey and Cairo back to North America to work on his project to create a city on a "natural port" he had "discovered," which later served Prince Rupert, British Columbia, Canada (founded in 1910, about two decades after Frewen's proposed development), immediately south of Ketchikan, Alaska. This dream, too, fizzled. [JEN, Vol. I, p. 254 and Vol. II, p. 284.]

In 1891, Moreton turned his attention to a gold-crushing machine he had patented to extract the wealth of Mashonaland, in South Africa. Among many others, Lord Randolph Churchill, Winston's father, bought some stock in this latest scheme. In England, the *Western Daily Mercury* noted that the invention was most appropriate for Frewen, "seeing that he is a prominent bimetallist and therefore anxious to crush gold as far as possible out of existence." [JEN, Vol. I, pp. 268–269.] When Clara Jerome, Moreton Frewen's mother-in-law, died in 1895, he was in Australia, involved in "another disastrous venture called Electrozone." [JEN, Vol. II, p. 50.]

Early in January of 1898, while still in India, the budding young author, Winston Churchill, turned his first book, *The Story of the Malakand Field Force*, over to his uncle, Moreton Frewen, to edit and pass on to the publisher, Longmans, Green & Company of London. When the book came out, Churchill was livid. He wrote his mother, Jennie, on 22 March, 1898: "...the revised proofs reached me yesterday and...I spent a very miserable afternoon in reading the gross and fearful blunders...In the hope of stopping publication I have wired Longmans..." He was too late and the book was published, warts and all. His lament continued: "Emendations made by Moreton...have the effect of making the passage as bald as if written by a Harrow boy." He harangued on unnecessarily capitalized words, misspellings ("fusilade, shrapnell, dissappointed") and misprints ("primiter for perimeter; causalities for casualties; seren for seven; purses for passes and last but not least this atrocity 'Babri' for babu, meaning an Indian clerk"). "Surely Moreton [who had spent some time in India] could not have even read this. If he did God help him." He concluded his assessment of his uncle: "I writhed all yesterday afternoon—but today I feel nothing but shame and disappointment...as far as Moreton is concerned, I now understand why his life has been a failure in the city [of London] and elsewhere." [TSMFF, Foreword, pp. ix–xii.]

On 3 May 1898, Winston wrote to his brother, Jack: "The gross and dreadful blunders which disfigure every page have caused me acute pain." To Winston's good fortune, Longmans proposed to reissue the book in their Silver Library series to be published in November 1898, only months after publication of the Frewen-edited debacle. Longmans allowed Churchill to re-edit the work. He "sent in corrections which required 196 hours of printer's work on the plates." [TSMFF, Foreword, p. xii.]

For all his faults, Moreton Frewen kept at his dreams until the end; throughout his life he maintained his contacts with the rich and famous of the world. He befriended the young and celebrated American author Stephen Crane shortly after the publication of Crane's *The Red Badge of Courage*. Crane rented Moreton and Clara Frewen's historic Brede Place home in Sussex and spent the last years of his life there. When Crane died in 1900 at the age of twenty-eight, Frewen led a successful fund drive to pay off Crane's debts and final expenses. [JEN, Vol. II, p. 245.]

Following a brief illness, Moreton Frewen died in 1917 at the age of sixty-four. [JEN, Vol. II, p. 350.] Some fifty years after his death, Allen Andrews penned Frewen's biography. Entitled *The Splendid Pauper*, it was published in America by Lippincott of Philadelphia and New York in 1968.

The fate of the Marquis de Mores: Following his departure from Medora in 1887, the marquis stayed a year in India and then moved on to a long stay in China, where he unsuccessfully attempted to negotiate favorable trade concessions for France with the Chinese government. He finally returned to France where, totally disillusioned with the French bureaucracy, he became somewhat of a revolutionary. In the process, he fought repeated duels, killing his opponent in at least one instance. According to Hagedorn, "he became a violent anti-Semite...and a radical Socialist." The marquis was once imprisoned for three months for his role in attempting to "incite the populace to violence against the army."

While all of this was going on, France and England were vying with each other for the colonial control of central Africa. The marquis, never short of grandiose ideas, conceived of uniting all of the Moslems in the world against England. In 1896, he hied off to Tunisia, intending to travel across the Sahara, meet up with the Arabs in the Sudan and incite them to do in the English. This time, Fate cut him short. He was ambushed at the well of El Ouatia and murdered. While legend has his corpse surrounded by "a ring of dead men," an Arab search party simply "found his body riddled with wounds and buried in the sand near a clump of bushes."

However he met his end, Antoine Marie Vincent Manca de Vallambrosa, the Marquis de Mores, was dead at the age of thirty-eight (1858–1896). As befitted his royal ancestry, his funeral in Paris

MARQUIS DE MORES, 1886
PHOTO COURTESY OF THE MONTANA HISTORICAL SOCIETY RESEARCH CENTER PHOTOGRAPH ARCHIVES, HELENA

was a noted public event. And so, as Hermann Hagedorn wrote, "the curtain fell on a great romantic drama." [RBL, pp. 449–450 and pp. 460–463.]

Contrary to Norton's observation that the Marquis de Mores abandoned Medora and Dakota Territory and never returned ("that was the last we ever saw of him"), Arnold O. Goplen, the senior foreman historian of the U.S. National Park Service, reported that the marquis did return to Medora in the spring of 1889 "and spent some time hunting there." Goplen also wrote that Madame de Mores, after her husband's death in 1896, "…maintained her contacts at Medora and kept the property there intact. She paid her last visit to Medora in 1903 and…was accompanied by her daughter, Athenais, and her son, Louis. She spent six weeks in Medora on this occasion." Madam de Mores died in Cannes, France, on 2 March 1921. As late as 31 December 1938, Louis Vallambrosa, one of the two sons of the Marquis and Madame de Mores, still owned "slightly over 1100 acres in Billings County, North Dakota." [CMM, pp. 64–68.]

Ebenezer and Louisa Slawson and their children: Ebenezer Slawson was born in Duanesburg, Schenectady County, New York, on 21 September 1824. Louisa P. (Green) Slawson was born 26 August 1831, also in Duanesburg. They were married in New York (probably in Delaware County), on 14 October 1849. They had four children who attained adulthood:

1. Imogene Slawson, born 17 May 1853, probably in Delaware County, New York. She married George F. Grant on 17 May 1873 in Osakis, Douglas County, Minnesota, and died at the age of forty-five on 18 July 1898 near Cashmere, Washington.

2. Frank Deloss Slawson, born 29 October 1857, in Delaware County, New York. Frank was killed by a falling tree in north-central Washington about 17 August 1939 at the age of eighty-one.

3. Elsie Slawson, born 26 November 1863, probably in Delaware County, New York. She married Owen Lovering of the Newlon settlement on the lower Yellowstone River on 1 January 1883. Elsie and Owen lived out their lives on the lower Yellowstone. Elsie died on 7 June 1927 at the age of sixty-three. Owen died in 1935. Both are buried in the Newlon Cemetery.

4. Willard G. Slawson, born 18 May 1866, probably in Delaware County, New York (he was shown on the Dawson County census as "Age 14" in June of 1880), married Mary Martha Van Blaricom on 10 October 1887. Willard abandoned Mary less than three weeks after their marriage. They had one child, a daughter, Emma Mabel, born 16 December 1887. Mary was granted a divorce in Ravalli County, Montana, seven years later on 10 October 1894. Following their separation, Willard lived for several years in Old Mission (Cashmere), Washington, either with or near his parents. Sometime around the time of the divorce in 1894, Willard left Cashmere and, according to a family member, was never heard from again.

Mary Van Blaricom vs. Willard Slawson: After walking the eighteen miles into Glendive from the Slawson ranch, fifteen-year-old Mary Van Blaricom filed her complaint against twenty-one-year-old Willard Slawson on 29 September 1887, Case No. 286 in Probate Court of Dawson County, Territory of Montana. It was recorded by James McCormick, Ex-officio Clerk of the Court:

Personally appeared before me the 29th day of September, 1887, Mary M. Van Blaricom, who being first duly sworn, complains and says: That one Willard Slawson, on or about April, A.D. 1887 at Slawson's Ranch in the County of Dawson, Territory of Montana, committed a misdemeanor in that said Willard Slawson did then and there by sexual intercourse with affiant caused her to be pregnant with a child and that he, the said Willard Slawson, is the father of said unborn child. That affiant is an unmarried woman and is now quick with child all of which is contrary to the statute in such case made and provided, and against the peace and dignity of the Territory of Montana. Said complainant therefore prays that a warrant may be issued for the arrest of said Willard Slawson and that he may be dealt with according to law.

Henri J. Haskell was attorney for the plaintiff. John Trumbull was attorney for the defendant. Josiah H. Ray was the judge. The misdemeanor complaint dated 29 September 1887 was amended to the crime of fornication when the Warrant of Arrest was issued on the 1st of October.

The following events are recorded as Case Number 12, in the Justice Court of Dawson County, Territory of Montana:

October 3rd, 1887 (No. 12)

Personally appeared before me a Justice of the Peace in and for Dawson County, this 3rd day of October, 1887. Mary M. Van Blaricom, who being first duly sworn on oath complains and says that one Willard Slawson on or about the 20th day of February, 1887*, and at diverse times thereafter at Slawson's Ranch, in Dawson County, Montana, had sexual intercourse with her and that then and there, between the 20th day of February, 1887, and the first day of April, 1887, did get her pregnant with child and prays that the said Willard Slawson may be apprehended and that he may be dealt with according to law.

[* Born 7 March 1872, Mary Van Blaricom was fourteen years old on that date. Willard Slawson, born 18 May 1866, was twenty.]

October 3rd, 1887 (No. 12)

Complaint taken and filed. Warrant issued and given to the Sheriff. Bail $800.00.

October 8th, 1887 (No. 12)

Warrant returned and filed with return of arrest thereon. Subpoena issued and given to Sheriff for the following persons as Witnesses for the Territory: Mary M. Van Blaricom, Dr. [A]. R. Duncan, Frank L. Johnson* and Mrs. Frank L. Johnson.* Mary M. Van Blaricom, the complaining witness, was duly examined by County Attorney H. J. Haskell, Esqr., in the premises and cross examined by Atty for Defendant [John Trumbull]. Territory rested. Attorney for Defendant then and there not wishing to continue further examination. Complaining of Witness, waives all rights to further examination. Argument by counsel waived by consent. The Court took the case under advisement and, after consideration of the same, orders that the defendant Willard Slawson be held in a good and sufficient bond for the sum of Eight-Hundred Dollars to appear at the next sitting of the District Court in and for the Fourth District of Montana. The prisoner was remanded into the hands of the Sheriff for safekeeping until such orders be complied with. Bail was given with Eben Slawson and E. W. P. Harvey as sureties. The sureties not considered sufficient, the prisoner was held for additional security. Now comes James Coram, who, as additional surety, signs the recognizance and justifies in the amount of the same. Defendant given his liberty.

[* The Johnsons left Glendive by wagon in May of 1887. They traveled across Montana Territory to Victor in company with Zachariah and Mariah Scribner. [See Footnote 318.] With relatively short notice, they must have returned to Glendive by train to testify at the Willard Slawson proceeding.]

In another document, No. 286 in the Dawson County Probate Court, Martin Newcomer of Glendive, a flour and feed dealer, is also shown as a surety. Defendant requested as witnesses Mrs. (Ebenezer) Slawson, and Owen and Mrs. Owen Lovering, the defendant's mother, brother-in-law, and sister. It had been reported two years before (YJ, 5 September 1885) that Martin Newcomer and E. W. P. Harvey, both of them sureties for Willard Slawson in this case, had served on the same federal grand jury in Dawson County. [Cited in TLW, p. 153 and p. 264.]

October 10th (No. 286 in Probate Court)

2 O'Clock P.M. Defendant in Court with his Counsel. Defendant requested a further continuance until Oct. 11th, 1887, at 10 O'Clock A.M. Granted by the Court.

Late in the afternoon of Monday, 10 October 1887, Willard Slawson married Miss Mary Van Blaricom. The event was reported in the *Glendive Independent* on Saturday, 15 October 1887:

MARRIED: SLAWSON–VAN BLARICAN *[sic]* -- Monday, October 10, 1887, Willard Slawson to Miss Mary Vanblarican *[sic]*, by the Rev. F. G. Boylan, at the M. E. parsonage.

The Marriage Certificate shows the two witnesses who attested to Willard Slawson's signature were Eben Slawson, the defendant's father, and John Trumbull, the defendant's attorney. [See Marriage Records, Dawson County, Glendive, Montana Territory.]

Fifteen days later, on 25 October 1887, the criminal charges against Willard Slawson were dropped:

By advice of the County Attorney, the above case was dismissed, a marriage ceremony having taken place between the defendant and the complaining witness. [Notes for Case No. 286 in the Probate Court, 25 October 1887.]

According to Mary's testimony in her divorce action, Willard Slawson disappeared only days after the marriage ceremony. In 1888, Willard surfaced in Old Mission (now Cashmere), Washington Territory, in the company of his parents, who had moved to Old Mission in that same year. Willard and Mary never saw each other again. Their daughter, Emma Mabel, was born in Glendive on 16 December 1887. The baby never went by the name of "Slawson." She was called "Emma Mabel Van Blaricom" until her mother married Herbert Eddy in Victor, Montana, on 26 April 1895. Thereafter, from the time she was seven years old, she went by the name of "Emma Mabel Eddy." Willard Slawson reportedly never saw nor ever attempted to communicate with Mary or the child.

Herbert Eddy and his apparent brother, William Eddy (also a resident of Victor), had also lived in Glendive during the 1880s. They were both survivors of a difficult home life, the children of a drunken and abusive father:

> Sarah Eddy, Plaintiff, against Wm. Henry Eddy, Defendant.
>
> The said action is brought to obtain a decree of divorce a viacule matramoni on the ground of cruelty, abuse and a failure to provide this plaintiff with the necessaries of life, also for habitual intemperance on your part. [GI, 5 July 1884.]

The divorce was granted in October, 1884:

> Sarah Eddy v. Wm. Henry Eddy, Divorce.
>
> Comes now the plaintiff Sarah Eddy with her Attorney W. Clark. Wm. Henry Eddy although called makes default. Sarah Eddy the plaintiff being duly sworn and was examined. Herbert O. Eddy sworn and examined. Decree granted. [Records, Clerk of Court. Dawson County, Territory of Montana. Court opened 1 October 1884.]

Herbert Othello Eddy was born on 1 August 1858 in Stratton, Vermont. When the family moved to Glendive is unknown, but he was twenty-six years old when he testified in his mother's divorce action.

Mary Martha Van Blaricom, age twenty-three, married Herbert Othello Eddy, age thirty-six, on 26 April 1895 in Victor, Ravalli County, Montana. Given their age difference, it seems unlikely that Mary Van Blaricom and Herbert Eddy were very well acquainted in Glendive. It is probable they only met after both of them had coincidentally moved to the Bitter Root Valley. They subsequently had five children, three boys and two girls, all born near Victor between 1896 and 1903. The last child, Flora Teresa Eddy (born in 1903) died in Victor in 1911 at the age of eight.

On 16 June 1916 the Eddy family left Victor, crossed the border at Sweetgrass, Montana, and immigrated to Canada. [Correspondence from Mrs. Jack Walter (nee Eleanor Rose Eddy) dated 25 March 1993.] Herbert Eddy died 25 June 1940 at the age of eighty-one. Mary Martha (Van Blaricom) (Slawson) Eddy died 26 February 1956 in Edmonton, Alberta, at the age of eighty-three. [HVBG, Family Group Sheet of Levi Van Blaricom.]

CHAPTER TWENTY-TWO

Some Good Friends

MRS. ANN TOWLE[325] WAS ONE OF MY favorite people. Whenever I was in Glendive and wanted to treat myself, I would go into Mrs. Towle's Merchant's Hotel and order up one of her excellent meals. She was a delightful English lady, and she would laughingly refer to my visits with her as "Towle Time" (as opposed to the usual English "Tea Time"). More than being a wonderful cook, she was an interesting person and her life touched many of Glendive's very earliest settlers. She spent many years in the company of one of Glendive's most important men, Henri Haskell, from whose library she would occasionally (with Henri's permission) lend me books.

She told me she was born in England in 1835. Her maiden name was Goodwin. When she was nine or ten years old, her parents came to America and settled in New Hampshire. She married there in 1862. In the spring of 1883, however, she left her husband in Lowell, Massachusetts, and came to Glendive in the company of her sister, Mrs. Charles (Hannah) Temple.[326] Shortly thereafter, she opened the Merchant's Hotel and Restaurant. She made no secret of the fact that she had left her husband back in Massachusetts where, she said, "he had plenty of women friends." Her daughter, Nellie, who was about twenty, had accompanied Mrs. Towle to Glendive and helped her mother at the hotel. Nellie was quite a pretty girl and she was an immediate social success. At the age of fourteen, of course, I had neither the maturity nor the money nor the social standing to be considered an eligible beau for Nellie, but I certainly remember fervently wishing those attributes could have been mine.

---

[325] According to correspondent John Steffen, Ann Towle's surname was pronounced "Toll." [Steffen letter dated 27 November 1995.]

[326] OTOL, p. 305.

My youthful judgment concerning members of the opposite sex was confirmed when Nellie, within weeks of her arrival, was being seriously courted by Henri Haskell, one of our local lawyers. It was a whirlwind romance. Married in June of 1883, they were given a grand reception by Mrs. Towle at her restaurant.

Henri and Nellie's first child died at birth in 1884. About a year later Nellie was pregnant again, and Henri and she were anxiously awaiting the birth that was expected sometime early in 1886. Just before that expected event, Mrs. Towle moved in with them. Nellie wasn't doing well, and the idea was that Ann could help out her daughter. During the course of the birth, both mother and child died within hours of each other. In a short thirty-month period, two babies and Nellie were lost. Both Henri and Ann were devastated and, each being left alone by Nellie's passing, they relied on each other to get through this trying period.

At Henri's insistence, Mrs. Towle continued to make her home in Henri's residence. Over a period of several months, Henri had taken quite a liking to Mrs. Towle and she to him. Now alone in Glendive, the hotel business was beginning to wear on her, yet she needed a means of support. Henri was a busy man who needed a cook and a housekeeper and a bookkeeper. And so it was that Mrs. Towle gave up her hotel and restaurant business sometime in 1887 or 1888 and stayed on with Henri on a full-time basis.

Henri deservedly became one of Glendive's most famous citizens when, as a Republican, he was elected Montana's first attorney general following our territory's admission to the Union as a state in 1889. It was during Henri's run for re-election that he narrowly beat Ella Knowles, the Populist candidate for attorney general and the first woman admitted to the practice of law in Montana. After Henri won, he offered Ella a job in the office of the attorney general. She must have figured that if you can't beat 'em, join 'em, for she soon accepted Henri's offer of employment. It wasn't long until she married Henri and moved back to Glendive with him when his second term expired at the end of 1896.

Mrs. Towle stayed on as the live-in housekeeper and cook for Henri and Ella. This arrangement worked out quite well for all concerned until, all of a sudden, Ella up and divorced Henri and left town.[327] Ella and Henri never had any children. Because Henri never remarried, he was the end of the Haskell line in Glendive. Mrs. Towle stayed on with Henri until her death in 1911 at the age of seventy-six. She and I had kept in touch after I moved back to Ohio and married in 1900. She wrote me a letter just about a year before she died.[328]

Although childless, Henri Haskell did leave a permanent mark in Glendive. It was Henri who applied the sobriquet of "Horse Thief Row" to Meade Avenue. Around the turn of the century, Henri had accumulated some land on the east side of town that he wanted to sell for upscale homesites. Bill and May Jordan were the first to break ranks when they bought property and built on the west side of town. Bill Jordan had been one of the early Texas cowboys to come into this country. He had shown up in the Terry country in 1884. He was one of those long riders I previously mentioned who stuck around and did well. His wife, May, had come up to Miles City by steamboat in 1879. She had busied herself in the hotel business in Miles City and Terry until she and Bill got married in Terry in 1888 and built their own hotel there that same year. In 1897, they bought the old Yellowstone Hotel in Glendive in a sheriff's sale. Things must have been going pretty well for the Jordans because around 1900, they bought the entire 700 block of Meade Avenue. In 1901, the same year they started construction of the spectacular Jordan Hotel in Glendive (it had both gas and electric lights, steam heat, and electric call bells), they built a beautiful home out on the sagebrush prairie abutting the Yellowstone River.[329]

That stretch of Meade Avenue where the Jordans built was originally part of the old Judge Allen[330] homestead. About 1906, Tom Hagan,[331] another noted horse and cattle breeder, built a

---

[327] Henri Haskell and Ella Knowles were married in San Francisco on 23 May 1895. [PMM, p. 474.] Their divorce is discussed briefly in CGL, p. 73.

[328] OTOL, p. 128 and p. 305. Norton's daughter, Ann Falor, stated that, as a child, she had seen correspondence from an Ann Towle.

[329] See "William and May Jordan" in Author's Notes following this chapter.

[330] See "Judge Joseph 'Wolf' Allen" in Author's Notes following this chapter for the biography of one of Dawson County's most colorful and energetic characters.

[331] Tom Hagan went from being a railroad fireman and brakeman for nearly ten years (1893–1902) to becoming one of Glendive's most prominent businessmen and investors. Some people (see "Thomas F. and Mary Hagan" by Fr. Barry Hagan in OTOL, pp. 118–119) have spec-

mansion on Brennan Street across from the Jordans. The next year, Elmer Herrick[332] sold his huge sheep outfit and moved into town. He bought half of the Jordan block and built an eighteen-room mansion right next door to Bill and May Jordan. While the road that ran in front of these three places was shown as Meade Avenue on the Merrill townsite plat, it was, in fact, simply a dirt track. These properties, including Elmer Herrick's lawn, ran clear down to the Yellowstone and so, in order to keep out the local livestock, Jordan, Hagan and Herrick fenced their lots from Meade clear to the river. Jordan built a picket fence around his home. Hagan went so far as to fence his entire acreage with wrought iron.[333]

Well, this was all too much for Henri Haskell, who had wanted these men to build their fancy homes on his property on the other side of the railroad tracks. Henri was a very bright lawyer, and while he was quite a wit, he also had a more serious side. Nobody was ever too sure which side of Henri was talking when he dubbed the exclusive development occurring out on Meade Avenue as "Horse Thief Row." He even went so far as to declare it highly unlikely that old Judge "Wolf" Allen had fought both Merrill and the Northern Pacific for title to that land just so he could set it aside "for the likes of horse thieves."[334] The Meade Avenue sign was never replaced, but maybe it should have been. The nickname took and the locals then referred to that stretch of Meade Avenue where the mansions were located as "Horse Thief Row" for a number of years—at least during General Henri Haskell's lifetime.[335]

While the construction of Elmer Herrick's home drove Henri

---

ulated that Hagan's wealth may have been assembled in part due to his unflagging political support of mining magnate William Clark. See *"Thomas F. Hagan"* in Author's Notes following this chapter.

[332] Elmer Herrick became vice president of the Exchange Bank, helped organize the First State Bank of Wibaux, and served on the Glendive City Council. [GTHG, p. 47. Also see OTOL, p. 134.]

[333] For a more detailed description of the Jordan, Hagan, and Herrick homes, see GTHG, pp. 43–47. Also see the map of *"Glendive Historic Sites"* in GTHG.

[334] There may have been more to Haskell's comments than simply good-natured humor. Haskell, as a staunch Republican, had been Montana's first attorney general. According to Hagan biographer Fr. Barry Hagan, Tom Hagan was an advocate for the election of William Clark, a Democrat, during one or more of Clark's notorious runs for the U.S. Senate from the state of Montana. [OTOL, p. 118.]

[335] GTHG, p. 33. See *"Ann Towle, Henri Haskell, and Ella Knowles"* in Author's Notes following this chapter.

Haskell "over the edge," so to speak, Elmer and his wife, Eloise, were very pleasant people. Elmer had come into the Dakotas in 1882. Along towards the early part of the winter in 1884, he and a partner had moved a large band of sheep from Dakota onto Cracker Box Creek, some twenty-five miles or so southwest of Glendive. One of Elmer's favorite stories was to tell of his first visit to Glendive on Christmas Eve night. It was well after dark when he and his partner pulled into town to get their winter supplies. They were driving a wagon pulled by a pair of mules. After they found the livery stable, the attendant flatly refused to take care of their mules—or anybody's mules, for that matter. The stable man got pretty upset, yelling that "they were the worst kind"; and Elmer wasn't too sure whether he meant "mules" in general or the people who used them. After paying for the privilege of taking care of their own mules at the stable, they walked downtown to find some food for themselves. The restaurants had all closed. They found about a dozen saloons with the hitching racks in front tied solid with horses waiting for their riders to stop celebrating—and that wasn't going to be soon on Christmas Eve night. The partiers had already licked the soup pots clean, the sandwiches were gone and the cooks had either gone home or were too drunk to care. All of the beds and rooms in town were full, already rented to the revelers. They returned to their wagon, got some jerky and hardtack, and went back to the nearest saloon and ordered two beers apiece. After finishing their "supper," they sneaked back into the stable, threw down some straw in the alleyway behind their mules, and went to sleep in their clothes. When they awoke the next morning, they were nearly "froze to the bone." Discovered by the stable attendant, he charged them a dollar for "the straw they had spoiled by sleeping on it." "Uncovered, unfed, unbedded, unkempt, unwashed, unwanted and unwelcome" was how Elmer always described his introduction to Glendive upon awakening that morning. "There just wasn't much of a reason to stay in Glendive," he would say, "but we did and it worked out okay."[336]

---

[336] Ann Falor, Norton's daughter, recalled the "uncovered...unwelcome" phrase as one of Norton's favorite quotes concerning early Glendive settlers. "He frequently used that expression. It came from a friend of his there in Glendive named Herrick." [Ann Falor interview in August of 1993.]

Elmer was a natural-born storyteller. He would tell stories that revealed something of the character of Glendive in the middle 1880s, that same period of time when all of my family was still living there. He told how there were no sidewalks, just a dirt path between the hitching rails and the storefronts. Depending on the time of year, the storefront "path" could also be ice or mud. He recalled that most of the men in town were railroad workers, but there would always be a smattering of cowboys and about an equal number of just plain hangers-on who had no visible means of support yet always seemed to have enough money for poker chips or women or anything else they considered "sporty." Elmer remembered that the horse races, many of them simply spur-of-the-moment affairs, were frequent. They ran them right down Merrill Avenue, the main street of town. You always wanted to watch out if there was any kind of a crowd in the street, because that meant a race was on and they would run right over the top of you. Finally, he told about the girls from the "red light" who roamed the streets in the neighborhood of the saloons that mostly faced Merrill Avenue. Although a couple of the proprietors wouldn't stand for women or minors at all, in general they could go in and drink right along with the men. There were no scruples about age either. That didn't mean they'd serve you when you were twelve years old, but if you could grow a whisker and you could pay for it you could get it—and that played out about equal for alcohol or for the demimondes.[337]

About sixteen years after Elmer showed up in the Glendive area he got married. That was in 1900, the same year as my own wedding. He married Eloise Goodspeed, an attractive young lady who had come out from Minnesota only a few months earlier to take a job as a clerk in the Douglas and Mead store. They got married in July and their wedding occasioned one of the few times I ever saw the Glendive ferry all decorated up. Elmer's ranch was across the Yellowstone, about forty miles outside of town. In order to surprise Eloise and to give her a memorable send-off to her married life with him, Elmer paid the ferryman to decorate the ferry all up with bunting and flags and banners. All in all, it

---

[337] OTOL, p. 134. "Demimonde" was a polite way of describing a prostitute in the 1880s.

was quite the sight and it proved to be an auspicious beginning for these two nice people.[338]

The other side of the Ann Towle story was, of course, the Temple family: Charles and Hannah and their five children.[339] Hannah Temple was Ann Towle's sister. Up until 1882, they owned a general store in Lowell, Massachusetts. They had saved up some money and then the "call of the West" got into Charlie's blood. He decided to take a year off, relocate himself, and then send back East for his family. Charlie, his brother-in-law, George Turner, and Ira Alling[340] drove a herd of cattle from Iowa to Belle Prairie in 1882. They built a log house out there and in the fall Charlie went back East to get his family.

While Temple was gone, Turner and Alling took up with Nathan Brown and his son, Jim.[341] The Browns were the earliest permanent residents on the east side of the Yellowstone and the Glendive area, and they knew this country like the backs of their hands. The four of them spent the winter of 1882–1883 hunting buffalo for hides, humps, tongues, and hindquarters. One winter's day, Alling and young Jim Brown loaded up and hauled a load of hides and meat back into Glendive, intending to trade for supplies. They got stranded there several days during a blizzard. In the meantime, that left George Turner and old Nathan Brown out in the camp, miles from nowhere, and they simply ran out of food. The only thing there was to eat was the front quarters of those buffalo they had killed earlier. Hunters almost never messed with the buff's front quarters, always leaving them to rot or to provide meat for the

---

[338] Elmer Herrick was born in New York state in 1862. He moved to Dakota Territory in 1882 and on to the Glendive area in 1884. He was about thirty-eight years old when he married Eloise Goodspeed. Through the years, he became a prosperous livestock grower and banker. He wrote his memoir in 1939, a year before Stephen Norton Van Blaricom told his own story. Elmer Herrick died in Glendive in 1945 at about the age of eighty-three. [OTOL, p. 134.]

[339] The Temples had five children when the family arrived in Glendive in 1883. Two more were born after their arrival, Carl on 1 April 1887 in Dawson County and Charlotte in Park City, after the family left the Glendive area in 1887. [OTOL, pp. 408–409.]

[340] See "Ira M. Alling" in Author's Notes following this chapter for the biography of this colorful character.

[341] In 1879, the Harpster family had wintered their numerous railroad-grading teams out on Belle Prairie. Since all of the Harpsters returned to Wisconsin that winter, the horses were apparently left under the care of Nathan Brown and his family. [OTOL, p. 345. Also see The Harpster Brothers manuscript by William Harpster in the Glendive Public Library.] See "Nathan Brown" in Author's Notes following this chapter.

coyotes and wolves, whichever event first occurred. Turner and Brown survived okay, but over the next decades, when telling and re-telling the story of their "survival," George Turner always relished the part about how careful they had been to cut out from around the coyote and wolf tooth marks on whatever well-aged meat they chose to put into their stew pot. "Of course," he would say, "it was well froze so that made our task a little bit easier." Old Nathan took the whole deal in stride and chalked their "survival" up as a rather unremarkable event and I don't believe he ever mentioned the subject once. He'd had a few suppers like that before.[342]

Charlie Temple returned on the train early in 1883 with Hannah and their children, Mrs. Turner, and Mrs. Towle and her daughter, Nellie. (Mrs. Temple, Mrs. Turner, and Mrs. Towle were sisters.)[343] He took Hannah and the kids straight out to Belle Prairie to the log house he and Turner and Alling had built in one of the coulees. The story goes that it rained hard the first night they got there and the dirt roof leaked like a sieve. The water poured in through their dirt roof onto their dirt floor, and so there they were in their new "home" standing in mud with more mud pouring in on their heads. I guess Hannah gave old Charlie the real "what-for." She said she was going to take the kids and head back to wherever they had come from, which, word had it, was a nice dry frame home with a shake roof in Lowell, Massachusetts. Needless to say, conditions improved pretty quickly, meaning Charlie put on a roof that didn't leak.

If Hannah had stormed off and gone back East, she would have passed their cows. They'd spent their winter walking their way back toward Iowa. Charlie, Alling, and Turner just turned their cattle loose for the winter and never checked on them once. After all, they reckoned, the cattle were branded and it was "free and open" range and that meant "no work." Well, during the winter of 1882–1883 those cows of theirs had headed off back east, the way they had come in. They crossed the Little Missouri on the ice, and had wandered fully half way across Dakota. Come spring, Charlie and George couldn't find their cattle for several weeks. They never did get all of them back. Not that it mattered

---

[342] A similar story is related in OTOL, p. 109.

[343] OTOL, p. 305 and p. 408.

too much, anyway, for the Temples lost all but seventeen head during the winter of '86–'87. Like the rest of the country, they ended up mostly broke. They sold the seventeen cattle they had left to Pierre Wibaux in the spring of 1887 for fifteen dollars a head and they left.

George Turner and his family had already moved from Glendive before the "killer winter" and I believe he was working for or managing a coal mine in Red Lodge.[344] When the Temples left Glendive, that's where they went, too. Hannah died of pneumonia in Red Lodge about ten years later. A couple of years after that, around 1899, I heard that Charlie re-married. About 1902, just after I left Glendive, he and his new wife returned to Belle Prairie, where it is my understanding Charlie died in 1905.[345]

---

[344] OTOL, p. 408.

[345] OTOL, p. 410.

CHAPTER 22–AUTHOR'S NOTES

William and May Jordan: Born in Texas in 1861, "Billy" Jordan was the scout for a herd of three-thousand cattle that were driven up the Chisholm Trail from Texas to the Powder River country of Montana in 1884. He was soon running his own ranch on O'Fallon Creek and, following the winter of 1886–1887, he began investing in real estate. Married in Terry on New Year's Eve of 1888, Bill and May Jordan opened their first hotel in Terry in 1889. In March of 1897 they purchased the old Yellowstone Hotel in Glendive. [GI, 3 March 1897.] The Jordans built their "palatial" home on Meade Avenue in 1901, the same year that they started construction of the Jordan Hotel in Glendive. May Jordan died in Glendive in December of 1928 at the age of seventy-three. Bill Jordan was living in Winter Park, Florida, when he died at the age of ninety-seven on 7 February 1959. For the biographies of Bill Jordan and May (McDonald) (Miller) (Zahl) Jordan see the chapter entitled "May Jordan: Surviving Hard Times in a Hard Country" in "Old Dawson."

Judge Joseph "Wolf" Allen: The true given names of Judge Allen are not known. He is variously noted as "James Joseph Allen" (OTOL, p. 31), "Joseph Wolf Allen" (TLW, p. 4), and "Joseph Allen" (in the 1880 census of Custer County). Official Custer County records showed him as "J. J. Allen" when he was appointed justice

JOSEPH "WOLF" ALLEN, JUNE, 1896
ILLUSTRATION BY JAMAICA JO

of the peace (which led to him being called "Judge" Allen). His obituary addressed him as "Joseph W. Allen." It is most likely that "Wolf" was a nickname applied after his 1866 arrival in Montana Territory to reflect certain aspects of his character. A hyperactive and rather fearless individual, he was born "at the mouth of the Little Redstone River" in Fayette County, Pennsylvania, on 17 February 1837. His family later moved to Marietta, Ohio, where he attended Marietta College. The Allen family then moved to Big Springs, Kansas, where, during the winter months, he studied law. He aligned himself with John Brown and Tom Lane to oppose the pro-slavery forces working to bring Kansas into the Union as a "slave State." He then served in the Union Army as a member of the 1st Kansas Volunteers from 21 May 1861 until August of 1865. [GI, 6 February 1904.]

In January of 1866 at Topeka, Kansas, Joseph Allen, age twenty-eight, married Sarah E. Wright, about age fifteen. From May through September of 1866 they trekked west, finally following the Bozeman Trail and ending up in Helena. He mined in the Helena area for a couple of years, and the couple's first child, a daughter, was born there. Not lacking a sense of destiny, they named the baby "Orofina" ("Fine gold"), but it appears that the child was the only fortune they found in Helena. According to some, Allen was a born journalist and during the early days of Montana he was interested in several of the newspapers" in the territory. Hoopes identified his involvement in publishing the *Bozeman Avant–Courier* from 1874 until 1877. [TLW, p. 4.]

Eleven years and six children after their arrival in Montana Territory in 1866, and being the hardy souls they were, he and his wife moved their family from Bozeman to the north side of the Yellowstone River opposite the mouth of the Big Horn River. That was in June of 1877, less than a year after the Custer massacre had occurred just a few miles away. They had a daughter, Sophie (later Mrs. Charles N. Mallett), born in Etchetah on 25 October 1877. Sophie Allen is generally recognized to have been the first white child born in Custer County, Montana Territory. In 1877 "Etchatah" was variously described as being located at the mouth of "Etchetah Creek" on the north side of the Yellowstone River about one mile downstream from the old "Fort Pease" or three miles downstream from the confluence with the Big Horn River or "about three miles below

Guy's store at Pease Bottom." "Etchatah Creek" may have been that creek in Treasure County now called Allen Creek, presumably named after Joseph Wolf Allen and his family.

It was on 6 December 1877 that the *Bozeman Avant–Courier* reported that a committee of citizens residing in the Yellowstone Valley opposite the Big Horn River had met at the behest of John C. Guy and J. W. Allen. The committee asked the Custer County Commissioners to create a township called "Etchetah" and to form road and school districts. They further requested that J. C. Guy be appointed constable and that J. W. Allen be appointed both justice of the peace and chairman of the school board. The outcome of the citizen's petition is unknown. There was a post office there from 1877 to 1892, but the place carried many names: Guy's Bluff; Guy's Landing; Sherman; and Sherman City. [TLW, p. 106 and p. 316.]

The 1880 census of 26 and 27 June recorded the Allens as residing in "Fort Custer Valley" (in the vicinity of modern Hardin, Montana; Fort Custer was located on the east side of the Big Horn River just south of the confluence with the Little Big Horn River):

Names	Age	Place of Birth
Joseph Allen	41	Pennsylvania
Sarah [wife]	29	Kentucky
Orofina	13	Montana [born in Helena about 1867]
Thomas B	12	Montana [born in Helena about 1868]
William R.	10	Montana [born about 1870]
Joseph	8	Montana [born about 1872]
Maggie	6	Montana [born in Bozeman about 1874]
Frank	4	Montana [born in Bozeman about 1876]
Sopphia	2	Montana [born in Etchetah, 25 October 1877]
Mattie	9/12	Montana [born about September 1879]

[1880 USC, Fort Custer Valley, Custer County, Montana Territory, Page 28, Dwelling Number 6. After their arrival in Glendive in July of 1880, Joseph and Sarah Allen had four more children. The last child, born in Glendive, brought them to an even dozen.]

Sometime in July of 1880, Allen and his family relocated his family from Custer Valley and squatted on the flat just above the mouth of Glendive Creek. Discovering that the railroad was going to turn and move south up the east bank of the Yellowstone, he quickly relocated between the Yellowstone River and the future railroad track, just north of the middle of what was soon to become the Merrill plat for the Yellowstone Land and Colonization Company, and filed a homestead claim.* He later successfully sued the Yellowstone Land and Colonization Company and the Northern Pacific Railroad for rights to the land. In 1893, fully thirteen years after his arrival in Glendive, the court awarded him clear title to eighty acres. [OTOL, p. 31. TLW, p. 4.] His daughter, Sophie (Mrs. Charles N. Mallett), recalled that when the NPRR finally did come through "they built [part of] the town on my father's homestead. Besides the depot and one store," she recalled, "the rest of the [earliest] town was saloons. The sidewalks were wooden planks on which the cowboys rode their horses [since] the street was bottomless mud in the rainy [spring thaw] season." [TLW, p. 213.] After the turn of the century, the mansions of so-called "Horse Thief Row" were built on Judge Allen's land. [OTOL, p. 134.]

> * Homestead claims required a government lands survey in order to be valid. The earliest surveys in the lower Yellowstone were not undertaken until Phineas S. Towne surveyed the Glendive townsite in 1880 and 1881. [See the original Glendive town plats dated 1881. Also see the article in RR, 15 April 1990.] Towne then continued his surveys, initially concentrating on the west side of the lower Yellowstone Valley between Glendive and Fort Buford. The Towne surveying project lasted for a number of years. It is of some interest to note that Dawson County records show land grants to the following parties dating prior to 1885: Merrideth Parsons in 1882; Joseph Allen, William Brake, John Butler, Jonas Hedges, Thomas Kean, Edward Marron, and W. Raymond, all in 1883; none in 1884; and only Martha Allen (no apparent relation to Joseph) in 1885. It could be that the dates reflect the date of the "claim made" with approval given retroactively following the survey dates. It is known, for example, that Thomas Kean filed his original claim to his Glendive property in Helena in 1872

while the site was clearly part of the Gros Ventre–Mandan–Arikara reservation. Kean's claim was also found to be valid in the court's 1893 decision relative to the sorting out of all the conflicting claims to the Glendive townsite. [See this subject in "Old Dawson."]

In August of 1880, it was "Wolf" Allen who successfully lobbied the Custer County Commissioners to create the massive "Glendive Township" as an administrative unit of Custer County. He got the commissioners to approve the boundaries of the new township to run east from the mouth of O'Fallon Creek to the Dakota border, then north to the Missouri River, and then south on the Yellowstone back to the mouth of O'Fallon Creek. Thus composed, "Glendive Township" encompassed a huge parcel of land, some in Custer but the vast majority in Dawson County. That task accomplished, he immediately got himself appointed justice of the peace for "Glendive Township," and named James Taylor his "Constable." The practical result of this rather astute maneuver was the formation of a sort of "Judge Allenland." All of this was done despite the fact that unorganized Dawson County was legally under the administration of Chouteau County and the county officials located in Fort Benton. It wasn't until the 18th of February of 1881 that the Territory of Montana transferred official control of Dawson to Custer County. [Refer to *"Dawson County"* in Author's Notes following Chapter 7.]

The Custer County Commissioners who participated in this ruse clearly suspected that Glendive would probably develop into a railhead of some importance, since Glendive was the first juncture of the Northern Pacific with the Yellowstone River. Since Dawson County was unorganized, the strategy had to have been that "annexation" of "Glendive Township" would result in the expansion of Custer County, and would ultimately remove that area from Dawson County. If and when Dawson County was ever organized, the Custer County thinking went, it would be sans all of that area east of the Yellowstone River. Further, such a strategy would have placed the Northern Pacific track from the border of Dakota Territory all the way to the west end of the Crow Reservation (then only miles from Bozeman) within the control and tax base of Custer County.

Sometimes, however, all of "the best laid plans of mice and men" go awry. The majority of the new citizens of Dawson County wanted nothing to do with the notorious corruptness so rampant in Custer County at the time and Judge Joseph Wolf Allen knew it. "To remedy this," Grace Gilmore wrote, "the pioneers took the reins into their own hands and called a special meeting September 9, 1881. J. W. Allen presided and James McCormick served as secretary. Ten of the largest property owners were selected. These ten chose a committee of three to draft a set of resolutions which were sent to B. F. Potts, Governor of the Territory of Montana, with the request that the matter receive his prompt attention." [IVEM, 10 October 1935.]

The organization of Dawson County was approved on 27 September 1882, and two weeks later the governor appointed the new county's officers (12 October 1882). The boundaries followed the original legal descriptions and "Glendive Township" and its administration, all put in place by Custer County authorities, disappeared overnight. When the county's elections were held in November of 1882, "James Allen" ran as a Republican to become the Dawson County representative to the Legislature of the Territory of Montana—but he was soundly defeated. [Gilmore in IVEM, 10 October 1935.] It had been a good two-year run (August of 1880 through 12 October of 1882) for Judge J. W. Allen, but it was over. [See "Glendive Township...The Town That Never Was" in "Old Dawson."]

Ever the entrepreneur and opportunist, "J. W. Allen," the *Bismarck Times* announced on 9 December 1881, "is opening a coal mine in this area, and is finding a ready market." This was the beginning of the large "Blue Jacket" mine located east of Glendive up Griffith Creek. The "Blue Jacket" was owned and operated by Norton's uncle, Frank Perry, from the fall of 1882 through the winter of 1886–1887 and for some time thereafter by Charlie Bowers.

In another interesting turn of events (considering his substantial personal interest in his homestead claim in the middle of the Merrill plat and the Northern Pacific land claims), the *Glendive Times*, on 14 June 1884, reported: "Judge Allen has become the U.S. Lands Attorney located at the corner of Merrill Avenue and Towne Street." [TLW, p. 4.]

While maintaining his many property interests in Glendive, Judge Allen moved north and, about 1901, acquired substantial holdings on the east side of the Yellowstone River in what had once been Allred County, North Dakota. Allred was a short-lived county that contained all of the alluvial flood plain of the Yellowstone River south of Dore, North Dakota, and immediately east of Fairview, Montana. By 1900, Allred had been incorporated into Billings County, and by the 1920 census the old Allred County area had become the northwest corner of McKenzie County. [IVEM, 10 October 1935. Also see MGFC, pp. 263–266.]

In 1904, fate dealt Joseph Allen one of the oddest of hands. He was on a business trip to Williston when the train stopped at a siding about a mile outside of the town. It was early February and a blizzard was raging. The judge, apparently believing the train had arrived at the station, disembarked. Several passengers saw Allen get off the train and reported him missing once the train started back up. A search party was sent back from Williston and, a few hours later, his frozen body was discovered. He was only a few days short of his sixty-seventh birthday. [GI, 6 February 1904.] "Jodie Allen [Joseph Allen, Jr., born in 1872] came in from his ranch on Redwater last Sunday, a messenger having been sent to his place with the announcement of his father's death at Williston last week. At first it was intended to bury Mr. Allen at Glendive, and a grave was dug and arrangements made for his burial, but the weather being very inclement it was finally decided to bury him at Buford [North Dakota], the funeral being held there last Saturday." [DCR, 11 February 1904.]

Sarah Allen lived until 1923. She died in Glendive at about the age of seventy-two. [IVEM, 10 October 1935.]

Thomas F. Hagan was born in Erin Prairie, St. Croix County, Wisconsin, on 22 October 1864, the son of John and Bridgit Hagan. He took a commercial degree from St. John's University in Collegeville, Minnesota. He married Mary Gavin in Erin Prairie, Wisconsin, on 12 September 1893. Traveling west on their honeymoon, they arrived in Glendive. Hagan got off the train and told his surprised bride, "We're getting off here for good." Mary reportedly took one look at the two blocks of saloons opposite the train depot and simply sat down and cried. Hagan's surprise announcement to his wife may not have been such a surprise to him. His sister, Catherine, was married to Ed O'Neil, who was an engineer with the Northern

Pacific working out of Glendive. [Norton Van Blaricom worked with Ed O'Neil. See Chapter 23.]

In 1896, Hagan, who was one of early Glendive's few citizens to hold a college degree, took a job as a brakeman for the railroad, a position he would hold for the next six years. It was also about this time he became politically involved working on behalf of William Clark, a Democrat, during one or more of Clark's notorious runs for the U.S. Senate from the state of Montana. One of Clark's memorable clichés was "I never bought a man who wasn't for sale." [See "Copper and Politics, 1880–1910," M/M, pp. 201–231.] It was during this period, around 1902, when he was about the age of thirty-seven, that Hagan acquired the Pabst Blue Ribbon beer license for the area—and his economic life took a dramatic change for the better. After nine years as a fireman and a brakeman, Tom suddenly quit working for the railroad. He became a director of the First National Bank (along with his neighbor, William F. Jordan) and a partner in the Koch Furniture Company, the Glendive Ice Company, and the Jordan Hotel Company (also with Bill Jordan). He soon bought a Glendive saloon and purchased large tracts of grazing and farmlands about five miles west of Glendive. He also began raising high-quality blooded horses.

After being the justice of the peace for some time, Tom Hagan served as Glendive's mayor from 1909 to 1915. Sources disagree as to when the Hagan house on "Horse Thief Row" was built and occupied. "Hagan's grand Neoclassical-style home was designed by renowned St. Paul architect Cass Gilbert and built in 1905." [GTHG, p. 45.] Hagan family historian, Fr. Barry Hagan, however, wrote: "In 1911 he and Mary…moved to their large home at 621 North Meade Avenue." Tom and Mary Hagan had four children. Of three sons, one graduated from Gonzaga University in Spokane, one from Montana State College in Bozeman, and one from Notre Dame. Their only daughter graduated from St. Catherine's College in St. Paul, Minnesota.

In 1916, Tom Hagan partnered with William F. Jordan and John F. Murphy to form the Jordan Hotel Company. While Jordan continued to own the real estate, the new company leased the property and managed the hotel's operations.

Thomas Hagan died 13 March 1924 at the age of fifty-nine, in Hollywood, California. His remains were transported to Glendive for burial in the Dawson County Cemetery. Two years after Tom's death, his three sons (Phil, Paul, and Gerald) negotiated the purchase of Bill Jordan's real estate interest in the Jordan Hotel, as well as his stock in the operating entity, the Jordan Hotel Company. Despite being a relatively wealthy widow, Mary Hagan went to work in 1927 as a housekeeper at the Jordan Hotel, the corporation of which she was then president. She stated she "preferred to wear out rather than rust out." When she died on 12 January 1946, her attic had a complete section filled with the classical literature she had read. Mary (Gavin) Hagan was buried beside her husband in the Dawson County Cemetery at Glendive. [See "Thomas F. and Mary Hagan" by Fr. Barry Hagan in OTOL, pp. 118–119.]

Tom and Mary Hagan's son Paul (born in Glendive on 17 June 1898), continued operating the Jordan Hotel Company until 1967. Even then he continued serving on the company's board of directors until his death on 2 February 1968 at the age of sixty-nine. It was only following Paul's death that the Hagan family sold their interests in the hotel. [See "Paul and Aimee Hagan" by Fr. Barry Hagan in OTOL, pp. 117–118.]

In the twentieth century, at Tom Hagan's old horse ranch on the west side of the Yellowstone, one of the more exciting archeological discoveries relating to the origin of the Crow tribe was made. Ethnologists long assumed that the hunter-gatherer, tepee-dwelling Crows were originally a part of the more horticultural Missouri River earth lodge dwellers, the Hidatsa. [DFIT, pp. 137–138.] "As one of several possible interpretations of the Hagen [sic] site near Glendive, Montana, where buffalo scapula hoes, pottery, and a single earth lodge site were found, William Mulloy has suggested its occupation by the Crows in process of transition from a horticultural to a hunting economy." ["The Hagen [sic] Site, a Prehistoric Village on the lower Yellowstone," *Publications in Social Science, No. 1*, pp. 99–102. University of Montana. Cited in DFIT, p. 138, Footnote 2.]

Ann Towle, Henri Haskell, and Ella Knowles—restaurateur, the state's first attorney general, and Montana's first lady lawyer: Ann Towle's maiden name was Goodwin. She was born about 1835 in England. At the age of nine, she immigrated with her family to the United States where they initially settled in New Hampshire. Her niece and biographer, Ann Fletcher, wrote in *Our*

Time, Our Lives that Mrs. Towle operated "the Merchant's Hotel and she also served meals. This building was located behind the Brenner Building." She left her husband in Lowell, Massachusetts, "where he had plenty of women friends, but she brought her daughter, Nellie, with her." [OTOL, p. 305.] Mrs. George Turner and the first Mrs. Charles Temple (Hannah) were both sisters of Ann Towle. [OTOL, pp. 409–410.] Ann was about forty-eight years old when she and daughter Nellie arrived in Glendive.

Henri J. Haskell was born 20 July 1843 in Palmyra, Somerset County, Maine. In 1862, age nineteen, he joined the 1st Maine Cavalry Regiment. His unit was soon attached to the Army of the Potomac, and in 1863 he participated in the battle of Gettysburg. Henri was discharged from the Union Army on 11 March 1865. He returned home to work on his father's farm and to recuperate from wounds received just prior to his discharge. In 1867, he moved to Marysville, California, where he studied law. He was admitted to the California bar in 1875. He practiced law in California for a year before returning to Maine in 1876. Haskell then practiced law in Pittsfield, Maine, for the next six years. [HD, p. 518.]

In 1882, Haskell moved to Glendive, where he "put out his shingle" to practice law in Montana Territory. He married Nellie Towle in Glendive in June of 1883. Henri was thirty-nine and Nellie was in her early twenties when they wed. Henri was well connected, and in 1884 his friend Wilbur Fisk Sanders employed him as the local attorney for the Northern Pacific. Also, between 1883 and 1887, Henri functioned as the deputy clerk of the Third District Court of the Territory of Montana. Henri and Nellie (Towle) Haskell had two children (born ca. 1884 and ca. 1886) both of whom died in infancy. Nellie died of complications following the birth of their second child.

At first named the deputy district attorney for Dawson County in 1887, Henri Haskell became the Dawson County district attorney the following year. [GG, p. 1.] On 20 January 1887, Father Lindesmith wrote in his diary that he "was driven from Glendive to the Wibaux ranch by J. [sic] J. Haskell, the prosecuting attorney and coroner of Glendive." The reason the two men traveled out to Pierre Wibaux's place together was to confirm the reported suicide of Emma D'Hellin, the maid servant to Mrs. Wibaux. [TLW, p. 153. FLP, p. 22.]

HENRI HASKELL

PHOTO COURTESY OF THE MONTANA HISTORICAL SOCIETY RESEARCH CENTER PHOTOGRAPH ARCHIVES, HELENA

Haskell, a Republican, was elected to the Montana Territorial House of Representatives in 1888 and was a member of the Montana State Constitutional Convention in 1889. In that same year, he was elected as the first attorney general of the State of Montana, a position he held for two consecutive terms. Henri was commonly known thereafter as "General Haskell." Following his 1892 election to his second term as attorney general, he hired his opponent, Miss Ella Knowles, the candidate for the Populist Party, to work in his office. Work soon turned to romance and, on 23 May 1895, Henri and Ella married. Henri was fifty-one and Ella thirty-four when they wed. Following their San Francisco wedding ceremony, the couple returned to Helena. In 1896, after Henri's second term as attorney general expired, they moved back to Henri's home in Glendive. [OTOL, p. 128. GG, p. 2. HD, pp. 519–520.]

Ella Knowles was born 31 July 1860 in Northwood Ridge, New Hampshire. She graduated from Northwood Seminary at the age of fifteen, and one year later she completed the teaching course at Plymouth State Normal School. She taught for four years and then entered Bates College at Lewiston, Maine, where she became "the first woman to participate in college debate and the first to hold an editorial position on the college magazine." [CGL, p. 64.]

ELLA KNOWLES

PHOTO COURTESY OF THE MONTANA HISTORICAL SOCIETY RESEARCH CENTER PHOTOGRAPH ARCHIVES, HELENA

Ella graduated *magna cum laude* from Bates in 1884 and moved to Manchester, New Hampshire, where she read law in the office of Henry E. Burnham. (Burnham was a distant relative of Henri Haskell). [HD, p. 519.] Following a year of teaching rhetoric and elocution at Western Normal College in Iowa, in 1888 she moved west, to Helena, where she taught for a year at Central School. She was then appointed principal at Helena's West Side School, a position she soon abandoned in order to continue her study of law in the Helena office of Joseph W. Kinsley. She passed the Montana bar exam and was admitted to the practice of law in Montana in 1889, but only after Council Bill No. 4 had been passed by the Montana legislature, which stated that individuals otherwise qualified should be allowed to practice as attorneys "without regard to sex...." Some correspondents, not seeing the broader implications of the bill, regarded the proposition as "a special bill meant solely for the benefit of Ella Knowles." Others felt that the presence of women in a court (where they could not be jurors or sit on the bench) "would do much to purify the atmosphere." Henri Haskell, a member of the judiciary committee, was particularly supportive of Council Bill No. 4. And so it was in 1889 that Ella Knowles became the first "lady lawyer" in the history of Montana. [CGL, p. 68.]

In 1892, Ella Knowles won the Populist Party's nomination for Attorney General of the State of Montana. That made her only the second woman in America's history to be nominated as a candidate for the office of any state's attorney general. [Ten years earlier, Marion Todd had been the Greenback Party's candidate for Attorney General of California. *Women Lawyers,* Robinson, p. 27, cited in CGL, Footnote 27, p. 70.] There was a potential problem or two with Ella's candidacy in Montana in 1892. The state constitution referred to the attorney general as performing "his" duties. Further, there was the more serious issue of whether she could legally run for and hold an office for which she, as a woman, could not vote. Montana Attorney General Henri Haskell, who was himself running for re-election on the Republican ticket, wrote the legal opinion which held that Ella could run for the office. [CGL, p. 70.] To make a long story short, Henri Haskell won re-election in 1892. In 1893 he appointed Ella Knowles his assistant attorney general. In 1894, they married. [CGL, p. 71.]

Sometime after Henri's second term expired in January of 1896, Ella and Henri moved to Henri's home in Glendive. Even after their marriage, Ella remained active in the Populist Party. "In 1896, she was a delegate to the Populist Party county, state and national conventions. She served on the Populist Party's national convention for four years. In 1896 and 1900 she took to the stump on behalf of presidential candidate William Jennings Bryan." [CGL, p. 75.]

Ella Knowles divorced Henri Haskell in 1902 and thereafter made her home in Butte. While in Butte she participated in some mining and claims cases, acquired some mining properties of her own, and was active in the International Mining Congress. She remained an avid supporter of women's causes the rest of her life. After suffering from a brief bout with an infection, Ella Knowles died in Butte on 27 January 1911 at the age of fifty. [CGL, p. 75. GG, p. 3.]

Ann Towle, the mother of Nellie, Henri's first wife, continued in her role as the housekeeper, cook, caretaker, and bookkeeper for Henri Haskell the rest of her life. Henri served as one of the attorneys who unsuccessfully defended Joe Hurst in 1899 and 1900 during the famed trial and subsequent appeal regarding the murder of Sheriff Dominic Cavanaugh. Around 1900, Henri purchased a large property on the east side of the Yellowstone, about ten miles southeast of Glendive, near the old railroad siding of Colgate. He was one of the first in Dawson County to install an irrigation pump in the Yellowstone. He raised cattle, sheep, horses, and hay on his property. [GG, pp. 3–5.] It was around 1907 or 1908, when Elmer Herrick decided to build his new and expensive home on Meade Avenue, that Henri coined the term "Horse Thief Row" to humorously describe the neighboring addresses of the well-to-do residents who were concentrating in that part of town. [OTOL, "Henri Haskell" by Sylvia Mickelson, p. 128.] Ann Towle died in Glendive in 1911 at the age of seventy-six. [OTOL, p. 305.] She was buried beside her daughter, Nellie, and Nellie's two children, in the Haskell plot of the Dawson County Cemetery. [GG, p. 2.]

In his later years, Henri spent much of his time on his ranch. Henri Haskell renewed his interest in politics, however, by successfully running as a Republican for the Montana House of Representatives in the fall of 1920. He had served only a little less than two months of his term when he died on 11 March 1921 at age seventy-seven. He was buried in the Haskell plot beside his long-time friend Ann Towle, his first wife, Nellie, and their two children. [HD, p. 520. Burial data from Rose Wyant interview, 10 November 2003.]

With over three-thousand books, Henri Haskell left the largest private law library in eastern Montana. Although he died intestate, he had often expressed his wish that the books be available for the use of other attorneys in the Seventh Judicial District (Dawson, McCone, Richland, and Wibaux counties). With the consent of the Dawson County commissioners, the collection was transferred from Henri's law office to the Dawson County Courthouse. There it was housed on the second floor where the clerk of the court served as librarian. The commissioners also agreed to purchase the books necessary to keep the collection up to date. [GG, pp. 5–6.]

Ira M. Alling was born in Dutchess County, New York, on 6 September 1860. He first arrived in Glendive on 3 March 1882 aboard a Northern Pacific train. There, the story goes, he ran into a young man named "Sailor." Finding no work (if they were really looking for work in any case), the two of them decided to go live on the banks of the Yellowstone on the south end of Belle Prairie "and eat fish for a while." Shortly thereafter another unidentified young man (Alling remembered him only as "Skippy") wandered into their camp, and Alling and Sailor decided it would be okay to take Skippy into their fold as well. Skippy, being totally broke, was ready to return to his former home in Pleasantville, Iowa, which he described in glowing terms as a regular "land of milk and honey." He convinced Alling and Sailor that, with Sailor's help, they could build a raft and float the Yellowstone and Missouri back downstream as far as Sioux City. (Obviously, anybody named "Sailor" would know all about building and sailing a boat, right? Yeah, sure!) Thus it was they built a "boat" (most people today would describe it as a raft) on "Harpster's bottom" out on Belle Prairie and decided to float back to "civilization."

They got the "boat" finished and stuck it in the river. Not caring much for the design or the quality of their new craft (which Sailor had designed and in whose construction he had been both supervisor and participant), Sailor reckoned as how they'd never make it. He opted out of the trip, although he did stick around long enough to help Alling and Skippy shove off. After he waved good-bye, Sailor dropped his hook in the river and went back to eating fish. Neither Alling nor Skippy had ever been in a boat or on a raft before in their lives. After being stranded on a snag in the Yellowstone for a day or two and nearly drowning each time they went through a couple of rapids, they quickly decided if they could only make it to Fort Buford they would beach their craft and walk back to Pleasantville from there. Wrong! The Missouri River's current shot them past Fort Buford and, like it or not, they were on their way to the next town—Bismarck—another three-hundred miles away. They nearly drowned a couple more times floating down the Missouri. They encountered so many other hazards (snags, eddies, and sandbars) they vowed that if they lived to get to Bismarck they would take the train the rest of the way to Iowa. They made that pledge despite the fact they had not a dime between the two of them. There was one other problem. As they had discovered at Fort Buford, they didn't know how to control their raft well enough to land it. If they could only make it to Bismarck they determined they would swim for it even if they had to abandon all of their worldly goods in the "boat." With no way to cook aboard their luxury liner, Skippy and Alling were getting real tired of eating raw river fish.

Well, fortune smiled on the adventurers. Another week or so of practice gave them the skills necessary to land at Bismarck. They quickly abandoned their craft by the simple expedient of shoving it back out into the river and letting it float away. (Just what is a "hazard to navigation," anyway?) In Bismarck, either they scrounged together enough money to buy train tickets or they hopped a freight to St. Paul. There they had a chance encounter with two new immigrants from the East, Charles Temple and his brother-in-law, George Turner. Temple and Turner had just arrived from Massachusetts, and Skippy turned his golden tongue loose on the two men. "[They] were on their way to Montana [looking] for [their] pot of gold," said Alling. "They, too, were taken in by Skippy's talk. They threw in with us [meaning Temple and Turner paid all of the expenses for the trip, including the one-way train fare] to return to Pleasantville, Iowa [Skippy's hometown], buy a little bunch of cattle, two saddle horses, a team and covered wagon." In Pleasantville, the day before their planned departure, they all learned that Skippy was called "Skippy" for a reason—he "skipped out" on them before the return trip started. Temple and Turner had paid Skippy for his assistance in assembling their herd and purchases, and apparently "Paid in Pleasantville" meant "adios" to Skippy. He wasn't about to chase a bunch of cows a thousand miles or so back to the Yellowstone.

Alling stuck with the deal. They trailed the cattle the thousand miles from Pleasantville, Iowa, to Belle Prairie by way of Pierre, the Black Hills, the Little Missouri country to O'Fallon Creek, then to the Yellowstone River, and back downstream to Glendive. After returning to Belle Prairie, "Turner and I," Alling said, "built a log shack close to the Browns for our winter home." (This was the "log home" to which Charles Temple brought Hannah and their five children in the spring of 1883. The roof leaked like a sieve and Hannah threatened to leave him on the spot. It quickly got repaired.) After they arrived, they turned the cattle loose on the unfenced Belle Prairie. Not familiar with the range, the cattle spent their winter drifting east, back toward Iowa. Temple and Turner spent much of the summer of 1883 trying to re-assemble their small herd. What they did put back together they lost during the blizzard winter of 1886–1887. "Most of them were found frozen and dead in the coulees that spring." Seventeen head were finally rounded up in the spring of 1887. They were sold to Pierre Wibaux for fifteen dollars a head.

Alling had met the Browns during his previous brief stay on Belle Prairie. Jim Brown and Alling were about the same age. When Charlie Temple returned east late in 1882 to gather up his wife and family, Charles Turner and Ira Alling and Jim Brown and his father, Nathan R. ("Squaw") Brown, teamed up and went out buffalo hunting for the rest of the winter. Alling eventually got into the livestock business himself, first as a partner with F. H. Merrill on Smith Creek in 1883. Later he bought the original Cheney location from Bill Cheney in 1886. Tom Forbes and Ira Alling then ranched together for a number of years on Hay Creek.

On 3 November 1897, Ira Alling married Minnie Hurst, the daughter of William Hurst, a well-known Glendive contractor and banker who had arrived in Glendive in 1881.

Following his marriage to Minnie, Ira's life began to settle down and his circumstances changed dramatically. Ira and Minnie Alling had three children, all boys, born between 1899 and 1906. Ira reportedly built the first wood frame house in what is now Sidney, Montana, in 1905. Following a stint of ferrying and employment as a teamster on the Glendive–Sidney stagecoach, he eventually became one of the organizers of the Valley Hardware Company, the Bank of the Valley (which later became First National Bank), the Valley Mercantile and Lumber Company, and the Sidney Provision Company. Ira Alling was one of the driving forces to separate Richland County from Dawson County in 1914. He later became one of the organizers of Day Land and Livestock Company, the majority stockholder in Alling Mercantile and Lumber Company, and was one of the original directors of the Montana Life Insurance Company.

Minnie (Hurst) Alling passed away in Sidney in 1932 and was buried in the local cemetery. In 1952, Ira died in Riverside, California. He was about ninety-two years old. He was returned to Montana and buried in the Sidney Cemetery beside his beloved wife, Minnie.

[CE, pp. 866–867. OTOL, p. 32. TLW, p. 4. There are several versions of the Ira Alling–Skippy story. See CE, pp. 866–867 and AIR, Vol. I, p. 245.]

Nathan Brown: Ira Alling was one of the few people to recall Nathan R. ("Squaw") Brown and his family as probably the earliest non-native residents of Belle Prairie, and perhaps the lower

Yellowstone. "I came to Glendive, Montana, in March of 1882. Squaw Brown of Glendive [originally] had a squaw for a wife and [they had] one child, Emma Brown. His [Indian] wife died. Later he married an Irish woman. Their oldest son was my age [about 21]. I lived with them on Belle Prairie 12 miles out of Glendive. That first winter we hunted buffalo. Young Brown and I freighted meat to the railroad and that's what grubstaked us." [CE, p. 867.]

It is known the Brown family was living on Belle Prairie during the winter of 1879–1880. The Browns apparently monitored the Harpster's herd of two-hundred or so draft horses when the Harpsters returned to Wisconsin for the winter. Owned by George Harpster's company, the draft horses were used to drag the "slips" (a large metal "scoop shovel" with a wooden handle on each side pulled by two or more horses) used in preparing the grade for the tracks of the Northern Pacific. Harpster would never have left such valuable horses to simply run loose and unattended on Belle Prairie for the entire winter.

Another piece of evidence placing Nathan Brown and his wife in Glendive early on is the undated letter from Daniel Brown of Miles City: "Grant Brown, First White Child born in Glendive, Montana, April 23, 1881...Father's name was Nathan Brown; Grant was one of twelve children in that family." [For the full text of this previously referenced letter, see "Grant Brown" in Author's Notes following Chapter 9.]

Although there is no evidence to support such a conclusion, one suspects that Nathan Brown was involved in the last vestiges of the fur trade in the lower Yellowstone during the 1850s. He had an Indian wife and one child, Emma Brown, and had then married a white (Irish) woman and had several children with her (among whom was Jim Brown, and Ira Alling mentioned him as being "about my age" or born around 1860). The one child (Emma) born to his Indian wife was older than Jim Brown. That means Jim Brown's older half-sister, Emma, was born in 1859 or earlier and that Nathan was married to the Native American woman in Montana late in the 1850s. The only whites in Montana in the 1850s were the last of the fur trappers and traders. Nathan Brown was probably born in the 1830s or earlier. During the later lawsuits surrounding the Merrill plat of Glendive, Nathan Brown was one of the many plaintiffs.

He claimed that he had resided at what later became the site of the NPRR water plant for "several years" prior to the coming of the railroad and Merrill in 1880 and 1881.

For whatever reason, the court must have dismissed Nathan Brown's lawsuit, for no originally platted deeds in Glendive go back in title to either Nathan or his apparent son, Michael Brown. (It could be that Brown never filed any of the proper paperwork. His name was not on any of the claims that were "proved up" in 1882, 1883, 1884, or 1885. See the asterisked discussion of homestead claims in the Judge Joseph Allen story on page 329.) Nathan R. Brown apparently died sometime during the lawsuit, since the claim continued only in Michael Brown's name for some years. The story by Ann Fletcher in OTOL (p. 409) references "Jim" Brown as Nathan Brown's son while the lawsuit only mentions Michael. It is unknown if "Jim" Brown and "Michael" Brown are one and the same (as in "James Michael Brown" or "Michael James Brown") or if "Jim" Brown and "Michael" Brown were otherwise related.

CHAPTER TWENTY-THREE

1888:
I Find a New Line of Work

I N 1888 THE LIVESTOCK BUSINESS was still busted. There just weren't a lot of cattle out there. I couldn't get on at the **W** that spring so I had to look for some other line of work.[346] There was a general merchandising company looking for a young man as a general factotum about the place, so I took that job for the summer. For some time, however, I had been thinking that I would like to try railroading. Like many boys of nineteen, I thought it would be great to be an engineer—a train driver. During that summer I made application for a job in the roundhouse, at that time the first step in an engineman's career. About the first of November 1888, they sent for me to come to work, and for the next eleven years I was a Northern Pacific railroader.[347]

One of the first jobs I was on after being promoted to fireman was picking up a wreck. In the late spring of 1889, the ice in the Yellowstone River was breaking up and going out. In doing so the ice had wrecked a bridge by knocking the pilings out from under it. An engineer was driving his freight train west in the night. He could see nothing wrong with the bridge and proceeded to cross it. The engine got across but the following thirteen cars went along with the bridge into the slough when the pilings gave way. There was a car of immigrant stock and goods in the lot. The west end of the car had the livestock, and the east end contained the

---

346 Unless otherwise indicated, the source for Chapter 23 is SNVB, pp. 38–40.

347 Norton Van Blaricom spent more than seven years as a roundhouse worker, brakeman, and fireman. It was sometime after April of 1896 that he became an "engineman" or "train driver." By 1898, he had become the hostler in charge of the trains and consists (the makeup and composition or arrangement of a train [TID, p. 484]) arriving and departing Glendive. His background was sufficient for him to get employment in 1900 as a master mechanic at the McKeefrey Iron Works in Leetonia, Ohio.

household goods. There was a ten-year-old boy sleeping in the car on the goods and, fortunately, that was the end above the surface of the water. The cattle and horses were flailing around and drowning in the water directly underneath, and there was no escape. It was absolutely dark as pitch, and it took some time for the rescuers to even discover the boy's presence, let alone rescue him. I have often wondered how that young boy must have felt during those solitary hours. He certainly knew that he had survived the train disaster, yet he remained alone and imprisoned in the dark of night with the watery sounds of the freezing Yellowstone swirling about him, and the terrible commotion of desperation, and the thrashing and throes of death of the animals underneath him. Just before dawn, they got him out by cutting through the end of the car. He didn't have a scratch on him.

Another time I was firing on a passenger run with an engineer I had worked with for two and a half years. I always considered him one of the best I ever worked with, but he was a cocky cuss. The officers of the road had issued orders that all the engineers should read their orders to their firemen. Well, he resented this as a reflection on his integrity. "Hell," said he, "if they think I can't read my orders and carry them out, why don't they fire me?"

He never once read me an order. He would hang them up on the order clip and I could read them myself, which I most always did.

It was a very unusual happening for a passenger train running on schedule to get a meet order with a freight train, but one day we did get such an order. Train Number 2 was to meet Extra West at Horton Station.[348] I read the order and thought no more about it. It was a beautiful day, and in the mid-afternoon Bill[349] whistled for Horton. The moment I heard the whistle, that meet order popped into my head. I could see that he was making absolutely no preparations to stop. I kept quiet and let him go until I could see that he couldn't possibly stop without running over the mainline switch. I finally yelled at him, "Bill, what about that meet order?"

---

[348] In 1883, Horton Station on the Yellowstone Division of the NPRR was located on the south side of the Yellowstone River about twelve miles west of Miles City. [TLW, p. 164.] To confuse matters, however, there was also a "Horton" on the Missouri Division of the NPRR in Dakota Territory located between South Heart and Fogarty (east of Little Missouri). [TLW, photographic section (pages unnumbered), "Northern Pacific R. R. route, Bismarck to Sentinel Butte, Dakota Territory, 1881."]

[349] "Bill" was probably William D. or "Bill" Norton.

Well, let me tell you, old Bill really hopped to it and did we ever scratch gravel! We had no more than got back to where he should have stopped in the first place than there that freight train was! It stuck its nose around the bend in the road and it was under a full head of steam. Although it's been almost fifty years since that happened and old Bill has long since got his last order, this is the first time I have ever told this story. It's just as well that people are unaware of all their narrow escapes from serious accidents on public transportation. They probably wouldn't use it as much as they do. Even after our near miss, Bill never did read me an order!

It was in June of 1894 that the great Pullman railroad strike started in Chicago. It fanned out from there and spread to the other parts of the country. It depended on where you were, but some of the activities of the strikers got pretty rough. The U.S. Army was called out to protect railroad property—tunnels, bridges, buildings, and the like. There were lots of murmurings here in Glendive about whether or not to support the Pullman men[350] when all of a sudden the Army showed up. They garrisoned the Glendive roundhouse, the rail yards, the station house, and the company hospital. Nothing came of it. The troops basically secured the town's railroad-owned facilities for about a month and then they left. I only mention this event because it is an odd feeling when you wake up one morning and discover your town occupied by soldiers. They weren't threatening in any way, but you could tell they meant business. The other unusual thing about the "occupation" of Glendive was that the soldiers were all blacks. Sometime around 1891, Negro outfits replaced the white troops at Fort Buford. The few white soldiers remaining at the fort called the new soldiers "Brunettes." Throughout the West, however, the civilians called them "Buffalo Soldiers" and the locals here in Montana Territory were no different. Around 1895,

---

[350] The community of Glendive was essentially in support of the strikers. On June 23, 1894, all seventy-five members of the Glendive Local of the American Railway Union, recently organized and led by Eugene V. Debs, walked off the job. A couple of days later the conductors, engineers, firemen, and other trainmen of Glendive vowed to support the union until the strike ended. "Act as a unit, have no divided councils and be prepared to fight to a finish," the *Glendive Independent* editorialized. The strike ultimately failed. [See *"Boycott: The Pullman Strike in Montana"* by W. Thomas White in *Montana The Magazine of Western History*, Volume 29, Number 4. October, 1979. pp. 2–11.]

Fort Buford closed down and all of the troops were transferred to Fort Assinniboine and other posts.[351]

On or about April the 25th of 1896, we suffered the worst snow storm I have ever witnessed in my life. I was firing on a passenger run. When we left our terminal at five o'clock in the morning the wind was blowing a gale. The air was so full of snow you could see nothing at all. We moved past strings of boxcars on sidings where I could reach out and touch them but I couldn't see them. The only way we could tell where we were was by the feel of the engine going over the various switches. We were just about halfway over the division coming to a station called Blatchford.[352] The engineer and I both heard something but could not tell what it was. I was standing on the deck and all of sudden I could clearly smell torpedoes.[353] I hollered to Hank[354] to shut her off and stop, which he promptly did. When we came to a halt, right there on the ground by my gangway stood a brakeman holding a red flag we never could have seen in that storm. He was the brakeman from a train coming in our direction, and he had put the torpedoes on the track to stop us. They had stalled on the mainline and had only been able to get half their train into the siding. The other half was still out on the line. If it hadn't been for this good old snozzle of mine, I couldn't be telling about this now, and the hundred or so people on our train would have been badly mussed up.

Before I leave the subject of railroading, I must tell you a little about one of Glendive's great engine men, Joel Gleason. Joel was in his mid-forties when I went to work for the Northern Pacific. He had been a railroad man all of his life and he had been an engineer for at least twenty years when I met him. It was Joel Gleason who drove the first train across General Rosser's ice bridge from Bismarck to Mandan in the winter of 1879–1880, and it

---

[351] See *"The 'Buffalo Soldiers' in Montana"* in Author's Notes following this chapter. Also see this subject in "Fort Union and Fort Buford–The Center of the World" in "Old Dawson."

[352] Blatchford station was located on the east (south) side of the Yellowstone River between Terry and Miles City. It was about three miles due south of the confluence of the Powder River and the Yellowstone [MAG, p. 64] and about twenty miles northeast of Miles City. Blatchford, one of the few places where the Yellowstone River could be crossed by ferry, was recognized in the press in 1885 as "a new town." [TLW, p. 26.]

[353] A "torpedo" was a flare.

[354] "Hank" was probably Henry E. ("Hank") Day.

was Gleason who ran the first passenger train on the Yellowstone Division between Glendive and Billings.[355] I was lucky enough to have been assigned as Joel's brakeman and fireman on many, many runs up and down the Yellowstone. He knew the workings of locomotives and consists inside and out and he gave freely of his vast knowledge. It was with his help and advice that I was able to become an engineer as fast as I did.

In 1888, Gleason made a real career move. I always believed that it was because he was tired of living out of the Commercial Hotel in Miles City.[356] Joel had always wanted a farm. In 1885, he'd gone into the sheep business on the side and he was doing pretty well at it. When Hank Tuttle finished his second term as Dawson County Sheriff in 1888, Joel decided to run for election to replace Henry. Joel was a well-known personality in Dawson County and he won the job of sheriff in a landslide. So Joel Gleason ended up being our sheriff for three full terms, 1889 through 1894. He kept his sheep ranch going and did quite well at that, too. Joel had opened a feed store and started raising some well-known and quality race horses. As I recall, he and his wife had six children. The Gleason family was still living in Glendive when I left in 1900.[357]

Another acquaintance of mine was Ed O'Neil. Ed was the oldest engineer in years of service on the Yellowstone Division. He became a Northern Pacific legend after I left. In 1906, he stayed with his engine and shut down the throttle just before he crashed into a freight train near Marsh. His engine was totally wrecked and he was made a cripple for life, but his passenger cars remained on the track and his passengers were saved.[358]

Besides O'Neil and Gleason, Bill Norton, and Hank Day, other early railroad engineers I recall were George Mott, "Crazy" Davis, Jack Snyder, and Alf White. These men all worked long hours on their various divisions, and a word or two should be said about how these men lived. Some of these engineers, like my brother

---

[355] OTOL, p. 110.

[356] TLW, p. 135.

[357] OTOL, p. 110.

[358] "When Ed O'Neil died in 1912, every engine on the division stopped for five minutes at the hour of his funeral to show respect and love for a fellow employee." [OTOL, p. 9.]

Fred's friend, Alf White, were married and had homes or even small ranches they returned to on their "off" days. Alf worked out of Dickinson, and his wife maintained their ranch just outside of town. Although known as the "Sweet Singer of Glendive" (he really did have a tremendous singing voice), Alf spent his railroad career based out of his home in Dickinson, and he eventually became the mayor of that city.[359]

Gleason, O'Neil, and Day, however, primarily worked the Yellowstone Division that ran between Glendive and Billings. (That stretch of track between Glendive and Bismarck was known as the Missouri Division.) Although they spent lots of time in Glendive, Forsyth, or Billings when they weren't working, the three of them basically called the original old Commercial Hotel in Miles City "home."[360] They roomed and boarded there for $7.00 a week. Their "rooms," located upstairs above the bar and dining room, were identical to the twenty or thirty other bed stalls that were simply separated by curtains. The "doors" were old bed sheets or canvas tent halves.[361] There was one bucket and a ladle to drink from, located in the sleeping area, and another bigger bucket and ladle in a small washroom. If you didn't use a washcloth, you just splashed the water out of the ladle and let it run off you onto the floor. All in all, the Commercial wasn't a place for the shy or persnickety, but the price was right and, more or less, the place was clean—and, as one of the old regulars described it: "You might see a mouse or two once in a while, but there waren't a lot of vermin."

The Commercial was a fairly typical accommodation in the early days. Built in 1878 as a one-story, split-cottonwood-log structure, it had a finished lumber face, It was located right by Wolf's Restaurant and Saloon. In February of 1880, Bill Reece bought the place and remodeled it to be a dance hall. It started out as kind of a big deal. The brass band from Fort Keogh played at the grand opening (but then the brass band from Keogh played

---

[359] Alf White and his wife made a serious effort to convince Fred Van Blaricom, Norton's younger brother, to allow them to adopt him. Fred lived with them for about a year. [FVBM.] The Whites are discussed at length in THWT.

[360] See TLW, p. 90 for H. E. Day, p. 135 for Joel Gleason, and p. 273 for Ed O'Neil.

[361] TLW, p. 71.

**STEPHEN NORTON VAN BLARICOM IN THE CAB OF
NORTHERN PACIFIC ENGINE NO. 291, FORSYTH, MONTANA, CIRCA 1898**

PHOTO COURTESY ELIZABETH FALOR CARDUCCI

at the opening of practically every new business in Miles City). The dance hall deal didn't really work out for Reece, however, for the simple reason that Doc Lebscher, the Miles City physician, soon shot and killed him. Harry Burgard and George Thomas then took over the place, and by the summer of 1881 they had added a second floor for the "bedrooms" and converted the first floor into a restaurant and boarding house.[362] That's when it became known as the Commercial Hotel. After the railroad arrived in Miles City in December of 1881, the Commercial became the overnight home two or three nights a week or more to many of the train crews.[363]

Alfonso Wolf had been working in Captain John Smith's saloon in Miles City since 1877.[364] Wanting to pull in some of the Northern Pacific men, Alfonso Wolf soon built his own hotel right next door to the Commercial, and he carried on quite a campaign to bring in the traveling crowd. His ads proclaimed "the finest location in the city with cool airy rooms with a magnificent view overlooking Tongue River and the mountains beyond." This was always curious to the locals since the Tongue was at least three blocks away and the only mountains you could see from Wolf's place were the bluffs of the Yellowstone River. Wolf eventually took over the Commercial Hotel for a while and leased it from Harry Burgard for a year or two. Old Alfonso was never shy. He once advertised that "all of the fat, sleek, and good-looking men in Miles City board at Wolf's."[365]

The original old Commercial Hotel burned to the ground in the spring of 1885. That marked the end of an era. By then, they were building hotels out of frame lumber. They had windows. They had walls between the rooms, and each room had its own door complete with hardware—doorknobs, deadbolts, and separate keys—and kerosene lamps. Some of them had inside plumbing. They were a far cry from the old Commercial, but, by then, civilization was finding its way to eastern Montana.

---

[362] Harry Burgard operated the Star Saloon in Glendive for a few months (August of 1883 through January or February of 1884).

[363] See *"The Commercial Hotel"* in Author's Notes following this chapter for the convoluted story of this historic old building.

[364] See *"Captain John W. Smith"* in Author's Notes following this chapter.

[365] See *"Alfonso B. Wolf"* in Author's Notes following this chapter.

CHAPTER 23–AUTHOR'S NOTES

The "Buffalo Soldiers" in Montana: The etymology of the term "Buffalo Soldiers" was neither as kind nor heroic as modern revisionist literature and the movies have made it. See TNC, p. 10.

"Beginning in July, 1891...an all-Negro outfit [the 25th U.S. Infantry Regiment] came in [to Fort Buford]. In May of 1892, as the white regiments were phased out, the infantry was supplemented by elements of the all-Negro 10th United States Cavalry. These regiments would serve as the post garrison until the final days." ["Fort Buford" in CE, p. 345.]

"The last official action requiring troops from Fort Buford occurred in the summer of 1894. The army was asked to intervene in a civil disturbance after employees of many railroads went on strike on June 26 in support of the Pullman workers in Illinois. In the Department of Dakota, troops were used to guard bridges and tunnels, as well as other railroad property. At Fort Buford, Commanding Officer T. J. Wint, three officers, and 103 men of the 10th U.S. Cavalry left for Glendive, Montana, where they guarded Northern Pacific Railway property. They returned to Fort Buford on August 8." [FBMF, p. 55.]

There was, in that same year, one other somber action the soldiers from Fort Buford were ordered to undertake. For twenty-five years or so, a rather large "renegade" band (meaning they weren't residing on their designated reservation) of Gros Ventres (Hidatsas) had lived near Fort Buford and up and down the lower Yellowstone River as far as Glendive. The Hidatsas had continued to live in the area with the full knowledge of the U.S. Army, the Indian agents, and the local settlers. That part of the country had been withdrawn from the Indian lands in 1880. In 1894 someone in the government determined that this sizeable group of two- or three-hundred souls should be "shipped back to where they belonged" on the Fort Berthold Reservation in North Dakota. (These were the Hidatsas who, under Chief Crow-That-Flies-High, had successfully confronted Winston and Shaw in 1879 when they had attempted to build a permanent store at the confluence of Glendive Creek and the Yellowstone while that land was still on the Gros Ventre–Arikara–Mandan reservation. [TLW, p. 136.]) The black soldiers "took them away in wagons amid protests and screams as they bundled them up and drove off [to the Fort Berthold Reservation]. Their lamentations and cries could be heard a long way." ["Fort Buford" in CE, p. 345.] On 1 October 1895, Fort Buford was officially retired from service. Reassigned to Fort Assinniboine (immediately southwest of Havre, Montana), the last troops departed Fort Buford on 7 November 1895. ["Fort Buford" in CE, pp. 345–346.]

The Commercial Hotel started out as the original store Charles Whitford Savage built in "Old Town" (Miles City) in January of 1878. It was a one-story structure built of split cottonwood logs with a dressed lumber front. The building was reportedly the first commercial structure in Old Town, which was renamed "Miles Town," then "Miles City." In the summer of 1878, it was picked up and moved to Miles City and located on the north side of Main Street between Fifth and Sixth, next door to Wolf's Restaurant (and what later became Wolf's Hotel). Thus, the ten lots that eventually constituted the Main Street side of the block by 1881 started with Charlie Brown's Saloon (complete with Charlie's live pet bear, "Ring," "a great favorite with the 'boys'") on the west corner, then Wolf's Hotel (and Saloon), and Savage's building that eventually became the Commercial Hotel (and Saloon). Next came Strader's Billiards Hall and Saloon, Isaac Orschel's (wholesale liquors: "scotch sunshine and cigars") and the Miles–Strevell Hardware Store.* Finally there was the Keg Saloon, Doc Lebscher's drug store and office, and, on the east end of the block, Charlie Savage's General Store (occupying two lots). [TLW, p. 37 and pp. 391–392.]

> * Miles–Strevell Hardware was owned by George M. Miles, a nephew of Colonel Nelson Miles, the commandant of Fort Keogh, and Charles ("Charlie") Nettleton Strevell, the son of Judge Jason W. Strevell of Custer County. Mrs. George (Helen) Miles was Charlie Strevell's sister. [TLW, p. 244–245 (Miles) and pp. 332–333 (Strevell).]

Charlie Savage was one of Miles City's earliest residents and a long time promoter of development in the area. He came into the Tongue River Cantonment in 1876 as a clerk for the military stores. He very quickly got into business for himself. After building substantial new buildings for his operations, he converted the old original structure to a saloon and dance hall and named it "The Cosmos Hall." Charlie sold it late in 1879 to Bill Reece. [TLW, pp. 74–75 (Cosmos Hall) and p. 308 (Charles Whitford Savage).]

William ("Bill") Reece was listed on the rolls of Custer's 1876 Dakota column as a civilian teamster. He had signed on at the Powder River supply depot on 24 April 1876 for the salary of $30.00 per month. He stayed on through the Sioux campaign and was a very early civilian resident of the Tongue River Cantonment. By January of 1878, the *Bozeman Avant Courier* reported that he and "Fitzsimmons" were the proprietors of the Varieties Theatre in Miles Town. A year later he had relocated his business, renamed it Reece's Dance Hall and Sample Room, installed a genuine Steinway piano, and offered a "faro bank" and "sampling rooms" where the patron could get "two shots of whiskey for two bits."

Around December of 1879, Bill bought the Cosmos Hall from Charlie Savage for $3,000, remodeled it into a 25-by-100-foot dance hall and saloon, and re-named it Bill Reece's Dance Hall. He reopened the place for business about 1 February 1880 and hired the Fort Keogh Brass Band to play at the grand opening. On the 18th of March, the *Bozeman Avant–Courier* reckoned he was clearing $100 per night.

Unfortunately, Bill Reece was already dead by the time the *Avant–Courier* reported his new bonanza. He and "Doc" Lebscher (Dr. Chester B. Lebscher), the thirty-year-old Miles City physician and coroner (formerly the physician at the Crow Agency in 1876 and 1877) had a shoot-out at Clara Clifton's "cat house" located at what is now Fifth and Main on 7 March 1880. Reece died two days later of gunshot wounds to the abdomen. (Bill died while under the care of the other Miles City physician, Dr. A. J. Hogg, whose office was located above Konrad Schmid's new harness and upholstery shop.) On 8 April 1880, the case was heard before Custer County Probate Judge John M. McBride (whose law office in 1882 was located "over Pat Gallagher's Saloon"). Clara Clifton and Lebscher himself were the star witnesses for Doc's defense. Clara, described as a "demimondaine," had lived in Miles City since 1879 after fleeing Bismarck, where she herself had been charged with "the crime of murder" in 1878 (a charge for which she was arrested when she returned to that town for a brief visit in 1882). After carefully listening to the witnesses, Judge McBride found that Lebscher had acted in self-defense.

When Bill Reece died in March of 1880, the dance hall property was taken over by his brother, Frank Reece. Frank sold the building on 2 July 1881 to George Thomas and Harry Burgard (the name is also seen spelled as "Beaugard" and "Beauregard") for the sum of $3,000. Frank then started his own place, Reece's Dance Hall, in another location, where there was soon "a general row which resulted in broken noses, etc." [BAC, 6 October 1881.] The dust-up in Reece's Dance Hall wasn't the only row in which Frank Reece was entangled. On 1 July 1880, Reece wrote an open letter to the editor of the *Yellowstone Journal* entitled "A. C. SWIFT." The editor published the letter in its entirety:

> When my brother William Reece was shot, before he died, he transferred to me his interest in our joint property and business, and told me that it had been his habit to contribute regularly to the support of our mother at home, and charged me as solemnly and tenderly as a dying man could, under no circumstances to forget her, or to let her know the means and manner of his death. I have cherished his wishes and in all things tried to do as my dead brother desired, and have been especially careful to afford my old mother no definite information of the circumstances attending his death, fearful it might break her loving heart.

> On Thursday last, I received a letter from her, saying that one A. C. Swift, who called himself a lawyer, had, without knowing her [and without] her solicitation, written her the story of my brother's killing, dwelling on every painful fact that could agonize a mother's sensibilities, and, in addition, telling her that I had 'got all the property,' and would 'beat her out of it,' but if she wanted to save herself, he, this thing Swift–to do the most dastardly thing I ever heard of– would throw the estate into court and save something for her. I want the people in this country to know how mean a man can be in hopes of making a dollar, and to what a dirty depth of conduct this man descends to forward his contemptable purpose. He is a dastard. He has, and ought not to have, no part with an honorable community. Let him follow the example of his associate. The [steamboat] Batchelor will be here to-day. Let him go if he would be wise. He need not stay to take somebody's horse.

> /s/ FRANK REECE.

On 9 July 1880, Tom Reece (Frank and the dead Bill's brother) arrived in Miles City. [TLW, p. 295.] Exactly what transpired between the Reece brothers and Clay Swift was not recorded, but two months later, in October of that same year, A. Clay Swift, attorney-at-law of Miles City, departed for Custer City, Dakota Territory. Shortly after Swift left, the *Bozeman Avant–Courier* reported that A. Clay Swift was, on 3 January 1881, admitted to practice law before the courts of Montana Territory. [TLW, p. 336.] And so it appears that Frank Reece was right in claiming that A. C. Swift only "called himself a lawyer." Although Mr. Swift had put his shingle out in Miles City, he had no standing with the Montana courts until some three months after he left the territory.

Harry C. Burgard, who purchased the hotel from Frank Reece, had been in Bismarck by 1873. According to some sources he was running a restaurant in Miles Town (the primitive civilian settlement adjoining the Tongue River Cantonment) in 1876. George Thomas, Burgard's partner, came into Miles City from Bismarck in 1880. He and Harry Burgard contracted and furnished two-hundred-and-fifty tons of hay to the Army at Fort Keogh. They also contracted wood to the fort in that same year. George Thomas took over management of the Merchant Hotel in Miles City on 11 February 1881. In July he partnered up with Harry Burgard and they closed the deal with Frank Reece on the old Cosmos Hall / Bill Reece's Dance Hall building.

Thomas and Burgard remodeled their new acquisition, added a second floor for sleeping rooms, and reopened the building in the first week of August 1881. The remodeled structure "has a spacious dining room of 25 by 30 feet and boasts 20–30 bedrooms" (which were actually sleeping stalls separated by curtains). [TLW, p. 71, citing the YJ of 10 August 1881.] Intending to cater to the railroad crews, the Thomas and Burgard operation was originally called The Northern Pacific Hotel. The railroad company, however, soon "pitched a fit" over the use of the name so the two proprietors grudgingly changed it to The Commercial Hotel. In any case, they continued to cater to the railroaders and the place soon became the popular location with the Northern Pacific crowd in Miles City.

[TLW, p. 42 (Harry Burgard), p. 67 (Clara Clifton), pp. 70–71 (Commercial Hotel), pp. 74–75 (Cosmos Hall), p. 162 (Dr. A. J. Hogg), p. 198 (Chester B. Lebscher), p. 291 (Probate Judge John J.

McBride), p. 294 ("Reece's Dance Hall" and Frank Reece), p. 295 (William Reece), and p. 340 (George Thomas). Note that "Reece" is occasionally spelled "Reese." See TLW, p. 162 and POY, p. 348. Dr. Hoopes, the author of TLW, alphabetized the name as "Reece." Since Frank Reece signed his letter to the *Yellowstone Journal* dated 1 July 1880 as "Reece," that spelling has been used herein.]

On 25 February 1882, the *Yellowstone Journal* reported that George Thomas had married Miss Maggie Schunert of Glendive. By January of 1883, Harry Burgard bought Thomas out of his interest in the Commercial Hotel, and in June of that same year L. C. Currier took Thomas out of the Merchant Hotel deal. The *Yellowstone Journal,* on 12 July 1884, reported that George Thomas was in Canada working on the construction of the Canadian Pacific Railroad. [TLW, p. 340.]

For whatever reason, Harry Burgard also decided to move on. Leaving the Commercial Hotel in Miles City under the management of a relative, Anton Burgard, Harry moved to Glendive where, by 18 August 1883, he was operating the Star Saloon. This is the same Star Saloon that was owned and operated by James Taylor when he was elected sheriff of Dawson County in November of 1882. Taylor had the place back by March of 1884 and Burgard returned to Miles City. [TLW, p. 42 and p. 338.]

Harry had kept the real estate but sold the business and inventory of the Commercial to Alfonso B. Wolf in September of 1883 for the sum of $5,000. Alfonso renovated the property, "spiffed up" the restaurant, and expanded the hotel's services to include the Brunswick Bar. Wolf also added an innovative twist to the hotel's restaurant. He accepted "non-resident boarders" (mostly train crews) and provided "table board only" for the sum of six dollars per week, utilizing a pre-paid punch card system. He also promoted the hotel's accommodations to both the traveling public and the railroad crews by providing "free bus and baggage" to and from the railroad station. [TLW, pp. 70–71.]

On 16 May 1885, Alfonso Wolf sold the business of the Commercial Hotel (the real estate was still owned by Harry Burgard) to Anton Burgard for $6,000 in cash. A week later, on 22 May 1885, a fire started in the hotel's Brunswick Bar and the entire hotel (along with the rest of the block of buildings on the north side of Main Street between Fifth and Sixth) burned to the ground. [TLW, pp. 70–71.]

And so it was that the favored haunt of the earliest Northern Pacific train crews who plied the rails between Glendive, Miles City, and Billings was no more.

A quick review of the buildings and the businesses that replaced the structures destroyed by the fire tells much about the general environment that helped lure the railroaders to the venerable and historic old Commercial Hotel. In addition to losing the hotel, John Carter's New Keg Saloon (that famously had three "Spanish booths" fully draped and enclosed for privacy) went up in smoke, as well as his pawnshop. Also gone were Richmond's jewelry store, and Carter's loan office, Drover House Saloon, and Courthouse Sample Room. The destroyed buildings on the block were rapidly replaced by a single large two-story brick structure named the Commercial Block. Later in the year, John Carter and Isaac Orschel occupied the new building. [TLW, p. 70.] It was announced on 22 August 1885 that Carter's part of the new block was to have a restaurant in the basement, a saloon on the first floor, and a hotel on the second floor. On 10 October 1885 Carter's part of the newly rebuilt block opened. His "new setup [was] called [the] 'European Hotel and Restaurant.'" [TLW, p. 55.] Orschel's store was an interesting combination of "clothing, general merchandise for men, liquors and cigars." Years before, back in the 1870s, Isaac Orschel was well known in Bismarck as being "a travelingman for a St. Paul liquor house." He was especially popular since he specialized in "scotch sunshine and cigars." [TLW, p. 274.]

It is unknown if Flick and Louie's (gambling hall and saloon), one of Miles City's "most popular corners," was rebuilt following the fire. [TLW, p. 115.] Flick's real name was John McTiernan, "one of the best known sporting men in the West." [YJ, 9 December 1882.] "Louie" was Louis Hainemann, a lesser-known gambler who, after the fire, offered up "bargain household furniture and saloon fixtures" even though they were "in a slightly smokey condition." [TLW, p. 148.] While it is known that McTiernan stayed on in Miles City (he also operated The Second National, a saloon just across the street from the Commercial Hotel), there is no further record of Hainemann.

The new Commercial Block gave Miles City its first display of electric light. The *Yellowstone Journal* reported on 23 October 1886:

"The new arc light shineth forth." On that same date the newspaper commented on the fact that the new electric lights in Miles City were not only a curiosity to the citizens, they drew the attention of the wildlife as well:

> A curious thing was noticeable a few nights ago, at the electric light near the depot. A flock of wild geese were attracted by the unusual brilliancy of the light, and, descending from their flight, circled around in close proximity to the globe, all the time calling their discordant cries. They kept up their circling for about half an hour, and then, alarmed at the approach of a train, took up their southern journey.

Captain John W. Smith, born in 1828, was an "old hand" in Dakota and Montana territories. In 1857, he was trading with the Indians near Fort Yates. He married an Indian woman there in that same year. From 1866 through 1868, he was the sutler at Fort C. F. Smith on the "bloody" Bozeman Trail. Reportedly fluent in the Sioux language, he was then the Indian trader at the Whitestone Agency until 1872. Smith was the sutler attached to Custer's expedition to explore the Black Hills in 1874. [TLW, pp. 321–322.] The BT reported on 21 and 28 July 1875 that Captain John W. Smith "is the post trader at Fort Buford." Smith was the sutler for Custer's expedition against the Sioux in 1876. He set himself up at the mouth of Powder River and waited there while Custer and the 7th Cavalry went on to meet their fate at the Little Big Horn. On 27 December 1876, the BT reported from Fort Buford: "Capt. John W. Smith is at Tongue River. He is doing a good business there. He also has a branch establishment at Glendive [Cantonment]." See a more complete biography of Captain John W. Smith in "Old Dawson."

Alfonso B. Wolf was born in Louisville, Kentucky, around 1833. His father was a baker and trained Alfonso in the same trade. Wolf showed up in Miles City ("Old Town") in 1877, where he managed Captain John W. Smith's restaurant (the predecessor of the Cottage Saloon), located on the northwest corner of the block facing the park bounded by Park (now Fifth), Main, Bridge, and Sixth. In 1878, he set up Wolf's Restaurant, an interesting combination of café, ice cream parlor, and saloon. In that same year he built Wolf's Hotel right beside his restaurant. In 1881, he tore down Wolf's Hotel and replaced it with the Merchant Hotel. He sold the Merchant in

August of 1882 and moved to his ranch some thirteen miles up the Tongue River from town.

Alfonso quickly became known as "the jolly granger" and was reported to be "growing 300 different fruit trees as well as fresh market potatoes." Wolf then leased the Commercial Hotel from Harry Burgard from September of 1883 until January of 1884, when he gave up the lease to Cotter and Kennedy. He then basically retired to his true love, farming, and he was reported to have harvested and brought the first fresh strawberries into Miles City in June of 1884. In October of 1885, his address was Cutler, Custer County, Montana Territory, where he owned and operated a road ranch known as Ten Mile House. At that location, Alfonso had his own greenhouse ("glass house") and raised chickens for both meat and eggs. After 1886, Alfonso Wolf dropped from sight. [TLW, pp. 373–374.]

CHAPTER TWENTY-FOUR

Some Old-Timers

TOO OFTEN MANY OF THE FIRST PIONEERS somehow become forgotten.[366] I would like to mention here a few of the early settlers who contributed to the settlement of Glendive, the lower Yellowstone, and the old original Dawson County.

No history of Glendive or the county could ever be written without the name of William W. Mabee.[367] His name must be inscribed therein in large red letters. Mr. Mabee was the proprietor and editor of Glendive's first newspaper, the *Glendive Times*. Brother Mabee arrived on the scene in 1880 when the sign was fresh—when all things seemed possible and a man might give his imagination full swing and no man could say him nay, for there was no past and the future was all before.

Mabee was a young man, a Canadian as I recall, and he took full advantage of the circumstances afforded him in this wide-open country. His powers of description were truly remarkable. When you finished reading one of his articles on the advantages of the Yellowstone Valley as a place of residence, one felt sure the Lord had indeed overlooked the place when He chose the Garden of Eden as the temporary abiding place of his first born.

In all seriousness—and quite aside from his promotional skills—to Mr. Mabee must go full credit for the preservation of much of the early history of the lower Yellowstone. His young and attentive eye saw many things and his crafted pen dutifully recorded them. He was but thirty years old when he departed

---

[366] The primary source for this chapter is a rather lengthy letter written by Stephen Norton Van Blaricom and published in the *Dawson County Review*, Glendive, Thursday, February 15, 1923, p. 1. The names of "Slim" Burdick and George Widmyer were added to complete the story of the early Glendive newspapers. Alex Ayotte was added to flesh out the story of W. W. Mabee. Harvey Hall was included to give due credit to the man and his wife who, along with the Griffin and Ward brothers, were probably the first commercial livestock operators in Dawson County.

[367] See "*William Wallace Mabee*" in Author's Notes following this chapter.

our community, yet he had been our record keeper for nearly six of our earliest years. The Yellowstone community owes this energetic and personable young man a great deal.

Despite his hectic schedule as chief reporter, editor, and publisher of his newspaper, the *Glendive Times,* Mr. Mabee enjoyed other activities. Among other things, he found time to court and marry Miss Effie Ayotte on Christmas Eve of 1882. Miss Effie was the beautiful daughter of Mr. and Mrs. A. P. Ayotte of Fort Buford.[368] Mr. Ayotte, the United States Deputy Marshall stationed at Fort Buford, played a prominent part in suppressing the evil-doers who infested the Missouri River and the Yellowstone Valley at that time.[369]

No newspaper could have been published without the skills of a typesetter, and Slim Burdick[370] provided them. A printer by trade, he set the first edition of the *Glendive Times* that Mabee published in August of 1881.[371] In 1882, he had his own newspaper, the *Yellowstone Press,* but that only lasted a couple of months. After that he set type for Joe Widmyer's *Glendive Independent* for a number of years.[372]

In the early business history of the town are the names of Douglas and Mead,[373] A. M. Coleman, Weeks and Prescott, Davis and Prescott,[374] Snyder and Savignac,[375] William Lowe,[376] and J. D. Sears.[377] These men were among the pioneers who were the

---

[368] Effie Ayotte, born 21 January 1864, was the daughter of Aleck Ayotte and his first wife, Caroline Woods. Caroline had died in 1876. "Mrs. A. P. Ayotte" at the time of Effie's marriage to Will Mabee was Georgiana ("Jennie") Brown, Aleck's third wife who was some fifteen years his junior.

[369] See *"Aleck P. Ayotte"* in Author's Notes following this chapter.

[370] See *"Gilbert N. ('Slim') Burdick"* in Author's Notes following this chapter.

[371] The first issue of the *Glendive Times* was published on 11 August 1881. [GHMT, p. 15. TLW, p. 211. HYV, p. 669.]

[372] See *"Joe Widmyer"* in Author's Notes following this chapter for the story of this remarkable journalist.

[373] See *"Douglas and Mead"* in Author's Notes following this chapter.

[374] See *"Weeks and Prescott (Will). Davis and Prescott (David)."* in Author's Notes following this chapter to sort out the somewhat complicated business relationships between Edward K. Weeks, David S. Prescott, William S. Prescott, and Hope S. Davis.

[375] See *"Savignac and Snyder"* in Author's Notes following this chapter.

[376] William Lowe was, in turn, a tinsmith and hardware dealer; a miner, adventurer and Indian fighter; a tinsmith and hardware dealer; a romantic who couldn't stay away from the West; a tinsmith and hardware dealer; and, finally, an undertaker, tinsmith, and hardware dealer. In later life he was frequently called Glendive's "Grand Old Pioneer." See *"The many biographies of William Lowe"* in Author's Notes following this chapter.

[377] See *"John D. Sears"* in Author's Notes following this chapter.

fibrous roots taking sustenance from the world as it passed by, yet helping and heartening all to build and settle in Dawson County and have faith in the future.

Of the cattlemen who placed their faith in the free range of the country and put their all in herds of cattle, the foremost were Pierre Wibaux and his **W** ranch, Henry Ward and his **101,** Scobey,[378] Cavanaugh,[379] Mr. E. P. Lovejoy,[380] Colonel Hodgson,[381] and many more with smaller herds. All of these people except Pierre Wibaux went down to defeat in the terrible winter of 1886–1887.[382]

Honorable mention should be given to Mr. and Mrs. Harvey Hall, the owners and operators of the Glendive Livestock Company. Mr. Hall was a very reserved man and he received little public recognition during his lifetime. However, he may have been, along with his wife, the ranch operator with the longest tenure in the livestock business in Dawson County, perhaps in all of eastern Montana. Mr. Hall and a Mr. Volkirk, both of Glendive, organized the Glendive Livestock Company in 1880, and that was almost certainly the first commercial sheep operation in Dawson County. They brought in a thousand head of Rambouillet sheep and located their ranch on CS Creek in what is now northern Wibaux County. The ranch eventually grew to hold some six-thousand head of Rambouillets. Mr. and Mrs. Hall bought Mr. Volkirk's interest in the ranch in 1901, and they continued to operate the property until they sold out in 1910 or 1911. That gave them some thirty or more years in the livestock business in Dawson County, all of that time in the same location.[383]

Of those whom I recall as the leaders in the religious life of the

---

[378] See *"Charles Richardson Anderson Scobey"* in Author's Notes following this chapter.

[379] See *"Dominic Cavanaugh"* in Author's Notes following this chapter.

[380] See *"E. P. Lovejoy"* in Author's Notes following this chapter

[381] See *"Colonel H. Hodgson"* in Author's Notes following this chapter.

[382] Stephen didn't have it quite right when he wrote: "All of these people went down to defeat in the terrible winter of 1886–1887." Charles R. A. Scobey remained in the cattle business for many years, concentrating his operation on the Fort Peck Indian Reservation. Dominic Cavanaugh was, during the winter of 1886–1887, primarily a horse breeder, and his animals came through the winter in good shape. Cavanaugh later became sheriff of Dawson County.

[383] Richard Moore visited the headquarters of the Glendive Livestock Company in 1908. He reported that the main structures at the headquarters were a sod house and sod sheep corrals. "Mr. and Mrs. Hall were still operating the ranch with the aid of hired men. Moore remembered Mr. Hall as a very reserved, aloof gentleman, who did not socialize with the neighbors." The Halls sold the ranch in 1910 or 1911. [TABC, p. 51.]

town, the name of the Reverend Coombe[384] comes first. He was a Methodist minister. The first church erected in town was a Methodist structure that stood just east of the old William Lowe homestead. It was built in either 1883 or 1884. The leaders of Reverend Coombe's church I recall were William Lowe, J. D. Sears, Mr. Ellison,[385] E. S. Rigby, [386] W. S. Prescott,[387] and Uncle Henry ("Joe") Freese.

Uncle Joe was a character. He was a very large man, well over six feet, a jovial Sunny Jim type, very bald but seldom wearing his hat on his head. He typically carried his hat in his hand, and when he was at work it could usually be found lying around somewhere. I recall that habit developed an interesting tableau once upon a time. Uncle Joe followed the carpentry trade. When they were building the first brick roundhouse in Glendive, Uncle Joe was helping put on the roof. As usual, his hat was lying out on the job by itself. A young man by the name of S. A. D. ("Sad") Westfall was also engaged in the work. He conceived the idea of having a little fun at the expense of old gentleman Joe. Watching for his opportunity, he drove a nail through the hat into the roof, fastening it securely. When the whistle blew for noon, the old man walked over to his hat and attempted to pick it up. The hat, however, seemed fully disposed to remain at rest. Ascertaining the cause, Uncle Joe reared up to his full six feet and, with a fire in his eye and a directness which no one

---

[384] "Brother Van [pioneer missionary W. W. Van Orsdel] made a visit to your locality in June 1882, and got the men together who formed the [Methodist Episcopal] Society. My first service in Glendive was on February 16, 1883." [Excerpt from a letter written in 1932 by the Reverend G. C. Stull then residing in Ocean City, New Jersey, and cited in OTOL, pp. 18–19.] The Reverend W. J. Hunter was assigned to Glendive, and on February 6, 1884, the articles of incorporation were filed with the Dawson County clerk of the court. The first trustees were William Lowe, J. D. Sears, W. H. Raymond, D. S. Prescott, and Henry Freese. [OTOL, p. 19.] Only brief mention of the "Reverend Coombe" has been discovered: "Rev. Wm. B. Coombe and wife have been visiting in Livingston." [GT, 13 September 1885.] "Wm. B. Coombe, Esq., is pastor of the M. E. Church." [GT, 6 December 1885.]

[385] "Mr. Ellison" may have been the Charles Ellison who, in 1884, built an icehouse for the Marquis de Mores in the "Old Town" section of Miles City. [TLW, p. 105.] The same man may also have been the G. W. Elesen who the YJ noted as a Glendive resident on 4 April 1885.

[386] E. S. Rigby may have been the "Professor Rigby" who, on 16 January 1886, moved his business college to the upstairs of the new Basinski building in Miles City. [TLW, p. 298.]

[387] William Prescott's apparent brother, David S. Prescott, was also involved early on with the Methodist Church in Glendive. "On my arrival [in Glendive] on January 19, 1883, I was met at the train by Brothers Lowe and Davy Prescott who told me I had better go on to Miles City as they had no means for taking care of me." [Letter from the Reverend G. C. Stull written in 1932 and cited in OTOL, p. 18.]

misunderstood, he loudly declared: "I am a Christian and I love the Lord...but I'm going to whip the Hell out of that possessed soul who nailed down my hat!" Well, young "Sad," obviously possessed by the Devil, was not forthcoming nor did anyone else see fit to turn him over to kindly Uncle Joe while he was in such a ministering state. I only tell the story now in the knowledge that Joe is probably now standing up there by St. Peter waiting for that evil-doing hat-nailer to show up in due course. God be with you, Sad!

While on the subject of the earliest pioneers, I should relate to you the story of Glendive's first "Pioneer Ball." The county had just been organized late in 1882, and the few settlers of our new town (which was still in the process of being built) wanted to celebrate. They decided to throw a dance and a midnight banquet on New Year's Eve. There were about twenty-five men to every female in the county so, to make it extra nice for the ladies, the committee sent off to St. Paul for flowers and printed programs. Each lady got one of each when she entered. Well, let me tell you there was no rest for those women for the remainder of the night. I can assure you that there were no "wall flowers." Young and old, homely or pretty, all fared the same and that was to dance continuously and sometimes with two partners at the same time. The most popular tunes were "The Virginia Reel" and "Pop Goes the Weasel," and I can't tell you how many times each one got played. When midnight finally arrived, everybody strolled over to Harry Helm's Bon Ton Restaurant, where the banquet was served. Every lady had two, three, or four escorts. After the supper, the fathers took all the younger ladies home, many of them being but twelve, thirteen, or fourteen. All of the older women, however, returned to the ballroom, where they danced until well after the dawn of 1883. Everyone was on their best behavior, and the sheriff and his deputies did a good job of keeping a lid on things. There wasn't even one fight as I recall—but that was one worn-out group of women who saw the sun come up on New Year's Day of 1883.[388]

---

[388] Grace (Bendon) (Marron) Gilmore took part in the "Pioneers Ball" of New Year's Eve, 1883. See *"The Pioneer's Ball"* in Author's Notes following this chapter for her recollections as a fourteen-year-old participant.

Another subject concerning old-timers and early Glendive is the name of the town itself. Interestingly, I don't recall that ever being a subject of conversation in the early years of the town. That's probably because those early settlers had enough to worry about without being concerned over the source of the name of the place. As the years have passed, however, I have received some inquiries on the subject.

Obviously, the townsite was named Glendive because it was located on Glendive Creek. Where Glendive Creek got its name is another question. There are a number of theories I have heard. I'll give you a couple of them here. If either one is true you'll have to judge for yourself.

The first story is that George Gore, an eccentric Irish nobleman, spent the winter of 1856 hunting buffalo and other game in the area. Accompanied by Jim Bridger, Gore remarked how much the confluence of Glendive Creek and the Yellowstone reminded him of his Irish homeland. He then applied the name of "Glendive" to the creek in honor of some location in Ireland. Successive people, including later army mapmakers, retained the name and thus it became Glendive Creek.[389]

The other story, which has some credence with the locals, is the most colorful. Somewhere along the line, about the time that George Gore was in the area, an old French trapper or Indian trader by the name of "Glen" or "Glenn" lived at the mouth of the creek or thereabouts and, in the course of his trading, he maintained a supply of liquor. The dictionary says a "dive" is "a disreputable resort for drinking or entertainment." Gore and others supposedly frequented the place and applied the term "Glenn's dive" to the location.[390]

There are even several versions of those two stories. One had George Gore giving the creek the name "Glendale" after someplace in Ireland and then "Glendale" got mispronounced into "Glendive." Others have old man "Glenn" selling whiskey in his "dive" to the fur traders and, later, to the cavalry. Another perhaps far-fetched version tells of old Glenn's "dive" being

---

[389] Marie MacDonald recounted the "George Gore" theory in GHMT, p. 9.

[390] The George Gore and the "Glenn's dive" stories are both related in GTHG, p. 2 and p. 4.

located right on the Yellowstone: A patron would come in by himself. Glenn would "bonk" him over the head and rob him. He would then dispose of the body by "diving" the victim out of the window straight into the Yellowstone where the "evidence" would be swept away.

Not one of the tales just related has ever been substantiated by a soul and they will go on, perhaps even more embellished, for the next hundred years. The one thing that seems certain is that there is apparently no other place in the world that carries the name "Glendive."[391]

---

[391] None of these popular versions of the source of the name "Glendive" are accurate. However, the name does appear to be unique. Global name searches have yielded no other location in the world with the name "Glendive." For a complete discussion of the origin of the name, see Glendive in "Old Dawson."

CHAPTER 24–AUTHOR'S NOTES

William Wallace Mabee was born 24 February 1857 near Simcoe, Ontario, Canada. He started training as a pharmacist in Canada when he was eighteen. He stayed in the druggist business for the next four or five years in Illinois, Iowa, and Michigan. He arrived in Glendive as a railroad grader and construction worker on 19 November 1880. He then worked as a railroad mailman between Glendive and Miles City until July of 1881. In that month, at the age of twenty-four, he went to Bismarck, where he purchased a Washington hand-set printing press and set up his newspaper business in the rear of the Hope Davis Drug Store in Glendive.

The first issue of the *Glendive Times* was published on 11 August 1881. [TLW, p. 211.] There was a brief flurry of competition from the *Yellowstone Press* for a week or two late in 1882. Mabee quickly bought a half-interest in the new competition and shut it down. [The BT, 19 January 1883, reported the *Yellowstone Press* operated for about two weeks in Glendive "and then went bust." See TLW, p. 379. Also see the biography of Gilbert N. "Slim" Burdick later in these Author's Notes.]

In one of his more memorable articles, Mabee tried his best to get young, single females to move into town: "Glendive offers special inducements for domestic help. Girls for dining room work are in great demand at excellent wages. There is also a 'right smart' chance to catch on to husbands. Come along, girls!" [GT, 21 April 1883.]

Promotional ideas published in 1883 regarding the opposite sex were unnecessary for Mr. Mabee himself. On Christmas Eve 1882, at the age of twenty-four, he had married U.S. Marshal Alex P. Ayotte's beautiful eighteen-year-old daughter, Effie. The wedding took place at the Ayottes' residence in Fort Buford. In February 1885, their first and only child, a daughter they named Jessie Maude Mabee, was born in Glendive.

Following the disastrous winter of 1886–1887, Will Mabee closed his newspaper down in the spring and left Glendive. He moved his hand-set press to Little Muddy, Dakota Territory (now Williston, North Dakota), and established a short-lived newspaper there. He sold out in 1889, and the purchaser carried the equipment to Minot. There the old *Glendive Times* press was used to print the *Minot Optic* (which later became the *Minot Daily News*).

In 1889, Mabee (then about thirty-two years old and already an experienced pharmacist) and his brother-in-law, Leon S. Ayotte, moved to Glasgow, Montana, and started that town's first drug store. Some four years later, about 1893, William Mabee and Effie divorced. Effie (Ayotte) Mabee took their eight-year-old daughter, Jessie, and eventually moved to Chicago. Her father, Alex Ayotte, and her stepmother, Jennie (Brown) Ayotte, had returned to Park Ridge, Cook County, Illinois, in 1891. There she eventually married Frank Devine. (Effie died in 1943 in Great Falls, Montana, at about the age of seventy-nine.)

One of the prime movers for the successful creation of Valley County in 1893, Will Mabee became that county's first clerk of the court in 1894 and he remained in that office until 1 January 1901. Will eventually got into the livestock business and moved to his ranch on Cherry Creek, five miles north of Glasgow, in 1895. Mabee married a second time on 1 December 1895, this time to a lady named Harriet Morgan. They had one son, W. B. Mabee. In July of 1899, Will became Glasgow's first Republican postmaster.

Early in 1931, William W. Mabee suffered a stroke at his ranch. Known as "W. W." to all of his friends, Mabee died in Glasgow on 2 April 1931 at the age of seventy-four.

[CE, p. 75 and p. 879. FITV, Vol. I, p. 508. Also see research of and family group sheets by Patricia Darling published in *The Last Leaf,* Sylvia Mickelson, Ed., Vol. I, No. 4, Spring 1991 and Vol. II, No. 3, Winter 1991/2. Special thanks to Patricia Darling of Dillon, Montana, for access to her records regarding Will Mabee and his related families.]

"Aleck" or "Alex" P. Ayotte: Born 21 September 1835 in Quebec, Canada, Alex Ayotte was orphaned at the age of eleven. He then moved to Rutland County, Vermont, where he was taken in and raised by an uncle, Pierre Ayotte. At the age of twenty-three he married fifteen-year-old Caroline Woods in Rutland County on 25 October 1858. Ayotte served in the U.S. Army during the Civil War. He was wounded, and during his hospital stay he contracted tuberculosis. Upon his discharge he returned home, where his wife and his oldest daughter, Jessie, immediately became infected with the dread disease. His wife, Caroline, died of tuberculosis in Rutland County, Vermont, in 1876. In 1877, Alex left Vermont and went to Fort Buford, Dakota

Territory, where he was the farrier and blacksmith for the cavalry unit stationed there. He left his three children, daughters Jessie (b. 14 June 1860) and Effie (b. 21 January 1864) and son Leon (b. 5 July 1866) in Vermont in the care of his wife's relatives. Jessie subsequently died of tuberculosis on 4 January 1879. She was eighteen.

Sometime around 1878 Ayotte was appointed the deputy U.S. marshal for the Fort Buford area (which then covered the western third of northern Dakota Territory and the eastern third of Montana Territory). According to *Glendive Times* publisher Will Mabee, Ayotte became "the terror of all evil doers." [GT, 22 March 1882.] It was also about 1878 that forty-three-year-old Alex married a young fifteen- or sixteen-year-old girl named Emma at Fort Buford. They had a daughter, born about August of 1879, whom they named "Jessie" (apparently in honor of his eldest daughter, Jessie, who had died in Vermont in January of that same year). The couple can be found on the 1880 census for Fort Buford. What became of Emma and baby Jessie is unknown.

What is known is that U.S. Marshal Alex P. Ayotte, age forty-five, married the beautiful thirty-year-old Georgiana A. (Jennie) Brown (born 23 February 1850) in Park Ridge, Illinois, on 9 November 1880. They moved to Fort Buford shortly after their marriage and brought with them Effie and Leon, Ayotte's two remaining children from his marriage to Caroline Woods. (Thus it was that Will Mabee met the fair Effie and married her in Fort Buford on Christmas Eve, 1882.) In 1883, Ayotte and Jennie built their famed two-story roadhouse (named "Ridgelawn" by Jennie) at what became the small community of Ridgelawn, located on the west side of the Yellowstone just south of the Fort Buford Military Reservation boundary. Their property was about two and a half miles west of the Yellowstone and about a mile south of First Hay Creek.

Aleck and Jennie Ayotte had three children: an unnamed boy born at Ridgelawn in 1883 and who died at birth; Ellen Lida Ayotte, born 16 August 1885; and Ethel Viva Ayotte, born 3 September 1888. It was also about 1888 when Ayotte left the U.S. Marshals Service and associated himself with Major C. R. A. Scobey up on the Fort Peck Indian Reservation. In 1891, Alex and Jennie and their two daughters left Fort Peck and moved back to Jennie's hometown of Park Ridge, Illinois (just outside of Chicago). Alex P. Ayotte died there of an "intestinal obstruction" on 30 October 1892 at the age of fifty-seven. Jennie later remarried. She died in Park Ridge on 14 January 1939 at the age of eighty-eight.

[CE, p. 75 and p. 879. FIV, Vol. I, p. 508. Also see research of and family group sheets by Patricia Darling published in *The Last Leaf,* Sylvia Mickelson, Ed., Vol. I, No. 4, Spring 1991 and Vol. II, No. 3, Winter 1991/2. Special thanks to Patricia Darling of Dillon, Montana, for numerous interviews and access to her records regarding Alexander P. Ayotte and his various families. See THWT for a more complete biography of this colorful character.]

Gilbert N. ("Slim") Burdick was born in Spring Valley, Minnesota, on 21 March 1858. Sometime during his early years he became a "printer's devil" and learned the trade of typesetting. Early in 1881, carrying only salt pork and crackers, he walked from Sentinel Butte, Dakota Territory, to Glendive in two days. He arrived at the Joseph "Wolf" Allen ranch just outside Glendive on 23 March 1881. Mrs. Allen served the twenty-three-year-old a supper of fresh hot bread and milk, a meal that earned Burdick's lasting appreciation. His first job was driving mules on the Northern Pacific grading work and he later became a cook for the grading crew (although that job only lasted for two days). Somehow he made the acquaintance of Will Mabee, who learned of his typesetting skills and hired him. Burdick then set the first edition of the *Glendive Times,* printed in August of 1881. He soon became the assistant editor of the *Glendive Times.* [OTOL, pp. 60–61.]

In the fall of 1882, Burdick and Bert Blake, a former employee of the *Yellowstone Journal* in Miles City, started a competing newspaper in Glendive. They named it the *Yellowstone Press* (not to be confused with the *Yellowstone Journal* that was published in Miles City). Mabee quickly bought out Burdick's interest in the *Yellowstone Press* and, by January of 1883, had closed down the competition. [HYV, p. 669.] By May of 1883, Blake was back in Miles City working as a reporter for the *Daily Press,* another short-lived newspaper that went out of business in June of 1884. This time, "Bert Blake, the chief reporter, left to go west." [HYV, p. 669. TLW, p. 26.]

After selling his upstart newspaper to Will Mabee, "Slim" Burdick took work as a Dawson County deputy sheriff under Sheriff James Taylor in 1882 and 1883. On 13 August 1884, Burdick married Miss Mary Theresa Rock in a ceremony performed by Father Lindesmith in Fort Keogh. Following their marriage, the Burdicks spent the next ten years farming. In 1894 they moved back into Glendive.

During his Glendive years, Slim Burdick worked at just about every job in town: From 1894 through 1898, he ran the Glendive ferry, worked for Joe Widmyer's *Glendive Independent,* and ran the Northern Pacific Railroad pump house. From 1898 to 1917, he was Glendive's justice of the peace while also working at the Douglas and Mead department store from 1898 to 1902. He served as the deputy county coroner in 1898. It was in that year that Slim convened the coroner's inquest into the murder of Dawson County's sheriff, Dominic Cavanaugh. It was his jury's findings that led to the indictment and, ultimately, the hanging of Joe Hurst in Glendive on March 30,1900. (Three of the six men on the coroner's jury were Henry Dion, Bill Jordan, and Elmer Herrick.)

From 1902 to 1908 Slim was in the cartage business and also handled Continental Oil's business in Glendive. In 1910, Burdick was elected as Dawson County Treasurer and from 1912 to 1917 he served as deputy county clerk and recorder. He later served as a Glendive city magistrate and was employed as Glendive's city weigh master. After spending more than fifty years in Glendive and the lower Yellowstone, Slim Burdick died at the age of seventy-seven on 27 April 1935. Slim and his wife, Mary (who died 20 January 1945 and who spent more than sixty years in the Glendive area), were buried in the Dawson County Cemetery. [See *"Gilbert and Mary Burdick"* by Leone Burdick Johns in OTOL, pp. 60–61.]

Joe Widmyer–Mr. Journalist of Dawson County: While it was William W. Mabee who established the first newspaper in Dawson County in August of 1881, Joe Widmyer arrived soon after. To complete the early Glendive newspaper story, Joseph R. Widmyer, born in Pennsylvania in 1860, started in the printing trade in Pennsylvania when he was seventeen. He worked for the Minneapolis Tribune for a short time and then, in 1883 at the age of twenty-three, he moved to Glendive. He worked for Mabee and the *Glendive Times* for a few months and then started a competing newspaper, the *Glendive Independent.*

The first issue of the *Glendive Independent* was printed on 14 June 1884. [OTOL, p. 322.] Between the two newspaper owners, Widmyer held a slight advantage. Where Mabee was a druggist by

JOE WIDMYER, CIRCA 1880
PHOTO COURTESY OF FRONTIER GATEWAY MUSEUM, GLENDIVE

training, Widmyer was a trained journalist as well as an experienced typesetter. Widmyer could compose his type while he was writing his story. He didn't have to hire anybody. To add a little fuel to the fire of competition between the two men, Widmyer was a Democrat while Mabee was a lifelong Republican. [CE, p. 75.] Marie MacDonald noted: "The rival editors exchanged insults and accusations in almost every issue. On behalf of Glendive, however, they sustained feuds with Miles City and Bismarck, campaigned to reduce the [size of the] Indian reservations, for Montana statehood [and] for a bridge over the Yellowstone River." [GHMT, p. 15.]

In 1886, following the election of Calvin Coolidge, a Democrat, as president of the United States, Widmyer was appointed postmaster of Glendive. When Mabee left in 1887, his *Glendive Times* ceased publication. Widmyer stayed on as postmaster and continued to operate the *Glendive Independent.* In 1889, he branched out into the furniture business and ran the combined businesses from his printing shop. In 1901, he built a large new building, with his furniture store and printing and newspaper businesses on the first floor and a public theater on the second level. He finally sold the *Glendive Independent* in 1917. In 1918, he started the *Glendive Free Lance* and wrote and published that newspaper for nine more years until his retirement in 1927.

Joe Widmyer wrote more about Glendive and the lower Yellowstone Valley than probably any other person. If one added together his years with the *Glendive Independent,* his earlier months with Mabee and the *Glendive Times,* and his last nine years writing the *Glendive Free Lance,* Joe Widmyer spent about forty-four years reporting, editing, and publishing the events and affairs of Glendive, the lower Yellowstone, and Dawson County. J. R. Widmyer died in 1935 at the age of seventy-five. He was buried in the Elks section of the Dawson County Cemetery. [OTOL, p. 322.]

Douglas and Mead: lifelong partners "and not a scrap of paper between them." Although one of Glendive's greatest promoters and developers, Henry F. Douglas basically worked out of St. Paul, Minnesota, later residing in Minneapolis. He never maintained a residence in Glendive, invariably staying with his brother-in-law, David R. Mead, during his brief visits. Although David Mead left town for a while in 1894 to assume direct control of their Fort Yates–Standing Rock Reservation trading post, he soon returned and managed their Glendive interests until his death in 1914.

Douglas was born in 1852 in Chambly, Quebec. In 1874, at the age of twenty-two, he married Elizabeth Mead, David Mead's sister. [OTOL, p. 14. GHMT, p. 14.] In that same year, he became the post trader at the Standing Rock Reservation at Fort Yates in Dakota Territory. [GHMT, p. 14.] The *Bismarck Times* announced on 11 June 1880 that, in addition to maintaining his post trading operation at Standing Rock, Douglas had become the sutler for Major Merrill's troops, who were guarding the construction of the NP between Bismarck and Glendive. "Mr. Douglas left for the front on Wednesday." [BT, 11 June 1880.] About the same time, he also became the commissary agent for the NP. He thus established a chain of tent stores supplying both the military and the construction crews as they worked west from Bismarck toward Glendive Creek. [GHMT, p. 14.] Douglas supplied his tent stores by ox trains coming out of Bismarck. [OTOL, p. 14.]

David R. Mead was born in Geneseo, Illinois, in 1848. He finished school in Geneseo and, around 1868, went to Winona, Minnesota, as an employee of the North Western Railroad Company. About 1876, he teamed up with his brother-in-law, Henry Douglas, in the management of the trading post at the Standing Rock Reservation in

Dakota Territory. [MISB, p. 1,114. USC, Fort Yates, Boreman County, Dakota Territory, 1880.] Sometime in June of 1880, he took over management of the Douglas and Mead tent stores as they followed the NPRR construction crews across Dakota and Montana territories.

By the middle of July 1880, Douglas and Mead were operating a tent store in "Old" Glendive. [TLW, p. 96.] As soon as it was decided to relocate the town, Douglas and Mead immediately built a log and canvas structure on South Anderson Avenue in the new townsite. Soon thereafter they constructed a wood-framed structure on the corner of Merrill and Towne. The Douglas and Mead Mercantile Company continued in business in Glendive until 1954. [GHMT, p. 14. OTOL, p. 14.] That building also served many years as the Glendive Post Office. [TLW, p. 96.]

Legend has Douglas being one of the founders of the Yellowstone Land and Colonization Company, and some biographers claim that "he built the first frame store on the townsite he helped to plan." [GHMT, p. 14.] Both statements are apparently in error. The *Bismarck Times* of 1 July 1881 noted: "Douglass *[sic]* has begun construction of a large two-story frame for his store." The same article, however, observed: "H. A. Bruns and Co. has erected two enormous warehouses and filled them with goods [and] Weeks and Prescott have put in a store front [with] a shingle roof and also set down a floor. [A] week ago there was not a single shingle roof or was there a single building with a floor in the entire community." [Cited in TLW, p. 378.] Neither was Glendive a townsite Douglas helped to plan: "Articles of Incorporation dated October 6, 1880, for the Yellowstone Land and Colonization Co. [YLCC] were filed by Lewis Merrill, James A. Burns, Henry J. Nowlan, William A. Mann and Herbert J. Slocum from Standing Rock, Dakota Territory. Raymond, Kendrick and Douglas were added in 1882. The new town was platted with ownership divided between YLCC and the NPRR." [Rose Wyman in OTOL, p. 11.]

Quite aside from "the first of this" and "the first of that," the local accomplishments of Douglas and Mead were significant. At the age of twenty-nine, Henry Douglas clearly envisioned that the struggling little settlement of Glendive needed the Northern Pacific to do more than simply pass through the town. Before the tracks reached the town in July of 1881, Douglas had already offered to furnish the bricks for a roundhouse if the NP would make Glendive a division point. The railroad accepted his offer and Douglas made good on it by building a kiln and firing the bricks right there. [GHMT, p. 15.] Construction of the original eleven-stall roundhouse was completed in March of 1883. ["Pages from the Past," Grace Gilmore in IVEM, 12 December 1935.] Douglas bricks were then used to build the railroad superintendent's house, the Dawson County Courthouse, and many other domestic structures in the town. [OTOL, p. 14.] Eleven more stalls were added to the roundhouse in 1890. The roundhouse eventually grew to forty-four stalls and employed one-hundred-and-twenty men in its various shops (mechanical, machining, carpentry, and painting). [GTHG, photo caption on p. 7. "Pages from the Past," Grace Gilmore in IVEM, 12 December 1935.]

In 1882 it was Henry Douglas who, at the age of thirty, shipped two-hundred-and-fifty-thousand buffalo hides from Glendive to the east. This shipment was the "last hurrah" for buffalo hunting in the west. [OTOL, p. 11.] Douglas was the first president of the Merchants National Bank, founded in 1883. David Mead was the bank's first cashier. It was also in 1883 that thirty-five-year-old David Mead married Miss Alice H. Bingham of Winona, Minnesota. After their wedding, David and Alice established their home in Glendive. [MISB, p. 1,114.]

In addition to the mercantile and bank, Douglas and Mead eventually operated the Glendive ferry and owned the lumberyard and a building materials store in Glendive. They got into the cattle business in 1904 by buying out the **HS** Cattle Company that had been founded in 1882 by Tom Hubbard and Henry Sampson and managed by Ed Marron. The **HS** at one time had been quite a large operation but Douglas and Mead bought the scaled down version and kept it that way. [GHMT, p. 14. OTOL, p. 14. TLW, p. 167. EBDC, p. 62.]

David Mead died in 1914 at the age of sixty-five or sixty-six. [OTOL, p. 14. USC, Standing Rock, Boreman County, Dakota Territory, 1880.] Henry Douglas died in Minneapolis on 23 June 1938 at the age of eighty-six. Elizabeth Dalgleish, the granddaughter of Henry Douglas, reported that during the lifetime relationship between the two men their business and partnership was conducted "without a scrap of paper between them." [GHMT, p. 14.] The Douglas and Mead store stayed in business until 1954.

Weeks and Prescott (Will). Davis and Prescott (David).
Edward K. Weeks and David S. Prescott were, by late 1880, operating their general merchandising store, Weeks and Prescott, on Merrill Avenue. [TLW, p. 363.] The *Glendive Times* noted on 2 December 1881 that William Prescott was "putting up a fine cottage in the YLCC development." The same article noted that William Prescott, like David (his apparent brother), was also "of Weeks & Prescott." Both of the Prescotts were early participants in the formation of the Methodist Church in Glendive. [See the Davy Prescott reference in OTOL, p. 18.]

On 12 October 1882, Edward Weeks was appointed by territorial Governor Potts to be one of the three original county commissioners of Dawson County (along with Eben Slawson and Robert Pontet). By 1883, Weeks was also operating E. K. Weeks and Co., a clothing and shoe store managed by S. M. Chapman. [TLW, p. 363.] While Weeks continued to be involved in the Weeks and Prescott general mercantile operation, by 1883 his sole partner was William S. Prescott. [TLW, p. 288.] Sometime between December of 1881 and mid-summer of 1883, David S. Prescott left the mercantile.

On 1 February 1884, the *Yellowstone Journal* reported: "D. S. Prescott is the cashier of a local bank" [in Glendive]. A little over a year later, on 25 July 1885, the *Glendive Independent* noted that David Prescott had become a druggist in Glendive in partnership with Hope Davis. Their firm was called Davis and Prescott. [TLW, p. 288.] This partnership was short-lived, however, and Hope Davis continued in the drug store business as a sole proprietor.

Hope S. Davis was born 14 September 1857 in Almont, Michigan. He attended the public schools there and apprenticed, at the age of seventeen, in the drug business. He arrived in Glendive early in 1881, and in July of that year he opened his drug store on Merrill Avenue between Bell and Valentine. [TLW, p. 89.] He immediately rented the back of his store to William W. Mabee and it was from that location the *Glendive Times* was published for the six years of its existence (August 1881 through the summer of 1887).

In 1885, Hope Davis married Ms. Nellie L. Farnum in Almont, Michigan. [TLW, p. 89.] Following their marriage in Michigan, Hope and his wife returned to Glendive, where he briefly partnered with David S. Prescott. [TLW, p. 288.] Hope Davis sold his drug store to J. C. Auld in 1888. Later, in partnership with his brother-in-law, Lovell Farnum (the brother of Mrs. Hope Davis), he bought the store back and operated it for many years. Hope and Nellie Davis were still residents of Glendive when their son graduated from high school in 1927. The Hope Davis drug store, operating as F and G Drug (and located at a different site than the original of 1881) was still in operation in 1988. [OTOL, p. 82.]

Savignac and Snyder: Benjamin A. Savignac was a native of St. Louis. He was residing in Kansas in 1868, in Fort Benton, Montana Territory, in 1879, and in Miles City by 1881. [TLW, p. 309.] R. W. Snyder was born in Kentucky in 1847. He lived there until he was seventeen, when he departed and lived in Kansas (in 1871), then Cheyenne, Wyoming, then Sidney, Nebraska, and finally the Black Hills. Around 1879, Snyder headed east where, in 1880, he met and married his wife, Nellie O'Connor, in Washington, D.C. He and his wife returned to the West, where he freighted and mined around Deadwood through most of 1881. Late in that year he loaded up his family, his widowed eighteen-year-old sister-in-law, Margaret (O'Connor) Elliot, and her small child, Louis, and, in company with his brother-in-law, Eugene O'Connor, joined a wagon train to Miles City. [TLW, p. 324. OTOL, p. 297. AIR, Vol. I, p. 219.]

Savignac and Snyder met in Miles City. They soon "partnered up" and surveyed their opportunities in Miles City and Glendive. In March of 1882 they purchased the Glendive Meat Market from Nick Comford. Comford had arrived in Glendive from the Fort Benton area and had the butcher shop up and running by June of 1881. [TLW, p. 70.]

Soon after their arrival in Glendive, Snyder introduced his young sister-in-law, Margaret, to Henry Dion, and the two were married on 7 September 1882 in Fort Keogh by Father Lindesmith, the Catholic priest assigned to the army post. The ceremony took place on Henry's thirty-sixth birthday. Margaret was nineteen. [See Author's Notes following Chapter 13 for the biography of Henry Dion.]

Ben Savignac married Adelia V. Gates in Glendive on 30 September 1883, sold his interest in the butcher shop to R. W. Snyder early in 1884, and left town shortly thereafter. Snyder sold the butcher shop, then known as Snyder and Hodgson, to Major C. R. A. Scobey in 1893. [TLW, p. 324. OTOL, p. 89 and p. 274.] Mrs. Snyder, her brother,

Eugene O'Connor, and ten other people (eight of the victims being the entire James Sullivan family) drowned during the ice break-up of 15 April 1899. Nellie (O'Connor) Snyder was fifty-one years old at the time of her death. [OTOL, p. 297. AIR, Vol. 1, p. 219.]

The many biographies of William Lowe could provide the material for an excellent case study to demonstrate how legends can magnify and how "facts" can change. There are nearly as many different dates and locations regarding William Lowe as there are biographies concerning him—and there are at least five. If all of William Lowe's biographies were accepted at face value, poor Will would have fought more Indians, prospected more mines, belonged to more vigilante groups, and ridden or walked more miles back and forth between Iowa and Montana than any other American in history. One of his biographers wrote that Lowe went back to eastern Iowa from western Montana to see his wife each and every year for eighteen consecutive years, from 1863 until he moved his family to Glendive in 1881. While there is little doubt that William Lowe led an adventurous life as a middle-aged man, the following summary is a "best guess" attempt at reconciling the many discrepancies found in his various biographies.

William Lowe was born in England on 17 February 1828. In 1843, at about the age of fifteen, he immigrated with his parents to Providence, Rhode Island, where he attended public schools. In 1853, he and his family moved to Canton, Jones County, Iowa, where William learned the tinsmith's trade. In 1856, at the age of twenty-eight, he married Ellen Baird in Providence. They made their home in Canton, Iowa, where he was a tinsmith and hardware dealer.

In 1864, age thirty-six, William left his wife and family in Iowa and went west. He ended up at Alder Gulch, Montana Territory. That same year he was a participant in a battle between sixty-five miners and a large number of Indians in the Powder River country. In the fall of 1866, he was among the survivors of a Sioux attack on twenty-five miners at Pease Bottom, on the Yellowstone east of Bozeman. In 1867, Lowe was reportedly one of fifteen men going down the Yellowstone from Bozeman to Fort Buford who were attacked by a large force of Sioux. (In this case, one of Lowe's biographers stated the group was headed for Fort Union in 1867. Fort Union, however,

WILLIAM LOWE
PHOTO COURTESY OF THE MONTANA HISTORICAL SOCIETY RESEARCH CENTER PHOTOGRAPH ARCHIVES, HELENA

had been sold by Pierre Choteau and Company to Hubbell and Hawley in 1864. In 1865, the trading goods were transferred to Fort Benton, and Fort Union was abandoned. In 1867, the Army bought the old fort, tore it down, and used the materials to construct Fort Buford, about three miles down the Missouri from the old Fort Union site. See POY, p. 85.)

Lowe reportedly mined at Alder Gulch off and on until 1867, when he moved to the area of Virginia City and mined there. In 1868 he moved his mining tools to the Madison River and then to India Creek. In 1869 and 1870, he moved around western Montana Territory and prospected at several sites.

In the fall of 1870, William returned to his wife and family in Canton, Iowa, where he again engaged himself in the hardware and tinsmithing business. The West, however, continued to beckon and, over the next eleven years, he made periodic trips to Montana Territory. Finally, in 1881 he sold out in Iowa and moved to Glendive.

Soon thereafter, his wife and three children followed (presumably after the NP began passenger service to Glendive in July of 1881). In addition to being the town's tinsmith and the operator of a hardware store, William Lowe also became the town's undertaker.* Hoopes stated that Lowe was the "public administrator" for Dawson County in 1885, the same year in which his wife, Ellen, died. After thirty-one years of residency, he died in Glendive on 26 May 1912 at the age of eighty-four. He was the town's oldest citizen at that time and he was respectfully referred to as "our Grand Old Pioneer."

> * The phenomenon of the hardware dealer also being the undertaker was not unique to Glendive. It extended to the neighboring community of Terry as well as many other towns in the west. "Mrs. [John] Stith kept a medicine cabinet filled with emergency supplies, which became a free dispensary. The first burial recorded in the [Stith] Hardware ledger was on October 1889 for $10.00. Five dollars of this was for the dray...the dray being the ambulance in those days. If the bereaved wished something nicer than a plain pine box, Mr. Stith would wire Glendive or Miles [City] for it. This service of the Hardware grew as the community developed until now a small fortune can be spent." [TDE, Section 3, p. 2.]

[GI, 20 June 1896. TLW, p. 209. OTOL, pp. 196–197. MISB, pp. 892–893. Biographical Sketches from HMS, pp. 461–462. CB, 28 January 1938.]

John D. Sears was born and raised in Delaware County, New York, in 1836. It was there that he became a cobbler and a boot and shoemaker. In February 1867, he was in the boot and shoe business in Yankton, Dakota Territory. During the Black Hills stampede of 1876 he earned a fortune selling and repairing boots and shoes in Yankton. He later entered the mining business, however, and lost everything. By May of 1881, Sears was in Glendive, where he opened up his boot and shoe store on Merrill Avenue. He was the first chairman of the Dawson County School Board. Sears Creek on the west side of the Yellowstone River was the site of his sheep ranch and is named after him. John Sears stayed in business in Glendive and the area until 1907, his seventy-first year, when he retired to Virginia. He died in Tom's Creek, Virginia, on 3 December 1932 at the age of ninety-six. [TLW, p. 314. CE, p. 771. PBSD/1. FVBM.]

Charles Richardson Anderson Scobey was born in Woodbury County, New Jersey, 12 July 1856. Scobey's father, Zephina Drake Scobey, was a Methodist minister. He moved the family from New Jersey to Fayette County, Iowa, when Charles was a child. Charles graduated from Upper Iowa University in the spring of 1875 at the age of eighteen and received his master's degree the following year. He started with the U.S. Mail Service in Fayette County in 1872 while he was a student. In 1876, following his graduation from university, he joined the U.S. government's railway mail service and served on the run between Chicago and Albert Lea, Minnesota, until 1883. He first visited Montana Territory in 1880. In 1883, he quit the government mail service and moved to Glendive. Over the next six years, Scobey was in the cattle business "having charge of three large cattle outfits on the Yellowstone and Missouri rivers, in two of which he was interested himself." [MT, 7 September 1923.] Charles R. A. Scobey was noted by Hoopes as "1886, Manager, Fayette Livestock Company, P.O. Glendive, MT." [TLW, p. 312.] In 1886 Scobey was elected and served in the Montana Territorial Legislature as the representative from Dawson County through 1888. [OTOL, p. 274.] "In 1887, C. R. A. Scobey had the government contract for beef for the Indian Agency. He brought the cattle in from Glendive. He operated from the Fort Buford area, but the cattle grazed mostly on the Fort Peck reservation."

On 21 December 1887, Charles R. A. Scobey, age thirty-one, married Elizabeth Jane Strachan, age seventeen, at Fort Buford, Dakota Territory. Elizabeth was the daughter of Sergeant and Mrs. John Strachan of Fort Buford. Born 25 April 1870, she was reportedly the first white child born at Fort Sill, Oklahoma Territory. When Sergeant Strachan was transferred to Fort Buford from Fort Sill (around 1876 or 1877), he had to leave his wife and child behind. Elizabeth Strachan and her mother made the trip by themselves, first in an ox cart train from Fort Sill, Oklahoma Territory, to Camp Supply, Dakota Territory, and then by paddle wheeler to Fort Buford.

In 1889, President Benjamin Harrison appointed Scobey the Indian Agent at Fort Peck. Former U.S. Deputy Marshal Aleck Ayotte worked with him there until Ayotte's departure in 1891. [CE, p. 879.] Scobey performed agency duties until 1893, and during this tenure he came to be known as "Major" Scobey, an honorary title that stuck with him through the rest of his life. In 1893 Scobey returned

CHARLES RICHARDSON ANDERSON SCOBEY, 1896
ILLUSTRATION BY ALEX AMEZCUA

to Glendive and bought the Snyder and Hodgson meat market. In 1894 he was elected superintendent of schools for Dawson County, and he returned to Glendive and worked in that capacity until 1898, when he was again appointed Indian Agent at Fort Peck, this time by President William McKinley. He was re-appointed to the post by President Theodore Roosevelt in 1902. Roosevelt knew Scobey personally and invited him to the White House to receive the commission. [RCTY, p. 39 and p. 130. MT, 7 September 1923.] He served as agent under Roosevelt until some time in 1904. [See HAST for a discussion of the specifics of Scobey's activities during his eleven years as the agent at the Fort Peck Reservation.]

"Major" C. R. A. Scobey and his wife, Elizabeth, had seven children: five daughters and two sons. One girl and one boy died young. In 1905, Scobey and his family left Montana. They initially moved to a farm by Lake Pomme de Terre in Stevens County, Minnesota. After seven years in that location they moved into the town of Morris, Minnesota (also in Stevens County). Scobey was a rural mail carrier from 1908 until a few months before his death. Charles R. A. Scobey died 2 September 1923 in Morris, Minnesota, at the age of sixty-seven. His wife, Elizabeth, died thirty-eight years later on 26 October 1961 at the age of ninety-one. [OTOL, p. 274.] Although he never lived there, the town of Scobey, today's county seat of Daniels County, Montana, was named after him. [RCTY, p. 130.]

Dominic Cavanaugh is credited with arrival in the Yellowstone country "in the early '80s; p.o. Glendive; brand OU; range Thirteenmile Creek." [TLW, p. 61.] Hoopes also showed a partnership of Cavanaugh and Duncan (Dr. Andrew R. Duncan, the NPRR physician in Glendive–see TLW, p. 99) in 1885. The *Glendive Independent* on 1 August 1885 reported on the "Duncan and Cavanaugh" partnership on Thirteenmile Creek. Cavanaugh was primarily interested in horses, consequently his ranch survived the winter of 1886–1887. In 1893, Dominic married Lillian Walmsley, whose family had homesteaded on nearby Morgan Creek in 1888. They had three children: two boys (Dominic, Jr., and Ray) and a girl (Esther).

Cavanaugh was murdered on Christmas Eve, 1898, while he was sheriff of Dawson County. That tragic event left his wife, Lillian, with three small children to raise by herself. Born 22 July 1872 in Butler County, Iowa, Lillian had moved with her parents to the lower Yellowstone in 1886. About twenty-one years old when she married Dominic Cavanaugh, she proved to be a resilient and self-reliant woman. The year following Dominic's death, Lillian sold her interest in the **OU** ranch to her brother-in-law, James Cavanaugh, and moved into Glendive. There she bought Miss Eleanor's Millinery Shop. In spring and fall, Lillian would travel to nearby communities with her stock of hats. In 1916, Esther Cavanaugh married Desmond O'Neil, the son of train driver Ed O'Neil. (Ed was previously noted in Chapter 23.) After some forty-two years together, Desmond died in 1958. Some time after Desmond's death, Lillian finally sold her millinery business in Glendive and moved in with her widowed daughter, Esther. Lillian was then more than eighty-five years old and had been selling ladies hats all over Dawson County and eastern Montana for more than sixty years. Lillian Cavanaugh died in 1963 at the age of ninety-one. Esther died in 1977. [OTOL, p. 65. AIR, Vol. I, pp. 213–214.]

E. P. Lovejoy came into the Glendive country in 1881 or 1882. He squatted on a claim on Sevenmile Creek and ran his cattle from Sevenmile to Thirteenmile Creek and on over the divide to the Redwater River. The lumber for Lovejoy's house was sawed in Minneapolis, shipped by Northern Pacific rail to Glendive and then hauled to his ranch some twenty miles from Glendive by horse and wagon. Dr. Lorman Hoopes reported that, in 1886, the E. P. Lovejoy Cattle Company (the **"Diamond L"**) [See MSD, p. 158] had its range on Sevenmile Creek with a "p. o. of Glendive." [TLW, p. 208.] Fred Van Blaricom reported that his brother, Norton, frequently worked for the **"Diamond L"** outfit.

The ranch failed during the winter of 1886–1887. Lovejoy, like many ranchers of that time and place, had no hay and most of his cattle perished. That next spring "he rounded up the remnant, swam them across the Yellowstone River, and sold them to Pierre Wibaux." It was in October of 1887 that the *Glendive Independent* reported: "E. P. Lovejoy is of the Diamond L." [GI, 15 October 1887.] Soon thereafter Lovejoy sold his buildings and squatter's rights on the Sevenmile "to an English nobleman who was in trouble with his family and was paid to stay out of England." Around 1898 the property was sold to Robert McNeeley and Bill Jones, two railroaders from Glendive. Isaac Evans bought the eight-hundred-and-forty-acre deeded parcel in 1910. The Evans family still owned the ranch in 2006 and the house built by E. P. Lovejoy in 1883 was still in use. [AIR, Vol. II, pp. 380–384.]

Colonel H. Hodgson: Little is know about "Col. H. Hodgson" and his brother. On 7 November 1885, the *Yellowstone Journal* reported "Hodgson and McClain, p.o. Glendive, Montana Territory; A. M. McClain and H. Hodgson; range is Clear Creek and Bad Route, Dawson County, M. T." Hoopes wrote: "In 1886 [McClain is gone and the operation] becomes H. Hodgson & Bro." [TLW, p. 161.] [See MSD, p. 155, for Hodgson's **"Keyhole"** brand.] However, Hoopes also reported A. McClain as a partner in both 1885 and 1886 and located at the same address. [TLW, p. 230.] No mention of any of the three men has been discovered following the winter of 1886–1887. One of the Hodgson brothers, however, may have been R. W. Snyder's partner in the Glendive meat shop (Snyder and Hodgson) when it sold to C. R. A. Scobey in 1893. It is difficult to perceive why Norton included Hodgson in his "foremost" list. The ranch was not noted as being an early cattle operation, nor was it noted for the number of cattle it ran. Perhaps Norton worked for the ranch from time to time and held Colonel Hodgson in high esteem.

The Pioneer's Ball of New Year's Eve 1883: Recollections of a fourteen-year-old. It may seem unusual today to read about a father escorting his fourteen-year-old daughter to a public dance attended primarily by adult males. A cursory review of marriage records in early Dawson County, however, reveals that the age of the bride was frequently fifteen or sixteen, with the husband between ten to twenty (or more) years older. (There were only ninety-four marriage licenses recorded in the entire 25,000-square-mile county during the first seven years [1882 through 1888] of Dawson County's organization.) Most of the early (pre-1900) Dawson County marriages involved brides who were teenagers. Unmarried females were few and far between. There simply weren't a lot of women in the county until the homesteaders started showing up en masse after 1900. Prior to 1900, the majority of "older" brides (meaning those over twenty years old) were local widows or divorcees, or "imports" from "the States"—married elsewhere by their Dawson County husbands and then brought to Dawson County following the marriage. The description of the ball attended by fourteen-year-old Grace Bendon may be of interest to the reader of today:

> My father promised to take me [to the Pioneer's Ball] and I think I was the happiest girl west of the Mississippi River and east of the Rocky Mountains. I thought about it day and night....Of course, I had a new dress. It was 'bottle green' with a high choker neck, long sleeves and a bustle. When the long-looked-for evening arrived, I walked into the ballroom on my father's arm as proud as a peacock! Each lady was presented with a flower and a dance program as she entered. There were about twenty-five men to one lady so the mad rush started the minute you received your program. [Sometimes the demand was so great] the lady would [share the same] dance with two partners. And, oh, how those pioneers could swing their partners! That is one of my early day recollections I have never forgotten. After [the banquet at] Harry Helm's Bonton Restaurant [was finished] many returned to the ballroom, but my father quietly escorted me to our little home in the badlands where I dreamed sweet dreams of my first ball on that never to be forgotten New Year's Eve. [Grace (Bendon) Marron Gilmore, "Pages from the Past," IVEM, undated but about New Years Eve, 1935.]

A year later, on Christmas Eve, 1884, fifteen-year-old Grace Bendon married Ed Marron, the twenty-eight-year-old manager of the **HS** ranch.

CHAPTER TWENTY-FIVE

1900:

Glendive to Salem

I N THE EARLY DAYS OF SETTLEMENT in eastern Montana, the ratio of the population was reckoned to be about seven males for every female. This, of course, did not affect the manners of the women that had come to the country as wives and mothers. The situation was quite different, however, with the single girls. It was easy to understand that they took full advantage of their opportunity to pick and choose. And who could blame them? Life in eastern Montana could be hard on a woman, hard on anybody for that matter, and Dawson County before 1900 was no place for any of the runts in the litter.

It was, therefore, probably natural that a young person like myself, without family or anyone else to recommend him, had to stay on the outer fringes of society and keep herd with the drags. As a result, my adolescence was devoid of all the pleasures and disappointments, happiness and sorrow common to that period in a boy's life. I must have been at least twenty-two years old when I had my first date with a girl. I am sure I could have met half of the crowned heads of Europe with less trepidation than I felt on that occasion.

Once my ship had set sail, however, I learned rather aptly for one who had lived for so long under that black cloud which is formed by feelings of inferiority. By the time I was twenty-five, I was quite a beau. I had a good job with the Northern Pacific Railroad. I had learned how to deport myself around the ladies, and I had learned how to dress fairly well. I had also been told that Mother Nature had been rather generous to me.

About 1896, I was firing a regular passenger run on the

Yellowstone Division of the Northern Pacific. We had a number of telegraph offices along the line, most of them manned by men operators. One day I happened to notice that one of these offices had a new lady operator. Passing that station almost every day, I began to notice that there was something different about this girl, something I could not define. She was nice, like sunshine after a shower, and she was possessed of a maidenly sweetness and modesty that held everything vulgar or shady at attention until it passed.

We never stopped long enough at that station for us to have the opportunity to get acquainted. I learned through reports, however, that her name was Maud and she was of Quaker ancestry. Quakers were a sect I had never come in contact with. I had always understood that the people of most religions were fine people, but, as the old song goes, "There is something about a Quaker...there is something about a Quaker"—or there was for me at least.

Well, fortune finally played into my hands. In the summer of 1898, this girl was transferred to our terminal office in Glendive. About the same time I was promoted to the job of hostler at the same place. It was her job to receive the orders from the dispatcher's office and deliver them to me. It was then I learned her name was Maud Elizabeth Griselle and she was from Salem, Ohio, where her family still lived. We both held our positions through the winter of '98–'99, and during this time we came to know each other well enough to decide that we would like to spend the rest of our lives together. We set our wedding date for the spring of 1900 and decided that our presence was no longer required in Glendive. She convinced me, instead, that Ohio was the land of our future. We returned to her old home in Salem, where we were married on the 5th day of April in the year of our Lord 1900.

It truthfully was a new and wonderful beginning.[392]

---

[392] The source for Chapter 25 is SNVB, pp. 40–41.

CHAPTER TWENTY-SIX

Maud Tells Her Story

D ESPITE WHAT MY HUSBAND HAS WRITTEN, I never really was a
Quaker. My grandparents on my mother's side were both
from old-line Pennsylvania families. My grandfather was a
staunch Quaker whose parents settled in the Quaker community
of New Garden, Ohio, in 1804. He met my grandmother when she
moved from Philadelphia to Ohio about 1825. My grandmother,
who had been raised in the Episcopal Church, joined the Society
of Friends when she married my grandfather in 1827. When
they moved to the town of Salem, Ohio, in 1855, she joined the
Presbyterian Church and remained an active member the rest
of her life. My grandmother, my mother and brother, and all of
my mother's sisters and their husbands and children attended
the Presbyterian Church. I was born in 1867 and for as long as
I can remember I attended both services, the Quaker with my
grandfather and the Presbyterian with the rest of my family. I
especially remember my grandfather's loyalty and adherence to
the Quaker faith, and as long as he lived I attended the Meetings
with him. I have always joked that during my childhood and as a
young adult I suffered from a real double dose of religion.

After I graduated from high school in Salem, I journeyed to
Philadelphia, where I attended the Philadelphia Academy of Fine
Arts. I loved the school. I lived in a boarding house with other
students, and there were relatives and friends in the area so I was
never lonely. I particularly enjoyed wood carving and painting in
both watercolors and oils. I continue to practice the skills I honed
at the academy.

My brother, Paul Hunt Griselle, was two years my senior.[393]
Since 1889 he had been residing in Bozeman, working as a

---

[393] See *"Paul Hunt Griselle"* in Author's Notes following this chapter.

telegrapher for the Northern Pacific. In September of 1890, Paul married Barbara Kerman in Billings, so Mother and I took the train west and attended the wedding. After the ceremony, my mother went home, and Paul, after a brief honeymoon, took his bride off with him to his new posting in Miles City. Since I had graduated from the academy in June, I had some time and decided to spend the winter in Montana with my brother and Barbara. Paul was rather well connected and, as a pleasant conclusion to my stay, we were invited to a reception and dinner at which the president of the Northern Pacific Railroad Company was to be in attendance. It turned out that the president was traveling alone, and I was his dinner partner for the evening. He kept putting forth the proposition that I should stay in Montana in the employ of his firm, the Northern Pacific. I told him that I had absolutely no skills that would lend themselves to the laying or maintenance of railroad track, and I pointed out that I had not the wherewithal to fire up or drive a train. My education at the Philadelphia Academy of Fine Arts simply had not prepared me for such an undertaking.

The president was quite good company and he persisted throughout the evening in his view that I must have some skill his company could use. Bookkeeping? No. Cook? No. Secretarial skills? No. Finally, almost in jest, I laughingly told him that my brother was not the only member of our family who was good with a telegraph key. Both my mother and I were most proficient in the Morse code and we could operate any kind of telegraph key then known. It had been my mother, after all, who had taught Paul the skills necessary to be a telegrapher. Within the week, the Northern Pacific offered me a job as a station telegraph operator out in the hinterlands of Montana. I viewed this offer with anticipation since it afforded me an opportunity for an independent and useful life. The idea, however, that I would entertain such a distant and uncivilized place as my future home dismayed my mother (and especially my grandmother) to no end, but eventually she consented. I purchased a Royal typewriter and quickly learned how to type. And so it was I ended up being a telegraph operator for the Northern Pacific Railroad Company for the next eight years.

I have spent much of my life answering two questions: The first has been how to spell my name: M-a-u-d, no "e." The second has always been: "How on earth did a nice girl like you ever learn how to operate a telegraph in such a rough place as the frontier in Montana?" The answer to the second question has always taken a little more time. My mother was a young woman, a schoolteacher, in Ohio at the beginning of the Civil War when a great many of the men of that state were called away to serve the Union. Around 1861 she volunteered as a telegraph operator and, after a training period, she worked in Ravenna and Kent, Ohio, and later in Corey and Union City, Pennsylvania. She continued to work as a telegrapher until she married in 1864. When my brother and I came along, she proceeded to teach us the Morse code. She would keep us entertained on rainy days by having us send messages to each other while we were located in different rooms of our large house in Salem. When we first started it was much like the children of today who pretend they have re-invented the telephone with two tin cans and a length of string or wire. It soon became quite exciting to us, however, for we learned that we could actually communicate with each other, and in a way that was an absolute curiosity and a perpetual torment to other children—and adults, too. Only our mother could read our secret written messages or understand what we were saying to each other once we got into our table-tapping conversations. By the time we were teenagers, we were quite proficient with either the tabletop or the telegraph keys that mother had acquired for us.

My first assignment in the employ of the Northern Pacific was in the village of Rosebud, Montana, and I arrived there on the 19th of April 1891. It was a small place built by the railroad for the housing of track maintenance crews who tended the rails between Miles City and Forsyth. Forsyth was some thirteen miles to the west, and Miles City was about thirty-two miles to the east. The only buildings were my telegraph shack, twelve houses, and a saloon. The telegraph office and the post office were combined so, since I worked at Rosebud by myself, I was to be both the telegraph operator and the town's postmistress while I was there.

It was during my stay at Rosebud that the Northern Pacific and I both discovered a very interesting phenomenon. The cowboys out around some of the more remote train stations had the annoying, destructive, and expensive habit of coming to whatever nearby saloon might be handy and raising a little whoopee. The aftermath would often be to shoot up the little telegraph office, make it full of holes, break out a window or two if there was one, and sometimes thrash up on the forlorn telegrapher. In general, they would commit periodic mayhem and, in the process, either accidentally or deliberately, damage or destroy the telegraph equipment. Despite my initial trepidation, I never experienced one instance of misbehavior on the part of my cowboys or the other male residents of the villages in which I was assigned. I always kept my distance, of course, but they invariably treated me with respect and courtesy, even if they were sometimes a little too inebriated to accomplish it with gentlemanly grace.

I must confess, however, to a certain degree of naiveté on my own part. One day a particularly inebriated fellow was on his way back to the ranch where he worked. As was common in those days the ranches absolutely forbid the presence of intoxicating drink on their property. Old Jake came up to my telegraph office about noon, on his way out of town. "Ma'am," he said, "I was a-wundrin' if'n you might not shtore thish here bottle-o'-vinegar for me until I get a shance to get back here into town. I'd shore appreshiate it if'n you could." Of course I said I would because I didn't think it would get back to the ranch in one piece anyway. Soon after that it started that everyone would leave their bottle of "vinegar" with me on their way out of town, and, sure enough, they never neglected to pick it up on their way back in.

In all my sheltered life, I had never seen, tasted, or smelled even a smidgen of whiskey. I often wondered what those cowboys did with all that "vinegar." Through my eight years there in Montana, believe me when I say I was told some of the most unique uses for "vinegar" that were ever dreamed up. My fame had spread from near to far, and wherever I showed up, even at some new and remote location, the "vinegar" bottles would come pouring in. I was well over thirty years old and safely back in Ohio with my husband when he laughingly explained to me one afternoon what had been in all those bottles. He explained that the Montana saloons in those times only sold whiskey by the bottle, never by the "drink" or by the "shot." And so it was that those homeward-bound cowboys usually had a bottle with a little extra "vinegar" in it. I had always understood that those cowboys had achieved their blissful state of inebriation while imbibing "goods" consumed at the saloon. It had never occurred to me that they were made tipsy from guzzling the contents of their "vinegar" bottles. I scolded Norton severely for his years of silence but I have laughed about it ever since.

Once the Northern Pacific discovered that the female presence could, under the right circumstances, have the effect of preserving some of their properties, they began to hire female telegraph operators on a rather consistent basis. Whether my experience alone provided the catalyst I do not know, but more women began to come on board. Not understanding the subtleties of my work until later, of course, I don't know if the railroad ever required any of the other lady telegraphers to provide "vinegar" storage as a part of their duties.

It was also at Rosebud that I invented my "hoop-mail" system. I would occasionally receive a message for a passenger on a through train. I couldn't stop the train, so I would cut a limb from a small willow tree and make a hoop by tying the tassel back around the limb about halfway down. I would make the hoop about eighteen inches in diameter, and that would leave the heavier bottom half of the limb hanging down. The result was a shape like a figure "9." I could tie the message on the "leg," and it also gave me a convenient handle by which to hold it out to the conductor as the train rushed by. He would simply run his arm through the hoop, gather up the message, and deliver it to the waiting passenger. The willow hoop was quite safe and could be used a number of times. Willow hoops soon became commonplace at the more remote stations.

After some five months in Rosebud, my next posting was to Miles City. I arrived there about 1 October 1891. This was a bustling railroad center and cattle- and horse-marketing town of about three-thousand people. Immediately adjacent to the town was Fort Keogh. The fort was a major military installation, so there were always lots of soldiers visible in Miles City. The telegraph office here was very busy, but the company allowed us to hire boys and young men to pick up and deliver messages, so aside from the walk-up traffic, we had very little contact with the citizens of the place. I also had the luxury of living in my own room in a boarding house situated conveniently near the telegraph office. As luck would have it, my brother, Paul, was still working out of that same Miles City office. I was fortunate that I had some time to spend with him and his new bride, Barbara, at their small cottage. Their first and only child, Frank Marsh Griselle, was born there on December 19, 1891, only days after I had been transferred to my next station. All in all, my life in Miles City was quite civilized, but I only stayed there less than two months.

My next duty was at Sanders, a small stop a little less than twenty miles west of Forsyth. Compared to Sanders, Rosebud had been a metropolis. Sanders was a very small cattle shipping point. There was a set of corrals and a loading dock, a water tank, my two-room telegraph office (I slept in the second room), and three Indian tepees. I stayed in this isolated location for some twenty months (from the 15th of December 1891, until August the 13th, 1893) and, except for the infrequent telegraph messages, almost all of my conversations were in sign language.

The Indian men, dressed only in breech cloths and moccasins, would occasionally come to the station house for a "visit." They loved the wide-brimmed hats I had brought with me for the practical purpose of protecting my face from the sun. I had decorated two or three of these with beautiful silk flowers, and the Indians became quite enamored with them. Through grunts and sign, the Indian men would ask as politely as they could to wear them. I finally consented to their persistent requests by setting one of my silk-flowered hats aside for their use. Of course, I could no longer wear it unless I wanted to share in their head lice. I solved that problem by setting the hat outside on a peg on the porch and affixing a small looking glass on the porch wall. They would then put on that hat, stand in front of the looking glass, and laugh themselves silly. This became a weekly event that provided much of our inter-tribal social activity during the rest of my stay in Sanders.

During the summertime, the mosquitoes in this area were quite numerous and ferocious. One day an Indian brought a very sick horse over to my office. The horse had been almost eaten alive by mosquitoes. Its eyes, ears, nostrils, and mouth were nearly swollen shut. I felt we had nothing to lose, so I concocted a "salve" made from mutton tallow and tar. The horse soon recovered. Following that, my "Sanders salve" was in wide demand along the Yellowstone for both man and beast.

I don't know how long the railroad would have left me at Sanders. My stay there was brought to an abrupt end on the afternoon of August 13, 1893. That's when the station caught fire and burned to the ground. The only things I saved were my telegraph log, my shotgun, and a three-piece mirror. Except for the clothes on my back everything else was a total loss. I took the next train through to Forsyth and took a few days off.

It was around the 20th of August of 1893 that I was transferred from the isolation of Sanders to the isolation of Pompey's Pillar. It was much the same as Sanders. While there were a few whites in addition to myself, the place was predominantly a scattering of a half-dozen tepees. There I worked twelve hours a day, seven days a week, and I was on call the other twelve hours. The water situation there was particularly bad. There was no well. A man would come around once a week with a twenty-five-gallon barrel of water he had dipped from the Yellowstone. That barrel had to last me an entire week, but in that location the Yellowstone was full of silt and it contained all of the dirt and decay known to the wild west. I would let the water sit for days to settle out the silt and then I strained and boiled whatever water I used for either drinking or bathing. In any case, it was a very unpleasant and unsanitary situation.

I slept in the two-room telegraph office at Pompey's Pillar just as I had done at Sanders. Personal security had never been an issue but, in any case, I had always kept at my bedside the long-barrelled shotgun the Northern Pacific's manager at Miles City had given me on my way through to the Rosebud station back in 1891. "You never know," he said, "when you'll need it for wild animals or cattle." Much of the range was still unfenced, and while the occasional cow or steer would wander into town they were no problem. It was that infrequent range bull that could make the hair stand up on the back of your neck. They were unpredictable and totally ferocious when they decided they were, as the cowboys said, "on the prod." Although I never once had occasion to use it in self-defense, I did become quite proficient with my trusty shotgun. Prairie chicken, once I learned how to cook it, became one of my frequent and favorite meals.

One night at Pompey's Pillar there was a continual thumping or stomping on my door stoop and a persistent hard rapping at my door. Startled awake, I grabbed my shotgun and my lantern and demanded, "Who's there?" There was no reply, but the disturbance stopped. I waited a minute or two and then cautiously cracked open my door. Suddenly, at about my eye level, a black, wet nose pressed itself into the crack of the door and levered it open. In walked a young adult white-tailed deer! It was as though he owned the place! As he pushed his way in against me, I pushed my way out against him. I peered in at him for some time as he paced about my office and bedroom, sniffing here and nudging there. He would occasionally stomp his little feet and paw at the floor but otherwise he did no damage. I tried shooing him out, but he steadfastly refused to be intimidated. I ended up spending the rest of the chilly night underneath the roof of my stoop while the deer occupied my cozy quarters. About dawn, I could hear a message coming in from a station some twenty miles or more to the east. It was an inquiry regarding a pet deer that had escaped its enclosure. Well, that explained why my guest had no fear of me. He was so totally used to humans that he thought he was one. Encouraged by the fact that my new white-tailed houseguest must be the culprit, I got him some water and a bowlful of horse-feed and placed them inside the office. He immediately quit his periodic pawing and stomping, ate his fill, and then followed me around like a dog for the rest of the day. About mid-morning, I wired back that Mr. White-Tail was, indeed, at my place and that we had become fast friends. The next day his owner, who lived about fifteen miles to the east, came by and claimed his wayward pet.

I had been in Montana almost continuously since September of 1890 when mother and I had come out to attend Paul's wedding. A little more than three years had quickly passed. During the middle of my stay at "the Pillar," my mother arrived for a visit and spent a few months with me. Her presence did much to relieve my growing sense of isolation. During this time we would receive plaintive letters from my grandmother contrasting the civilization, the culture, and the conveniences of Ohio to the desolation of this remote outpost to which I had consigned myself in the wilderness of Montana. Mother and I did take a break in March of 1894 and went to Portland, Oregon. I will confess that this trip did provide me with a sense of relief to be among large groups of people where I could speak English and hear English spoken. There was also plenty of fresh water to drink, hot water for baths, and flush toilets. I was able to truthfully write my grandmother of all of the "culture and civilization" I absorbed during this trip. My career and duty called, however, and I did not feel any remorse at leaving Portland and returning to the more remote environs to which I was becoming accustomed.

I left Pompey's Pillar on July 24, 1894, after a stay of some eleven months. Following a month in Howard (midway between Forsyth and Sanders) and an uneventful four months in Billings, I was transferred to Forsyth in January of 1895. One of the disadvantages of working in the smaller stations was that I rarely became acquainted with any of the regular train crews. The trains came through on a frequent basis, but in the smaller stations to which I was variously assigned, they only stopped infrequently and then just for minimal amounts of time. Forsyth, however, was a railroad town where the trains often changed engines and the crews stayed over. I worked the night shift from seven in the evening until seven in the morning. Unlike Miles City, where we hired young boys to deliver our messages around town, the situation in Forsyth was that we generally delivered our own messages. There was no street lighting in Forsyth in those days, so my only means of light was my trusty railroad lantern. I could be seen at all hours of night wandering around Forsyth, just my lantern and I, headed for the train yard to call on a conductor, an engineer, a fireman, or a brakeman with their assignments and instructions for the next day. In addition to these duties, I would provide temporary relief to the telegraphers at small stations all over eastern Montana. During my two-year stay in Forsyth, I was assigned to several small stations on the Yellowstone Division and elsewhere for a few days at a time.

In the summer of 1896 I took a trip to San Francisco. I had long wanted to see the city where my aunt, Elizabeth Griselle, M.D., had practiced medicine during the 1870s. She had experienced some difficulties and many adventures as an early female physician in central California, but she loved the city and her many lavish descriptions of the beauty of the place had long fascinated me. The Northern Pacific provided me with introductions and off I went. I stayed at the YWCA, rode the cablecars and streetcars, saw the Pacific Ocean for the first time, went to Yosemite National Park, and ate foods that were totally new to me. My horizons were expanding. After two glorious weeks I bundled myself back up and returned to Forsyth.

I had seen Norton Van Blaricom out at various stations a number of times, but the first time I ever met my husband-to-be was in Forsyth early in 1896. He was working as an engineer on the run between Glendive and Forsyth, and I would deliver his schedules and work orders to him. That didn't last long since, on March 21, 1897, I was transferred to the station at Huntley, between Pompey's Pillar and Billings. That posting lasted eight months, until November 27, when I was assigned to the division office in Glendive. Among my jobs was to relay messages from the dispatcher's office to the station's hostler. In this case, late in 1898, the hostler became the same handsome and polite young man I had met a couple of years earlier in Forsyth. He was intelligent and a hard worker, and, while direct, he was not forward or presumptuous at all in his manner. By mid-summer of the following year we had decided that we would continue this life's journey together. It was a decision concerning which I have never had occasion for one day's regret.

In the fall of 1899, after eight years of service, I quit my job as a telegrapher for the Northern Pacific and returned to Salem, Ohio, where my mother was still residing. In March of 1900, Norton joined us and he and I were married there on the 5th day of April.[394] He went to work right away in nearby Leetonia for the

---

[394] Stephen Norton Van Blaricom was born 4 April 1869. He married Maud Elizabeth Griselle the day after his thirty-first birthday. Maud (born 27 July 1867) was thirty-two on the date of the wedding. One suspects their wedding date of 5 April 1900 was selected so Stephen would be recorded as only one year younger than Maud.

McKeefrey Ironworks as a master mechanic and stayed in their employ for several years. We were able to buy our little farm from Mr. Levi Strailey in the spring of 1903. We had saved our money so we were able to pay his asking price of $5,000 in cash and we have lived here since that time.

Our first child, Austin Paul Van Blaricom, was born in Salem on June 30, 1901. Tragically, our little fellow died shortly after his first birthday. Mary Abby was born on November 19, 1903, after we had moved to the farm. John Phillip was born on January 30, 1909; Robert Perry on August 19, 1910; and our last child, our daughter Anna ("Ann") Elizabeth, was born on July 17, 1912.[395] All of our children are now grown and happily married, and we are the proud recipients of six grandchildren. We intend to now live out our lives on Norton's "little farm," warm in the comfort of each other and our family.

Ours has, indeed, turned out to be a life in which we have lived "happily ever after."[396]

---

[395] Ann Van Blaricom, Stephen and Maud's fifth child, was born two days after her mother's forty-fifth birthday. (Three of Maud's four surviving children were born after her fortieth birthday.)

[396] Chapter 26 is the result of a lengthy interview with Ann (Van Blaricom) Falor—the youngest of the four children of Stephen Norton and Maud (Griselle) Van Blaricom—on 4 February 1994. Additional facts were gathered from an article about Maud entitled "Telegraph Operator Now Enjoys Many Hobbies" printed in the SN in 1951 (no month or date on clipping). Elizabeth (Falor) Carducci, Ann Falor's daughter, also provided dates and other helpful information in a series of interviews from 23–26 June 2006.

CHAPTER 26–AUTHOR'S NOTES

Paul Hunt Griselle: Educated and trained as a dentist, Maud's brother, Paul Hunt Griselle, was born 3 June 1865 in Salem, Ohio. He had survived a tremendous fall at university that had produced some broken bones and a ruptured lung, an injury that ultimately hampered his career in dentistry. Early in 1889, after a stint as a dentist, he secured work with the Northern Pacific Railroad as a telegrapher. On 23 March 1889, he was sent to Bozeman and worked the telegraph there until Christmas. Around New Year's Day of 1890 he was transferred to Rosebud and worked there until his marriage to Barbara Kerman in Billings on 19 September 1890. He was then posted to Miles City through 1891. (Paul and his sister, Maud, were both working in Miles City in October, November, and December of 1891.) Paul and Barbara's only child, a son named Frank Marsh Griselle, was born there on 19 December 1891. The NP purchased a railroad in Wisconsin, and sometime in 1892 he was transferred to the station in Waukesha. Following that, he was the dispatcher for two years in Missoula.

In July of 1895, he decided to give dentistry another whirl and established a practice in Helena. Again, his recurring physical problems intervened and the practice simply proved too demanding. He returned to telegraphy and became a dispatcher for the Santa Fe Railroad at San Marcial, New Mexico. The lung he had ruptured during his fall at dentistry school continued to plague him. Paul Griselle died in 1916 at about the age of fifty-one. He was buried in Salem, Ohio. Frank Marsh Griselle, the only child of Paul and Barbara (Kerman) Griselle, grew up and became a telegrapher.

[Special thanks to Elizabeth (Falor) Carducci for sharing her unpublished genealogical research regarding the Falor and Griselle families.]

**STEPHEN NORTON VAN BLARICOM,
GLENDIVE, MONTANA, CIRCA 1892**
PHOTO COURTESY OF ELIZABETH FALOR CARDUCCI

**MAUD GRISELLE VAN BLARICOM,
FORSYTH, MONTANA, 1897**
PHOTO COURTESY OF ELIZABETH FALOR CARDUCCI

CHAPTER TWENTY-SEVEN

Years of Correspondence

O N THE FIRST DAY OF JANUARY 1904, my younger brother, Fred, got married and settled down. He married a wonderful woman, Luella May Geyer, and they have remained in the Bitter Root Valley since that time. Through the years Fred and I have maintained an infrequent but rather lively correspondence. Most of the letters conveyed the usual information concerning our family's welfare and activities. Occasionally, however, we wrote to each other simply for the entertainment of it, testing the other's wit.[397]

Salem, Ohio
September 22, 1926

Mr. Fred Van Blaricom
Hamilton, Montana

Dear Brother Fred,

Yours of recent date received. I suppose, as usual, you are short of rain. We could spare you some, at least enough to fill your bathtub. The avoidance of necessities under the excuse of drought can, as we both know, prove to be an isolating experience. We are having an over abundance of water here and the weather is very warm, all of which combines to create a sort of tropical atmosphere. This, of course, is highly stimulating to vegetable growth, especially so to the vines.

The road supervisors hereabouts are complaining bitterly about the farmers allowing their pumpkin vines to grow out into the public roads where they have become

---

[397] Both letters reproduced in this chapter are from the files of Emma (Van Blaricom) Freeze, Fred Van Blaricom's oldest daughter. Copies of the letters are in the possession of the author.

a menace to traffic. And, too, they have taken to the frequent roadside trees, so numerous in this country, so sparse in yours. The trees are now loaded with pumpkins and the woodpeckers have taken to pecking at both the pumpkins and their vines. They will work on them until they both drop...the pumpkins from the weakened vine and the woodpeckers full to the brim. This condition is so prevalent that it is downright hazardous to travel our roads without a co-pilot along to constantly survey the sky. Numerous people have reported narrow escapes from falling pumpkins and falling woodpeckers.

We did not plant any pumpkins this year, but planted, instead, one hill of a variety of small squash. That has given us trouble enough. Daughter Anna took a few seeds out to the garden to plant. She says that she noticed as she was going out the back door of the house that the seeds were beginning to swell. She prepared a small hill and pushed the first seed in with her finger. Germination was instant, the sprout pushing her finger out of the ground. It startled her, so she jumped up and started to run. Looking backwards, she saw the vines were slowly gaining on her, so she started to yell for me to come to her assistance. Both the boys and I happened to be nearby in the barn. Hearing her call as if in distress, I hurried to see what was up.

Taking in the situation at a glance, I saw that we would need more than our bare hands on a monster like that. I called to the boys to bring their pitchforks and do it in a hurry. While they bravely tackled it from the front, I grabbed a mattock and quietly circled to the rear where I succeeded in severing it at the root. This action lasted no more than three minutes, yet the next day when cleaning up the dead vines we found seven good and edible squash. Needless to say, that is the last squash that will be planted here under weather conditions such as we are having this summer.

At such a time I am almost willing to admit that there are compensations for living in a country like yours. But then I remember how it really was and I reflect that one could only be content there when one knew no better.

Your Brother,
S. N. Van Blaricom

October 20, 1926
Hamilton, Montana

S. N. Van Blaricom
Salem, Ohio

Dear Brother Stephen:

Yours of the 22nd ultimo received. I am glad to hear from you at any time and read about what it is that you remember and how it is that you reflect. I must say that your memory has proven to be more stable than your imagination. I, of course, can believe anything of a country with a climate, soil or water that will develop an imagination like yours over the short period of twenty-six years.

You seem to have developed an idea that yours is the only country which can create unusual circumstance. I will admit that here in Montana we shun such uninteresting things as growing pumpkins or squash for thrills. However, if I might have your ear for a moment, so to speak, I should like to relate a little event that happened here this last fall. To my mind, this activity provided much more of a sporting proposition than fighting mere squash and pumpkin vines.

You will remember from your last visit here, now so many years ago, the old Curlew orchard and its location at the mouth of a canyon on the mountainside. You will remember also that a creek runs along below the orchard with a high rock wall on the opposite side. This year the orchard was set with a very heavy crop of extra-large apples. Just before picking season, something in the nature of a small tornado blew down the canyon and it hit the orchard hard. It stripped every apple from the trees and hurtled them down the steep slope where they crashed against the rock wall on the opposite side of the creek. You will remember that the Curlew orchard is quite large and I suppose there was a pile of crushed apples fifty feet deep and a quarter of a mile long lying there in that creek, fermenting in the sun. For a full ten days the creek was dammed up by the apples, but below the pile it was running full bore, full to the brim with hard cider. That creek, as you know, empties into the Bitter Root River.

No one had thought of any serious consequences, but two or three days after the storm some boys reported seeing some whitefish out on a sand bar in the Bitter Root dancing the can-can. At the time it was thought that the boys had probably been swimming in the creek of cider and had swallowed too much of the liquid themselves. Reports soon multiplied, however, of strange and weird actions being perpetrated by the fish in the river. Some of the sandbars were, in fact, being worn smooth by whitefish doing the Charleston. The salmon, on the other hand, were becoming downright aggressive. There were some reports of people being chased by these large fish with seemingly murderous intent.

One tenderfoot from your town in Ohio, I think maybe he said his name was John W. Gates (or maybe it was Yates, I don't remember), was here during the "cider run." He saw several large old mama salmon cavorting around on one of the Bitter Root sand bars and it gave him the real fish hunger. He bethought himself to catch one and take it along over to his night camp. He assayed to approach them under cover and to get between them and the water. He figured surprise would be on the side of him and his net.

Well, he need not have bothered. Those old mama salmon were full of eggs and were on their way home to roost. Topped off with that apple juice, they feared neither man nor his majesty. Old John W. Gates from Ohio escaped being bitten to death by those salmon only by the mere fact that his wife had the presence of mind to remain in the car. She held the door open while he roared in pursued by that pack of snapping salmon. He slammed the door, peered back out at those leering fish and said, "Let's go home, ma. I never liked salmon anyhow."

That pile of apples is now nothing but a heap of rotten pumice, so inspiration no longer flows from it. Things along the river are now back to normal again but you never know what this fall might bring.

Brother, I am worried by the evident lack of your old time spirit. Is it senility or a softness resultant from dwelling in a condition of continual swamp that permits you to be content with pumpkins and squash as the theme for a story about your country?

Regardless of the state of your mental affairs, I will, of course, be glad to hear from you at any time. They say that writing or otherwise expressing yourself can be a means of providing useful therapy.

Best regards,
Fred

CHAPTER TWENTY-EIGHT

1940

I N 1900 we returned to the area of Maud's old home in far northeastern Ohio, very near the border with Pennsylvania. We have lived the last thirty-seven years here on our little farm near Salem. We have raised our family of four children, two boys and two girls, of whom we are justly proud.[398]

Last year, on April 4, 1939, I reached my three score and ten. Seventy years! I consider myself in excellent condition for that age. I have no organic troubles whatsoever. I sleep well and I can eat whatever my appetite dictates. The only thing I notice is the passing of relatives and friends. Walter Hilliard died the other day. Not from anything in particular. Just worn out. Walter was four months older than me. How near, I wonder, am I to the end? Constitutionally, I am sound as a nut and I can still do a good half-day's work so I am not particularly concerned. My biggest regret is that I have not seen more of my brothers and sisters. I have seen my youngest brother, Perry, but once in the last forty-some years. When he was small I had much of the care of him and I would like to see him once more before our final separation.[399]

Next month, on April 5, 1940, Maud and I will mark the fortieth anniversary of our partnership. We are both deep in the shadows of life's end, yet I enjoy so much now the coming of each day and I view with special fondness all the memories of days long past.[400] Some times have been monumentally difficult—the death of my mother in 1882, the death of our first child, Austin Paul, in

---

[398] SNVB, p. 41.

[399] Norton never saw his youngest brother, Perry, after Norton's trip west in 1917. Perry Van Blaricom died in Seattle, Washington, on June 20, 1942. There is no evidence that he ever saw his sister, Alice, after her departure from Glendive in 1887. Diary of S. N. Van Blaricom: 4 April 1934, 4 April 1939, 11 June 1940, and 20 June 1942.

[400] SNVB, p. 41.

1902 when he was less than a year old, the great flu epidemic of 1918, the ten weeks in 1921 when I thought I had the grippe[401] but actually suffered near death from malaria, and the first years of the Great Depression in 1933 and 1934. Other times have brought greater or lesser rewards—when Maud and I fell in love in 1899, our marriage in 1900, when we were able to buy our farm in 1903, the healthy births and raising of our four children, our first battery-powered radio in 1922, electricity installed in our home in 1934 (two plug-ins so we could have two electric lights), the happy marriages of all four of our children...and now, a sprinkling of grandchildren.[402]

Thus it has been that while times have not always been easy,[403] other times have brought great joy. A very wise man, a famous industrialist, once told me: "If we were all good and had always known only good, how would we know that we were good? If we were all prosperous and had only known prosperity for all of our lives, how would we know that we were prosperous?"[404]

Man has always strived against adversity and he has always dreamed of a Utopia in which all things which torment him would be eliminated, little realizing that should he ever succeed in this ambition, his world would rapidly turn to ashes. Difficulties are necessary to the realization of a full and complete life, just as are the best times we have ever known. If we stood in the sunshine always, never knowing darkness or shadow, how would we appreciate the beauty of a sunrise as we do now?[405]

Perhaps the Truth of Life, or maybe its greatest lesson, lies in the simpler things: the gentle touch of a grandchild, the smile of greeting from a neighbor, a warm and understanding look

---

[401] "Grippe: An acute febrile contagious virus disease identical with or resembling influenza." [TID, p. 1,000.]

[402] Diary of S. N. Van Blaricom: 27 October 1918, 5 April 1921, 23 October 1922, 15 March 1934, and 10 May 1934.

[403] In his diary entry of 15 March 1934, Norton made a telling observation regarding the hard times of the Great Depression: "There is no profit in anything we do. Times are very dull [but] we have not found it as difficult (as others have) to get along...principally for (the reason that I was used to living with the) lack of money when I was a child."

[404] From an undated article written by Stephen Norton Van Blaricom in the *Salem News* (Ohio). The clipping is accompanied by other articles that fix the year of publication as 1926.

[405] Undated *Salem News* article by SNVB.

between loving people. These are the simple things that add so much to the texture of Life, and I know these things. Often when I wake of a morning I find Maud's head lying on my arm and it pleases me.[406]

Finis.

S. N. Van Blaricom

---

[406] SNVB, p. 41.

CHAPTER TWENTY-NINE

Journey's End

The Obituary

THE SALEM NEWS, MONDAY, JUNE 18, 1945:

Stephen Norton Van Blaricom, a prominent Salem farmer, was found dead of a heart attack at his home on the Franklin road about noon Saturday. He was 76 years old. Members of the family found him in a tool shed where he had walked after getting the morning mail.

A native of Waterville, Minnesota, where he was born April 4, 1869, he was the son of Levi and Sarah Van Blaricom. He had resided here for 45 years, having moved to Salem from Victor, Montana,[407] where he was a locomotive engineer for the Northern Pacific railroad. In his early boyhood he was a cowboy in the West.

Following his marriage here April 5, 1900, to Maud Griselle, he took employment as a master mechanic at the McKeefrey Ironworks at Leetonia. Afterwards, he turned to farming.

Mister Van Blaricom was the first president of the Columbiana County Farm Bureau, was a past master of the Columbiana County Pomona Grange, was a charter member and past master of the Perry Grange, and was on the county visiting board. He also had been active for 26 years in Perry township election affairs and served as the presiding judge in the township precinct for a number of

---

[407] Stephen Norton Van Blaricom died on Saturday, 16 June 1945. His obituary erroneously states that he moved to Ohio from Victor, Montana, when, in fact, Norton and Maud returned to Ohio from Glendive. Although Norton at one time owned some land next to his father's farm near Victor, neither he nor Maud ever resided there. All of Norton's siblings did live in the Bitter Root Valley in or near Victor or Hamilton at one time or another and that fact, perhaps, confused the author of the obituary.

years. He also was a member of the Sons of Veterans and the Oddfellows Lodge and attended the Presbyterian Church.

Besides these activities he was recognized as one of the best amateur astronomers in the district.

Surviving are his wife; two daughters, Mrs. W. H. Falor of Salem and Mrs. A. G. Harrison of Columbus; two sons, John of Salem and Robert of Huntington, West Virginia; six grandchildren, three sisters, Mrs. Effie Waylett of Hamilton, Montana, Mrs. Mary Eddy of Iola, Alberta, Canada, and Mrs. Alice Hyatt of Yakima, Washington.[408]

Funeral services will be held at 2:30 P.M. at the Arbaugh-Pearce funeral home in charge of Dr. R. D. Walter. Burial will be in the Grandview cemetery. Friends may call this evening at the funeral home.

The Diary. Two Final Entries:

The Diary of S. N. Van Blaricom, June 16, 1945:

The past few days have been warm and wet. Everything is growing, trying to make up for lost time." [SNVB.]

Dad died of a heart attack about 11 AM...just about two hours after he wrote the above. He had not felt well for some time but the heart attack was quite unexpected. He had gone for a walk and apparently felt tired and sat down in the tool shed to rest. John found him there when he went out to call him for dinner." [Anonymous.]

An Eloquent Eulogy:

Farm and Dairy, Salem, Ohio. June, 1945 (byline–*The Rambling Reporter):*

So Mr. Van is gone. It must be so---I saw his body placed in the ground, heard the minister offer words of consolation to the circle of friends and neighbors gathered about the grave. Yet for me, he will never be completely gone. Part of my thinking, of my outlook on life, will always be influenced by the ideas of Stephen Norton Van Blaricom.

---

[408] The obituary curiously mentions all three of Norton's sisters: Mary, Alice, and Effie, who were living at the time of his death in 1945, but omits any mention of Fred Van Blaricom, the one brother who survived him.

Yet I was not a close neighbor, not really a close friend. There were dozens who knew him better. And there are dozens who, although they realize that 76 is a good old age and that life past there is uncertain, were nevertheless shocked at the news.

Mr. Van was a fairly good farmer, yet not the best. He made a comfortable living for his family, yet his income was not as high as could be boasted by some of the neighbors. But there was one thing in which he truly excelled, and that was in the art of living. He enjoyed living, and he made life just a little more interesting for those with whom he came in contact.

I'm not sure but what that isn't the greatest success of all.

Mr. Van was a positive kind of man. He had convictions in many matters, and he would state them boldly, yet usually he gave no offense when his ideas didn't coincide with the other fellow's. And he could change his mind. He read widely and usually he was fundamentally right.

He had that rare gift of weaving humor into his remarks, and of saying a thing so directly and briefly that it stuck with a fellow. In a meeting he could make a statement on almost any subject and give the audience something to think about. You might disagree completely with what he said, yet still feel that he had added something to the meeting. This was such a gift that it might have made of him a great orator or a great writer.

He was a great example of the truth that a college degree is not a requirement for an education. A degree might—and should—hasten the process and give a fellow a broader foundation on which to build, but to my mind Mr. Van was better educated than most college graduates.

In later years (I knew him only in the last ten years of his life) he was more and more interested in the laws governing Life. The natural law, that is. He had seen a great industrial civilization develop, and some of the aspects of that troubled him. Mr. Van was born in a backwoods cabin in Minnesota, and he knew exactly what the early settler faced in trying to tame the woods and establish an income and a farm. He saw the electric trolley, the automobile, the airplane, the radio through birth and infancy. Will any of us living today ever again see such changes in the ways of living? He saw our topsoil being ruined and washed away, and was one of the first to climb on the bandwagon of soil conservation.

He will be missed by many. I have thought about it, and tried to analyze the things that made him so outstanding in the art of living, and I have come down to two facts which stood out in his life:

He was always curious, always interested in the things about him: he wanted to know why; and

He liked people and he was tolerant to their failings. I never once heard him make a belittling remark about a neighbor. Some people he liked better than others, of course, but to him they were all individuals, and all equally deserving of respect and tolerance as individuals. He genuinely liked everybody.

And there we have, I think, a pretty good constitution and its by-laws for a successful life. In the case of Mr. Van, it was a lifelong presentation.

MAUD

Maud Elizabeth (Griselle) Van Blaricom, the naïve "Presbyterian–Quaker" girl, a graduate of the Philadelphia Academy of Fine Arts and perhaps the first of Montana's lady telegraphers (1891–1899), lived another twenty years after the death of her beloved Norton. She died in Akron, Ohio, on February 5, 1965, at the age of ninety-seven. Maud was buried next to Norton in the Grandview Cemetery not far from their "little farm" near Salem, Ohio.

And so ended an uncommon journey.

Some would believe it had just begun.

Great Love is a miracle.

[THE END]

Levi Van Blaricom and the 4th Minnesota Infantry

At the age of nineteen, Levi Van Blaricom enlisted as a private in "I" Company of the 4th Regiment of Minnesota Infantry Volunteers (commonly known as "the 4th Minnesota Infantry Regiment" or simply "the 4th Minnesota") on 18 December 1861. He served until the regiment was disbanded in St. Paul on 5 August 1865.

Regimental records show he was a participant in the following engagements. In 1862, the siege of Corinth, Mississippi; the battle at Iuka, Mississippi; the Battle of Corinth, Mississippi; the Mississippi Central Railroad Campaign; and the Battle of Oxford, Mississippi. In 1863, the Yazoo Pass Expedition, Mississippi; the Battle of Champion Hills, Mississippi; the Battle of Jackson, Mississippi; the assault on Vicksburg; the siege and fall of Vicksburg (where the 4th Minnesota was the first Union regiment to enter the city); and the Battle of Chattanooga, Tennessee.

"When we left Fort Snelling, Minnesota, on April 20th, 1862, we had 22 wagons, 4 ambulances, 132 mules, 60 horses, 941 enlisted men and 59 officers." [HVBG, p. 99.] On 31 May 1863, a little over a year later, sitting in the trenches outside of Vicksburg (which surrendered on 4 July, 1863) they counted their resources again. Only 9 wagons, 2 ambulances, 52 mules, and 12 horses were left. 382 enlisted men and 17 officers were present and 22 of them were listed as "sick." [H4M, pp. 224–225.] 559 men and 42 officers had been killed, wounded, captured, or died of illness in thirteen months of service. Others not falling into those categories were in hospital somewhere convalescing from ailments ranging from chronic diarrhea to severe rheumatism to heat stroke and dehydration.

In December of 1863, while the regiment was stationed

at Huntsville, Alabama, Levi was thrown from the back of a "liberated" mule and dislocated his hip. He was sent north to a hospital in Washington City (now Washington, D.C.), where he spent four months recuperating. Never fully rehabilitated, he limped the rest of his life.

The U.S. Army had already sent Levi back to Huntsville when, on 2 May 1864, the regiment returned from a month-long furlough in Minnesota. 17 officers and 241 men returned to duty. Although they were sent reinforcements from time to time, the regiment never did return to anywhere near its original strength. Due to his disability, Levi was assigned as an ambulance driver or wagon teamster for the rest of the war.

Reassigned to General Sherman's army that had taken Atlanta on 1 September 1864, the 4th Minnesota took part in the bloody defense of the rail intersection at Allatoona, Georgia, on 5 October. The battle was ferocious. Alonzo L. Brown, historian of the regiment, described the scene:

> The rebels threw themselves in heavy masses against our outer entrenchments, and after a desperate hand-to-hand struggle fairly pushed our men from their rifle pits. With fearful yells they came sweeping down the road and entered the town. The Mississippi regiments charged and almost got between Companies "A" and "I" [the latter being Levi's company], but our men, without any protection whatever, poured double-shotted doses of cannister and musketry into the howling enemy. They charged four more times over the same ground but were as often broken and driven back. The artillery piece between Companies "A" and "I" was worked until every single gunner was killed or wounded severely. When the rebels discovered they could not win by direct assault they hid themselves behind every stump or any other place of shelter and kept up a murderous fire. The air literally rained bullets. We had received a new flag previous to the battle. After the fight, we counted 192 bullet holes in it. At around 4:00 PM the Confederates learned that major reinforcements sent by Sherman were on their way and the whole Johnny division left before they could arrive. The engagement had

lasted some seven hours [from about 9:00 AM until 4:00 PM]. The Confederates left 331 dead on the field, lost 411 as prisoners, and had over 1,000 severely wounded. The Union defenders lost 142 dead, 353 wounded and 212 missing. Every Union field officer on the western side [of the railroad tracks] with the exception of two were either killed or wounded. Brigadier General John M. Corse, the commanding officer of the Union forces at Allatoona, had been severely wounded in his face. The next day he sent a rather remarkable telegram to General Sherman: "I am short a cheekbone and an ear, but am able to whip all Hell yet! My losses have been heavy.–Corse." [H4M, synopsized from pp. 311–323.]

Following Allatoona, the regiment then marched as a part of Sherman's 60,000-man army "from Atlanta to the Sea" and participated in the capture of Savannah on 21 December 1864. On 1 January 1865, General Sherman announced: "We have one more campaign before us." They then marched north through eastern Georgia, central South Carolina, and North Carolina. It was at Goldsboro, North Carolina, where the 4th Minnesota finally rested and encamped from 24 March through 9 April 1865. Regimental historian Alonzo L. Brown recorded a letter he had received from First Lieutenant John G. Janicke of "G" Company describing the regiment's condition when it arrived at Goldsboro:

The misery the regiment was in will be remembered by everyone. Our undergarments and our uniforms are in tattered shreds. Both officers and men are half-barefoot, nay, half-naked. We are all lousy, heavily bearded, unbathed for a month, and the rags we wear are caked with mud and stinking with swamp grime. Finally, on April 2, 1865, we were issued new uniforms and good, new shoes. We were ordered to burn our old clothes and bury them in the ground. [H4M, synopsized from pp. 382–383 and p. 394.]

Back on the road on the 10th of April, Sherman headed for Raleigh. The soldiers learned on the 12th that Lee had surrendered to Grant on the 9th at Appomattox. "The woods around us seemed to be full of Confederate deserters." [H4M, p. 399.]

The 4th Minnesota was selected by General William Tecumseh Sherman to lead the Army of the West, 62,000 strong, in the victory parade down Pennsylvania Avenue in Washington City on 24 May 1865. From the time they hooked up with Sherman's army just outside of Memphis, Tennessee, on 18 July 1864, the 4th Minnesota (like the rest of Sherman's soldiers) had marched, slogged, fought, and foraged its way 1,549 miles through the heart of the South. Only eleven months had expired during the march from Memphis to Atlanta to Savannah and up the coast to Washington City. "On 24 July, 1865, the steamboat *Northern Belle* pulled into the dock at St. Paul. Of the 1,602 officers and men who served in the 4th Minnesota at one time or another during the Great War of the Rebellion, the last 560 men remaining in the regiment [Levi Van Blaricom among them] disembarked. 'We were fed supper in the capitol building itself.' Allowed to return to their homes, they came back to St. Paul on 5 August 1865, where they received ten months back pay and their discharge papers." [HVBG, pp. 96–105. See H4M and MCIW, Vols. 1 and 2 for the complete history of the 4th Minnesota Infantry Regiment.]

APPENDIX 2

The Van Blaricom Immigrants of 1634 and Their Descendants

NORTH HOLLAND TO NEW NETHERLAND (1634) TO
NEW CAESARIA (NEW JERSEY) (1654);
PENNSYLVANIA (1782); OHIO (1802 and 1805);
INDIANA (1846); IOWA (1853);
MINNESOTA (1855); MONTANA (1882)

Lubbert Gijsbertzsen (born 1601 in Blaricum, North Holland), his wife, Divertje Cornilesse (born about 1602 in Beemster, North Holland), and their three children, Gijsbert (born about 1624 outside of Beemster), Thys (born about 1628 near Rijp, North Holland), and Jan (born about 1632 in Blaricum), arrived in Rensselaerwyck, New Netherland (near *t'Fort Orangie,* now Albany, New York), on 20 July 1634 aboard the Dutch West Indies ship *de Eendracht* (*The Unity*). Lubbert Gijsbertzsen (pronounced "Gysbertsen") was under a three-year contract as a wagonmaker and wheelwright to Kiliaen van Rensselaer, the *patroon* of Rensselaerwyck (Rensselaer Village). [HVBG, p. 62.]

Following the Dutch naming system, the male children's last names were Lubbertsen (Lubbert's son). Lubbert, however, was a fairly common Dutch name so the youngest child, Jan—Stephen Norton Van Blaricom's lineal ancestor—clarified it by noting the town of his father's birth. Thus he was called Jan Lubbertsen van Blaricum. When the English replaced the Dutch government in 1664, the social rules changed as well. In Dutch, when Jan said his name was "Jan Lubbertsen van Blaricum," he was saying (and his Dutch contemporaries knew he was saying) that he was "Jan, Lubbert's son, the Lubbert from the town of Blaricum in North Holland." (That distinguished him from Jan Lubbertsen van Amsterdam, or Jan, Lubbert's son, the Lubbert from Amsterdam.) The English, on the other hand, heard "Jan Lubbertsen van

Blarkum" and, following their naming pattern, simply believed what they heard. Thus, over a generation or two, "Van Blarcom" (or van Blaregan, van Blarkum, van Blarcom, van Blaricum, van Blaricom) became the fixed surname of Jan's family and their descendants. [HVBG, p. 65.]*

> *Roger Hunt noted: "Beginning about 1706...'Van Blarcom' rapidly became the surname of all family members." On 4 September 1711, Magdaleentje, Jan Lubbertsen's wife, died. The death and burial was recorded as "Madalena, wife of Jan Lubbertsen Van Blarkum" in the Old Bergen Church. The baptism of Pieter, the son of Madalena and Jan Lubbertsen, was recorded as "Pieter Janse" on 6 May 1665, yet the estate of Pieter Janse was probated by his son, John Van Blarcom, on 31 May 1749. Gerrit Van Blarcom (born 2 November 1707), the son of Pieter Janse (Van Blarcom), was the first known ancestor of Stephen Norton Van Blaricom to have gone by that surname all of his life. [HVBF, p.41, p. 43 and p. 53.]

Twenty years after the family's arrival in New Netherland, Peter Stuyvesant, the peg-legged administrator of the Dutch West Indies Company, signed a grant on 5 December 1654 conveying title to fifty morgens (about one-hundred-and-six acres) of land on Bergen Neck in Nieuw Caesaria (now the Greenville area south of Jersey City, New Jersey) to Lubbert Gijsbertzsen. About 18 September 1655, Bergen Neck was subjected to attack by about fifteen-hundred Indians. Lubbert was one of "about 50 Christians [who] were killed or murdered." [HVBG, p. 64.]

Jan Lubbertsen Van Blaricom, then about twenty-three years old, somehow survived the massive Indian attack. From 1657, Jan was frequently involved in the Bergen militia as an officer. Numerous documents refer to him simply as *"jans Captijn"* (indicating his rank as a captain). Under the terms of an apparently arranged marriage, Jan wed Magdaleentje Theunis van Voorsthuysen (Madeline Theunis, from the village of Huysen, North Holland) on 7 June 1659. Some researchers speculate she was a remote cousin to Jan. It was from that marriage that, many generations later, Stephen Norton Van Blaricom and his siblings descended. [HVBG, p. 65.]

[See the ancestral charts following Appendix 9 for the Van Blaricom descendants of Lubbert Gijsbertzsen through Stephen Norton Van Blaricom.]

By 1654, Jan Van Blaricom settled in New Jersey. His wife followed a short time later, and there his descendants stayed until just after the Revolutionary War. Jan Lubbersten Van Blaricom died in Bergen, New Jersey, after 1711; his son, Pieter Janse Van Blaricom (born 6 May 1665 in Bergen) died in Bergen County, New Jersey, after 1720; Pieter Janse's son, Gerrit Van Blaricom (born 2 November 1707 in Hackensack, Bergen County), died in Paramus, New Jersey, after 1761. Ideologically split by the Revolution, the Loyalist part of the family migrated to Canada while those who supported the Revolution, the Continentals, stayed on in New Jersey. In 1782, however, Stephen Norton Van Blaricom's great-great-grandfather, David (1) Van Blaricom (the son of Gerrit Van Blaricom), branched off by himself and moved his wife and children from New Jersey into the mountains of central Pennsylvania, not far from Sunbury on the Susquehanna River. [HVBG, pp. 65–73.]

DAVID (1) VAN BLARICOM:
THE MOVE TO PENNSYLVANIA (1782)

David (1) Van Blaricom was born in Hackensack, Bergen County, New Jersey, in 1739. In 1761, at the age of twenty-two, he enlisted in Captain Lent's Company of Orange County, New York, and served the colonies during the French and Indian War. Around 1765, he married Elizabeth (some surmise her surname was Parrelman) and they had three children: Jacomyntje, Gerrit, and Jacobus, all born in Paramus, New Jersey. About 1771, they moved to Shrewsbury Township, Monmouth County, New Jersey, where their last five children, a girl and four boys, were born between 1773 and 1781. (Samuel Van Blaricom, Stephen Norton's great-grandfather, the fifth son and seventh child of David (1) and Elizabeth Van Blaricom, was born in Shrewsbury on 2 March 1777.) It is generally believed that David (1) fought with the Continentals at the Battle of Monmouth (28 June 1778), although no documents exist to prove that legend. In 1782, in a move that separated himself and his wife and children from the rest of the greater Van Blaricom clan, David (1) moved to

Catawissa Township (near the modern townsite of Mifflinville), Northumberland County, Pennsylvania. [HVBG, pp. 68–73.] Six years later, in 1788, two of the older boys, Gerrit and John, accompanied the Symmes party down the Ohio River to North Bend, the first settlement in southeastern Ohio. Gerrit was twenty years old at the time. John, his younger brother, was all of thirteen. A few years later, Cincinnati took root just to the east of the North Bend settlement. [HVBG, pp. 60–73.]

Some fourteen years later, around 1802, David (1) and Elizabeth and another son, Peter, followed Gerrit and John to the developing area near Cincinnati. Their youngest son, David, Jr., soon followed them. Their four other children had married in Pennsylvania and remained there. A veteran of both the French and Indian Wars and the American Revolution, David (1) was still living in Delhi Township near Cincinnati in 1820. David (1) was then eighty-one years old. When he and Elizabeth died or where they are buried is unknown. Family legend has David (1) living to be ninety-four years old. Since he lived only a couple of miles from David, Jr., it is likely that David (1) (and perhaps Elizabeth) is buried in an unmarked site within the now overgrown and unmaintained "Van Blaricum Cemetery." That cemetery is located on private property a short distance from "Van Blaricum Lane" (apparently named after David, Jr.) a few miles west of Cincinnati. David, Jr. (1779–1864), and both of his wives are buried there. [HVBG, pp. 72–73.]

GERRIT VAN BLARICOM AND JOHN VAN BLARICUM: PENNSYLVANIA TO OHIO (1788)

Gerrit Van Blaricom and John Van Blaricum were brothers to Samuel Van Blaricom, Stephen Norton Van Blaricom's great-grandfather (see below). Gerrit Van Blaricom accompanied the first Symmes settlement party into southwest Ohio in 1788 and lived in or near the pioneer community of North Bend, the village on the Ohio River that preceded modern Cincinnati. Gerrit (born in 1768) married Betsey Rudisill in North Bend on 12 December 1793. He was frequently mentioned in Symmes' personal correspondence. [HVBG, pp. 71–72.]

John Van Blaricum (born about 1775) left home at the young age of thirteen to accompany his twenty-year-old brother, Gerrit, on the Symmes expedition to North Bend, Ohio, in 1788. A little more than two years after Gerrit married Betsey Rudisill on 12 December 1793, John married Betsey's sister, Mary Anne Rudisill (on 26 June 1796). Later, John and Mary Anne were among Indiana's first settlers. His name was entered on the first census of Dearborn County (USC, Indiana, 1807). Although Dearborn County then covered what is now the eastern third of modern Indiana, the census contained barely more than one-hundred names. (The Dearborn County census contained only adult male names—they could have been bachelors or heads of families.) By 1821 he and his wife and ten children had moved to the new town of Indianapolis. [HVBG, p. 78.]

John Van Blaricum became well known as a somewhat cantankerous blacksmith, being "the first in Indianapolis to lay a plow, steel an ax, make a grubbing hoe, or shoe a horse." He was apparently a real character. His activities in Indianapolis were described by John H. B. Nowland in his 1870 book that bore the "brief" title of *Early Reminiscences of Indianapolis with Short Biographical Sketches of its Early Citizens* (cited in HVBF, p. 135, and HVBG, p. 78):

> The old man [John Van Blaricum was forty-six in 1821] was very clever if you could get on the right side of him, but very few had the good fortune to do so. A gentleman went to his shop to have some work done, which he needed very much. Van Blaricum told him he would not stop to make a nail for his coffin.

> He claimed the same right [of freedom] for his hogs, geese and cattle as he did for himself [and that was] to do as he pleased. It was during the lawsuit [over the murder of Captain John Cain's dog which John Van Blaricum, believing that the dog had harassed his pigs, had shot dead in Cain's front yard] that it was proved his hogs had been seen in the second story window of Hawkins' Hotel.

> On [another] occasion his geese had got into trouble [and were chased off by some of the local boys]. He said he would slay every boy in the settlement [of Indianapolis]

the age of six years and under. He would commence with John Nowland [the author], and when he got to the Carter boys he would [kill them first and then] take the old man with them.

It was John Van Blaricum who [at the age of fifty-six] in 1831, whipped the captain of the steamboat General Hanna and cleared the boat of the balance of the crew.

He [John Van Blaricum] died at his residence in the year 1850 [at the age of seventy-five]. Like everybody else, he had many traits of character...[except in his case] some were bad and some were very bad.

SAMUEL VAN BLARICOM AND THE FAMILY STRASSER: PENNSYLVANIA TO OHIO (1805) TO INDIANA (1844)

Samuel Van Blaricom (born 2 March 1777 in Shrewsbury, New Jersey), the fifth son and seventh of the eight children of David (1) and Elizabeth Van Blaricom, married Mary Ann Strasser (born April 1781 near Eckville, Pennsylvania) about 1798 in Northumberland County, Pennsylvania. "Strasser" (pronounced "Straw-sir") was probably the original Austrian and, later, Palatinate German spelling of the family name. Johann Nicholas Strasser, the immigrant (who also went by his nickname of "Honnickel" Strasser), was listed as "Johann Nickel Strass" on the passenger list of an English ship, the *Samuel*. At about the age of twenty, he left Europe from the Dutch port of Rotterdam, traveled via the port of Cowes on the Isle of Wight and arrived in Philadelphia on 11 August 1732. Land Warrant No. 55 for one-hundred-and-fifty acres in Philadelphia County, Pennsylvania, was issued 19 September 1738 to "Johann Sdrasser." This original holding was near present-day Eckville in an area then known as the "Allemaengel," a 2,000-acre tract set apart for the personal use and disposal of Thomas Penn, one of the three sons of William Penn. [HVBG, pp. 73–74.]

Honnickel married Maria Elizabeth (surname unknown) about the same time he purchased his Allemaengel farmland in 1738. They proceeded to have ten children (seven daughters and three sons) and lived out their lives near Eckville. Maria died in 1783 at the age of sixty-two and Honnickel died in 1790 at about age seventy-eight.

The Allemaengel, settled almost entirely by German immigrants, was a hotbed of activity during the French and Indian War (1754–1768). Six of Johann Strasser's eight immediate neighbors residing on the Allemaengel Road were killed by the Indians. "A list compiled by Captain Wetherhold on 21 December 1757 listed 56 persons killed by Indians in the Allemaengel area, with 10 more taken prisoner. In the month of February alone, 15 or 16 were killed in the area." [HVBG, p. 75.] Since the entire area of the Allemaengel was barely over three square miles, these were horrendous statistics.

About 1784, Johann Henry Strasser (born 24 August 1758 near Eckville, Pennsylvania), the youngest of the three sons of Johann Nicholas ("Honnickel") Strasser, moved his family from the Allemaengel to Penn Township in Berks County. About 1789, he moved to Catawissa Township, Northumberland County, and that is where his eldest child, daughter Ann Mariah (Mary Ann), met and married Samuel Van Blaricom. [HVBG, pp. 73–76.] By the late 1700s, some members of the greater family had Anglicized the spelling of the name to "Strawser" while others retained the "Strasser" spelling.

In 1805, some three years following the departure of David (1) and Elizabeth (Parrelman?) Van Blaricom to the Cincinnati area, Samuel and his family, in the company of his wife's greater family, the Strassers, left Pennsylvania and settled in the newly opened lands of Adelphi, Ross County, Ohio, about fifteen miles northeast of Chillicothe. In 1816 Samuel and his family left the greater Strasser clan and established themselves two miles away in nearby Hocking Township, Ross County. In 1818, Hocking County was formed, and the place where Samuel and his family were located became Salt Lick Township, Hocking County, Ohio. In 1825 forty-eight-year-old Samuel and his now extended Van Blaricom family moved to Wapakoneta, Shelby County, Ohio. (Johann Henry Strasser died in Adelphi, Ohio, in 1829. His wife, Margaret (Speakman?) Strasser died in Adelphi shortly after her husband's death.) Nineteen years later, in 1844, the Van Blaricoms moved again, this time to Liberty Township, Fulton County, Indiana. [HVBF, pp. 76–77.] Samuel died in Liberty Township in 1856 at the age of seventy-nine. Mary Ann died there eight years later at the age of eighty-three years and eight months.

DAVID (2) VAN BLARICOM:
INDIANA (1844) TO IOWA (1853) TO MINNESOTA (1855)

Stephen Norton's grandfather, David (2) Van Blaricom, was born 1 January 1800 in Catawissa Township, Northumberland County, Pennsylvania, the oldest child of Samuel and Mary Ann (Strasser) Van Blaricom. David migrated with his family to Adelphi, Ohio, in 1805 and on to Ross County (later Hocking County) in 1816. David married Mary Ann Reed in Ross County on 21 May 1823. Following the move to Wapakoneta in 1825, David's brother, John (born 10 November 1805 in Ross County, Ohio), had married Nancy McNamer in Shelby County on 3 June 1830. Both David and John and their growing families had stuck with their father's larger clan for the move to Liberty Township, Fulton County, Indiana, in 1844. Finally, in 1853, the two brothers decided to move off on their own. David (2) was then fifty-three years old and John was forty-eight. The two men first moved to Appanoose County, Iowa, located in the southern part of the state on the Missouri border. Two years later, in 1855, they moved north and landed in Le Sueur County, Minnesota. [HVBF, pp. 134–137. HVBG, pp. 80–81.]

Sixteen years later, in 1871, John led his large clan of at least twenty-eight people on the long trek to Washington Territory. They arrived in the Walla Walla country in the fall of 1871. Nancy (McNamer) Van Blaricom, John's wife, died there in 1872. After a series of brief layovers, the family settled in northwestern Oregon. They helped establish and name the town of Vernonia, and many descendants of that line of the family live in Oregon today. John Van Blaricom died in Vernonia, Columbia County, Oregon, on 27 December 1890 at the age of eighty-five. [HVBF, pp. 195–208 and Family Group Sheet 464.]

David and his clan stayed on in Minnesota. David died on 22 October 1878 in Waterville, Le Sueur County, Minnesota, at the age of seventy-eight. David's wife, Mary Ann (Reed) Van Blaricom died at the home of her son, Phillip, in Long Prairie, Todd County, Minnesota, on 14 April 1884 at the age of eighty-one.

LEVI VAN BLARICOM: MINNESOTA TO MONTANA (1882)

Levi Van Blaricom was the tenth child of the eleven children of David and Mary Ann (Reed) Van Blaricom. Born near Wapakoneta,

Shelby County, Ohio, on 12 September 1842, he moved with his family to Liberty Township, Fulton County, Indiana, in 1844; to Appanoose County, Iowa, in 1853; to Kilkenny, Le Sueur County, Minnesota in 1855; and, finally, to Waterville, Le Sueur County, in 1857. During his time in the military with the 4th Minnesota Infantry Regiment (18 December 1861 through 5 August 1865) he served in Missouri, Tennessee, Arkansas, Mississippi, Alabama, Georgia, South Carolina, North Carolina, Virginia, Washington, D. C., and Kentucky. Following his return to Minnesota and Waterville, he married Sarah Susan Johnson on 22 March 1866. They lived in Waterville (1866–1872), Long Prairie, Todd County, Minnesota (1872–1878); Lake Jefferson, Le Sueur County, Minnesota (1878–1880); and returned to Waterville in 1881. By the time Levi and Sarah moved to Glendive, Montana Territory, in April of 1882, they had eight children. Stephen Norton was the eldest, born in Waterville in April of 1869. Their ninth and last child, Sarah Effie, was born in Glendive on 9 July 1882, just weeks after their arrival. Sarah Susan, Levi's wife died of typhoid fever in Glendive on 25 September 1882, only four months after they arrived in Montana. Levi followed the greater family to Victor, Ravalli County, Montana, in 1888. His journeys through his childhood, the Civil War, and during and after his marriage to Sarah allowed Levi to see more of America than any other Van Blaricom until the onset of World War I. He died in Victor, Montana, on 22 September 1902 at the age of sixty years and ten days. Many of Levi and Sarah's descendants still live in the Victor–Hamilton–Missoula area.

The Johnson and Norton Lines

John Johnson of Roxbury, Massachusetts Bay Colony, came with the famed Winthrop fleet that landed at Salem on 22 June 1630. Captain John Johnson was the first clerk of the Ancient and Honorable Artillery of the Massachusetts Bay Colony. Founded 13 March 1638, it is the oldest military organization to have originated in North America. It was in Captain Johnson's house that much of the gun powder (seventeen barrels) for the colony was stored, and when his home burned in 1645 "all was suddenly burnt and blown up...and shook the houses in Boston and Cambridge, so that men thought there had been an earthquake." [HVBG, pp. 132–134.]

The early Johnson family history presented rather tragic stories from time to time, with many of the family's members killed or kidnapped by the Indians. Captain Isaac Johnson, John Johnson's son (and Stephen Norton Van Blaricom's direct ancestor) was killed in the "Great Swamp Fight" during the Narragansett Expedition of 1675. [HVBG, pp. 134–137.]

John (3) Johnson married Grace Morris in Woodstock, Connecticut, in 1743. Her grandmother was Elizabeth (Bowen) Morris, a granddaughter of Griffith Bowen and a direct descendant of Maynerick (Maynerch), Lord of Brecknock (ca. 1020–ca. 1080), whose son Blethyn married Otten, the daughter of the King of South Wales and from which marriage the American Bowen line descends. [HVBG, pp. 141–143.] Another notable member of the Morris family was Commodore Charles Morris, the commander of "Old Ironsides" (the USS *Constitution*) during its battle with the *Guerriere* in the War of 1812. [HVBG, p. 146.]

Lemuel Johnson (born 14 March 1750, the son of John (3) Johnson and Grace Morris Johnson) married Jerusha Norton in Middletown, Connecticut, in 1772, and added another colorful line to the Johnson family. The Nortons can be traced to Sharpenhoe, Bedsfordshire, with the birth of John Norton in 1440. His great-grandson, Thomas (2) Norton, married the daughter of the notorious Archbishop Thomas Cranmer and, in 1571, was elected to Parliament from London, "wherein he served a number of sessions." In 1581 he was made the *archicarnifex* (rackmaster) of London: "The character of his inquisition is shown in his treatment of Alexander Briant, whom Thomas (2) Norton told before he was racked that *'if he wolde not for his dutie to God and the Queene tell the truth, he should be made a foot longer than God had made him.'*" Falling out of favor with the crown, Thomas (2) Norton died only days following release from his second period of incarceration in the Tower of London in 1584. [HVBG, pp. 152–153.]

Stephen Norton (1) Johnson (born about 1788 probably in Deerfield, New York) was the fourth son and last child of the eight children of Lemuel and Jerusha (Norton) Johnson. He married Susan E. Blair in Lorain County, Ohio, on 4 December 1820. The name of Blair is Celtic in origin and is found in Scottish accounts from the 11th century. It was with the accession of James I (1603–1625) that Ireland was offered up to Englishman and Scot alike at such low prices that thousands were induced to make the migration. Better, reasoned the crown, to be Scot and Presbyter than to be Irish and Papist. Alexander Blair and an unnamed brother arrived in County Antrim, Ireland, about the year 1610. Legend has them coming from Ayrshire, Scotland. Alexander settled in Glendarmot, County Antrim, while the brother took land near the village of Aghadowey, also in County Antrim. James Blair (born in 1641 or 1645) was the first of the Blair line born in Aghodowey. With many of the Blair family among them, the Scots from Aghadowey chartered five ships and, emigrating from Londonderry, arrived in Boston, Massachusetts, in August of 1718. The family remained in Massachusetts until Thompson Blair and his wife, Esther (Perkins), moved themselves and their ten children to Lorain County, Ohio, in 1815. [HVBG, pp. 163–168.]

Stephen Norton (2) Johnson, the second child and second son of the five known children of Stephen Norton (1) Johnson and

Susan E. (Blair) Johnson, was born in Amherst, Lorain County, Ohio, on 2 April 1826. He completed school in Amherst, married Janette Mary Beardsley on 29 October 1848, and proceeded to complete his medical education. In addition to being a physician, he was also an accomplished musician. He enlisted in the 4th Minnesota Infantry Regiment at the beginning of the Civil War. The regiment was mustered on 23 December 1861 at Fort Snelling. On 2 January 1862, only ten days after going on active duty, Stephen Norton (2) Johnson died of pneumonia at the age of thirty-five. [HVBG, pp. 170–173. Also see H4M, p. 543.]

Zachariah and Mariah Scribner

Zachariah Scribner was born in New Hampshire in 1819. [HVBG, p. 194.] Zachariah and Mariah Janette (Beardsley) Johnson (*nee* Janette Mary Beardsley), born 1828, were married 6 February 1867 in Waterville, Le Sueur County, Minnesota. According to Marilyn Scribner, a descendant of that marriage, Zachariah was a widower who had one son from his first marriage. That child was an adult by the time Zachariah re-married. The Scribner–Johnson marriage occurred eleven months after the marriage of Mariah's sixteen-year-old daughter, Sarah Susan Johnson, to Levi Van Blaricom. Already the mother of five children from the Johnson marriage, Mariah then proceeded to have five more children with Scribner (the first of whom died young), all of whom were contemporaries with the children of her eldest daughter, Sarah Susan (Mrs. Levi) Van Blaricom. [HVBG, p. 176.] The ten children of Mariah Janette (Beardsley) (Johnson) Scribner, birthed over a period of twenty-five years, were:

1. Sarah Susan Johnson, born 5 December 1849, Amherst, Lorain County, Ohio
2. Mary Jane Johnson, born 31 March 1852, Kinderhook, Pike County, Illinois
3. Frank LaFayette Johnson, born 10 November 1853, Amherst, Lorain County, Ohio
4. Martha May ("Muz") Johnson, born 1859, Waterville, Le Sueur County, Minnesota
5. Norton Stephen Johnson, born 21 June 1862, Waterville, Minnesota
6. Baby Boy Scribner, born 1868, Blooming Grove, Minnesota (died at birth)

7. Clarence ("Cad") Scribner, born 1869, Blooming Grove, Minnesota
8. Charles Scribner, born 1871, Blooming Grove, Minnesota
9. Charlotte Scribner, born 1872, Lake Jefferson, Minnesota
10. Minnie Scribner, born 1874, Lake Jefferson, Minnesota

Zachariah Scribner died in 1901 at the age of eighty-two and was buried at Victor, Montana. Mariah Janette (Beardsley) (Johnson) Scribner died near Riverside, Okanogan County, Washington, on 23 April 1911 at the age of eighty-four. She was the first of many of her family to be buried in the Riverside Cemetery. [HVBG, p. 177 and p. 191.]

APPENDIX 5

The Families of Reed and Hinton

Mary Ann Reed, the wife of David (2) Van Blaricom and the mother of Levi Van Blaricom, was born 25 November 1802 in Bourbon County, Kentucky. She was the eldest daughter of William Reed and his second wife, Martha Hinton. William Reed was born in County Tyrone, Ireland, on 12 December 1751. He immigrated to New Castle, Delaware, in 1773. He served with the Continental Army at various times and locations throughout the Revolution. He died in Auglaize County, Ohio, in 1841 at the age of eighty-nine. [HVBG, pp. 80–81.]

Martha (Hinton) Reed, despite her common circumstances and impoverished life, descended directly from Eruald de Hynton, one of two Hynton brothers who accompanied William the Conqueror when he successfully invaded England in 1066. Thomas Hinton III (1574–1635) was a direct descendant of Eruald de Hynton. At the time of Thomas III's death in 1635, he was reportedly the wealthiest commoner in England. He was the majority stockholder and Director of the famed Virginia Company of London. It was through his direct efforts and management that the Jamestown colony was founded in 1610 and thereafter maintained. Despite many trips between England and Virginia, none of the Hintons settled in North America until 1653 when Thomas Hinton IV (1600–1683) immigrated to Virginia. In 1666, he established the family in Maryland and for several generations they were wealthy and successful planters around Chesapeake Bay. Thomas Hinton VII (1739–1821) was Martha Hinton's father.

For reasons unknown, Thomas Hinton VI disinherited his eldest son, Thomas Hinton VII, and upon his death left the Hinton estate of Sapling Ridge (in Anne Arundel County, Maryland) to his second son, James Hinton. Thomas VII broke with the family and headed out into the wilds near Paris, Bourbon County,

Kentucky, in 1792. Thomas VII had at least eleven children from two marriages and it is not apparent that any of the children were literate.

Martha Hinton, the daughter of Thomas VII, was thirty-two years old when she married William Reed, the forty-six-year-old Ireland-born widower, on 15 January 1798 in or near Paris, Bourbon County, Kentucky. She died around 1820 in Delaware County, Ohio, at about age fifty-four. [HVBG, pp. 82–92.]

Mary Ann Reed, the mother of Levi Van Blaricom, was the first child of the Reed–Hinton marriage. She married David (2) Van Blaricom on 21 May 1823 in Adelphi, Ross County, Ohio. Mary Ann and David had eleven children, six boys and five girls, born between 1824 and 1844. Levi, Stephen Norton Van Blaricom's father, was the next-youngest child, born 12 September 1842 in Shelby County, Ohio. Mary Ann died in Todd County, Minnesota, at the home of her son, Phillip, on 14 April 1884. She was eighty-one years old. She was buried in the Long Prairie cemetery. [HVBG, pp. 80–81.]

APPENDIX 6

The Beardsley and Hanchett Families

Stephen Norton Van Blaricom's grandmother, Mariah Janette Beardsley was born Janette Mary Beardsley on 11 February 1827 in or near Amherst, Lorain County, Ohio. She was the fifth of six children born to James Harvey Beardsley and Sarah (Hanchett) Beardsley. [HVBG, p. 131.]

William and Mary (Harvey) Beardsley, the immigrant ancestors of Janette Mary, were married in Ilkeston, Derbyshire, England, on 26 January 1632. They and their three children arrived in Boston harbor aboard the good ship *Planter* around the first of June 1635. In 1639, William Beardsley and his wife and children were among the seventeen families who left the Massachusetts Bay Colony and established themselves at what became Stratford, a location recognized to have been the fourth white settlement in Connecticut. William Beardsley served eight sessions (1645–1658) as a deputy to the General Court of Connecticut. In one of his more ominous acts, William Beardsley and two others were ordered by the General Court in 1651 to "pursue the execution of justice" in Stratford by hanging "the witch Goody Bassett." [HVBG, p. 113.] Although he died in June of 1661 at the relatively young age of fifty-six, his descendants served with distinction in the French and Indian War, the American Revolution, and later conflicts. [HVBG, pp. 108–128.] The Beardsley family stayed in Connecticut, with side migrations to Rensselaer and Dutchess counties, New York, until James Beardsley, a Revolutionary War veteran, settled in Vermont sometime before 1840. James Harvey Beardsley, the son of James Beardsley and Harriet Warner, was born 20 September 1798, in New Fairfield, Connecticut. Why James Harvey Beardsley settled in Ohio early on was not recorded. Perhaps his father, James Beardsley, utilized his service in the Revolutionary War to take a land claim in Ohio and then moved back east to Vermont, leaving his son and his son's family in Ohio. It is only known that James Harvey Beardsley married Sarah Hanchett about 1819 in Cuyahoga County, Ohio.

The Hanchett family of Janette Mary Beardsley's mother was also an old line of New England. John Hanchett appeared in Boston records in 1634. His younger brother, Thomas Hanchett, from whom Mary descended, first shows on the record being granted a "home-lot" in Wethersfield, Connecticut, in 1642, "having reached the age of majority." The Hanchett family remained in Connecticut for several generations until they joined the many Salisbury families who started investing in land in Vermont about 1761. Ebenezer Hanchett remained in Connecticut, but his son, Jonah, along with his family moved back and forth between New York and Vermont. It was Ebenezer Hanchett, Janette Mary Beardsley's great-grandfather, who owned the foundry involved in forging the massive chain that, during the Revolution, was stretched across the Hudson River to preclude the British fleet from advancing beyond West Point. Sarah Hanchett, Janette Mary Beardsley's mother, was born about 1798 around Pleasantville, New York. In 1817, Jonah Hanchett, Sarah's father, utilized his Revolutionary War pension (land rights) and settled his family in Ridgeville, Cuyahoga County, Ohio.

Sarah Hanchett moved with her family to Ohio in 1817 and married James Harvey Beardsley about 1819 in Cuyahoga County. [HVBG, pp. 128–132.] Janette Mary Beardsley was born 11 February 1827 in Amherst, Lorain County, Ohio. She was the fifth child and second daughter of the four sons and two daughters of James Harvey and Sarah (Hanchett) Beardsley. [HVBG, pp. 131–132.] At the age of twenty-one, Janette Mary Beardsley married Stephen Norton (2) Johnson, a physician, in Akron, Summit County, Ohio, on 29 October 1848. [HVBG, p. 171.] They had three daughters and one son prior to the death of Dr. Johnson at Fort Snelling on 2 January 1862 at the age of thirty-five. Dr. Johnson's death made Janette a widow at the age of thirty-four. Pregnant when her husband died, Janette gave birth to a fifth child, Norton Stephen Johnson, on 21 June 1862 at her home in Waterville, Minnesota. [HVBG, p. 171.]

On 6 February 1867, Janette Mary (Beardsley) Johnson married

Zachariah Scribner. She changed her name to Mariah Janette Scribner and she and Zachariah had five more children, three boys and two girls. See Appendix 4 for the marriage to Zachariah Scribner and Mariah's descendants of both her Johnson and Scribner marriages.

Phillip E. Van Blaricom, Levi's Brother

Phillip E. Van Blaricom was born in Shelby County, Ohio, on 5 October 1840. He was the ninth of the eleven children of David (2) and Mary Ann (Reed) Van Blaricom. He was immediately older than Levi (born 12 September 1842) and Arlinda (born 7 August 1844), the girl who disappeared during the Great Sioux Uprising of 1862, only days after her eighteenth birthday.

Phillip, twenty-one, along with his cousin, Samuel Van Blaricom (John's son), twenty-three, enlisted as a private in Captain S. Ramsdell's Company of the Sauk Centre (Stearns County) Volunteer State Militia on 25 August 1862 and served with this unit through 10 October 1862. Formed as a self-defense force to protect the citizens of Minnesota during the Sioux uprising of that year (17 August–26 December), the Ramsdell unit disbanded on 25 October 1862.

On 11 October 1862, Phillip joined "B" Company of the First Regiment of (Minnesota) Mounted Rangers in which he served as a private until the unit mustered out on 9 November 1863. The Rangers were part of General Sibley's 1863 expedition sent out to the Dakotas in pursuit of the Minnesota Sioux who had fled west. They engaged the Indians on 24 July at the Battle of Big Mound (or "Big Hill") and followed up with two more skirmishes on 26 July (the Battle of Buffalo Lake) and 28 July (the Battle of Stony Lake), all three events occurring in Dakota Territory. Sibley's force reached the Missouri about five miles south of the present site of Bismarck on 29 July. Three days later, the force headed back for Minnesota, where it disbanded on 9 November 1863.

Phillip married Roxie J. Bailey in Waterville, Le Sueur County, in 1864. They had six children before Roxie's death in Long Prairie, Todd County, Minnesota, on 5 March 1874. Five years later, on 12 June 1879, Phillip married Mathilda (Mary) Yarno and they then had eight more children.

About the time of Roxie's death in 1874, Mary Ann (Reed) Van Blaricom, Phillip and Levi's mother, came to Long Prairie and lived out her years with Phillip and his family. When Levi and his family gave up on the Todd County settlement and moved back to Le Sueur County in 1878, Phillip and his family stayed on at their farm near Gutche's Grove in Reynolds Township. They never left. (William, Phillip's eldest son, inherited the farm upon his father's death in 1925.)

In the summer of 1883, Ernst, the sixteen-month-old child of Phillip and Mathilda, tragically drowned. "The father was off in the field and the mother was weeding in the garden when the child fell into the well. She left her work to get a drink at the well where she discovered her child floating on the water." [TCA, 31 July 1883.]

Phillip, who outlived all ten of his siblings, died at his home on 30 June 1925 at the age of eighty-four. Phillip's second wife, Mathilda (Yarno), five of the six children from his first marriage, and seven of the eight children from the second marriage survived Phillip at his death. He was buried next to his mother, Mary Ann, in the Long Prairie cemetery. A single large granite tombstone marks the graves of Phillip and his second wife, Mathilda. Although her gravesite is visible immediately adjacent to Phillip's grave, Mary Ann's wooden marker has long since disappeared.

[HVBG, pp. 175–176 and Family Group Sheet for David (2) Van Blaricom. MCIW, Vol. I, pp. 519–524, p. 528, and p. 794. LPL, 9 July 1925. TCA, 18 April 1884.]

APPENDIX 8

David Cass Van Blaricom, Brother of Stephen Norton

David Cass Van Blaricom was born 24 April 1870 near Waterville, Le Sueur County, Minnesota, the second son and second child of the nine children of Levi Van Blaricom and Sarah Susan (Johnson) Van Blaricom. David was twelve years old when his mother died in Glendive on 25 September 1882. Shortly after her death, he wandered off to the southeast following a ranch job and ended up in Deadwood City, Dakota Territory. There he got a job helping bullwhackers haul freight into the Black Hills during the winter. David occasionally returned to Glendive and, after the greater family left in the spring of 1887, he spent the winter of 1887–1888 in Glendive with his father, Levi, his married but abandoned fifteen-year-old sister, Mary, and her new baby, Emma Mabel.

This remnant Van Blaricom/Scribner group left Glendive and traveled to Victor, Montana, in 1888. David then proceeded to work in Victor and wander back and forth between Victor and his old haunts of Glendive and Deadwood City. After a few years, David settled in Victor, where he became a coal contractor to the Northern Pacific Railroad. He married Maria Ella Chilson in Victor in 1894. After having six children between 1895 and 1911 (their daughter, Augusta, born in 1898, lived until 1959; of the other five children only one lived a month past birth), Ella died in 1912 coincidental to the birth of their seventh child. The baby was born at noon, and mother and child were both dead by 3 P.M. Maria Ella (Chilson) Van Blaricom and the unnamed baby were buried together in the Victor cemetery in a common coffin.

About 1914, David married a widow, Alice Lucinda (Fulkerson) Mowatt, who had three children of her own. They then had two children, a daughter who died young and a son, Clarence (born

1917 and who was still living in the 1980s). David Van Blaricom died of diabetes on 19 May 1921 at the age of fifty-one. The local headline dated 27 May 1921, read: "Victor Man Dead. David Van Blaricom died last Thursday at the Cottage Hospital in Santa Barbara, California, where he went last fall in the hopes that he would regain his health." His body was returned to Victor for burial.

[HVBG, Family Group Sheets, "David Cass Van Blaricom, 25 April 1870–19 May 1921." Also see unidentified newspaper obituary (probably a Hamilton newspaper) of David Cass Van Blaricom dated 27 May 1921.]

Ancestors of Stephen Norton
Van Blaricom

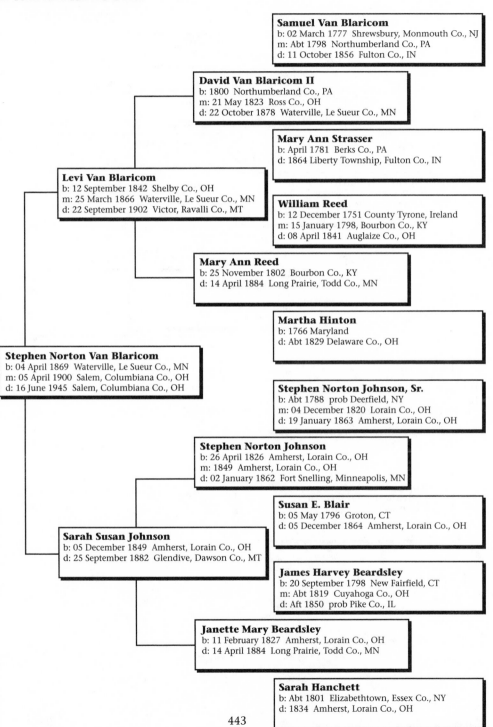

Samuel Van Blaricom
b: 02 March 1777 Shrewsbury, Monmouth Co., NJ
m: Abt 1798 Northumberland Co., PA
d: 11 October 1856 Fulton Co., IN

David Van Blaricom II
b: 1800 Northumberland Co., PA
m: 21 May 1823 Ross Co., OH
d: 22 October 1878 Waterville, Le Sueur Co., MN

Mary Ann Strasser
b: April 1781 Berks Co., PA
d: 1864 Liberty Township, Fulton Co., IN

Levi Van Blaricom
b: 12 September 1842 Shelby Co., OH
m: 25 March 1866 Waterville, Le Sueur Co., MN
d: 22 September 1902 Victor, Ravalli Co., MT

William Reed
b: 12 December 1751 County Tyrone, Ireland
m: 15 January 1798, Bourbon Co., KY
d: 08 April 1841 Auglaize Co., OH

Mary Ann Reed
b: 25 November 1802 Bourbon Co., KY
d: 14 April 1884 Long Prairie, Todd Co., MN

Martha Hinton
b: 1766 Maryland
d: Abt 1829 Delaware Co., OH

Stephen Norton Van Blaricom
b: 04 April 1869 Waterville, Le Sueur Co., MN
m: 05 April 1900 Salem, Columbiana Co., OH
d: 16 June 1945 Salem, Columbiana Co., OH

Stephen Norton Johnson, Sr.
b: Abt 1788 prob Deerfield, NY
m: 04 December 1820 Lorain Co., OH
d: 19 January 1863 Amherst, Lorain Co., OH

Stephen Norton Johnson
b: 26 April 1826 Amherst, Lorain Co., OH
m: 1849 Amherst, Lorain Co., OH
d: 02 January 1862 Fort Snelling, Minneapolis, MN

Susan E. Blair
b: 05 May 1796 Groton, CT
d: 05 December 1864 Amherst, Lorain Co., OH

Sarah Susan Johnson
b: 05 December 1849 Amherst, Lorain Co., OH
d: 25 September 1882 Glendive, Dawson Co., MT

James Harvey Beardsley
b: 20 September 1798 New Fairfield, CT
m: Abt 1819 Cuyahoga Co., OH
d: Aft 1850 prob Pike Co., IL

Janette Mary Beardsley
b: 11 February 1827 Amherst, Lorain Co., OH
d: 14 April 1884 Long Prairie, Todd Co., MN

Sarah Hanchett
b: Abt 1801 Elizabethtown, Essex Co., NY
d: 1834 Amherst, Lorain Co., OH

Ancestors of Samuel Van Blaricom

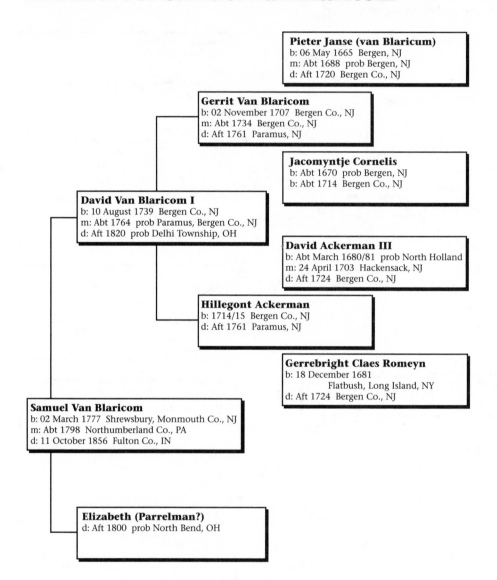

Pieter Janse (van Blaricum)
b: 06 May 1665 Bergen, NJ
m: Abt 1688 prob Bergen, NJ
d: Aft 1720 Bergen Co., NJ

Gerrit Van Blaricom
b: 02 November 1707 Bergen Co., NJ
m: Abt 1734 Bergen Co., NJ
d: Aft 1761 Paramus, NJ

Jacomyntje Cornelis
b: Abt 1670 prob Bergen, NJ
b: Abt 1714 Bergen Co., NJ

David Van Blaricom I
b: 10 August 1739 Bergen Co., NJ
m: Abt 1764 prob Paramus, Bergen Co., NJ
d: Aft 1820 prob Delhi Township, OH

David Ackerman III
b: Abt March 1680/81 prob North Holland
m: 24 April 1703 Hackensack, NJ
d: Aft 1724 Bergen Co., NJ

Hillegont Ackerman
b: 1714/15 Bergen Co., NJ
d: Aft 1761 Paramus, NJ

Gerrebright Claes Romeyn
b: 18 December 1681
          Flatbush, Long Island, NY
d: Aft 1724 Bergen Co., NJ

Samuel Van Blaricom
b: 02 March 1777 Shrewsbury, Monmouth Co., NJ
m: Abt 1798 Northumberland Co., PA
d: 11 October 1856 Fulton Co., IN

Elizabeth (Parrelman?)
d: Aft 1800 prob North Bend, OH

Ancestors of Pieter Jansen Van Blaricom

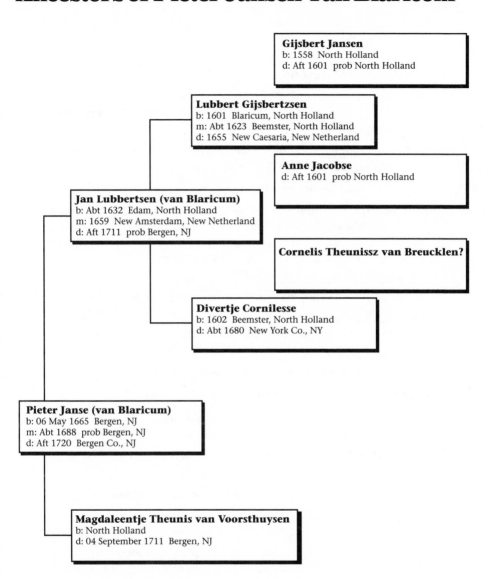

Gijsbert Jansen
b: 1558 North Holland
d: Aft 1601 prob North Holland

Lubbert Gijsbertzsen
b: 1601 Blaricum, North Holland
m: Abt 1623 Beemster, North Holland
d: 1655 New Caesaria, New Netherland

Anne Jacobse
d: Aft 1601 prob North Holland

Jan Lubbertsen (van Blaricum)
b: Abt 1632 Edam, North Holland
m: 1659 New Amsterdam, New Netherland
d: Aft 1711 prob Bergen, NJ

Cornelis Theunissz van Breucklen?

Divertje Cornilesse
b: 1602 Beemster, North Holland
d: Abt 1680 New York Co., NY

Pieter Janse (van Blaricum)
b: 06 May 1665 Bergen, NJ
m: Abt 1688 prob Bergen, NJ
d: Aft 1720 Bergen Co., NJ

Magdaleentje Theunis van Voorsthuysen
b: North Holland
d: 04 September 1711 Bergen, NJ

BIBLIOGRAPHY

1. Unpublished Materials

Book A, Dawson County land transfer records, 7 June 1901. Dawson County Courthouse. (Indenture between Sarah E. Allen and William F. Jordan, p. 360)

Bopp, May. Unpublished genealogical research regarding John Burns and family. Cogswell, North Dakota. 1994.

Brown, Daniel M. Unpublished letter, November, 1984.

Burkart, Jordan V. Unpublished genealogical research regarding William F. Jordan, Mary (May) (McDonald) Jordan, Maud (Miller) (Bogart) Miller, Nellie (Miller) Miskimen, Lillian (Miller) Bendon, and Irene (Jordan) (Burkart) Schafer. Los Angeles, California. 2003.

Carducci, Elizabeth Falor. Unpublished genealogical research regarding Maud (Griselle) Van Blaricom. Auburn, California. June, 2006.

Case Number 12, Justice Court of Dawson County, Territory of Montana. (Complaint filed by Mary M. Van Blaricom. Warrant Issued.)

Case Number 286, Probate Court of Dawson County, Territory of Montana. (Territory of Montana vs. Wilbur Slawson.)

Cashmere Cemetery Records, Cashmere, Washington.

Certificate of Death of May Jordan. Bureau of Vital Statistics, State of Montana.

Certificate of Death of Nellie M. Miskimen. Bureau of Vital Statistics, State of Montana.

Certificate of Death of Irene Schafer. Bureau of Vital Statistics, State of Montana.

Custer County Marriage Applications, 1888. Custer County, Montana.

Darling, Patricia. Unpublished genealogical research regarding Alexander P. Ayotte, Caroline Woods, Georgiana A. Brown, and their descendants. Dillon, Montana. July, 2003.

Divorce Complaint, Mary Miller vs. Frederick Miller. Custer County 1st District Court. Custer County, Territory of Montana. 6 June 1881.

Divorce Complaint and Decree, Sarah Eddy vs. Wm. Henry Eddy. District Court of Dawson County. Session of October, 1884.

Divorce Decree, Mary Miller vs. Frederick Miller. Custer County 1st District Court. Custer County, Territory of Montana. 8 October 1881.

Divorce Decree, May Jordan vs. William Jordan. Dawson County, Montana. 9 September 1914.

Document Number 79546, Book 8-33, Records of Dawson County, Montana, 8 November 1916. (Land transfer of Sara A. Jordan and William F. Jordan to Charles E. Miller.)

Falor, Ann (Van Blaricom). Notes of interviews with H. Norman Hyatt, August, 1993, 4 February and 6 February 1994, Akron, Ohio. Correspondence dated 16 August 1999.

Freeze, Emma Maud (Van Blaricom). Notes of interviews with H. Norman Hyatt. August, 1992.

Gilmore, Grace. "Biographical Sketch of Henri J. Haskell ('General')." Undated manuscript. Glendive Public Library.

Grand Army of the Republic, Descriptive Book for the Thomas L. Kean Post Number 12 [Glendive], Department of Montana. Entries from 1885 through 1894. Glendive Public Library.

Harpster, William A. "The Harpster Brothers." 1950. Glendive Public Library.

Herrick, Elmer. "The Memoirs of Elmer Herrick." Undated manuscript. Glendive Public Library.

Hyatt, Alice Janette (Van Blaricom). Notes of interviews with H. Norman Hyatt. 1954, 1957 and August, 1960.

Hyatt, Harold Chandler. Recorded interviews with relatives and others. ca. 1965–ca. 1977. About 300 pages transcribed. Much remains on tape recordings only. In possession of H. Norman Hyatt, Yakima, Washington.

Hyatt, H. Norman. "The Hero Was Throw'd...But the Horse Was Tamed. Book Two in the Quaternion of the History of Old Dawson County. The Biography of Fred Van Blaricom." Work in progress. Yakima, Washington.

_____. "The Naming of the Tributaries and Sites of the Lower Yellowstone River. Book Four in the Quaternion of the History of Old Dawson County." Work in progress. Yakima, Washington.

_____. "Old Dawson. Book Three in the Quaternion of the History of Old Dawson County." Work in progress. Yakima, Washington.

Johnson, Dr. Stephen Norton, Estate of. 1862. Le Sueur County Courthouse, Le Center, Minnesota.

Marriage Records. Dawson County Courthouse, Glendive, Montana.

Powell, Ada. Notes of interviews regarding Henry Tuttle and family. Hamilton, Montana. 2005.

Probate Number 7174. Estate of May Jordan. Dawson County Courthouse. March, 1929.

"Proceedings of the Board, School District Number 1, Dawson County." In the administrative office of Glendive High School, Glendive, Montana.

Ray, Tom. Unpublished papers. ca. 1940–ca. 1960 (many undated). In the archives of the MonDak Heritage Center, Sidney, Montana.

Receipts of the Clerk of the Court, Dawson County, Montana. 21 January 1886.

Starr, Clarence. Location of the Blue Jacket Coal Mine on Glendive Creek. Interview with correspondent John Steffen, Glendive, Montana. February, 2002.

Steffen, John. Glendive, Montana. Letters, correspondence, and interviews, 1990–2007.

Van Blaricom, Frederick Alfred. Original handwritten manuscript. ca. 1949. In the possession of daughter, J. Merle (Van Blaricom) O'Brien, Seattle, Washington. Copy of original in possession of H. Norman Hyatt. Various transcribed, typed and copied unpublished manuscripts in the possession of H. Norman Hyatt, Yakima, Washington, and other Van Blaricom family members. Typed copy of one version in Glendive Public Library.

_____. Correspondence to S. N. Van Blaricom. 20 October 1926. Copies in possession of Emma (Van Blaricom) Freeze, Hamilton, Montana, and H. Norman Hyatt, Yakima, Washington.

Van Blaricom, Stephen Norton. Unpublished, typed and copied memoirs and manuscripts. ca. 1940. In possession of daughter Ann (Van Blaricom) Falor, Akron, Ohio. Various copies in possession of H. Norman Hyatt, Yakima, Washington, and other Van Blaricom family members. One version of typed copy in Glendive Public Library.

_____. Unpublished first draft of letter to Gene Autry. 22 February 1942. In possession of Emma (Van Blaricom) Freeze, Hamilton, Montana. Copy in possession of H. Norman Hyatt, Yakima, Washington.

_____. Correspondence to F. A. Van Blaricom. 22 September 1926. In possession of Emma (Van Blaricom) Freeze, Hamilton, Montana. Copy in possession of H. Norman Hyatt, Yakima, Washington.

_____. Diaries, 1914–1945. In possession of David Norton Van Blaricom, Charlotte, North Carolina. Copy in possession of H. Norman Hyatt, Yakima, Washington.

Works Progress Administration (WPA) files. ca. 1930–ca. 1935. Collection "received from Prof. Burlingame," Dawson County Library, Glendive, Montana.

2. Published Materials

The Career of the Marquis de Mores in the Bad Lands of North Dakota. Arnold O. Goplen. (Reprinted from North Dakota History, Volume 13, Number, 1 and 2, January–April, 1946.) State Historical Society of North Dakota.

A Chronological Record of Events at the Missouri-Yellowstone Confluence Area and a Record of Interments at the Fort Buford, Dakota Territory, Post Cemetery. Ben Innis, compiler and editor. Fort Buford 6th Infantry Regiment Association, Williston, North Dakota. 1971.

Empty Boots–Dusty Corrals. Nancy Thiessen. Self–published. 1986. Copy in Glendive Public Library.

Fort Buford and the Military Frontier on the Northern Plains, 1850–1900, Larry Remele, Editor. State Historical Society of North Dakota, Bismarck. 1987.

Glendive, Montana: Northern Pacific Division Point (Draft). Lorenz P. Schrenk. Dawson County High School Library, Glendive. Undated.

Haskell Descendants Elected Delegates to Montana's Constitutional Conventions. Undated pages (pp. 518–521) from a manuscript. Author unknown. Frontier Gateway Museum, Glendive.

The History of the Van Blaricom Family. Roger D. Hunt, Gresham, Oregon. 1994.

Hoofprints from the Yellowstone Corral of the Westerners, Volume 22, Number 2, Fall–Winter, 1992.

Hyatt and Van Blaricom: A Brief History and Genealogy of the Ancestry of Nathan Lee Hyatt and Alice J. Van Blaricom. H. Norman Hyatt, Yakima, Washington. 2000.

Indiana Territorial Census, 1807.

The Last Leaf. Sylvia Mickelson, Editor. Volume I, Number 4., Spring, 1991.

_____. Volume II, Number 3, Winter, 1991/92.

_____. Volume II, Number 4, Spring, 1992.

_____. Volume III, Number 2. (No quarter indicated.)

Map of the Yellowstone and Missouri Rivers and their Tributaries. 1876. Raynolds, Capt. William F. (1859–1860 survey) with additions by Maj. Gillespie (1876 edition), Walter M. Camp, and Brig. Gen. Wm. C. Brown. South Dakota Historical Society–State Archives. Copyright 2004 Lifelong Learning Project.

Minnesota, Dakota and Montana: The Pioneer Route. Northern Pacific Railroad Company brochure. Winter, 1881.

Minnesota Territorial Census, 1857.

Montana. Map by George F. Cram. 1883. Denver Public Library, Western History Collection. CG4240 1876.GS. Copyright 2004 UM Lifelong Learning Project.

Montana. Map by Rand McNally and Company. 1898. Bitter Root Valley Historical Society, Ravalli County Museum, Hamiliton, Montana. Copyright 2004 UM Lifelong Learning Project.

Montana Atlas & Gazetteer. Topo Maps of the Entire State. DeLorme Mapping. Freeport, Maine. First Edition, Third Printing, 1994.

North Dakota Atlas & Gazetteer. Delorme. Yarmouth, Maine. First Edition. 1999.

POST-AGE. History of the mail service of Dawson County, Montana. Ell Waldon Schloss. Glendive, Montana. 1980.

Ranchers, Railroaders and Retailers of Glendive: Their Houses and Families, 1881–1930. Schloss, Anderson, and Melby. Wibaux, Montana. 1985.

Senator George J. McCone, 1852–1929. Compiled by Orville Quick for the McCone County Museum, Circle, Montana. 2001.

Synopsis of Old Glendive Newspapers, 1882–1910. R. N. Scherger, Compiler. Glendive Public Library.

Terry Does Exist–A History of Southeastern Montana Copied from Old Records by B. Stith (reprinted on the occasion of the Terry Centennial 1882–1982). Terry, Montana. 1982.

Towne, Phineas C., original survey maps of Glendive and Dawson County. (1881–1885 and selected later dates.) Glendive City Hall. Dawson County Courthouse. Montana State Historical Society, Helena, Montana.

United States Census, 1870, Dawson County, Montana Territory.

_____, 1870, Fort Randall, Dakota Territory (Unorganized).

_____, 1870, Little Sauk, Todd County, Minnesota Territory.

_____, 1880, Billings County, Dakota Territory.

_____, 1880, Custer Valley, Custer County, Montana Territory.

_____, 1880, Custer County, Montana Territory.

_____, 1880, Dawson County, Montana Territory.

_____, 1880, Fort Buford, Wallette County, Dakota Territory.

_____, 1880, Fort Custer Valley, Custer County, Montana Territory.

_____, 1880, Fort Yates, Boreman County, Dakota Territory.

_____, 1880, Miles City, Custer County, Montana Territory.

_____, 1880, Spruce Hill, Douglas County, Minnesota

_____, 1900, Glendive, Dawson County, Montana.

_____, 1900, Ward Township, Ravalli County, Montana.

_____, 1910, Glendive, Dawson County, Montana.

_____, 1920, Glendive, Dawson County, Montana.

Whistler, Lieutenant Colonel, Joseph Nelson Garland, telegram to General Alfred H. Terry who forwarded to Adjutant General, Washington, D.C. 1884. Reprinted in *Our Times, Our Lives*, p. 708. 1989.

The Woods Family and Related Families. Arthur L. and Florence P. Woods. Omak, Washington. 1965.

3. Newspapers

Bad Lands Cowboy. Medora, Dakota Territory.

Billings Gazette. Montana.

Bismarck Times. Dakota Territory and North Dakota.

Bozeman Avant–Courier. Montana Territory and Montana.

Cashmere Valley Record. Cashmere, Washington.

Circle Banner. Montana.

Dawson County Review. Glendive, Montana.

Dawson County Review and the Yellowstone Monitor. Glendive, Montana.

Glendive Daily Ranger. Montana.

Glendive Independent. Montana Territory and Montana.

Glendive Independent and Dawson County Review. Montana.

Glendive Times. Montana Territory.

Independent Voice of Eastern Montana. Glendive, Montana.

Long Prairie Leader. Minnesota.

Morris Tribune. Minnesota.

Ranger Review, Glendive, Montana.

Ravalli Republican. Hamilton, Montana.

Salem News. Ohio.

Terry Tribune. Montana.

Todd County Argus. Minnesota.

Western News. Hamilton, Montana.

Yellowstone Journal. Miles City, Montana Territory and Montana.

Yellowstone Press. Glendive, Montana Territory.

4. Articles

Ayotte and Brown families, family group sheets. Patricia Darling. *The Last Leaf,* Volume I, Number 4, Spring, 1991, and Volume II, Number 4, Spring, 1992.

"Boycott–The Pullman Strike in Montana." W. Thomas White. *Montana the Magazine of Western History,* Volume 29, Number 4. October, 1979, pp. 2–11.

"Charley Russell, Cowboy Artist." Bart McDowell. *National Geographic,* Volume 169 (1). January, 1986.

"The Chisolm Trail." John Rossel. *Kansas Historical Quarterly,* Volume 5, Number 1, February, 1936, pp. 3–14.

"Crossing the Gender Line: Ella L. Knowles, Montana's First Woman Lawyer." Richard B. Roeder. *Montana: The Magazine of Western History,* Volume 32, Number Three, Summer, 1982, pp. 64–75.

"Interesting Letter on Very Early Glendive History." John S. Truscott. Undated letter to Mrs. Frank P. Fleming. Published in unidentified newspaper. Undated. Clipping on file in Mondak Heritage Center, Sidney, Montana.

"O.S.B. Eli Washington John Lindesmith: Fort Keogh's Chaplain in Buckskin." Louis L. Pfaller. *Montana: The Magazine of Western History,* Volume XXVII, Number One, January, 1977, pp. 16–23.

"Pages From the Past." Grace M. Gilmore. A series of articles in *Independent Voice of Eastern Montana*. Glendive, Montana. October, November, December, 1935.

"Pierre Wibaux and the W-Bar Ranch." Donald H. Walsh. *Montana: The Magazine of Western History,* Spring, 1955, pp. 2–15.

"The Rambling Reporter." *Farm and Dairy.* Monthly. Salem, Ohio. June, 1945.

Sidney History. Kemmis, Walter D. and Ira L. Bendon. Untitled and undated newspaper article, item #64 and item #68, MonDak Heritage Center. Sidney, Montana.

Van Blaricom, Stephen Norton. Letter to the *Dawson County Review*. Glendive, Montana. 15 February 1923.

_____. Untitled article in the *Salem News*. Ohio. Undated. ca. 1926.

_____. Untitled article in the *Salem News*. Ohio. Undated. ca. 1932.

"Telegraph Operator Now Enjoys Many Hobbies." Pearl Walker. *Salem News*. Ohio. 1951.

"The Winter of 1886–1887: The Death Knell of the Open Range." John E. Mitchell and Richard H. Hart. *Rangelands,* Volume 8, Number 5, October, 1986.

5. Books

50 Years in the Saddle: Looking Back Down the Trail. 3 Volumes. Manfred Singnalness and 50 Years In The Saddle Committee, Quality Quick Print, Dickinson, North Dakota, and Associated Printers, Grafton, North Dakota. 1990.

The American West Year by Year. John S. Bowman, General Editor. Brompton Books Corporation. Greenwich, Connecticut. 1995.

As Big as the West: The Pioneer Life of Granville Stuart. Clyde A. Milner II and Carol A. O'Connor. Oxford University Press, New York. 2009.

As I Remember. Volume I and Volume II. Mrs. Morris (Gladys Mullet) Kaufmann. Sweetgrass Books, Helena, Montana. 2006.

Atlas of the North American Indian. Carl Waldman. Facts on File Publications, New York and Oxford, England. 1985.

Audubon and His Journals. Edited by M. R. Audubon and E. Coues. Charles Scribner's Sons, New York. 1897.

Battles and Skirmishes of the Great Sioux War, 1876–1877. Jerome A. Greene. University of Oklahoma Press, Norman. 1993.

The Beef Bonanza, or How to Get Rich on the Plains. James S. Brisbin. Self–published. 1881.

Bitter Root Trails IV. The Victor Community. Bitter Root Valley Historical Society and the Victor Heritage Museum. Stoneydale Press, Stevensville, Montana. 2007.

Bitter Root Trails, Volume I. Bitter Root Valley Historical Society. Professional Impressions, Darby, Montana. 1982.

Boots and Saddles. Elizabeth Custer. University of Oklahoma Press, Norman. 1961.

A Brief History of North Dakota. Herbert Clay Fish and R. M. Black. American Book Company, New York. 1925.

Bury My Heart at Wounded Knee. Dee Brown. Holt, Rinehart and Winston, New York. 1970.

Captain Cook. Alistair MacLean. Doubleday & Company, Inc., Garden City, New York. 1972.

The Champion Buffalo Hunter. Victor Grant Smith. Edited by Jeanette Hortick Prodgers. Falcon Publishing Company, Inc., Helena and Billings, Montana. 1997.

Chronicles of the Yellowstone. E. S. Topping. Reprint by Ross & Haines, Inc., Minneapolis. 1968.

Compton's Encyclopedia. 21 Volumes. William Benton, Publisher. 1972.

Compton's Pictured Encyclopedia. 15 Volumes. F. E. Compton & Company, Chicago. 1945.

The Conquest of the Missouri. Joseph Mills Hanson. Stackpole Books, Mechanicsburg, Pennsylvania. 2003. (A. C. McClurg, Chicago. 1909.)

Courage Enough–MonDak Family Histories. Bicentennial Edition. Richland County, Montana. 1975.

Cowboy Lingo. Ramon F. Adams. Houghton Mifflin. New York. 2000. (Original copyright 1936.)

The Dig Tree. Sarah Murgatroyd. The Text Publishing Company, Melbourne, Australia. 2002.

Five Indian Tribes of the Upper Missouri. Edwin Thompson Denig. John C. Ewers, Editor. University of Oklahoma Press, Norman. 1961.

Footprints in the Valley. 3 Volumes. Glasgow Courier & Printing, Glasgow, Montana. 1991.

Fort Benton: World's Innermost Port. Joel R. Overholser. Self-published. Fort Benton, Montana. 1987.

The Fur Trade of the American West, 1807–1840. David J. Wishart. University of Nebraska Press, Lincoln/London. 1979.

A Ghost Town on the Yellowstone. Elliot Paul. Random House, Inc., New York and Toronto. 1948.

Glendive, the History of a Montana Town. Marie Peterson MacDonald. The Gateway Press, Glendive, Montana. 1968.

The Great Northwest. Henry J. Wisner. Putnam & Sons, New York. 1883.

A Guide to Historic Glendive. Montana Mainstreets Series, Volume 2. Montana Historical Society Press, Helena. 1998.

Hanging Around the Big Sky: The Unofficial Guide to Lynching, Strangling and Legal Hangings of Montana, Book One. Tom Donovan. Portage Meadows Publishing, Great Falls, Montana. 2007.

Harvest of Grief. Annette Atkins. Minnesota Historical Society Press, St. Paul. 1984.

The History of the Assiniboine and Sioux Tribes of the Fort Peck Indian Reservation, Montana, 1800–2000. David R. Miller, Dennis J. Smith, Joseph L. McGeshick, James Shanley, and Caleb Shields. Fort Peck Community College, Poplar, Montana, and the Montana Historical Society Press, Helena. 2008.

History of the Fourth Regiment of Minnesota Infantry Volunteers during the Great Rebellion, 1861–1865. Alonzo L. Brown, Editor. (Facing pages missing but presumed to be printed in Minnesota.) 1892. Originally the property of Levi Van Blaricom; then Alice (Van Blaricom) Hyatt; now H. Norman Hyatt, Yakima, Washington.

A History of the Mexican War. Robert Selph Henry. Bobbs–Merrill Company, Indianapolis and New York. 1950.

A History of Minnesota. William Watts Folwell. 4 Volumes. Minnesota Historical Society, St. Paul. 1926. Revised edition 1969.

A History of Montana. 3 Volumes. Merrill G. Burlingame and K. Ross Toole, Editors. Lewis Historical Publishing Company, New York. 1957.

History of Montana, 1739–1885. 3 Volumes. Michael A. Leeson, Editor. Warner, Beers & Company, Chicago. 1885.

History of Montana and Biographical Sketches. 3 Volumes. Helen Fitzgerald Sanders. Lewis Publishing Company, Chicago and New York. 1913.

History of the Northern Pacific Railroad. Eugene V. Smalley. Putnam & Sons, New York. 1883.

An Illustrated History of Stevens, Ferry, Okanogan and Chelan Counties. Western Historical Publishing Company. 1904.

An Illustrated History of the Yellowstone Valley. Western Historical Publishing Company, Spokane, Washington. 1907.

Jennie. The Life of Lady Randolph Churchill. 2 Volumes. Ralph G. Martin. Prentice-Hall, Inc., Englewood Cliffs, New Jersey. Volume 1, 1969. Volume 2, 1971. Reprints by Signet, New York, Volume 1, 1970. Volume 2, 1972.

Joseph Culbertson's Indian Scout Memoirs 1876–1895. Joseph Culbertson. M. D. Trout, Editor. Van-Allen Publishing Company, Anaheim, California. 1984.

The Journals of Lewis and Clark. Bernard DeVoto, Editor. Houghton Mifflin Company, New York. 1953. Copyright renewed 1981. Foreword by Stephen Ambrose. 1997.

Kaleidoscopic Lives: A Companion Book to Frontier and Indian Life. 2nd Edition. Joseph H. Taylor. Privately published. Washburn, North Dakota. 1902. Republished as *Frontier and Indian Life and Kaleidoscopic Lives* by The Washburn Fiftieth Anniversary Committee, Valley City, North Dakota. 1932.

Land of the Dacotahs. Bruce Nelson. University of Minnesota Press. 1946.

Legends and Lies. Dale L. Walker. Tom Doherty Associates, Inc. New York. 1997.

Longitude. Dava Sobel. Walker and Company, New York. 1995.

Lord of the Plains. Alfred Silver. Ballantine Books, New York. 1990.

Map Guide to the U.S. Federal Censuses, 1790–1920. William Thorndale and William Dollarhide. Genealogical Publishing Company, Baltimore. 1988.

The March of the Montana Column: A Prelude to the Custer Disaster. Lieutenant James H. Bradley. Edgar I. Stuart, Editor. University of Oklahoma Press, Norman and London. 1991.

Minnesota in the Civil and Indian Wars, 1861–1865. Two Volumes. The Board of Commissioners, Editors. Pioneer Press Company, St. Paul, Minnesota. 1890. 2nd Edition, 1899.

Montana, A History of Two Centuries. Michael P. Malone, Richard B. Roeder and William L. Lang. University of Washington Press, Seattle and London. Revised edition. 1991.

Montana, Its Story and Biography. 3 Volumes. Tom Stout, Editor. The American Historical Society, Chicago and New York. 1921.

Montana, the Land and the People. 3 Volumes. Robert G. Raymer. Lewis Publishing, Chicago and New York. 1930.

Montana Man. Wilbur C. Tuttle. Avalon Books, Thomas Bouregy and Company, Inc., New York. 1966.

Montana Stockgrowers Directory of Marks and Brands, 1872–1900. Van Dersal & Conner, Helena, Montana. 1900. Reprinted by the Dawson County Bicentennial Committee, Glendive, Montana. 1974.

The Mystic Warriors of the Plains. Thomas E. Mails. Doubleday, Garden City, New York. 1972.

Names on the Face of Montana. Roberta Carkeek Cheney. Mountain Press Publishing Company, Missoula, Montana. 1990.

The Northern Pacific, Main Street of the Northwest. Charles R. Wood. Superior Publishing Co., Seattle. 1968.

The Negro Cowboy. Philip C. Durham and Everett L. Jones. Dodd, Mead, New York. 1965. First Bison Book Edition, University of Nebraska Press, Lincoln and London. 1985.

Our Times, Our Lives. Dawson County, Montana. 1889–1989. Dawson County Tree Branches, Rose Wyman, Project Chairman. Artcraft Printers, Billings, Montana. 1989.

The Plainsmen of the Yellowstone. Mark H. Brown. University of Nebraska Press, Lincoln and London. 1961.

Progressive Men of the State of Montana. A. W. Bowen & Co., Chicago. 1902.

Riel, A Life of Revolution. Maggie Siggins. Harper Collins Publishers, Toronto. 1994.

Roosevelt in the Bad Lands. Hermann Hagedorn. The Theodore Roosevelt Nature & History Association, Medora, North Dakota. 1921. Reprint, 1949.

Roosevelt County's Treasured Years. Leota Hoye, Editor. Blue Print and Letter Company, Great Falls, Montana. 1976.

The Splendid Pauper. Allen Andrews. Lippincott, Philadelphia. 1968.

The Story of the Malakand Field Force. Winston S. Churchill. Longmans, Green & Co., London. 1898. Re-released by Leo Cooper in association with Octopus Publishing Group plc, London. 1989.

Strange Empire. Joseph Kinsey Howard. William Morrow and Company, New York. 1952. New material edition, Minnesota Historical Society, St. Paul. 1994.

Tales Along Beaver Creek: A Chronicle of Wibaux County, Montana. Irene James Jones. Wibaux Pioneer–Gazette, Wibaux, Montana. 1976.

They Came and Stayed. Rosebud County History. American Revolution Bi-Centennial (1776–1976) Committee of Rosebud County. Forsyth, Montana. 1977.

Third International Dictionary. Noah Webster. G. C. Merriam & Company, Springfield, Massachusetts. 1964.

This Last West. Lorman L. Hoopes, M. D. Dr. Lorman L. Hoopes in cooperation with SkyHouse Publishers, an imprint of Falcon Press Publishing Co., Inc., Helena, Montana. 1990.

Trials and Triumphs. Rosebud County. Dorothy Tate Spannagel and Janet Spannagel Guptill. Forsyth, Montana. 1994.

Typhoid Mary. Anthony Bourdain. Bloombury, New York and London. 2001.

United States of America's Congressional Medal of Honor Recipients and Their Official Citations. R. J. (Bob) Proft, Editor. Highland House II, Inc., Columbia Heights, Minnesota. Third Edition. 2001.

Up the Missouri with Audubon: The Journal of Edward Harris. Edited by J. F. McDermott. University of Oklahoma Press, Norman. 1951.

The West That Was. John E. Eggen. Schiffer Publishing, Ltd., Atglen, Pennsylvania. July, 1991.

The West That Was–From Texas to Montana. John Leakey with Nellie Snyder Yost. Southern Methodist University Press. 1958. Bison Books, University of Nebraska Press, Lincoln. First printing, October, 1965.

We Pointed Them North. E. C. "Teddy Blue" Abbott and Helena H. Smith. Farrar and Rinehart, New York. 1939.

Wheels Across Montana's Prairie. Prairie County Historical Society. Terry, Montana. 1974.

Yellowstone Command: Colonel Nelson A. Miles and the Great Sioux War, 1876–1877. Jerome A. Greene. University of Nebraska Press, Lincoln and London. 1991. Reprint, University of Oklahoma Press, 2006.

Yellowstone Country. Richard R. Hein. Self-published. 1979.

Yellowstone Red. Tom Ray. Dorrance and Company, Inc., Philadelphia. 1948.

INDEX

Boldface page numbers indicate illustrations. Modern state abbreviations are given only for non-Montana locations.

NORMAN HYATT was born in Yakima, Washington, and raised on a cattle ranch in eastern Washington. A Stanford graduate (B.A., M.A.), he descends from early pioneers of Oregon, Idaho Territory, Washington Territory, and Montana Territory. *An Uncommon Journey* is his first book. He and his wife, Karen, reside in Washington.